Resources for Teaching

MAKING
LITERATURE
MATTER

An Anthology for
Readers and Writers

Second Edition

Resources for Teaching

MAKING
LITERATURE
MATTER

An Anthology for
Readers and Writers

Second Edition

John Schilb
Indiana University

John Clifford
University of North Carolina at Wilmington

Joyce Hollingsworth
University of North Carolina at Wilmington

BEDFORD/ST. MARTIN'S   Boston   ◆   New York

7 6 5 4 3 2
f e d c b a

For information, write: Bedford/St. Martin's, 75 Arlington Street, Boston, MA 02116
(617-399-4000).

ISBN: 0–312–40162–0

Preface

We designed *Making Literature Matter* to be a flexible pedagogical tool that provides students with help in developing their reading and writing abilities, as well as literature for them to read and write about. But the book is ultimately only a tool, and no text, no matter how carefully constructed, can substitute for a patient and attentive instructor willing to guide individual students through the reading and writing process. For such hard but rewarding work, an instructor's relationship with students is crucial to making the course a success. We hope that *Making Literature Matter* will help you negotiate the challenges of teaching students to read more attentively and write more skillfully, and we hope that the resources in this manual will make your efforts more productive and perhaps easier.

We begin by presenting two sample syllabi, the first for a composition course emphasizing writing about literature and the second for a literature course emphasizing reading skills such as interpretation and evaluation. We then discuss teaching strategies for Part One, where students learn basic concepts about writing, especially argumentative writing, and about the four genres of literature presented in the book. Supplementing this discussion is an annotated bibliography of sources that you might consult for further ideas about teaching rhetoric, argument, literature, and literary theory.

The rest of this manual — the bulk of it — comprises commentary on the literature in Part Two's anthology, "Literature and Its Issues." We include a discussion of every selection in the anthology, plus commentaries on how every selection works with others in its cluster. Generally we have tried to keep our comments focused on the issues raised by the questions we ask in the anthology, but when appropriate we provide further discussion, which we hope will be useful in raising other issues in the classroom.

Contents

PART TWO:
Literature and Its Issues   25

PART ONE

Working with Literature

Constructing the Course: Sample Syllabi

Both of the sample syllabi that follow are designed for a fifteen-week semester. The first of the two here is for a composition course built around literature. The second is for an introduction to literature course with a writing component.

English 103: College Composition: Writing and Reading

This is a one-semester writing course for students who place out of the two-semester writing requirement. The syllabus should work just as well in a second-semester composition course, where you may choose not to assign any of the genre-specific chapters (4 through 7), instead moving directly from the two opening chapters to the anthology of literature in Part Two.

The course begins with an introduction to Part One, "Working with Literature," before moving on to the five chapters of Part Two, "Literature and Its Issues." In a fifteen-week course, we have found that the two weeks spent preparing students to write using literature is time well spent.

A. The First Two Weeks. During this time, students are introduced to four key ideas:

1. Cogent "meaning-making" is more likely to occur in a literate environment of reading, responding, writing, discussing, and more writing.
2. Arguing about literature is a process of inquiry that entails revision reason, and reexamination.
3. Finding literary topics to write about involves asking questions.
4. Writing is best thought of as a process involving exploring, planning, composing, and revising.

The first idea, about "meaning-making," is the foundational structure for the course. We read, write, discuss, write, make comparisons, and write again. It is in this cycle of literate acts that good writing is most likely to occur. A discussion of Chapters 1 and 2 is also valuable in introducing students to reading comparatively — the basis for the cluster within the thematic chapters of Part Two. The two poems by Wright and Lohre (Chapter 1) can be read in class, perhaps the first day, as can the first writing exercise on page 9.

The second idea, about argument, can also be introduced the first day with an overview of "Thinking Critically: The Value of Argument"(p. 15). The key terms (**issues, claims, persuasion, audience, evidence,** and **warrants**) can be blended into an informal discussion of argument by giving examples from the three poems about work. A fuller discussion will be more useful after students have read this section at home.

The third idea, about the recent concerns of literary studies (p. 38 ff), seems especially likely to benefit students. A class discussion of the writing exercise on page 41 will help students see the multiple topics that are possible in writing about literature.

The fourth idea, about process, is central to any writing course. Chapter 3, "The Writing Process," then, deserves some attention. Although we assign this chapter for home study, at this point students need to understand only the general principles of exploring, planning, composing, and revising. Working out the logistics and details is what the course is about. We always need to remind ourselves that many concepts about writing tend to confuse students. We find it best to begin with a reasonable overview. The specifics will come as the class works through the book.

The two-week introduction continues with an examination of the writing process applied to specific literary works. This syllabus uses only one of the four chapters that deal with writing about genres (Chapter 5, "Writing about Poems") as a model for how the writing process can proceed. You can ask the class to read the six poems twice, and then assign the exploring exercise on page 120. Then read the various responses from students. It is especially useful for students to read Michaela's freewrite (p. 121) and to discuss its merits and ways she could revise it. Michaela's final draft is a good example of how to combine rigorous argument and analysis without losing sight of her initial personal response. Each instructor should make individual decisions about how much time to invest in clarifying the key terms (mentioned above). These ideas are merely the means to an end and not an end in themselves. The goal is to help students produce strong, serious writing, not obsess about terminology.

B. The Heart of the Course. The syllabus centers on Part Two, "Literature and Its Issues," and devotes nine weeks to four of the five chapters. Students write an essay (four typed pages) for each chapter. They begin with Chapter 12, "Living in Families," and they can work through several clusters in class; it is not possible to work with all the clusters, of course, but students can read other clusters on their own, responding in their journals to questions. Students spend two to three weeks on each essay, from exploring to revising. For Chapter 12, the following clusters are discussed in class: "Memories of Family,"

"Reconciling with Fathers," "Mothers and Daughters," "Siblings in Conflict," and "Not a Simple Decision." Depending on the time, you may want the class to read one other cluster.

The syllabus allots time for covering Chapters 13, 14, and 15 ("Teaching and Learning," "Loving," and "Doing Justice") in the same way, leaving the last two to three weeks of the semester for work on Chapter 16, "Confronting Mortality," and a concluding research essay of six pages.

C. The Conclusion of the Course.   Our last chapter is the focus of a research essay. After students have covered about half of Chapter 15, "Doing Justice," they can be asked to choose one of the research-oriented "Writing about Issues" prompts at the end of each cluster to develop into a longer paper. You may want to consider assigning Appendix 2, which deals with the longer, more traditional research paper in some detail.

D. Classroom Procedure.   In covering the individual clusters, you may want to begin by assigning the "Before You Read" questions for discussion to raise the students' awareness of the issues involved and help focus their attention. Even if all the reading is assigned for home study, you may want to have students read poems in class and ask them to write after reading. You can have them alternate between specific questions from "Thinking about the Text" and "Making Comparisons" to an open freewriting. Have them record their responses in a journal, which can be checked periodically. In general, you want to begin the class by asking for volunteers to read their responses as a way to open a discussion of possible writing issues.

E. Writing Assignments.   Each cluster ends with four "Writing about Issues" assignments. Students cannot do them all, but our intention was to give instructors a choice, depending on the focus of the course. In a junior-level essay-writing course you may prefer exclusively to emphasize argument, but in the lower-level course it's better to combine elements of argument with personal response, using the literature we read and personal experience as evidence. The assignments are merely prompts; authentic writing comes out of the rich literate texture of reading, writing, discussion, and journal writing. Students tap into that environment for topics that interest them. In the "Living in Families" chapter, for example, the assignment is simply to pick one of the "arguing" assignments in one of the clusters.

F. Semester Outline
Week 1	Introduction: "What Is Literature? How and Why Does It Matter?" (Chapter 1), "Reading and Thinking about Literature" (Chapter 2)
Week 2	"The Writing Process" (Chapter 3), "Writing about Poems" (Chapter 5)
Weeks 3–5	"Living in Families" (Chapter 12): Memories of Family, Reconciling with Fathers, Mothers and Daughters, Siblings in Conflict, Not a Simple Decision
	• **Essay 1 due**

Weeks 6–7   "Teaching and Learning" (Chapter 13): Recalling Lessons of Childhood, Teaching Youth about Society, Losing Innocence, Charging a Teacher with Sexual Harassment, Learning in a Colonial Context, Narrators Giving Advice
• **Essay 2 due**

Weeks 8–9   "Loving" (Chapter 14): True Love, Romantic Dreams, Completing the Self through Love, The Appearance of Love, Affairs of Love
• **Essay 3 due**

Weeks 10–11 "Doing Justice" (Chapter 15): Community Justice, Psychiatric Injustice, Racial Injustice, Punishments, Revenge
• **Essay 4 due**

Weeks13–15 Conclusion: "Confronting Mortality" (Chapter 16): Fighting for Survival, Reflecting on Killing Animals, Escaping Life, Making Literature Matter for September 11, 2001
• **Essay 5 due**

English 200: Introduction to Literature

In adapting the preceding syllabus for a course that stresses literature, instructors can spend less time on Part One (one week) and work through more of the chapters. It's still a good idea to have students write before they read and ask them to answer selected questions from Thinking about Text and Making Comparisons. Three short papers (two to three pages) are assigned, spaced over a fifteen-week semester. The topics are flexible; essentially any of the prompts seem appropriate. The two courses are similar, but in the Introduction to Literature course the emphasis is more on reading skills such as evaluation and interpretation rather than on developing topics for essays and direct writing instruction. *Making Literature Matter* was developed to facilitate either emphasis.

Week 1   Introduction: "What is Literature? How and Why Does It Matter?" (Chapter 1), "Reading and Thinking about Literature" (Chapter 2), "The Writing Process" (Chapter 3)

Weeks 2–4   "Writing about Stories" (Chapter 4), "Living in Families" (Chapter 12): Memories of Family, Reconciling with Fathers, Mothers and Daughters, Siblings in Conflict, Not a Simple Decision, Family Tragedy

Weeks 5–7   "Loving" (Chapter 14): True Love, Courtship, The Appearance of Love, Affairs of Love, Romantic Illusions, Is this Love? Love as a Haven?

Weeks 8–9   "Teaching and Learning" (Chapter 13): Teaching Children about Society, Losing Innocence, Charging a Teacher with Sexual Harassment, Learning in a Colonial Context, Narrators Giving Advice

Weeks 10–12 "Doing Justice" (Chapter 15): Military Justice, Psychiatric Injustice, Racial Injustice, Revenge, Confronting Sin, Misfit Justice

Weeks 13–15 "Confronting Mortality" (Chapter 16): Fighting for Survival, Reflecting on Killing Animals, Escaping Life, Reviewing Someone's Life, Making Literature Matter for September 11, 2001

Teaching Writing along with Literature

We have designed *Making Literature Matter* primarily for courses that integrate literary study with writing instruction. We realize that such courses can be difficult to teach. In particular, class members may become so involved in discussing literary texts that attention to their own writing slides off the agenda. To thwart this possibility, try to make writing part of as many class periods as possible. For example, you might have students freewrite about a particular work before or during a class and then ask for volunteers to read their efforts aloud. Throughout our book, we present many questions and writing assignments that can serve as the basis for brief composing exercises, as well as for more sustained papers. Needless to say, when students contribute their own writing to class discussions, they are participating more actively than they otherwise might.

Helping Students with Argumentation

In many respects, our book encourages students to engage especially in argumentative writing. We devote much of Part One to it, laying out and demonstrating key elements of argument like issues, claims, audience, evidence, and warrants. Our explanation of argument in Part One acknowledges to students that they may have trouble grasping what *warrants* are. We hope that our discussion of the term makes its meaning clear. But here we suggest that you also allow an ample amount of class time to help your students understand what *issues* are. In fact, this concept is often harder for students to grasp than the concept of *claims* is. Remind your class that an issue is a question that can have more than one answer. Stress that a worthwhile argument addresses a genuine and interesting issue. Have students review the various kinds of issues we list. At the start of your course, your students might write with a sense of grammar and organization but focus on elaborating noncontroversial theses. They need practice in discovering issues so that their writing will contribute to real or possible debates rather than merely state the obvious. To sense the possible issues that a literary work can provoke, students have to develop the habit of asking questions. Point out to your class that question-posing is a vital part of discussion. Students who usually feel they can speak only when they have answers may welcome your announcement that questions are valuable, too.

Discussion and Debate

Your students will become more proficient in their *written* arguments if you give them plenty of opportunities to discuss issues and advance claims in *oral* arguments. Consider requiring members of the class to make oral reports on particular authors. You might even call for entire panels on particular issues, authors, and texts. Another possibility is to break the class into small groups and require each group to collaborate on a particular task and to report back to the class on their findings. Bear in mind that small groups are unlikely to be productive if the task you assign them is vague; try to make it precise as well as manageable. Students can also get valuable practice in discussion if you have them undertake various kinds of role playing, even when the text under consideration is not a script. For example, you might have students enact a meeting of characters from various short stories.

Of course, a looming possibility in a class on argumentative writing is the staging of debates. And certainly you can arrange for groups of students to advocate conflicting judgments about a character, for instance. Yet although class debates can be exciting, sometimes they encourage opinions less nuanced than those you want to see in your students' writing. If your class does end up taking simplistic polar positions in a debate, leave some debriefing time in which you encourage more complex views to emerge.

Peer Review

Quite possibly you will also want to integrate writing into your class periods by devoting class time to peer review of students' writing-in-progress. Such review can effectively take place in pairs, but many instructors prefer to set up entire peer review groups. Students can remain in the same groups throughout the term; then again, many instructors like to change group membership from time to time. Some students will be comfortable reading drafts aloud to an audience, whereas others prefer to distribute their drafts and have the audience read them silently. Neither procedure is necessarily better, we think. You might let each group or the class as a whole choose which procedure to adopt.

Admittedly, many students need help formulating review responses that will be genuinely helpful to the writer. In fact, the typical peer reviewer is afraid to offend. We recommend that reviewers fill out a sheet that contains questions reflecting your criteria for the particular assignment you have given. Moreover, these questions should make clear that the reviewer is responding to the text and not to the writer's personality. We tend to discourage reviewers from directly giving advice; we think they will help the writer more if they focus on rendering their impressions of the text at hand. Occasionally you may want peer review groups to look at work that is considerably less than a full-fledged draft. After all, writers need opportunities simply to test their provisional issues, claims, and evidence, which may take the form of sentences or paragraphs rather than entire papers.

Teaching the Genres

We group most of the literary selections in *Making Literature Matter* by genre as well as by theme. Hence, teachers who prefer to stress elements of genre can easily do so. Even if you prefer a thematic approach, you probably will want to familiarize your students with some of these elements. Therefore, here we offer suggestions for teaching genres. First we discuss short fiction; then we turn to poetry, plays, and the essay. In each case, we refer to examples of the genre found in Part One of the book.

In our experience, students are far more ready to discuss the *content* of literature than they are the structural properties of literature, which much genre analysis emphasizes. We suspect the general public is similarly inclined. Whereas many critics in academe like to ponder a work's symbolism, its plot design, or other technical aspects of it, most readers outside the academy attend more to the text's personalities, events, and ideas. These readers tend to share Kenneth Burke's notion that literature is "equipment for living"; they are not so concerned about its particular nuts and bolts. When you refer to elements of genre in class, your students are likely to be more receptive if you introduce just one or two terms at intervals rather than bringing forth several at once. Students may even lose sight of literature if they have to focus on mastering a whole critical lexicon for it.

We believe that elements of genre are best taught as means to an end rather than as ends in themselves. Our book envisions a course aimed above all at helping students become more adept as arguers, whether their arguments wind up focusing on literary form or on literary content. Indeed, throughout the book we encourage students to think of their own arguments as a fifth genre, one just as important as the other four. No doubt they will learn characteristics of literary genres more easily if you point out how they can develop claims about these elements in their writing and class discussions. For instance, they will be keener to learn poetic meter if you show them how it can be the subject of the paper you have just assigned on several poems about work.

How much should you talk in class about the term *genre* itself? That is up to you. Probably most of your students will already have a rough sense of what the term involves. They will know that literature is often divided into fiction, poetry, and drama, although many of them will not immediately assume that it includes essays. To get your class thinking about genres in literature, you might first ask students to identify various film genres, since most Hollywood movies fit into easily recognizable categories. You might even ask how films are classified at local video rental stores, which are conspicuously arranged by genre.

You may want to point out that a genre can be described in various ways. When we discuss genres in Part One of the book, we refer mostly to their technical or formal aspects. In addition, you might note that some writers and literary theorists have associated certain genres with particular kinds of subject matter. For instance, in his book *The Lonely Voice*, short-story writer Frank

O'Connor argues that the short-story genre has often dealt with characters who live on the margins of society. (Try testing his claim by having your class read O'Connor's story "Guests of the Nation," which we include in Chapter 15, "Doing Justice.") In his book *The Situation of Poetry*, Robert Pinsky argues that much Romantic and post-Romantic verse investigates whether the speaker can ever really commune with the physical universe. Similarly, it has often been observed that a great many poems display an individual human being reflecting on the passage of time (the topic of a cluster of poems in Chapter 16, "Confronting Mortality").

You might also have your class situate genres historically, attending to ways genres have reflected or influenced specific societies and eras. To begin this contextualizing, try asking your students to identify genres on screen or in print that have recently changed as a result of changing social conditions. For example, because of massive media coverage of real-life sex scandals like the Clinton/Lewinsky affair, television soap operas can no longer hook viewers simply by presenting fictional hanky-panky. Meanwhile, the growth of Generation X as a consumer force has encouraged an epidemic of youth-oriented TV series like *Dawson's Creek* and *Buffy the Vampire Slayer*. In part because more people surf the Internet and more moviemakers rely on computer technology, Hollywood has produced several science-fiction/fantasy films that examine issues posed by virtual reality (e.g., *eXistenZ*, *The Matrix*, *Pleasantville*, *The Truman Show*). And now that the communist menace has faded, spy novelists like John LeCarré have been forced to invent new villains.

You will have to decide how much to discuss *subgenres* of short fiction, poetry, drama, and the essay. For each of these main genres, you can point out smaller topical categories. In fact, this is what we do with our clusters in Part Two; there, for example, we suggest that certain works of short fiction can be usefully grouped and analyzed as stories about revenge. You can also refer to subgenres based on form. In the case of poems, for instance, we feature numerous examples of the sonnet and the villanelle, and our drama selections include both Greek and Elizabethan forms of tragedy. Again, though, students need to feel that any generic classification they engage in has some larger purpose, such as helping them write more incisive arguments about particular texts.

Stories

Of all the literary genres featured in the book, probably students will be most familiar and comfortable with this one. Most likely they will have read several works of fiction beforehand, in school if not on their own. In addition, they will have developed some sense of narrative conventions through viewing films and TV shows as well as through listening to songs with story lines. Thus, when you identify elements of short fiction for them, often you will be helping them grow conscious of characteristics they intuitively know. Feel free to bring their tacit knowledge to the surface by encouraging them to compare the fiction they are reading with stories they have already encountered in popular culture. When teaching Rebecca Brown's story "The Gift of Sweat" (p. 86), for example, ask your class to compare it with AIDS narratives they have seen on the screen. You might even invite them to compare Brown's tale with journalistic reports about AIDS, including stories about such HIV-positive celebrities as Magic Johnson.

We find that of all the elements of this genre, students are most eager to discuss plot and character. Try asking your class to analyze at least a few stories using Alice Adams's formula ABCDE (Action, Background, Climax, Development, Ending), which we apply in the book to Brown's story, to William Carlos Williams's "The Use of Force" (p. 80), and to Eudora Welty's "A Visit of Charity"(p. 82). Few of your students are apt to know this formula; in fact, we have never come across it in any other introductory literature textbook. Yet Adams's scheme — devised not by a literary critic but by a veteran short-story writer — illuminates the plot structure followed by many pieces of short fiction. Furthermore, by using it as a benchmark, students can trace how other short stories prove unconventional in design. Of course, your class first needs to be familiar with the plot of any story it discusses. Despite our exhortations to the contrary, we have found that students tend to read an assigned story only once before coming to class, so their memories of plot details must often be refreshed. You might start your class session on a story by having students write and exchange brief summaries of its plot. Reviewing their digests, they may discover they do not agree in their identifications of the story's key actors and incidents, including the story's turning points. Such differences in understanding may then spark lively debate.

In Part One of our book, we define short fiction as "the art of the glimpse," a phrase we take from the veteran short-story writer William Trevor. Some stories feature quite dramatic events; for example, Frank O'Connor's "Guests of the Nation"(p. 1091) climaxes with a double execution. Yet other stories mostly present subtle "glimpses" into their characters' lives, and even a dramatic story may have quietly resonant moments. Some of your students may need help seeing the potential significance of a story's lower-key passages. Take the last two words of Rebecca Brown's story: "I ate." These seem ordinary words; furthermore, the narrator's tone seems muted. We would argue, though, that her act of eating is an important signifier in the story. It indicates her ultimate willingness to accept gifts from the man she has tried to help; also, eating is an age-old ritual of communion. To help your class sense implications like these, you might first ask students to list occasions when the declaration "I ate" is an ordinary, commonplace, unremarkable speech act. Then you can explicitly encourage them to consider how the particular context of Brown's story gives this statement more depth.

A good, quick way to discover what your class thinks about a particular story's characters is to have students write down three adjectives for each. You can then go around the room and have each student read aloud the adjectives he or she has devised. Next, you can ask the class to identify and elaborate whatever commonalities and divergences have emerged. You can use this "round robin" method of character analysis to initiate class discussion or revive it. You can even conclude the period by asking whether anyone's adjectives have changed as a result of hearing class members' adjectives. Remember, though, that character analysis is not always the best approach to a story, even if it does come naturally to students. You may find it more productive to have your class address other facets of the story first.

If characters in a story seem to act unpleasantly, irrationally, and/or unproductively, a number of your students may scorn them. Actually, a great deal of modern fiction (and drama, for that matter) centers on characters whose nature and circumstances strike many students as worse than their own. The great literary critic Northrop Frye helps put this situation in perspective. In his 1957 book *The Anatomy of Criticism*, now regarded as a classic account of genres, Frye traces various kinds of heroes that have figured in literature down through the centuries. The first kind was "a divine being," the hero of *myth*. The second was "superior in degree to other men and to the environment of other men"; this was the hero of *romance*. Then appeared the hero who was "superior in degree to other men but not to his environment"; this prototype, Frye argues, was "the hero of the *high mimetic* mode, of most epic and tragedy, and is primarily the kind of hero that Aristotle had in mind." Closer to our own time, there emerged the *low mimetic* mode; this mode features a hero who is "superior neither to other men nor to his environment," so that audiences "respond to a sense of his common humanity." Finally there is the hero of the *ironic* mode, who seems "inferior in power or intelligence to ourselves, so that we have the sense of looking down on a scene of bondage, frustration, or absurdity" (33–34).

Frye seems to refer exclusively to *male* heroes, thus leaving open the question of how much his categories apply to females. Yet many of the short stories we include in this volume fit into his so-called ironic mode. Reading Welty's story, for example, your students may believe that Marian and the adult women she encounters in the rest home are "inferior in power or intelligence to ourselves," caught up in "a scene of bondage, frustration, or absurdity." Even with this perception, a class analyzing Welty's characters may feel compassion rather than contempt. Nevertheless, quite possibly you will encounter animosity toward these characters, as well as toward those in our book's other ironic narratives.

If some of your students do rush to condemn characters, their attitudes may still provoke good discussion, especially if other members of your class are willing to defend or identify with the targets. Often, however, moralistic dismissal is hardly productive at all. At such times, you have various options. To get your students to at least provisionally identify with a character they criticize, you can invite them to report occasions when they have acted similarly or been tempted to. With a little prodding, for instance, many people will recall feeling nervous and uncertain visiting a nursing home, and they may also remember moments during their childhood when they were as self-centered as Marian. Or you might play devil's advocate, openly proclaiming that you yourself hesitate to indict the characters outright. You also have the option of shifting the discussion from judgment of the characters to analysis of their functions in the story. For example, rather than solicit your class's opinions of the querulous roommates in Welty's story, you might ask how these women serve as obstacles and/or discoveries for Marian. Another conversational tactic is to sketch Frye's history of narrative modes and ask students to supply other examples of the low mimetic mode. You might point out, too, that works of literature enable us as readers to study the complexities of people, whereas we might feel pressured to make snap judgments about them in real life. You can add that works of literature are often *most* worth reading when they complicate an audience's understanding rather than just confirming its righteousness. You might even conduct a "thought experiment" in which all of your students try writing nuanced claims about Marian and her ilk. Bear in mind that many students who offer complex character analyses in class are tempted to be more reductive in their writing. Composing a manageable argument on paper, they suspect, requires claims simpler than those they have put forth in discussion. You may have to remind them that, if anything, a written argument about a work is usually more interesting and credible when it shows that the work is *not* easily decoded and judged.

When discussing the plot of a story in class, usually students need not be concerned with the verb tenses they use. But when they write a paper about the story, you will want them to recount its events with a tense that is consistent. Unfortunately, many students wind up shifting tenses in their papers about short stories. They move back and forth between past and present, as if they cannot make up their minds which to employ. In Part One, we advise students to try sticking with present tense when they write about a fictional character's actions. Whether or not you agree with us, point out to your students what tense you want them to adopt.

Because short stories are short, you may be tempted to have your students read several for a given class period. We find, however, that less is more. That is, we are more likely to engender substantial analysis of a story if we do not make it compete for time with many others. A good limit is one or two per hour. You can, in fact, deal with several if you divide the class into small groups, assign each a different story to analyze, and then conclude the period by having each group report its analysis to the whole class.

Plan to spend at least one class period helping your students understand the role that point of view plays in short fiction. Let them know that a story may or may not feature a character who expresses the author's own thinking. In particular, indicate that a first-person narrator does not necessarily speak for the author; indeed, such a narrator may even be unreliable. You might acknowledge, too, that reliable first-person narrators may still withhold some of their thoughts from the reader. Such is the case with Rebecca Brown's narrator, who waits until near the end of the story before stating what she has found in Rick's kitchen.

Few of your students will be prepared to define or identify free indirect style, although it appears in many stories. Therefore, take time to explain this device. In our Part One discussion of short fiction, we demonstrate free indirect style by citing a passage from Welty's story that exemplifies it. Another way of familiarizing students with this style is to have them write brief passages of their own that use it. Actually, you can have your class practice various modes of narration, including reliable first person, unreliable first person, and direct address to the reader (see the Narrators Giving Advice cluster in Chapter 13, "Teaching and Learning").

Poems

Many students suffer what we call "poetry anxiety." Quite simply, they fear this genre. In part, they do so because they find many poems elusive in meaning, hard to figure out. To them, the average poet seems almost willfully difficult. But another reason for their unease with poetry is their feeling that whenever they study this genre they will have to learn many new technical terms. Of course, your class may also include students who love to read poetry, as well as students who have actually written some. You can even invite the poets in your class to bring in samples of their work. Still, when you first turn your class to poetry, it would be a good idea for you to begin by asking your students their general attitude toward it. Let the anxious ones know that you understand their concerns, even as you submit that reading poetry can be pleasurable.

We suggest, too, that you proceed slowly as you introduce your class to the genre's technical features. How many of these features should your students learn? Quite a few instructors believe that the study of poetry should involve extensive practice in technical analysis, so that students develop an ability to identify any poem's particular meter and rhyme scheme. If you are dealing with multiple genres in your course, though, you may not have time for such work. Also worth considering is the level of the course. When our classes consist mostly of first-year students and sophomores pursuing majors other than English, we do not make them regularly engage in scansion. Rather, we draw their attention to various issues raised by particular texts, especially so they can find topics for their own writing. We elaborate on matters of meter and rhyme when we feel they are especially important to a given text's meaning and impact.

We recommend that, whenever possible, you have students read aloud in class the poems to be discussed. Oral delivery helps both reciter and audience sense a poem's sound patterns, while also giving everyone a chance to identify other aspects of it that they may have missed in their first reading. After a poem is read aloud, you can go around the room and ask all of your students to note anything about it they have newly recognized. Needless to say, your reciters will vary in their degree of elocutionary skill, but the practice in speaking is worthwhile for all of them. If they mispronounce a word or substitute another for it, you can patiently correct them.

In our experience, students need help detecting how various words in a poem relate to one another. The task is especially difficult for them when the related words appear in different stanzas. Encourage your students to range back and forth over the entire text, looking for distant connections. Prod them to consider, for example, how the end of the poem is linked to its beginning. We have also found it useful to have students circle what they deem the poem's most important word; usually, interesting discussion ensues as they defend their choices. A worthwhile exercise, too, is having students identify the major stages or phases that the poem moves through, which may or may not coincide with its stanza breaks.

We believe that when students are asked to interpret one of the poem's images, they should be encouraged first to think of all possible associations with it. In the case of Frost's "After Apple Picking" (p. 189), for example, you might put the word *apple* on the blackboard and invite students to point out various things it has signified or evoked. Eventually you can invite them to consider which of their associations fit this specific text. Some of your students may be wary of attaching much figurative meaning to a seemingly simple word like *apple,* whereas you yourself may be inclined to pack it with symbolic import. In fact, poetry tends to be the genre that students most see as in danger of English teacher overreading, the one that leads our own students to ask, "But could the author really have had all those meanings in mind?" The best answer to this question, we think, came from the poet Michael Collier when he visited one of our classes. Collier's poetry tends to rely on seemingly plain words like *water*. He said, however, that readers invariably make all sorts of associations with such a common term when it appears in a poem. He acknowledged, too, that several of these meanings may suit the poem well, even if the writer didn't think of them while composing it.

In Part One, our section on poetry as a genre presents poems that feature a first-person speaker. Actually, much of the poetry in our book does so, and contemporary poets seem very much drawn to the "I." Some of your students may automatically identify the "I" of a poem with its author, but we suggest you emphasize that the two may need to be distinguished. Of course, certain poems do seem autobiographical. But as we point out when we discuss issues of history in Part One, even Milton's poem about his blindness (p. 37) may be presenting just one aspect of Milton rather than his complete, authentic self. You may find, as we have, that unless a first-person poem clearly indicates otherwise, many students refer to its "I" as male. This tendency is not all that disturbing when the poet is male, but it is troubling when the poet is female. In one of our classes, for instance, many students used the masculine in referring to the "I" of Maxine Kumin's "Woodchucks" (in the first cluster of "Doing Justice"), even though the poem seems based on Kumin's own experiences as a farmer. When asked why they made such a gender choice, some students revealed a continuing attachment to the generic male as a pronoun, while others assumed that the poem's gun-wielding farmer had to be a man. If this situation arises in your class, take the opportunity to discuss with your students the various criteria they can use in determining a speaker's gender. Our own view is that if the text of an "I" poem leaves the speaker's gender unclear, the critic should write as if the gender of "I" is the same as the author's. But this is only our default strategy, for we realize there may be justifiable departures from it.

Because your class will not have time to read all the poems in our book, you will have to be selective in the ones you assign. Various principles of selection are possible. We recommend, though, that you introduce students to all sorts of forms. We find many of them unacquainted with blank verse, even though contemporary poets are fond of it, and several of our students have more or less assumed that a poem must rhyme. Your class can learn much when you present examples of poetry that test narrow definitions of the genre. Consider assigning, for example, Carolyn Forché's dramatic prose poem "The Colonel" (p. 1304).

Plays

When you teach a play, you have to decide how much you will present it to your students as a blueprint for production rather than as simply a text to be read in class. Our own inclination is to make our classes always aware of the play as a script to be performed. There are numerous reasons for stressing its theatrical dimension. For one thing, doing so gives students a better sense of how interpretations can be consequential; after all, performers' understanding of their parts influences their enactment of these characters on stage. Furthermore, referring to actual or hypothetical productions of the play helps students see the material conditions that can affect literature. Susan Glaspell created dramatic intensity when she confined the onstage action of *Trifles* (p.290) to the Wrights' kitchen, but no doubt she also relied on a single set because that is what companies like her Provincetown Players could manage in the small theaters where they performed.

The best reason, however, for treating a play as a script is to get your students up on their feet and actively participate in class. Let students read scenes aloud, or better yet, assign groups to rehearse scenes and then stage them. You can even assign the same scene to different groups; most likely, their different renditions of the scene will inspire your class to talk about how interpretation shapes performance. When students work together on scenes, they will also see how learning can be collaborative.

Do not be afraid of letting a male character be played by a woman, and vice versa. The results may be fascinating. Moreover, such reversal can be good preparation if the class is going to discuss David Henry Hwang's M. Butterfly (p. 908) — a play that deals with gender confusion — or a play by Shakespeare, whose female characters were originally played by men. If you teach *Hamlet* (p. 1185), you might point out that in modern times the title role has been played by several actresses, including Sarah Bernhardt, Judith Anderson, and Diane Venora. Perhaps you will want your class to consider, too, the current willingness of many professional theater companies to cast a role with someone of another race than the playwright probably had in mind. Sometimes the casting is deliberately provocative, as with the numerous modern productions in which Shakespeare's Caliban is played by a black man. On other occasions, the casting purports to be "color-blind," as when the black actor Paul Winfield played Falstaff in a Washington, D.C., production of *The Merry Wives of Windsor.* (In fact, Winfield replaced actress Pat Carroll in the role.) You may know that "color-blind" casting was debated by black playwright August Wilson and white theater critic Robert Brustein in New York City's Town Hall in 1997. While Brustein supported the practice, Wilson criticized it, arguing that it diverted America from establishing more theater companies that perform black dramatists' plays with black actors. Your students may be interested in pursuing this debate. If you teach Lorraine Hansberry's *A Raisin in the Sun* (p. 226), you might ask them what they think about casting whites as the Younger family.

Perhaps some of your students will have acted in high school or college. Some of them may currently be theater majors. Try beginning your discussion of drama as a genre by inviting students to report their own acting experiences. You might go further and ask them to report performing experiences of any kind, as a way of beginning to analyze what is involved in making presentations to a live audience. You can also invite students to recall plays they have seen rather than acted in. Do not be surprised, though, if several students report that they have rarely or never seen live professional theater — all the more reason for having your class actually perform. You might encourage your students to see current productions of your college's theater department and even consider arranging a group visit to one.

You may want to augment your discussion of a play by showing a filmed version in class. For most of the plays in our book, film versions are readily available on video. Various audio recordings of Shakespeare's *Hamlet* (p. 1185), are in circulation as well. Students can learn much from watching or listening to an actual production but can grow passive if forced to be simply an audience for prolonged periods. Often a thoughtful discussion can result when students are asked to analyze just a film clip or two. For instance, you might have your class compare Kenneth Branagh's "To be or not to be" soliloquy with Laurence Olivier's or Mel Gibson's. Or before showing a film clip, you might have some of your students perform the same scene; later the class can compare the two versions. Most film adaptations of plays modify the original script, and your students might evaluate changes they spot.

Much of what we have said about teaching short fiction applies to the teaching of plays. In particular, as with short stories, you may find students contemptuous toward a number of the characters they encounter in plays. If this situation occurs, try following some of the strategies we suggested using with short fiction. But with plays, you have an advantage: You can ask someone criticizing a character to perform that character, an exercise that encourages the student to investigate the character's various human dimensions.

In our Part One discussion of plays as a genre, we refer to changes in theatrical conventions. Quite possibly your students will express discomfort with the language and format of *Oedipus the King* (p. 495), *Antigone* (p. 541), and *Hamlet* (p. 1185). When you teach any of these plays, there will be times when you have to explain conventions at length. But keep trying to find points of contact between the play and things that your students have experienced, read about, or heard about. In Part One, we stress that even so-called realistic plays like *Trifles*, *A Raisin in the Sun*, and *'night, Mother* (p. 141) observe certain conventions. Calling attention to these modern theatrical devices may prepare your class for plays that seem less immediately accessible.

Essays

You may be reluctant to teach the essays in our book, suspecting that this genre is not as "literary" as short fiction, poetry, and drama. But as we indicate in the text, quite a few essays show many of the same qualities traditionally associated with the other three genres. Indeed, you may want to emphasize that nonfiction is less a window on the real world than an artful representation of it, exhibiting many of the same techniques of craft that one can find in fiction. Furthermore, reading essays can serve as a bridge between the literature your students encounter in our book and the writing you have them do. Even if you demand that their writing eschew explicitly personal reflections like those of June Jordan and Alice Walker, familiarizing your students with essays expands their rhetorical repertoires. They grow aware of strategies and techniques that can, to some extent, shape their own prose.

Unfortunately, we find that most students have had little previous experience analyzing essays. At best, they have taken an English class that included a brief unit on this genre. We also have had scant formal training in essay analysis, and the same may be true of you. Moreover, we find that published theories of the essay do not dwell much on specific features of specific texts. Instead, their tendency is to exalt the genre in broad terms. Hence, more than with the other genres in our book, your class's approach to the essay will include evolving a critical lexicon for it. We try to help by identifying typical elements of essays in Part One.

Many instructors report that their students often refer to essays as "stories." We, too, find this to be so. We have already indicated one reason why students resort to this term: They have not been trained to identify the genre's own particular characteristics. Another reason, we suspect, is that many essays do feature quite a bit of narrative. We recommend that when you move to discussing essays, you spend at least one period reviewing with your class the different amounts and functions of narrative that particular essays entail. Help students distinguish moments of pure storytelling in an essay from moments when the text is more devoted to argument or philosophical reflection. Get them to identify, for example, the claims that Jordan and Walker make, in addition to the narrative sequences these essayists spin. Worth noting, too, however, is *where* in the text the claims appear. As Douglas Hesse has pointed out, often an essay achieves its intellectual force precisely by embedding its claims within a compelling and credible narrative.

You and your class may desire to discuss the extent to which, and the sense in which, a particular essay is "true." Some of your students may simply accept the text's veracity; others may be skeptical, disposed to regard the work as fiction. We encourage our classes to consider how even avowedly objective writing is still a selective, crafted representation of the world. We also suggest that essayists deserve at least some leeway when they attempt to render their past experiences, conversations, and thoughts. At the same time, we acknowledge that readers approach essays and short stories with different expectations. In an important sense, they are willing to accept short stories as fabrication, while being suspicious of essays that seem bent on falsifying the writer's life.

Probably your students will better grasp the craft of essays if you let them try, even briefly, to write a personal account like Jordan's and Walker's. In our experience, many students enjoy practicing the essayist's present tense, even when the experience being described has perhaps already occurred. Scott Russell Sanders's "Doing Time in the Thirteenth Chair" (p. 1114) is an especially good example of how the present tense can give readers a "you are there" feeling. Also worth discussing are the various ways in which an essay can seem relevant to a wide audience even when it dwells on the writer's own life. If and when your students draft their own essays, you can have them consider how successful they have been in making their experience count for others.

Annotated Bibliography of Resources

The following is a list of books and articles that we have found especially useful in teaching literature and composition courses. They have influenced, too, our work on *Making Literature Matter*. The list is necessarily selective; particular items on it may lead you to other good resources for your pedagogy. We have divided the list into three categories: (1) texts on basic principles of rhetoric and argument, (2) texts that engage in rhetorical analysis of literature and/or discuss argumentative moves that literary critics make, and (3) texts that relate literary theory and/or pedagogy to the teaching of writing.

Basic Principles of Rhetoric and Argument

Aristotle. *On Rhetoric: A Theory of Civic Discourse*. Ed. and trans. George A. Kennedy. New York: Oxford UP, 1991.

> Although an ancient treatise (dating from c. 333 B.C.E.), this remains an illuminating guide to basic principles, and most contemporary theorists of rhetoric and argument continue to build on it. Kennedy's edition is accessible as well as sound and up to date in its scholarly apparatus.

Bitzer, Lloyd F. "The Rhetorical Situation." *Philosophy and Rhetoric* 1 (1968): 1–17.

> A key document in contemporary theorizing about rhetorical situations. Still worth consulting even though subsequent writers on the subject have pointed out some problems in Bitzer's framework.

Bizzell, Patricia, and Bruce Herzberg, eds. *The Rhetorical Tradition: Readings from Classical Times to the Present*. Boston: Bedford Books, 1990.

> The best compendium we know of primary sources in rhetorical theory through the ages.

Crosswhite, James. *The Rhetoric of Reason*. Madison: U of Wisconsin P, 1996.

> Winner of the Modern Language Association's Shaugnessy Award, this is a lucid and thoughtful defense of written argument as a form of reasoning.

Ede, Lisa, and Andrea Lunsford. "Audience Addressed/Audience Invoked: The Role of Audience in Composition Theory and Pedagogy." *College Composition and Communication* 35 (1984): 155–71.

> Clarifies various possible senses of the term *audience*.

Emmel, Barbara, Paula Resch, and Deborah Tenney, eds. *Argument Revisited, Argument Redefined: Negotiating Meaning in the Composition Classroom.* Thousand Oaks, CA: Sage, 1996.

Includes many thoughtful essays that apply current strands in argument theory to the teaching of writing.

Fulkerson, Richard. *Teaching the Argument in Writing.* Urbana, IL: National Council of Teachers of English, 1996.

Good introduction to various theories of argument. Written expressly for teachers of writing.

Lamb, Catherine E. "Beyond Argument in Feminist Composition." *College Composition and Communication* 42 (1991): 11–24.

Despite its title, this article does not go "beyond" argument but rather proposes a collaborative model of it while incisively critiquing "monologic" forms.

Lynch, Dennis A., Diana George, and Marilyn Cooper. "Moments of Argument: Agonistic Inquiry and Confrontational Cooperation." *College Composition and Communication* 48 (1997): 61–85.

Detailed presentation of a framework for composition teaching that stresses argument as inquiry.

Perelman, Chaim, and Lucie Olbrechts Tyteca. *The New Rhetoric: A Treatise on Argumentation.* Trans. J. Wilkinson and P. Weaver. Notre Dame, IN: U of Notre Dame P, 1969.

A landmark in contemporary theorizing about rhetoric, especially argument. Details many strategies of informal logic and makes a cogent case for seeing argument as intertwined with considerations of value.

Toulmin, Stephen. *The Uses of Argument.* New York: Cambridge UP, 1964.

A significant influence on textbooks about argument, including ours. Foundational especially in its discussion of claims and warrants.

Rhetorical Analysis of Literature and/or Discussion of Argument in Literary Criticism

Eagleton, Terry. *Literary Theory: An Introduction.* Minneapolis: U of Minnesota P, 1983. 2nd ed. 1996.

Lucid and witty survey of various schools of literary theory. Concludes by recommending they be replaced with a rhetorical approach to literature.

Fahnestock, Jeanne, and Marie Secor. "The Rhetoric of Literary Criticism." In *Textual Dynamics of the Professions: Historical and Contemporary Studies of Writing in Professional Communities.* Ed. Charles Bazerman and James Paradis. Madison: U of Wisconsin P, 1990. 76–96.

Invaluable survey of the kinds of issues and argumentative moves that literary critics undertake.

Fish, Stanley. *Doing What Comes Naturally: Change, Rhetoric, and the Practice of Theory in Literary and Legal Studies.* Durham, NC: Duke UP, 1989.

Includes many essays that show the pervasiveness of rhetoric in literary criticism and theory.

Frey, Olivia. "Beyond Literary Darwinism: Women's Voices and Critical Discourse." *College English* 52 (1990): 507–26.

A forceful call for less agonistic forms of argument in literary studies.

Graff, Gerald. *Beyond the Culture Wars: How Teaching the Conflicts Can Revitalize American Education.* New York: Norton, 1992.

———. *Professing Literature: An Institutional History.* Chicago: U of Chicago P, 1987.

Graff's 1987 book is an excellent chronicle of debates among literary critics since the modern founding of the discipline. His later book recommends ways of teaching such conflicts in undergraduate classes.

Levin, Richard. *New Readings vs. Old Plays: Recent Trends in the Reinterpretation of English Renaissance Drama.* Chicago: U of Chicago P, 1979.

Negative about current practices in literary criticism but cannily analyzes the field's typical argumentative moves. Especially good on the impulse to "thematize."

MacDonald, Susan Peck. *Professional Academic Writing in the Humanities and Social Sciences.* Carbondale: Southern Illinois UP, 1994.

Winner of the College Composition and Communication Book Award, this is an incisive empirical comparison of scholarly discourse in literary studies with writing in other fields.

Mailloux, Steven. *Reception Histories.* Ithaca: Cornell UP, 1998.

———. *Rhetorical Power.* Ithaca: Cornell UP, 1989.

Two books by a theorist dedicated to showing how both literature and literary criticism function rhetorically.

Sosnoski, James J. *Modern Skeletons in Postmodern Closets: A Cultural Studies Alternative.* Charlottesville: U of Virginia P, 1995.

Identifies impasses created by current forms of argument in literary criticism. Recommends that the field practice a more communal discourse.

Sullivan, Patricia A. "Writing in the Graduate Curriculum: Literary Criticism and Composition." *Journal of Advanced Composition* 11 (1991): 283–99.

An empirical study of graduate students attempting to practice the rhetoric of literary studies. One of relatively few works on this subject.

Tompkins, Jane. "Fighting Words: Unlearning to Write the Critical Essay." *Georgia Review* 42 (1988): 585–90. Rpt. in *West of Everything*. New York: Oxford UP, 1992. 227–33.

Drawing on personal experience, Tompkins calls for more civil argument in literary criticism.

Turner, Mark. *Reading Minds: The Study of English in the Age of Cognitive Science*. Princeton: Princeton UP, 1991.

Advocating "cognitive rhetoric," this book focuses on metaphor as a way of linking literature and other discourse to human beings' everyday acts of perception.

Veeser, H. Aram, ed. *Confessions of the Critics*. New York: Routledge, 1996.

A collection of essays examining the recent turn to autobiographical criticism in literary studies.

Relating Literary Theory and/or Pedagogy to the Teaching of Writing

Atkins, G. Douglas, and Michael Johnson, eds. *Writing and Reading Differently: Deconstruction and the Teaching of Composition and Literature*. Lawrence: UP of Kansas, 1985.

A bit dated in its enthusiasm for deconstruction, this anthology still presents many useful suggestions for connecting literary theory to the teaching of writing.

Berlin, James. *Rhetorics, Poetics, and Cultures*. Urbana, IL: National Council of Teachers of English, 1996.

This posthumously published book is a thoughtful overview of how the three terms in the title have historically been related. Suggests many ways of making composition classes sensitive to the social and historical contexts of literature and other discourse.

Berlin, James, and Michael A. Vivion, eds. *Cultural Studies in the English Classroom*. Portsmouth, NH: Boynton/Cook, 1992.

Contains several essays that integrate literary study, writing instruction, and cultural studies.

Bleich, David. *Know and Tell: A Writing Pedagogy of Disclosure, Genre, and Membership*. Portsmouth, NH: Boynton/Cook, 1998.

The latest book by a veteran theorist of writing and literature offers numerous examples of how to combine the two subjects.

Booth, Wayne. *The Vocation of a Teacher: Rhetorical Occasions, 1967–1988*. Chicago: U of Chicago P, 1989.

Collection of essays by a highly influential advocate of combining literary study with instruction in writing and rhetoric.

Cahalan, James M., and David B. Downing, eds. *Practicing Theory in Introductory College Literature Courses*. Urbana, IL: National Council of Teachers of English, 1991.

Many essays in this collection include interesting writing assignments about literature.

Donahue, Patricia A., and Ellen Quandahl, eds. *Reclaiming Pedagogy: The Rhetoric of the Classroom*. Carbondale: Southern Illinois UP, 1989.

Includes several essays that merge literary theory with composition theory.

Horner, Winifred Bryan, ed. *Composition and Literature: Bridging the Gap*. Chicago: U of Chicago P, 1983.

Though published in the early 1980s, this is still a useful anthology of essays on ways to overcome the institutional divide between composition and literature. Many of the contributors are leading scholars in both fields.

McCormick, Kathleen. *The Culture of Reading and the Teaching of English*. Manchester, Eng.: Manchester UP, 1994.

Insightful recommendations for teaching students how to read literature critically and explore its various cultural dimensions through their own writing.

McQuade, Donald. "Composition and Literary Studies." In *Redrawing the Boundaries: The Transformation of English and American Literary Studies*. Ed. Stephen Greenblatt and Giles Gunn. New York: Modern Language Association, 1992.

Incisive overview of the relations between composition and literary studies in English departments.

Miller, Susan. "What Does It Mean to Be Able to Write? The Question of Writing in the Discourses of Literature and Composition." *College English* 45 (1983): 219–35.

Provides a model for analyzing both the production and reception of texts, including student writing as well as published literature.

Pope, Rob. *Textual Intervention: Critical and Creative Strategies for Literary Studies*. New York: Routledge, 1995.

Delightful presentation of assignments that help students learn about literature by encouraging them to write extensions and alternative versions of particular texts.

Scholes, Robert. *Textual Power: Literary Theory and the Teaching of English*. New Haven, CT: Yale UP, 1985.

This now-classic book on the roles of composition and literary studies in English departments calls for such departments to affirm writing instruction more and proposes a useful way of analyzing literary texts.

Young, Art, and Toby Fulwiler, eds. *When Writing Teachers Teach Literature: Bringing Writing to Reading*. Portsmouth, NH: Boynton/Cook, 1995.

A collection that constantly emphasizes the integration of literature and composition.

You may also be interested in four of our own books:

Clifford, John, ed. *The Experience of Reading*. Portsmouth, NH: Boynton/Cook, 1990.

Clifford, John, and John Schilb, eds. *Writing Theory and Critical Theory*. New York: Modern Language Association, 1994.

Harkin, Patricia, and John Schilb, eds. *Contending with Words: Composition and Rhetoric in a Postmodern Age*. New York: Modern Language Association, 1991.

Schilb, John. *Between the Lines: Relating Composition Theory and Literary Theory*. Portsmouth, NH: Boynton/Cook, 1996.

PART TWO

Literature and Its Issues

| 12 |

Living in Families (p. 315)

MEMORIES OF FAMILY (p. 317)

BELL HOOKS

Inspired Eccentricity (p. 317)

In this piece of autobiographical nonfiction, bell hooks provides an example of the genre at its best. She describes characters, her grandparents Sarah and Gus Oldham, who are three-dimensional and unexpected. And although she interprets their recurring behaviors in the most loving and respectful light, she shows their weaknesses as well. As her title states, they are inspirations to her, but they are not icons. They are, as she tells us, eccentric — different. The author takes pride in their reversal of the conventional roles men and women are expected to take in their community. Her grandfather, seen as passive and henpecked by adult family members and neighbors, is "calm and gentle" in a way that nurtures the child and inspires her to become a writer and a pacifist. Her grandmother seems mannish to those around her, speaks her mind, and carves out her own space. The illiterate, older woman's verbal virtuosity feeds the writer as well; her independence makes possible "bell hooks," the bold feminist who chooses to write her name — borrowed from this grandmother's mother — in an eccentric way and to "talk back" to a culture that has long made it difficult for women of color to find voices of power. Hooks emphasizes that it is not one or the other of these grandparents who have shaped her own identity but the two together, a combination that she says burns as hot as the black coals in their fireplace.

While the author traces individual lessons she learned from family members, her interpretations of their influence are seen from the perspective of an adult who teases out the strands of her own personality, based on values that she

25

holds important. Adults do not always teach what they think they are teaching, even those who consciously consider such things. But bell hooks writes an autobiography here, examining her values and priorities and searching out possible sources, laying out a narrative line — or perhaps the branching narrative lines of a family tree. She knows she seems eccentric to most people, and she likes it that way. She barely touches on her "painful childhood" in this excerpt from her autobiography, but she does mention often being punished. The reader may suspect she was punished for the very traits that she now sees as her strengths, character traits that she may still be trying to justify by writing about them. Like the quilts that her grandmother made, hooks's autobiography is skillfully pieced together in vibrant detail to create something of use and beauty. Students will find many details that contribute to the dominant impression she seeks to project. Perceptive readers will also question the author's views of her grandparents, asking whether the perceptions of the townspeople might have some validity as well. In the writer's attempt to explain her own outspoken individuality, critical readers may discover tensions within the text as well as in the family it describes.

BRENT STAPLES

The Runaway Son (p. 323)

When writing about the life of an individual and the family influences that have shaped that person, the writer must choose what to include and what to leave out. Brent Staples builds his autobiographical narrative around family patterns of loss and separation that continue to haunt him, selecting the family experiences that, taken together, may explain rather complex feelings. The irony implied in the title and opening paragraph of this autobiographical narrative may eventually surface for students who stick with it to the end. Others will wonder when he will finally get to the point and may complain that he seems to veer from his stated thesis. Often Staples does seem to be rambling, and the reader wonders when he will finally reveal the pivotal event that explains his attitude toward innocently wandering children and their distracted mothers. Perhaps he means to contrast this image with the legacy of runaway sons, runaway fathers, and the profound loss of childhood that were a part of his family history. As his narrative ends, the writer has escaped into education and is accused of running away from his family, perhaps from who he is. Many readers will recognize, however, that the true experience of being a son has run away from *him*, as it had from his father before him. Furthermore, since the writer himself is not the only son who runs away in this narrative, issues may be raised about the implications of the title. Who does run away in this story? What causes the narrator's childhood to be lost?

By framing his essay as he does, Staples gives adult perspective and meaning to an appallingly difficult childhood. Without this adult voice, the overwhelming impression would be of a cycle of abandonment and near-neglect in which children are forced into responsibilities that rob them of the security of childhood. Themes might focus on poverty and dysfunctional families. The issues of race and class arise from the beginning images of women and children who are explicitly white and prosperous, who are encountered at beaches and museums and near the doctor's office where the narrator goes for a yearly check-up. Staples implicitly lets us know that he frequents such places, can afford to go to the doctor even when he isn't sick, and is recognized as an equal by the mother whose child he "rescues." His descriptions of childhood come as a shock after this. His scenes are vivid with sensory details that recall long walks to the outhouse alone, mornings building fires, and his sister's burned body. His last paragraph includes another sister's accusation that he has abandoned his own people. Since his fantasies of rescue center on the children of privilege rather than ten-year-olds like himself, questions could be raised about his choice to escape the cycle of loss by shirking the responsibility to rescue those who truly need his help. Must he do this for his own protection? Is he an Uncle Tom?

Because Brent Staples and bell hooks share racial, class, and regional backgrounds and were born a year apart, it would be interesting to look at their differences in terms of gender. Given the complexity of families, the argument could be made that too many variables exist, that their experiences were not the same, and that conclusions made on this basis would not be valid. It may be argued, however, that gender is significant for the writers: Staples identifies his gender in his title, and hooks makes much of being a loud woman seeking the genesis of this character trait. If the child in Staples's essay had been a daughter forced to take over the household in the absence of parents, her story might recall the trials of Cinderella. Would the female Staples, lacking hooks's nurturing grandparents, have hoped for a prince to rescue her rather than turning to education? Would a male bell hooks still feel the need to find the familial source of his independent streak?

As students speculate about the changes the writers would make in their childhood experiences, some might argue that difficulties may be what gave these people the strength to become who they are and that they would change little. Both writers acknowledge the importance of grandparents, however, and this may be where we would look for changes if the writers could exchange childhoods. Staples implies that if his father had drawn the education-oriented grandfather as foster father, his character and his family's future might have been much different. And although she celebrates her grandparents' eccentricity, hooks may have allowed her grandmother an education and her grandfather a wider respect. Because the writers acknowledge the complexity of self-image and family influence, students may be able to justify several answers to the question of their attitudes. Overall, hooks seems defiantly proud of who she is but may attribute her character too much to inheritance. Staples seems even more defensive and more ambivalent about his family, even as he acknowledges the power of the past.

N. SCOTT MOMADAY

The Way to Rainy Mountain (p. 331)

This essay has an interesting publishing history, having appeared first as a magazine article and then as the word of a character in a novel, as the introduction to the writer's autobiography, and as a frequently anthologized essay in college writing textbooks. Many students have read it in high school. The essay is highly organized, though students often complain that it lacks focus because it is not a linear, chronological narrative. The narrator begins and ends at Rainy Mountain in the summertime and moves through time and space, interweaving history, myth, and family experience as he goes. Family is central to his story because Momaday journeys into the history of his father's tribe, the Kiowa, and because he uses his grandmother to tie together the diverse strands of the story. The result is coherent, intricate, and uniquely Native American.

By seeing through his grandmother's eyes, Momaday personalizes the historical events, and his vivid sensory images also bring readers into the story, giving a sense of movement down mountainsides and visions of religious ceremonies no one has seen for years. He causes us to feel the heat and to hear his grandmother's voice in prayer. We may recognize that it is an illusion that we can truly see as we think another might see, especially when separated by experience to this extent, but the attempt can open the mind to alternative ways of defining the universe, and Momaday's concrete and specific language keeps us from moving too far away from the senses. Some distances are hard to bridge: few students have seen a heated anvil, and some need help thinking through the word *deicide*, though the symbolism and cultural ramifications quickly arise as discussion proceeds. Words work as important cohesive devises in this essay, with repetitions and parallel constructions linking ideas together in a way that approaches poetry. In addition, the writer uses his grandmother to bridge gaps that he could not close on his own; he can take her back to childhood to view historical events or have her recount a myth.

By blending genres he makes us see that these ways of seeing overlap and intertwine, especially in families and especially in this specific culture. Furthermore, he refuses to privilege one sort of text over another: folklore and history are equally legitimate or indeterminate. He evokes Aho as a person, especially in his observations of her at prayer, and yet although his reverence for her extends to a reverence for the heritage she represents, Momaday still observes Aho as an outsider. Some may argue that he romanticizes Kiowa values or that assimilation has been so intrusive that we have no way of really reading Kiowa values, much less going back to any of them. In his penultimate paragraph, Momaday hints that this may be so. His metaphors speak of death, and he notices how small his grandmother's house now seems.

LOREN EISELEY

The Running Man (p. 335)

Like Brent Staples in the similarly titled "The Runaway Son," Loren Eiseley gives what at first may seem a rambling account of childhood events in "The Running Man," and both essays share the situation in our anthology of being pulled out of the context of longer autobiographies. The bewildering reference to the "Colorado cabin" in the opening sentence, for example, makes more sense when we realize that Eiseley had been confined there during an illness, and the reading is further enriched when we discover that the author has left home as a young (running) man and stolen rides on trains as a hobo. The incident in the abandoned house gains resonance when we come to know that Eiseley was the child of his father's second marriage and that he has a half-brother fourteen years older who is a stranger to him. Although his family may be more eccentric than most, students may relate to his need to escape into the outdoor world and to flee the parent who seems so odd in comparison to others. It has been said that one of the tasks of growing up is to accept the fact that one's family and upbringing are unique: we all are peculiar and isolated in some way. Students will easily recall times when their parents were an embarrassment to be escaped, such as when the taunt "I hear your mother calling you" was a challenge to the emerging sense of self. Class discussions will provide many examples of this common life experience.

When introducing Eiseley to undergraduate students, instructors may want to read excerpts from *All the Strange Hours*, from which this essay is taken, or from other books that capture the essence of his writings about the place of human beings in the universe of nature, like *The Immense Journey* (1948) or *The Star Thrower* (1978). Readers who enjoy Henry David Thoreau or Annie Dillard will respond to passages that find the naturalist Eiseley locked in eye-to-eye contact with a baby fox, dancing with frogs, speculating on the language of dolphins, or exploring fossil-laden limestone caves. Like many writers in this genre, Eiseley raises questions not only in geology, biology, and paleontology but also in philosophy, religion, psychology, and sociology. Coming to paleontology relatively late, as a graduate student, Eiseley first wrote for publication as a poet. His first published poem, however, is about a spider and owes much to his childhood interest in nature. Much of his prose, with its vivid sensory imagery and deep symbolism, reads like poetry. It is not surprising, therefore, to find Eiseley saying, as he explores humankind's isolation from other communicating animals in his essay "The Long Loneliness," that writing is our great strength and our great source of alienation from nature. "Man without writing cannot long retain his history in his head," Eiseley explains. "His intelligence permits him to grasp some kind of succession of generations; but without writing, the tale of the past rapidly degenerates into fumbling myth and fable. . . . Only the poet who writes speaks his message across the millennia to other hearts. Only in writing can the cry on Golgotha still be heard in the minds of men." While the issues raised by such linking of nature, autobiography, and religion in this quotation are complex, they are common to the genre of nature writing.

Such issues also link the writing and philosophy of Eiseley to that of W. H. Auden, who figures as a catalyst for Eiseley's thinking in "The Running Man" and who wrote an introduction to an edition of Eiseley's *The Star Thrower,* the book in which "The Long Loneliness" appears. Auden was an important English poet who worked in the early to mid-twentieth century and whose poetry has been widely anthologized and posted on the Internet. His poem "In Praise of Limestone (May 1948)" undoubtedly moved and influenced Eiseley and works well in an introductory literature classroom when read intertextually with Eiseley's autobiography.

Eiseley himself provides some autobiographical, geographical, and historical context as he takes his time answering Auden's question about what public event he first recalls. His inductive organization of the essay also forces the reader to think about issues of public versus private experiences. Searching for a public event analogous to Auden's childhood memory of the 1912 sinking of the *Titanic*, Eiseley at first seems to fumble as he recalls the first "running man" of the essay, the escaped convict — an event that qualifies as public because it would have been recounted in newspapers and discussed by the adults in the community. Readers are given many private memories along the way, and by the time we are told of the writer's own uncomfortably public yet private experience of becoming a running man himself, we have a clearer idea of its significance. And because we hear early in the essay of his mother's own intermittent running away to various jobs during his Nebraska childhood, the essay acquires unity by the end, in spite of its "indirection" as the discourse in the middle seems to ramble aimlessly.

Context is critical because Eiseley comes across as odd, and readers need to work to find commonalities with him. While most children have ignored the call of a parent, most have never run away and been chased by a witchlike mother as their friends gawked. The immensity of the Nebraska fields adds to a sense of isolation and provides space for running as other places may not. Many students will recall a large park or playground, beach, or series of backyards as they bring up memories of the outdoor adventures of childhood. They can understand Eiseley more fully if they see a wider landscape. Because many of this excerpt's details are taken outside of their context in the autobiography *All the Strange Hours*, they may confuse readers. In fact, we often ask students to focus their essays on a central main idea and avoid the sort of "wandering" that is displayed in Eiseley's essay. Even so, we might encourage skilled but formula-bound writers to experiment with less linear styles in which they link ideas in a thematic fashion.

The real focus may involve the intertwining of Eisley's memories and guilt about his achievement of autonomy at the expense of his mother and their ultimate linking of him to her. While this may not seem at first to be a typical "American narrative," it has affinities with much literature of the American West in which the isolated individual, especially the "American man," must forge his own way outside of community. Eiseley, as an academic and a writer of literary prose, may not be the expected "rugged individualist" of the mainstream American narrative, but his very oddness alienates him from family and community in a way that is particularly American. His specific act of running in shame from his mother thus takes on symbolic significance. As all of us must do, he breaks the parental bond to gain a separate identity. This happens over time and even into adulthood. Indeed, Eiseley said at one point that he was fifty years old when his youth ended. And his obsession with his mother and with the failure of love that she represented for him continued throughout his life. Perhaps his telling of the story eases his isolation at the same time it marks his separate identity.

Taken together, all of the essays in this cluster show facets of the American story. Two of the authors, bell hooks and Brent Staples, are African American, and yet their autobiographical narratives are set in different regions. Staples captures the working-class North, and his narrative is claustrophobic in its depictions of city streets and indoor scenes of children taking care of each other. The South of his father's childhood seems similarly closed in. These men must run away to escape families that are as hard to live with as Eiseley describes his as being. Hooks grew up in the South in a different sort of American community, a segregated one in which everyone minded their neighbors' business and ostracized nonconformists. Yet both hooks and Staples, whether embracing family or escaping it, are proud of their "inspired eccentricity" and the ability to gain strength and individuality from embarrassing relatives and difficult experiences. N. Scott Momaday, on the other hand, writes from the less individualistic Native American tradition. Nevertheless, he finds himself in his search for connection with a broader history and extended tribal family in a landscape in which his grandmother's house stands in isolation in a scene in which "there is no confusion of objects in the eye, but *one* hill or *one* tree or *one* man" (emphasis his). Certainly all of these texts deal with isolation and the centrality of the individual "self" alone in his or her odd particularity, an important theme in American literature.

This individuality is something that Americans both admire and seek to hide. The last lines of Eiseley's essay bring out this point. We separate ourselves from the family culture in order to "belong" to the wider culture — one in which a real man cannot be ruled by a witch mother or perhaps by any woman. And to admit this intertwined failure and success at breaking the bond is somehow "savage" but necessary for Eiseley. Perhaps to write is to isolate oneself fully, to belong neither to culture nor to nature, as Eiseley suggests in "The Long Loneliness." Like running from one's mother, writing both breaks and binds, and the knowledge of this can be a motivating, perhaps a compelling, force for writing. Perhaps because his setting is the American West, Loren Eiseley's tone seems more closely connected to that of Momaday than to the evocations of family and neighborhood of the Staples and hooks essays. Although hooks describes a grandmother as difficult as Eiseley's mother, her tone is loving and admiring, while Eiseley still seems to wrestle with bitterness and guilt. Staples is more rejecting of family than hooks and more closely resembles Eiseley in his conviction that one must sometimes run away from family in order to survive the dysfunction and pain.

Reconciling with Fathers (p. 343)

LUCILLE CLIFTON

forgiving my father (p. 344)

Lucille Clifton's extended analogy between paying one's bills and seeking emotional resolution between father and daughter begins with the language of blunt earnestness. The speaker has been thinking hard. She has come to a conclusion. After many years of delay, it's time for a resolution. Although both her parents are dead, Clifton's speaker focuses on the continuing emotional tug of unresolved pain and disappointment. Both the speaker and her mother had tried to get emotional nurture from the father, but, as she notes, he had never been capable of such commitment. He was too needy himself to give to others, a trait that apparently ran in his family. In the analogy, the father never had emotional reserves to give but was instead an "empty pocket" to the women who hoped for more. In the last stanza of the poem, the speaker suggests that she is trying to be rid of the exhausting blame game. She realizes that he can give her noth-ing, then or now. In a kind of neutral reconciliation with herself, she will have nothing more to do with his memory. Neither parent can supply emotional resti-tution or ultimately satisfy her. Her epiphany that her desires are futile leads to as much "forgiving" as she is capable of giving her father.

The answer to Lucille Clifton's question in line 21 — "what am I doing here collecting?" — seems to be "wasting my time," since the last two lines strongly suggest that no emotional support is forthcoming: no money, no "pay-day." The speaker seems to suggest that we should face reality, that her father was incapable of giving more than he had, which wasn't much. Her realization that there will be "no accounting" suggests that no matter how she tries to ration-alize the situation, it's over. But one could make the case that this poem is a way of settling the emotional tension once and for all. The poet is imaginative in sus-taining the analogy from start to finish. Students could be asked to suggest other financial terms she could have used, such as *interest, hoarding,* or *stealing.* They might also be asked to supply connotations for "old dead man" as a way of understanding the poet's attitude. The main contradiction arises as she asks a dead man to pay up, to give what is no longer possible. It is finally resolved by claiming that both parents are "in debtor's boxes," without the resources to pay anyone anything. Some students may see her acceptance of this fact as the way she finally forgives her father, whereas others may argue that forgiving is more problematic, perhaps even closer to forgetting.

ROBERT HAYDEN

Those Winter Sundays (p. 345)

If we assume that the speaker of Robert Hayden's poem "Those Winter Sundays" is the author himself (or a 1920s contemporary), we find ourselves in a Sunday morning atmosphere that may seem alien to students' recent child-hood experiences. Students accustomed to central heating may not at first rec-ognize the deprivation and effort implied in making "banked fires blaze" in a wood- or coal-burning stove, furnace, or fireplace to make the day's activities possible in a drafty house in Buffalo, New York. Hayden makes it clear from the first line that it is a *daily* sacrifice that the father makes: "Sundays *too* my father got up early," the speaker says (emphasis added). There is a priestly, almost god-like, quality to the everyday "offices" that the adult speaker, looking back, can view with awe, though the child of the past cannot. The word *offices* here has connotations of religious service, and we are meant to see not only the impli-cations of the title but also other ways in which the father's labors are sacra-mental. The speaker does not invite us to be overly idealistic or sentimental, however; we are given both the freshly polished shoes and the "chronic angers of that house," both the physical pain of daily labor and the archetypal wonder of creating fire.

The realization that the father is keeping his family alive ("breaking" the cold) — through his Sunday fire making but more important through his work throughout the week — is echoed in the last lines of the poem. Repetition of the phrase "what did I know" makes the last sentence more a lament than a question. An answer would consider the difference in perspective that comes with adulthood: an acceptance of ambivalence perhaps or an awareness that experiences may be interpreted without necessarily assigning blame or assuming guilt. The ambiguities and gaps in the text leave readers room to interpret the poem in the light of their own family dynamics; the working-class nature of the poem's setting provides a context that might add depth to discussion. Images in the poem, such as the repetition of synonyms for *breaking*, gain significance in the context of hard times. The poem's tone suggests personal regret, coupled with the evocation of a specific historical and socioeconomic setting beyond the child's understanding or control.

Although Robert Hayden and Lucille Clifton, both African Americans, describe similar situations in terms of social class, Clifton's tone is less forgiving — some might say more realistic — at least on the surface. Whereas Hayden conveys images of coldness, hints at conflicts he does not reveal, and cloaks the father's labor in heroic significance, Clifton hotly calls names and explodes with anger at her father's "needy" heritage. Clifton addresses her father directly and berates him openly for his failures; Hayden seems to explain his seemingly unloving father to others, placing the shortcomings on himself. Switching to third-person pronouns might have lessened Clifton's accusatory tone but would have robbed her poem of its power. If Hayden addressed his father directly, the poem might edge into sentimentality but would certainly lose the subtle sense of love communicated not by words but by inarticulate actions, actions we need to see. In the rhetorical questions asked in the poems, both poets seem to realize the futility of settling accounts completely with their fathers. Each might answer with the resolve to make some sense of it and then let go.

THEODORE ROETHKE

My Papa's Waltz (p. 346)

The images in "My Papa's Waltz" contrast to each other in ways that defy a simplistic reading. Students who would sentimentalize the relationship must deal with the undercurrent of danger implied by the connotations of the words *whiskey*, *battered*, *beat*, and even *death*. The household is brought into chaos, and the mother clearly disapproves. Yet those who jump to conclusions of child abuse — a frequent reaction among students — must account for a verb like *romped* and for the child's holding onto his father rather than struggling to get away. In fact, it is the child who holds on "like death" — an ironic simile — and the father whose hands show signs of injury and wear, perhaps a reversal of what might be expected of an abuser. Still, those who argue that the father is an abuser could say that it is the knuckle that is battered. Are these the scars of a man who works hard, or has he been injured by striking something — or someone — with his fist? No, the poem is characterized by playfulness, the sentimentalist could respond. The title refers to the father lovingly as "My Papa," and the regular rhythm and rhyme have a dancelike quality. Father and son participate together in the dance, while the mother — not, we may note, *mama* — stands aside, unwilling to "countenance" such behavior. The formal word used to describe her face invites the connotations of stern disapproval while neatly providing the rhyme. The sense of male solidarity in the rough and dangerous play that excludes the woman may be a subtext worthy of discussion.

With its contrasting imagery of play and danger, the poem expresses both fondness and bitterness, both fear and affection. Such a text invites an issues-based approach. Word choices would strengthen the argument for fond remembrance and affection: If *romped* became *fought*, the meaning would be unambiguously violent; if *waltz* were changed to *dance*, a specific word with romantic and civilized connotations would become a generality allowing less safe, more carnivalistic interpretations — a war dance, perhaps, or the disorder of a whirling dervish. But the poem invites readers to remain open to a more complex reading and may provide an opportunity for teachers to assure students that it's okay to change our views as we write about a text or discuss it with others.

If Roethke had called his poem "forgiving my father," much of the ambiguity and complexity would have been lost. Lucille Clifton can use the word *forgiving* because her tone sounds angry and unforgiving: the use of the word therefore contributes a needed irony to her poem. Both Roethke and Robert Hayden are less open, however; both hint at mixed feelings, intertwining fear and love throughout their poems. Although it may be going too far to say that they miss their fathers, their poems are nostalgic. The three poems express complex feelings about the fathers they describe, but Roethke's speaker reveals the least about what he really thinks, leaving it for the reader to respond to the experience he shows.

SHIRLEY GEOK-LIN LIM

Father from Asia (p. 347)

For most of us, becoming adults involves a movement away from the family and culture of childhood, a questioning of the ideologies and common sense of our parents. We must distance ourselves at some point in order to grow. Yet the feelings involved are complex, a mixture of anger, loss, and guilt, a tangled knot of emotions. Shirley Geok-lin Lim expresses such feelings, which are compounded by the realities of a separation East and West that is equally complex. The first image of the poem, the father's hands as empty bowls, evokes images for an American reader of the empty bowls in television commercials for Third World charitable causes. We want to reach out and help. Yet for the speaker, the need is an emptiness that will eat her up. As the poem proceeds, the rejection of the father by the daughter, of the homeland by the emigrant, is searingly painful. Can she really mean she has learned nothing from him, that such profound distance must be maintained? In succeeding lines, she speaks of her father and/or Asia as a "ghost / who eats his own children" and "who loved his children." Does parental love devour? Imperial China, with a reasoning more like ours than we like to admit, saw itself as the "center of the world," as Lim points out. To move away from our own ethnocentrism may be painful, but the poet implies that going back would be to enter into a cycle that destroys.

The narrator's heritage haunts her, even though she renounces it as one might renounce a false god. Her use of hyperbole, screaming that she will not be held by her heritage, shows its power over her. Her attempts to escape the past lead only to vivid images of pain. Perhaps she writes to shock her audience into deromanticizing Asia, perhaps she writes so that we will protest that she is wrong, or perhaps she writes only to express the intensity of the inevitable loss of culture that comes with change. The repetition of the image of dust in the last line implies a grinding down that repeats itself like some inevitable karma, a renunciation that goes on forever without redemption. This image, like those throughout the poem, expresses the antithesis of life and growth.

If Lucille Clifton's speaker looks at the grave of her father and angrily finds it futile to expect him to give to her, Lim's takes her anger a giant step further and flees across "two oceans" to escape the father whose poverty demands so much of her. Clifton's father is an empty pocket, Hayden's tries without thanks to keep out the cold, and Roethke's spins him dangerously off to bed; Lim's father is emptier, more sacrificial, and more dangerous than any of these. He is a frightening abstraction, and forgiving does not seem to enter into her thinking at all. The easy answer would be that her attitude is the least healthy of the four, but taken figuratively, the impulse to free ourselves from the past — or at least to recognize its power over who we are — is worthy of consideration.

EXORCISING THE DEAD: CRITICAL COMMENTARIES ON SYLVIA PLATH'S "DADDY" (p. 349)

SYLVIA PLATH

Daddy (p. 350)

Often the voice in a poem is quite different from the poet's own, and students need to go beyond the tendency of novice readers to see all poetry as an emotional outpouring of the poet's soul. The poems of Sylvia Plath, however, invite a biographical approach. As a confessional poet, writing as part of a 1950s and early 1960s attempt to bring the life of the poet into the text, Plath incorporated images of her personal psychological struggles into her poetry. For this reason, her poetry might first be approached in the context of the post–World War II society in which she came of age, when the Holocaust and other abuses carried out by fascist movements were within recent memory. Before the cultural changes of the late 1960s, including the resurgence of the women's movement, the expectations placed on most daughters were rigidly prescribed. Fathers tended to be authoritarian, and husbands to control the lives of their wives and children. Thus contextualizing the poem may help current readers understand the tone and imagery of "Daddy" and allow them to respond thoughtfully to the alternative views of critics.

Like the speaker in Lucille Clifton's poem "forgiving my father," Plath's persona angrily rails at a dead man who has left the business of fatherhood unfinished. His early death has made it impossible for her to challenge her father's power over her self-image through his approval, disapproval, or indifference. She has therefore been unable to function as an adult. Because he is absent, she feels, she has replicated the father/daughter relationship in her marriage. If she is to break out of the victim position, she must kill the inner father who has caused her to be self-destructive.

Because her own father was of German ancestry, Plath metaphorically portrays the father in the poem as a Nazi and the daughter as a Jew, appropriating the imagery of brutality and war for her own personal purposes. This bothers many readers. Other similes seem extreme as well: He is a "black shoe . . . a bag full of God . . . a devil." But images of his replacement, perhaps her husband, seem even more severe, and students may want to discuss the extent to which she is really angry with her father or with someone else. Although Plath claimed that the poem was not her own story, she wrote it on the day her divorce papers arrived. Could blaming her father actually be her way of masochistically blaming herself for the difficulties of her marriage, of remaining a victim who tortures herself with guilt? The poem's assertion that "Every woman adores a Fascist" recalls the I-must-have-asked-for-it thinking of abuse victims.

The childish language of the poem may trivialize it for some; it is interesting that even the bits of German she chooses to interweave are one-syllable words a child would learn. If Plath is describing her inability to escape a role she acquired in childhood, however, the juxtaposition of baby talk and brutality makes sense. The poem seems less about the rebelliousness of young adults and more about the ways in which we may continue to play out the dramas of childhood. Plath seems to refer to her earlier attempt at suicide in the poem, and she would kill herself by sticking her head into a gas oven a few months later, an interestingly symbolic act when considered in terms of her Holocaust imagery here. That she would leave her young children to deal with a loss similar to the one she laments in the poem seems ironic but may simply reflect a deeply held belief that the loss of a mother could not possibly be as important as the loss of "Daddy."

Critical Commentaries:

MARY LYNN BROE, From *Protean Poetic:*
The Poetry of Sylvia Plath (p. 353)
LYNDA K. BUNDTZEN, From *Plath's Incarnations* (p. 356)
STEVEN GOULD AXELROD, From *Sylvia Plath: The Wound*
and the Cure of Words (p. 357)
TIM KENDALL, From *Sylvia Plath: A Critical Study* (p. 362)

Before reading the critical interpretations of Sylvia Plath's poem, students may need to brainstorm their own ways of seeing it as more than the autobiographical ranting of a middle-class woman unable to come to terms with her neuroses. Because the father's body seems to lie across the American continent, is this young woman living in England protesting that her home country is as fascist as the Third Reich? Does the final scene of villagers dancing remind us of carnival with its implications of overturning authority? What images and words are repeated, and what could this symbolize? Students might look back at the list of issues on the front inside cover for additional questions they could raise about Plath's text.

Mary Lynn Broe sees the speaker of the poem as an actor playing out a scene of exorcism that doesn't quite work. Broe calls the poem "self-parody," implying that Plath is laughing at herself and inviting the reader to see the irony between the intensity and incantation of the speaker's words and the paltry results of her actions. Lynda K. Bundtzen, on the other hand, while also seeing the speaker as a dramatic persona, uses quotations from Plath to argue that the poem is "a figurative drama about mourning" that describes feelings the poet has already conquered. She is no longer a comic victim, but a victor. Steven Gould Axelrod goes beyond the other critics to say that the poem is about woman as writer, its imagery metaphorically describing the poet's attempts to find her voice in a world of words dominated by men. Tim Kendall, on the other hand, uses Plath's words from her journals and other sources to posit that the poet repetitively acts out her victim role with herself as psychoanalyst as much as writer. He points out that while she plays the Freudian games of transference and *fort-da* (peek-a-boo), the ambiguity of the poem's last line leaves unanswered the question of whether she succeeds in escaping through her self-therapy. An important factor in our interpretation of Plath's poem involves how closely Plath the victim and Plath the powerful, "aloof" psychotherapist correspond to each other.

Readers will have different ideas about which critic best answers the poem's perplexing questions, though teachers steeped in literary theory may feel that Axelrod opens up issues of feminism, patriarchy, and the literary canon that give the poem's angry tone a broader context. Axelrod's movement beyond the specifics of the poet's family life differs strikingly from the more limited interpretations of Broe and Bundtzen, but the critics agree that "Daddy" is a staged representation rather than an autobiographical confession of the emotional turmoil of Sylvia Plath herself. Tim Kendall, however, links Plath's performance more closely to autobiography, and many students, while they balk at accepting Freudian explanations, will find his discussion of the poet's persona more closely fulfilling their desire to see the poet and the speaker as the same person.

MOTHERS AND DAUGHTERS (p. 367)

TILLIE OLSEN

I Stand Here Ironing (p. 367)

Readers tend to have strong reactions to texts by Tillie Olsen. Many feel that she challenges class- and gender-based societal barriers, whereas others see her as simply making excuses for failures to overcome them. In her nonfiction book *Silences*, published in 1978, Olsen supports her assertion that both men and women of the working class were long denied political, intellectual, and literary voices by the realities of labor and survival. Olsen was in fact instrumental in bringing texts written by women back into print and into the literary canons of universities during the 1970s and beyond. "I Stand Here Ironing" blends fiction, dramatic monologue, and autobiography. Many of the details of the story echo details of Olsen's early life as a working mother during the 1930s and 1940s.

Today's college students, living with many of the benefits brought about by social movements propelled by Olsen's generation, sometimes have trouble understanding the narrator's situation. In one memorable presentation in an introduction-to-literature class, a student saw Emily as retarded and the narrator as obsessive-compulsive, as evidenced by the fact that she is ironing! A show of hands revealed that several students had never seen their mothers iron. Ironing as a metaphor for oppressive but necessary work may therefore be an elusive concept for young readers. An equally simplistic reading sentimentalizes the characters as victims of poverty, reducing them to cardboard cutouts.

The ambiguity of the ending's optimism or pessimism suggests that the issues are more complex than they appear on the surface. The narrator despairs at ever being able to explain why her daughter needs help, but she holds out hope that the girl will find her own way if she is empowered by self-knowledge. A critique of social conditions is implicit in the text, while the narrator explicitly sorts out her failings as a mother. She may be trying to forgive herself, and this issue — of where personal responsibility ends and societal responsibility begins — may be the major theme of her story. Students could explore other perspectives by acting out an imagined conference among the characters mentioned in the story, perhaps even bringing Emily's father, stepfather and grandparents into the mix. Reactions to the first-person voice of the narrator vary, with some students sensing an effort to impose a narrative line on fragmented memories and others dismissing the narrator as a whiner. The narrator may resist a conference with the teacher because she wants to avoid blame, but she seems primarily to resist an intrusive and profitless discussion that would oversimplify complex issues. She also hints that the power for change is not in the mother but in the daughter herself.

AMY TAN

Two Kinds (p. 373)

After Amy Tan discovered that her mother had been forced to leave three living daughters in China, rather than the dead twins that play a climactic part in "Two Kinds", she had fears that her mother would drop her for the "good" China daughters. These fears compounded the already difficult relationship that lends realism to the stories of *The Joy Luck Club*, from which this story is taken. A trip to China with her mother helped Tan place these fears into perspective, however, when she found that her mother was just as critical of her half-sisters, dashing their dreams of the nurturing mother they had fantasized about having. For Tan, writing her mother's stories has become both a way of finding her own voice as a writer and a way of coming to terms with her painful resistance to the older woman's controlling personality. Learning to forgive herself for being the wrong kind of daughter, the disobedient kind, has been a major task for Amy Tan. She says, however, that learning to forgive herself has helped her to forgive her mother as well.

Because the cultural differences between the mother who came of age in China and the daughter born in America are so obvious, the writer admits that the cultural and generational differences are difficult to sort out. These factors and her mother's great personal losses intensify their struggles. Asian American young people maintain that the cultural expectations of their parents still cause similar difficulties in some families, and non-Asian students may recognize their own families in the story as well. Americans who travel to other countries, Tan included, realize that social mobility is more possible here, but we cannot say that race, gender, and other differences do not matter. Perhaps the little Chinese girl can be a prodigy, but she cannot be Shirley Temple. The argument does not settle the matter for either character. The mother is wounded deeply but still cannot accept her daughter as she is; the narrator becomes the wrong kind of daughter but discovers the power of her own will. We know less about the mother's feelings since we see and hear her through the eyes of the daughter, whose thoughts we are allowed to share. Dialogue and descriptions of body language bring the mother to life, as do anecdotes of her failed attempts to create a "prodigy" of her daughter. The characters are dynamic but remain locked in their struggle with each other.

The mothers in the stories by Amy Tan and Tillie Olsen provide a sharp contrast between oppressive control and frantic neglect. Olsen's narrator wishes for her daughter to be empowered and to find her own way. The mother of Tan's narrator seeks to empower her daughter by directing her life, and does not see the irony in this attempt. Both mothers unintentionally reject their children, but love and want good things for them. Because the stories are told from different points of view, it's hard to say which daughter has the more difficult life. We know more of the pain of Tan's narrator, but we know that she grows up to be successful and that she wins the battle for selfhood. We are less sure about Olsen's Emily. It may be that living with an overpowering mother is more intense but less painful than living without one.

ALICE WALKER

Everyday Use (p. 382)

One of the major themes of Alice Walker's short story "Everyday Use" is the indeterminacy of history and identity, especially for African Americans. Walker's characters raise issues about what constitutes a family's heritage. As autobiographers must, we all identify the major events in our lives and the characters representing our ancestry by choosing those that fit into the narrative line we have chosen for our story. We look back at the poem we wrote in third grade and interpret this as a signpost along the road to the career in English studies, foreshadowing the budding literary giant we hope to become. Since we didn't become Michael Jordan, we omit the hours perfecting the free throw on the basketball court, or we reinterpret them as evidence of perseverance. We choose our ancestors as well, literary or otherwise. Alex Haley finds the West African *griot* and the courageous Kunta Kinte as he explores his *Roots* and writes the text that becomes a culture-changing miniseries on television. Never mind that some of the details are borrowed; this narrative explains Alex Haley to Alex Haley.

As we approach Alice Walker's story, we might ask students to tell about ancestors — genetic or chosen — that they claim as their own. Alice Walker picks fiction writer and folklorist Zora Neale Hurston, a Harlem Renaissance literary figure who gave voice to the African American storytellers of the rural South. But she also searches out the strengths of her mother and other remarkable, everyday women of Minnie Tallulah Grant Walker's generation — and earlier generations — who paved the way for the independent African American woman who strides through today's world. These are the women who worked in the homes and took care of the children of white families or labored on farms to battle for the education and equality — and survival — of their own children. Most of the students coming into our college classrooms today know these women, if they see them at all, as elderly neighbors and grandmothers, and their struggle seems far away.

Like the mother in "Everyday Use," many women of Alice Walker's mother's generation found ways to send one or two promising children away to college. As often happens in working-class families, regardless of race, the hard-bought education sometimes separates the young person from people back home, and what was intended to uplift may lead to conflict and isolation. In her poem "For My Sister Molly Who in the Fifties" (in *Revolutionary Petunias* [New York: Harcourt Brace Jovanovich, 1973]), Walker describes the gradual move of a college student away from her roots. From reading stories to her family and trying to make changes in the household, the sister moved on to

> Another life   With gentlefolk
> Far less trusting
> And moved and moved and changed
> Her name
> And sounded precise
> When she spoke   And frowned away
> Our sloppishness (18)

African American students born in the 1980s feel far removed from the afros, the daishikis, and the earnest quest for black pride of their parents' 1960s and 1970s youth and glimpse images from the period perhaps in the stereotypes of television reruns. Ironically, though "Everyday Use" could be taught until recently as a contemporary view of conflicting values about history, today's students need a historical context to understand the characters in Walker's story and the issues of concern to them, including the trendy Dee/Wangero, who now seems dated to many readers.

Although we are meant to see Dee and her male companion as pretentious and ironically humorous, Alice Walker's treatment of them in 1973 was not applauded by all African Americans. She was questioning blind political correctness before the term was invented, and there was a risk involved in holding black pseudo-intellectuals up for ridicule. What was to stop white Americans from interpreting her text to mean that a person of color is ridiculous unless he or she remains in poverty and ignorance? In this context, we should raise the issue of audience and purpose. This is not a text written to explain black folks to the white reading public but a text about cultural issues within the African American community. Readers who are not African American can also be cruel to family members, however, and thus miss much of value in their own heritage. The story thus has universal applications. We may also benefit from the reminder that there is no one monolithic "African American community."

Most readers will agree that Walker visualizes an audience that needs to be reminded that family and community values are not to be discarded simply because one acquires an education. There is history that we read in books, and this is good. As a writer and speaker, Walker has shown that she knows this sort of history. She has lived in Africa, and the topics of her writing are international. In her imaginative fiction she has traveled as far back in African history as one can go, which means she has traveled as far back in human history as one can go. But there is a history that is not found in books or formal archaeological and anthropological studies, and this sort of history is good, too. This is oral history, the true if not always factual history of folklore, the material history that can be touched in a handmade quilt or churn or bench, and the living history of parents and grandparents.

While a valid argument could thus be made that Dee, in her newly awakened consciousness about African American history, has more in common with the writer Alice Walker than the stay-at-home Maggie ever could have, Walker makes Maggie the more sympathetic character. Walker calls on us to feel compassion for Maggie from the second paragraph, in which Mama, the narrator, indicates than Maggie has been burned and that she is in humble awe of her sister. Because the narrator clearly has more tender feelings for the damaged sister, we more readily accept her "everyday use" of items of material culture over the museum curator's impulse that would take them out of context. Maggie is a part of folk culture while Dee is a romantic — disconnected — collector. Mama is hostile to Dee because she recognizes the rejection and coldness behind Dee's motives.

Dee seeks her roots because this activity is in style, and she is more concerned with style than substance. She thus misses her chance to see the more immediate history that her mother could pass on to her because hypocrisy and arrogance blind her to its value. Most college readers can understand Dee and would probably feel more comfortable having coffee with her than with the formidable narrator and her pathetic daughter Maggie. We'd be more likely to hang the quilt on the wall than to put it to everyday use. Looking at a portrait of Alice Walker, we *know* she would not join them in a dip of snuff. But we can imagine her sitting in a nearby rocking chair, really listening and learning.

Rather than opposing "getting back to one's roots," Walker seeks to open the eyes of educated African Americans like herself to the emptiness of doing this in isolation from the living people in one's family and the immediate ancestors whose memories they preserve. Walker's characterizations of Maggie and Dee therefore border on the symbolic two-dimensional traits of allegorical figures. Her characterization of Maggie seems more balanced than that of Dee. While Maggie is portrayed as a sympathetic character who carries on the traditions and remembers family members as real people, we see her limitations. If she is Cinderella, her Prince Charming has "mossy teeth," and she carries on the tradition of dipping snuff, details not likely to reassure us that the quilts will be preserved in her hands. Walker paints Dee with an even broader brush, however, allowing us to see only the pretentious arrogance and superficiality that Mama finds so distressing. We do not know what she is thinking as a child when she watches with concentration as the house burns or why she has so desperately tried to educate the people around her as an adolescent. Mama puts a negative connotation on these actions, but they could be interpreted as love and concern. She might have portrayed Dee as an insecure person searching for her identity, and Mama might have found a way to force Dee to listen to the oral history that gives the objects meaning beyond their value as folk art. A less positive view of Dee might have painted her actions as even more deliberate than they seem in the narrative as it now stands. Dee seems uncomprehending rather than deliberately evil. Like white liberals who exhibit unconscious prejudice while thinking they are free from any taint of racism, Dee shows by her attitude toward her mother and sister that she does not truly value her African American culture.

The problem with Dee is that she comes to take, not to share in her true heritage. She gives the distant kiss on the brow instead of the full embrace. She grasps and insists and belittles. Her self-esteem depends on pretense, and she must protect herself from her true history and identity. Like many African Americans and others who acquired names reminiscent of slavery or colonial domination, Dee has chosen a new name. This can be a positive act, an assertion of independence from a constant reminder of oppression and stolen identity. But Walker seems critical of Dee's choice to do this. Perhaps she opposes the superficial, imitative, faddish quality behind the decision for some people.

For Dee, the impulse differs on the surface from slavish assimilation into white society, but underneath lies a similar falseness and fear. Dee and her friend *pass* for political thinkers who celebrate their African roots, but they *bypass* the living family heritage. Walker has the narrator remind us how much is owed to the hard-working people who lived and created in between the romanticized African ancestor and the beautiful, educated woman of the late twentieth century. Their names deserve to be continued and put to everyday use. But the newly christened Wangero denies this honor to the Dees in her ancestry. Students interested in exploring the social and historical issues raised by the discussion of Alice Walker's texts might turn to other texts in our anthology that deal with similar issues. They might compare Dee with Beneatha Younger in Lorraine Hansberry's *A Raisin in the Sun* (p. 226); compare the place of the quilt in bell hooks's "Inspired Eccentricity" (p. 317); or compare generational conflicts in texts by Nikki Giovanni (p. 485), and writers in the "Living in Families" chapter. We can have them research contemporary African American and Caribbean writers to determine how many have chosen new names and what reasons they give for the change.

The conflict in values between Maggie's and Dee's joint desire for the quilts raises the definition of culture. Dee represents "high culture" and art. To people who see culture in this way, Maggie and the narrator are uncultured. The work of family members is not art but craft and is desirable because it is quaint and currently in vogue among sophisticated people. Maggie, however, knows how to make quilts. She values them because they are links to people she has known and valued, her grandmother and her aunt. She uses the education they have given her to create new ones. She is willing to give them up because she has the memory without needing a material reminder. She knows the stories behind each object because she has paid attention. The creators are not anonymous to her. Her mother remembers the hands that have worn the marks on the churn.

The narrator does not share the story of the blue piece of cloth from the Civil War uniform or the knowledge that Dee's name goes "back through the branches" much farther than the younger woman realizes. Dee has cut herself off from the family tree and chosen other ancestors. She devalues Maggie's keen memory, saying that her "brain is like an elephant's." Their difference highlights the difference between recorded history (fixed in writing or displayed on museum walls) and oral history and folklore (worn and constantly changing with everyday use). It is easy at this point to see these views of history as being in conflict, and the narrator must choose between their competing values. But the question is complex.

We may look back to "In Search of Our Mothers' Gardens" (p. 163) in which Walker describes being inspired by an exhibit in the Smithsonian Museum, a quilt created by an anonymous black woman. Obviously, if the quilt had not been hung on a wall, Walker would not have experienced it. In "Everyday Use" Walker has her narrator choose the way of human love and compassion, choose to value the one who needs uplifting rather than the one who unwittingly takes on the role of spoiler and oppressor. To Dee the quilt is an object, just as the man who accompanies Dee looks at the narrator as an object, "like somebody inspecting a Model A car" — and just as their ancestors were objects to slave traders and slave holders.

The symbolism of the quilt now seems important to Dee, standing (as we have seen in "In Search of Our Mothers' Gardens") for the art of working women. The irony, of course, lies in our recognition that she values the working people who have created the artifacts but not the working women in front of her face. The symbolism of the quilt could be expanded to stand for America itself. The cliché of the melting pot does not capture the reality of an American culture that is not homogeneous but made up of separate subcultures that retain their identities. Like a quilt, the colorful scraps are sewn together but form one functional whole. While this image of diversity is striking, however, we should recall that it comes close to Booker T. Washington's metaphor in his Atlanta Exposition Address in 1895 in which he argued that blacks and whites should remain separate but equal, like the fingers on a hand, one in social responsibility but segregated in all other ways. W.E.B. Dubois strongly disagreed, arguing for full integration and equality of opportunity. Students may think of metaphors that more closely capture the fluidity and overlapping of subcultures within American society, perhaps coming up with organic examples or examples from computer technology. The issue of whether affirming ethnic differences helps or hinders the American fabric is a complex one. While emphasizing genetic and so-called racial differences, accepted as essential categories that cannot be changed, can lead to dangerous social results (as it did in Nazi Germany), a recognition of the different historical and cultural experiences of ethnic groups can enhance understanding and add to the richness of all our lives. Seen in microcosm, America is a culture made up of diverse families, a fact to which any newly married couple — even though they come from similar ethnic groups —

can attest as they negotiate holiday traditions and details like who keeps the checkbook and which way to hang the toilet paper. We reject some family values and fight for others.

At one point in the story, the educated daughter proclaims of her former identity as Dee, "She is dead." For her, culture and family history are reduced to lifeless commodities, things that can *belong* to her but are no longer filled with the memory of life that gives them value to Maggie and the narrator. Dee has been influenced by her education and by the political movements of the time, as represented by the farming collective that operates in the neighborhood, one of many efforts to organize people and to better economic conditions in the South. Her friend makes it clear that he is not involved in this sort of active labor. The implication is that he wears the trappings of black pride but doesn't allow the philosophy to sink in to the extent of helping others or breaking a sweat. Dee seems to be influenced by him. But she has always been concerned with whether or not something was in style, had even refused the quilts as "old-fashioned" when she left for college.

Few readers would suggest that Dee should be like her mother and sister; what she needs most is to learn to respect them and to find out who they are and what they know and value. This is not easy. Walker has given them qualities that have figured in racist stereotypes and have been used in some African American groups to sort by social class. The narrator and Maggie are dark-skinned. Numerous people of color have spoken of the "paper bag rule" or the "blue vein society" that kept women out of debutante balls and social clubs if their skin was a shade darker than the bag or too dark to see the vein on the inside of the wrist. The beauty criteria of white society thus continued to oppress and influence class even in social arenas where no whites were involved. Dee, on the other hand, is a golden girl — light-skinned, intelligent, strong-willed. The mother anticipates her visit as if she were a famous movie star, even fantasizing about a television meeting in which she herself becomes miraculously lighter-skinned and less heavy.

Her weight also contrasts with Dee's trimness, which reaches even to her "neat" ankles and feet. The narrator is so heavy she has difficulty moving. This makes her look like the stereotype of "Mammy" in *Gone with the Wind*, a Bertha-type housemaid and cook, or an Aunt Jemima. We learn that she works like a man. She is the image of the black woman as the "mule of the world" who shoulders all the burdens and takes all the abuse. We can admire and respect her strength while we understand that Dee would not want such a difficult life for herself, nor would we, nor — we can assume — would Alice Walker.

While mothers often side with daughters with whom they are more politically or culturally sympathetic, the reverse sometimes happens, as well. Working class mothers are often less forceful than the Mama of this story and would not have been able to stand up to a daughter like Dee. If the values of the dominant culture had been internalized by Dee's Mama (as they may have been by Dee before she encountered people proud of their African heritage), she may have despised herself and her daughter Maggie. There are elements of this indicated in the early scenes of Walker's narrative in which Mama imagines herself to be lighter skinned, less heavy, and quick with the repartee of television talk shows. The narrator of the story would be intellectually capable of identifying with

Dee, but she chooses the traditional values of her family, one of which seems to be compassion for the underdog. Basic human kindness seems to be lacking in Dee, and this is what finally causes Mama to side with the daughter who needs her. Although most mothers try to be equally supportive of each of their children, children seldom see it this way. Quite often, parents favor the successful child. Others, however, spend an inordinate amount of time with the child whose needs seem most compelling, often to the detriment of other, seemingly more independent, children in the family.

We feel compassion for Maggie. She may remind readers of Celie in Walker's novel *The Color Purple* in her shyness and the extent of her pain. Her life is limited not only by her burns but by her future with the husband with "mossy teeth in an earnest face." Students sometimes ask if Dee has set the fire that burns down the hated house and damages her sister. The story does not reveal this, and there is no sign that the narrator suspects such a thing, but we notice that Dee is absorbed in her own thoughts rather than the injury to her sister even then. She seems more self-absorbed than evil, and this seems to be the message that Walker sends to those who have escaped unscathed, perhaps including herself. Open your eyes and ears. Respect those who have endured labor and pain. By making Maggie a burn victim, Walker insists that we feel compassion for her rather than seeing her as backward or stupid. Some readers see the story as an allegory of the conflict in values between intellectuals and the working class that makes their success possible. Others argue that it is about shaping an identity for oneself as changes take place in society and fooling oneself by donning trendy masks rather than dealing with real issues. It has been interpreted as a reversal of the parable of the Prodigal Son. Other critics interpret the narrator's attitude toward Dee as idolatry that she comes to see as false. We can focus our reading on the character of Maggie and empowering her mother achieves by supporting her.

Most readers will take the story seriously, though they recognize the humor and irony. Certainly there is nothing funny about the image of Maggie's arms sticking to her mother or about the rejection the other women feel from Dee. But we laugh when the narrator humorously refuses to understand the name of the man who comes with Dee. She first pretends that she confuses his name with the greeting — meaning *Peace be with you* — that she has heard used by people at the collective farm; then she mispronounces his Muslim name to sound like he's a barber. This makes him look ridiculous, as does Dee's African greeting, which we know she does simply to show off. The characters are exaggerated, and the hyperbole makes us smile. On the other hand, hints of a real political situation are understated. The narrator has gone out of her way to see the farmers guarding the collective with rifles after whites poison their cattle. This contrasts with Dee and her companion, who play-act at fighting oppression while others do the work. The narrator seems justified in her evaluation of Dee's world as characterized by lies and make-believe. She speaks of Dee's reading to everyone as if it were a punishment. It is as if she reads *at* them rather than *to* them, using reading as a weapon. But don't we value reading and make-believe? Do we agree with the definition of fiction as *lies*? We may be left with the question of how far Alice Walker may have reeled us in with an unreliable narrator and convinced us to accept her value judgments as correct.

It is always difficult to predict how a child will respond to different styles of parenting. The mother in Tillie Olsen's "I Stand Here Ironing" blames her poverty as a single mother for the emotional neglect of her child, but the mother in Alice Walker's "Everyday Use" is also poor and seems to be on her own as a parent. Both mothers lack a true bond with their eldest daughters, however, and try to puzzle out the reasons why. The mother in Olsen's story sees her daughter Emily as "homely" during the long years she has not been close to her, though she thought she was a beautiful baby and recognizes her "now-loveliness" as a young adult. Her monologue paints a picture of a child suffering from the low self-esteem that stems from always feeling inadequate and unwanted in her mother's life, despite the older woman's guilt-driven rationalizations. Dee's mother, on the other hand, has always seen Dee as beautiful, though she is bewildered and frustrated by Dee's strong-minded bossiness. Dee has been allowed to rule the family. Emily has not been a full member of her family.

In spite of these differences, both are outsiders. Had Dee been brought up by unloving surrogates rather than her mother and had her teachers failed to recognize her abilities, she may have become more bitter and vindictive, but she may have been less self-absorbed and demanding. Olsen's narrator ends by blaming society, saying that Emily has been "a child of her age, of depression, of war, of fear." Dee, growing up a generation later, benefits from her own turbulent age and is shaped by the civil rights movement and the subsequent black power and black arts movements. As a gifted African American woman, Dee would have found few avenues for her talents in the early twentieth century and would have found herself frustrated and angry, trapped in a society that offered little help for people of color or of the working class. Ironically, it is her success that separates Dee from her mother, while Emily's life has been characterized by failure.

If Dee had been the elder sister of Amy Tan's "Two Kinds," her alienation from the family would have been even more profound. The older sisters in this story have died in China, but Tan's real half-sisters had been left behind. If Dee were brought up like the protagonist of Tan's narrative, her behavior might have been much the same, since both girls have an independent spirit and reject the values of their mothers. Dee, without the pressure to become a prodigy, actually becomes one, but this is not what her mother seems to want.

Taken together, the three narratives of this cluster demonstrate three different responses to a generational conflict in values. Emily seems to have bad luck, suffering illness that only complicates the division between mother and daughter. After a lifetime of unintentional rejection, she seems to be coming into her own, choosing the life that suits her, rejecting the academic world that tries to supply pat answers to complex issues. Emily, like Dee, could come to reject her mother's values, but the story's ending indicates that perhaps she will not, that her mother approves of Emily's independent action and does not want a passive daughter. And Emily's wry comment about her mother's constant ironing hints at an understanding of the reasons her mother has neglected her and an acceptance that this is just the way her mother is, a woman constantly working. One could see her comedy, however, as a way of turning pain into art. Although Dee could be seen as doing something similar by hanging quilts on the wall, she fails to recognize the pain of her sister. Emily's motives seem to run deeper. The

daughter in Amy Tan's story seems closer to Dee, and perhaps the major difference in our evaluations of the two exist in the point of view of the stories.
Because we hear Tan's story from the daughter's perspective, readers may have
more empathy for her than we do for Dee. Looking from the outside, we might
see the pleasure of the daughter in Tan's story when her mother gives her the
piano as similar to the nostalgia Dee seeks to gain from the artifacts of her childhood home. But unlike Emily, who does not get enough from her mother, and
Dee, who overachieves to please herself, Amy Tan's protagonist feels that she is
mothered too much and reacts by refusing to give her mother what she wants,
effectively rejecting the older woman to maintain her own identity. If the child
is Tan herself and the narrative a veiled autobiography, one could argue that her
attitude is quite similar to Dee's attitude in terms of art, since Tan takes her culture and turns it into art. She differs, however, in that she allows us to see her
own shortcomings and in her adult understanding of her mother's actions. Her
use of her ethnic heritage in art does not objectify but shows respect, even when
describing her complex feelings about her family.

Of the daughters in the stories, readers will find Dee the least kind. The
daughters in the stories by Tan and Olsen seem less cruel. Most readers will find
Tan's narrator the kindest in the end, since we know her thoughts and see that
in the long run she cares about her mother while insisting on her own autonomy. Dee's sister Maggie seems perhaps to be the kindest character in the stories,
but her willingness to completely efface herself and her needs in favor of her sister stems from an attitude of worthlessness, and it could be argued that one must
have a certain amount of power for kindness to be meaningful.

Dee may be the smartest daughter if we use academic ability as a measur-
ing rod, but she is blind to the deeper significance of the objects she seeks to col-
lect and to the value of the people of her childhood. She may not be as smart as
she thinks she is. The daughters of the other stories, on the other hand, may be
smarter than they think. The narrator of Amy Tan's story reveals depth and critical thinking that supersedes the trendy knowledge that Dee demonstrates.
Emily, too, may reveal self-knowledge by choosing acting over academics. She
may be brilliant, but school has hampered rather than enhanced her potential.
Dee is arguably the most ambitious of the daughters in these narratives. All seek
to be the person they define themselves to be, however, rather than conforming
to their mothers' ambitions for them.

A case could be made that each daughter is troubled, and certainly the
mother-daughter relationships are not bringing any of them self-esteem. Emily
may seem to be in the most danger of having a troubled life, but she is the
youngest when we encounter her. Amy Tan's character is a good candidate for
least troubled because we observe her working out her rejection of her mother.
Dee does not seem capable at this point of doing this, and she continues to reject
her mother, thus rejecting a part of herself. Because she has suffered so much
rejection, Emily may have the hardest time succeeding in life and in love, since
we often tend to replicate our childhood experiences in love relationships. Tan's
character should bring the same sort of self-examination and insight into other
relationships, but no one will own her, and she may see domination where it is
not intended. Dee seems to have found a partner as pretentious and superficial
as herself. She may succeed on the surface but keep flitting to the next trend and

the next man, respecting what she reads but never quite seeing the reality around her. While the mothers must take responsibility for their actions toward their children and how they turn out, most readers will agree that adult sons and daughters need to reevaluate the attitudes they have developed from childhood perceptions and take responsibility for their own responses to parental actions.

SIBLINGS IN CONFLICT (p. 390)

TOBIAS WOLFF

The Rich Brother (p. 391)

As this story ends, the older brother imagines the voice of his wife calling him to account for his brother. "Where is your brother?" is a question of biblical proportions, and the circumstances here recall at least two similar stories. After killing his brother and thus committing the first murder, the eldest son of Adam and Eve is asked this question by God, and he (Cain) answers, "Am I my brother's keeper?" Much later, Jesus describes two brothers in the parable of the prodigal son. In the parable, the younger son wastes his inheritance in riotous living, and the conforming elder brother is furious when the slacker is welcomed home with ceremony. In Wolff's story, the elder brother seems to accept that he must be his brother's keeper in spite of its injustice. Ironically, the younger brother's prodigality is too Christian for the Christians, and his riotous living is generous and naive to the point of holy idiocy. Still, a bit of doubt remains for Pete that the prodigal may be rewarded with the fatted calf after all. "What a joke if there really was a blessing to be had, and the blessing didn't come to the one who deserved it, the one who did all the work, but to the other." The title begs the question of which brother is the rich one. Pete has all the trappings of prosperity, but Donald is the one who gives everything away, the one who acts with largesse, the one who invests.

The language Wolff uses to describe Pete identifies him as the typical, money-grubbing bourgeois salesman, a literary character we have learned to view with contempt. Donald is the dreamy romantic that we expect to have unexpected wisdom. The hitchhiking Webster seems sinister and even Satanic at first, identifying the darkness as "Stygian," and we expect some terrible thing to happen. Later, when Pete hears a twig snap in the woods as he leaves his brother on the road, we wonder if the terrible thing will now take place. Webster's story of Peru smacks of the formula of romantic adventure, and we agree with Pete that it is not credible. But we view it all from Pete's point of view, and we can't be sure what has happened. Like Pete, we expect the ironic ending, a true climax to the story, but we're left in the middle of the road. Rather than give stock answers based on our past reading of fiction, we might respond by questioning the formulas we have come to expect. Pete and Donald do not fit the stereotypes of fiction when examined closely. Pete, the practical brother, appreciates the mystical experience of skydiving, whereas Donald, the spiritual searcher, questions its cost. There is a mixture of mutual dependency and rivalry between the brothers that surfaces as they sleep or pretend to sleep, as children or adults. The young Pete strikes the young Donald, who turns a blind eye; the adult Pete dreams his brother guides him in his blindness; Pete sleeps while a mysterious contract is made between Donald and Webster. And the reader is left in the dark to fill in the gaps where the issues may really lie.

JAMES BALDWIN
Sonny's Blues (p. 404)

Like the protagonist of Tobias Wolff's "The Rich Brother," the elder brother in "Sonny's Blues" must deal with the question of being his brother's keeper. And although the story stands on its own as a narrative about family relationships, the phrase takes on metaphorical significance in its African American context. Brothers, in James Baldwin's Harlem, must be there for each other but can sometimes only stand and watch. The story begins as the schoolteacher protagonist's younger brother has gone to prison for using heroin. He tells us that his students remind him of his brother, and we walk down a Harlem street with his brother's friend. In a flashback, his mother reveals in their last conversation that his father had seen his own brother maliciously killed by white people in a car that was speeding down a road like an uncontrollable force. We see inside bars and look out the window at gospel meetings where participants call each other brother and sister. Other flashbacks reveal class conflicts within the extended family, and dialogue often carries the story line and the debate between brothers. Baldwin both shows and tells a parable about letting one's brother be who he must be, within both the family and the community.

The story belongs to the elder brother at the beginning, and we continue to see through his eyes. We get to know Sonny better as the brothers' dialogue proceeds, however, and by the end the story belongs to him, as the title has indicated all along. Both brothers are dynamic characters, and we see them struggle — less with each other than with forces beyond their control, the "darkness outside." Their dying mother places the responsibility for Sonny on the older brother, but he is forced by World War II to shift this responsibility to his wife's family, and Sonny must reckon with the judgment of the middle class and deal with his brother's expectations without his presence. In this case, to be one's brother's keeper may be to deny him the freedom to keep himself. At the end of the story, as Sonny plays his music, his brother is finally able to listen to him. This happens as he recognizes that the men playing the blues with Sonny function as a family tuned in to each other, as the real brothers have failed to be. Perhaps our sense of responsibility for our siblings limits our ability to see them as separate from ourselves.

Baldwin's characters come closer to understanding each other in the closing scene. They have talked throughout the story, but music and gesture communicate more in the end. Wolff's brothers are less articulate and less able to find real closure, though perhaps this is because we leave them at a different point in their relationship. Students might want to discuss popular psychology studies about birth order as they look at the conventional older brothers and their passionate siblings. It may be that parents, by making the older child somehow responsible for the younger, subtly suggest the roles that the children will play. Students will choose their own answers to the possible themes of these stories, even going beyond obvious family issues to social, political, or religious ones.

ART OR FAMILY?
RE-VISIONS OF *THE GLASS MENAGERIE* (p. 427)

TENNESSEE WILLIAMS

Portrait of a Girl in Glass (p. 429)

Tennessee Williams says at one point in this autobiographical story about his sister that she is not "foolish" but that "the petals of her mind had simply closed through fear." In fact, he has no way of knowing if Laura is retarded or not, since in the 1920s such a diagnosis would have been made only in the most extreme cases, most likely if a family member had become a behavior problem.

Because mental retardation was connected in the public mind with sexually transmitted diseases, with the "bad blood," or with genetic factors that were passed down as a result of incest, the social stigma of having a daughter or sister who was "foolish" would have justified denial. Perhaps this explains why Williams gives the corresponding sister character in *The Glass Menagerie* a more obvious physical disability.

People like Laura — who were limited but appeared to be innocent and shy — often did enter the community, learn to do simple jobs, marry, and have families. Laura's mother is desperate to provide for her, either by preparing her for an acceptable job or by finding a potential husband. While Williams paints his mother's domineering and unrealistic attempts at managing his sister's future as laughable and foolish in their own way, he has an escape — though he admits that he sometimes feels remorse for leaving. Readers might take issue with the interpretation of Laura as mentally slow, and students may choose instead to see her as Williams does — as filled with enclosed wisdom and too delicate and beautiful for this world, much like the figures in her glass collection.

While their mother seems to be trying to give her daughter roots and wings, the family that Williams describes seems more like a trap. Mother is concerned that Laura conform to society enough to take care of herself or to find someone to take care of her and not that she will have a fulfilling and happy life. The narrator himself works at a job he dislikes to contribute money to the family. Not until he is fired — for wasting work time and materials writing poetry — does he break away from the family to go out on his own. Both young adults are trapped in this story in a world that does not value them.

Laura, however, steals moments of freedom. She smiles when she is sick enough to be confined to bed and has permission to skip school. Laura's glass collection also represents an escape from a world whose demands she cannot face. The glass is fragile, like Laura, and catches the light in a beautiful way.

Like Laura, it serves no practical purpose but requires a great deal of care and is constantly under the threat of being broken by minor stresses. While the narrator is perhaps the only person able to appreciate Laura, he chooses not to sacrifice himself for her — spending his time in the dark, polishing bits of glass to no end.

The story of the vicious Chow dog who attacks the cats below Laura's window serves as an analogy for what would surely happen to Laura if she were forced into the world to fend for herself. The culture of Depression-era America in some ways required a ferocious quality in its survivors. Furthermore, the narrator's mention of the Chow hints at possible violence in Laura's early childhood. We have assumed that her innocence is congenital, but the narrator does not tell us much about the violence of the drunken father who has absconded. Because complex problems often have complex causes, we may not want to speculate excessively about child abuse, the parenting that these children have received has brought little comfort or joy.

When he speaks of bringing the "lamb-like Irishman" to meet his mother and sister, Williams implies that an animal is being led to a blood sacrifice. Because his mother is so eager to find a man for her daughter, the narrator sees her as ready for the kill. Jim, the guest, seems as innocent as Laura in his own way, and it takes a while for him to catch on that he has been invited as a gentleman suitor for Laura. Laura accepts him as part of a story, opening up because she sees him as the "Freckles" of the sentimental novel she has read and reread. But while her mother and brother stand in awe while she dances with Jim, Laura remains childlike and is unconcerned, probably unaware that a courtship has been imagined and then thwarted by the revelation that Jim has a girlfriend.

By having her read *Freckles*, Williams not only makes Laura's acceptance of Jim plausible, but he shows that she is intelligent enough to read and that she has chosen a reality to believe in, the reality of the sentimental novel in which conflicts are resolved and everyone turns out to be okay. Laura's question about the stars is presented as profoundly creative, but it is also the sort of question a child would ask. Laura can recall the letters on the typewriter keyboard at home but cannot apply the knowledge at school. Her mental status therefore remains ambiguous: she may be an idiot savant, or she may be profoundly intelligent but too emotionally fragile to be understood. Certainly, many bright students can recall the frustrations of learning to type, a skill one learns through practice, not through memorizing keyboards.

Perhaps Williams tells this story of his young adulthood to justify his leaving his family. It is hard to see how his remaining at a warehouse job would have helped his mother and sister in the long run. He may be trying to persuade us or himself that he made the right decision. More likely, however, he replays the trauma of leaving because he is still trying to figure it out himself. Williams identifies with his sister in that both of them seem unsuited for a culture that requires a person to think only of where the next meal is coming from. Laura with her collection of glass figures and her brother with his poems scratched on the tops of shoeboxes are both artists whose concerns make them misfits in a mundane, uncomprehending family and social milieu.

TENNESSEE WILLIAMS

The Glass Menagerie (p. 437)

Tennessee Williams has woven many autobiographical elements into his play *The Glass Menagerie*. The playwright had to interrupt his education to work in a shoe factory; his father, who belittled the son's artistic temperament, was a traveling salesman; his mother was a genteel southern lady; and his sister had a mental illness. Williams sees the question of autobiography in his play as problematic, however, as he shows by the poetic and philosophical comments woven into descriptions of the *dramatis personae* and stage directions as the play begins. He explains to us that we are to pity the mother and see her tenderness even as we laugh at her. He makes explicit the symbolic and metaphorical connection between Laura and her fragile collection of glass animals. He tells us that Tom will have to escape from this trap and that the gentleman caller we are to meet is just "a nice, ordinary young man." He goes on to give the reader the historical and cultural context for the play. But more importantly, Williams reminds us that memory is elusive and tricky and that the line between fiction and nonfiction unclear. He has Tom narrate, calling him "an undisguised convention of the play" and giving him lines that analyze the symbolism of various characters. By showing us the framework of the writing, from the beginning he presents the text as a literary object. As readers we may object, as Tom does when his mother tells him how to eat, and may challenge the playwright's analysis of his own text and his advice to us on how to take it.

By giving us the social context, Williams makes Amanda's desperation to find a husband for Laura seem less neurotic than we might otherwise judge it to be. Yes, she's obsessive, but she also has to worry about how to keep the lights turned on, and women don't have many financial options in this time period. We recognize Laura's emotional fragility and the symbolic nature of the glass menagerie and realize that, like the unicorn, the lightest touch will break her. Her giving of the unicorn to Jim seems more a giving up of hope and love; she has given herself to him in their dance, and there will not be another gentleman caller in her life. Perhaps this is a realistic view of a hyperbolic family. Visitors to the American South are sometimes shocked to find what they thought were the exaggerated eccentrics of fiction having histrionic conversations in the next booth at the breakfast house. Tom truly loves his sister, and she continues to haunt his thoughts after he leaves. That the writer grieves for his broken sister is documented and undoubted. Perhaps the play is for Rose and the final line echoes the words of Tennessee Williams himself. Like Tom, he must say good-bye. It is interesting that Jim at one point says to Laura, "If you were my sister. . . ." Outsiders sometimes can see what to do, while family members continue to spin in circles. Students, at a time when they are finding a place in the world outside of family, may have more to say about the need to break free of destructive, or simply familiar, family cycles.

Williams gives more social and political context in the play than he give in "Portrait of a Girl in Glass," (p. 429). In his detailed stage directions and in Tom's asides to the audience, he explains influences of the outside world. The setting in the play is grittier than that of the essay, even while being less realistic, as Williams points out. He speaks of "vast hivelike conglomerations of cellular living-units that flower as warty growths in overcrowded urban centers" and calls their inhabitants "fundementally enslaved." But the difficulties of the Depression of the 1930's are part of the plot, as well. Amanda, the mother, may seem to live in the glow of a Mississippi girlhood in which she had numerous gentlemen callers, but she uses her connections at the D.A.R. to make contacts so that she can eke out a living selling magazine subscriptions. The poetic Tom is trapped in a warehouse job and ends by escaping to the merchant marines. Laura logically should be trained for a job that women can do — secretarial work — or she must marry. Few choices are available to this family that finds itself in the working class in spite of the family's remembered affluence.

Besides implicitly showing us more fully the difficulties on the domestic front, Williams reminds us explicitly in the play that we are in the era of Fascist and Nazi takeovers that preceded World War II. He mentions the Spanish Civil War and the Fascist attack on Guernica, events passionately discussed by intellectuals of the time, many of whom traveled to Spain to help the resistance. Students need to do research or be provided with context for the time period so that they are able to grasp the frustrations and concerns of the times. Laura's fragility and Amanda's fluttery Southern belle charm compare startlingly with the imminent Rosie the Riveter. Their reality is being shattered like glass.

Besides the increase in social and political context clues, Williams made many changes when he adapted the autobiographical narrative "Portrait of a Girl in Glass" into the drama *The Glass Menagerie*, changes that affect the atmosphere of the play and our interpretations of the characters. One of the most striking changes is in the character of Laura. The vague and mentally limited young woman of the story is still painfully shy and different but is more articulate within the walls of the home. Her handicap is now a physical one but is still a forbidden topic: Mother does not allow Laura to be called "crippled." Although Laura is also crippled emotionally, she seems to be a sensitive, thinking human being subject to what we would now call panic attacks. When Laura meets "Freckles" in the story, it is as if a character in a book has come to life, but she accepts this and seems to have few expectations beyond the dance. She accepts his engagement with aplomb, explaining it to her upset mother in her own enigmatic way. When the Laura of the play meets again the love of her life, the high school hero she has built up in her mind, however, her disintegration is complete when her fantasy suddenly comes to life and just as suddenly is crushed. The Laura of the play is a touching character for whom we feel empathy. The Laura of the story is less compelling and tragic because we find her mysterious wisdom harder to grasp, just as the author does. The change at the end — from pieces of glass in the story to the snuffing out of a candle in the play — may have much to do with the visual nature of drama. Lighting has played a large part in the stage directions, and the darkness that comes from the candle's being blown out can be seen as symbolic. Quite simply, it may be easier to see. On the other hand, the symbolism of the glass menagerie and the broken unicorn have played their part at the drama's climax, when Laura realizes that Jim is lost to her.

GRANDPARENTS
AND LEGACIES (p. 485)

NIKKI GIOVANNI
Legacies (p. 485)

From her first recognition as a poetic and political voice of the black arts movement of the 1960s and 1970s to her current involvement with young people as a professor at Virginia Polytechnic Institute, Nikki Giovanni has celebrated and articulated her African American heritage. Rather than following the literary and cultural traditions of white America, Giovanni uses the rhythms and vocabulary of her family and neighborhood in both her message and in the way she delivers it. Like many black people of her generation, she seeks to recover and preserve a distinctive, powerful family and cultural history and to express it to her contemporaries and their children and grandchildren. Her grandmother, Louvenia Watson of Knoxville, Tennessee, is for the poet a tangible link with this heritage, and Nikki Giovanni — now grandmother age herself — serves as such a link to younger people. The poem expresses a strong sense of this continuity, going all the way back to West African customs and ways of being in the world. We therefore need to see beyond the everyday images of the poem to the longer chain of human experience they may symbolize.

In a similar way, the dialogue of the poem has surface meaning, but the granddaughter, at least from the poet's distance, hears instead something unspoken in the dialogue. Although she seems to reject it, the child holds the legacy too dear to spoil it with everyday use, is afraid — superstitiously or otherwise — to touch the gift that her grandmother wants to pass on to her. Folklore can be a way of doing something, such as making rolls. The child seems to be thinking of a more spiritual, mystical link. When the grandmother wipes her hands, she seems to give up on the idea that children will ever be able to grasp the legacy their elders want to give, but we know that the poet has recognized the motives of both generations. What is passed along cannot be articulated by either.

Pride is an important concept in the poem and in the ideology of the poet; being proud of one's heritage is her implicit message. The compressed, idiomatic language and conversational rhythms, although not formally structured, are nevertheless poetic and help prove her point that *this* way of writing poetry — this African American way — is just as legitimate as any other, is in fact part of the legacy. Linguists tell us that the surface meanings of words form only a part of the story of any given discourse. We might encourage students to think of times that they have spoken at cross-purposes with older family members, knowing but not acknowledging that what was said was simply a code for something of deeper significance.

WILLIAM CARLOS WILLIAMS

The Last Words of My English Grandmother (p. 486)

When the most American of poets makes a point of putting his *English* grandmother into the title of a poem, it's fair to question why. Actually, William Carlos Williams did have a paternal English grandmother, his father having been born in England and his mother in Puerto Rico. His parents immigrated to Rutherford, New Jersey, where the poet was born and spent most of his life. Williams takes the language and imagery of his poetry from the sounds and sights of this small town. Much of his poetry has a medical connection, since Williams was a pediatrician who made house calls and cared for people in the hospital. His methods are firmly based in theory, however, though less in literary theory than in that of the visual arts. Like many artists and writers of the early twentieth century, Williams was profoundly affected by the objective approaches to reality he saw in modernist paintings exhibited in the 1913 Armory Show. Like a nonrepresentational artist working with pigments, Williams sought to present words and images without commentary or narrative that would tell the audience how to interpret them. He maintained, furthermore, that rather than search for "poetic" material a poet should take his images from ordinary life and may write about anything that gives him amusement or that is deeply felt. In this poem, we catch a few glimpses of a dying grandmother, and though we are not told of it, an unsentimental but deeply felt compassion seems implicit in the poet's choice of images.

Growing old tends to strip away the need to be tentative and polite about one's needs. Readers will see the grandmother through the eyes of their own experiences, but she says, in what the speaker describes as a moment of clarity, that young people "don't know anything." Perhaps we will not really see what the doctor/poet is able to describe — her renunciation of everything but her own hunger and pain. The last lines of the poem indicate that she is past caring about the objects of the world. There is a profoundly physical nature to the concrete images of the poem — "the rank, disheveled bed"; the old woman snoring and complaining; the fuzziness of her vision — suggesting the reality of the body to one who is dying. Nothing outside of the body really matters. The text invites us to raise issues about a sick person's right to decide about medical care, the desire of the elderly to be cared for at home, and the ramifications of the euthanasia debate.

The grandmothers in this poem and in Nikki Giovanni's "Legacies" both state that young people are unable to understand their elders. Each poet, at least from the distance of adulthood, does understand, however. Each is able to communicate to the reader the crossed communications of an earlier time. It would be difficult to make a case for exchanging the situations or the grandmothers. Each poet makes a point of ethnicity. Yet readers who are not African American can imagine the child who wants to bypass homemaking skills for the memory of the grandmother who magically made rolls as no one else could. And people without English grandmothers can relate to the grandson's problems in Williams's poem. In our comparison of the women themselves and in our speculations about whether they might get along, we are hampered by the vast differences in their situations. At this point, Williams's grandmother is doing the work of death and would be oblivious to the woman of Giovanni's poem, who continues her work as the living center of a household.

ALBERTO RÍOS

Mi Abuelo (p. 488)

At the personal Web site of Alberto Ríos, information on the poem "Mi Abuelo" can be found in a section devoted to helping students with research. This is a testimony, perhaps, to Ríos's philosophy of education and his dedication to dialogue and to what he has termed the "language of listening." Accompanied by a picture of his grandfathers, Margarito Calderón Ríos, a broad-faced man with a bushy moustache who fought in the Mexican Revolution, Ríos has posted his reply to a student who asked for help with a presentation on the poem. This reply illuminates some of the poem's imagery and provides a bit of the poem's background. We find that "Mi Abuelo" is a companion poem to another sestina about Ríos's grandmother, "Nani." While Nani was an important figure in his early life, Ríos's grandfather died before he was born. But the poet felt connected to both grandparents and found ways to communicate with both of them.

Like Richard Rodriguez, who describes a similar experience in "Aria," Ríos recalls being punished for speaking Spanish at school, even on the playground. Speaking Spanish was a bad thing to do, and he lost his ability to speak his first language until relearning it (though he says it actually had not gone away) in high school and college. Since his Nani could not speak English, Ríos explains that he learned a language that used gestures and eyes as well as a language based on her nurturance: "she would cook, and I would eat." While Spanish is his first language, the early nonverbal language that he used in his interactions with his grandmother is a true first language that we all learn. It is "a language we can all claim together, or reclaim: it's the language of listening" and is not unlike "the language of art and science, of kissing and architecture." This goes beyond simply hearing the words that someone is using to express ideas and feelings: it includes "finding meaning" in both verbal and non-verbal dialogues.

Ríos is able to listen not only to the languages of food and kissing but to the whispers of his dead abuelo. As Ríos has explained in an interview, in his father's Mexican cultural heritage the border between the living and the dead is not as fixed as it is in his mother's English traditions. Growing up celebrating the Día de los Muertos (Day of the Dead,) Thanksgiving, and Memorial Day, he came to feel that the grandfather who had died before he was born was "part of every family gathering" and an important figure in his life. So he listens for his abuelo to speak to him from the grave and interprets his language for us.

Perhaps because as a historical personage high in the army of the Mexican revolution he is a powerful figure in family folklore, or perhaps simply because he is dead, the grandfather evokes ambivalent feelings in his grandson. Ríos knows how the man looks in a photograph on his grandmother's wall, which he says is sometimes the only scrap of reality he has about him. At this point, his abuelo would be literally a flat, two-dimensional character. But as he listens, the writer fleshes out the corpse and imagines him to speak mysterious things. Abuelo seems to be able to predict the future. But if he is wrong, this is a false prophecy: can the great man be wrong? More frightening than deliberate lies might be his seeming omniscience even though he lacks power and knowledge. If the ancestor figure is "at best . . . a liar," then perhaps he is at worst weak, mistaken, and self-deceived.

Another alternative to being a liar, of course, is to be a teller of truths. Some readers may feel that this is the worst-case scenario the speaker fears — that the vocalizations he hears from the grave are true, that his abuelo communicates something about reality. When the corpse says *my hair is a sieve* over and over again, the narrator is angry and shouts to the dead grandfather that he is not a sufficient ancestor, implying that he is not a whole man. The phrase may disturb him because it seems meaningless and yet is repeated. Does the dead man mean that everything sifts through into his head? That he knows all? He justifies himself with the strange statement that he "has served ants." Ríos explains that this line is autobiographical, that he remembers seeing an anthill on his abuelos's grave the first time he visited it as a child and wondering if the ants had gone into the grave and eaten his grandfather's body. The dead man confirms this.

The implications of this image, however — taken with the lines in which el abuelo speaks of hills as *"slowest waves"* and the speaker sees him as a "ripple-topped stream in its best suit, in the ground" — is that the man in the grave has become an integral part of the natural world. According to Ríos, this sense of being a part of the environment is embedded into the Spanish language, whereas in English we must often use the pronoun *I*, creating a sense of separateness from and responsibility for acting on the environment. So while the grandfather seems odd and crazy, his words may carry this sense of oneness with the earth.

The grandson discourses with his dead grandfather about the woman they both love — "his wife," who is the poet's Nani. He also relives the old man's childhood memories and his struggles to find home remedies rather than trust doctors: these imagined memories are based on stories passed down in the family. Those of us who did not know our grandparents share this frustrating imaginative task of sorting out the stories of their lives and our consequent heritage from bits and pieces. When the poet says that his grandfather "speaks through all the mouths in my house," he says something about how we learn about our ancestors through oral tradition and through the assumptions about reality that are passed down in families without our even being aware of them. The grandfather lives on through the voices of his family, whether or not they realize they are continuing to pass on his words.

Margarito Calderón Ríos is an imposing presence, even in death. This can be a positive notion. On the other hand, an important element of critical thinking involves bringing the unquestioned assumptions of family lore to light for examination. We can encourage student readers to become more aware of the influences of family and culture on their thinking, and to communicate with their ancestors and bring them into perspective. When the speaker of the poem says that his grandfather's "fever has cooled now," we may take this in an ironically literal way: a corpse is cold and can no longer experience passion. The statement may be taken to mean, however, that the grandfather's panicky repetition of the phrase *"my hair is a sieve"* can now be calmed as the poet acknowledges its truth — that everything sifts for all of us — and as the language of listening frees the ghost to rest in peace. The last lines may indicate that the poet wants to continue his dialogue with the dead man, since he says, "I look down the pipe, sometimes." On the other hand, when he looks down the pipe in the final lines, he leaves us a visual image rather than the auditory ones encountered earlier in the poem. Perhaps now that his grandfather is "an ordinary man" to him, he can communicate with him through vision — using something like the language of gesture and eyes he shared with his grandmother.

LINDA HOGAN

Heritage (p. 490)

As a Chickasaw, Linda Hogan has a heritage that is a mixed bag, and in this poem she hints at the multiracial history that complicates it. Originally from the Southeast, the Chickasaws were considered one of the "civilized tribes" and were known in the nineteenth century as slaveholders whose cruelty almost matched that of their white neighbors. At the same time, they sometimes welcomed runaway slaves, and both blacks and whites were known to marry into the nation, with children given full recognition. None of this prevented the government from seizing Chickasaw lands, however, or forcing the relocation that took the nation, including Hogan's ancestors, to Oklahoma. Later, when oil was discovered on new Chickasaw lands, white speculators often married Native American women to gain title to mineral rights, further victimizing their families. Hogan traces her blond coloring to such a marriage, explaining why she describes "white breasts that weigh down / my body" and why she calls her "whiteness a shame." Images of deathly white contrast with images of black and brown throughout the poem, with both oil and tobacco — important substances in Chickasaw history — recurring as ambiguous stains. The poem's last stanza recalls a history of dispossession, a heritage of ambiguity and confusion of self, a compass that points in two directions at once.

Homelessness seems to be a negative concept at first, but the last stanza raises questions. The grandmother says that "it is wise to eat the flesh of deer / so you will be swift and travel over many miles." This hints at a tradition that predates the "civilized" farming life of the nineteenth century and that sees the return to wandering as an ironic return to Chickasaw roots. Hogan uses her elder relatives to find both a personal heritage and a link to the larger history of Native America, a history that is largely one of loss. The black saliva spilling onto her from her grandmother's snuff can is a startling image, but it becomes "sweet black liquid like the food / she chewed up and spit into my father's mouth / when he was an infant." Anthropologists have speculated that the origin of kissing in human society may stem from mothers and grandmothers chewing up food for recently weaned children, and the concept may be touching if we can get past our knowledge of hygiene. Tobacco in Native American tradition is "medicine" to cleanse the body and "medicine" in a magical and religious sense. The image of being covered by night can be comforting. Still, much bitterness and justifiable anger emerge as Hogan looks at her "heritage." Like Hogan, readers who are honest will at least find ambiguities in their family histories.

Hogan's poem, like her family history, is complex. When oppressor and oppressed exist together in our bloodlines, how do we avoid the self-hate that Hogan seems to battle? Perhaps others deal with the conflict by choosing which ancestors to internalize. Nikki Giovanni, brought up in Ohio, didn't come to know her Tennessee grandmother well until she was a teenager, but she took the older woman as a symbol of strong, black womanhood. Like Linda Hogan, Alberto Ríos describes a family steeped in a mixed heritage. Ríos communicates with strong grandparents from the Spanish and indigenous peoples of southern Mexico in the poem we find here, but he acknowledges that he has celebrated holidays from his English heritage, as well. Like Hogan, Ríos sifts through thes multiple influences and seeks out the voices of his ancestors.William Carlos Williams doesn't bring up his Puerto Rican grandparents in the poem about his English grandmother. Hogan's poem, however, says as much about the ancestors she does not mention as those that she describes. She *becomes* the white ancestor who causes the sufferings of her family.

The last two stanzas of Hogan's poem differ from the earlier stanzas in perspective, and their seeming flatness may reflect the attitude of an observer who has stepped outside of the picture for a moment, much as Williams does in his poem. It may be, however, that Hogan's voice becomes particularly Native American in these stanzas, taking on the tone of orally transmitted wisdom. The tones of Ríos and Giovanni are those of adults making sense of the legacies of their grandparents' spiritual connection to themselves, though there are echoes of the child in both. In each poem, the speaker/poet is dynamic, and the ambiguity allows the reader to be involved in sorting out the heritage the poet describes.

GARY SOTO

Behind Grandma's House (p. 492)

The images of his childhood in Fresno, California, permeate both the poetry and the prose of Gary Soto. Known as a children's writer as well as a poet, he relates stories about streets surrounded by junkyards and tire factories and about being a Hispanic boy playing baseball and attending Catholic school. The Mexican American families of Soto's childhood world are poor but hardworking role models who survive without compromising their values. Because his father died in a factory accident when Soto was five years old, the influence of the extended family of uncles and grandparents — already prominent in traditional families — becomes essential to his upbringing and important in his writing.

Students may not recognize the poems' images from the 1960s. There's Bryl-creem, with its "Kookie, Kookie, lend me your comb" connotations, recalling a television show that featured advertisements for this "greasy kid stuff" hair cream, needed for the Elvis-like ducktail hairstyles of the bad boys in the barrio. The speaker collects glass Coke bottles to return them for refunds, to get money in his pockets. He seeks the trappings of power, and in his imagination he practices being a man who conquers men. The poem ends with a punch line, the punch delivered through the ironic medium of his grandmother. He thus dispatches the macho ideal with self-effacing comedy.

Most readers, male and female, have acted out similar childhood fantasies. We remember both the naiveté and the desperate longing to be grown-up and powerful that lay behind our bravado. Most college students enjoy discussing their grandparents as well and often have just recently gained the distance needed to admit that the older people have both strengths and flaws. In childhood, grandchildren's attitudes range from awe — even fear — to the conviction that grandparents are children like themselves, perhaps co-conspirators. Gary Soto's ten-year-old protagonist has a grandmother who inspires awe, since she is obviously in control of the situation. But there's a sense of equality here, too. After all, she throws the sort of punch we'd expect from another boy. She knocks him and us abruptly into the reality of her commonsense world. The verisimilitude of Soto's concrete detail places us in a particular time and place, and this sense of reality is ironic in the context of his playacting machismo, the minutiae cutting him even more down to size. The profanity lends authenticity but also contributes to the plot of his small narrative. His words, and the noise and vandalism that accompany them, cause the grandmother's action. Although he does not provide an explicit moral, the speaker is able to select events that tell this story, and the poem's existence implies a lesson learned, perhaps that *pride goeth before a fall*, literally.

Some American subcultures, including Hispanic ones, have long traditions involving extended family roles, whereas others privilege the independence and privacy found in nuclear families. However, even in mainstream American culture, many grandparents now play a major part in child rearing, helping with money or time, and sometimes actually serving as primary caregivers. Although some older people still move into what have been called *golden-age ghettoes*, the needs of working families, volunteer efforts, and delayed retirement keep some grandparents actively involved in their families. Many now communicate with distant grandchildren by way of the Internet. Although the rule of autocratic matriarchs and patriarchs has waned, respect for elders may be reviving in American culture. When the grandfatherly Pope John Paul II made a papal visit in 1999, for example, his most loyal and vocal cheerleaders were young adults. What are the ramifications of children rebelling against the more liberal ideals of their parents' generation to make common cause with conservative grandparents?

In Gary Soto's poem, we see the single exchange between the boy and his grandmother, and whether we see her action as admirable or as child abuse depends as much upon an understanding of irony as on cultural perspective. We can guess that he admires her greatly. Nikki Giovanni's narrator also admires her grandmother, even though she seems disrespectful. We know this because she tells us. Alberto Ríos is compelled to respect and heed his grandfather, a hero of the Mexican revolution. But he is frustrated by possible shortcomings and by the fact that the old man is dead and his imagined words sound crazy. As he comes to his own peace with his abuelo, a more poetic and spiritual respect seems to come as well. And respect for the gritty old English grandmother comes through in William Carlos Williams's description of her strong-minded battle with those who interfere with her dying. Linda Hogan is honest but accepts her heritage. Whereas inexperienced writers tend to sentimentalize or demonize, these poets give glimpses of complex individuals, and readers can see any of the grandchildren as respectful. None are idealized, though Nikki Giovanni and Alberto Ríos move in this direction by describing spiritual links. Alberto Ríos does not deal explicitly with gender issues in his poem about his grandfather, though the close relationship the men have with the woman in both their lives, Ríos's grandmother, is an integral part of the poem. It is only through the memories of Nani's household that the grandfather is remembered. The woman links the generations of men. Although women can relate as well as men to the main idea of Gary Soto's "Behind Grandma's House," the child's male gender is a crucial fact. The poem deconstructs myths of manhood through the action of a strong woman. If a grandfather struck a girl child pretending to be a beauty queen, we would have a very different story.

A FLAWED FAMILY: A COLLECTION OF PLAYS BY SOPHOCLES (p. 494)

SOPHOCLES

Oedipus the King (p. 495)

In his *Poetics*, written in the fouth century B.C.E., the Greek philosopher Aristotle defined tragedy as "an imitation of a noble and complete action, having the proper magnitude." The language of tragedy, according to Aristotle, should be elevated beyond ordinary speech, employing what modern audiences would see as elements proper to poetry. Trajedy is presented in dramatic rather than narrative form and "achieves, through the representation of pitiable and fearful incidents, the catharsis of such pitiable and fearful incidents." For Aristotle, *Oedipus the King* was the epitome of Greek tragedy.

Richard Janko points out in his introduction to *Aristotle's Poetics* (Hackett 1987) that the interpretation of Aristotle's concept of *katharsis* usually taught in schools is that "advanced by Jacob Bernays, the uncle by marriage of Sigmund Freud, in a famous essay published in 1857." This "medical model" centers on the effect that the play has on the emotions of the audience: By stirring our emotions, the play allows us to work them out safely and be healed from our bad feelings. Freud himself, of course, developed the concept of the "Oedipus complex" during his own self-analysis and underlined the lines in his German translation of Sophocles' play in which Jocasta delivers the ironic statement, "Many a man before you, in his dreams, has shared his mother's bed" (1074–1075). For Freud, the catharsis of *Oedipus the King* is powerful because it replicates a subconsciously recalled family drama that we have all experienced — to replace one parent in the affections of the other.

Later scholars challenge Bernays's view of catharsis as simplistic. The pleasure derived from drama is intellectual, they maintain, and has to do with the working out of the plot, and while emotions are aroused, a well-structured drama keeps them in balance. In this interpretation, catharsis thus links the intellect and the emotions as the audience engages in critical thinking and learns more about what it means to be human. The result is what has been called an "intellectual clarification" that takes place as we think about the issues raised in the play — as we *make literature matter.*

This intellectual definition of *catharsis* is closely related to current thinking about *hamartia*, the "tragic flaw" that the hero is supposed to possess. The issue has been raised that Oedipus and other tragic heroes are not so much hampered by deliberate sin or by something essentially wrong within their moral beings, as traditional interpretations imply, but by a failure of critical thinking, a miscalculation, a missing of the mark. Catharsis actually comes as the cause and effect of the plot works itself out, having to do with dramatic irony and the entertainment and intellectual satisfaction we derive from the play. While Oedipus cannot escape what the gods plan for him, he does not seem to deserve such punishment, and the interest of the plot lies in his futile attempts to avoid the very sins that bring him down.

In fact, Oedipus and other tragic heroes must be noble (*spoudaios*). This does not necessarily mean, as Shakespeare and his contemporaries assumed, that the hero must be a king or queen, though Oedipus is high-born, but that heroes must not deserve what happens and must be human beings that we can look up to in some way. This causes us to identify — to realize that such things could happen to us, as well. We pity Oedipus because he does not deserve his awful fate, and we experience the dread, however fleeting, that we can't escape what God or fate or random luck has in store for us. Because he is the quintessential intellectual, a man who uses his brains to save the city from the Sphinx by solving her riddle, we realize that if he can't outwit fate, we probably can't do it either. However, Oedipus's failure to "get it" and to put together the truth of his identity adds greatly to the ironic satisfaction for the audience. Paul Roche explains in the introduction to *Oedipus the King* in his translation of the plays of Sophocles that the tragic flaw in this "upright character . . . is the lever for his destruction, but the irony is that it does its work, trips him up, through his finest qualities; in Oedipus, his honesty and courage."

While Roche states that Oedipus's tragic flaw is related to his courage and honesty, he might have added that the flaw is closely related to the hero's intellect and to the search for truth that it compels. Oedipus is above all a person who seeks to know, to figure things out so that he can carry out the proper actions and avoid sin and its consequences. When we first meet him, Oedipus desperately wants to know how to save the people of Thebes from plague, and he seeks the help of the gods in doing so. But when the messages of the gods don't make sense, he creates his own scenario, imagining a narrative in which others are to blame for his problems. He acts on faulty knowledge throughout the play, propelling the plot and creating the dramatic irony. The search for truth has the highest priority for Oedipus, but he is unable to connect the dots.

Most readers will agree that Oedipus should have been more adaptable and less driven, especially in his relationships with other men. Perhaps he could have found a way to avoid killing the man at the crossroads in spite of the attack, and he certainly could have waited for proof before accusing Tiresias and

Creon. A man with the prophecy of incest hanging over his head perhaps should marry a woman of his own age. Oedipus's problem may be less that he is driven to search for truth than that he seems driven to act on incomplete, ambiguous information. His tragic flaw may be that he thinks he knows it all. The gods don't like this quality, a mixture of arrogance and impiety that the Greeks call *hubris*. While modern audiences may not understand the concept of impiety, since we more often praise writers and performers for being irreverent, most of us still recognize the truth of the cliché *pride goeth before a fall*.

There seems to be little free will allowed in the world of Greek tragedy, and although the personality and character of Oedipus drive the plot of the play, his fate is decided in childhood — perhaps before he is born — and he has done nothing to deserve such terrible punishment. The issues here are related to the question of why good people suffer, and the answer seems to be that people may get cancer, lose their lives in automobile accidents, or even commit suicide in the midst of depression through no moral shortcomings of their own. Like Africa in the grip of an AIDS epidemic in the early twenty-first century, the city-state of Thebes in Sophocles' play has come under a plague. The assumption is that some sin has caused the "pollution" leading to illness and death. But often such a reason cannot be found, and modern audiences would insist that the king's unintentional sin is far removed from anything that could have caused the people to be ill. We might also insist that finding the cure should not be confused with assigning blame.

Even though we know Oedipus' knowledge to be faulty, his altruism as he seeks salvation for his people shows Oedipus to be a man who has grown into his job. Like the gunslinger in the traditional western movie, Oedipus has at first saved Thebes as a by-product of his own self-interest and personal achievement, but now it has become his top priority.

While the case can be made that Oedipus is a rigid character who keeps making the same mistakes, many readers see him as a dynamic character, especially as he goes through changes in his thinking about fate and about his place in society. There is also an ironic change in Oedipus in terms of blindness and knowledge: when he can physically see, he seems unable to grasp the truth, but once he knows the truth, he blinds himself. While he has always wanted to know the truth, he no longer desires to see reality, since it is too terrible to bear. Where he has been arrogant, he now is ashamed to face with open eyes his parents in Hades or his children on earth. Although he has briefly shared Jocasta's impiety and has spent his life trying to dodge Apollo's power, he now realizes that the gods cannot be challenged. A man of action, he now walks with a cane and — as many scholars have observed — has lived out the riddle of the Sphinx: his "walking on three legs" recalls the image and adds a final twist of irony for an audience that knows the story.

Many readers will fail to find the experience of reading this play cathartic in the traditional sense because the evidence seems so convincing that it is difficult to see ourselves in a similar situation. Yet as we have discussed above, many of us have had experiences in which we fail to recognize the clues that seem so clear after the truth has been revealed. Readers able to see Oedipus as an honest, courageous, intelligent man struggling to do right and avoid doing harm find themselves relating to his pain and to the injustice of the curse the gods have placed on him, through no fault of his own. We may more easily experience catharsis in the sense that current scholarship gives it, however, appreciating the way the causes and effects within the plot are worked out while we think about the issues involved and experience the dramatic irony. We are entertained and educated, leading to an intellectual balancing of pity and fear that many would call catharsis.

The "complete action" of Sophocles' plot in *Oedipus the King* all comes together in a satisfying way; the plot itself is worked out as events come to their inexorable climax and resolution in the tragic exile of Oedipus for the good of the city. But the terrible fate of Oedipus and his family at the play's end seems too extreme for many readers, and they do not think that the pity they feel for Oedipus benefits them in any way. They may feel that the actions of the gods are too arbitrary — even too evil — to elicit a sense of fear. Untroubled by a need to avoid blasphemy, their emotions may more closely approach anger at the gods and contempt for Oedipus and the other characters for becoming their pawns. It may help to remind readers that the fate of Oedipus, though couched in a moral universe they do not accept, is not unlike the experiences of survivors or victims of events like the terrorist attacks of recent years. The head chef of the restaurant on the top floor of the World Trade Center survived because he decided on the spur of the moment to stop by the optical shop on a lower level to have his prescription changed; a young Israeli soldier died in the bombing of a bus because he'd left home early to fill in for a friend who needed to run a similar errand.

SOPHOCLES

Antigone (p. 541)

In other places in our anthology, students have been exposed to the concept of persona in poetry, used to describe the speaker of a poem who is obviously not the poet. The term originally referred to the masks worn by the exclusively male actors in Greek drama to indicate to the audience who they were supposed to be. When a man acted the part of Antigone, Ismene, or Eurydice, therefore, gesture and voice were all that were available to him as he sought to suspend the disbelief of his audience. The audience was called on to imagine it, to be an active participant in reading the human emotion portrayed. The more we allow ourselves to become involved emotionally in the drama, the more likely we are to experience catharsis, the "cleansing" that comes as we work out feelings of pity and fear as we share in the conflicts of the characters in the play. As we have seen in our discussion of *Oedipus the King*, catharsis may also involve the intellectual satisfaction we derive from thinking critically about the issues raised as the plot comes to its climax and resolution. Issues of cause and effect arise as the characters are thrown into conflicts by the decisions they make in the face of destiny. In *Antigone* the moral family obligation to bury the dead and to cry out in mourning is one of the few public roles allowed to women, one the Athenian establishment in the home city of Sophocles historically sought to control and limit. The tension of the play exists between the human laws of government — an arena of exclusive male dominance — and the emotional imperative of honoring the death of a loved family member, thus preserving traditions of family and religion — activities important to women. This reality of Greek life underlies the conflict between Antigone and her uncle, Creon, who has become king of Thebes on the death of her brothers.

If students are reading only *Antigone*, instructors will want to provide more background about Antigone's father, Oedipus, and the reasons behind the situation that Oedipus's children experience. Some students will have heard Oedipus referred to in psychology classes as the archetype for the desire that every little boy presumably feels to get rid of his father and be united with his mother. Reading *Oedipus the King* along with *Antigone* enriches both stories, however. We might also suggest that students find a copy of *Oedipus at Colonus* on the Internet and read this as well.

The trilogy is best read in chronological order according to the events that take place. *Oedipus the King* presents the plot that sets the later events in motion and, as can be seen from reading our entry on the play, provides an introduction to all of the aspects of Greek tragedy in the classic form that Aristotle advocated. *Oedipus at Colonus* develops the story a bit further, taking Oedipus to Athens where we see the loving care that his daughters, Antigone and Ismene, give to the blind, elderly exile. This middle play also introduces the conflict between the two sons of Oedipus, explaining that Polynices has cemented an alliance with Argos and that they are going to the seven gates of Thebes to reclaim the city from Eteocles, the brother who has driven Polynices out. Creon, the brother of Oedipus's mother and wife, Jocasta, is still very much in the picture as Eteocles's mentor, and he seeks to bring Oedipus back to Thebes so that he can die there. Polynices also wants the banished Oedipus back. This desire is explained by an oracle predicting that the results of a battle will be affected by proximity to the tomb of Oedipus. The old man thwarts this with the help of the gods, entering the underworld at a secret place revealed only to Theseus, the king of Athens, who must tell only his successor.

These plays, though each can stand alone as a complete action, provide a rich context for understanding the characters of *Antigone*. When Antigone is described hanging in the tomb in which Creon has buried her alive, with her beloved, Creon's son Haemon, clinging to her after stabbing himself, readers cannot help but recall descriptions of the dead Jocasta, who hanged herself after learning of her incest with her son Oedipus, and of Oedipus blinding himself by stabbing his eyes with Jocasta's brooches. Readers of the earlier plays will recall throughout *Antigone* the primal sin that Oedipus has inadvertently committed, bringing additional curses to his progeny, who are both his children and his siblings. We will remember that Oedipus has cursed his sons explicitly for their perceived failure to help and honor him. While at Colonus he has emphasized that his daughters have thus been forced to care for him as sons should have done, going out into the world while the young men have stayed at home. This sets the stage for Antigone's actions in the play named for her.

While the plays can be read in the order of their events, we should mention that they were not written in this order. Antigone's story came first, *Oedipus the King* was written later when Sophocles was in his fifties, and the tale of the elderly Oedipus came last, first presented soon after Sophocles's death in his seventies. Audiences would have known about the tragic happenings in the family of Oedipus, however, and would have enjoyed the dramatic irony as characters learned of them for the first time.

Instructors will want to provide more background about Antigone's father Oedipus and the reasons behind the situation his children experience. Some students will have heard Oedipus referred to in psychology classes as the archetype for the desire every little boy presumably feels to get rid of his father and be united with his mother. Instructors who are unfamiliar with the story can find it in any number of reference books about classical Greek mythology. The actuality of Oedipus inadvertently committing this primal sin brings a curse upon his family; in addition, during his old age and blindness, Oedipus has cursed his sons explicitly for their perceived failure to help and honor him properly. One tragedy leads to another in this family.

To Antigone, the daughter of Oedipus and of Oedipus's mother, Jocasta, another monstrous event seems about to take place. Her brothers have killed each other contending for control over their dead father's city, Thebes. Their uncle Creon, in his role as the new king, will not allow proper burial of Polynices, the brother who had allied with a competing city in his attack. Both Antigone and Creon have seemingly valid reasons for their actions. The king feels that it is proper to deny glory to Polynices by leaving his body unburied because this nephew has committed treason against the city, even though such handling of a body is not the tradition in their city. Antigone, however, operates under an ethic that sees lack of burial as a horror, going against religion and tradition.

There may be personal grounds for Antigone's obsession as well. It is a woman's duty to care for family members in death as in infancy. Creon's action further denies to her the only public voice and participation in ritual a woman is allowed in ancient Greece. Women are not citizens, but Creon devalues women even beyond this, telling his son Haemon that "there are other furrows to plow." Women are interchangeable, he implies, and Antigone, Haemon's betrothed, is less than nothing, even though she is a king's daughter. Creon accuses her of hubris, the overreaching pride that brings the anger of the gods, because she challenges male authority. He sees her as irrational and insane. But he too is arrogant and habitually acts in rash anger rather than taking the time to reason out his actions.

Scholars debate how *Antigone* fits the traditional elements of tragedy. How can Antigone be a tragic hero, since she is a woman? Would the audience have been moved to pity by her desire to bury her brother, or would they have seen her as a hateful feminist dangerously out of control? Interested students can look up descriptions of Greek tragedy and debate the issue of tragic flaws and other qualities of the hero to determine if Creon fits the role. Some argue for Haemon, who plays a small but important role, dying for the love of a woman and the shame of his father's actions. Students will be reminded of Romeo and Juliet on a grander, more intense scale.

Haemon's conflict with his father is warranted by his belief in reason as opposed to rigidity and unbridled emotion, his respect for the gods, and the importance of considering the will of the people. He therefore stands between the obsessions of Antigone and Creon. Like Antigone he disobeys the ruling authority. He comes close to committing patricide like Oedipus. If Haemon is the hero of the drama, perhaps this willingness to overturn the order of society and family is his fatal flaw in the eyes of Sophocles and his immediate audience. He ends as a suicide after failing to stab his father, Creon, and his death leads to catharsis as his mother (Eurydice) commits suicide and his father cries out in mourning and guilt. The chorus drives home the point that suffering can lead to wisdom.

Modern readers tend to see Antigone as tragically heroic and as an early feminist who stands up for what she believes is right. Students may see her as determined, idealistic, passionate, and loyal. Others may feel that she is obsessed, shrill, and hysterical (a word with pejorative connotations toward women). We sympathize with her and see her as morally superior to Creon, though cultural differences may stand in the way of our understanding of her intensity about this particular subject. Some readers may feel that at some point she loses moral authority as the issue becomes more a matter of defying Creon than burying her brother. We have more difficulty sympathizing with Creon. He seems especially irritating when he is accusing people of being money hungry. He constantly shifts blame. He flies off the handle easily and allows matters to escalate as he rigidly holds his ground. Perhaps, at the end, when he has lost his whole family, we feel pity for him and hope he will gain the wisdom the chorus speaks about.

Antigone's sister, Ismene, comes across to modern audiences as lacking in courage, though she tries to stand with Antigone by sharing the blame for something she didn't do. She comes in for some harsh judgment from her sister, but she is following the rules and traditions set out for women to follow. She is also aware of the tragedies the family has already endured and shies away from yet another public shame. Ismene is a good girl. The first audience for this play might have seen her as more normal than the manic Antigone.

The chorus is the unified voice of the elder statesmen of the city, and its wisdom varies. When Creon announces that he will not allow Polynices to be buried, the chorus agrees, going against its better judgment in the face of his power and determination. This shows the chorus's imperfection, as does its handling of Eurydice at the play's end. The chorus hopes that she will retire to her quarters to work out her feelings in private, and it watches her go, even though it partially suspects that she will harm herself. Often, however, it interprets events for the audience, mixing its reading of the current situation with philosophy. It tells us about the nature of mankind, the gods, and fate. It recalls historical events and genealogy. Students who have read William Faulkner's "A Rose for Emily" (p. 969) may see in the first-person-plural perspective echoes of the Greek chorus, interpreting events surrounding Miss Emily as normal citizens would have explained those surrounding the royal personages of Greek tragedy. We might also remember that Faulkner's story involved an unburied body, with the heroine taking a stand quite different from Antigone's.

Most viewers of Sophocles' tragedy prefer the Greek tradition of keeping the actual violence offstage. Creon entering with his son in his arms is a moving scene, evoking our pity more strongly because we only hear the telling of the events that lead up to it. We do not need to see the struggle between father and son to feel the agony of a man whose father has killed the woman he loves, nor do we need to see Eurydice slashing herself in grief to recognize the suffering of a mother who has lost a son. Students may disagree, having observed realistic violence in films, on television, and in video games. The Greek audience had probably seen more death than most modern, Westerners do. But we have become emotionally hardened through experiencing violence and death vicariously, and catharsis becomes more elusive. Although students will think of many examples of violence in slasher movies and films in similar genres, the most vivid recent evocation of realistic violence may be the movie *Saving Private Ryan*. Students could argue for the importance of showing such violence in historical reenactments so that we understand the enormity of war. Others say that the opposite will happen, and we will yawn at seeing yet another televised image of an actual war, perhaps even complaining that the angle is not quite right, undercutting the realism.

The responses of modern audiences to *Antigone* will also differ, depending on their personal contexts. A mayor of a city, like Creon, would have to weigh the consequences of backing down once a stand has been taken. Creon does not want to appear to be a weak leader, so he stays firm. While the reaction of the populace to his treatment of Antigone indicates that he may have been applauded if he had given his nephew Polynices a proper burial, their reaction had they not been struck by her pathos might have been critical. The crowd is often fickle. For Creon to admit that he has been wrong to leave the body of his nephew on the battlefield would expose himself as fallible and would allow people to question his authority. When he is finally convinced by Tiresias to do the right thing, it is too late, an experience many analytical people know well. A mayor might relate to Creon's dilemma, realizing that it is important to show leadership and stand by decisions. On the other hand, he would also realize that he should listen to the people. Haemon makes an excellent point when he reminds his father that people will say things in private that they might keep from authority figures, and elected officials might be reminded to choose advisors who hear the true feelings of the voters.

Creon also says at one point that he would die before he'd be governed by a woman, a statement that sets off alarms for feminists. A feminist reading would closely analyze the interactions among the men and women of the play to determine warrants for the characters' actions. Because she has been thrust into the world through the tragedies of her family, Antigone has learned to make her own decisions, standing up for higher laws and challenging the decisions of a tyrant. Although this leads to her death and precludes any chance she has of marrying Haemon and having children, she does effect change, since the people of the city see her actions to be right and Creon's treatment of her to be unjust.

By allowing her this victory, Sophocles shows Antigone to be a rebel fighting against injustice. No middle ground seems available to her because of Creon's rigidity. Yet her sister Ismene contends that Antigone is a firebrand even before she goes head to head with Creon, and she seems to seek a confrontation with her uncle even as Ismene counsels moderation.

Although Ismene is willing to die with her sister when her crime is revealed, Antigone will not allow her to share responsibility for her actions in giving their brother a proper burial. Ismene wishes to share blame, but Antigone interprets the situation as one of triumph and will not share it. Feminists often disagree on how militant their actions should be and on how much moderation can be used before falling into submission and settling for second-class citizenship. Rebels might applaud Antigone's actions, while conformists might join Ismene and plead that the dictates of the city be followed or that matters be taken care of quietly, avoiding open defiance. Had Antigone been willing to concede on this point, she could have become the wife and mother of kings, since she is engaged to marry Creon's son Haemon.

Some readers will find this a trivial matter on which to take a stand. They might ask why a lifeless body can't be disposed of in the way that seems most practical, especially since some people die alone in isolated areas and are never buried or cremated. But such opinions depend on culture. A religious leader in an orthodox faith would understand the significance of both Creon's actions and Antigone's response. Given the culture, Creon's actions in leaving the body in the hot sun (a fact emphasized in the play) is a profound insult, and Antigone takes it exactly as it has been intended. Creon has sent a message about the value of Polynices as an enemy, but Antigone sees this as contempt for her brother as human being and the son of her tragic father. To refuse him burial is to treat him worse than an animal. Although we might think such ideas are outdated, recent news items recount the shock and sadness of families whose deceased members had been warehoused by the owner of a crematorium in Georgia. And we may recall the great care and reverence with which the remains of people killed in the collapse of the World Trade Center towers were recovered. It may be that our present context is more positive toward Antigone's attitude than it might have been a few years ago.

As we compare the tragic flaws of Oedipus and his daughter Antigone, we find that they have much in common. Both are determined to do the right thing, and both courageously place themselves in harm's way for others. Oedipus begins his search for truth in the opening scenes of *Oedipus the King* because he wants to save the people of his city. Antigone passionately takes what she believes to be honorable actions in burying her brother. The tragic flaw — or miscalculation, as current scholarship might have it — may be their extreme foolhardiness in proceeding alone. Many readers would see this as admirable. Oedipus acts on incomplete, ambiguous information. Antigone, on the other hand, seems to have a good grasp on the situation, and she piously seeks to obey the higher laws of the gods above those of the tyrant of the city. Perhaps, in the view of her culture, she oversteps her place, since a woman is not supposed to assert herself in such a way. Putting aside our feminist leanings, we might ask why she didn't go to Haemon, her betrothed and Creon's son, with the problem. However, it seems unlikely that Haemon could have changed Creon's mind or kept the plot from working out as it did. This is tragedy, after all.

Just as Oedipus in trying to outsmart Apollo's oracles maneuvers himself straight into killing his father and marrying his mother, Antigone, in trying to bury her brother, causes herself to be buried alive. Similarly, Creon and Oedipus both seek to be good rulers. Oedipus, however, seems more directly concerned with serving the people of Thebes, even while lashing out in frustration because he cannot fathom that he could be the cause of the moral pollution that brings about the plague. Creon's main concern seems to be maintaining his image as a firm ruler, even when his son tells him that the people think he has made a mistake. Both are alike, however, in their stubborn refusal to listen to advice with which they disagree and in the rashness of their actions and orders. Both accuse others of selfish motives when they are criticized. Indeed, if Creon is the hero of *Antigone*, his flaws of character seem more obvious and his sins more intentional than those of the undeservedly doomed Oedipus.

If we are looking for satisfying endings for tragedies, both plays wrap up the strands of their plots admirably. The body count is larger in *Antigone*, with each event leading inexorably to the next. Creon seals Antigone in the tomb that should hold her brother, she hangs herself, Haemon stabs himself for love of Antigone, and Eurydice hangs herself because her son has stabbed himself. All of these events occur just after Creon realizes his mistake — his *hamartia* or tragic flaw — too late to stop the suicides.

Sophocles times the characters' revelations of the truth to maximize suspense, irony, and suffering. *Oedipus the King*, with its theme of knowledge and blindness, ends appropriately with Oedipus, who now sees the truth for the first time, blinding himself. Readers will differ about which ending is more satisfying. We might ask them to take the question a bit further and consider whether *Antigone* provides a fitting ending for the trilogy.

NOT A SIMPLE DECISION: CULTURAL CONTEXTS FOR GWENDOLYN BROOKS'S "THE MOTHER" (p. 581)

GWENDOLYN BROOKS

The Mother (p. 583)

Students who have read Lorraine Hansberry's play *A Raisin in the Sun* (p. 226) will recall that one of its characters, a married woman, decides on an abortion for economic reasons. The Younger family of Hansberry's play lives in the Bronzeville neighborhood of Chicago, a real community of African American families at the time that both Hansberry and her contemporary Gwendolyn Brooks were living and writing in the Chicago area. In the 1940s, when "The Mother" was written, Brooks was perfecting her art in the poetry workshop in Chicago's South Side Community Arts Center and was describing ordinary people with honesty and compassion. In her 1944 collection *A Street in Bronzeville*, she painted a portrait of her neighborhood. Her purpose was to show "that Negroes are just like other people; they have the same hates and loves and fears, the same tragedies and triumphs and deaths, as people of any race or religion or nationality." The quotation strikes us as sadly revealing. Why should this articulate poet have to justify the common humanity between her subjects and her readers?

Later, after meeting Amiri Baraka and other black literary thinkers at a conference in 1967, Brooks would worry less about explaining African Americans to an establishment audience and would express more forceful anger at racism and sexism. Her style would change as well. In "The Mother" Brooks uses rhyme but is already experimenting with varied rhythm and line length, motivated in part by her admiration for Langston Hughes. The speaker of the poem addresses the children that she has lost to abortions. Like Ruth Younger in *A Raisin in the Sun*, the narrator does not abort because she is selfish or because the timing of her pregnancies is inconvenient. She chooses not to complain or shift blame, only hinting that she has not willingly chosen their fate. She tells them, "Believe that even in my deliberateness I was not deliberate. / Though why should I whine, / Whine that the crime was other than mine?" (lines 21–23). She grieves but rejects self-pity. To understand the speaker of this poem, we must take social and historical issues into account. Some students, often African Americans, do not grasp the vast differences between the opportunities available in the ghettos of a rigidly segregated America of the 1940s and those open to college students sixty years later. It is true that the people who live in the high-rise urban-renewal projects that replaced the neighborhood of Bronzeville face problems even more debilitating than those of earlier generations and that racial prejudice and injustice still exist. But if we imagine a situation in which reliable birth control and access to medical care were not available at the same time that social services for families were virtually nonexistent, perhaps we will judge less harshly.

Readers may find the speaker of "The Mother" brave, enduring, sad, grieving, longing. These ghostly children haunt her, much as the ghost of her child haunts Toni Morrison's Sethe in the novel *Beloved*. In Morrison's story, a woman kills her living child rather than have her returned to slavery. Brooks's speaker imagines nurturing these babies and apologizes for taking away their identities and their lives from birth on through to natural death. The speaker must sacrifice her desire to mother all of the children she conceives presumably because she does not have the resources to raise them. The poem does not make abortion seem like a good thing. But it doesn't argue against it, either. Abortion must be available to her because she has no other choice. The implied argument is implicitly directed toward a culture in which she is forced to deny herself children.

In the poem's first stanza, the speaker uses the second person to imply that the experience she describes is common to many people. The focus is on the mother's experience. She describes the loss in negative terms: here's what you don't get. She lists some of the everyday joys of motherhood, ending in line 10 with a delicious sensory image that captures a feeling most parents know, the desire to "Return for a snack of them, with gobbling mother-eye."

The second stanza shifts to first person, as the speaker makes the loss concrete as she speaks to her aborted children. She seeks a definition of what she has denied to them in a series of parallel clauses beginning with *if* followed in turn by the verbs *sinned, seized, stole,* and *poisoned*. But she does not claim that abortion is the equivalent of sinning, seizing, stealing, or poisoning; she only says that *if* this is the case, then she did not intend these deeds. She goes on to seek her definition of abortion in what has happened to them, rather than what she has actively done. She says at first that they are "dead," tacitly accepting the equation of abortion and murder. Then she revises her judgment to suggest that perhaps they were "never made," going with the definition of the embryo as not equivalent to a baby. Finally, she decides that they "were born, . . . had body, . . . [and] died." The "damp small pulps" of the first stanza are redefined as children who had a life, albeit an abbreviated one. This mother insists that she must come around to the "truth," to speak plainly rather than trying to duck the responsibility for her decision.

In the third stanza, Brooks's speaker begs her aborted children to understand that she loved them. The repetitions intensify the force of the feeling, and the rhythms remind us of the rocking movements of a mother comforting an infant. The isolation of the one word *All* in the poem's final line is powerful. Perhaps this mother, like many, has living children that she is able to bring up but has chosen to give up others as her responsibility to them. If this is the case, the final word is more touching, since mothers usually do love all of their children and would not want to choose between them. When the speaker pleads for the children to believe her, repeating the word three times in the course of the poem, she reveals the fear that they or some other judge will not believe her when she says that she did not mean to take anything from them, that she does love them. It is unlikely that she reiterates her love for them three times for any reason beyond emphasis and the symmetry of poetry, though we might guess at deeper reasons. Perhaps she has aborted three children. We know that there are at least three, since she uses the word *all* to refer to them. Perhaps each declaration of love is for one of the poem's stanzas, since she says between the first and second statement of love that she "knew" them, and it is in the second stanza that she works out the logic of their nature.

The feelings that the speaker expresses are those of a loving mother, and most readers will grant her the title. A few may judge her as insincere or engaged in an unhealthy obsession. If we knew this woman, we would try to find counseling for her so that she could work these feelings through. But if the abortions have not been her choice, as seems to be the case, then we understand her grief. It would be difficult to adapt this poem enough for it to make sense as a father's mourning for his unborn children, though certainly men experience a sense of loss if they have wanted a child that the mother chooses to abort. Though he wouldn't be able to communicate the physical sensations of longing to bear a child or to nurse one at the breast, he might ache to hold the child in his arms, to carry her on his shoulders, or to peek in for that second look at him asleep. If the father has shared in the decision for similar economic reasons as those implied in the context of the poem, we might expect his distress to be profound. But if he has usurped the decision and is similarly explaining it to the aborted children, we are likely to judge him harshly. The imposition of abortion on a woman's body is as oppressive as forcing her to carry the child to term.

The balanced voice of this poem, filled with *pathos* but calling on our reason *(logos)* and our sense of *ethos*, is a powerful piece of persuasive writing that helps the reader understand the narrator's decision. Therefore, this cluster could be used in a composition class to illustrate the use of all three avenues used to reach an audience.

We still might have questions for the speaker, however — the most frequent in classes being whether Brooks herself had abortions, and is speaking from direct experience. We need to reiterate that what matters is that the persona of the poem has had this experience. Whether Brooks has felt this in her body or has developed a great deal of empathy for other women, the power of the poem remains. By placing it in a cluster that emphasizes the social ramifications of bringing children into a hostile world, we focus on this interpretation of the poem.

Aside from moral questions and sincere opposition to abortion that instructors should handle with respect but try to keep on an intellectual level, students may raise questions about medical and psychological repercussions of abortions, especially in colleges that offer majors in these fields. Student research in this area could add depth to class discussions. Questions may also be raised about the differences between legal and illegal abortions and their effects on the woman and her family. Research might also focus on resources available to women and girls seeking counseling about abortion as well as help that exists for those choosing to carry their babies to term. Students may find statistics comparing adoption data for various ethnic groups.

We might also look at ethnic differences in acceptance of abortion, adoption, and other options. Many African Americans, for example, strongly oppose the adoption of black children by white parents, using both logical and viscerally emotional warrants: to see a dark-skinned child being petted or disciplined by white parents evokes uncomfortable pictures of plantation slavery and issues rise about the ability of such parents — however well-intentioned — to bring their adopted child into full adulthood in a historically racist society. In a diverse class, students often share the feelings they encounter about these issues in their home communities.

Our social and personal contexts will color readings of the poem and determine whether we see Brooks as a defender of abortion or an attacker of it. We should remind ourselves as discussion leaders that some of our students have experienced abortion firsthand and will struggle to maintain emotional equilibrium, especially if they do not wish to share their personal histories with the class or if there are strong anti-abortion advocates represented in the group. Some students, however, privately share their experiences with their instructors and choose to write about the issue or present analyses of the poem to the class. This would not be a subject for a mandatory assignment or for small-group discussions that we cannot control, since emotions tend to be intense on both sides of this issue. Her balanced, credible voice makes Brooks's poem a useful one for dealing with this tough issue, however, and will help us to remind our students that persuasion is often most effective when we acknowledge that the other side includes reasonable, decent human beings who disagree with our solutions to a complex problem. We may continue to disagree with the opposing view but perhaps may come to understand it.

CULTURAL CONTEXTS:

THURGOOD MARSHALL, *The Gestapo in Detroit* (p. 584)
LEON F. LITWACK, *Hellhounds* (p. 588)
RALPH GINZBURG, From *100 Years of Lynching* (p. 591)
PETER M. BERGMAN, *Snapshots from History* (p. 595)

While citizens in Detroit, Michigan, like those of many other cities with a history of racial conflict, are working hard to head off conflicts — replacing traditional "Devils' Night" mayhem surrounding Halloween with "Angels' Night" activities, for example, and increasing the number of African American police officers to more closely approximate the racial make-up of the city — the mistrust and resentment of police officers remain in many neighborhoods. When W.E.B. Dubois predicted in the 1890s that the problem of the twentieth century in America would be that of the color line, he was correct, though many people of good will, both black and white, have labored to find solutions. Yet police departments continue practices like racial profiling into the twenty-first century, and many African Americans consider attitudes of police officers to be racist, even as official policies change.

Ironically, as we enter an era of terrorism from extremists outside traditional black and white categories, debate swirls around racial profiling of people of Middle Eastern and South Asian descent. Sikhs, members of a religious minority originally from India, have complained, for example, that anyone wearing a turban has become targeted for abuse, and businessmen of Arab descent have been asked to leave airplanes simply because pilots feel that they looked like terrorists. Detroit, with a large Islamic population, must deal with such new problems, as well. As Hispanic people become the largest "minority" group in the United States, they also become the focus of suspicion, and language differences complicate their relationships with law enforcement officials. Will African Americans suddenly find themselves acceptable as long-time citizens band together in new manifestations of prejudice? Or will new groups of people, especially people of color, simply become members of a larger outsider category?

We hear the question constantly raised in the first decade of the new century: "How are we to protect ourselves if we don't find ways to identify dangerous people before they hurt us?" According to some anthropologists and sociologists, prejudice is endemic to humanity and has developed as a defense mechanism needed for survival. Yet as beings capable of reason, we must constantly reevaluate such impulses, questioning the warrants underlying our fears.

Police departments often try to teach their members to overcome ingrained prejudice and to avoid placing crime suspects in racial (and other) categories, but people in situations they perceive to be dangerous must react quickly, often without thinking their actions through. Even assuming that individual police officers sincerely want to avoid racial profiling, life experience and instinct can override logic and can lend a gang of policemen to imagine a dark-skinned Amadou Diallo in a shadowy corner in the night to be reaching for a gun rather than identification and then to fire forty-one bullets at the unarmed, innocent man. There is something primal, something atavistic, about such "overkill."

Considered from the perspective of people who have experienced racial profiling directed against themselves or their family members and who know well the history of white on black racism and brutality in the United States, the police officer — especially the white male police officer — becomes the dangerous outsider to instinctively fear. This becomes problematic, since law enforcement officers have the weight of governmental power behind them and have the authority to use force. Furthermore, they are supposed to protect all law-abiding citizens and often are needed in crime-ridden communities by the very people they mistakenly abuse. The sense of injustice in the community then intensifies the rage and frustration.

In Detroit, a history of violence between blacks and whites continues to color perceptions. Written in 1943, Thurgood Marshall's account excerpted here deals with the riots that took place that year during World War II home-front activities in Detroit, which had become such an important producer of wartime materials that it was called the "arsenal of democracy." Many defense workers were African Americans who were considered more useful in this capacity than as soldiers and sailors in a segregated military, though as we can see from Marshall's text that many did serve in the armed forces. Many blacks had migrated to Detroit in the early part of the twentieth century as the auto industry grew, and the city's black population had increased from 5,741 in 1910 to over 200,000 by the mid-1940's. But little thought was given to where these workers would live, and a great deal of conflict took place over the years surrounding the issue of segregated versus integrated housing, with real estate agents at one point openly ranking potential residents by "degree of swarthiness."

In 1967, forty-three people died in one of the most deadly outbreaks of racial conflict of a chaotic decade. Ironically, city government cited the "over-reaction" of police during the 1943 riots as their reason for staying out of the affected neighborhoods as violence escalated in 1967 and the role of rumor then as the reason for news blackouts during the later riots. As we can see in Thurgood Marshall's description, however, it was not police overreaction but their misplaced actions, their virtual participation, that fueled the 1943 riots; and it could be argued that factual news information could have countered the rumors that fed anger and fear through their historically oppressive connotations.

As a U.S. Supreme Court Justice from 1964 until 1991, two years before his death, and as the constitutional lawyer who argued the successful *Brown v. Board of Education of Topeka* in 1954, which resulted in the elimination of legally segregated public schools in the United States, Thurgood Marshall's voice carries a great deal of authority for readers today. In 1943, however, Marshall's article in *The Crisis*, the newspaper of the National Association for the Advancement of Colored People, would have reached a smaller sympathetic audience. Most white readers in America would not have been as open as NAACP members in the 1940s or as audiences today to the *ethos* projected by Marshall. Nevertheless, the voice that we hear is credible for reasons beyond the ethical appeal that depends on the speaker's authority and the shared values of the audience.

Marshall uses both *logos*, appeals to logic and intellect, and *pathos*, appeals to emotion, to convince his audience that the actions of the police played a major role as they unfairly handled minor incidents and stood by as rumors escalated into combat between mobs of whites and blacks. While he qualifies his statements with words like *usually* and *much* rather than engaging in oversimplified absolutes, Marshall makes it clear from his opening sentence that he considers defects in the "attitude and efficiency of the police" to be the most important of "many underlying causes." He plunges immediately into this claim without engaging in vague or general statements as a preliminary, lending an aura of straightforward, no-nonsense authority to the argument from the start. The writer is not wasting our time with extraneous issues, and whether or not we agree with him at this point, most readers are inclined to give him a chance to explain why he believes the assertion he makes.

As we have seen in *Making Literature Matter*'s definition, each argument has two parts — a claim and support for that claim. Marshall gets the claim out of the way and proceeds quickly to provide specific examples to back it up. As he proceeds, he continues to maintain a balanced voice, conceding that "there are several exceptions" to the police brutality and inefficiency that he describes in the essay. While students sometimes see this as a weakness, such anticipation of opposing argument and acknowledgment of its validity actually strengthens the credibility of the speaker, showing him to be balanced and thoughtful.

Students can learn a great deal from the argumentative techniques Marshall uses to convince readers that the police caused the riots to be worse. He employs subtle pathos, for instance, to take advantage of feelings that his readers have about World War II. Beginning with the title, he compares the police force of Detroit with the Nazi Gestapo. Even now, sixty years or so later, the term *Nazi* is loaded, perhaps even more than was true at the time, since we know more about concentration camp atrocities than the American public knew during the war. Marshall further links patriotism with his own cause when he offers a "typical" example of police brutality: "A Negro soldier in uniform." While what happened to this soldier was probably typical — he is knocked out by a policeman's club after stumbling into the riot area inadvertently and being ordered to run and must be taken to the hospital by bystanders — but it is unlikely that the typical victim of police brutality in the riots was a soldier. The example is designed to stir the protective emotions most reader would feel toward one of "our soldier boys" who had been away fighting for freedom and to evoke outrage at the police actions, implicitly positioning them as enemies, even though the Nazi connection is only implied in this anecdote.

Marshall also appeals to the emotions of a readership sympathetic to the historical abuses directed toward Negroes. He relates the rumors that wrongly accused black men of rape. Such rumors originally stirred the emotions of the nineteenth- and early twentieth-century white mob, which fantasized salaciously about black men's sexuality, particularly with white women. But when Marshall relates the details of the rumor, he also stirs emotions. This is a story long used to justify lynching, and Marshall's audience knows its ugliness and danger. We refer our students to the poem "Afterimages" (p. 1178) by Audre Lorde in another cluster of *Making Literature Matter* in which the writer refers to the 1955 murder and mutilation of fifteen-year old Emmett Till that made a wider audience aware of this dangerous link between sexual fear of and brutality toward black men, and we assign the Leon Litwack entry about lynching photography (p. 588) that directly follows Marshall's text. Even stronger emotions would be evoked by the rumor of a black woman and her baby being thrown into the river by whites: what could move us more than the image of a baby being harmed? And the incident again recalls actual events: bodies of murdered blacks in the South, the victims of vigilante justice, were often found in rivers. Finally, Marshall repeats several times the story of people being forced to run, and then being attacked from behind. He emphasizes their innocence; though looting has occurred, he tells us that this happens only later and that accusations of looting were used to justify brutality. He relates incidents in which the white mob follows the lead of the police, telling their victims to "run, nigger, run."

The words that Marshall uses are heavily loaded with connections to slavery, and we must recall that many readers in 1943 would have heard parents and grandparents recall punishments dealt to rebellious or fugitive slaves, since the Emancipation Proclamation had been declared only eighty years earlier. The white people who take part in the riots in Detroit, once a destination of freedom on the border with Canada, remind the African American audience of "patrollers" who used such words while running down escaped slaves. Although he couches them in logical terms, referring to "affidavits" in which people swear that the events are true, Marshall nevertheless chooses words and examples calculated to convince his audience through pathos.

In his preface to *Without Sanctuary: Lynching Photography in America*, excerpted here, Leon F. Litwack provides historical background for the gruesome photographs of lynchings collected by the book's editor, James Allen. Some instructors might want to share these disturbing pictures with students, since they present an important aspect of American history that was acceptable enough in their time to form a genre of popular art. A copy of the book could be passed around, or the short movie or series of slides accompanying the exhibit of some of the photos that was displayed in Atlanta in 2002 may be downloaded and shown in class or assigned as homework (http://www.journale.com/withoutsanctuary/main.html).

Several photographers in the early twentieth century marketed these images of hanging bodies in various states of mutilation: sometimes burned, sometimes bullet-ridden, sometimes with body parts cut away, sometimes charred or burning. The pictures often show smiling bystanders, including women and children. The pride on faces is at times reminiscent of that displayed by hunters or fishermen posing with a trophy — the big fish hanging from the scale, the broad-antlered elk lying dead under the boot.

We can imagine these postcards occupying the niche now filled by lurid magazines, videos, and images on the Internet showing grisly scenes of death. While we may view them with horror, perhaps with fascinated interest at their inhumanity, we can't imagine a friend sending one for our entertainment. And yet the addresses and notes on the back of the picture postcards usually indicate that of the sender was at the event or was offering an exciting piece of news from home. One photograph was found in a family album, along with other pictures of grandma and grandpa. Another chilling image in Allen's collection is framed along with a chunk of hair cut from the body of the lynching victim.

Many victims are white men, some are women, and while most are from the South and the West, one of the most horrifying and popular images is from Indiana. One, from Minnesota, shows the bodies of three black men who had come through town with a circus and, as strangers, had been the "logical" suspects when a crime was committed; they were later exonerated. The image that Allen says struck him most profoundly was that of the lynched Leo Frank, a Jewish factory owner thought to have raped and killed a thirteen-year-old worker, the "Little Mary Phagan" of the folk song, in Atlanta, Georgia, in 1913 — a case that led to both the revival of the Ku Klux Klan and the formation of the

Jewish Anti-Defamation League. "It wasn't the corpse that bewildered me as much as the canine-thin faces of the pack, lingering in the woods, circling after the kill," Allen claims in his introduction to the collection, and he goes on to wonder about the photographer himself, the voyeur who made the experience available for public view. "I believe that the photographer was more than a perceptive spectator at lynchings," he explains. "The photographic art played as significant a role in the ritual as torture or souvenir grabbing. . . . Lust propelled their commercial reproduction and distribution, facilitating the endless replay of anguish. Even dead, the victims were without sanctuary."

A legitimate objection to viewing these photos could be made on privacy grounds; although these people are long dead, their bodies, often naked and marked with abuse, perhaps deserve to rest in peace. Litwack's complete essay includes material that is more explicit and horrific than the text our students will read, but the examples included here are perhaps more dramatic because they do not overwhelm us. They allow us to see individuals rather than hanging bodies. Still, perhaps we let ourselves off too easily by denying the full impact of their reality. Maybe the images should be seen, just as the frail skeletons of Holocaust victims should be seen, lest we forget.

By confronting the historical facts, readers may become aware of new manifestations of prejudice and vigilantism. We may also come to understand the determination of African Americans to prevent a return to such a cultural environment. We could demonize the white mob, arguing that their savagery and brutality make them less than human and therefore nothing like us. But the lack of guilt in the faces in the crowds in lynching photographs can be accounted for by their profoundly different reading of events. They see themselves as people who have accomplished a righteous act, as defenders of innocent, valuable victims who have been wronged by brutal animals incapable of human feelings.

We might want to recall our reactions to the attacks on the World Trade Center, the Pentagon, and the airplane over Pennsylvania on September 11, 2001. What would we wish to happen to the people who planned such terror? By calling them "evil ones" or "animals" could we be allowing ourselves to think like the mob? And more important, can we distinguish between terrorists and innocent people of Arab descent or Islamic faith? People on news talk shows on television and radio even blithely suggest that torture is justified if it results in information that prevents further terrorism against the United States. Allen, the collector of the photographs, analyses their effect: "These photos provoke a strong sense of denial in me, and a desire to freeze my emotions. In time, I realize that my fear of the other is fear of myself. Then these portraits, torn from other family albums, become the portraits of my own family and of myself. And the faces of the living and the faces of the dead recur in me and in my daily life." Not only must we identify with the victims of lynching in these historical images from the American family album, but to truly learn from them we also must identify with the faces in the brutal crowd. We are human, too, and may also identify with Allen as he tells us, "With each encounter, I can't help but think of these photos, and the march of time, and of the cold steel trigger in the human heart."

The four newspaper articles we have excerpted from Ralph Ginzburg's book make an interesting contrast. The first, taken from a 1926 issue of a newspaper in Missouri, a hotbed of racial violence at the time, strikes the reader as surprisingly fair to the accused man. It uses the word "alleged" to describe the crime and includes the shocking fact that the child was not examined until the day after the lynching. Unlike many newspaper accounts, this one does not play up the victimization of the young accuser but openly suggests the girl was merely frightened and that the young man was innocent. A bit of quick research explains the angle: the *St. Louis Argus* was a Negro newspaper.

Even more revealing is the narrative account from the *New York World-Telegram*. Because the source is a New York publication, the pathos evoked for the lynched man does not take readers by surprise, but we do find the tone and structure of the narrative more similar to fiction than we might expect a newspaper article to be. Although the story begins as newspaper accounts are supposed to begin, in a deductive way that places the main idea in the first lines, the reporter immediately announces in a conversational tone that he will now move into inductive organization, telling the story "from start to finish." His plot proceeds as one event leads to the next, and he even includes dialogue. The opening sentences are short and dramatic, hitting like bullets. If we don't remind ourselves that the story is true and horrific, we might find ourselves enjoying the narrative action as the frightened man clings to cell bars and other objects to avoid being carried out by the members of the mob. Descriptive details are vivid as the narrator shows onlookers leaning against buildings calmly watching and laughing at the botched hanging and the agonizing death by burning. The narrative captures the scene with the same disturbing reality as the postcards described by Leon Litwack in the text preceding this one in our anthology (p. 588). The *New York World*, purchased by Joseph Pulitzer in 1883, had long been known for sensational journalism and good storytelling, and Nelly Bly had pioneered investigative reporting for this periodical in earlier decades. *The World* had become known for its "yellow journalism" and its competition with the Hearst newspapers. Written in 1933 after the *New York World* had bought out the *Evening Telegram*, this article therefore stands in the Pulitzer tradition as it seeks the strongest impact and undoubtedly succeeds in selling papers. It is a compelling story that stirs our compassion.

The matter-of-fact delivery of the *Galveston Tribune* article from Texas is quite different in tone. Striving for an objective journalistic voice that keeps to the facts, the reporter gets the "who, what, when, where, and how" into the early paragraphs. And we are told why, as well. The "negro" has been "charged with associating with a white girl." While we are accustomed by now to hearing of accusations of rape leveled against victims of lynching, this time the charge is the immoral practice of what laws forbidding it called *miscegenation* — interracial dating. The article doesn't give a great many details about the killing or the state of the body, aside from the facts that the man had been hanged and shot. The story seems really to be about the abduction and the deputies who lost their man to the "howling mob" that somehow managed to figure out where to place their roadblock. The story is slanted in a way that makes the sheriff's men seem like the heroes of the piece. They are clearly outnumbered and are shown to have done their best to protect the man in their custody. But we hear nothing of the identities of the individuals who participated as part of the "howling mob" or the crowd "eight men deep" at the roadblock.

The article ends instead with speculation about the perpetrators of what the

Galveston Tribune writer sees as the real crime, the individuals named in the headline: "White Girl is Jailed, Negro Friend is Lynched." The deputies themselves seem to be the reporter's primary sources of information, and nothing about the writer's tone questions their complete veracity. We are given the number of people in the crowd (200), the number of miles south of town the deputies were stopped (27), and the exact time the body was found (2:00 A.M.), but no facts appear that could convict anyone of murder for killing a man whose only crime seems to have been dating a woman with her consent. Although the article has the trappings of credibility, readers are justified in questioning it. The warrants on which the writer depends are so incredible to current readers that the story has an eerie quality: here is a world in which a girl is imprisoned and a man hanged and shot for being friends or lovers, but three deputies have a great adventure and exhibit their bravery (though they fail in their assigned task) while a faceless crowd of 200 commits a horrible murder with hardly the bat of an eye from anyone.

Finally, the account in the *Macon Telegraph* in Georgia actually reports on the lynching *before* it happens and offers an agenda that interested observers could follow to take in all of the events of Claude Neal's torture and death. We again enter a surreal world in which horrifying events are anticipated with a matter-of-fact tone, as if they were the most normal things in the world, like preparations for a homecoming dance, a championship game, or a Fourth of July picnic. Like the Texas reporter, the Georgia writer uses the pejorative word "mob" and seems to stand a bit apart from the lynching preparations as an objective reporter of the facts. But he gives much space to the announcement of the "Committee of Six" — though like the Texas reporter he does not share the conspirators' names — and public reaction to the committee's plans. Can he be writing with an intentionally ironic tone? It is tempting to believe that he must be. The flat statement that the first item on the program is to take "the negro" to the home place of his alleged victim, a white female, where "he will be mutilated by the girl's father" sounds like satire, and its macabre tone would be grimly funny if this were a wry barb ridiculing men who would calmly mutilate — probably castrate — a person who has not yet been tried for a crime he is only being held "in connection with." But he is speaking of the father of a murder victim, so satire is unlikely; this would be cruel. Whether the writer's tone is serious or ironic, the facts seem to be uncontested. These people plan to carry out an execution, and no one seems willing or able to stop it. Even the attorney general of the United States and the governor of Florida are powerless or absent from the scene. Again, the details read like satire. Surely the last line — that the governor is "'out of the capital" and can't be reached" — is meant to inspire our outrage as the details of good satire must. But, again, we can't be sure that this is so. The lynching of Claude Neal did indeed take place the following day.

While the lynchers intended that African Americans be terrified by these public displays of power, reactions by both blacks and whites would have varied. There can be no doubt that terror had its effect in many ways, girding up codes of behavior, whether legally sanctioned or simply accepted as custom and so-called common sense. People who wanted to live were less likely to demand equal rights if visibility might lead to false accusations, torture, and death. While women might meet in clubs to oppose lynching, few were likely to break the law and actually interact with people of another race, especially black men; therefore, we can imagine that dialogue among members of different races was severely hampered.

Most readers find the history of lynching almost beyond belief, and few of us have read about it in detail. American history courses in high schools touch on issues of slavery and the civil rights movement, but the long eras of Reconstruction and Jim Crow segregation in between the 1860s and the 1960s blur for students, and they often seem to assume that the time period was shorter. African American professors are often frustrated, though not surprised, to find that college students — whether they are black or white — cannot envision the racism that ruled many communities well within the lifetimes of middle-aged teachers.

To ignore African American history is to proceed in ignorance about important issues that have shaped American thought. One instructor was bitterly amused when a student referred to "Malcolm Ten" in a class discussion of an excerpt from *The Autobiography of Malcolm X*. While this mistake is not typical, students have little awareness of the situation that Malcolm X and Martin Luther King addressed and little sense of their differences. Many high school and college teachers may be equally uninformed about this part of our history. Reading and discussing primary sources such as the ones in this selection and viewing the images in the previous selection can go far toward filling in the gaps in our educations.

Peter Bergman's book *The Chronological History of the Negro in America* is the source for the excerpted material here, providing a partial timeline of events and statistics from 1935 to1945. The "snapshots" we find in this factual family album, therefore, illuminate the Great Depression and World War II eras. Much of the information also adds context for the earlier entries in this cluster of *Making Literature Matter*. For each year, for example, a one-sentence paragraph tells how many Negroes were killed by lynching during the year. Although every year has a few lynchings, even after the war effort refocuses the nation's attention on an outside enemy, the year 1935 has an appalling eighteen deaths by lynching, a figure interpreted in another entry to be "one in every three weeks." Readers will recall Ralph Ginzburg's collection of newspaper articles from the preceding decade (p. 591) and the horrifying examples on the postcard photographs described by Leon Litwack (p. 588). This text also revisits the Detroit riots that Thurgood Marshall described in his *Crisis* article (p. 584) and credits him with requesting redress for police damage. It shows that riots occurred in places like Harlem, New York; Mobile, Alabama; and even a military base on the island of Guam. Statistics about housing, welfare, and education recall the problems of the grieving mother of Gwendolyn Brooks's poem (p. 583). Throughout, the reader is struck by the inequalities evident in the raw data of history. Usually, Bergman leaves the reader to interpret the facts presented so starkly. Juxtapositions sometimes suggest connections but just as often seem unrelated. This excerpt shows facts most relevant to issues raised by the other entries in this cluster.

Readers will have differing reactions to this reading. While statistics can be dry and English majors often skip over them, the facts here begin to pull readers into their implications as we move further into the text. We have students circle three sentences or three longer passages that they find particularly striking. Some readers find the anecdotes most compelling, finding it interesting that a soldier figures as a character in the short narrative describing the genesis of the Harlem riots in 1943. We recall that Marshall uses a soldier to relate his "typical" example of police brutality during the Detroit riots that same year. Others find their attention caught by statistics that reveal inequalities appalling in their arbitrary unfairness. Such injustice occurs in education, as the amount of money spent on all-white schools consistently exceeds that spent on educating African American children. It happens when relief is granted, with white welfare recipients receiving a larger amount of money than blacks. Inequalities surface in data about voter registration, housing, government policies and political parties, unemployment rates, and the sort of jobs open to Negroes in both the military and civilian spheres. It is startling to see that 95 percent of the 165,000 Negro men serving in the United States Navy during 1943 were kitchen workers.

A young pregnant woman living in Chicago's Bronzeville, the setting for Brooks's poetry and Lorraine Hansberry's drama (p. 226), or in Detroit's Black Bottom or other neighborhoods described in Thurgood Marshall's *Crisis* article would be justified in expecting that her child would have a life filled with deprivation, humiliation, injustice, and fear. The incident described by Leon Litwack in which a pregnant woman is lynched and has her eight-month-old fetus torn from her body and crushed is atypical but has symbolic significance in the light of these snapshots of horrors. Bergman's repetition of lynching statistics, accounts of Ku Klux Klan activities, and anecdotes pointing out torture and brutality by law enforcement officers would fill an expectant mother with terror for her newborn. When Brooks's speaker says, "I loved you all," her love takes in all of the people represented by the facts and statistics outlined here. The child who is not allowed to read the books in a library because libraries are for whites only may also become one of the poet's abortions, the loved one whose potential is lost because of unreasoning hate.

While some people argue that looking at the negative aspects of history "stirs up" racial tensions and rage, we maintain that such negative history needs to be foregrounded in our educational system. Americans have many sources of pride, but a history based on sentimental nostalgia for the *good old days* ignores reality and bases American identity on a lie. As Marshall points out in his article about the police, even there we can find exceptions. We might recall the women's group in Florida organized to oppose lynching or the senators who proposed the bill lost in filibuster that would have put teeth into an antilynching law. And we also might recall that while many attitudes from our racist past remain, times have changed to such an extent that we hardly recognize the America we see in the texts collected in this cluster.

FAMILY TRAGEDY (p. 603)

KATE BRAVERMAN

Pagan Night (p. 603)

In the closing paragraphs of "Pagan Night," Kate Braverman raises an issue by repeating the same unusual word. At this point, she has carried the reader along with her protagonist — if we can call such a passive, acted-on character a *protagonist* — to the knowledge that Sunny will probably abandon her baby. Having moved into the future tense for several paragraphs, the character continues to live in a fantasy of what might happen and has not yet taken the final step. But she has come to a final decision. For Sunny, life consists of accepting the inevitable, of letting things happen. And this final action will be the nonaction of abandonment rather than infanticide. If the baby dies, as it will, this is simply destiny. Braverman tells us as Sunny stands on the railroad trestle that "she will think of ineluctable trajectories" and in the following paragraph that she thinks of the "ineluctable destiny" of Moses, another abandoned baby. The word *ineluctable* comes from a Latin word that has connotations linked with wrestling matches: when the loser is pinned to the ground and cannot struggle clear, he is in an ineluctable position. The denotation of the word according to one dictionary is "not to be avoided, changed, or resisted."

One way to begin this cluster in *Making Literature Matter* might be to have students look up the word. One professor led into the story by discussing the word, and then reading "Pagan Night" aloud rather than assigning it. Braverman's poetic imagery invites such a reading. As in another narrative about a woman struggling with a postpartum crisis, Charlotte Perkins Gilman's "The Yellow Wallpaper"(p. 1149) the evolving logic of the main character does not accommodate a quick skimming of the story. We need to be swept along with her in order to understand.

Still student readers tend to ruthlessly condemn Sunny and refuse to accept any suggestion that they could ever think in this way. The issue thus devolves into whether Sunny should have had an abortion or instead have placed her baby for adoption. She should leave Dalton, they insist, get a job, get daycare, get counseling. Centering on the view of life that leads to her passivity and then reading the story with attention to details helps to ward off the easy, moralistic judgments that often characterize pro-life versus pro-choice debates. Hearing it without knowing that it will be about infanticide makes it easier for students to see that Braverman's theme may suggest something about making choices that goes beyond abortion versus motherhood. How does a person fall into the fatalism and passivity that Sunny demonstrates? Why is her happiness dependent, like that of a latter-day Cinderella, on a handsome prince who now seems to be destroying himself as well as the woman and child he should, according to the warrants of most readers, nurture and protect?

As the title of this cluster suggests, a "family tragedy" is taking place. Advocates of abortion choice often cite child abuse to support their arguments, and while the logic may be faulty — many abused children are born to parents who think they want them — details of Braverman's story suggest that we should consider it in our discussions. Sunny's decision to go to San Francisco and pursue dancing rather than nursing has something to do with escaping the influence of her father. When she compares Idaho to Los Angeles, why does Sunny's description of the city where she lived briefly as a child include the unexpected observation that its "air reminded her of what happened to children in foster homes at dusk when they took their clothes off, things that were done in stucco added-on garages with ropes and pieces of metal and the freeway rising in the background like a cheap sound track"? The paragraph starts with more general, though still disturbing, comparisons to "the rancid gleam like spoiled lemons that coated everything in a sort of bad childhood waxy veneer flashback." What seems at first to be an attempt at poetic metaphor stumbles into horrific detail, hinting at personal experience.

Our discussion might therefore consider what happens to abused children when they are adults. Often, they replicate the abusive relationship, choosing partners who treat them badly. Dalton uses Sunny, selling her possessions while keeping his own, buying drugs and alcohol rather than food and diapers, and forcing her to choose between his fitful peace and her child's welfare. Some reason exists for Sunny's extreme passivity, her fatalistic view that everything *just happens*, words that appear often enough in her thoughts to raise issues of repetition for readers. Young girls and boys who are sexually abused often embrace this sort of passive acceptance as a way of getting through horrific experiences they are powerless to stop, waiting for it to be over.

Braverman's narrative, moving as it does into future tense and fantasy atmosphere at the end, does not tell us for sure that Sunny will abandon her baby, and a few readers hold out hope that she will not be capable of this action or that someone at the zoo will call social services rather than offering peanut butter sandwiches. Others feel that since her action will really be a nonaction, part of the "sequence of erasures and absences" she speaks of at the story's end, she will inevitably let the baby slip away into the river or leave it in the weeds. We may question whether she will do this because she loves Dalton or because it is the easy way out.

Neither of the young people in this story actually engages in critical thinking about their options or makes real decisions. Sunny's sense of herself is tied up with the men in her life; her early decisions have been made as a rebellion against her presumably abusive father, and her thinking now revolves around keeping Dalton pacified. She lacks the autonomy to be her own person, and she engages in magical thinking, spending most of her time in vague fantasies. Rather than a woman making choices, she seems much like the adherent of a cult engaged in a process of renunciation. She has abandoned herself to a hazy "pagan night" that allows her a Bacchanalian lack of control. The band's name works on this level in the narrative as well as on many others. "Pagan Night" carries connotations of a time spent in a dreamlike state of nature, outside of oppressive rule-bound religions. Dalton, who reads about "primitive" religions, seems to feel that they can live off the land, be part of nature in the way that he imagines people in simpler cultures to do.

In this context Braverman includes the image of the encaged snow leopard. Many readers have encountered the much anthologized essay entitled "Snow Leopard" by Peter Matthiessen, who recounts, as a Zen Buddhist exercise, his experiences on a trip to the Himalayas where he hopes to spot a snow leopard, an animal that symbolizes the freedom of the elusive creature totally adapted to and at home in its natural environment. Written in 1973, Matthiessen's essay illustrates a view of the natural environment that seeks to find holiness and spiritual illumination in its beauty and power and to enter the timelessness of the present moment in its contemplation.

While Dalton may be imagining himself as someone like Matthiessen, his actions are self-indulgent rather than idealistic. For Sunny, wrapped up in

Dalton's needs, the "pagan" aspect has at first meant sexual freedom and adventure, perhaps, but has come to mean a confused enthrallment to this petty deity in the form of a rock singer. In one scene, he takes her by the hand, and she feels that she is "walking into a yellow . . . of simultaneity and symbols and some arcane celebration she can vaguely sense." This sounds like a religious experience, as does the eucharistic eating of fish eyes that makes her think "of rituals, primitive people, the fundamental meaning of blood." But all of this remains vague, reminding us perhaps of the psychosis of the woman in Gilman's "The Yellow Wallpaper" entrapped into forced passivity, and the baby's crying jolts Sunny out of her reverie.

Braverman's couple doesn't succeed in living out their pagan ideals. Calling on African customs, Dalton seems to use the naming ritual, or his deliberate evasion of the rituals as an excuse to exclude the baby as a possible human being. Although some ethics experts, most notably Dr. Peter Singer of Princeton, now argue that the disposal of infants less than one month old should be considered a matter of parental choice, American jurisprudence and most readers disagree. While many societies do permit infanticide (or what is now termed *neonaticide*, the killing of a newborn), such drastic actions usually grew out of cultural responses to famine or strongly held beliefs about the danger or inferior value of a disabled child, a twin, or even a female. The naming ritual in African cultures, on the other hand, provides a way for the father of the child to endow it with spiritual significance and to assert his paternal responsibility for its upbringing; a man who refuses to give his child a name for self-serving reasons would be censured by the community. By showing us Dalton's attitude, the author separates him from the "primitive" men he claims to follow; her details about him paint him as a thief and an addict whose priorities can always be rationalized to justify what he wants at the moment. Like the Dalton gang members, for whom Braverman may have named him, the young man may imagine himself to be a romantic outlaw, roaming the west with his girlfriend like Bonnie and Clyde. He seems to keep his guns because he has the notion of being the mighty hunter who feeds himself and his mate, but his "pagan" ideals are impractical. He may be suffering and agonizing over their situation, but we are given no indications of this by the author.

If it "takes a village to raise a child" (an African truism Dalton ignores), Sunny and Dalton deliberately place themselves outside that extended support group. Aside from small acts of kindness to the young mother so obviously in need, no one seems to intervene. By going into town, Sunny tries to protect Dalton from the baby. She may also protect the baby from Dalton, though she does not say this, especially if we consider that her thoughts sometimes veer toward child abuse. But what she does, in effect, also without realizing it, is make herself visible. Yet no one really helps. Often, individuals suffer because others in the community are reluctant to invade their privacy.

Optimists might imagine an epilogue in which someone saves the baby, at least. In spite of Sunny's ominous thoughts about child abuse in foster care, we can imagine a scenario in which he is rescued and brought up with loving attention to his needs. We might ask, however, if the community could help Sunny, too — and even Dalton.

We might see this young trio as the nuclear family carried to the extremes of dysfunction. They carry out the traditional roles: Dalton imagines himself as the hunter and fisherman, while Sunny does the woman's work of caring for the child and gathering handouts. They are alone, isolated from support groups that could teach them how to be parents and ease the burden by babysitting or providing work. Like Andrea Yates, the Christian mother convicted of drowning her five children in a bathtub in 2001, the pagan Sunny is expected to do it all by herself. Not only do young parents need chances to see good parenting models, they need the companionship of other adults, and they sometimes need drastic intervention. While Sunny's situation goes beyond the norm, her feelings may not be as foreign to those of many desperate young parents as we might at first assume.

T. CORAGHESSAN BOYLE

The Love of My Life (p. 612)

The news event that T. Coraghessan Boyle says will break our hearts is the story of nineteen-year-old college students Amy Grossberg and Brian Peterson, who spurred national debate in 1996 when Amy gave birth in a hotel room and Brian disposed of the baby's body in a dumpster. Grossberg was sentenced to two and a half years in prison, while Peterson originally received eight years but served only eighteen months because much of the time was suspended due to his testimony against his girlfriend. The couple had begun their ordeal by sticking together but eventually came to blame each other.

Many writers, both liberal and conservative, tackled the issues raised by the event. While an estimated 250 newborns are similarly disposed of every year in the United States, this story was striking for several reasons. The parents in this case were affluent, white, college students who exhibited a shockingly naïve combination of panic and denial as they successfully hid the pregnancy but failed to think through how they would handle the birth. With access to college libraries and an Internet with virtually unlimited information about the facts of parturition, the two young people did not realize that the afterbirth needed to be delivered, and when Amy returned to her dorm, the resulting hemorrhaging forced a trip to the emergency room, where the question of the baby's location was immediately raised.

Another fact that made the item newsworthy was the "chivalry" of Brian Peterson, who stood by his girlfriend as she insisted that a visit to an abortion clinic might cause her mother to find out and as she used all the energy she could muster to push the reality of her pregnancy out of her mind. It is unprecedented, according to experts, for the boyfriend to help deliver and dispose of a newborn; such mothers are stereotypically poor, uneducated, alone, and without a support system. Some analysts of the news story posit that having Brian's support might have encouraged Amy to avoid other sources of counseling and help, however.

Always having been the perfect daughter, Amy's greatest concern was that her mother would discover that she had betrayed her parents' trust perhaps by sexually transgressing or by not being cautious but especially by derailing the life they'd planned. Psychiatrists involved in the court cases argued that Brian and Amy were trying to maintain their family image as good kids. One explained that parents send their children the message that they carry the family reputation on their shoulders, implying, "You are my success story. You cannot fail because it is not you failing, it is me failing." Students might want to read Maxine Hong Kingston's "No Name Woman" (p. 1138) in another cluster in *Making Literature Matter* to see a similar cultural mechanism working openly in China. Furthermore, psychiatrists say, to have an abortion or to take the newborn to a safe place like a hospital emergency room would mean taking an important adult step on one's own. Perfect kids can't do this without discussing it with mom and dad first.

Some writers pointed out the "magical thinking" that led Amy and Brian to have unprotected sex, and and to assume that the consequences did not apply to them, to hide the pregnancy, and to hope that everything would be solved on its own. Merle Hoffman, an advocate for women, insisted that sex education campaigns are "no bulwark against the powerful influence of desire, impulsivity, and the youthful sense of invulnerability. Nor are they a protection against the lack of self-determination and sexual empowerment that plague many young girls and women."

The trials led to proposed laws seeking to allow newborns to be left at hospitals with no questions asked. (It is unclear how such a law would provide needed medical care for mothers.) Proponents of lesser penalties for infanticide argued that in England mothers who kill their infants usually receive psychiatric help rather than criminal charges; they propose that manslaughter be the charge rather than murder if a mother kills her own newborn child. Others, like bioethicist Dr. Peter Singer of Princeton and psychology professor Dr. Steven Pinker of the Massachusetts Institute of Technology, argue more extremely that infanticide has evolutionary value, is practiced in widely varied cultures, and should be a matter of parental choice.

Most student readers condemn the characters in T. Coraghessan Boyle's adaptation of this story in "The Love of My Life" (p. 612), just as China and Jeremy have expressed contempt for *"those breeders that bring their puffed-up squalling little red-faced babies to class."* To get pregnant is to class oneself with the stupid people, and China is especially determined not to do that as she keeps careful watch over her class ranking to the last, even naming individuals she'd be ashamed to have finish ahead of her. Such attitudes are not uncommon in a class of college students, and most students will relate to the desire to keep one's life and career on track. Most also can relate to being swept up in the moment and failing to use birth control on a camping trip, though others will argue that they could have limited intercourse to the two condoms, engaging instead in oral sex, or that they could have taken a day to drive back to town.

However, while understanding that accidents happen and that China and Jeremy should not derail their lives by becoming parents, most readers find it difficult to relate to the altered state of mind that allows someone to halt all problem solving and planning once the pregnancy is discovered. Boyle goes far toward helping us to see how this could happen by focusing on the glow of first love, itself a surreal experience with few ties to reality, and by dropping in references to television and movies. When we first meet the lovers, they are caught in a situation that allows them to play house during an ice storm. Because of the weather and Jeremy's mother's absence, they have permission to occupy a dream world of togetherness like the one China sees in sexy movies. Later, the camping trip represents a different reality, especially since it happens during spring break, a carnival time when rules are suspended. To Jeremy, Boyle's narrator tells us in the first paragraph, being in love was "like being immortal and unconquerable, like floating." These words capture both their sense that nothing bad can happen in their cocoon of love and the essentially passive nature of their relationship. In a state in which we are accustomed to just letting things happen, floating in a romantic but protected bubble, it is easy for events to take over.

Like Kate Braverman's "Pagan Night" (p. 603), Boyle's story might be more effective if we do not know what will happen beforehand, but it will be difficult to allow our students this experience in the context of the anthology. We know that a "family tragedy" will take place, and the lead-in question gives away the infanticide plot. We may ask them when approaching the question about Boyle's narrative strategy in the opening scenes to imagine how an unprepared audience might respond. He begins with a great first line that encapsulates the nature of their relationship, and he then goes on to describe first love between clean-cut, good kids whose parents give them love, attention, and approval as a couple. That they rent slasher movies is a nice touch: these films take off from the folklore and urban legends of teenagers and often mix the sexual titillation of young couples on lovers' lanes with gory violence. Later, when reality sets in and they desperately try to get through China's labor and delivery, they still relate their experience to the movies: the baby is like the horrible creature in "Alien" that occupies a human body and bursts through suddenly, covered with gore. If we know what will happen later in the story, the phrase "teens have sex, and then they pay for it in body parts" seems a bit over the top, but it may seem like subtle foreshadowing if we do not know the ending. The underlying message of slasher movies and the folklore they draw on is exactly that sex has dire consequences and the irony works best if we keep this in mind.

Boyle may be reminding us, too, that teenagers, especially those in the throes of first love, are oblivious to any negative circumstances that could come from their actions. Life is like a movie in which the camera only shows the glow and skips over the clumsiness and the body odor. First love often does not survive simply because it is based on fantasy, and we can imagine China and Jeremy under other circumstances moving on in college to new relationships as they mature and see each other from new perspectives, as they share fewer experiences together.

Long before the end of the story, Jeremy has fallen out of love, even though he continues, perhaps out of habit as much as responsibility, to be a loyal boyfriend. With an irony typical of his style, Boyle has his young male protagonist dreaming of fishing as he is shaken out of sleep and arrested for killing his newborn child. Perceptive readers will recall that Jeremy had made a point on the trip to the lake to leave his fishing pole at home to make sure he would devote every minute to China. This detail, perhaps more than any, reveals the change in Jeremy's feelings toward his girlfriend. It is ironic, as well, that he has pushed the event so far from his mind at this point that he cannot link his arrest with any action on his part more serious than traffic violations. If, as we are told at the story's beginning, love makes one feel immortal and unconquerable, Jeremy now knows that really bad things can happen to him, and that he can be brought into hellish defeat.

China, on the other hand, is still in love, though her lawyer and parents have apparently decided that she will testify against Jeremy, claiming she thought she'd had a miscarriage. Yet the reader recalls, as Brian Peterson claimed Amy Grossberg said in the real life version of the story, that China screams at Jeremy, "Get rid of it." Now China is back home with decisions being made for her, and she continues to live in the unrealistic glow of first love, recalling at the story's end her first sexual experience with Jeremy as if it were the scene in a movie. It seems unlikely that this couple can or should reunite; Jeremy faces a court trial at which China will testify against him (a scenario that reverses the actual story), and China seems to have slept through the whole experience, still hiding its reality from herself.

While Jeremy in Boyle's story and Dalton in Braverman's "Pagan Night" may have similarities, we know more about Jeremy because Boyle does not limit his narration to the female protagonist. If anything, we know more of Jeremy's point of view than we do of China's, since he is the one called on to solve the problem. Yet Jeremy comes across as a person struggling to do the right thing, though we may fault him for not breaking China's confidence at some point to insist on outside help. Dalton, on the other hand, is judged by many readers to actually be the problem. Sunny must take action or make decisions that cater to Dalton, but the opposite situation prevails between Jeremy and China. The pregnant China, in a state of denial and panic, is a ticking time bomb that Jeremy fails to defuse. Neither man sees value in the life of his baby, though Jeremy is haunted by the imagined breath that is never taken. Perhaps Dalton also is haunted by his son's cries, and this may be why he insists that he be freed from them. Both refer to the baby as *it* to avoid seeing it as human, and both have philosophical justifications for disposing of an unwanted child: Dalton argues that some African cultures do not acknowledge the child as human before it is named, and Jeremy insists that he should get a medal for being a responsible person who does not add to overpopulation.

Neither Dalton nor Jeremy seems capable of seeing himself as a father or of even considering that he should nurture and protect the baby or find someone who can; instead, the infants are garbage or things that make noise. Their attitudes toward the women in their lives differ dramatically, however, a fact figured symbolically — and ironically — in both stories by a fishing pole. Jeremy chooses to leave his fishing pole behind when they go on the camping trip, sacrificing this symbol of masculinity to focus on China. Conversely, we can be fairly confident that Dalton has traded Sunny's jacket for a fishing pole. While Dalton may do this to acquire food for both of them, his planning does not take into account the coming of winter or Sunny's right to her own property, and his acquisition of the fishing pole and decision to keep his guns symbolically show him asserting his masculinity with no consideration for his lover or his child.

While we might see the actions of Jeremy and Sunny as springing from love, many readers raise issues about the definition of love in the context of these stories. Does Sunny love Dalton, or does she more closely resemble a battered woman emotionally dependant on an abusive partner? Why do they remain together if Dalton does not love Sunny in some way? Does he depend just as much on her slavish, groupie-like adoration of him as she does? Is the romantic fantasy that China and Jeremy play out together really the sort of mature love on which lifelong relationships are built?

Other problems, especially unresolved feelings about parents, play a part in the decision-making processes (or their absence) in these stories. Although we do not know about Dalton, readers can see that all the other characters still either depend on the good opinions of their parents or act in response to or rebellion against them. All deliberately avoid seeking help from adults in the community, struggling instead to hide problems and keep their independence or their good reputations.

GAYS AND LESBIANS IN FAMILIES (p. 626)

ESSEX HEMPHILL

Commitments (p. 626)

During the last years of his life, before he died of the complications of AIDS, Essex Hemphill was not reticent about his homosexuality. Above all, perhaps, he was a poet who wanted to be seen and heard. Although "Commitments" speaks explicitly of silences and of the family relationships that depend on masking his true identity, the longing to be seen and heard sets its tone. He refuses to remove himself from his place in the family, even though he knows that someday some family members will want to literally cut him out of the picture. The opening lines hint at his coming death, and we hear the echo of a cliché about the eternal quality of the soul in his assertion "I will always be there." It sounds like a reassurance, but it is also a declaration of his intention. It says, "I'm here." And it is not his dead body but his "silence" that will be "exhumed" — dug up from the grave — perhaps when people know him without his mask of practical invisibility, perhaps when he is dead. He names relationships and gives pictures the typical details of a backyard picnic in which the foods identify a family with roots in the American South.

But to echo the silence of his earlier stanza, line 16 adds a spatial equivalent of silence; his "arms are empty," childless. And the hopes of his aunts to see his wedding are empty, too. If he could marry the person of his dreams, these aunts might not attend the wedding, and if they did, they would not throw rice, the symbol of fertility in marriage. After giving us a vision through the camera lens at holiday celebrations, he repeats his image of empty arms, juxtaposing it with an elaboration upon emptiness: "so empty they would break / around a lover" (lines 26–27). The image is enigmatic, the word *break* making us think of voices breaking in sadness, of vulnerability so fragile it could shatter, or of longing so demanding it would hold on too tightly and break as a result. Although he is part of the family in a pragmatic way, he tells us that he is "the invisible son" (line 32), contrasting emptiness again with the permanent visual record of the photographs and the appearance that all is well. As an African American,

Essex Hemphill was familiar with the metaphor of wearing a mask, but his poem subtracts by presenting images of emptiness, rather than adding a protective identity. Like the "invisible man" of Ralph Ellison's novel about the African American struggle to be recognized and made truly visible, Essex Hemphill as a homosexual man in an African American family evokes the tensions of visibility and invisibility, of silence and poetry.

Although questions implicitly give students the impression that they can come up with an answer to explain the conflicting statements in "Commitments," assure them that sometimes a poem may be *about* the conflicting feelings and tensions in a situation. Perhaps we will want to create a different definition of *invisible*, one that takes the possible allusion to Ellison into account or that considers a misreading of who one *really* is as a part of invisibility. A part of the person he is has been buried with his silence, and perhaps will come to light. But things dug out of graves cause fear and disgust, and he is realistic enough to know that his relatives will not welcome the visible breaking of his silence.

In the second stanza, the poet is describing an image in a photograph, not an action, and no verb is needed. The image is so American and so normal we expect to smell the apple pie. Hemphill contrasts this normality with his inability to be completely part of it. His mention of a lover in the middle of this family scene reminds us that his would be a lover, not a husband or a wife. There seems to be a real desire for a place in the family and a concomitant longing for children of his own. Heterosexuals sometimes have problems imagining homosexuals as real people who have desires unrelated to sex. A recognition of the loss he feels as someone who simply does his duty can help readers who do not have gay friends or relatives to see gay men and lesbians as three-dimensional.

The word *commitment has* multiple connotations that the class can discuss. The commitment of marriage is suggested, and we may question whether he feels that this is the commitment that his family implicitly requires of him, as well as the commitment to produce children. He clearly feels that his participation in family life is secondary, even though he is always there for his family in a practical way. In some of the lists that students make to determine what commitments the narrator's family owes to him we can expect to find something like *the insight to see his value as a person* or *the courage to accept him as he is.* Teachers also should remember their responsibility to encourage a safe classroom atmosphere that privileges diversity, allowing legitimate dissent without permitting expressions of prejudice, even when veiled as jokes or platitudes. Perhaps our students' lists will suggest further specific commitments they need from us.

KITTY TSUI

A *Chinese Banquet* (p. 628)

Many Asian American writers speak of conflict when their loyalties to family values and traditions run counter to the separate identity they have developed in the dramatically different world outside of the home environment. Often the family is their only link to the Asian part of their heritage. Amy Tan, David Henry Hwang, Maxine Hong Kingston, and others have taken the stories of grandparents, aunts, and friends of the family as themes for their exploration of what it means to be an American whose roots reach into China. Living as a lesbian or gay man complicates the matter of heritage for an Asian American young person. Even the most Americanized Chinese people of earlier generations tend to look with disapproval upon a gay lifestyle, seeing it as unnatural. Evangelical Christianity has played a large part in forming the value systems of some families, and some condemn homosexuals with communist labels of "decadence and bourgeois false consciousness." Kitty Tsui is Chinese American; she grew up in Hong Kong and England but has lived in the United States since she was sixteen. In the title of her 1983 poetry collection *The Words of a Woman Who Breathes Fire*, Tsui asserts her complex identity. She is first a poet, a person who uses *words*, usually English words, but sometimes Chinese ones. She is also a *woman* who celebrates the bodies and spirits of women. She is, in fact, a sort of superwoman, a bodybuilder who exudes strength, health, and beauty. And she is a *woman who breathes fire*, a self-proclaimed dragon lady who reappropriates the Western stereotype of the dangerous and exotic Chinese woman and uses its connotations for her own purposes. Rather than serving as the subject of white male fantasy, the dragon lady *breathes fire* and thus becomes the dangerous counter to the romantic knight who lives out his fantasies by rescuing damsels in distress. This dragon gets the girl and dismantles the fantasy.

"A Chinese Banquet" describes the same sort of setting that we encountered in Essex Hemphill's descriptions of a gathering of his African American family. But Tsui is less accepting of her invisibility in her Chinese family, perhaps because she has not been assigned the role of helpful son but of ungrateful and disappointing daughter. Some of her family's disapproval is culture-specific, as we have seen in Amy Tan's "Two Kinds" (p. 373), and does not have its source specifically in her being lesbian. But Tsui's sense of loss focuses more on the partner who has deliberately been left out than on her loss of family continuity. In spite of her usual skill with words, she is unable to tell her mother how important her lover is to her, how she wishes to bring the woman she loves into all the parts of her life, including her family. In many families, even when a member's homosexuality is open, the seriousness and commitment of relationships tend to be dismissed. One openly lesbian young woman relates that when her first long-term relationship with another woman broke up, her mother minimized the pain she was feeling, acting as if she'd lost a college roommate rather than suffering something akin to divorce. If the son's or daughter's lover can be kept out of sight, even parents who intellectually acknowledge the relationship can emotionally deny the reality of the bond between committed lovers of the same sex, dismissing it as friendship alone. It's likely that Tsui's mother does this, understanding subconsciously but not wanting to admit that her daughter loves another woman.

The conversations at the banquet are aimed at telling the young woman who she should be and what she should do. She imagines telling her mother who she really is, what she really wants. The foods and the manners at the banquet are Chinese. Although boundaries exist in non-Asian families, the traditions of this Chinese American family contrast with the narrator's other reality, showing that the gap she must bridge to get their approval is wider than it might be in other ethnic groups. The phrases that are repeated — "it was not a very formal affair," "she no longer asks when I'm getting married," "not invited" — all have negative structures, are denials of something. Contrasting ironically with the narrator's statement, the details of the banquet indicate what most of us would consider a formal affair, and she presumably has no corsage because she has no escort, not being involved in the formal affair of marriage. Within her mother's silence about marriage lies its opposition. Her mother no longer asks the question, but the question exists beneath its absence. The one "not invited" is conversely the one who is most present to the narrator, the one to whom she addresses her poem. Because she does not use capitalization, the poem also gives a sense of internal monologue.

Like Kitty Tsui, Essex Hemphill would like to bridge the boundaries in his family. His repetition of images of arms indicates this, since arms physically bridge the spaces between people — draped around a shoulder, hugging, holding, reaching out — and are a natural symbol of human connection. In this context, it is interesting that Hemphill uses the verb *break* to speak of arms around a lover, since we might guess that it is his heart that *breaks*. The connotation communicates the same feeling but subverts the cliché. We find visual images in Tsui's poem, as we do in Hemphill's, but other senses are important, too. We hear a great deal of talk, and we feel and taste the foods at Tsui's banquet. The difference in effect is considerable when Tsui directly addresses a specific lover, whereas Hemphill refers to an anonymous and abstract one. Tsui's poem is about relationships and the anger and loss she feels when her love cannot be accepted as legitimate and integrated into her heritage. Hemphill's emotion is a vague sadness that seems more directed toward his place in the family tree and the loss he feels about not being seen for who he is.

MINNIE BRUCE PRATT
Two Small-Sized Girls (p. 630)

Like Kitty Tsui and Essex Hemphill, the poet and activist Minnie Bruce Pratt finds herself in conflict with the values of the culture into which she was born. Hers is the dilemma of a child of the rural American South who loses much by breaking away from traditional mores. Pratt lost her parents, her extended family, and her children as well. Her book *Crime Against Nature*, from which this poem is taken, deals with the consequences of the legal term echoed in its title. It was because she was a lesbian that custody of her sons was granted to their father when her marriage was dissolved, and the threat of possible conviction for "crimes against nature" was used as a club to keep her from fighting the court's ruling. Pratt had already been involved in feminist activism when in graduate school at the University of North Carolina at Chapel Hill and had helped to establish women's collectives in the nearby towns of Durham and Fayetteville. She identifies herself as part of a group of "anti-racist, anti-imperialist Southern lesbians."

Along with lesbians and gay men who transform the pejorative *queer* to make it a proclamation of pride, Pratt explores definitions of gender but is also passionate about issues of race and all forms of discrimination. She refuses to accept cultural stereotypes about the body, whether they deal with gender, sex, or ethnic origins. She resists inflexible definitions within the gay and lesbian community, arguing that to criticize some lesbians as being too *butch* and others as not being true lesbians is to fall into the trap of discrimination and oppression. As a Southerner who has taught at traditionally black colleges, Pratt resists biologically determined definitions of human diversity. "I can't be the only one," she writes in a short story, "who grew up trained into the cult of pure white womanhood and heard biological reasons given to explain actions against people of color, everything from segregation of water fountains to lynching." She challenges any attempts to place people into such predetermined categories. Although her poetry has political implications, she explains that she began to write poetry not because she had "become" a lesbian, but because of something more personal: "I had returned to my own body after years of alienation."

Students will differ in their beliefs about "crimes against nature" in terms of sexual behavior. Inevitably, students will speak of ancient laws — even current laws in some states — prohibiting sodomy and making illegal certain heterosexual practices within marriage. In 1999, Pratt's home state, Alabama, was debating the legalization of sex toys and aids for medical purposes, with many politicians arguing that since they might be used outside of heterosexual marriage such devices should remain banned. We might want to extend the question outside of the sexual arena. How might a person unfamiliar with the term and its history in America attempt to define "crimes against nature"? As war, perhaps? Or as environmental destruction? Pratt's nature imagery in the poem evokes a hot summer on an Alabama farm, but it also shows the kudzu devouring everything and the wildfire that they set blossoming like some brilliant growth. The garden imposes order on nature, just as the girls turn corncobs into the images of human beings. We can encourage students to explore the symbolic connotations of sensory details that seem at first to be here only for verisimilitude. An issue might be raised about the nature of the kudzu vine, for example, an all-enveloping vine that is not native to the South.

The first numbered section of the poem shows the cousins as little girls on their grandmother's farm. In the second, we see them as adults linked to the earlier scene by certain images — Grandma's bedspread, "rough straw baskets" like the corncobs of their youth, kudzu — and we discover that both have endured custody battles. Pratt compares her "crime against nature," a sexual transgression, to her cousin's desire for a garden, somehow symbolic of her freedom of action. This too has been deemed a crime against nature, an unreasonable demand for a woman to make. The third section of the poem places their different attitudes in political perspective but has a sense of futility; they have traveled different paths but are accused of transgressing, of stepping out of their preordained "natural" roles.

The sections reveal a progression of awareness. Pratt begins with the vague busyness of little girls doing what they have seen others do, moves on to their break with tradition in the present, and ends with the philosophical realization that no matter what path they took, they have been "made wrong." The phrase has a double meaning. They have been made to *seem* wrong, though they have not done anything wrong. But they have also, in the culture's implicit value system, been *made* wrong; with female bodies, they are vulnerable to judgments about how they must behave in the world. A definition of cousins may be made without referring to parents at all; they are people who share a grandparent. The girls are like their mothers at first, shaping their babies from the natural materials at hand. In the second section, we see a shared heritage in their grandmother's crocheted bedspread. But in the final section we see their true heritage, the grandmother who doesn't condemn their fire but instead washes them up after it. Women do this for each other in Pratt's world. Age-mates, the daughters of sisters, provide support; grandmothers give unconditional comfort. Their pain as they think about losing children indicates that family ties are important. But rigid family roles are called into question as arbitrary and unjust.

Both Kitty Tsui's speaker in "A Chinese Banquet" and Minnie Bruce Pratt's in "Two Small-Sized Girls" address women, but their messages are different. Tsui's poem is at times a love song to a person who shares a passionate relationship with the narrator. Her futile desire to find a place for her lover in her family precipitates the poem. Pratt's narrator has a sisterly relationship with the woman addressed in her poem, and they share similar injustices. There is no indication that her cousin is lesbian, and we do not know from this poem how their mothers feel about the behaviors that cause them "guilt from men." Both poems share, however, the sad realization that transgressive female behavior separates family members, sometimes irrevocably. And both resist the culture's belief that such transgressors are worthy of the punishment they receive.

All three narrators in this cluster search for what Pratt's poem calls "kernels of fire deep in the body's shaken husk." Essex Hemphill's narrator is aware of his empty arms and wants integrity as a family member rather than the two-dimensional role of duty. Kitty Tsui's hates the silences behind her mother's words and wants to fill them with truth. And Minnie Bruce Pratt's knows that women must follow the substance of their own bodies and of their desires to walk free and to tend their own gardens without interference.

| 13 |

Teaching and Learning (p. 634)

RECALLING LESSONS OF CHILDHOOD (p. 636)

CATHY SONG

The Grammar of Silk (p. 637)

Both multiethnic and multilingual, Hawaiian culture is sometimes open, sometimes insular. Some residents of the state, when filling out forms, have to add extra lines to proudly include every ethnic group represented in their ancestry. Other families keep to the received traditions of the islands or continents their ancestors left, living and working with people who look and speak much like themselves. Many are personally or vicariously involved in the revival of the Hawaiian language and culture that was submerged beneath nineteenth-century missionary teachings. The groupings are multiple and shifting — Native Hawaiians, Asians with varied histories, American military families of many shades and accents, and tourists. It may be a cliché that America is less a melting pot than a salad bar, but Hawaii epitomizes this mix of individual flavors. Or perhaps a better metaphor is the crazy quilt, sewn together from many scraps of life. This would be an appropriate trope, since quilt making has long been an important craft in Hawaii. So when Cathy Song juxtaposes *grammar* and the communal business of fabric shopping in her poem, she does it within a rich linguistic and cultural context.

The learning that Song describes takes place in an informal community institution, the Saturday sewing school for girls. Grammar, too, is learned informally. Linguists tell us that the human brain seems to be wired for the rules of language and that we learn these rules without being able to articulate them consciously. We internalize the speech patterns we hear as children, and these patterns influence how we see ourselves and the world. In much the same way, the girls at Mrs. Umemoto's sewing school learn the rules of what it means to be a woman in a particular society. Sewing, like being a woman in Hawaii, is a language that one learns, and the seamstresses who know it well are "like librarians to be consulted" (line 20). The "mothers and daughters paused in symmetry" are themselves a pattern (line 31). The pattern books are holy texts, like the "stone tablets" of the Bible, a book that provides patterns for lives (line 30). The fabrics "have titles" (line 42), and the remnant the narrator's mother chooses is a "composition" (line 46).

But whereas a composition may be defined in terms of writing, the word takes on added connotations in the final lines of Song's poem, reminding us that patterns can be released into moments of music and freedom. The narrator, looking back, realizes that more was being learned than sewing in Mrs. Umemoto's "pleasant" basement with the "Singer's companionable whirr" (line 8). The sensory images, mostly auditory and tactile, connect the narrator with the women and girls engaged in sewing as a communal activity. They also connect her with history and the traditions of art; the silk inspires awe, "as if it were a piece from the Ming Dynasty" (line 35). The poet is Korean and Chinese, though we might note that the teacher's name is Japanese. It is the continuity that is important, and gender overrides ethnicity. The narrator puzzles out the possible meanings the activity has for the women, now that she can step outside the childhood experience. Beneath images of community, history, and art, she uses words like *sanctuary* and *refuge* to suggest what sewing might represent for these women as individuals.

Song frames her poem by beginning and ending with the experience of sewing itself, but she takes us to the fabric shop in the four middle stanzas. The beginning and end have a meditative quality; sewing, even in a group, is an individual experience, much like the music she compares it with. In the middle section, the rules of sewing are learned in a communal way. Students will have their own interpretations of the mother, but her longing for solitude is explicit in the poem. There may be an implicit desire for individuality and autonomy as well. Though the poem seems mostly positive about the activities of girls and women at the sewing school, the emphasis on grammar, a subliminally learned set of rules, raises the issue of the place of women in a traditional society. The seamstresses in the fabric shop are *like* architects, according to the poem, but they may not think of expressing their art and skill in a less domestic fashion.

Hawaiian culture differs from that of much of the contiguous U.S. Immigration has taken a different pattern, giving Asian and Pacific Rim history and culture a more prominent place than in most states east of California. More important to the poem, however, may be the history of the islands themselves. One of the first changes that English and American Christian missionaries demanded of Hawaiian culture was that the people clothe themselves more thoroughly. Sewing, therefore, became an important activity for women. Many students may come from cultures where textile arts are traditionally female activities that pass down community values. Several texts in this anthology emphasize the importance of quilts or other handmade heirlooms for African Americans or for whites of certain regions. Although Hawaii may be the most ethnically cosmopolitan of states, many strongly held traditions date back to issues of the eighteenth and nineteenth centuries. Many children and adolescents go to schools like Kamehameha, Iolani, and Punahou, private institutions established by church or royal family members to provide formal education for specific groups. Although these schools have broadened their goals in recent years, and although the U.S. government has formally apologized to the indigenous peoples of Hawaii for the forcible seizure of their lands and culture, both formal and informal education teach patterns that owe much to the history of colonial-style conquest. In the midst of this, however, people transform received patterns into strengths, using them both for community and for individuality.

JULIA ALVAREZ

How I Learned to Sweep (p. 639)

Julia Alvarez came to the United States from the Dominican Republic as a ten-year-old girl. She was from a traditional family that expected her to grow up to be a housewife. However, being female in the well-to-do family of her childhood in the Dominican Republic meant living in a compound filled with sisters, aunts, and maids that handled household chores. After moving to America when her father fled political imprisonment or execution in their home country, Alvarez was surprised that she missed the extended family and prosperous circumstances she'd taken for granted. She also encountered prejudice and social isolation, which she had never experienced before coming to America. Alvarez describes the impact of immigration on a child: "The feeling of loss caused a radical change in me. It made me an introverted little girl." Finding her place in the spaces between two languages, she knew as a teenager that she would become a writer, and she speaks eloquently of the power of stories to change us and to help us create meaning. Alvarez weaves her life experiences into stories and poems, often writing about family relationships. Both her knowledge of women in the midst of change within traditional families and her experience with the impact of war and revolution underpin this text, which is from a poetry sequence ostensibly about housekeeping.

Although the speaker of "How I Learned to Sweep" claims that this is a skill her mother never taught her, readers understand that many of the things we have learned were never an explicit part of our education. When she says that she knew what her mother expected, however, the statement is ambiguous. Are we meant to understand that she has picked up the art of sweeping without training? Or are other values being taught? Most students have experienced being kept busy as children so that they are distracted from thinking about serious matters. A child born in 1950 would be a teenager or older when the Vietnam War was being viewed in American living rooms every evening. Is Alvarez expected to do housework rather than dwell on current events because young women need to be distracted from such things? The point may simply be that she should make herself useful, rather than sitting and watching television when the floor is dirty. Whatever the reason, the speaker juxtaposes the act of sweeping and the content of the news program to say something beyond housework.

The poem begins with a regular rhythm and rhyming couplets. The rhythm is much like sweeping, and the rhyme, almost doggerel, gives the action an everyday triviality. This contrasts with the unrhymed descriptions of the televised war scenes in the middle of the poem that are at the same time more realistic and more surreal than household activities. When the poet returns to sweeping, she returns to rhyme for a time. In the closing lines, she has alternate lines rhyme *breath* with *death*. It is ironic that the metaphor of sweeping up the results of war alternates with her mother's innocent praise of her handiwork. In reality, she does not learn to be comfortable with sweeping sacrificed lives aside, as the president may be doing in his television speech. Students will have heard before that Vietnam was the first televised war. Since the advent of twenty-four-hour-a-day news on cable television, war has become even more immediate, as we know from events in Eastern Europe, the Middle East, and Africa in the 1990s. The usual response of teenagers might be to switch to MTV. Alvarez's Vietnam-era girl could have turned on the radio to listen to rock and roll. But her attention has been caught, and the metaphor her mind creates has the sort of power Alvarez attributes to story. The sweeping becomes a frantic obsession, a spell to make death disappear. The mother fails to see the underlying cause of her daughter's success in sweeping. She values cleanliness, orderliness, obedience, and industry.

But the poet may be telling us that reality is messy, that to make reality disappear along with the dust is not as worthy of praise as the mother thinks. The mother easily turns off the news of war but values a tidy house and a daughter who pays more attention to housework than to politics. Studies of Hispanic college women in the 1990s revealed that many still have problems making families understand the importance of focusing on schoolwork. Many parents feel that daughters should be available to help their families first and that college can be dropped to drive a grandparent to a doctor's appointment or to prepare for a family occasion. Students may think of times that they have encountered such conflicts between family attitudes and personal or political priorities, and many will recall being praised by their parents for motives far different from those they really feel. Parents and children may usually sweep away just such differences in worldview, especially when the child knows that the metaphors that bring issues to life can never quite be articulated in a way the parent will understand.

The use of rhythm and rhyme structures a poem, enclosing thought and dictating the readers' pace more directly than the open structure of free verse. The overall effect of Cathy Song's "The Grammar of Silk"(p. 637) is interior monologue. We have a sense of the narrator as an adult musing about the meaning of sewing in the lives of her mother and her friends. Alvarez allows her narrator less distance in "How I Learned to Sweep." Her intermittent use of rhyme pulls us into the action of the moment, as the young woman works out her feelings toward death and war in a physical way. In Song's poem, *sanctuary* and *oblivion* are words connected with peace, a temporary respite from the pace of motherhood and other domestic responsibilities. For Alvarez, oblivion would have less positive connotations. The cleanliness that her narrator achieves as she tries to sweep away the war is a sort of oblivion, an effort to forget reality. But the activity has not been peaceful but frantic, and her mother's happiness with it seems petty and misguided in contrast. Since to receive sanctuary one must flee from the dangers of life, this too would run counter to Alvarez's theme.

The tone that the poets take toward the mothers they describe shapes our interpretation of their actions. Most readers probably sympathize with the busy mother of Song's poem, who must find moments of solitude and creativity in between the activities of life and who teaches her daughter the meditation of work. But we only know what the narrator guesses about her mother's motives, seeing her only from this romantic point of view. The mother of Alvarez's poem may be much like Song's mother, but we see her from a less positive perspective. The daughter learns on her own that work and emotion are interrelated, that sometimes the work we do has symbolic meaning beyond — perhaps opposing — its obvious meanings. But the result is ironic. The mother remains ignorant of her daughter's profound insights about the horror of war, and the reader remains ignorant of the mother's true motives and thoughts. Though some students will protest that the mother is simply practical and the daughter up in the clouds, we can only guess at the mother's thoughts while we overhear the daughter's.

FORREST HAMER

Lesson (p. 641)

Poet and psychologist Forrest Hamer writes that he feels lucky to have been an African American growing up in the South in the 1960s. In fact, when he was an undergraduate at Yale, he felt out of his element, since his rural upbringing set him apart from other black students and he was not yet comfortable with the white establishment. He remembers his childhood as happy and secure. The strength of his parents and grandparents brought him through in a time and place when prejudice could have challenged his confidence and self-esteem. The setting of "Lesson" is a Mississippi highway, a frightening place for a black family to drive through during the specific years of the poem's events. Students may need some orientation, perhaps looking through periodicals from these years or examining pictorial histories and documentaries of the civil rights movement. Freedom rides, bus boycotts, and lunch counter sit-ins had begun a few years earlier, and the South was in the midst of voter registration drives. Some students may have seen movies like *Mississippi Burning* and may realize that "outside agitators" were harassed, even killed. Others might remember reading about violence on the highway at the time of the march on Selma or seeing taped footage of protesters being attacked by police using fire hoses and dogs. It would take only a small misstep for strangers like Hamer's father to become suspect. Current readers may find it odd that the family sleeps by the side of the road in such dangerous territory, but finding a motel or even a place to eat would have been a problem in the days of "whites only" signs. Hamer has related that even at home in Goldsboro, North Carolina, the children would fill up on water before going downtown on shopping trips, since it was difficult to find a water fountain that Negroes were allowed to use. Many such childhood experiences make their way into his writing.

His father, too, is an important figure in Hamer's poetic imagery. His father's two tours in Vietnam greatly affected the family, and the changes he saw in the older man after his second return home led Hamer into psychology as a career. If the date of this trip is indeed "1963 or 4," U.S. military involvement in Southeast Asia was just beginning to build up, and Vietnam was indeed "a place no place in the world" to most Americans. To the extent that we know the personal and historical context of the narrator's childhood fears, the poem becomes ironic and powerful. The narrator fears one danger, the very real domestic violence of a 1960s hot summer, but we know that it is the other, unknown danger his father faces in Vietnam that will have the most impact on him. He has said that his father came back a different man, so if — as it seems here — the poet and the voice in the poem are the same person, he really does come to lose the father he needs, and the noises in the dark take on new meaning.

There is an opposition between two lessons in the poem, the one recognizing that his father is not omnipotent against all the dangers of the world and the other realizing that the boy "needs [his] father with him." Perhaps the difference is related to the two major issues of the 1960s, civil rights and Vietnam. The adult narrator knows that his father and other family members have succeeded in bringing him through the wars of prejudice, but he knows that something in his father was lost to him through the war in Vietnam. Could it be the fear of losing a father rather than any concrete danger to himself that requires a boy to keep his father near him? If so, the lesson is singular, as the title indicates. If a father is not all-powerful, the son will have to keep him safely at hand. As a psychologist, Hamer understands that children feel responsible for protecting their parents and that at the root of separation anxiety lies a fear of loss. What is a premonition for the boy is known history to the man who relates the story, and the poet uses this difference in knowledge to create irony for the reader.

By isolating the word *Noises* in line 9, the poet forces us to pause and listen. When he uses the word again, he has just implicitly conjured up for readers the image of soldiers in the jungles of Vietnam, sleeping on the ground and listening for danger. He describes the boy as "fixed against noise," and we think of fixed bayonets. From the distance of a new century it may be easy to claim that the father should not have gone to Vietnam, should instead have been there for his son. Students who are quick to judge may be led to consider the consequences for the family if the father had deserted the military. Wouldn't he have been lost to them in another way? During the Gulf War of the 1980s many of the soldiers who were deployed with reserve units were not fathers but mothers, some with very young children. Debates about whether a child needs a father or a mother tend to depend heavily on pathos. We need to steer students toward using psychological studies and other hard evidence to back up their assertions rather than let them depend primarily on emotion and personal experiences that may or may not be representative.

In each of the poems in this cluster, children learn lessons that involve their parents. But we do not see the parents intentionally teaching these lessons. Cathy Song's speaker in "The Grammar of Silk" (p. 637) speculates that her mother takes her to the sewing school because she wants her to learn how to carve out these times of peaceful concentration when the mind and body work together as one. She believes that the older woman gives her daughter what she would wish for herself. On the other hand, the mother in Julia Alvarez's "How I Learned to Sweep" (p. 639) does not teach her child about housework or about the metaphors of death. She merely sets the learning experience in motion by accident, and the result would be bewildering to her if she realized that her daughter has actually learned the enormity of war along with her sweeping. Like most of the teaching that parents actually do, the lesson that Hamer's father teaches in the incident described in the poem is unintentional. Most parents don't tell their children that they are invincible, but children make that assumption. Nor do fathers usually tell sons that they are afraid, that they are powerless to protect their children or themselves from war and hatred. Instead, children learn as Hamer describes in his poem, adding up clues from restless sleep, stories they've heard, on the tension in a father's listening body.

As they consider the question of how the poems might be different if written by the parents, students might try writing poems that express the parents' point of view. Song's mother, given time, might speak as her daughter does, but as her life stands, her words might be quicker, with no nonsense. She has been described in terms of music, so perhaps we could expect lyricism in compressed form. Perhaps she would write a haiku in calligraphy. The mother in the Alvarez poem might write greeting-card verse in cliché form. But perhaps this is unfair. She might describe her pride in her daughter, so quick to learn how to make a room spotless with no formal training in the art of sweeping. Or perhaps we will learn that she knew what was going on in her daughter's mind all along, but she knew the child must work it out for herself.

Hamer's father might finally talk about Vietnam; his son said that the father tended to deflect such conversations to the subject of Korea. We might learn what he was thinking that night in Mississippi, what he was feeling about leaving his son. Although Hamer's poem is historically realistic, he only hints at what Vietnam will do to the country and to this family, leaving us to our own associations. In fact, if we assume that the boy in the poem is not identical to the boy who was Forrest Hamer, we can imagine scenarios other than the autobiographical one. The father might run to Canada, for example. Or he might die in the war.

The girl watching television in the poem by Alvarez ironically has more information than the boy who lies near a man who will actually participate. She describes the familiar television image of rescue helicopters, but as she begins to describe the men as dust falling from the sky too quickly to be swept up, the experience becomes surreal, almost a vision. The sheer numbers overwhelm her. Hers is a sudden realization, an epiphany that only begins with the specificity of the television image. His is dread, a presentiment of some lurking, unseen danger to the one soldier who really matters. Although Hamer's poem is more realistic, both poems depend on a grasp of historical events.

TEACHING CHILDREN ABOUT SOCIETY (p. 643)

JAMES AGEE

A Mother's Tale (p. 644)

James Agee graduated from Harvard University in the year that Franklin D. Roosevelt was first elected president of the United States: 1932. As the world entered into the Great Depression and it was becoming apparent that the economy was not going to correct itself, FDR pushed through the programs of the New Deal, transforming the social institutions of the country. Agee, with photographer Walker Evans, used an equally revolutionary approach as a reporter for *Fortune* magazine. The book that grew out of his series of documentary articles was *Let Us Now Praise Famous Men* (1941). The book presents the stories of three families of tenant farmers in the rural South in a way that reveals their battles to survive the starvation and appalling deprivation of the Depression.

Rather than preaching, however, Evans's black-and-white photographs and Agee's poetic narratives invite readers to come to their own conclusions while allowing their subjects to retain their dignity.

The effectiveness of this style of educating the public seems obvious to readers now, but Agee was the father of this sort of journalism. Students interested in issues raised by Agee's content or style in "A Mother's Tale" will profit from an examination of this ground-breaking text. They might look at other texts of the period, such as John Steinbeck's *Grapes of Wrath* or the movie based on the novel. Our context for reading the story should also consider Agee's Marxist perspectives and his possible use of the cattle to symbolize workers of the world who should unite against the system that markets their labor and destroys their lives. The foregrounding of death in Agee's thinking is also important. His father died in an accident when he was a child, and this event shaped both his life and his writing, resulting in the novel *A Death in the Family*, published in 1957 after his death. At the time "A Mother's Tale" was published, Agee himself was near death. He had lived as an iconoclast in almost every realm of his life, once saying, "I know I am making the choice most dangerous to an artist in valuing life above art." For Agee, the idea of "pie in the sky by and by" was one way men in power could fool people into accepting oppression, and the true reformer would relieve suffering in the real world by forcing us to look it straight in the eye.

Although "A Mother's Tale" reads like a fable with its talking animals, it uses narrative techniques to suggest that reality must be faced with open eyes rather than with platitudes or self-deceptions. The cattle are dominated by a false consciousness that contributes to their exploitation and destruction. Some students will be offended by the incongruity of cute animals and violent content, and others will not get beyond the surface, perhaps seeing the story as an indictment of eating meat. The class could look back at Philip Levine's "What Work Is" in Chapter 2 (p. 117) and be led to compare the men in line for jobs with the cattle in line at the abattoir. Levine has said of this autobiographical experience that he realized the people in the employment office had deliberately forced unemployed men to wait two hours to see who had the desperation or docility to wait it out. Like Agee's cattle, the unemployed workers are at the mercy of a system that sees them only as so much meat. Going further to look at other Levine poems, especially those that feature animals, can illuminate Agee's method. Both writers, to use Levine's words, "give voice to the voiceless," and their twentieth-century working-class parables can be used intertextually. Some students will object to Agee's implication that belief in heaven is for uncomprehending cattle. The One Who Came Back will seem like a Christ figure to them, warning them away from Hell. But we might also think of the trains that took Holocaust victims to their deaths. After all, this story was written soon after World War II, and it could be read as an indictment of Nazism.

Regardless of the historical or religious implications, Agee is pessimistic about the ability of his characters to learn from the experiences of others or from the mistakes of the past. The mother cow passes on the tradition, but her lack of knowledge makes her narrative less convincing to the audience within the story. She is not a true believer, so her tale has the quality of a ghost story or of folklore, used, as she admits, "to frighten children." She moves in and out of belief as she alternately gets caught up in the story and then remembers her audience.

There is irony for the reader, since we know that cattle are taken to slaughter in this way and that man is not a kind, paternalistic protector of cows. The mother is unwilling to accept the consequences of true belief, however, because this would mean rebellion for the adults and death for the calves and yearlings. Readers familiar with Toni Morrison's *Beloved* might think of slave women who were willing to kill their babies rather than allow them to live in slavery. As the class discusses the views of The One Who Came Back, we might raise the issue of how far individuals would be willing to go to save themselves or their children from oppression. Those who reject his views should consider how power might be gained when a group finds itself as powerless and bewildered as these cattle.

TONI CADE BAMBARA
The Lesson (p. 659)

Like her young protagonist in "The Lesson," Toni Cade Bambara remembers a childhood in which strong female figures educate younger women and girls. In her most recent book of essays, *Deep Sightings and Rescue Missions*, Bambara quotes one mentor, Miss Dorothy: "Colored gal on planet earth . . . know everything there is to know, anything she/we don't know is by definition the unknown." The older woman teaches the child how to tell stories based on her inner knowledge, and Bambara says that she "taught me critical theory." Later, Bambara would recognize the older woman's advice in her reading. She was taught that stories must be culture specific, that to speak is to assume responsibility. She learned that her stories must be based in the narratives of freedom that make up the oral and literary history of African Americans. Her goal is to "lift up a few useable truths" in a "racist, hardheaded, heedless society." Her voice is thus both political and personal, and she takes seriously the responsibility to pass on what she knows. In "The Lesson" the narrator learns, but the reader is taught as well.

Because the voice of the story moves into present tense in the second paragraph and speaks much as a young girl would speak, the age of the narrator matters little. She has enough distance to choose her details so that we see her begin to realize what Miss Moore wants her to learn from the trip to the toy store, and we see her at the end going off alone to absorb the lesson. Like Paulo Freire, whose pedagogical theory influenced Bambara, Miss Moore knows that one of the purposes of education is to wake up those who are oppressed, to make them see their circumstances so that they can rise up against them. The West African proverb that *it takes a village to raise a child* — that the education of children is the responsibility of everyone with something to share — is central to Bambara's philosophy. In the fragmented culture of slavery, this precept became even more important than it was in Africa before people were forcibly brought to America. Mothers were often strangers who worked from dawn to dark, and elderly women too old to go to the fields cared for the children of many mothers. Furthermore, it was against the law in many states to teach slaves to read and write, so lessons had to be passed on in any way possible.

Traditions that worked for survival and freedom in desperate times continue because children need role models and people who will prod them to think.

For many students, Miss Moore's efforts make her seem like a busybody who interferes in family matters. Bambara, whose experience included many such women, would disagree. She and other members of the black power and black arts movements of the 1970s believed strongly that neighborhood programs must be established to teach children about their heritage and about wrongs that need redressing. Miss Moore has a political agenda, to show the children the inequality that will make them angry. Students may suggest that simply pointing out the problem does not guide the children into finding solutions, does not really empower them. Miss Moore's audience rejects much of what she says because they see no means of acquiring desks for their rooms or microscopes for observing bacteria. Her distance from them, the air of authority that keeps even the adults from addressing her by a first name, makes it difficult for her to build common ground with her audience. They find her boring and have their own agendas. But her Socratic method "contaminates" the youth in her charge into seeing that their lot is unfair, though their reactions vary. Rosie Giraffe's sour-grapes comment — "White folks crazy" — misreads Miss Moore's lesson, accepting the cultural difference without openly admitting the injustice. Mercedes also misreads, thinking the unreachable toys will soon be available to her. Flyboy ignores the issue and doesn't puzzle out the reasons for his weariness. Sugar articulates the philosophy behind Miss Moore's lesson, but there's no sign that she is as distressed by it as the narrator, who internalizes it and makes it her own in the story's final sentence. Race plays a large part in the story, and Bambara would maintain that all stories must be seen in the context of their cultures. But class plays perhaps a more important role in "The Lesson" since it is the economic issue that is most explicitly addressed.

In both stories of this cluster, children are taught lessons about society that are not comfortable ones to learn. In fact, most of the children resist the teachings, misreading or ignoring them because their reality is too hard to face. In James Agee's "A Mother's Tale" (p. 644) the children cannot accept their oppression and looming death, and we realize at the end that they will continue as always to accept and even welcome their fate. There is more hope for Miss Moore's charges, but only one or two will take the hard lesson to heart and find a way to take action. When teachers use such an approach, we sometimes say that their aim is to lead their students into a state of "cognitive dissonance," the awareness that one must work out a way of taking in an uncomfortably new idea. Teachers who challenge us in this way, shaking up our worldviews, make us uncomfortable, but the learning that we acquire becomes our own. The approach of this course is, in fact, a confrontational one. We want students to find their issues in literature and in life and to do the hard work of thinking them through. We want them to examine preconceived assumptions, to explore the reasons for their discomfort with certain ideas, rather than ignoring them or quickly explaining them away. By trusting them with their own intellectual space, we run the risk that only a few will "get" the lesson we think they should. Bambara's teacher succeeds only when she uses this method; her lectures are ignored as educational propaganda. The mother cow is less aware. She passes on the story of her culture but doesn't quite believe it herself. Both try to make the younger ones aware of oppression, however, and both care deeply about the welfare of their audience.

Writing Agee's story from the perspective of one of the calves would be difficult, since the irony of its last line depends upon the young audience not really understanding the point of the story. The mother cow herself is the dynamic character of her story; she is the one who is moved by the horror she only partly accepts as possible. In Bambara's story we share Sylvia's emotions and know that the lesson has struck her deeply. Because we listen to her resistance, her vow to "not be beaten" is more compelling. We know that she does not simply parrot an answer to please a teacher but that she sincerely owns this knowledge and that this ownership will empower her.

LOSING INNOCENCE: RE-VISIONS OF LITTLE RED RIDING HOOD (p. 666)

CHARLES PERRAULT

Little Red Riding Hood (p. 666)

Charles Perrault's tale of "Little Red Riding Hood" begins with a close extended family of women taking care of each other and showering affection on the little girl of the youngest generation. But hints of problems occur in the second sentence, since the mother is "excessively fond" of the child and the grandmother is said to have "doted" on her. The implication for readers in the 1600s, long before the Romantic period's idealization of childhood in the early 1800s, would have been negative. This child is spoiled and perhaps vain and therefore can be expected to come to a bad end.

Coming from the country, Little Red Riding Hood is at a further disadvantage. She is sent into the world to do good works but is little prepared for the dangers along the way. The women of the story seem to share a loving, compassionate community among themselves. Little Red Riding Hood is in fact on an errand of mercy. But the women are too trusting. While there are vague hints that "some woodcutters" provide protection, the wolf manages to get around this male authority fairly easily through deceit. Readers in the twenty-first century might quickly extrapolate to the dangers for young girls wandering into chat rooms on the Internet or hanging out in malls.

The connotations of rape in the grandmother's house are clear. The wolf intrudes into the innocent family love among the three generations of women, first devouring the grandmother out of hunger and teasing and consuming Little Red Riding Hood seemingly for dessert. Both women die because they are too trusting, and some readers might question whether they are truly as innocent as they appear to be. It is rather shocking when the wolf's invitation for the girl to get into bed — presumably with her grandmother — elicits the response of disrobing. We can imagine adults enjoying the naughty connotations of the scene while children giggle at the series of questions as they eagerly await the "All the better to eat you up with" of the well-told tale. The ignorance of the females in the story provides a satisfying irony, since we know what will happen and pick up on the sexual nuances but the characters do not.

In fairy tales, young women are both innocent and pretty, a stereotype of women in European and American cultural history that portrays women as vulnerable and desirable to men. While much has changed about women's roles in society in the centuries since Perrault wrote, images of women in magazine advertisements and television commercials perpetuate this subconscious view of women as beautiful objects to be used for men's sexual pleasure or to raise men's status by serving as trophy wives or mistresses. Class discussion can benefit from viewing video presentations on images produced by Jean Kilbourne and others. Students also might find Internet images from Frank Cordelle's "The Century Project" — a photographic display that challenges the slick, infantile images of women perpetuated in popular culture. Models and women in advertisements are usually portrayed as physically perfect, sometimes as anorexic, sometimes with unrealistic Barbie doll curves. Like Red Riding Hood, actresses in movies are seldom "homely." Students in groups can be asked to cast a movie based on the story of Little Red Riding Hood.

Although the story has much comic potential, however, the issue is serious: our definitions of men and women are shaped by subliminal messages, and our ability to interact with each other without playing fairy-tale games is hampered by them. We might as easily critique the images of men in the tale: one male is a predatory wolf, who feeds his hunger through deceit; others are protectors that are supposed to defend the public against the wolf but because they are busy working they do not save the women from death (or a fate worse than death) in this particular narrative. (And though it may take us a bit off track, environmentally minded students may question the images of wolves as villains and woodcutters as heroes!)

Perhaps the mother could have given the naïve Little Red Riding Hood and her sickly grandmother some concrete help, had she been on the scene. But like the dead mothers in the tales of Snow White and Cinderella, this potentially strong character is removed from the scene. In fact, she is responsible for throwing the more vulnerable females into danger, and we may question why she chooses not to accompany her daughter on the walk through the woods and not to serve as a caregiver to her mother. In Perrault's world, perhaps she has been removed by her position as a (presumably) married woman or by her need to provide for the family. More telling is the disappearance or nonexistence of the father. In most traditional fairy tales, the father's absence or complicity leaves the child open to danger, often from a stepmother or witch.

We may want to return to the issue of education and raise the question of Red Riding Hood's age and her preparation for the world outside her home. If she is a thirteen-year-old surfing the Internet or hanging out at the mall, her parents have some culpability, but the story also becomes a parent's nightmare. On the other hand, if she is a college student, the story might be more relevant to our readers. We all know students who come to college with little understanding of how to manage their lives without the supervision of Mom and Dad. Students might suggest the role that parents should play in preparing adolescents for college and then letting them go, sharing what they wish their own parents had done differently or have done particularly well. They can also tell us of friends who seem most like the characters in the story — perhaps the ones who gather rosebuds until early morning when a paper is due, who fall for the line of every predator who comes along, or who even play the role of the wolf. The adjectives that students choose to describe Little Red Riding Hood show that they tend to judge her rather harshly or to see her as comic, evaluations that seem to be in the spirit of Perrault's text. Perhaps she is, as students point out, so stupid she deserves to die, though Disney fans tend to be surprised at the ending and the wolf's swift finishing off of the grandmother. Often students are horrified that the violent tales of Perrault and the Grimm brothers were so long told to children, but we might recall that children love scary stories and often understand the moral, especially when it is given so explicitly. Perhaps children need to know that unthinking decisions can lead to death: we don't want them to run into the street or to help the "nice man" find his puppy, setting themselves up for harm. The deaths of Perrault's narrative seem appropriate because they emphasize the danger.

The "moral" at the end may undercut the story's impact by bringing it out of the forest and into the ballroom of upper-class French society of the seventeenth century. But it does raise an important point. Children taught to avoid "strangers" often do not know what a stranger really is. They tend to picture monsters, like the wolf with his huge arms and frightening teeth, rather than the more charming predators who court them with subtle compliments and deceptions that take advantage of their vulnerabilities. He makes the point for "well bred young ladies" — perhaps some of our college students, both male and female — that the dangers of trusting too easily are not confined to such obvious situations as forests and wolves.

JACOB AND WILHELM GRIMM

Little Red Cap (p. 669)

While the Charles Perrault version of "Little Red Riding Hood" (p. 666) seems to be aimed mostly at "well-bred young ladies" susceptible to seduction by male predators at the French court in the late 1600s, Jacob and Wilhelm Grimm's tale, adapted from those told by German peasant women, imagines a less sophisticated audience. Modern parents might be reluctant to tell their children stories with this degree of violence, but the Grimms' "Little Red Cap" is more childlike than Perrault's in terms of sexual innuendo. In both tales, the wolf devours the grandmother and the female child, and this gobbling up of women by a fearsome but clever predator can be equated with rape. Perrault clearly gives his audience a cautionary tale, laced with a certain amount of adult humor: his characters are gullible, and their fate comes as a direct result of their trusting natures. Wolves exist, the narrative implies, and if you are not prepared to deal with them, you die, and the wolves win.

This symbolism is buried in the Grimm version, making its message less clearly about sex. The Grimm version of this story has more to do with "do[ing] everything just right," staying on the path of righteousness and obeying one's mother. Even though the young girl goes astray and the old woman in her weakness allows the wolf in the door, redemption comes in the form of a good man, and the evil character is punished, not the foolish ones whose intentions are good. Here we have the "fairy-tale ending" with which we are familiar, and we can imagine that in a few years the brave woodcutter's son will be rewarded for his father's bravery with marriage to a wiser Little Red Cap, and all will live happily ever after.

At the beginning of their tale, the Grimms emphasize how sweet and likeable Red Riding Hood is. She is the good little girl that female children are expected to emulate. Unlike the child of Perrault's version, who is depicted as spoiled and overly "doted" on, Little Red Cap is loved by everyone and has been given training and discipline. We hear her mother instructing her on how she should mind her manners. But like Perrault's Little Red Riding Hood, this girl also lacks knowledge about how to deal with deception in the world away from home. This omission in her education makes her vulnerable to the wolf, who — with veiled sexual connotations — is attracted to her being a "sweet young thing" and imagines that she "will taste even better than the old woman." Even when Little Red Cap goes astray, she thinks about gathering flowers for her grandmother.

In terms of narrative, Grimms' storytellers would find it difficult to allow such a sympathetic protagonist to die in the way that Perrault's foolish heroine does. The audience, especially one composed of children, is delighted when the good but temporarily wandering child and her grandmother are cut from the belly of the beast intact, still good but no longer innocent. For this unlikely scenario to succeed, the characters who are saved must be likeable — otherwise their salvation would be less satisfying and even harder to believe. As the story stands, justice is served because the innocent victims are saved and the perpetrator of the crime is executed. Furthermore, the experience empowers the women so that they may save themselves in the future, making them dynamic characters who change as the cause and effect plot of the narrative develops.

Ironically for modern readers, Little Red Cap is drawn from the path of righteousness because her eyes are opened to the beauty of nature. For audiences in around 1800 — as the Romantic period in art, music, and literature was beginning to flower in Germany and other European countries — the conflict between traditional moral virtues and the sublime awe of untamed nature would have been more problematic than it may be for twenty-first century readers. For Grimms' readers, the idea that the beauties of nature should be sought out and enjoyed was revolutionary, and for earlier tellers of the folk tales such a thought would have bordered on sin. Wilderness was something to be tamed and brought under God's control: woodcutters cleared the tangled growth of sinful nature to create the parks and gardens of Christian civility and order. Being swept up in the beauties of nature would have been judged by some listeners to the tale to be as dangerous spiritually as being swept up in the pleasures of sexuality. As products of the Romantic movement of the early 1800s and the environmental movements of the late 1900s, today's readers have a "commonsense" view of nature as uplifting and find it difficult to understand how powerful the "commonsense" fear and distaste for untamed nature was for an earlier audience.

At the same time, people did respond to the beauty of nature, even though they viewed it as forbidden fruit. Therefore, the symbolism of a young girl's straying from the path to "gather rosebuds" relates to her dangerous discovery of herself as a sexual human being. While modern audiences may not "blame" Red Riding Hood for either discovery, we need to imagine audiences who would and examine both their warrants and our own.

We also need to problematize the views of women revealed in the story. The society that we meet at the beginning of both the Perrault and Grimm versions of Little Red Riding Hood seems to be centered on the female members of a family, with fathers, brothers, and grandfathers nowhere to be seen. When the first male figure enters the picture, he takes the dangerous form of a ravenous wolf. In Perrault's version, this is the only depiction of a male. Although wood-cutters are mentioned as a deterrent that causes the wolf to be more sly in his machinations, they do not appear on the scene to miraculously save the women from the predator. In the Grimm version, on the other hand, the woodcutter saves the women from death, even after they seem to be ruined. So in "Little Red Cap" some men are not beasts but heroes who notice when a situation does not seem quite right. While the story could have had the mother come to the rescue, it doesn't.

The message may be that women need men to save them, encouraging passivity on the part of women and the desire to be a rescuer on the part of men. Certainly, many other Grimm tales carry this message: in "Cinderella" and "Snow White," for example, handsome princes come to the rescue of persecuted women, and marriage is seen as a happy ending that solves all problems. Perhaps, however, rather than assuming that the message is one we would now see as negative — that women are too weak or foolish to save themselves without the help of a man — we could see "Little Red Cap" as demonstrating the reality that women usually cannot enclose themselves in a society that ignores the presence of men. Indeed, ignoring their existence may lead to danger when women instead trust those who would do them harm. The women of the Grimms' story actually learn to fend for themselves by the story's end: the heroine does not marry the woodcutter, and the women carry on as an autonomous group, benefiting from the knowledge acquired by their experiences.

As we have noted already, although the Perrault and the Grimm versions of Little Red Riding Hood share the same plot, subtle differences exist between the two tales. Perrault's female characters are more gullible, weaker, and less likeable than the Grimm brothers' women. The Perrault characters are quickly killed by the wolf and do not return to life to exact revenge or to learn from their mistakes. The women in the Grimms' version become as violent as the wolf himself and are in no way passive victims of male predators. They become self-sufficient and work together to keep themselves safe. Nor are men always villains in the Grimm story: the woodcutter plays his role but does not dominate the action, and the wolves come across finally as creatures less clever and more driven by insatiable desires that lead to cruel but appropriate deaths at the hands of their intended victims.

The Grimms' version seems to be less about sex than Perrault's and more about the serving up of justice. When the wolf invites Perrault's Little Red Riding Hood into bed with him, adult readers can nudge each other with salacious pleasure while the children shiver with delicious goose bumps. The Grimms' version is more overtly violent at the same time that it is less realistic. Having the wolf jump out of the bed blunts the sexual symbolism and makes this less a story of seduction and more a story of an outright attack. But death, like sex, is similarly skirted in the Grimm story. While the power of good is foregrounded, the power of evil is somewhat denied, making the cautionary effect of the Grimm tale perhaps less dramatic than that of the Perrault version.

The device of having the women return to life in the Grimm version may deliver an unrealistically optimistic view of life. If the hunger of the wolf stands for the compulsion to rape, then the easy recovery of the women may imply that one can bounce back from an attack and be made stronger than before. On the other hand, the Perrault version implies that evil wins, perhaps even applauds the fact while pretending to give advice to young ladies. While some may argue that the use of violence by the women in the Grimm version undercuts any positive message the story holds and that the *deus ex machina* of the woodcutter is unrealistic, the overall theme offers more room for action and problem solving and thus may offer more useful tools for learning than the simple cautionary tale of Perrault.

ANGELA CARTER

The Company of Wolves (p. 673)

While the traditional folk tales about Little Red Riding Hood warn young women not to stray from the path of conventional morality and obedience, the feminist retelling by Angela Carter, "The Company of Wolves," first published in 1977, complicates the story's message by turning it upside down. Carter's Red Riding Hood embraces the wolf and the wolf nature within herself as she seizes her own sexuality.

In the movie version of Carter's "The Company of Wolves," the story begins with the Little Red Riding Hood of this version, Rosaleen, dreaming of the death of her conventional, judgmental sister, Alice, who is attacked by wolves as she runs in fear through the forest. Should some people stay on the path, since not everyone possesses a moral compass or the ability to deal with ambiguity? Is it okay to become a predator oneself and to devour others? Carter's Little Red Riding Hood attacks the wolf and tames him, and the argument can be made that she thus falls into a dangerous fantasy that kills many marriages. She seems unconcerned about her grandmother's death, an attitude that may trouble some readers. However, if we see all of the characters of Carter's narrative as part of the young woman's own psyche — which the dream premise of her screenplay version of the story invites the audience to do — we might argue that the voice of the "old wives' tales" that hamper women's freedom and sexuality need to be silenced.

Much in our interpretations of the Little Red Riding Hood stories depends on the age of the audience. No ethical person would deny that children should be kept safe. Yet we have seen with the revelations in recent years of molestations of children by priests and other trusted authority figures that recognizing predators is not an easy matter and that what seems like a safe path of obedience and morality may be as dangerous as the "bad neighborhood" represented by the forest. In both the world of the folk tale and the world of today, however, young people reach a point when they must strike out on their own and enter into adult relationships. While Perrault's "Little Red Riding Hood" warns girls about the dangers of seduction and the Grimm version ends with women banding together to protect themselves against predators, neither seems to admit that girls grow up and enter into sexual relationships, whether through their own desires or through society's overt or subtle admonitions to marry and produce children. The stories may mean to discourage the former and protect women for the latter. But for most women, heterosexual relationships happen eventually, and the Little Red Riding Hood narratives provide little guidance for moving beyond the fear of sexuality to a mature relationship with a man who is neither all wolf nor all woodcutter, neither destroyer nor protector. Perhaps Carter, by setting some of her transformations of humans into wolves at weddings, implies that marriage itself can become a dark and dangerous wood for the naïve, both for women taught to fear men and for men who fear domestication, men "too shy to piss into a pot."

Carter's narrative gives us several episodes about wolves before bringing us to the story that most closely resembles the Little Red Riding Hood of the folk tales. In her screenplay, Carter has these stories told in the girl's dream by her grandmother. These, therefore, are the cautionary tales meant to teach the budding young woman to stay on the path of morality and to be on guard against predators. But from the beginning, although the narrator tells us that the wolf is "carnivore incarnate" and beyond reason and redemption, she also hints that the wolf simply follows his nature and responds to his hunger. When hunters cut off the paws of the trapped animal, the reader is more likely to feel empathy for the creature than to side with the brutal humans of the story. When we think of *paws*, we think of our pets, and the connotations of the word raise issues about distinctions between wild animals and the ones we feel at home with.

When the wolf turns into a human being, the narrator drives home her point that predators are not always easy to recognize and that wolves are not always what they seem to be. When the voice of the storyteller tells us that we "could count the starveling ribs through their pelts," the reader's compassion is further aroused. Creatures that are starving are dangerous, of course, but they are also victims. We need to ask whether this compassion we feel for an animal (or human being) that is hungry for food, the natural drive of the carnivorous predator, corresponds to the sexual symbolism. The fear of rape and the awakening desire of teenaged girls become mixed in thrilling fantasies.

But the issue should be raised: does stalking with rape in mind really equate to stalking because one is starving for food? The symbolism requires that one view the issue from the point of view of a victim. This is the very position that Carter's text challenges. The story of the missing bridegroom complicates matters further. The narrator again encourages us to feel sad for the wolf, and we see the man compelled to leave his bride for the forest as a more sympathetic figure than the uncomprehending woman who is so quick to remarry. While some students will remind us that she does the "sensible" thing by taking another husband, others will argue that she should have followed the voice of her mate into the forest rather than simply waiting under the covers, even if this meant death. Her first husband seems to think so. The matter-of-fact narration continues as we are told that both men abuse the woman for what they see as unfaithfulness.

Readers may find irony in this episode or may be angry that the writer does not condemn it. This is how things usually are between men and women, the story seems to say in its medieval voice. But the anecdote about the woman with two husbands prepares the audience to accept the different woman who later takes the far from sensible action of embracing her wolf lover, contrasting the passive victim with the eager participant who demands equality.

While the narrative is composed of several episodes, these are tied together by observations about wolves that are told in the present tense and evoke a sense of timelessness. This technique does not explain all of the tense shifts in the narrative, however; in fact, Carter changes tenses at least eighteen times in the course of the story, sometimes for just one line. She begins the story in the present tense, describing the qualities of wolves. This conveys a sense that her statements express universal truths. But we cannot be sure of who the speaker is. Perhaps it is the grandmother, a possibly unreliable narrator. A hint of this occurs when she breaks into past tense for half a sentence, telling us that "there was a woman once bitten in her own kitchen as she was straining the macaroni." The trivial detail of the example undercuts its value as evidence, giving the narration the flavor of the cautionary folk tales we have already seen in this cluster. This is directly followed by the imperative sentence that provides the thesis for the grandmother-like narrator's argument: "Fear and flee the wolf; for worst of all, the wolf may be more than he seems." The first anecdote follows, in the past tense, and we find a wolf first described as an individual. This is closely followed by a one-paragraph story telling of a witch transforming a wedding party into wolves, also presented in the past tense.

These anecdotes, along with the more complex story of the missing bridegroom, seem to be offered as evidence. Their past-tense delivery implies that these events indeed happened and are facts that could be verified. The bridegroom story is interrupted, however, by a beautifully evocative paragraph in the present tense that expresses the inherent despair of wolves. The missing bridegroom anecdote is followed by the storyteller's voice giving information in the present tense again, starting in paragraph 20 with the suspiciously unreliable words *They say.* Instructors might want to take the opportunity here to discuss the credibility (and the lack of attribution) of sources in the narrator's argument. In the movie version of Carter's story, the devil's ointment that is mentioned in passing in the story is delivered to an innocent young man by the prince of darkness, whose chauffeur is Little Red Riding Hood in a blonde wig. Here, however, we are given a series of short proofs that wolves are sometimes actually men, and the reader is given the useful information to avoid naked men spotted in the woods.

The shift in tenses therefore affects the narrative pace as well as the point of view, serving to stop us with this short declarative sentence set apart in its own paragraph in the midst of seemingly timeless description. The story moves into past tense until the wolf arrives at the grandmother's door. It then moves into present tense as we experience the violence through the old woman's eyes. The sexual connotations are made explicit here, and after we see the wolf's huge genitals, the story shifts suddenly to past, then present, and then past tense again as the wolf attacks the grandmother. The form again enhances the content as panic is implied by the narrative action. Shifts in tense continue as the story comes to its climax, both in terms of plot and the actual events of the story. Most of the

reverse seduction is told in present tense, but the changes in tense — and therefore in perspective — occur closer together at the story's end.

After the young woman seizes her own wild nature, refusing to listen to "the
old bones under the bed" — the old wives' tales that urge women to stay on the
path far away from their own sexual pleasures — the narrative moves from past
tense to present tense for one line and then for the first time to future tense. This
sentence implies that the girl and the transformed wolf indeed have a future and
that her overturning of the story's expectations will lead to a mutual taming
mixed with a mutual wildness. The result is peaceful as we are told in the past
tense that the blizzard did die down as predicted. The story ends with an image
in the present tense and a happy ending as the girl "sleeps in granny's bed,
between the paws of the tender wolf."

This Little Red Riding Hood differs in many ways from the naïve girls of the
earlier tales, and we are told explicitly that she deliberately delays her arrival at
her grandmother's house so that she will lose the bet and be forced to kiss the
wolf. Although she may not know exactly what will happen, she knows by instinct
that to become a woman she must step past the grandmother's admonitions
against female sexuality. There is a fine line in Carter's story that students should
discuss. Does she mean for us to believe that young girls wish to be seduced and
that the rapist can be tamed by turning his seduction around on him? Or does it
mean that women are capable of making their own decisions about sex? Where
does the line exist between actions that are bold and powerful and actions that
are dangerous or exploitative? Where is the line between rape and the sort of sexual fantasy women enjoy reading about in romance novels?

Some radical feminists believe that all heterosexual relationships are destructive to women and would argue that Little Red Riding Hood falls into a dangerous and self-destructive game, deceiving only herself that she is in control of her
own sexuality when playing around with a wolf. Medieval thinkers, on the other
hand, saw women as either virginal saints or dangerous sexual beings intent on
tripping up men who were trying to stay on the path of chastity. Readers of the
Middle English text *Sir Gawain and the Green Knight* might be struck by the
motif of the wager with the kiss as the payoff. In the medieval story, the virginal
young knight is tempted by the worldly woman in a castle deep in the forest.
Carter's switch of predators is therefore not unprecedented and in fact falls into
an ancient hatred of women prevalent in early Christian thought. By embracing
the values of the forest, Carter's Little Red Riding Hood in this interpretation
rejects Christianity and accepts the attitudes of pre-Christian European religions.
What students feel is Little Red Riding Hood's state of mind as she dawdles on
the way to grandmother's house may depend on their thinking about these issues.

The "company" of wolves of the title is called a "congregation" in an early
passage of the story. While the presence of this group of soul mates surrounding
the wedding bed represents nightmare in the early episodes of the story, which
are told from the grandmother's point of view, the wild couple finds them a
source of strength. The story may be telling us more about wolves than about
Little Red Riding Hood. The wolves are indeed more important than the girl,
but she becomes one of them when she accepts her nature. Carter's long
descriptions, poetic in effect, emphasize the nature of wolves, and students will
find many from which to choose details that show the wolves as more than sim-

ply evil predators. While some readers find the ending unsettling and conclude that the girl has become heartless, especially since she does not seek revenge for her grandmother's murder, others enjoy its eroticism and evocation of female power and male humanity. Some may be bothered by the eating of lice, especially because she does it "as he will bid her." They may be disturbed by the implication of domination here, similar to that in the earlier story in which the bridegroom returns to order his wife to cook for him and to call her a whore. Others will enjoy the sensuality of the image and appreciate the mutuality of the "savage marriage ceremony." The word *savage* has come to be pejorative and prejudicial but originally came from the Latin word for forest, and it carries appropriate connotations of natural wildness. Marriage is about sex and about love, and Carter's ending implies that it's okay to be wild, celebratory, and at peace about enjoying both.

Perrault's tale of Little Red Riding Hood presents a wolf who is male, predatory, and irredeemably evil. Men are out to get you if you stray from the path, and if they get you, you are a goner. If the wolf's attack symbolizes rape or seduction, we conclude, then a woman thus ruined is destroyed in society's eyes forever. The wolf is a coward who is cautious of woodcutters and forced to be sly to avoid being controlled. His eating of the grandmother is explained by his not having eaten in three days, but this fact seems to be offered to explain why he is able to dispatch her so quickly, not to cause us to empathize with his hunger. The wolf wins, and we are not meant to applaud him but to fear him as we should fear those like him who would cause us to stray from the path of obedience and morality. Perrault's version also hints that women who have been doted on by their mothers and grandmothers may be more vulnerable to such predators. In the dual version collected by the Grimm brothers, the wolf seems a bit more three-dimensional. He is still a cowardly deceiver, but he seems overwhelmed by his insatiable hunger and ends up as a victim of the avenging women. He also is ineffectual: the women are only temporarily victimized; saved by the woodcutter, they live to take revenge on both the offending wolf and another threatening wolf in a future story. Although a modern audience accustomed to movie monsters might find the fearsomeness of the Grimm wolf mixed with pity for his plight as a victim, earlier readers would have seen his fate as just and as a clear sign that goodness triumphs in the end.

Carter's image of wolves is much more complex. We are encouraged to see them as individuals who become victims themselves, who suffer from starvation, and who are ultimately redeemable if rightly understood and loved. Students will find many details to back up such an assertion. Carter's version of this folk tale is feminist because it refuses to accept the stereotypes of the female victim and the male predator. Furthermore, she rejects the premise that women must be protected from sexuality. Many feminists strongly agree with the point of view taken in "The Company of Wolves" and call for a full acceptance of female power, often with the addition of pre-Christian religious imagery that draws on a similar iconography from Europe or Africa. To be human is to live fully in one's body, these women would say, whether male or female. Other feminists might feel more comfortable with the strong political action of the epilogue to the Grimm version of the story. Rather than buying into the "happy ending" with the marriage ceremony — even a "savage" one — they approve of the solidarity of women who exact justice for the wrongs done in the past, working together to see that hard-won knowledge about the world is passed on and that predators are eliminated.

These feminist thinkers might define *feminism* as a community working together rather than as one in which individual women care more about seizing their own pleasure with men than righting wrongs done to their grandmothers. Issues may be raised about the place of the grandmother in feminist thought. While older women often paved the way for equality for women, others perpetuate the "old wives' tales" and traditions that hold women back. We might think of other stories, like "Cinderella" and "Snow White," in which women persecute each other. Feminists like Estes would advise women to kill the sort of grandmother in their own psyches that continues to internalize cultural oppression and to act as the inner predator that drains energy better used for living. Perrault's narrative seems most diametrically opposed to feminism. It assumes that women are infantile and vain, vulnerable to danger if they stray from the path of righteousness even in the pursuit of natural beauty. Nature is dangerous and women's nature is weak in the traditional tales, a view that is antithetical to feminist thought. Many will find Carter's twentieth-century version of Little Red Riding Hood more realistic than the earlier narratives because her views of women, men, and nature seem more commonsensical to us. Modern readers don't usually like tales with morals, preferring more subtle approaches, and they may find the characters too simple to be real — either all good or all bad.

Little Red Riding Hood, perhaps, has captured the interests of readers and listeners for so many generations because she goes astray, if only because she is naïve. But her innocence may pose barriers to readers who see her actions as simply too stupid to apply to them. A good case can be made, however, for the irrelevance of *reality* when applied to fairy tales. Carter has sometimes been categorized as a writer of "magical realism" and has claimed to be influenced by South American writers like Jorge Luis Borges. Some students might want to follow up on this issue of genre and discuss whether unrealistic stories may help us to think from fresh perspectives more easily than straightforward narratives. Some psychologists and philosophers feel that fairy tales contain a deep reality that evokes archetypes to which all human beings respond, while structural literary theorists have studied them in depth to determine aspects of all good narratives. Considering issues of realism in the Little Red Riding Hood stories may therefore lead students into more scholarly and personally valuable territory than they might at first expect.

OBSERVING SCHOOLCHILDREN (p. 682)

LOUISE GLÜCK

The School Children (p. 682)

Louise Glück has written that although poems take details from autobiography and the experiences of everyday life, the voice of the poem transcends the specifics of the poet's individual life. For the writer and later for the reader, the connotations of the words in poems change and move away from the incidentals of their original creation. Glück therefore feels free to create her own mythic, surreal world in her poems, moving through time and space. In addition, her attitude frees the reader to create personal meanings and to be an active and flexible interpreter of the poem's imagery. We might explain to our students as we discuss "The School Children" that issues do not always have to be resolved, nor do we need to reach a consensus about the interpretations of literary texts. Sometimes *both/and* is preferable to *either/or*. Readers often find mythological symbols in Glück's poetry. Some students will be familiar with the labor of Hercules in which he seeks the apples of the Hesperides. In contrast to the male hero of the myth, however, Glück's poem tells us in lines 2 and 3 that the "mothers have labored / to gather the late apples" for their children, and we may think of the added connotations of the word *labor* to describe childbirth. The diction of the last stanza carries the biblical tone of edict or prophecy with its parallel clauses beginning with *and* and using the formal verb form *shall*. This poet is often characterized as dreamy, and we find this quality also in "The School Children" as the speaker moves back and forth from schoolroom to orchard.

To be truly universal, a writer must be particular. The poet pictures this group of schoolchildren vividly, though sparely, and we can imagine the rural setting where apples grow and both mothers and children seem to be trapped. But most of us have experienced the rigid demands of conformity regardless of where we grew up, and our first encounter with it often occurred at school. When we are told in line 8 that "they" are orderly, we automatically look back to the last noun phrases for referents, and we may be surprised to find in the next line that the pronoun refers to the nails on which the children hang their clothes. The speaker could have been referring to the teachers — labeled only by the vague, formal designation "those who wait behind great desks" (line 6). But this leads to another problem with a pronoun. Does *those* mean teachers? But surely the apples are not meant to fulfill the apple-for-the-teacher requirement? Do the women pick apples as workers for a fruit company that has executives who sit behind desks? Alternatively, the pronoun *they* in line 8, a collective pronoun capable of containing any number of referents, could refer back to everyone in the earlier stanzas — children, mothers, and *those* teachers or other authority figures. All are orderly, like the nails; all remain in their designated places. In academic essays, as students support their arguments in an orderly way, we will undoubtedly call them to task for failing to make clear the referents of their pronouns.

Ambiguity can be misleading, even dangerous. (Just recently, a neighbor called to ask if someone could come to the hospital to pick up his child for the night. Speaking of his wife, he said, "Mary was in the hospital visiting her mother, and she had a heart attack." It was much later that his neighbors realized with shock that his wife and not his mother-in-law needed emergency cardiac care.)

But poets can break rules concerning ambiguity, and we love them for it. Meanings become multilayered, and we see commonplace events as having a newly discovered intricacy. The indeterminacy of the poem will lead to different interpretations of its theme. It is possible to support the assertion that the poem is about the children or even about the teachers who impose this order upon the young and seem to wield so much power over the lives of the mothers who defer to them. But the mothers seem most active in the poem, and we know the most about how they feel.

Still, we might ask for whom the mothers " a way out." If it is for their children, then perhaps the focus changes again. Glück might suggest that the fuzzy focus exists for a reason; that the lives of teachers, children, and mothers are interrelated; that the whole notion of focus is reductive. Though the focus may be unclear, the colors are as sharp and the lines as spare as a Piet Mondrian painting. Aside from the gold of the apples and the gray of the limbs, the colors are primary red, blue, and yellow, colors we associate with the crayon boxes of early childhood. The red and gold of the apples have a magical feel, and the gray limbs signify the bareness of winter and the depression of mothers who have few resources — "so little ammunition" — to use in the battle for their children. The word *ammunition* comes as a surprise in a poem that has not raised issues of war to this point. Is the conflict between the mothers and the teachers who now have charge over their children? Is the conflict the economic one we might expect in the imagery of a more overtly political writer than Glück? We only know that the mothers' efforts are intense, since they "scour" the orchard, a word that recalls the "labor" of the first stanza.

Other phrases are puzzling. The construction "instruct them in silence" seems to be an oxymoron; surely one must communicate in order to teach. The apples of the mothers, on the other hand, are "like words of another language," silent objects that speak but perhaps cannot be deciphered (line 4). Or it may be that the children do understand the labor of their mothers, but now must learn the language of school. The lives of these children have a peculiarly inarticulate quality, and we do not hear them at all. Most of us at some time have encountered teachers who did not understand the community in which they taught or who thought that children should be seen and not heard. In a 1980s movie, a teacher known for handing out worksheets and then retreating behind a newspaper dies during class. The punch line is that none of his students notice.

TOI DERRICOTTE

Fears of the Eighth Grade (p. 683)

The reader's first reaction to Toi Derricotte's "Fears of the Eighth Grade" may be skepticism about its basic premise that middle-school children's greatest fear is dying in a war. Students may question the context of the discussion or the relationship between these young adolescents and the adult who raises the issue of fear. In fact, some psychologists say that a major fear of teenagers is talking to adults, and they warn their colleagues that members of this age group are reluctant to reveal their true feelings. One list of the most common fears of adults, teens, and older children puts common fears in order: public speaking, making mistakes, failure, disapproval, rejection, angry people, being alone, darkness, dentists, injections, hospitals, taking tests, open wounds and blood, police, dogs, spiders, deformed people. Fear of dying in a war doesn't even make the top ten. A closer look at the statistics supports Derricotte, however.

Although war is not a major fear for children younger than eight or adolescents older than fifteen, it does affect older elementary and middle-school children. Events in the news such as kidnappings, school shootings, and wars cause great distress for children in this age group, and they feel powerless to do anything about such threatening forces. Our images of war take forms learned in childhood. The children of the 1940s and 1950s recall fears of bombs dropping from the sky; boys drew detailed pictures in crayon showing airplanes fighting in the sky. The jungles and helicopters of the Vietnam War preoccupied the next generation. Ironically, children growing up in the 1990s and the early years of the new century may return to the images of air battles and bombings that characterize their parents' wars.

Although "Fears of the Eighth Grade" was published in 1989, it is difficult to place it in time. The "somewhere else" of the second stanza, where women and children gather "at the gates of the bamboo palace," belongs to a generation that sees war in jungle images. Perhaps the default template for war is the poet's own, war being something that happens in an Asian, South American, or African location far from a safe America. Our college students may raise issues about this, arguing that the narrator's assumptions may beg the question of the reality of war for everyone, even those who imagine they are safe in a "little box of consecrated land" (line 9). Some may feel that the last stanza implies that the children are able to see things that adults miss and that when the speaker exclaims "How thin the veneer!" in line 13 she tacitly admits that war can happen anywhere. We can discuss how Americans might deal with war in our own country, how attitudes might be different if our mothers were the ones crying or we were the ones without toilet paper. Those who plan to use this poem in classroom discussion can build the question What things do you fear? into early questionnaires so that they can have the data for this discussion. We have also asked new students, What issues do you think will be most important in the twenty-first century? to get a sense of their values and to orient them to the focus of the course. Most do not mention war, though discussion often raises terrorism issues.

Even in our politically and religiously conservative region, most college students dismiss biblical prophecies of Armageddon or any great conflagration that pits ultimate good against ultimate evil. But Derricotte is speaking symbolically when she uses the word from the biblical text Revelation, as the writer of that text undoubtedly was doing as well. Her contrasting images in the final stanza support her contention that the trappings of civilization are ephemeral. Our students may be old enough to remember how quickly the Soviet Union shattered into pieces and how they needed to memorize strange new names for political entities. Televised images of the effects of war in Bosnia-Herzegovina or Serbia will be fresh in their minds, and they will recall the swiftness with which events moved. One day in 1999, only dedicated news junkies could find Kosovo on a map, and the next day NATO was dropping bombs and President Clinton was vowing not to send in ground troops.

Derricotte's poem captures the pervasive possibility of war, a potential force that lies beneath everyday life. She implies that children may be sensing something that we are no longer able to see. This may be a romantically Wordsworthian interpretation of childhood, but this does not mean that such fears should be dismissed. Most educators of eighth graders, aware that children see both real and fictionalized violence daily on television, address the issues of war more than they did in the past. Several excellent novels dealing with events of World War II are on reading lists for middle-school students, and teachers may use these as a springboard for discussions of current events. Recently, the journal of a young girl in Sarajevo was published and widely read by American schoolgirls the age of Derricotte's students. Some of our college students may argue that children should be sheltered from such knowledge, and will even object to having to discuss "politics" in a freshman composition or literature class such as ours. Others will recognize that discussing fear — or any other issue — brings it into the realm of critical thinking, where it can be understood and perhaps used to strengthen our ability to solve the actual problems it represents. Students need places where they feel safe to do this. Middle school is the time of preoccupation with horror and the macabre. It may be that children of this age use the imagery of violence to work out fears that are only tangentially related to those they articulate to adults.

The students in Derricotte's "Fears of the Eighth Grade" bring their fears into the light of discussion, and the narrator imagines their visions of Armageddon. The mothers in Louise Glück's "The School Children" (p. 682) work desperately to find the way out of something for themselves or their children, but the narrator leaves the nature of their fears undefined, and her use of the word *ammunition* seems oddly out of place. The emphasis on violence in both poems may be appropriate, but Glück's final lines force us to go back and reinterpret the poem to take the intensity of the image into account. In Derricotte's poem, the structure follows the narrator's thought processes. In the first stanza, we listen in on the discussion in the classroom. The two short middle stanzas move us into the narrator's mind as she reacts to the unexpected response of the eighth graders to her questions. In her final stanza, Derricotte's narrator goes on to imagine what the children see in their minds, moving into the imagery of apocalyptic vision and horror movie. The move is from the realistic to the symbolic. The four stanzas of Glück's poem interweave the realistic and the symbolic, but she also begins the first stanza with a sharply defined image of schoolchildren and moves in the last stanza to biblical syntax and diction that connotes warfare. The emotional impact of both endings leaves the reader unsettled.

Although the persona who narrates Derricotte's poem may be a teacher or a guest in the classroom, the children's voices and the narrator's reaction to them are the focus. This is not a teacher-centered classroom but one in which the children participate. Glück's teachers are like gods who impose order and silence and who must be appeased with offerings. The difference is significant. Our students may think back to their experiences in classrooms where teachers were autocrats and compare these with classrooms where students were encouraged to get involved with their own learning. As college instructors, we may be surprised to find that some students are more comfortable with teachers who supply them with correct answers rather than with teachers who require them to take responsibility for their own critical and creative thinking. We should challenge them to examine their attitudes toward authority.

PHILIP LEVINE

Among Children (p. 685)

Philip Levine is a prize-winning poet who has been called the "poet of the factory floor." Having grown up in the gritty industrial city of Detroit, Michigan, during the Great Depression, Levine writes passionately of working-class people. He remembers deciding, while working beside these men and women in various types of factories during the 1950s, that he must "find a voice for the voiceless." Like Tillie Olsen, who writes of the silences of women and working-class men, Levine recognizes that much is lost to literature and intellectual thought by the demands of work in a capitalist society. Like James Agee and Walker Evans, who during the 1930s sought to reveal the plight of tenant farmers, Levine celebrates the dignity and worth of his subjects by presenting them in a concrete and forthright style. His narrative voice speaks with plain words and the rhythms of everyday American speech. Rather than reaching for flowery metaphors or mannered allusions, Levine's poetry is content-oriented, depending on the authenticity of voice and the clarity of image.

This does not mean that his poems are lacking in allusions or that his voice is devoid of sophistication, however. Like many working Americans, Levine's speaker does not fit a stereotyped blue-collar image. He is a man who thinks, who sees. Students encountering Levine's writing for the first time sometimes miss its complexity because it reads so effortlessly. The poet would appreciate the ease of reading but would want his issues to be considered. In *The Simple Truth* (1994) he tells us in verse:

> Some things
> you know all your life. They are so
> simple and true
> they must be said without elegance,
> meter and rhyme
> they must be laid on the table beside
> the salt shaker. . . .

Though his style is simple, the depth of his philosophy is not. We need to encourage our students to dig deeply into Levine's texts and to look at his poetry in collections and in other sources outside this anthology to see how motifs repeat and enrich each other.

Students will find a variety of adjectives to describe the poem's narrator, but *compassionate, angry,* and *pessimistic* might come to mind. He cares about the children and longs to inspire and strengthen them. But we can sense righteous indignation in his descriptions of their already coarsened bodies and pessimism in his knowledge of "what is ahead." We also sense some distance from the families he describes; he is wise and philosophical in a way that the children and their parents may not yet have discovered. His reference to the Bible might lead students to characterize him as religious, although he claims to be an anarchist in both religion and politics. Nevertheless, the case could be made that he is a profoundly moral and ethical thinker. It might be useful to discuss the difference between being religious and being ethical. The narrator assumes a great deal about what the children think and feel. He characterizes them as victims. The intense image of torn wings in lines 5 and 6 jerks us to attention after we have seen the ten-year-olds nodding off to sleep in the opening lines.

It seems unlikely that the poet was allowed into the hospital nursery ten years ago, but his description makes us identify with the babies. The imagery of "their breaths delivered that day, / burning with joy. . . . / on the hardest day of their lives" (lines 30–38) is too perfectly worded to paraphrase. He imagines the babies to be joyful, filled with wonder, brave, and optimistic. This contrasts dramatically with the pessimism of the poem's beginning and the renunciation of its ending lines as he imagines them as adults. By placing his schoolchildren in the city of Flint, Philip Levine particularizes them and emphasizes the working-class circumstances of the poem. They could be school-children in any number of other, similar places, even nearby Detroit, but the name *Flint* lends connotations to the situation, making the setting even more gritty and hard-edged. He also mentions the town of *Paradise*, an ironic name in this context, since the future he foresees for the children is not an idyllic one.

Like Toi Derricotte in "Fears of the Eighth Grade" (p. 683) and Louise Glück in "The School Children" (p. 682), Philip Levine echoes the Bible in "Among Children." Increasingly, college students do not catch biblical or classical allusions, and therefore many nuances of literature in the traditional canon are inaccessible to them. Although we do not need to reopen cultural literacy debates at this point, even a poet like Philip Levine, who has the stated agenda of breaking elitist idols, relies on some shared knowledge. Most scholars would be forced to look up the reference to the horse galloping joyfully into battle, but our students may also miss the connotations of the poet's mention of Job, and they may be frustrated. Searching out the sources of the poet's cultural and personal allusions can add to our enjoyment of reading. When Levine mentions "oranges" in line 25, for example, his fans might think of a later poem, "The Mercy," in which he tells the touching story of his immigrant mother as a little girl being given an orange:

> She learns that mercy is something you can eat
> again and again while the juice spills over
> your chin, you can wipe it away with the back
> of your hands and you can never get enough.

Some readers may argue that the narrator does not take active steps to help these children. But isn't it the duty of a poet to create change through the showing and telling of his words? When he says in the ending lines "I bow to them here and whisper / all I know, all I will ever know," doesn't he take the largest step of all by passing on his knowledge, by educating us as well as them?

Because Glück does not use the pronoun *I* at all, "The School Children" is the most visual and lyrical of the three poems in this cluster. Like Archibald MacLeish, who says that "a poem should not mean but be," Glück presents her poem as an object to be experienced rather than a rhetorical argument to be understood. Derricotte uses the first person in the first two stanzas of "Fears of the Eighth Grade" but drops it as she moves into reverie and imagines what the children see. She seems to be addressing the audience at first, but early in the second stanza we begin to have a sense that we are overhearing her thoughts. In

"Among Children" Philip Levine may also be talking to himself, but he tells us of his feelings throughout. He raises issues for us to think about. In fact, he speaks directly to his audience, telling us, "You can see" (line 10). The effect is less of interior monologue than of dialogue with a hint of persuasion. Perhaps Levine's poem depends more on context than Derricotte's or Glück's, but one could argue that all are both specific and universal.

A representative example can say much about a group, can be convincing evidence. The specificity of Levine's poem makes its evidence more compelling, since we could go to Flint and observe the children of factory workers to see if things have changed. And we could extrapolate the results to other children of factory workers if his example is indeed representative. The same can be said of the specifics of Derricotte's poem. A bit of research verified that her assertion about her particular eighth-grade class was consistent with psychological studies. Glück, on the other hand, is less specific, leaves more unanswered questions. We might find through research where the poet has lived, where she might have observed the people and the apple trees of her poem, but we would still be guessing. Ironically, this makes the poem more universal in that the individual may create his or her own reading. But culturally it is less universal, since we are limited to the images of the poem and cannot apply them with confidence to other settings. Levine looks at his fourth-grade children in the context of their whole lives, and this makes his poem significantly different from Derricotte's, which keeps us in the present tense of eighth graders' fears about war. But how can we read about children and war without also looking ahead a few years to a time when the thing they fear could come to pass? Glück's poem could go either way. One reading would have it be a snapshot of the present. But the connotations of the word *labor* when juxtaposed with motherhood hint at a changing relationship between mothers and children as the children file into the school. And the poem also looks ahead, since the mothers seek an escape. Levine's poem has a broader perspective, but the others may not be as time specific as they seem at first reading.

RESPONDING TO TEACHERS (p. 688)

LANGSTON HUGHES

Theme for English B (p. 688)

"Theme for English B" by Langston Hughes raises issues about the writer of a poem (the poet) as opposed to the persona of a poem (the speaker) who may or may not represent the poet at the time of the writing. Students tend to see all poetry as confessional, the outpouring of a soul in the throes of emotion. In fact, those who write poetry often do so to express themselves. But Langston Hughes, especially at the time this poem with its twenty-two-year-old narrator was published in 1949, was deeply involved in experimentation with different voices in both his poetry and his prose. Hughes was then in his late forties and was a well-known and much-celebrated writer who had chosen to live in Harlem. His satirically comic figure Jess B. Semple was articulating the issues within the Negro community of the 1940s and 1950s in a balanced voice that ranged from pain to hilarity but was never beaten or shrill. He had long been trying out blues voices and was experimenting with female narrators. Of Indian, French, and African ancestry, Hughes grew up with various members of an extended and mostly dysfunctional family in the American Midwest. Unlike his narrator in "Theme for English B," he was born in Joplin, Missouri, and went to high school in Cleveland, Ohio, where he was a gifted student and the only "colored" person in his class. He had traveled to places like Mexico, where his father lived, and to New York, Africa, and France before he and writer Zora Neale Hurston joyfully toured the American South in the summer of 1927. By the time he wrote the poem here, he had also been to Spain during the Spanish Civil War and to Russia as part of the socialist fervor of the early 1930s.

Having pointed out the differences between Hughes and his narrator, however, we may find many similarities between the narrator of "Theme for English B" and the Langston Hughes who arrived by steamer in New York in 1921 to study mining at Columbia University. Columbia is "on the hill above Harlem," as is the college of the poem. The talented, light-skinned Hughes was not the only Negro on campus, but he lived in an otherwise all-white dormitory after initially staying at the Harlem YMCA. He soon was spending all his time with the writers and artists of Harlem, however, meeting W. E. B. Du Bois and other stars of the Harlem Renaissance and becoming an important participant in this heady intellectual and artistic community. To the fury of his father, who saw education only as a way to make money and who had no respect for poets or for his own African American roots, Hughes left school and became a writer who celebrated his race.

From the distance of adulthood, Hughes has his narrator encounter a typical assignment for a college freshman, the autobiographical narrative. When a similar assignment was given a few years ago in a graduate seminar, at least two students rebelled and wrote essays that resisted the reductive nature of the assignment. Yet their resistance created what may have been the most revealing responses. One woman wrote a poetic piece that touched on the shifting nature of identity, and another wrote an angry explanation of why she could not write an autobiographical essay, in the process writing an essay defining who she was *not*. The assignment as stated in Hughes's poem recalls the "non sequitur" of William Shakespeare's character Polonius in *Hamlet*, that if one is only true to oneself, then it is not possible to be false to any man. But it doesn't follow as the night the day that writing something *true* is that simple. The narrator of the poem critiques the assignment, sounding for a while like Walt Whitman's *Leaves of Grass* as he moves into the street for his self-definition and then pulls even the instructor into the mix.

Even today, to be white in America is probably to be *more free*, especially when the white person is the person in authority, as in the college classroom. In mainstream American culture, white people are the default human beings, with everyone else being defined in contrast to this definition of "normal" humanity. People of color are *different*, are *other*. Of mixed race, Hughes saw himself in the "tragic mulatto" category, not quite accepted as black or white. When a young Langston Hughes traveled to Africa, the black people who lived there would not accept him as being like themselves. They looked at his golden skin and softly curling hair and laughed, "You — white man." America still struggles with the artificial divisions that the history of slavery creates between human beings.

Students who are interested in exploring this topic further might begin with Toni Morrison's brief nonfiction study *Playing in the Dark: Whiteness and the Literary Imagination* (1992). According to Morrison, much of literature until very recently was directed toward a white audience, even when written by African American authors. This is often true of Langston Hughes, as we hear him constantly speaking to the white person looming just outside the picture, defining and explaining his race to the stranger. But this poem consciously defies the white audience, admitting the impossibility of defining oneself as separate. The rhyme scheme is interesting in this context. The poem imposes the structure of rhyming couplets at the beginning and the end, when the paper is assigned and when it is presented to the professor. This frames the lively rhetoric in the middle that sometimes addresses Harlem, sometimes moves into a jazzy alliteration — as in the "Bessie, bop, or Bach" of line 24 — even occasionally rhymes as if by accident. Hughes often reworked material that was written in earlier years, and he may indeed have turned in a response to an assignment much like this one. We hope that the teacher likes the narrator's impertinence; good writers can get away with challenging the rules. But in 1921 or 1949, and perhaps even today, for college students who are not Langston Hughes, drawing outside the lines entails risk.

LINDA PASTAN

Ethics (p. 690)

Our students come to college with their own ethical codes built from experiences both in and out of schools. But many may be examining these "commonsense" assumptions for the first time. Marshall McLuhan once said that we aren't sure who first discovered water, but it's unlikely to have been a fish. One of the tasks of education is to learn to see the water, to confront the warrants for our beliefs. Ethics can be studied at the college level in introductory and advanced courses in departments of philosophy but may also be a component of other disciplines. Business majors usually must study the ethics of advertising, contracts, and so forth, and scientists look at the issues and principles that affect biology, technology, the environment, and other areas where standards of conduct must be debated and applied. Medicine, law, religion, psychology, political and social sciences: students of all these disciplines must deal with profound ethical dilemmas. Many of the issues from other discourses find their way into our English classrooms, with argumentative research papers addressing abortion, assisted suicide, animal rights, capital punishment, marijuana legalization, genetic engineering, and a myriad other issues currently being debated in other classrooms and dorms. When we ask our students to define an *issue* as a question about which reasonable people may disagree, we are asking them to make ethical judgments as well as logical ones. The root of the word *ethical* is *ethos*, the same word that we use when discussing the need for writers to appeal to common values or for readers to judge credibility and tone.

Debates rage about the teaching of ethics at the high-school and elementary-school levels. The directive approaches to teaching virtues and morality popularized by William Bennett and other moral conservatives vie with the discursive, decision-making approaches to "values clarification" epitomized by Lawrence Kohlberg and other liberal sociologists and educators. As our college students tackle these opposing viewpoints, they have the opportunity to examine their own reasons for choosing one over the other. Many readers will feel that the teacher's question is inappropriate, that to merely present ethical dilemmas without presenting criteria for making decisions may give teachers insight into the way children think but does nothing for the children. While her theory may have been discursive, designed to force her students to think, the teacher's approach has been ironically prescriptive. She could have seen the narrator as a creative thinker rather than labeling her as a person who refuses to accept responsibility.

Kohlberg maintains that we pass through stages as we develop values over time. In the preconventional stage, children accept what they are told and are good either because their parents expect it or because they will be rewarded or punished for their behavior. Adolescents may advance to a conventional stage in which they are loyal to groups with which they identify, deferring to the consensus of the family, the gang, the church, and the school. Adults, especially those who consciously think about ethics, may move into a postconventional stage in which they question internalized group loyalties and norms and develop principles that promote universal ideals of justice, human rights, and the greater good for all people. This begs the question of whether values are universal or relative, an issue that lies at the heart of the debates.

The theme of Pastan's poem about ethics also addresses the issue of the stages of life and how our worldviews may change over time. She uses images of fall and winter because she knows they will make us think of the latter stages of life. The children seek the answer that will please the teacher and perhaps earn them the reward of a good grade. The narrator soon learns that divergent thinking will be punished. One year, the narrator thinks of her grandmother, perhaps calling on the norms of the family group to help her make the decision. Now, as an adult, she sees the whole exercise as reductive, viewing the issue in the light of universality and viewing herself at one with both art and nature. Her description of the Rembrandt painting captures the colors and the use of light but goes beyond surface detail to speak metaphorically and to critique the differentiation between art and life that the teacher's question assumes. The description is subjective, perhaps discarding both logos and ethos in favor of pathos, the emotional component of argument. Her last line resists the whole exercise of teaching children by presenting them with ethical dilemmas. Like many critics of current teaching approaches to ethics, Pastan may object less to the discussion of ethical issues in the classroom than to the inductive method that presents children only with the problems. Philosophers have developed several approaches that could be made available to children and adults to help them solve the problems presented. They might be taught to ask which alternative will lead to the most benefit and the least harm, which most closely respects the rights of all involved, which avoids both favoritism and discrimination, which advances the common good, or which will make us better people. All of these questions are value laden, but we may also admit that bias can never be eliminated and therefore should be conceded. Some people who work with children argue for the power of narrative and poetry in the teaching of ethics, pointing out the long tradition in many cultures of using parables, fables, proverbs, and songs to illustrate principles of conduct or to raise questions about values. Linda Pastan's approach is finally an artistic and literary one that may still avoid confronting difficult choices but that raises new issues for our consideration.

The narrators of both Pastan's "Ethics" and Langston Hughes's "Theme for English B" (p. 688) resist the assignments imposed on them by their teachers. Both feel that the assignment seeks to reduce a complex issue — a person's true identity, the relative value of life versus art—into simple terms beyond the capability of adults, much less young people, to articulate. Hughes's teacher imparts to his students the truism that most writing teachers have used: Write what you know! But Hughes has his own agenda and wants to say something about the oneness of humanity, the vitality of Harlem, and the inequities implied in the whole situation of white teacher and black student. Pastan also seeks to transform the teacher's question, to make it her own. Writing as an adult looking back, she critiques the warrants underlying the posing moral conundrums to children, continuing to resist what she sees as a false dichotomy. She, too, ends with a celebration of oneness, something that she implies can come only with maturity. Her leap to a later stage in life is significant to a reading of the poems. We must do research to realize that Hughes the poet is speaking from the distance of maturity, and readers therefore may see his narrator as immature and cocky, a slacker just trying to avoid the intellectual work of the real assignment by being flippant and artistic. Pastan explicitly invites us to assume that she now has the maturity and the freedom to object to the teacher's assignment. Students might decide that she cannot get off the hook this easily, that her vague sense of oneness may be beautiful but still "eschews / the burdens of responsibility" (lines 15–16).

Characterizations of Pastan's and Hughes's poems as pessimistic or optimistic will depend on the readers' interpretations of tone. Pastan undoubtedly has a pessimistic attitude toward the efficacy of placing tough moral responsibilities on the shoulders of children or of reducing life to either/or choices. But she seems optimistic about the interrelationships between the aspects of life that people consider as separate. Hughes also sees life as of one fabric and seems optimistic about Americans being part of each other. But there may be an irony and defiance in his tone that undercuts the seeming optimism. The knowledge that Langston Hughes is not the voice of the poem may lead us to see that the poem's narrator is actually naive, limited, and unreliable. If he is trying to be cheerful and to put the best face on the anger that simmers underneath, then Hughes's poem is profoundly pessimistic.

HENRY REED

Naming of Parts (p. 692)

Known primarily as a writer for BBC radio, Henry Reed wrote only one book of poems, *A Map of Verona*, published just after World War II in 1946. The most famous of the poems in this volume is called "Lessons of the War," and

"Naming of Parts" is the first section of this poem. It was reprinted in 1970 with additions, but by then "Naming of Parts" had become the most popular British poem to come out of the war, and many people of Reed's generation can recite it by heart. The poet explains that he wrote it as a joke to amuse his fellow recruits. According to William Scammell's entry on Reed in *The Oxford Companion to Twentieth-Century Poetry* (1994):

> Its good-natured humour, broad sexual innuendo, and lyrical evocations of nature make it instantly memorable. By juxtaposing dry and faintly absurd technical language about the cleaning of guns with the immemorial goings-on of flowers and bees in spring, Reed dramatizes both the ridiculousness and boredom of war . . . and its relationship to the awkward, unbalanced lives of the individuals helplessly caught up in it. (445)

In the context of our poems on teaching and learning, "Naming of Parts" neatly contrasts an instructor's intentions and the student's transformation of them as he learns his own lessons from the teacher's presentation.

If we read Reed's double-voiced poem aloud, it is easy to believe that the author was involved with radio broadcasting, since it is particularly auditory. Students who have grown up in liturgical churches might be reminded of the responsive readings in which the leader reads a line and the congregation responds in unison. Two good readers in the class could be asked to study the poem and to perform it, choosing the places where the voice of the drill instructor ends and the voice of the recruit begins. Or the class might replicate the call-and-response method used in church, with one side of the class reading about the guns and the other about the flowers and bees. Adults seldom get a chance to read aloud to each other, and many students find it a particularly satisfying experience, especially at schools where a strong drama or film studies major is offered.

Students should have little trouble contrasting the voices and finding adjectives for them. Sometimes we hear the military regular characterized as masculine and the responding voice as feminine. We might want to discuss issues raised by this contrast. Much of the enjoyment of the poem is lost if readers do not understand that the voice of the recruit is ironic, even mocking, whereas the voice of authority, the voice of war, is deadly serious. Readers may wonder if the reader means to be making sexual puns. We should assure them that the poet certainly does mean to be talking dirty. What's more, there may be a great deal of significance to the coupling of guns, a phallic symbol, and flowers, the sexual organs of plants, in the same poem, especially since the switch from one to another occurs in midline. In addition, the poem moves from the lyricism of the Japonica blossoms in the first stanza to the violent and clumsy "assaulting and fumbling [of] the flowers" by the bees in line 23. The movements become more violent in each stanza until in the final lines the recruit (or the poet?) repeats lines from earlier stanzas almost incoherently. Readers can decide how far they wish to take the sexual imagery at this point. Although current readers may interpret the poem as antimilitary, Reed may simply intend it as the sort of inside joke that can occur in any group of workers where a particularly self-important person in a position of authority becomes the surreptitious target of a talented and witty mimic. Nevertheless, the poetic voice of the recruit is privileged while those who would worship the weapons of war are ridiculed. The poet uses white space to set off the final line of each stanza. Both the indentation and the space between stanzas emphasize the statement and slow the pace. The effect is a full stop. When the voice of the instructor begins again in the new stanza, he is not responding to the inner voice of the recruit but beginning a new point in his lecture. By contrast, when the recruit's interior monologue begins each time, it begins in the middle of a line and is enjambed with the first voice. Because the voices are not engaged in dialogue but in separate monologues, this arrangement is particularly telling. The inner voice of the student responds to the spoken words of the instructor, but the instructor is ignorant of what the student really thinks. The repetition also serves as emphasis, but with each repetition the line accumulates connotations. The effect is of an echo but an echo that is changed, its meaning transformed into an antithesis.

The most obvious difference between Reed's "Naming of Parts" and the previous poems in this cluster, Langston Hughes's "Theme for English B" (p. 688) and Linda Pastan's "Ethics" (p. 690), is the setting of the learning situation. The narrators in Hughes's and Pastan's poems respond to assignments given to them at school, whereas Reed's protagonist reacts to the absurdity of military training in what amounts to a garden. Ironically, Reed's recruit really needs the information he is given, whereas the school assignments come across as sophistry. Some college students have served in the military and recognize the earnest, single-minded instructor as a character who in some respects only exists in this particular setting. But most readers have experienced classrooms or work situations in which the teacher or trainer relayed information according to a boring, detailed script and had no tolerance for questions or deviations. Although the teachers of Hughes's and Pastan's poems ask for a response from their students, they may have fallen into set patterns as well. Hughes's professor makes a perhaps unwarranted assumption that autobiography is possible in a theme for English B, and Pastan's teacher presents the same ethical dilemma every year. Reed is concerned with naming, and Hughes contends with the idea of defining oneself. Both seem to be saying that life is more complex than these teachers assume. Pastan struggles with her teacher's demands that she make distinctions when she prefers to see wholeness. All challenge their teachers and change the rules; Reed plays with the meaning of words, making love not war from the words of his teacher.

WALT WHITMAN

When I Heard the Learn'd Astronomer (p. 693)

Walt Whitman will not be new to most of our college students. He is arguably the most influential poet that America ever produced and is a pivotal figure between the romanticism and decorum of the early nineteenth century and the modernism and experimentation of the twentieth. He created his own rhythms from everyday American speech and Italian opera, from newspaper journalism and the Bible. Although "When I Heard the Learn'd Astronomer" might mislead readers into jumping to the conclusion that he was against science, Whitman was a great believer in science and an early proponent of the theory of evolution. In the preface to his long, unprecedented celebration of human individuality, *Leaves of Grass*, in 1855, Whitman writes, "Exact science and its practical movements are no checks on the greatest poet but always his encouragement and support." In a list that includes astronomers with sailors, travelers, anatomists, chemists, and geologists but also with phrenologists, spiritualists, and lexicographers, Whitman calls such scientists "the lawgivers of poets" whose ordering of reality forms the infrastructure of poetry. But he goes on to place matters in their proper order: "In the beauty of poems are the tuft and final applause of science." In terms of our cluster on teaching and learning, it seems clear that to Walt Whitman the student is expected to outshine the teacher, to transform science into poetry. Mysticism and science overlap in Whitman's worldview, as they did for many in the nineteenth century. He can see in the Milky Way galaxy the same oneness that he sees linking himself and the universe, and the stars are to him "the visible suggestion of God in space and time." The short poem "When I Heard the Learn'd Astronomer" incorporates in one long, eight-line periodic sentence many of the elements of Walt Whitman's philosophy and prosody.

Whitman's formal schooling ended when he was twelve years old, but he was indeed "learn'd." He sharpened his writing skills as a printer and a newspaper reporter and read widely, referring to the writings of most of the world's religions and to philosophers from Plato to Leibnitz, Hegel, and Kant. He traveled from New York to New Orleans and back. His first publication was praised by Ralph Waldo Emerson and criticized by Henry David Thoreau. He was a force to be reckoned with throughout most of the nineteenth century, and much of the literature of the twentieth century defers to him in some way. Nevertheless, in spite of his own learning and his respect for science, the word *learn'd* has a pejorative tone in this poem; the precision and logic make him suddenly "tired and sick." Whitman must escape from logos into the pathos of mysticism and beauty. The effect of the anaphora, the repeated parallel structures of the first four lines, is often characterized as biblical or sermonic. In this context, however, it seems to emphasize the point-by-point logic of the lecturer as he piles up evidence. When contrasted with the flowing diction and syntax of the last four lines, the repetition of the word *When* projects the poet's sense of frustration, the increasingly longer sentences stretching out the lecture interminably. We might ask students what the poet's reaction suggests about using formulaic approaches to writing arguments or about relying on hard evidence alone to persuade an audience.

Whitman uses a periodic sentence, a form of syntax that does not become grammatically complete until the final line of the poem. The result is inductive, like a mystery story. The reader is kept in suspense and must think ahead throughout the poem to anticipate the revelation at the end. In the first four lines, the narrator hears an empirical argument; at the end, he observes for himself and wraps himself in silence. The easy assumption will be that he proposes another method of education than the scientist's. But we know that Whitman saw science as the father of poetry, at least in 1855. Perhaps, ten years later, he resists the oppressive precision of science that is isolated from beauty. His gazing at the stars is a typically romantic response. He may not learn a great deal about astronomy, but he may learn other things that he values even more. Whitman must use words to convey the "perfect silence" of his last line, and we may argue that this sometimes most talkative of poets contradicts himself. But the word *silence* is placed just before the white space at the bottom of the page where the poem ends, after all the words that precede this last image. The effect on most readers is exactly what Whitman intends, that deep breath of satisfaction at the aptness and beauty of the scene, the unfettered poet out there in communion with the Milky Way. But the poet is wily. Every word has been precise, the structure of the poem as deliberate as any astronomer's chart.

Among the four poems of this cluster, Whitman's narrator is the only student who actually walks out on the teacher. But all the students walk out in one way or another. The young college student of Langston Hughes's "Theme for English B" (p. 688) challenges his teacher by, in a Whitmanesque way, putting the universe, including the professor himself, into his autobiography. Though he does not walk out on the teacher, he walks out on the assignment, choosing, like Whitman before him, poetry over prescribed structure. The older narrator of Linda Pastan's "Ethics" (p. 690) finally walks out on the assignment after many years, echoing Whitman's rejection of cold logic in her revelatory ending. Henry Reed, like a great many students, hides in plain sight; he is present in body but transforms the meticulous details of weaponry into poetry. Whitman, as an adult attending a lecture, has a perfect right to come and go; the others are more or less compelled to remain. Although Whitman does not directly quote the lecturer, he gives us a fairly good idea of the nature of the lecture. Each poem is less about the teacher's words than about the narrator's use of them in his or her own thinking. The narrators find the assignments "uncomfortable" for more or less unaccountable reasons. Whitman's adverb in the line "How soon unaccountable I became tired and sick" is telling. The narrators react against logic, against any *accounting* of reasons and details. They privilege what they obviously consider a higher understanding of reality that is silent and somehow more natural and unified than the compartmentalizing of reality their teachers insist upon. Some readers may agree. Others may question their pathos as vague and baseless, insisting that outside of poetry one must *account* for one's claims.

ROSEMARY CATACALOS

David Talamántez on the Last Day of Second Grade (p. 694)

Students in teacher education programs need to post a copy of Rosemary Catacalos's evocation of "David Talamántez on the Last Day of Second Grade" beside their bathroom mirrors to read every morning. It wouldn't hurt for college instructors to read it from time to time either. It has been more than two decades since Mina Shaughnessy's 1977 *Errors and Expectations* gave instructors of basic writing at the college level the practical insights we needed to help our students improve their own writing. They make mistakes, she says, "not because they are slow or non-verbal, indifferent to or incapable of academic excellence, but because they are beginners" (5). They see writing as a *trap* — as

Shaughnessy terms it — or a test for which we refuse to provide clear-cut questions, rather than a means of communicating real ideas to real people. If we look together at patterns of errors, we can help them find these for themselves as they edit and proofread late drafts. Like David Talamántez's spelling, errors in college essays tend to have a logical basis that students can learn to spot with attention.

Before this, however, we have to get past the fear of judgment that has become connected with writing for so many students. Some have overcome this and made good grades by writing according to the set patterns laid out for them, giving the teacher exactly what the directions require. "But what did I do wrong?" they demand, when their mechanically perfect but lifeless essays earn them a B- in their first semester of college. We try to work through issues of form and content in conferences and emphasize that writing is a process, that our nebulous ideas and fragmented logic seldom fall into beautifully organized prose in the first draft. Discovering their own content and form through writing is a new experience for many students, who assume we are unorganized and unable to articulate exactly what we want them to write, as previous teachers have done.

Accountability issues have placed high-school and elementary-school teachers in a difficult position. Standardized testing of writing works against all that we have learned about critical thinking and the need for form to follow content. To make their school's percentages look good on the test, students must reduce a complex issue quickly to an oversimplified thesis statement, then follow specific guidelines about how many points to make. In recent formulas that middle-school teachers must follow in one state, even paragraphs have a predetermined form, beginning with the obligatory topic sentence, but also dictating the degree of specificity of the following set number of sentences. This practice ignores studies showing that professional writers seldom follow such rigid order and that a large percentage of paragraphs in published prose do not have topic sentences. Unfortunately, some college instructors carry this prescriptive pedagogy into higher education. One teacher at a community college measures margins, counting points off for misalignment. Another has students place the main ideas in the paragraphs of a published essay into a formal outline with Roman numerals, letters, and so forth in the same way she breaks them down, with a topic sentence and exactly three points in each paragraph.

Grammar, punctuation, and spelling also count heavily with these instructors. Students quickly learn to keep their essays short and safe, avoiding any risk that will cut into the grade. This makes grading simpler, but the focus at college thus becomes similar to what we see happening already to David Talamántez in elementary school. Creativity and originality are squelched. Rather than being allowed to enter the academic dialogue with a fresh perspective on the issues being discussed, they must concentrate instead on semicolons. In the 1970s when composition theorist Lil Brannon taught in Wilmington, North Carolina, the local newspaper quoted her in an interview as saying something like "Grammar and punctuation are the last thing we worry about in a college writing class." Angry letters to the editor followed. The writers thought she expressed contempt for proper English and that contempt epitomized all that was wrong with liberal education. They saw a defiance of standards bordering on a Socratic contamination of the morals of the young.

What she meant, of course, was that we first get the ideas down on paper somehow, not letting issues of correctness make us tense or limit our thinking. We don't censor ourselves, understanding that we may learn something interesting from that wild thought about why birds are warm-blooded, even if we are technically wrong. Then we organize and rethink, perhaps get some more ideas and throw away a few others or save them for other essays. We test the quality of our evidence or examples and then make connections and clarifications to help the reader follow the argument or narrative. Then we tinker with sentences, and finally — as the last thing we worry about — read to make sure we have used the conventions that will make it easiest for our audience to understand our ideas without distractions.

It isn't that linear, of course, and computers make the process a bit different, inviting even more backtracking and shifting of materials. They also allow spell-checker howlers like *cereal killer*. Some lazy or overextended students might throw together something at the last minute and expect to get the A their work received in high school. And some have both talent and solid grounding in critical thinking before they come to college; they construct cogent essays with admirable style. But most students dread having their writing judged as much as we dread judging it. And too many college students can relate experiences at school that battered their spirits. If this is true of those who succeed, imagine the struggles of those like the little boy in Rosemary Catacalos's poem who experience such negative evaluations consistently.

Catacalos creates in David Talamántez a character who seems real. Even after being told that he is a composite, we still see him vividly and feel that we know him, because she gives details of his personality. We watch him in action and hear his voice. We have seen his artwork and know how he thinks: his warrants for knowing that birds are warm-blooded have to do with their lively movement and the complexity, which is of their expression. We are hurt that the teacher is unable to see the beauty and creativity of his mind, its liveliness and complexity, which is so like his warm birds. We are conscious of his ethnicity because he has an Hispanic surname, because we see a few details of the neighborhood, and because he has difficulty with written English, spelling it just as he hears it. But most second graders have some difficulty with the spelling of English, a notoriously inconsistent language. The "whole language" approach to reading and writing takes this into account, allowing students to invent spellings so that they are not slowed down as they first begin to write. But David's teacher doesn't cut him any slack, nor does she seem to take his probable bilingual learning situation into account.

Although in some ways it is important that English is probably not David's first language, the experience is not confined to his being Chicano. He could as easily be limited by an English dialect or by cultural or class differences that separate him from mainstream American speech and concepts. He could simply be a child whose learning style differs from the one privileged by an obviously unperceptive teacher. Studies have shown that evaluations of a student's work can be influenced by misinformation planted by researchers. If the teacher is prejudiced, even unknowingly, against Mexican Americans, her bias clouds her expectations of David's abilities. Other forms of bias might affect expectations of other students.

This teacher assumes that everything belongs in its proper place and should be done in the proper way. Neatness counts. Creativity and originality are punished. Rules are important. So are correct spelling and "nice details." Readers readily conclude that the teacher values conformity. In her classroom, students learn rules rather than critical and creative thinking skills.

David, when we first meet him, may be angry, but he is most of all determined to make "his mark," to shout out his name to the world. There is something triumphant about his contribution of language to the world. He "publishes" his literary and artistic creations like broadsides or flyers thrown from an airplane. If David were a part of speech, he would be an active verb, and readers might count the verbs and other references to movement in the poem. By inscribing his name in place of the teacher's evaluation of him, he reclaims his identity, replacing the negative minuses of his grades with the positive "yes" of his worth. His voice rings out confidently and his affirmation is large, unlike the small letters he uses for schoolwork. He has not been beaten down yet. But readers usually characterize this poem as sad. Perhaps this is because we hurt for children who suffer judgments from teachers who fail to recognize their strengths. "But we should have standards," teachers object. We might answer that students do need to learn language skills that will help them in life but that it is not necessary to ignore the value of a child's identity while teaching him. Interested students might review "Aria" by Richard Rodriguez (p. 752) for another view on the role of teachers in giving a Mexican American child a voice of his own. Some readers of Catacalos's text maintain that bilingual education would help David to express himself in a more familiar language while learning skills in English.

But the issue seems more universal. It involves a difference in philosophies about education. School boards and principals can influence the type of teacher who is hired, screening for attitudes that fail to take difference into account. Teacher training programs have a great influence, as do English departments at universities. Many teachers try to find something positive to say before raising a negative issue with a child or her parents, a policy that tends to build self-esteem and good will. Some activists call for the elimination of grades altogether. We might ask our college students how they think such an action would affect their current learning experiences. If they think they would expend little effort, we might ask them if the result would be the same for young children, eager to learn and create. Most of us recall thinking of grades as somehow involved with good or bad luck or the teacher's personal dislike or affection for us. This is especially true of evaluations of writing or art, since our identity is so closely bound up with such efforts. Some teachers think like the computer, sticking to the rules and disregarding the differing purposes of poetry and prose, along with any other difference.

The enjambment of the poem gives syntax importance, since we keep reading to the end of the sentence for the sake of meaning. Nevertheless, punctuation and line breaks allow smaller units of discourse. In the middle of the first line, for example, we have the phrase "whose mother is at work" set off by commas. This gives us an indication of David's family life, since he is going home on his own and his mother will probably not be home until later. The commas emphasize this fact, but the poet just mentions it in passing, not explaining anything but instead leaving it for us to simply note, perhaps to think of it later as we see the drawing of the crowded dinner table with "To mush noys!" We see that perhaps David could be valued more as an individual even in his family, though this is just a fact of his life, not something that is singled out for judgment. Enjambment allows the smallest of pauses to occur at the end of each line, thus emphasizing by the white space the words that occur in these spots. For example, the first line could have come to a full stop at the end of the word *mark*, and we do pause there, left for a fraction of a second with the idiom "leaves his mark," meaning to make a difference in the world. But the indented phrase that comprises the second line modifies the meaning. Therefore, we see that the syntax and the punctuation and line breaks maintain a tension between the headlong action of the text's narrative and the more measured and intermittent pace of the poetry.

Charging a Teacher with Sexual Harassment: Cultural Contexts for David Mamet's Oleanna (p. 697)

DAVID MAMET

Oleanna (p. 699)

David Mamet's postmodern drama *Oleanna* affects audiences much like a Rorschach test. As we try to decipher the inkblots, our readings reveal as much about our own assumptions as they do about Mamet's characters. The play's gaps and contradictions make it less ambiguous than indeterminate, and the text could support directly opposite assertions about many of its issues. Important information is left out, and we are taken by surprise by the dynamics of the characters. What happens to Carol between the first and second scene, for example, to change her character from a seemingly shy and insecure student to a wielder of power? Who are the members of her "group," and what can we assume about their influence over her? What is she about to reveal to John when the final telephone call of the first scene interrupts, ending their conversation? In many ways, this text deals with critical reading and with rhetoric. The two main characters, the unseen members of Carol's group and the tenure committee, John's family and personal connections, and the readers and viewers of the play all read and misread the situation and the characters' words. Sources of authority are questioned. Carol wants John's book pulled because her group objects to its being used as a "representative example" of the thinking of the university community. Both characters refer to the texts that they have produced, citing them as textual evidence. Each character reads beneath surface meanings and jumps to conclusions about what the other intends by his or her words, projecting personal feelings and experiences into their interpretations. John, in particular, repeatedly assumes that he knows what his student is thinking and feeling, and he constantly silences her by interrupting and anticipating her words. He assumes facts that are not evident. But in a typically professorial manner, he finds her writing imprecise. And both the reader and Carol herself agree that the writing is vague in a way that is typical of student writing, Carol characterizing it as "pathetic." The word has a double meaning, of course, and we are left ironically unsure which one she intends. She may be making a self-evaluation that positions her as an incompetent victim, helpless before the difficulty of the course. But she might be speaking of her rhetoric.

We find examples of all three of Aristotle's types of persuasive appeals in Mamet's play: logos, ethos, and pathos. In later scenes we see Carol using logical, hard evidence to build her case against John, though we have seen with our own eyes that the facts are taken out of context. The play deals with the nature of power and discourse in the university and critiques the theories of education and the philosophical poses that are cynically, carelessly, or manipulatively professed by both teachers and students. To some readers, the professor is the worst sort of chauvinist, the unaware bigot who is self-deceived into thinking that he is tolerant. To others, the female student is an example of political correctness run amok. The situation is a junior professor's nightmare, and there is a dark humor and irony to the play for anyone who has spent any time in a university setting. Like the contemporaneous television series *Third Rock from the Sun*, which operates on the premise that the best cover for a creature from an alien planet is as a university professor, *Oleanna* could take place only in this stuffy little office where the dialogue sounds all too normal.

John's philosophy strikes uncomfortably close to home for many of us. He feels that the educators of the past have failed young people, and he is cynical about the assumption that education can be the salvation of the working class. He believes that he wants his students to think for themselves, to put ideas into their own words rather than constantly taking notes and parroting their professors. He is idealistic, identifies with his students, and believes that he wants to help them. He objects to the confrontational approach that seeks to instill cognitive dissonance, to engage in hazing. He enjoys performing in the classroom and trying to solve his students' problems in a personal way. But our student readers will find many ways in which he fails to put his theory into practice and times when his attempts to apply principles backfire. His cynicism devalues what he does, he does not allow his student to finish a thought, and his attempts at establishing common ground go awry. Carol, on the other hand, wants to be told what to think, insists that she has done what he told her to do, has bought and read his book. Eventually, she sees education in terms of groups rather than individuals. She seizes control and forces confrontation.

Ironically, many students identify with John rather than with Carol, missing the ways in which he compromises and undercuts his own ideals. They react against her inversion of the power structure and what they perceive as her irrationality, even paranoia. Actually, she is at times hyperrational, blindly relying on her evidence and on written texts. Some readers see Carol as a survivor of child sexual abuse that causes her to seek victimization, citing her bristling at John's contention that he is not her father. The epigraph from Samuel Butler at the beginning and Carol's submissiveness at the end may support this contention, since they hint at self-blame. The class issue is important to other readers, and the second epigraph, from a folk song according to Mamet, mentions slavery. But which character is the slave? And slave to what? Carol's motives are problematic, and although she hints that she has overcome great difficulties to get to college, we are not told what they are. At the end of the first scene, she seems about to reveal something about herself that might have helped both John and the reader to understand, perhaps heading off the events that follow. But John is too self-absorbed to hear her, and this fact may explain a great deal.

Students usually blame the group to which Carol refers for her change in attitude and for the escalating political interpretations of John's words and actions that reverse the dynamics of power as the play proceeds. She instructs him to "consult the report" with its loaded words, characterizing his words and actions as "sexist," "elitest," "classist," "self-aggrandizing," "theatrical," "deviations from the text," and "pornographic." She accuses him of being patriarchal. (She would protest that these are not accusations but proven facts!) By the third scene she is pronouncing sophisticated evaluations of the power relationships in John's classroom and in her conferences with him. Although she may be parroting the rhetoric of the group, a case might also be made for a real change. Perhaps the group has succeeded in making her education meaningful to her by *telling* her what to think. She is no longer an individual but a representative example, has found in the group the sort of indoctrination she desires.

John, on the other hand, personalizes education and fails to realize his place as part of groups and systems or the political implications of his theories. He also fails to realize that he is often a walking cliché. When Carol objects in the final scene that John knows nothing and believes in nothing, we see that she has a legitimate complaint, that his fine theory is a veneer covering vagueness, hypocrisy, and egotism. When he violently finds the strength of his convictions at the play's end, Carol seems to accept his evaluation of her, perhaps finally getting from him the imposition of power that she wants. Many readers will be troubled by the sadomasochistic implications of the closing lines and may raise issues about the relationships between sex, violence, and power. Mamet's use of fragmented dialogue and the intrusions of personal telephone calls into what should be an academic setting are particularly appropriate to this play. They demonstrate John's inability to listen to Carol or his wife, thus providing insights into his character. Because we know more about his personal aspirations and motivations, readers usually find John more three-dimensional and easier to relate to than Carol, who seems peculiarly flat and symbolic.

CULTURAL CONTEXTS:

ANITA HILL and CLARENCE THOMAS, *Statements to the United States Senate Judiciary Committee on October 11, 1991* (p. 729)
HOWARD GADLIN, From "Mediating Sexual Harassment" (p. 739)
ROBERT M. O'NEILL, "Protecting Free Speech When the Issue Is Sexual Harassment" (p. 746)

Many of us remember vividly the United States Judiciary Committee hearings in which Supreme Court nominee Clarence Thomas defended himself against charges of sexual harassment levied by his former employee, Anita Hill (p. 729). Especially because most of the proceedings took place over a weekend, millions of Americans watched them at home on TV. Even though a significant

portion of the public believed Thomas rather than Hill, and the Senate eventually ratified Thomas's appointment to the Court, the hearings greatly increased
the country's awareness of sexual harassment. Also, quite a few people disliked
how Hill was treated by the Judiciary Committee, which was composed entirely
of white men. In the following year, this dismay proved consequential when a
record number of women were elected to the Senate. Furthermore, in recent
years, surveys have repeatedly shown increasing support for Hill's version of the
truth.

Perhaps all or most of your students will be unfamiliar with the
Hill/Thomas dispute. You probably will need to clarify the hearings' basic facts
as well as the issues that came up for debate. Try to avoid lecturing at length
about this historical event, however, especially because the class's main aim is to
explore how the case relates to Mamet's play. A good concept to focus on is timeliness — or, to use a term from classical rhetoric, *kairos*. As we noted above, the
hearings were able to seize public attention in part because they were shown on
TV at a time when many Americans could tune in. Moreover, Hill had difficulty
proving Thomas guilty for two reasons that involve timeliness: (1) her accusation appeared at a very late point in the confirmation process, after the initial
hearings had concluded; (2) rather than accusing Thomas immediately after his
harassment, she had continued to work for him and made her charge years later.

Timeliness figures, too, in the narrative structure of Mamet's drama.
Playwrights always have to determine the time span that their play will cover,
and this determination often involves deciding how best to create excitement. In
the case of David Mamet's *Oleanna* (p. 699), you might point out, tension develops partly because Carol accuses John of sexual harassment at the moment in
his career when he is being considered for tenure. Most important, we have
included Hill and Thomas speeches here because the timing of the hearings
affected the reception of Mamet's play. Mamet has been cagey about how much
he himself was thinking of the hearings when he wrote the play. As we note in
our book, he says that he had already written a version of the first act beforehand,
but he thereby leaves open the possibility that the hearings influence his completion of the work. Certainly *Oleanna*'s initial audiences were thinking of the
Hill/Thomas controversy when they saw the production. Given this situation,
you might ask students to identify a historical event that shaped their response
to a particular text, even if the work was written before the event. You might
remind them that certain movies made before September 11, 2001, weren't
screened until much later because their subject matter wound up resembling
events of that day. You might observe, too, that after the Hill/Thomas hearings,
many people saw sexual harassment charges as necessarily involving the hearings' he said/she said structure, which seems to require either the accuser or the
accused to be totally innocent. In Mamet's play, however, both John and Carol
can be seen as flawed.

Spend some time on Hill's and Thomas's actual speeches, which are interesting in part because each of these two people tries to make a persuasive argument through personal narrative. With each speech, ask your class to identify
particular strategies the speaker uses to convince others that his or her story is
true. Probably someone will note that Thomas relies much on sheer anger to
convince his audience that he is the victim of a false complaint. You might point

out that in rhetoric, the use of emotion as a persuasive appeal is called *pathos*.

In Mamet's *Oleanna*, the words *unwanted* and *unwelcome* in the definition of sexual harassment depend upon the state of mind of the victim, placing much of the power in her hands. Carol's evidence refers to all of the points in the section describing which behavior may constitute sexual harassment, and she uses its jargon, accusing John of "misuse or abuse of power or hierarchal authority" in almost these words. She keeps written records and goes to advisors, her "Group." She bypasses the informal grievance process, however, going straight for the jugular and contacting the tenure committee that has power over his career, reputation, and economic welfare. Ask students to research the process at their college or university and compare the texts the university distributes with the one here. We might consider whether a student would be allowed to take her case directly to the tenure committee and whether John's colleagues would be so quick to accept Carol's version of the events if they were at our school. Does anyone in the class know a person who has been harassed or accused of harassment? What happened as a result?

Howard Gadlin, in his case study of Joanna from "Mediating Sexual Harassment" (p. 739), privileges informal resolutions of sexual harassment issues but maintains that the threat of formal proceedings, even if unspoken, can be used as a tool to make mediation work. Both the student and the professor have their reputations on the line and can be harmed by a formal hearing that becomes public knowledge. When considering mediation, Joanna must deal with her reluctance to meet her harasser face to face; he could have aggressively denied her accusations and possibly talked his way out of them. As Gadlin points out, he could have played the "role . . . of the misunderstood professor," as John's tenure committee undoubtedly believes he does. Since harassment is difficult to prove, Gadlin's contention that formal procedures usually favor the harasser makes mediation sound like a good solution. However, in Mamet's *Oleanna*, John and Carol engage in behavior that should never occur; they meet alone to discuss the matter without a mediator, allowing the situation to escalate. The best mediation for the characters of Mamet's play might require each to allow the other to speak without interruptions or attempts to *read* or *misread* the words of the other party.

In his article from *The Chronicle of Higher Education*, Robert M. O'Neil (p. 746) concludes by focusing on the issue of definition. He maintains that tolerating sexual harassment is not an issue but that deciding what constitutes sexual harassment is. This gives us the opportunity to have students recall the definition of an *issue* as "a question about which reasonable people may disagree." Some students might argue with the teaching practices of Dean Cohen as O'Neil describes them in his second paragraph. The complaints that Cohen's student registers could be made about many college teachers, including those using this anthology, which often deals with adult themes. Furthermore, we often make our students uncomfortable as we provoke them to engage in critical thinking. O'Neil's readers do not know from the facts as they are outlined the full context of Cohen's teaching methods.

Sometimes it is not the actual content of a course but the teacher's tone that students find disturbing. And we have seen from Carol's use of the facts in *Oleanna* that facts alone do not always give a true picture of events as another participant or observer would interpret them. Sometimes students, after engaging in many uninhibited discussions of sexual content in past literature classes, will find one class particularly uncomfortable. The problem is not always one we can identify easily; in one case, the elderly male professor seemed more titillated and embarrassed than intellectually stimulated by the content of the course and seemed to think that he was being daring. His students, on the other hand, found his comments quite naive. The issue of sexual harassment never arose in outside discussions of the course and would not have seemed warranted, since no comments were directed at individual students and the atmosphere was not hostile. Like the language of the harassment policy at Cohen's school, the discomfort was vague and imprecise. O'Neil suggests that the classroom environment is hostile when offensive language is directed at one or more students in a way that makes them uncomfortable. Even this might be misinterpreted, however. Who is to decide what is "germane to the subject matter" of a given course? Since we have witnessed both Carol and John misquote or misread each other, students might argue that Carol could have made her case no matter what the guidelines. John, however, might have learned from O'Neil's suggested process what sort of comments would be likely to offend students like Carol and perhaps could have saved his job and his freedom.

COMPARING SCHOOL CULTURE WITH THE CULTURE OF HOME: CRITICAL COMMENTARIES ON RICHARD RODRIGUEZ'S "ARIA" (p. 751)

RICHARD RODRIGUEZ

Aria (p. 752)

Although his essay "Aria" and the commentary that accompanies it in this cluster were written in the 1980s, the issues they raise are still very much alive, and so is Richard Rodriguez — alive and, as usual, kicking against all sorts of conventional definitions. He is a contributing commentator on PBS's *NewsHour with Jim Lehrer*, a much published feature writer for newspapers and magazines, and the author of a second book of essays, *Days of Obligation: An Argument with My Mexican Father* (1992). He continues to be a burr in the saddle of many Mexican Americans, and students often stage protests when he is invited to campuses to speak. He still objects to bilingual education and affirmative action, even turning down university teaching positions because he felt that they were offered to him because of his ethnicity. Richard Rodriguez is in many ways a contradiction. Seen by many non-Hispanics as representative of Mexican Americans, he is actually an iconoclast, constantly at odds with those who advocate for Hispanic causes. He is openly homosexual, yet gay and lesbian issues have only recently played a part in shaping his public persona, and he resists the characterization of homosexuality as a lifestyle, suggesting instead that it is an "emotion." He argues for using the dominant language of cultural literacy, but his doctorate is in the literature of the English Renaissance, an era characterized by the triumph of the vernacular over the cultural literacy of Latin and Greek. His most popular texts speak in eloquent English about topics that surround his non-English ethnicity.

Rodriguez feels that he has been empowered by his command of the English language but claims that he is not an Anglophile. If Spanish suddenly becomes the language of public life in the United States, then he says that he will support the dominance of Spanish in the schools. What he objects to is an education that isolates children from the whole of tradition. He claims that the point of education is not to build self-esteem but to teach children what they need to know, to connect them with people who are unrelated to them but are a part of who they can be. This can and should be uncomfortable for learners. He insists that assimilation is inevitable, that the very act of asserting one's ethnicity is a peculiarly American act. The same is true for individuality in Rodriguez's thinking; to be unconventional is to be conventionally American. In his view, multiculturalism as it is expressed on most college campuses is a political pose, allowing only trendy and politically correct differences rather than true diversity. True to his agenda of paradox, Rodriguez asserts his independence by embracing the mainstream. He says of the book *Hunger of Memory: The Education of Richard Rodriguez,* from which "Aria" is taken, that it was written as a sort of protest. It was "my objection to the popular ideology of that time: my insistence that I am this man, contrary to what you want to make me: my declaration of myself, of my profession — political and personal."

Because he writes beautifully and with confidence, Rodriguez may so skillfully persuade readers with pathos and ethos that they do not hold his logic to the usual standards. Though his title "Aria" may seem at first to refer to the sounds of his early, private Spanish language, necessarily lost, he says, to the public English language, the musical title more likely refers to his speaking out and to his writing style as well. An aria is a lyrical solo, and Rodriguez insists on singing alone. We need to ask our students if his conclusions follow from the personal experiences that he relates. Even by his own definitions, Rodriguez is not a representative example when it comes to language learning. Why is it not likely that he acquired his skill with language around the dinner table as the family played word games in Spanish? He says that he was a bilingual child, and most linguists would maintain that his language learning occurred long before he finally spoke up in class. Can students imagine other scenarios in which he could have learned the "public individuality" of skill in English without losing the joy of Spanish? Some people might argue that his whole life has been shaped by the attempt to recover what he lost rather than by the voice he gained, since he continues to write about his identity first as Mexican American and lately as Indian. We might also ask if students who would grow up to be math majors would have been as well served by the author's educational experiences, or would this type of schooling have only worked for children who would become English majors? Do students feel comfortable with letting Rodriguez constantly equivocate, making up his own vague definitions? His tone is sad, nostalgic, and filled with paradox as he tries to convince us that his "awkward childhood does not prove the necessity of bilingual education." But why doesn't it? Does it *prove anything?* Many readers understand the sense of loss he conveys when he talks about his parents. No one would contend that children should be denied the language skills that will help them achieve, but many readers take issue with his conclusions that separating them from their home culture is the way to do this.

Although Rodriguez faults "middle-class ethnics" as romantic, some students might assert that Rodriguez uses sentimentality to get us on his side. Many of our students at regional or community colleges are first-generation college students who understand the dilemma of choosing between the person they are at school and the very different person their parents see at home. During the "Ebonics" debates that made the news in the 1990s, many prominent African American writers were eloquent in their appeals to teach children to skillfully use Standard English. On the other hand, it is interesting to hear properly academic English professors who grew up with regional dialects change register in a social or family group from *back home*. Most instructors in college English classes will probably agree that language plays a crucial role in education and that speaking out in class is important. Students may differ, however. The quiet one in the back of the class sometimes surprises us with the depth of her written work. Actually, many may have found that to speak in class is to meet with the sort of "public individuality" that peer pressure sometimes squelches. They have learned to keep their opinions to themselves. The vague generalities and platitudes that we read in student papers may reflect an attempt at consensus, a communal voice. Rodriguez may have a point. To think critically and to speak in one's own voice can be isolating, but profoundly rewarding.

CRITICAL COMMENTARIES:

RAMÓN SALDÍVAR, From *Chicano Narrative* (p. 762)
TOMÁS RIVERA, From "Richard Rodriguez's *Hunger of Memory* as Humanistic Antithesis" (p. 763)
VICTOR VILLANUEVA JR., From "Whose Voice Is It Anyway?" (p. 765)

Ramón Saldívar, in this excerpt from *Chicano Narrative* (p. 762), maintains that Richard Rodriguez's narrative "Aria" (p. 752) serves the interests of political conservatives. Many readers will agree, but others will applaud Rodriguez for challenging political correctness. Underneath his narrative lies the assumption that the only way for a member of an ethnic minority to gain power is to adapt to the dominant culture at any cost. If bilingual education does not empower children who do not speak English, then the government does not have to spend money on such programs. If individual effort, simply learning how to speak up in class, can result in the achievements of a Richard Rodriguez, then why juggle limited opportunities to implement affirmative action? *Those* people just need to speak English at home with their children, so that the children will be able to learn at school, goes the argument. By linking the speaking of English to acquiring a public voice, Rodriguez devalues other languages. Why not study Shakespeare *and* Cervantes, Faulkner *and* García Márquez?

The unspoken implication that English is better than other languages plays into the hands of uninformed or racist Americans who use the English Only movement to cover prejudice against brown people. This is especially problematic when Rodriguez is seen as a representative voice of Hispanic peoples or when readers encounter only one text isolated in an anthology. Much of his writing celebrates the strength of Mexican culture, especially its Indian heritage, but most students will only read this essay. His project is to problematize, to complicate, to create metaphors and ironic oppositions that shock his readers, perhaps for his own self-aggrandizement but perhaps because he really believes what he says. But he is also reductive, sometimes so caught up in creating new oxymorons that a close examination reveals his rhetoric to be meaningless or fallacious. Because he is articulate, vocal, and prolific, many readers are misled into thinking that Rodriguez speaks for a community when in fact he is idiosyncratic in the extreme.

There may come a time with any individual when the choice must be made between home and school. Rodriguez maintains that the break he experienced is true for every child, not just for those whose private and public languages differ. For many readers, however, not just Hispanics, the essay "Aria" dishonors Rodriguez's parents and ethnic heritage in a shameful way. In fact, Rodriguez's mother wrote him a letter asking that he not write about family matters in this way. Some would contend that to destroy the language of a people is to commit cultural genocide and that when the Irish nuns require the family to speak English at home they engage in a colonial enterprise ironically reminiscent of the sort Ireland itself has endured. Tomás Rivera's critique (p. 763) of the book from which this essay is taken uses Spanish verbs of being to explain that Rodriguez chooses the lesser alternative. In the process, he demonstrates even for English-speaking readers the power of the Spanish language for analysis. Many foreign language instructors are sold on the total immersion technique, however, and some students will insist that only in this way will a child have the incentive to learn the language that will give him a voice in the wider community.

Victor Villanueva Jr., in "Whose Voice Is It Anyway?" (p. 765), responds to the philosophy of Richard Rodriguez by pointing out the institutionalized economic inequalities that historically accompanied the creation of minority ethnic groups as opposed to the free movement of immigrants. He suggests that quite often a racial distinction also exists, with skin color playing a more dominant role than most members of mainstream society are willing to admit. Villanueva recounts the joking of his friends and the stereotypes that they reveal. Rodriguez, along with many others, has pointed out that the image of the lazy Mexican still exists in spite of a work ethic that rivals that of the Puritans. The CEO of Black Entertainment Television recently said in an interview that people in parking lots frequently assume that he is a chauffeur. On the other hand, we know of one blond South African immigrant who, even with a limited education and a working-class British accent, is immediately assumed by most Americans to be highly cultured and finds many doors opened to her in spite of her colossal rudeness. However, Rodriguez, in *Days of Obligation*, points out the power of indigenous peoples to overcome conquest because cultures have a way of merging. Looking at his own Native American skin and features and those of Mexicans, he asks, "Where is the Conquistador?" The Indians seem to have won the DNA war, even though in many ways Spanish has conquered in the language arena. Ethnicity is complex and constantly in flux, and the direction of assimilation is not fixed. Perhaps the best way to ensure that minorities have an equal opportunity to overcome the barriers of the past is to do exactly what we are engaged in at the moment. Awareness of the issues may be a first step toward attitude changes that accumulate over time. Rodriguez may best serve as a reminder that ethnic groups are not monoliths in which everyone believes the same way. By taking political action of the sort Rodriguez would oppose — multiculturalism in the readings of university students, for example — perhaps we can overcome some stereotypes, making understanding possible and increasing opportunity.

LEARNING IN A COLONIAL CONTEXT: A COLLECTION OF WRITINGS BY JAMAICA KINCAID (p. 767)

JAMAICA KINCAID

Girl (p. 768)

The writings of Jamaica Kincaid immediately raise issues of genre. How are readers meant to interpret these texts? They seem to be short stories or essays or chapters from novels. Yet we can imagine setting them on the page as poetry, choosing line breaks in the quick pauses between breaths, emphasizing the repetitions and collocations. Kincaid's texts also cannot be classed as fiction or as nonfiction. Her stories of mothers and daughters are undoubtedly autobiographical, set in her native Antigua or an island setting much like it, or following the life of a character who, like herself, has left such a place. But she sometimes shifts the details around in time or creates a character from a composite of several real people. Some of her narratives began as stories about her mother's childhood, whereas others are her own. She has said that she does not aim to be factual, but she does aim to be true. We might explore her distinction, perhaps considering it in terms of David Mamet's *Oleanna* (p. 699), in which a character presents the "facts" in a way most will agree is not true. Kincaid writes of intensely close relationships between women and girls, but she cut off communication with her mother for many years after immigrating to the United States, renewing the relationship partly because she wanted her children to know the strong grandmother. The older woman's influence was overwhelming to Kincaid's sense of identity and her ability to grow, and she found it necessary to break free. Many college students can relate to her need to escape the dictates of childhood. Like many Caribbean and African American writers, Jamaica Kincaid chose a new name for herself when she began finding her own voice as a writer. She grew up as Elaine Potter Richardson. Ironically, she gives many of her characters variations of this name. To change one's name is a profound political and personal act, especially for a woman who has struggled for her own identity in the midst of colonialism and sexism. "Girl" is the first story in her first published book, *At the Bottom of the River*, and was the first of many stories to appear in the *New Yorker*, where she also published much nonfiction.

Although "Girl" might aptly be labeled a dramatic monologue, students will find several of the traditional elements of the short story here. The story has a protagonist, though we hear her voice only in the two places highlighted by italics, where she summons up the courage once to defend herself and once to ask a question. And the story certainly has an antagonist, the prevailing voice of the mother. Conflict takes place. The mother gives advice, but she also pronounces evaluations of her daughter in an inexorable stream, like the current at "the bottom of a river," as Kincaid's book title implies. The undertow is so strong that the daughter must eventually leave, but this does not happen until later. At this point, the glow of childhood is being destroyed by the nagging obligations of puberty and adolescence. The fifth item in the catalog instructs the girl in one of the rules of menstruation, and the worries about her future as a slut surface soon after.

Women now in middle age, even younger women in traditional cultures, usually are able to pinpoint the year they discovered that to be a woman was to be judged and limited by the culture. A recent study suggests that the self-esteem of American girls tends to take a nosedive somewhere between the ages of nine and fourteen unless concerted efforts are made to see that they find areas of achievement and acceptance. Have our female college students experienced this? What solutions do they suggest for younger girls? Readers will find it interesting that the voice of oppression is female. Our discussions might consider how mothers internalize a culture's evaluations of women as inferior or bad and pass them on to their daughters. Defenders of pornography often cite the women who cooperate with their own exploitation and seem to enjoy it. Do students think this is a related issue?

Male students are often fascinated as the women in the class relate the experiences of middle school and high school. We should ask men to consider how these hierarchies — from which they benefit — came to be and why they continue to be so powerful. We might also introduce them to some of the literature on colonialism and its metaphors and implications. What do women and conquered peoples have in common?

Kincaid's writing style allows the reader to hear the voice of oppression as the girl hears it, as one long harangue that effectively silences her. This may explain why the story is written as one long sentence. The indiscriminate order of the items in the mother's list make us see that her teaching is a recurring event, so pervasive that it washes over the girl every minute of her life. The effect for the reader is shock with a twist of irony when abortion has equal weight with cold cures and fishing. This is a practical matter that a young woman must be told about, especially if her mother fears she will be a slut. It also indicates what we know to be true of many traditional cultures; women can follow certain procedures to subvert the rules that limit choices. Some might argue that this subversion still entails loss, however. Preventing pregnancy depends upon either purity or early abortion. The mother is teaching the girl how to survive in a specific time and place, but most readers will realize that this girl will escape into a culture where her mother's "common sense" must be unlearned. We might have students relate the advice their parents have repeatedly given them and consider what sort of culture this advice assumes. Or might television or music be the current disseminator of cultural lore in the United States?

JAMAICA KINCAID

Columbus in Chains (p. 771)

"Girl" (p.768) and the other stories of *At the Bottom of the River* describe the education a parent passes on to her child in formal and informal ways; Jamaica Kincaid's novel *Annie John* adds the influence of the school and the structures of colonialism. Annie is a bright, feisty nonconformist. She is competitive and wants to be recognized for her achievements. She is honest, telling us of her evil thoughts and her teasing of classmates without shame. Kincaid writes within a long tradition when she tells her story from the point of view of a naïve child, allowing readers to experience irony as they see a reality that still escapes her. Although she is limited as a narrator by her age and by her circumstances as an Afro-Caribbean child under British colonial rule, Annie John's unique view of the world is in some ways more trustworthy because she is open and honest.

Annie is taught the worldview of the British empire. Its goal is to turn her into a loyal, unquestioning subject. There is no question of adapting the superior British view to the needs of the children; these are facts for them to memorize, not issues raised for critical thinking. Rewards and punishments are used to motivate. Most of our students will recognize that such pedagogy is "good" for teaching conformity, though some will argue that the education Kincaid received makes it possible for her to write as she does.

Students might want to compare Kincaid's implicit criticism of her Anglican education with Richard Rodriguez's acceptance of an equally confining Catholic one in "Aria" (p. 752). Whereas Rodriguez believes that he had to devalue the culture of his family to grow, Kincaid's narrator resists the education that positions her as the descendant of slaves.

Her caption for Columbus, although innocent, reflects her attitude of resistance. Perhaps the illustration of Columbus in chains is meant to evoke empathy, to show that even great men may be tragically misunderstood. But the humor of her mother's sarcastic comment about Pa Chess sets off intertextual connections in the mind of a divergent thinker. The educators do not see the irony of presenting to the descendents of slaves and oppressed peoples the image of a white man in chains on a ship. The narrator refuses to be reverent about the historical figure who symbolizes the destruction of both Caribbean and African cultures.

Like many Caribbean and Native American thinkers, Kincaid does not see Columbus as a hero. To most adults in North America, the European explorers were introduced as achievers, brave men who came to an essentially vacant land and created a great civilization. Even though today's college students may have a less chauvinistic view, they may still feel that education should give us role models at the expense of complexity. History textbooks in elementary and high schools often oversimplify for the sake of time and space on the page, and the desire to uplift and inspire students tends to encourage the perpetuation of myths. Have our college students experienced this, or do they see a trend toward romanticizing indigenous peoples while demonizing figures like Columbus? We do not hear the voice of the teacher Miss Edwards. Kincaid may choose to allow us to see her through Annie John's eyes as more symbol than individual.

At the end of the story, Annie's mother lies to her. She is given the native breadfruit but is told that it is some exotic food from Belgium so that she will eat it. In the last image of the story, she sees her mother as a crocodile. At school, also, the child is given a lie rather than something of value, as the educational system pretends that the doctrines of British colonialism will sustain the child of Africans and Caribbean Indians.

The child in "Girl" is given a stream of instructions about how to be a woman. But the implicit message that she is bad underlies the mother's words. In "Columbus in Chains" a girl resists the messages she receives about her value as a person, especially a dark-skinned subject of the British empire. These messages underlie the rules and formal instructions of the school. The children may be different. If they are, we might expect Annie John to resist the teachings of her mother. But the difference may lie instead in the situations. Annie John is confident at school; because she is so bright, she has a voice, in spite of her teachers. But she seems to be more submissive at home. She seems left out of the joyful interactions of her mother and father, and she does care what they think. The two times we hear the voice of "Girl" she protests or questions, and this behavior is consistent with Annie John's personality. The sassy behavior that makes us like Annie is the sort of behavior that the mother in "Girl" thinks will make her daughter a slut. Kincaid often writes of the loss of paradise that comes when girls goes through puberty, when they lose the close symbiotic bond with the mother that characterizes childhood. The foreign colonialism is comparatively easy to resist, but the lore of womanhood that also positions the girl is harder to overcome. The young woman internalizes both, both contribute to her identity, but she will ultimately have to struggle and break with the power of both sorts of education to become her own person.

JAMAICA KINCAID

On Seeing England for the First Time (p. 777)

Following the stories in which we meet a young girl much like Jamaica Kincaid as she learns and resists the lessons of home and school on the island of Antigua, Kincaid's essay "On Seeing England for the First Time" allows us to see some of the results of this education in the woman's thinking. Kincaid takes the reader through her education on England and her changing views of the country so long held up to her as the epitome of civilization, culture, and scenery. A well-known experiment conducted in the early twentieth century in the United States found that young African American girls consistently chose white dolls over dolls that looked more like themselves. They had received the message of the culture that white was prettier and more normal, more human, than their own dark skin. The same sort of message was given to West Indian children of Jamaica Kincaid's generation. England's was the default reality; everything else had to be defined in contrast to it. Kincaid takes us through her education about England, both the formal education and the more powerful informal education. She speaks of first seeing it consciously on a map and then seeing it in historical terms. But it is the privileging of its culture in everyday life, the tone with which it is described, its pervasiveness as the language of reality, that are most powerful. She is affected not only by the way she sees England but also by the way England constructs her view of the world and of herself. However, Jamaica Kincaid, like her fictional protagonists, resists this influence. She speaks of filling up with hatred the gap between the myth and the reality of England. Colonialism and slavery have intended her "erasure" as an individual, and she in turn wants to erase England and its power over her. Her tone asks her audience to feel her outrage and her sense of loss at having been taken over body and soul by England long before she was born.

The narrator of the essay is as open about her negative feelings as is the narrator of *Annie John*. Students might find her too negative, feeling that she is too tough on the current residents of England, people who have done her no harm. After all, she has kept her independent spirit. But the childhood assumptions about the superiority of everything English result in a devaluation of the culture from which she comes, as she points out in paragraph 6. All lessons both in and out of school teach the Afro-Caribbean child to feel ashamed and less worthy because her home and her very self are so different from the English ideal. As Kincaid describes her trip to England, she reminds us of slavery, prejudice, and the ways in which people show contempt for others. After describing in paragraph 14 how her friend changes her behavior and attitude in England as her status is devalued, Kincaid departs from chronological order to show the reader her own reaction to the "slavish, reverential, awed" tones of a salesman as he shows her the prince's crest. Perhaps her organization becomes more topical in this final section of the essay because she wants to drive home her point about oppression for arbitrary reasons. What she finally *sees* in England is the power of colonialism and institutionalized racism over the individual. She subtly points out that personal prejudice, which she admits to feeling along with rage and disappointment, differs from the power "to do evil on [a] grand scale" as England has done by its organized subjugation and colonialism of the hearts and minds of people.

Because it is written as nonfiction, and because the voice of the narrator is that of a bitter adult, readers may feel less compassion for the real Jamaica Kincaid of "On Seeing England for the First Time" than they do for the children who speak in her fiction. Perhaps they take her more seriously. Kincaid's adult voice usually makes white students uncomfortable, since they feel she is directing her anger toward them. In this context, her fantasy in paragraph 12 about enslaving the white people of England and making them more like herself bears examining more closely. She ironically says that this would make them more like the people she loves and implies that they would be improved and helped, or humanized, by becoming slaves. This may remind some readers that the Christianizing of Africans and other "primitive" peoples was long an excuse for enslaving and indoctrinating them for their own good. "Could I resist it?" she asks. "No one ever has." Similarly, in paragraph 10, she compares her obsession with England and the gap between its myth and reality with Columbus's experience. As she describes him in the essay, he is still the "Columbus in chains" of *Annie John*'s picture, enslaved by the difference between his fantasy about what he'd found and its reality. Although it is not explicitly colonial, we could argue that the short story "Girl" nevertheless reflects customs and traditions of slavery. A conflict is evident between "benna," the music with roots in West Africa and the Caribbean, and "Sunday school," an institution of the Anglican or Methodist church. The mother teaches her daughter how to iron the khaki pants that her father wears, an item of British colonial culture. She is taught how to set a table properly. The household chores are women's work, but are also the work of the servant.

TEACHING THROUGH LITERATURE (p. 786)

DAVID WAGONER

The Singing Lesson (p. 787)

Whenever our students say a text is *about* life or *about* death, our first reaction may be to scream out the word CLICHÉ. David Wagoner's poem "The Singing Lesson" is obviously an extended metaphor *about* life, however, and it ends with intimations of mortality. He says that life is like singing, and here's a lesson on how to do it properly. Before assigning the poem, we might ask students to come up with their own metaphors for life and to think of others they have encountered in their reading. Many students have read William Shakespeare's *Macbeth*, for example, or discussed the life-and-death symbolism of Robert Frost's poetry. Such activities give us a chance to bring up the concepts of *abstract* and *general* versus *concrete* and *specific*, encouraging students to take abstraction into account in both their critical reading and their own writing. Some may recall a 1999 music video called "Everybody's Free (To Wear Sunscreen)" that humorously parodies the clichés of advice columns and bestsellers filled with warm, fuzzy aphorisms. Set to music by Australian film director Baz Luhrmann, the song's words had circulated on the Internet as a commencement address purportedly by novelist Kurt Vonnegut, who liked it but didn't claim it, before being correctly attributed to *Chicago Tribune* newspaper columnist Mary Schmich. Students may still be able to find the column itself, sometimes still credited to Vonnegut, and also parodies of the parody.

Each generation probably has its own additions to the wise advice genre. Rudyard Kipling's "If" comes to mind from an earlier century, as do the biblical Proverbs of Solomon from an earlier millenium. Children of the 1960s may remember the poster of *Desiderata* printed in fake calligraphy on yellowed vellum look-alike paper for that natural look. We probably won't share with our students the parody of *Desiderata* posted by Sean Sullivan on the Internet: "Go placidly amid the noise and haste and remember what peace there may be in sleeping through breakfast. Do not speak the truth; it merely upsets the neighbors. Listen to others, even the dull and ignorant; they assign your grade and sign your paycheck."

Wagoner's "The Singing Lesson" is a dramatic monologue ostensibly spoken by the maestro to his student. When he speaks of *posture, resonance,* or *measures,* he uses the vocabulary of formal voice training. But it soon becomes apparent that he is speaking of more than singing. The first three lines might refer only to singing, but the word *compromise* hints at something more. The words begin to take on added connotations at the end of the third line when Wagoner transforms the expected cliché *best foot forward* into "best face forward" and immediately follows this with the loaded phrase "willful hands." As the poem progresses, we begin to understand that he is referring to an attitude toward art, life, and finally death. The content of the poem deals with the transforming of breath into song, the ironic "inspiring and expiring moments" of line 11. The poem's form echoes this by alternating long and short lines. He models the transformation of prose into poetry, reminding us of both poetry and death with the words "final end-stopped movement." We also see the swift movement of the music director's hands as he signals the end of the song. Although the poem does not rhyme, it does follow its own advice to "Keep time." Perhaps he chooses not to rhyme because the singer makes his own song and does not have a script to follow, only instructions about moderation. Most of the sentences are long and complex. This too models the breathing of a singer, but it also emphasizes by contrast the one short sentence of the poem: "Take care to be heard." The effect is like a musical staccato, each one-syllable word separate and clipped.

The emphasis on singing with constant vigilance about the audience may be ironic. If the poem is about life, it is about a life lived in public, even in the most private of moments. It is about a life constantly being evaluated. One who is not careful about how he presents himself to others is "asking for it." Do students feel that this is realistic advice about how to live? Or is Wagoner's persona limited by an overly conforming worldview? Is he saying that art requires walking this fine line of moderation, a constant adjustment that finds ease and beauty in order?

THEODORE ROETHKE

The Waking (p. 788)

To attempt an analysis of Theodore Roethke's villanelle "The Waking" is to risk a reduction that goes against its paradoxical message. From its first line, the poem is deliberately indeterminate, resisting the *knowing* that it speaks against. If we read the poem by feeling it, letting it take us where we "have to go," we sense that we understand it in some mystical way. Yet the poem is written in one of the most structured of closed forms, its meter and rhyme scheme precisely determined. What seems free and effortless depends upon great care in construction, revealing knowledge of prosody that stands in opposition to the poem's apparent message. The content is equally mysterious. What does the first phrase actually mean? Does he wake *in order* to sleep? Or rather than waking to the verbal form, the infinitive *to sleep*, does he awaken to some entity that he labels *sleep*, the noun? The first possibility implies that the waking life is a sort of sleepwalking state that he must rise and take part in. Feeling takes precedence, even in the world of daylight, and he goes through life as a joyful zombie. The second possibility implies that he has come to realize something about sleep, maybe about death. He blesses the "Ground" and speaks of the "lowly worm."

For most readers, these images carry connotations of the grave. He is slowly coming to realize the reality of it. He doesn't have a map, doesn't know exactly which way to go, but that's okay. Perhaps the speaker of the poem is on the edge of dying. The first line of the quatrain that ends the villanelle hints that he is ill, recovering from a sickness or a hangover that makes him shake. Roethke was hospitalized several times for alcoholism and mental illness, and he saw such breakdowns as opportunities to gain spiritual insight. He felt a bond with other visionary poets who struggled with the line between reality and mysticism. This poem may reflect the influence of Dylan Thomas, who died in 1953, the same year "The Waking" was published. Thomas's famous villanelle "Do Not Go Gentle into That Good Night" (p. 1477 in the "Confronting Mortality" chapter) addresses his father as the older man is on his deathbed. Perhaps when Roethke says that we must "learn by going where to go" he answers those who speak to the dying. We might question the identity of the person he directly addresses by the pronoun *you* in lines 7 and 14. The word *lovely* in the last line of the fifth tercet makes us think that he may speak to a woman, but the word could refer to the beauty of the experience of being alive — in the "lively air" — before "Great Nature" has her way.

One of the hallmarks of lyric poetry is repetition and echo. Rhyme is most familiar, but assonance, consonance, alliteration, rhythm and meter, even the repetition of whole lines or groups of lines that we find in refrains, play a part in our response to poetry. Often the effect is subliminal. Roethke's repetition of lines, in keeping with the rules for writing a villanelle, are easy to recognize, especially when the form has been explained. They are especially effective in a poem like "The Waking" because they help us find our way in a circling motion that seems to drift in and out of sleep. We replay the action as we do the events of a dream that we try to reenter in the state between sleep and waking. We do not know the way, so the repetitions help us learn as we go. But echoes also occur in other ways. Again according to the conventions of the villanelle, the meter repeats the rhythms of iambic pentameter and the rhyme is limited to the two echoes of the long *o* and the *r* sounds. Roethke departs from this rhyme a bit, with near rhymes allowing slight differences. More subtle is his use of alliteration, the *sl* sounds of the beginning line or the *f*s of the second; his assonance, such as the repetition of the *ee* sounds of *sleep, feel*, and *fear*; or the consonance of *lively* and *lovely*. All of the echoes work together with the content to produce a sense of unity between inner and outer realities, sleep and waking, death and life.

The paradoxes of Roethke's poem play into this unity as well. Opposite meanings intertwine in the same line. The poem violates logic by equivocation and vague, undefined terms. We wouldn't stand for such lack of cogency in an argument. But Roethke's poem makes the point that intuition may be a higher sort of learning. Like the devices of the poem, the lessons of life and death may come to us in subliminal ways, through our physical senses. Analysis may discover the patterns underneath, but we respond to them even before logic enters the picture. When Roethke breaks the pattern of the villanelle, the contrast makes us pay attention, especially since he does it to address someone he calls "you" and links with the narrator "me." Although this unseen listener to the dramatic monologue may not be the reader, the effect of this direct address, along with his earlier use of the pronoun *we*, personalizes the poem, lessens the distance. Consequently, when he urges us to learn as we go, most readers will feel that we should at least consider his advice.

Writers who let the content lead them along, writing by enjambment and coming back later to tinker with the finished freewrite, will respond to Roethke's suggestions about learning. Others, perhaps those who like to write from a pre-planned outline, will raise issues about the practicality of learning by doing. Some might contend that we can follow the paths blazed by those who have gone before, rather than fumbling in a half-sleep to find our way alone. The answer might be to point out that Roethke does not assume himself to be alone; he even asks his listener which of "those so close beside me" he or she is. This sort of learning can take place in a college course, but it requires a spirit of inquiry and a tolerance for ambiguity. Anyone who gets hooked on the joy of the chase in the course of research or who has found insights in the midst of brainstorming or who has written her way into uncharted territory knows the sort of creative learning that Roethke seems to advocate. For teachers, it requires giving students a great deal of responsibility for their own learning and helping them find the courage to think for themselves, making the assumption that they are willing and able to make. Even then, we may owe them the tools of logic and convention. After all, it is within a highly formal, intellectually ordered structure that Roethke suggests intuitive learning.

When he calls on "Great Nature" in the fifth tercet, Roethke seems to imply that there is a higher power that controls human life and death, especially death. He uses capital letters in two other places aside from the beginnings of lines, in the apostrophe "God bless the Ground!" in line 8 and when he says "Light takes the Tree" in line 10. Both nouns refer to nature but seem to have religious significance. The ground may have multiple meanings, since it could refer to the earth beneath our feet as we walk, the grave we are going toward, or the ground of being that is connected with God. The tree may also be a link to nature. For Roethke, growing things have great spiritual significance. Both the form and the content of "The Waking" imply that there is a natural oneness between life and death at the point when we intuitively let it be.

Although Theodore Roethke's "The Waking" is more formal in structure than David Wagoner's "The Singing Lesson," the tone and content of Roethke's villanelle make it seem freer than Wagoner's less traditionally formal poem. Roethke's narrator accepts the intuitive path toward the process of living and dying. Wagoner's narrator seeks to achieve equilibrium through a carefully maintained set of instructions for performing life and death in an artful way that will be clear and approved. Both are aware of the paradox involved. Both poets instruct. Roethke is less precise but brings his "student" into the awareness of the journey, advising him or her to "take the lively air" and to learn by going. The narrators of the two poems instruct in different ways. Wagoner's stays out of it, at least explicitly, speaking directly to an audience addressed in second person. He may intend to maintain his distance as an instructor, inadvertently slipping into the ironic personal revelations as his monologue takes its course. He may, in fact, be addressing himself. Roethke's narrator, on the other hand, takes the reader by the hand by including both first- and second-person pronouns, sometimes even referring to "we." Our students might consider the rhetorical effects of finding common ground with the reader, as Roethke literally seems to do, as opposed to presenting directives, even symbolically and metaphorically rich ones like Wagoner's.

ELIZABETH BISHOP

One Art (p. 790)

The editors of the selected personal correspondence of Elizabeth Bishop gave their 1994 publication the title *One Art: Letters.* The title is borrowed from the villanelle that she wrote in the 1970s, not long before her death, a text that possibly struck someone as epitomizing her experience of life. Bishop certainly knew about losing. Her father died when she was eight months old, and her mother was lost to her soon after through her institutionalization for mental illness. A lesbian in a time when it was difficult to be open about this in the United States, she lived happily with another woman in Brazil for around fifteen years. But that woman committed suicide, as did another lover. Unlike her contemporaries Robert Lowell or Theodore Roethke, Bishop reveals little of her personal life in her poetry. Although "One Art" is more autobiographical than most of her work, she maintains her distance with wry understatement, choosing not to be openly confessional.

A perfectionist, her poems are precisely crafted but not usually as formal in structure or as dependent on rhyme as the villanelle. She said at one point early in her career that her aim as a poet was "to say the most difficult things and to be funny as possible." In life she refused to allow anyone to see her take too seriously, though she took her work so seriously that her output was smaller than it might have been. She held poems back from publication as she searched for the exact word to express an idea or convey an image. Donald E. Stanford points out in a book review in the Winter 1994 *Sewanee Review* that Bishop does not usually raise political or social issues in her poetry. "She was an artist, not a propagandist," he says. Nevertheless, critical readings will undoubtedly reveal issues for our classes to discuss.

With its five tercets and final quatrain, "One Art" has the structure of a villanelle, and the rhyme scheme follows its traditional conventions. But like much of Elizabeth Bishop's poetry, its tone is conversational, and its rhythm departs from the strict iambic pentameter. Bishop also varies the refrain, subtly changing each statement about the existence of "disaster" so that we move gradually and ironically from the denial of the first tercet to the forced admission in the final quatrain that losing "may" affect her after all: "*Write* it!" the voice orders in parentheses. Her tone begins with dismissive bravado, as the narrator proposes to teach her audience the proper way of losing. The tone grows progressively more serious and ironic as the losses become greater, though the sardonic humor remains. By the end of the poem, she is becoming honest about her grief at losing the person addressed, possibly to death, though she still admits only to the appearance rather than the reality of disaster.

We can use autobiography and the motifs that recur in Bishop's poetry to understand some of the losses. The loss of a mother's watch in line 10 reminds us that Bishop may have had only mementos of a mother hospitalized when she was five and separated from her until her death when Bishop was at Vassar. The loss of houses, important in her poetry, also may symbolize the loss of mother or of other loved women. The loss of a continent may recall her loss of Lota de Macedo Soares, the Brazilian woman with whom she shared a home in South America. Part of the practice for losing as detailed in the third stanza seems to require that we give up our dreams for relationships, homes, and "where it was [we] meant / to travel." As a woman who traveled the world and who had lost houses and people, Bishop knows that this renunciation is tougher than she pretends. We might accept her advice if we desperately wish to protect ourselves from the losses that come with living and loving, but the issue can be raised that we would lose even more.

Coming at the end, the rhetorically sound spot for the most important example, we are startled to hear the sudden inclusion of the person addressed — "you" — within the catalog of lost items. The emotion grows stronger. Pain? Anger? Affection, certainly. We try to picture the person who has been lost and wonder if she has simply left or if she has died. Again, we might recall the mother who unintentionally abandoned her daughter as she battled her own demons in the asylum or the lovers who abandoned the poet through their suicides. Her denial that either is a disaster would be ironic. Many readers find the break from the villanelle form dramatic as it allows the voice of the not so gentle muse to intrude. The effect is consistent with Bishop's method. She says the difficult things, but she remains *funny* in her own acerbic way. In recent years, poetry therapy has become a psychological tool. To call what Bishop does therapy would be to oversimplify. Still, the voice of reality that forces her narrator to admit her denial in spite of her inherent tendency to protect herself is the voice of health and honesty.

Although both David Wagoner in "The Singing Lesson" (p. 787) and Bishop in "One Art" assume the pose of teaching a lesson, both seem to be speaking as much to themselves as to the audience. Both show irony, as well, since the speakers reveal their own attempts to carry out the programs they advise to be less than perfect, perhaps achieved at great cost. Both seem in rigid denial as they protect themselves from the revelation of loss or vulnerability, either to others or themselves. Wagoner's narrator speaks to an implied listener in a dramatic monologue, but his own metaphorical revelations are more important to himself and the poem than is any reaction from the student he presumably addresses. Like many teachers, he talks at rather than to the student, beginning with the content of the course but wandering off into his own concerns. Bishop's narrator seems at first to be more like Wagoner's didactic music teacher, beginning with the quotidian and then moving to the poetic. But in Bishop's final stanza, we suddenly realize that the person addressed is not a student but an intimate who has been lost. Logically, we can assume that if she is lost the person is not in the room with the narrator. We know that Bishop was a prolific letter writer, once admitting that given time she'd do nothing else. Perhaps she is writing a letter to her unseen audience, speaking to herself within parentheses as she briefly recalls her love and then orders herself to write.

NARRATORS GIVING ADVICE (p. 792)

JONATHAN SWIFT

A Modest Proposal (p. 792)

From its root meaning of "a dish of mixed fruits," the term *satire* describes a text in which humor and criticism mix in a way that is sometimes gentle, sometimes biting. The satirist walks a fine line. Without the humor and the unexpected twist of irony, satire becomes abusive invective or mournful jeremiad. Rather than persuading its audience to seek solutions, invective tends to make us defensive. When the humorous barbs are intended to hurt someone, to vent bad humor, or to show off, we might characterize them as sarcasm rather than satire. Satire seeks to teach in an indirect manner that causes its readers to reach their own conclusions about the severity of a problem. The satirist uses wit to open our eyes to abuses and to subvert social and political institutions that need changing. Satire is less a genre than a tone that can occur in virtually any mode of human speech or writing: poetry, prose, drama, fiction, or nonfiction. College students have most probably encountered it in comedy routines or in movies and television shows.

Because it depends on the audience's understanding of political and social situations that are specific to a certain time and place, satire can become quickly dated and may require some historical or cultural orientation. British humor is often lost on Americans, for example, and jokes in other languages seldom translate well into English for similar reasons. Some of Jonathan Swift's satire — some of the mock travel tale *Gulliver's Travels*, for example — is inaccessible to most current readers because the individuals and situations that inspired the humor are long dead. "A Modest Proposal" continues to find an audience, however. We get Swift's point that what is done to oppressed peoples is as cruel and unfeeling as the ironic suggestion that those in power eat the children of the poor. That we recognize this so readily may not be a good sign. Enough prejudice still exists against the poor to make Swift's argument meaningful, though most readers will insist that *we* are not oppressors. Although Ireland is no longer wracked by the sort of starvation and deprivation that existed in the eighteenth and nineteenth centuries, large groups of people in the Third World are in great need. Can students imagine this argument applied to people in inner-city slum neighborhoods, to illegal immigrants, or to others who are said to place a burden on the welfare system? Could we as easily substitute homeless people or drug addicts or poor southern rednecks? How different is this proposal, which we recognize as ridiculous, from attempts in modern history to find "final solutions" to deal with minorities through concentration camps, "ethnic cleansing," and other forms of genocide? At the time of Swift's writing in 1729, the institution of African slavery was being developed in the Americas, with its worst abuses still a century away. Native Americans were already being displaced, eventually to end up on lands that would provide little sustenance, leading to the starvation and squalid living conditions that still exist on some reservations. It isn't surprising to find the narrator crediting an American with the idea of consuming the young of an oppressed people.

Swift's narrator in "A Modest Proposal" claims that everyone involved with the problem of poverty in Ireland would benefit from an organized program that paid mothers to suckle their young for a year and then sell them to be used as food. He begins his argument by presenting the problem in a reasonable and compassionate tone, calling on his readers to consider the pathetic state of the children of the Irish poor. He appeals not only to pity but to the accompanying fear of crime and treason. He says that he wants to provide for the children, to prevent begging, even to prevent abortion. He logically outlines his program for alleviating poverty, giving statistics, citing medical studies, providing specific cost assessments, and suggesting procedures by which his plan may be carried out. In paragraph 29, he catalogs the benefits of his plan and maintains its superiority over other possible solutions to the problem. He lends a sense of balance to his argument by his qualification that the eating of older children would not be practical, since the boys are likely to be tough and the girls would be lost as breeders. What's more, as he points out in paragraph 17, this would not be cost effective and there might be objections that this "a little border[s] upon cruelty; which, I confess, has always been with me the strongest objection against any project, how well soever intended." He further assures the reader of his objectivity in his closing sentence, explaining that he does not stand to gain from his own proposal, since he has no children to sell and does not anticipate having any in the future.

His argument is thus a masterful mix of logos, pathos, and ethos. It might be a useful exercise to divide the argument into sections and have students find other such examples of well-developed rhetoric. The warrants underlying his argument assume that his readers will want to find a compassionate solution to poverty, but the point of the satire is that he proposes this solution as a compassionate one. We may have students specifically explore the assumptions he makes about the poor: for example, the assumption that they will welcome the chance to make a few shillings by selling their babies. The implied warrant is that the poor are not really capable of loving their children. But as we look at the argument as satire, we might shift to his warrants about the rich. He explicitly states at one point that since landlords already devour the parents, they should have the first chance to eat the children. Underlying the whole text is the warrant that compassion is not being exercised in England's treatment of Ireland's poor, that the current policies essentially devour the lives of these downtrodden people for selfish reasons.

"A Modest Proposal" is highly ironic. Broadly defined, *irony* refers to the recognition of a reality that differs from the appearance presented; it depends on opposition and double meaning. Verbal irony is perceived when the actual words used are opposed to the intended meaning. Dramatic irony occurs when an opposition exists between the words of a character and the different reality recognized by the audience. Situational irony is more difficult to define, though we recognize it when we encounter it. Events occur in a way that contrasts with what might usually be expected to happen, but there is an appropriately absurd quality to the divergence that provokes a grim smile. Swift's readers may begin to recognize irony when the narrator refers to human mothers as "dams" and "breeders." Although he seems to care about the plight of the poor, he slips into the terminology of a livestock dealer. The ironic tone becomes obvious, of course, when he relates the claim of his American friend that children are delicious. Even this outrageous proposition is delivered in a reasonable, rhetorically sound tone. It is our recognition of this contrast between the appearance of logic and the reality of cannibalism that produces the ironic response. The verbal irony is sustained throughout the text, since most readers understand that the author, Jonathan Swift, means just the opposite of what his narrator says. His purpose is to make his contemporaries see that political and social policies are figuratively eating up the people of Ireland and that no one seems to have compassion for them. A case can be made for dramatic irony if we look at the narrator as a man who thinks he is making a reasonable argument but does not realize that his underlying warrants are horrifying and obscene. For intelligent readers of good will who recognized Swift's ironic tone, "A Modest Proposal" must have been profoundly moving in its time. Actually, some readers believed that Swift was serious in his proposal and were outraged by the essay. Even readers who understand his purposes may think his images of flaying and otherwise abusing children are unwarranted. History shows that abuses continued in Ireland long after 1729. Still, because they can be extrapolated to other situations in which the problems of society are being mishandled, Jonathan Swift's satires have long outlasted his sermons as an Anglican dean. They provoke readers to think for themselves in opposition to the surface meaning of the text.

DANIEL OROZCO

Orientation (p. 799)

Fans of Scott Adams's comic strip "Dilbert" will recognize the small, weird world of cubicles in Daniel Orozco's short story "Orientation." We might want to take advantage of this intertextuality by introducing Orozco's story with a few representative clippings of Dilbert's difficulties in the work place, following the lead of the readers of the thousand or so newspapers that carry the comic strip daily. The strip hits close enough to reality to appear on doors and offices all over the country — even the world — and its creator makes a fortune from the use of the characters in corporate training programs. No one believes that he or she is like the pointy-haired boss who fakes any understanding about what the company really does, but readers always feel they have worked for him. Nothing in Dilbert's world is just or fair; in fact, the one thing that he can count on is the arbitrary rule of the absurd. He can't expect his coworkers to work as a team or to provide support. One character warns, "I can please only one person per day. Today is not your day. Tomorrow's not looking good either." Incompetence is to be expected. "I love deadlines," a worker says. "I especially love the swooshing sound they make as they go flying by." One law of work maintains, "Anyone can do any amount of work provided it isn't the work he/she is supposed to be doing." Clichés are transformed to express the irony of the corporate hierarchy: "To err is human, to forgive is not our policy." False religions abound, and a devil dressed in a red suit and carrying a large spoon in lieu of a pitchfork shows up at times when naive workers dare to hope for fairness or recognition.

Students who have been operating under the delusion that the completion of their formal education will lead to autonomy and automatic success may miss some of the irony in both Adams and Orozco. But they may recognize the traits of human nature that tend to come out when people feel that they are power-less or that the work they do has little meaning. We might have students look back at Marge Piercy's poem "To be of use" (p. 180) and consider the contrast between the total immersion in work that she describes and the arbitrary rou-tines of Orozco's "Orientation" and Adams's "Dilbert." Have they considered the importance of *meaningful* work in their future plans?

Though most students have not been office workers, some may have gone through similar orientations at school or at work. At community colleges and at many regional branches of state university systems, nontraditional students may be coming to college because they do not find their work meaningful and want a more satisfying way to make a living. They may be trying to escape the sort of rigid atmosphere that the story reveals. The language of the narrator in Orozco's story is as impersonal as the computerized voice mail the worker will be required to use, but he manages to get the office gossip through nevertheless. He advises hypocrisy and noninvolvement rather than the sort of joyful or determined effort Piercy's poem celebrates.

But the details of Orozco's story exaggerate absurdly while his narrator delivers the monologue in short sentences in a deadpan tone. This discrepancy and the contrast between the narrator's recitation of the rules of the corporate machine and his matter-of-fact hints at bizarre, idiosyncratic tragedies among the workers produce the same sort of irony we see in "Dilbert." The office gets more unusual as the orientation proceeds. Office crushes are elaborately unre-quited, one worker is a serial killer, another has stigmata and the curse of prophecy, one seems to be bulimic and emotionally haggard, another has an autistic child, and a male worker lurks in the ladies' room. But the new employ-ee is admonished not to let on that he/she knows of these things, though the nar-rator spills it all. Because he does not seem to draw the line between the details of the work situation and the dramatic specifics of his coworkers' lives, and because he coolly passes along the most intimate secrets to a total stranger, the narrator reveals his own character. Readers may detect passive aggression in his seemingly unemotional narrative. But perhaps he simply does not care, has become a cog in the machine. It is interesting that the beautiful view he pres-ents to the new employee is limited, its natural elements hemmed in by other buildings that literally reflect the deadly corporate routine. The order of the nar-rator's statements matter. The aberrations of the office staff get progressively more bizarre, though his tone does not change. Interwoven with the orientation of the new worker to the rules, revelations of the workers' strange behavior increase the reader's sense of irony.

Both Jonathan Swift's "A Modest Proposal" (p. 792) and Orozco's "Orientation" feature unreliable narrators who pronounce the most horrific facts in a reasonable and logical tone. Swift's proposal of cannibalism comes fair-ly early in the argument, and he focuses on supporting it, but Orozco's revela-tions about his coworkers' troubles build gradually, interwoven with what pur-ports to be his true agenda of orienting the new employee to the job itself. Of course, it is altogether possible that the narrator is pulling the leg of the new employee and that the other workers are perfectly normal people. New doctors in a medical clinic familiar to this writer were routinely hazed. They would receive charts for bogus patients with names like "Duck, Donald," whose symptoms became more and more incredible ("webbed phalanges, unusually fluffy epidermal formations") until the intern caught on. Readers may raise issues about whether the size of the audience assumed by each narrator makes a difference.

Swift's mock argumentative essay follows the conventions of the genre it imitates, aiming for a balanced tone and seeking to appeal to the intellect and to the emotions of its audience. Orozco's chatty narrator speaks in a more informal setting. We can imagine him ticking off the points he is supposed to make as he goes through the guidelines for orienting a new worker. But the gossip slips in, much as digs against Jews or Americans do as Swift's narrator speaks. The narrators seem much alike, and we can imagine Swift's social reformer as the promoter of office morale. Perhaps he would propose that since their personal emotions lead to so many problems, all office workers should undergo lobotomies and spend their nights in suspended animation in their cubicles in space suits that preclude the need to provide restrooms at all.

PAM HOUSTON

How to Talk to a Hunter (p. 803)

Pam Houston revels in having outdoor adventures and writing about them. After graduating from Denison University in Ohio, she rode across Canada on a bicycle, then wound up in the western United States, where she supported herself with odd jobs and worked on her doctorate at the University of Utah. But she also writes in her nonfiction essays about meandering through water lilies and hippos in Botswana, going whitewater rafting through Cataract Canyon and Satan's Gut on the Colorado River, and galloping horses through wide, open fields. She dismisses her bravery: "You think I spent three summers leading hunters through Alaska because I like watching guys like David Duke shoot sheep? No. It was because if I didn't go with my boyfriend, somebody else would. I wanted to win." This may be true but does not explain a continuing way of life. Naive readers may want her to get the man, but more experienced readers may root for the woman herself, wanting her to claim her independence. Her emphasis is interesting in this context. It is less the acceptance of the man than the competition with the other woman that is foregrounded in her disclaimer. She wants to *win*. She also takes the opportunity to make a political statement with her dig at former Ku Klux Klan member–turned–Republican David Duke.

A similar subtext turns up early in the story "How to Talk to a Hunter" when she relates the questions her female protagonist, addressed in the second-person "you," avoids asking herself and simultaneously comments on her perplexity about why anyone would like country music or the Republican Party. Houston implies that she knows her way of life is not politically correct, and her texts raise their own contradictory issues. We might consider the differences between the environmental movement that many students find appealing and the conservation movement dear to hunters. These discourses can be as different as the rhetoric of Greenpeace and that of the National Rifle Association. If she is a graduate student like the writer, the woman is saturated with the urge toward critical thinking that demands that she eschew the tendency to see in black and white. The hunter lives in a different world, one where the truisms are those of country music, political conservatism, and physical exploits. Do readers feel that Houston's narrator is struggling with the issues raised by these differences and what they mean to her as a woman? Can we be sure that the hunter is not also having mixed feelings?

The narrator is intelligent, educated, and liberal to the extent that she knows she should be asking questions and raising issues. She is sensual, honest with herself, reluctantly romantic. She hears the voices of reason but decides not to heed them. Several voices are heard in the story: the narrator, her female friend, her male friend, words from her education and reading. We hear the "coyote woman" on the answering machine, and we are told of what the narrator's lover, the hunter, does and does not say. The words of her friends and her education enter into dialogue with the narrator and the reader, like a Greek chorus that helps us define and elaborate on the ambiguous interchanges between herself and her lover. The story, as its title implies, is about communication, about what lies underneath the surface of what is said between these lovers from different discourses. Because we are allowed to overhear her dialogue, readers respect her intelligence, but some may end up feeling that she doesn't make much use of it. We may question whether she is a dynamic character who changes in the course of the story by finally "letting go of fear" or whether she allows herself to be lulled out of language and self-determination by his "humming in [her] ear." Maybe both things happen. Perhaps she accepts the relationship as temporary and understands that this is okay, that she does not need monogamy or commitment.

Whether or not the story engages in gender stereotypes begs the question of, Which stereotypes? Certainly the hunter comes across as a typical American *type*, the survivalist mountain man out to prove his masculinity by conquering the wilderness and as many women as he can. And true to the usual assumptions, it is the woman who desires commitment. Other stereotypes tag men as rational and women as irrational, however. A case might be made that the female narrator engages in quite a bit of rationality; she just decides to discard it. We may also want to question the reliability of the narrator. Does she make unwarranted assumptions about her lover's infidelity and reluctance to commit? We have no way of knowing, since we have only her interpretations.

Student writers might find a more pertinent issue by exploring the animal imagery in Pam Houston's story. She begins by juxtaposing her own skin (or the skin of the woman she addresses as "you") with the hide of a moose the man has carried "soaking wet and heavier than a dead man, across the tundra." She ends with the howl of the dog accompanying her musings during or just after sex. Her rival has the last name Coyote. Are the women in this story stereotyped as the *hunted*?

For women who read the story, the narrator's use of the second-person pronoun is effective, bringing the reader into the story as if she were describing a universal — or at least a culturally common — story about the communication between men and women. Since the struggle between sexual desire and rationality is an experience familiar to many readers, we may find ourselves nodding our heads. Yes, this is what it's like, we think. The word *talk* in the story's title is echoed throughout. The narrator talks to "you," perhaps to herself. But she also talks about talking and not talking. She reads the syntax of his speech for gaps and oppositions. She notes his ambiguity — "I feel exactly the same way" — in response to her declaration of love, and she echoes it later when he admires her body. We might have students note all the instances when the narrator engages in metalanguage, talking about talk or about the disjunction between what is said and what she believes is meant. She tells us what questions she does *not* ask. Overall, she tends to approach love as a text to be subjected to critical analysis. A few romantic readers may approve the final lovemaking as a happy ending. Others will argue that the howl of the dog and the acknowledgment of the shortness of the days project a mournful feeling. Are we meant to see her as winning? Or does she give up the fight?

Although both Daniel Orozco's "Orientation" (p. 799) and Houston's "How to Talk to a Hunter" use humor, Houston's narrator sardonically recognizes the irony of her situation, deliberately creating the humor at her own expense. Orozco's narrator seems oblivious to the humor. The irony lies in the recognition of the audience that his tone and his content do not match. Some readers cannot get past the horror of Jonathan Swift's subject matter in "A Modest Proposal" (p. 792) far enough to perceive any humor in it. But others find it humorous for the same reasons we find "Orientation" grimly funny. Irony — the unknowing discrepancy between the words and the reality or the conventions and the their unexpected negation — can be intellectually satisfying in a way that seems so apt that we must smile. The distance of the narrators from their stories constitutes the main difference among the three narratives in this cluster. Houston's narrator focuses on her own situation, though she does imply that it has some universality by using the pronoun *you*. Orozco's narrator does not directly tell us about himself, focusing instead on his coworkers. Swift maintains the most distance of all, proposing a solution to a sociopolitical issue that ostensibly has little to do with him; he mentions his own situation only to convince us that he is a disinterested party. Each story is highly ironic. Although we have touched on the distinction among types of irony in the teaching suggestions for this cluster, we might have students look up definitions in handbooks of literature or other sources before characterizing the irony of the narratives as verbal, dramatic, or situational.

| 14 |

Loving (p. 810)

TRUE LOVE (p. 812)

WILLIAM SHAKESPEARE

Let me not to the marriage of true minds (p. 813)

William Shakespeare's Sonnet 116 seems at first to celebrate the enduring qualities of love between husband and wife. It is, in fact, often recited at wedding ceremonies, an appropriate setting for a poem whose first lines echo the marriage vows in *The Book of Common Prayer*. It is written in one of the most structured of forms, in what has come to be known as the Shakespearean sonnet, though Shakespeare was not the first to use it. Although this poem was published — probably without his permission — as part of a sequence of 154 sonnets in 1609, it may have been written earlier. In 1598, a writer mentioned Shakespeare's "sugared sonnets among his private friends"; imitating and transforming the conventions of the Italian sonnets of Petrarch had become a popular pastime in literary and court circles of the late 1500s. Petrarchan sonnets held strictly to conceits describing unrequited love for an idealized woman leading ultimately to religious transcendence. English writers often toyed with these conventions, however, and Shakespeare inverted conventions and used the poems for wordplay and argumentation about the nature of love and change — and about rhetoric and writing as well.

The form of the Shakespearean sonnet keeps the fourteen lines of the Italian sonnet, but its three quatrains followed by a final couplet allow the poet to form an argument that reaches its conclusion in the last two lines. Predominately iambic pentameter, each line follows the patterns of normal English speech and therefore has a natural ring to its audience, while the *abab cdcd efef gg* rhyme scheme provides a satisfying pattern and sense of closure. However, a closer look at this poem, which seems to proclaim constancy, reveals a series of oppositions that challenge an easy interpretation based on surface sound and sense. Within its closed form, this sonnet rocks back and forth with irregular meter, double meanings, puns, and indeterminate negations. Does the speaker mean to say in the opening lines that he should hold his tongue when the priest asks if anyone knows any impediment that would prevent the marriage, that he is unwilling to concede that such impediments exist, or that they actually don't exist? Is this a traditional marriage ceremony, a platonic marriage of minds, or — since this sonnet is in the part of the sequence in which most poems are addressed to a man — an argument about a homoerotic relationship? What sort of logic is implied in the second line: "Love is not love"? Even though the enjambment leads to a qualification, a sense of paradox remains. Furthermore, each sentence contains a negative or an absence: *Not, not, remove, no, never, unknown, not, not, never,* and *no* continue to pile up oppositions. Contrasted with this emptiness of *not-love,* the word *impediment* seems unusually solid, and the conventional enemy time is personified as an inexorable automaton that mows down everything within his *compass,* recalling the circling hands of a clock that signal human aging. Love, on the other hand, receives a negative personification — is defined as a not-fool — and seems peculiarly distant and impersonal. The only positive metaphors for love in the poem are linked closely to their opposites: The solitary channel marker, while not shaken, merely "looks on," and the guiding star cannot really be known.

Having conceded the poem's rhetorical ambiguity, most readers would still undoubtedly be pleased to have such enduring love proclaimed to them. The last lines seem to indicate, however, that the speaker may be defining true love rather than declaring it, since he makes it explicit that he is offering a scientific or rhetorical proof. There's a logical conundrum implied in the words "I never writ." Some *I* wrote these lines, but perhaps the speaker is a persona or mask that the poet assumes, and this is the sort of equivocation we often see characters use in his dramas. And the closing line may have either a compound subject or a compound predicate. That is, the poet may mean to say that if his argument is fallacious, then "no man" has ever fallen in love; that he, the poet, never loved a man; or that he never loved "no man" (woman).

Line 12 projects arguably the most powerful image of the poem. Juxtaposed with images of time and of sea voyages, the image of a love that lasts until "the edge of doom" reminds us that we are reading a text written when oceans and continents were being explored and time was being measured in ways never accomplished before. Enduring to the end of the world and going to the ends of the earth may both be implied in such a metaphor, but looking over the edge of either reveals nothingness. Inverting the argument that lovers should seize the day while beauty and youth allow love to flourish, Shakespeare seems to say that love is more lasting than this, and many readers of romance novels and fairy tales will agree without further question. Although we may still agree that this is a beautiful definition of love after reading it more critically, however, we should hold the poet to his challenge in the last lines to examine his evidence. He may be saying that such love does not really exist.

ANNE BRADSTREET

To My Dear and Loving Husband (p. 814)

As the wife of the governor and the mother of eight children in the Puritan Massachusetts Bay Colony of the 1640s, Anne Dudley Bradstreet wrote at a time when few women were literate, much less published poets. Most women in colonial America would have been unable to read what Bradstreet had written, even if her work had been published there. However, she had received a good education in England, as the daughter of a well-connected Puritan family. When a male relative had a number of her poems published in London, in a collection called *The Tenth Muse Lately Sprung Up in America*, she found a wide audience. After her death, her polished versions of these poems, along with several new ones, appeared in *Several Poems Compiled with Great Variety of Wit and Learning, Full of Delight*. The book titles, neither chosen by the poet herself, would be worth analyzing: the first offering a lively identification of gender coupled with classical and poetic allusion, and the second a gender-neutral evaluation or advertisement of the texts themselves.

Bradstreet's poetry hints that some Puritans were not as austere as law codes and sermons sometimes indicate. Although it would be considered a sin to place physical love and other pleasures of the earth above God, many members of Christian communities saw such things as gifts from God, even as earthly patterns of spiritual truths. The biblical Song of Solomon, for example, with its sensual imagery was considered to be an allegory of Christ the bridegroom and the church, his spiritual bride. In "To My Dear and Loving Husband," the poet uses less explicitly passionate but similar imagery. Her poem opens with the image of two being one, alluding to the biblical assertion that marriage causes a man and woman to become *one flesh*. References to gold and riches of the East recall the language of Psalms and Proverbs in praise of God's wisdom, as well as the Song of Solomon's more erotic images. Bradstreet ends her poem with a prayer that her husband be rewarded for his love toward her and that their earthly love be replicated in some way in the afterlife.

Although the sentiments may seem like naive clichés to current readers, there's no reason to believe they were not deeply felt. As a devout woman, Bradstreet gains permission to be passionate within the bounds of religion and marriage, and the poem has the ring of freely given devotion to her husband, as if he were God. We can be confident that she is not compelled to write by any outside force, since she is doing something unusual by composing poetry as a woman in a woman's voice. In the context of her given situation, she seems to have an independent identity, in spite of her poem's theme of oneness. In fact, Bradstreet was often left alone to manage her household, since her husband's duties took him away for long periods of time, and Massachusetts was a true frontier, filled with physical hardship and danger. The universal danger of two becoming one, of course, is that the submissive partner may become submerged in the more dominant personality and thus lose autonomy and personhood. Students will probably think of religious institutions and organizations that still encourage women to be subservient to men. They may also discuss why abused partners sometimes remain in destructive relationships, maintaining that they still love their abusers. Bradstreet's poem implies that her conjugal love and her husband's are mutual, though, even within the institutionalized patriarchy implied by its theme.

Like the poet's life, the poem is tightly structured and simple. Most of the poem is written in rhyming couplets of iambic pentameter, with only slight variation from the regular beat of five feet per line — that of one unstressed syllable followed by a stressed one. When the line ends with a stressed syllable, as happens here, we call the line masculine. The last two lines move away from this rhythm, however, giving them a tentative sound, especially coupled with the word *may* rather than *will* or *shall*. With one exception, the rhymes are true, and most of the diction is simple and direct, Bradstreet's plain speech in keeping with her Puritan life. As a Calvinist, she might be expected to speak of predestination and grace rather than *recompense*, but rewards and punishments figure prominently in sermons of the day, and therefore the religious parallels hold true as she tries to think of ways to repay her husband for his love. There seems to be much joy in this marriage; thus her use of the word *persevere* is puzzling. Perhaps Bradstreet means that love is predestined rather than earned but that a couple must also keep working at it, since faith without works is dead, according to the Puritan view of salvation.

Anne Bradstreet's religious vision of love is quite different from William Shakespeare's secular view in Sonnet 116 (p. 813), although both touch on the impossibility of ever doing enough for love. We can imagine Bradstreet agreeing with Shakespeare's contention that love endures "to the edge of doom" and that it is something very solid and sure that nevertheless cannot be fully expressed. Their major differences lie in the responses their speakers have experienced from the objects of their love and in the sources of their imagery. Shakespeare speaks to a changeable lover who doesn't seem to know what love is, and he can only grasp for negative definitions linked to images of science and logic. He works within the conventions of the poetic and philosophical theories of his day and subverts them at the same time. Bradstreet uses hyperbole to describe her husband's value to her, and she uses images of faith to develop themes of earthly and heavenly love. She accepts the social and religious conventions of Puritan culture and writes within that context. Ironically, whereas Bradstreet seems happier and more sincere, Shakespeare's complex imagery of time's tyranny and love's elusive persistence is more original and strikes us as more realistic and appropriate, perhaps because it is less sure of itself. Living only a generation or two apart, both poets lived in times when forever was a seldom-questioned reality. Bradstreet undoubtedly took for granted that Protestant theology was correct and that everyone would spend eternity in heaven or hell. Shakespeare and his contemporaries in Elizabethan England were much concerned with the ravages of time, possibly as a result of the queen's concern with aging. That love might not even last a lifetime, much less forever, is a frequent theme. At the same time, Shakespeare can mention doom in a sonnet and expect to be understood, and he can people his plays with ghosts; both concepts presume that life continues after death.

E. E. CUMMINGS

somewhere i have never travelled (p. 815)

An unusually structured and grammatical poem for e. e. cummings, "somewhere i have never travelled" nevertheless uses vocabulary in the poet's idiosyncratic way. As always, reading cummings involves breaking a code, which we can only touch on in a short introduction. The experiments with syntax and typography that characterize cummings's poems reflect cubism, futurism, and other modern visual art movements. He is also keenly aware of sound, and much of his diction depends on the musical rhythms of American speech, the punning qualities of the language, and the often highly personal and carefully crafted connotations that he attaches to words. Words for him carry inherent positive or negative qualities, and the connotations of pathos and poetry are opposed to the denotations of logos and common sense. The specific and concrete tends to be privileged, whereas generalities and agreed-upon conclusions are considered deadly. He especially likes words like *alive, Spring, suddenly, young, new, yes, touch, small, frail, guess, dare, open, dream,* and others that symbolize positive movement and energy. He knows the meaning of *is,* contrasting its immediacy with the negative *knows* or *reasons. Who* is individual and thus good, but the rhetorical *which, how,* and *because* move into reductive explanations that he abhors. Although cummings was strongly grounded in literary theory and was influenced by Ezra Pound to choose his words carefully, he deliberately traveled the path of extreme individuality. Thematically, his poetry sets the courageous, joyfully spontaneous "anyone," the protagonist of another popular cummings poem, against the oppressive conformity of what he calls "mostpeople." Only this sort of human being is capable of an authentic emotion like love.

So when cummings begins this particular poem with the vague and negative "somewhere i have never travelled," he contrasts it with the positive "any experience," using two words that indicate specificity and spontaneous awareness. To be alive is a hyperbolic experience for which love is necessary. He explicitly compares his lover's touch to that of "Spring," the only capitalized word in the poem, contrasting with the lowercase *i* of the speaker, and his opening up is obviously positive. We should avoid the easy reading that would see the closing-up images of the third and fourth stanzas as negative, however. The word *death* in the lexicons of some poets might denote something negative, but for cummings it may indicate another positive living experience. Addressing his readers, cummings speculates in his introduction to *New Poems,* "if *mostpeople* were to be born twice they'd improbably call it dying . . . you and i wear the dangerous looseness of doom and find it becoming." Other paradoxes in the poem also are consistent with the poet's view of reality. The synesthesia of line 19, "the voice of your eyes is deeper than all roses," mixes several senses together, defeating reason. The whimsical personification of the rain as having hands in line 20 would be laughable if read literally rather than for a beauty that appeals somehow to our senses rather than to our intellects. And although "the power of your intense fragility" in line 14 sounds like an oxymoron, it implies that true power is not to be equated with force or strength. This fragility's "texture / compels me with the colour of its countries," the speaker says, calling upon synesthesia again to pull the reader out of logic and into the immediate world of the senses. The sensory — and sensual — images of the poem hint that love is located at the point of touch where senses intersect and that our understanding of it is essentially physical.

Whereas William Shakespeare uses intellectual images in Sonnet 116 (p. 812) and Anne Bradstreet (p. 814) uses religious ones, cummings borrows the natural symbolism of the flower that stands for physical love but he carries it beyond cliché. At times, the speaker is the tightly closed fist of a budding flower opened by the lover, who is compared to spring, but he later speaks of the woman's "intense fragility" and its color, as if the lover herself were the rose.

Cummings is closer in spirit to Bradstreet in the intensity of the two lovers becoming as if they were one person. Inexperienced readers may prefer Bradstreet's simplicity, and some students will relate to her faith. Other readers will delight in the word play of cummings, and some will hate his anti-intellectual ambiguity. Most students will probably find Shakespeare the most difficult of the three because his complexity is complicated by historical distance and differences in language.

Although each poet uses the concept of a love that lasts forever, each poem reveals a different perspective on what *forever* might actually mean. Bradstreet's *forever* is in the hands of an omnipotent God who may honor the husband and wife in heaven if they persevere in their love for each other. Shakespeare's *forever* depends on a lonely, one-sided constancy that endures in the face of loss, uncertainty, and change. Still, his definition of the relationship as a rare but perhaps possible "marriage of true minds" holds out hope. Cummings sees *forever* as part of an eternal *now*, experienced by individuals who are able to be alive and open to each moment.

Worldviews and tastes in poetry are both personal and culture-specific, but open-minded readers can step into experiences that are new to them. If Bradstreet and Shakespeare encountered the poetry of cummings, they might be startled at first. The Puritan Bradstreet might be offended by the content, whereas the master of the sonnet and blank verse, Shakespeare, would be offended by the form. But Shakespeare, as a questioner of rhetoric and a lover of wordplay, would undoubtedly understand cummings's motives. And Bradstreet, as the mother of eight, had experience with the physical expressions of love. Because this poem appeals to the senses and is comparatively free of allusions, the poets of the past would seem at least as likely as our students to respond to it as individuals and would need no crash course in modernism.

WISLAWA SZYMBORSKA

True Love (p. 816)

Some students have trouble uncovering irony, but they should have no difficulty detecting it in Szymborska's "True Love." Most college student, want to believe in true love and will be immediately skeptical of the narrator's questions, "Is it normal, is it serious, is it practical?" Indeed, the author's opposition of true love with practicality never does seem serious. Szymborska's narrator is miles from the bitter satirical irony of Jonathan Swift's "A Modest Proposal" (p. 792); in fact, she almost seems to be winking at the reader from the start. And this balancing of playful irony and sincerity gives the poem its charm and romantic credibility. Although the narrator does ask these questions, they seem rhetorical, simply part of her pretend outrage at the "billing and cooing" behavior of the lovers. Today's college students seem a bit more conservative than those of past generations, but few will take seriously the narrator's worry that lovers give a bad example for those hoping we "stay within bounds." Few of us expect or want romantic love to be sensible or practical. A good deal of our literary heritage and certainly our popular culture champions romantic couples who have found their one-and-only. Indeed, Szymborska finally abandons her playful curmud-geonly tone in the last three lines of the poems to make her serious assertion that true love does exist and that those who have it know it. Only those who "never find true love" adopt the attitude that our narrator has been affecting. By impli-cation, life is hard without true love.

Certainly e. e. cummings (p. 815) would have appreciated the indirection, irony, and playfulness of "True Love." And we assume William Shakespeare (p. 813) would also since he is a master at all three of these poetic approaches. Anne Bradstreet (p. 814) seems more direct and less fond of irony, but she surely would agree with the affirmation of true love.

EDNA ST. VINCENT MILLAY
Love Is Not All (p. 818)

Edna St. Vincent Millay's sonnet is an interesting companion piece to Wislawa Szymborska's, (p. 816) employing as it does the same ironic indirection, the same thematic turn-about from a seeming rejection of love to an affirmation and acceptance of romantic love. Like Szymborska, Millay plays off the opposi-tion of practicality with love. Using such basic human needs as food and drink and such necessities as good health and "a floating spar" to a drowning person, Millay reminds us that romantic love is not conventionally practical, but she does so only as a set-up for lines 7 and 8, where she uses hyperbole to turn the poem on a dime. Even if love is not practical, she says, people are "making friends with death" not for lack of food or drink or decent medicine but for want of love. These lines might be an exaggeration, but clearly death from a broken (and per-haps a lonely) heart is part of our conventional lore about romance. Students might be interested in discussing this claim about dying for love or the lack there-of. And no discussion of love in our current critical climate can ignore the claims of social constructionists that our beliefs about romantic love are ideologically sit-uated in specific cultural and historical moments. Some students might resist this postmodern notion, claiming instead that romantic love is universal and a prod-uct of nature not nurture. But if indeed people are dying for lack of love, either position can use this grim situation as evidence for their argument.

In the second part of her sonnet, Millay continues her indirection by spec-ulating again that practicality will win the day, claiming that under intense duress ("moaning for release") or in dire need of peace or food she would renounce love. But again her turn-about is swift, plain, and emphatic. Renunciation is, possible she must admit, but then "I do not think I would" might be cited as understatement. Millay prefers love — and by implication an intimate night — to food. So much for practicality's "You cannot live on love alone." If this were an actual, practical situation, we must assume Millay would indeed choose food, but the poetic sentiment about love's life-sustaining power is her primary concern.

Asking students to compare the claims that are made by the five poems might result in some interesting differences, but on some levels the poems in this cluster seem remarkably similar in their thematic adherence to the convention of true love's enduring desirability. Perhaps this is not remarkable at all since all five poems were written in comparable ideological climates, at least in terms of their commitment to the reality and passionate intensity of true love. Shakespeare's London, Bradstreet's and cumming's Massachusetts, Millay's New York, and Szymborska's Krakow are obviously different places, but for all their historical, social, religious, and political variations, they are also clearly identifiable as sites where the Western tradition of affirming romantic love is already centuries old. Students will be able to note the differences as they are asked to demonstrate how these poems are original and thoughtful reiterations of a received tradition that is not in danger of being eclipsed. From Shakespeare's line, "Love is not love" to Millay's "Love is not all," students can be asked to note how similar arguments can be presented in poems that speak to and echo one another and that remind us how diverse and similar our cultural heritage is.

ROMANTIC DREAMS (p. 820)

LESLIE MARMON SILKO

Yellow Woman (p. 820)

In the montage of texts that make up Leslie Marmon Silko's 1981 book *Storyteller*, from which this story is taken, the writer presents a mixture of autobiographical, fictional, and mythical retellings of the stories of her life as a member of the Laguna Pueblo Tribe of New Mexico. Like many indigenous storytellers, Silko weaves together past with present, dreamlike legend with the mundane verisimilitude of everyday life. She has said that, for her native culture, time is not linear but is like an ocean that surrounds us. The past does not remain past but ebbs and flows into the present. In "Yellow Woman" a young wife and mother, living in a Pueblo household that includes her mother and grandmother, encounters a mysterious stranger. We meet her *in medias res* (in the middle of the story) as she awakens on a riverbank in a sensuous scene with a man who may be a Navajo cattle thief from a neighboring reservation or may be a *ka'tsina*, a mountain spirit. She realizes that she too may be a character in the myth that her dead grandfather used to tell her. She acts out the part of Yellow Woman, the heroine of a ritualized captivity story. Depending on the point of view we decide to take as readers, we may see her as the victim of a seduction, as the embodiment of an ancestral fertility figure, or as a housewife living out a romantic fantasy. The story is disturbing as a rape fantasy, but a sense of freedom surrounds her abduction as well, as she throws off conventions and follows the nature spirit — her own nature, perhaps — to the top of the mountain. Her will seems suspended in a surreal way that follows the logic of myth: "I did not decide to go. I just went. Moonflowers blossom in the sand hills before dawn, just as I followed him." She moves as we do in dreams, forgetting to leave when she intends to go home, and finally going home when she means to go uphill to Silva's place because going downhill seems safer at the moment.

As in her novels, *Ceremony* and *The Almanac of the Dead*, Silko retells a myth in *Yellow Woman* to question the nature of reality and the nature of personal, family, and tribal identity. Though it throbs with danger, the world of Silva, with its intense and sometimes bloody images, puts the narrator in touch with something missing in an inverted world where the younger generation teaches the older how to make Jell-O.

Throughout the story, the woman gives reasons for her actions, but they don't really explain the actions they claim to explain. She stops pulling away from him, she tells us, "because his hand felt cool and the sun was high." She decides that he must be a Navajo because he is tall or because he steals. At one point, she assures us that he has heard her approaching him; she knows this because he speaks to her without turning. She knows that she cannot be Yellow Woman because they have just met the day before. She knows she can escape but stays to eat because she "knew it would be a long walk home."

In each case, her attempts at logic reveal that the opposite may be true. She goes because she wishes to go, believes that he really is a *ka'tsina* with supernatural knowledge and that she is Yellow Woman, wishes to stay in this place where senses are heightened and she finds herself "standing in the sky with nothing around . . . but the wind." Linear thinking does not work in this world, which evokes the colors and circular mazes of sand painting. She goes with him because she enters the reality of the myth.

Her story does not end "happily ever after," as students may expect from their experience with romantic stories in Euro-American culture. Though she stays longer, even the original Yellow Woman of the Pueblo legend returns to her family eventually rather than continuing in an eternal state of romantic adventure. Nor does the story end with her reaping the consequences of sin. The story does not judge the actions of Yellow Woman as a morality tale might, and rather than "learning her lesson" she will simply continue her life as she left it. In mainstream culture, people often try to live out variations on the Cinderella theme that tells every woman she will find her prince if she is beautiful, patient, and good. Equally powerful is the gothic "beauty and the beast" romance in which the tormented hero is converted into a prince by the insightful heroine who comes to understand him. Advertisements create their own ministories in which romantic fulfillment is achieved by buying the right product or looking the right way.

Although college students may gain insight into their assumptions by discussing "Yellow Woman" as romantic fiction, its origins as a myth give it cultural significance for people within the tribe, and its symbols and meanings may elude others. Silko's cousin, Paula Gunn Allen, has complained of Silko's novel *Ceremony* that it appropriates Laguna Pueblo lore that should not have been shared with outsiders, and the issue of whites stealing yet another possession of native peoples is a legitimate one. Myths are tied to origins, to the shared values passed down within a community, to ethos in the classical sense of the term. Perhaps any good story taps into the human need to understand and order the universe. Stories tell us who we are and how we are to behave within a culture. But they also provide us with the enjoyment of reading a well-told tale, and Silko's use of specific details adds to this experience. Students will find many examples, from the tamaracks and willows of the opening sentence to the screen door and Jell-O in the final paragraph. Details contribute to the sense of reality but also serve to reveal characters and to show the state of mind of the narrator. Especially vivid are the piglike description of the white man that Silva apparently kills, the violent and bloody images connected with Silva himself, and the enhanced sensitivity of Yellow Woman's perceptions of the natural setting.

JAMES JOYCE

Araby (p. 828)

The influence of James Joyce on writing in the twentieth century cannot be overemphasized. He consistently appeared at or near the top of lists of the most important books of the last century. Speaking of the complex and almost indecipherable *Finnegans Wake*, Joyce wryly boasted that his aim was to "keep the critics busy for three hundred years." In *Ulysses*, another novel that continues to keep critics and college students occupied, he allowed his characters internal dialogues that had never before been attempted to such an extent, fragmenting reality into multiple points of view and writing styles. He also dealt with sex and other bodily functions in ways that caught the attention of censors, and the first editions of his books had to be smuggled into the United States. More troubling to many readers, however, especially those in his native Ireland, were his irreverent criticisms of the Catholic Church and the nineteenth-century Western morality. However, in the semiautobiographical novel *A Portrait of the Artist as a Young Man*, Joyce presented himself as a man seeking a higher morality, ending with one of the most memorable lines in literature: "I go forth to encounter for the millionth time the reality of experience and to forge in the smithy of my soul the uncreated conscience of my race." Even though Joyce may have realized the overreaching irony contained within this statement of his hero, Stephen Dedalus, he nevertheless tried to live it in his writing.

Although James Joyce lived most of his life as an exile from Ireland, his fiction evokes Dublin and the countryside and schools of his childhood and adolescence. The short story "Araby" is found in the collection entitled *Dubliners*, a series of portraits intended to reveal the city itself. Each of the stories culminates in its protagonist's experience of what Joyce termed an "epiphany," a sudden spiritual manifestation of insight and understanding. The action of the story takes place within the consciousness of the character and the reader and is meant to reveal some aspect of reality. In "Araby," the young protagonist seeks a romantic ideal, much as knights of earlier literature sought the Holy Grail, and discovers that his pursuit and its object — his religion — have been trivial and false.

At the end of the story, the boy's "eyes burn . . . with anguish and anger." The reasons for his emotions are revealed earlier in this final sentence. He has been suddenly struck by the realization that he is a "creature driven and derided by vanity." He has seen Mangan's sister as a pure and beautiful goddess. She is a figure of fantasy rather than a real girl, much like the Virgin Mary adored in The *Devout Communicant* or the romantic objects of knightly devotion in *The Abbot* — both books he has found in the room of the dead priest who formerly occupied his house. A third book in the priest's library, *The Memoirs of Vidocq*, a collection of sexually suggestive detective stories, may have contributed a more carnal slant to his thoughts about Mangan's sister, however. Heretofore, he has sublimated his lusts to something he has interpreted as holy, has carried the thought of her through the vulgar streets of Dublin as if it were a chalice, like the most sacred symbol of the Catholic mass, the transformed and transforming blood of Christ. By conflating the two symbols, Joyce suggests that both are equally false idols, thus critiquing both romantic love and the church. At Araby, agreed by many to represent the Vanity Fair of John Bunyan's *Pilgrim's Progress* where Everyman is tempted to buy cheap substitutes for true religion, carnival inverts the ideal of romantic love for Joyce's protagonist. The empty banter of the people at the fair, presumably already initiates into the world of adult sexuality, makes his elevation of love suddenly seem tawdry. Joyce seems to imply that to believe in anything is shameful, and this implication may reflect his philosophy.

Like most of his writings, "Araby" reflects autobiographical events in the author's life; we know that he lived for a time on Richmond Street and that a traveling bazaar named Araby visited Dublin in 1894, when James Joyce was a twelve-year-old boy. Readers may feel that Joyce takes the naiveté of his youth too seriously, that his rejection of conventional attitudes toward love and religion is too extreme, especially when based on an event so insignificant on the surface. Most of us have made mistakes like this, however, and still blush to remember obscure humiliations that no one else noticed at the time. Our closest friends would be bewildered by the power these memories still have over us. Joyce's epiphanies are based on just such trivialities, and he might suggest that we examine these experiences for the manifestation of reality contained within them, that we take off the blinders of false consciousness. The beginning of this short story describes Richmond Street as "blind," meaning that it is a dead end but suggesting an obvious metaphor about the people who live on such streets. At the end of the story, the boy's blindness has been overcome, though he is ironically blinded with tears. He feels anguish but also anger that he has been fooled by romantic ideas. Beyond the story of a boy who becomes aware of his false illusions, however, "Araby" insists on an interpretation that connects love and religion equally as types of muddled and confining ideology. An interpretation of Joyce's texts must also consider what is being said about Ireland's collective false consciousness. In James Joyce's thinking, the same institutions and beliefs that diminish individuals also limit cultures.

The boy in Joyce's "Araby" and the young wife in Leslie Marmon Silko's "Yellow Woman" (p.820) inarticulately act out the myths of their respective cultures. Joyce's character is the hero of an Arthurian legend, a seeker after a version of the holy grail. He sees the object of his search as something pure, an emblem worthy of his chosen lady, herself an object worshiped from afar. The reader realizes that the protagonist has idealized the Dublin schoolgirl and the sordid carnival to a ridiculous extent, but the boy does not realize this until the end. In a similar way, the female protagonist of "Yellow Woman" moves through a romantic dream, failing to shake herself out of it even as the reader sees the danger and the underlying brutality to which she has exposed herself. It is less clear that she frees herself from the power of the myth than it is with Joyce's character. When she arrives home to the tableau of the older women preparing

Jell-O, she is faced with the most prosaic of images, much as Joyce's character is faced with the trivial chatter of the street fair. But the Jell-O, representing the undermining of traditional culture, can be seen as a contrast to the mythological world.

While it is clear to informed readers that Joyce means his character to reject the idealism of myth, Silko leaves the way open for Yellow Woman to return to the romantic, mythological world if the opportunity again presents itself. Perhaps the knowledge that she can return to the world of story is her epiphany. If so, the result is the opposite of the epiphany in which Joyce's character recognizes with shame the unreality of idealism and religion. The door to myth remains open to the Pueblo woman but slams shut for the Irish schoolboy. Whether we find one story more realistic than the other may say as much about ourselves as about the narratives.

Readers steeped in the "realism" of Western culture may find "Araby" more realistic, perhaps recalling moments when they came to understand that the idealistic values they had learned in books and religious teachings were not absolute ones accepted by all people. Readers open to alternative views of reality might feel that Joyce's character is too easily robbed of his mythology, agreeing with Silko that the worlds of reality and myth actually do overlap.

JOHN UPDIKE

A & P (p. 833)

If the minutiae of the daily lives of John Updike's characters seem trivial and their preoccupations self-absorbed, this may be the fault of the culture rather than the writer. Updike has been a prolific recorder of the details of American middle-class existence since the publication of his first fiction in 1959, and he continues to tell our stories forty years later. Readers tend to love Updike or hate him. Students who read "A & P" sometimes say it's the best story they have ever read. These are usually nineteen-year-old young men who work part time at grocery stores to earn money during their first year at college. Many students, typically young women who spend a lot of time at the beach, are highly offended by the suggestion that Sammy is anything but a sexist pig. Critics are similarly divided on a more sophisticated and ostensibly objective level. Updike, however, is not a trivial thinker. Interested in philosophy and theology, Updike joins Franz Kafka, Henrik Ibsen, and W. H. Auden as an avid reader of the equally prolific Søren Kierkegaard (1813–1855), the father of existentialism. Seen as the first philosopher of the subjective individual and opponent of "the system," Kierkegaard coined the term "leap of faith" to describe the sort of daring move into a new consciousness that we see Sammy make in Updike's story.

Like many of Updike's characters, Sammy seems more to stumble and fall his way into his future rather than to actually leap. Students often think that Sammy has ruined his chances by a foolish act, using as evidence the final sentence where Sammy realizes "how hard the world was going to be . . . hereafter." We might ask them, however, if coming to such a realization is a bad thing. If Sammy is an incarnation of Updike, as many of his protagonists are, will he really be better off as a version of the grim supermarket manager Lengel, unable to perceive beauty or to think independently, or as the writer and thinker he will become? Remembering Kierkegaard, we can see Sammy's angst as a natural reaction to newly found freedom, and freedom can lead in a positive or a negative direction. That direction is up to Sammy and falls outside the story, though we should not let that fact stop our speculations about his future.

Although Sammy's reasons for quitting may be based on romantic illusions, the result of his quitting leads to his new, more realistic view of life. Underneath, his quitting may have less to do with the girls than with his reluctance to be one of the trivial name-brands of the A & P, catalogued with great specificity in the story. The customers are characterized as sheep, the workers look like conforming chumps, and the items for sale are as tawdry as the wares of James Joyce's bazaar in "Araby"(p. 828) or in John Bunyan's Vanity Fair in *Pilgrim's Progress*. Sammy quits because he pursues, in his crude way, the romantic ideal of individuality. Has he, like the protagonist of "Araby," sought a pure ideal only to realize that the pursuit was vain? Students might want to consider times they have done the right thing for the wrong reasons. Undoubtedly, Sammy is selfish if he quits a job his parents approve of just to gain the attention of girls who hold him in contempt if they notice him at all. But students should be challenged to examine the concept of selfishness as problematic.

Ultimately, the story for both Updike's and Joyce's young knights is not about the ladies — the queens, the false goddesses — that they seek to worship and please but about their own changing perceptions of themselves. Students of the 1960s, who read "A & P" in its first years after publication in *Pigeon Feathers and Other Stories* (1962), may list different priorities than their children do in the early twenty-first century. Breaking free from a conforming society sounded seductively good to Updike's age-mates and the generation directly following him. Current students in our regional branch of a state university often state openly that they are in college solely to prepare for a well-paying career. They have trouble understanding Sammy's dilemma, and most feel that he has his priorities out of order when he quits his job. Sammy, to the extent that he admires the girls for reasons of social class, reveals materialistic values of the same sort, however. This equating of the moneyed class with value may be the false consciousness that corresponds in Updike's American story to the religious dominance in Joyce's Irish one. When Sammy leaves that symbol of homogenized, commercial America — the A & P — he escapes what many of our students actively seek, a job with a secure if limited future.

Although we would like to think that the gains obtained by the social movements of the 1960s and 1970s have removed stereotypes about class and gender, students will be quick to tell us that the time frame of the story has less to do with adolescent thought than we would hope. Women are more likely to notice and to challenge sexism in the story, but most students agree that Sammy's attitudes still prevail among the young people that they know. However, we might want to grant him an ironic chivalry that — though misplaced — is preferable in Updike's estimation to the suppression of individuality. The final paragraph takes Sammy outside of the supermarket, and he is able to see the kind of life he has escaped — easy, safe, sheeplike, and paralyzing. Perhaps some students will maintain that, in this case, hard is better.

Comparing the three characters at the end of the stories in this cluster takes us back to the cluster's title, "Romantic Dreams." Each character — Yellow Woman in Leslie Marmon Silko's story by the same name (p. 820), the boy in Joyce's "Araby," and Sammy in John Updike's "A & P" — acts within a dreamlike world of fantasy, based on the stories and the assumptions of his or her specific culture. Yellow Woman seems to change the least. Her journey into myth has moved her closer to a part of herself as an individual and as a strand of a vanishing tribal identity. She is less interested in personal awareness than in continuity with her grandfather and with the people of the stories. The false thing is the Jell-O of the present, not her unexpected and oddly passive interlude into passion and danger. She'll do it again if drawn back into it, but it does not represent a quest.

The young men of the other two stories are active seekers of romance, however, and they both end in a state of disillusionment with the assumptions of their cultures. Individuality and its accompanying alienation are foregrounded in both Updike and Joyce, with the limitations of culture being something to be avoided or changed. The passivity of Silko's heroine, while recovering Laguna myth, is disturbingly similar to that of thirteen-year-old girls of many cultures, and class discussion might address the ramifications of fantasies that portray young women swept up dreamily and helplessly into relationships. Both men and women will recall times that they had unrealistic fantasies about a person or worshipped someone from afar, as the boys in Joyce's and Updike's stories do. The real "anguish and anger" — but also the epiphany — come when we act on the fantasy. Both Updike and Joyce end their stories on a note of realization that the world will be profoundly different for the protagonists not only because of their actions but, more importantly, because of their changed perceptions of reality.

COMPLETING THE SELF THROUGH LOVE (p. 838)

DIANE ACKERMAN

Plato: The Perfect Union (p. 839)

At first, a reading of *Symposium 5*, the section of Plato's dialogues that inspires Diane Ackerman's analysis, invites our laughter. To begin, Plato places the story in the mouth of Aristophanes, a comedian, rather than giving it to a more serious member of the discussion. Then Aristophanes begins by asking his friends to laugh with him, not at him, as he tells his story, a "please don't kick me" sort of request that immediately invites us to disobey. The story, as he tells it, is ridiculous, the original humans described as perfectly round spheres with four legs, four arms, etc., rolling around the earth like so many hamsters in plastic balls. Furthermore, Zeus threatens that if they continue to be impertinent, he'll slice them again, and they'll have to hop around on one leg, a slapstick image. "He spoke and cut the men in two, like a sorb-apple which is halved for pickling," Aristophanes tells us, using a simile that hardly invites respect for the poor things. This reads like the script for an episode of *Monty Python's Flying Circus*. But with the pathos of the divided creatures clinging to their other halves, afraid to unclasp to eat or care for themselves, human beings begin to look a bit tragic, though still ridiculous. And when he begins to discuss "soul mates," we recognize a familiar idea that has its source here in Plato's *Symposium*.

Ackerman, a poet as well as an essayist who explores the importance of the body and its senses in all aspects of human life, accepts the longing for oneness that Plato's dialogue assumes. But she finds its source instead in the oneness the unborn child experiences with its mother. She frames her discussion of Plato's *Symposium* and its religious, mythological, and literary correlatives with a reference in the opening paragraph to a child waiting for a good-night kiss and a poetic image in the closing paragraph of a child in the womb. Both Plato and Ackerman begin with the assumption that the longing for union with a perfect "other half" is an essential quality of humanity, begging the question of whether this premise is true. Still, Ackerman's science-based reasoning has logic on its side and seems free of the doubleness of Plato's comic narrator, whom we may not be expected to take seriously. She takes many examples from literature, and she is a poet, a fact that Plato's student Aristotle would say also gives her a double voice.

We probably can believe Aristophanes when he speaks of the supermanliness of men whose mates are other men, offering the evidence that "these when they grow up become our statesmen, and these only, which is a great proof of the truth of what I am saying." This requirement for public office might change some things if applied in today's United States! Ackerman asserts, on the other hand, that the human need for complete union finds its genesis in the power of women to carry children and to give birth, undercutting the Platonic assumption that males are superior. Using Plato's logic, the ultimate fulfillment of Ackerman's yearning child would be incest with its mother, whether it is male or female, a variation on Sigmund Freud's Oedipus complex. Students may question whether these ideas about finding wholeness through love explain something innate to human beings or reflect assumptions that are acquired as part of a culture.

The idea that Ackerman is talking about wholeness rather than love is supported by her discussion of religious practices that seek union with God and by her use of the mother and child bond as the underlying reason behind the longing for such wholeness. Yet she fails to develop an equally tenable idea that the union of egg and sperm is part becoming whole in microcosm and that the child who develops from this union carries just as much of the father's biological essence as the mother's. Watching the doubling of cells under the microscope recalls the splitting of Plato's spherical beings, and oneness begins to look quite multiple at this level. Ackerman doesn't try to puzzle out the differences between homosexual love and heterosexual love as Plato does, though she acknowledges a biological heritage in which the sexes coexisted in one body, but she concentrates instead on the "osmotic yearning" precipitated by being torn from one's mother's body at birth.

The question of whether this yearning manifests itself as physical or spiritual begs the question of the nature of spirituality as something apart from the human body. Most students have experienced both sexual longing and religious searching, and most are of an age when they are particularly vulnerable to both. Cults succeed in recruiting members through exploiting this need for ultimate belonging. Romantic ideas about human love can lead to equally destructive situations. Readers might question whether Ackerman's "pinnacle" refers to a long-term relationship with a soul mate, as Plato implies, or a rare achievement that one encounters in rare, brief moments of intense unity with any human being in the right time and place.

ANDREW SULLIVAN

The Love Bloat (p. 843)

Andrew Sullivan certainly seems to be enjoying himself, debunking with gusto such a cherished cultural icon as the Valentine card and all that it implies about romantic love. It might be interesting to ask students what they think Sullivan means by "serious" in line 3. After all, Aristotle, Montaigne, and Shakespeare are not simply serious; they are iconic geniuses. But Sullivan is using a broadsword here, not a scalpel, to chop down what he calls Valentine's Day "Hallmark pedestal." We assume he is referring to the unreflective and often sentimental clichés that are common in such cards. Perhaps sentimentality is an obvious target for intellectuals, but many students will resist his insistence that romantic love is an invention of Rousseau's that helps fill the empty emotional center of bourgeois life and that we are being diverted by the "phony adrenaline" of sex and the narcissism of romantic love from important civic and personal matters such as "truth and honor and power." Most students will not buy it.

Sullivan knows his argument is a tad outrageous ("O.K, so maybe I just broke up with someone"), but such self-consciousness does not slow him down. Amusingly, he establishes rhetoric's common ground with his audience by claiming that for "99 percent of us, relationships are, at best, useful economic bargains." This is a risky rhetorical strategy since surely more than one percent of his audience will think of themselves as in a loving relationship.

In between his one-line zingers ("It's all promise with the delivery of the postal service"), Sullivan makes a series of cogent observations. "Excessive expectation" can cause disappointment in relationships, and hoping that love will cure all our ills ("a personal and cultural panacea") is bound to have "doleful social consequence." And perhaps most perceptively, Sullivan suggests that friendship, affection, caring, and civility are crucial elements of a successful relationship. For all Sullivan's hyperbole and occasional over-the-top rhetorical flourish, his main point is well worth serious discussion — that love is more than erotic adrenaline and that romantic love cannot, over time, conquer all. In that sense, Sullivan, at the end of the essay, seems quite trustworthy. Mature students will readily see that romantic love can be fool's gold, but they will also argue that a caring friendship and romantic love do not have to be mutually exclusive.

COURTSHIP (p. 846)

CHRISTOPHER MARLOWE

The Passionate Shepherd to His Love (p. 846)

The subject of popular legend in his lifetime and in the years directly following his violent death in 1593, Christopher "Kit" Marlowe continues to live in the popular culture at the edges of literary studies some four hundred years later. In the 1999 movie *Shakespeare in Love*, playwright Tom Stoppard has a young Shakespeare's competition with Marlowe and his hasty exchange of identity with him lead Shakespeare to believe that he is responsible for Marlowe's being stabbed in a tavern brawl. Stoppard cannot be unaware of the latest wrinkle in the ongoing debate about the authorship of Shakespeare's texts, which maintains that Marlowe's death was a hoax related to his espionage activities in the intrigues between Catholic and Protestant factions. The theory, suggested in 1993 and circulating internationally on the World Wide Web ever since, suggests that a deal was worked out in which the politically compromised Marlowe would seem to be killed, disappear, and then reemerge from some Renaissance version of Superman's telephone booth with a new identity as . . . you guessed it. If true, all of the works of Shakespeare were actually written by Kit Marlowe, the Canterbury shoemaker's son with a Cambridge education and a reputation as a spy and atheistic practitioner of the black arts. Students might enjoy the historicist task of tracking down the myths, legends, and fiercely held beliefs about Marlowe both in his time and in later ones.

We have evidence of the popularity of Marlowe's pastoral lyric, "The Passionate Shepherd to His Love" (first published in 1599, six years after his death), in the great number of parodies and responses to it that still exist from the early 1600s, when his life and death were still fresh in living memory. In addition to those included in our anthology, John Donne's teasingly sweet variation "The Baite" might intrigue students who are interested in fishing as foreplay, and Shakespeare's comical use of several lines in "The Merry Wives of Windsor" may add fuel to the "Marlowe Lives" controversy. Marlowe's poem reflects his interest in classical themes and is undoubtedly inspired by his translations of Ovid's *Amores* from Latin into English. His setting is Arcadia, with its idealized shepherds and milkmaids living idyllic lives in a trouble-free, natural paradise where love and work are uncomplicated. Such fantasies must have provided a welcome contrast for stressed courtiers during these years surrounding the beheading of Mary, Queen of Scots, threats from political and religious factions at home and abroad, and the anxiety about the future that accompanied the aging of Queen Elizabeth I. The poem's structure may have contributed to its popularity as well, its rhyming couplets in regular iambic tetrameter making it easy to memorize.

"The Passionate Shepherd to His Love" continues to be a much-read poem today, both through its obligatory inclusion in high-school and college anthologies and through its informal and voluntary circulation on the Internet, a good barometer of current popular culture. The argument is what literary folk would later call a romantic one, projecting an idealized portrait of love. But we know that Marlowe was not himself a simple shepherd, and we can assume that the persona of the poem masks a sophisticated man of the world who realizes that the argument is more charming than logical. The argument will probably succeed to the extent that the lady to whom it is addressed is willing to play the simple milkmaid to Marlowe's simple shepherd.

Even in this idyllic setting, a closer examination raises issues about the world of reality outside of paradise. He imagines making her shoes "for the cold" (line 15), hinting that the season may not always be springtime. And although some of his construction materials — like gold, amber, and coral — are lasting, the flowers and leaves will quickly fade, and two types of materials are inextricably intertwined. The whole enterprise, his dressing of her, reflects both his erotic desires and the economic reality that women depended on men for the clothing they wore. Students might question whether the shepherd's beloved, if she relents, is more seduced by the shepherd or by what he says he will do for her. Seen from an economic perspective, the seduction seems more of an exchange of one commodity for another, the setting and the beautiful trappings traded for sexual favors. Issues may also be raised about the *carpe diem* convention itself. In the Old Testament, Ecclesiastes 8:15, contrary to some other biblical passages, counsels us that there is nothing better for us to do than "to eat, to drink, and to be merry" — a *carpe diem* philosophy that is antithetical to the Puritanical worldview. Students will be familiar with the tension between these philosophical forces in American culture. The same force also battled in Marlowe's London, with the theaters constantly struggling to stay open in the face of religious and moral arguments against them.

Our discussion of the persuasive techniques of the passionate shepherd could also examine the ways in which advertising and other aspects of popular culture try to sell us on the idea of seizing the day for their own purposes.

SIR WALTER RALEIGH

The Nymph's Reply to the Shepherd (p. 848)

Probably the closest England came to a Renaissance man, Sir Walter Raleigh was deeply involved in the issues of his day. He survived the changing fortunes of a courtier subject to the whims of Queen Elizabeth I to eventually be imprisoned by King James I for high treason in 1603. Before and during his time in the Tower of London, where he wrote a history of the world, Raleigh was a writer and translator of both prose and poetry. Often active in commercial ventures of the sort that planted colonies in the Americas, Raleigh tended to write for self-promotion. The long title of his book about his holdings on the South American continent begins *The Discoverie of the Large, Rich, and Beautiful Empire of Guiana, with a Relation of the Great and Golden City of Manoa (Which the Spanish call El Dorado).* . . . The title's hyperbole strikes symbolically persuasive chords that the author hopes potential investors will hear, but the story is an especially well-written exploration narrative. Other prose reflects a practical interest in war and naval expeditions, not surprising for a man who lived during the age of exploration and the invasion of the Spanish Armada. The arts of persuasive rhetoric are important to Raleigh for pragmatic reasons, since even poetry dedicated to the queen can help him remain in favor at court.

Like many poets of his time, Raleigh experimented with the Petrarchan sonnet, an Italian form whose conventions elevated the speaker's lady to a position of worship, a position quite in keeping with that of Elizabeth I. Raleigh's poems reveal his wit and rationality, and he seems to have enjoyed poetry as an intellectual game, played always in the context of his social and political surroundings. This is especially evident in his refutation of Christopher Marlowe's "The Passionate Shepherd to His Love" (p. 846). Raleigh critiques the shepherd's argument, and comes to the conclusion that Marlowe's poem is "in folly ripe, in reason rotten" (line 16). He attacks the ethical and pathetic appeals of Marlowe's poem with the sharp logic proposed by his persona, a woman wise about the effects of time. He implies that a girl would have to be really young and naive to buy Marlowe's argument. Appropriately, these poems are sometimes given the titles "The Milke Maids Songe" and "Milk Maids Mothers Answer."

The key words in Raleigh's refutation are *if, then,* and *but.* The shepherd has offered the milkmaid a deal, and she makes her counteroffer. "Here are my terms," she implies. "See if you can meet them." Since she sets him an impossible task, her counterargument amounts to a refusal of his proposition, for the pragmatic reason that the kind of love he offers will not last. The ambiguity of line 22 raises the issue of how love is to be defined, however. We may agree with the preceding implication that youth does not last, though it is couched as a conditional rather than a declarative statement, but whether joys become dated depends on our understanding of the definition of *joy.* As a true rhetorician, though, Raleigh would probably accuse us of equivocation. The thrust of his argument is that this particular experience of love is fleeting. The tone of Raleigh's poem mocks the impractical idealism of Marlowe's; like a true adman, the speculator who wrote his hopeful account of gold in Guyana knows a con when he hears one. The speaker of Raleigh's poem has a tinge of stereotype about her, though, and this may also be part of the joke. She is a woman as familiar to readers as Chaucer's earlier Wife of Bath, a woman who wishes above all to be empowered by her sexuality, not seduced because of it. Raleigh's poem also stereotypes the young male lover, assuming that his love will last only as long as the flowers he offers his nymph.

Raleigh's poem follows Marlowe's stanza by stanza, refuting each bit of evidence offered by the shepherd to prove love's pleasures. He subverts the *carpe diem* theme by using its basic assumption about the brevity of life to come to a different conclusion, that erotic love will not last any longer than youth will, and a wise woman will not be fooled into thinking otherwise. Raleigh's speaker wants something more lasting. In Marlowe's poem, nature seems pleasant and comfortable, with images of flowers and jewels that sparkle with color and light and birds that sing with the intricate melodies of springtime. The shepherd plucks wool effortlessly to make his love a dress, an especially unrealistic image for anyone who has seen how filthy sheep can become or has thought about the steps involved in getting wool from its raw state to the finished garment. And we wonder, with all this work he cuts out for himself, weaving and embroidering her garments, when he will find time for lovemaking. That Raleigh misses the chance to refute this may betray his gender or his class. Women and men involved in the wool industry wouldn't be expected to let this pass.

The seasons have changed in Raleigh's poem, though, and the floods and cold of winter cause everything to wither and die and the birds to stop singing. He doesn't mention the warm shoes or wool dress of Marlowe's poem, but they didn't seem very practical, anyway. And this is Raleigh's point, of course. Love is not simply a romantic promise. We can assume that Sir Walter Raleigh knew something about love, since he jeopardized his position at Queen Elizabeth's court to marry Elizabeth Throckmorton, and their marriage endured his later long imprisonment. His wife was allowed visits to his apartments in the Tower of London, and a son was conceived in this confined setting, one that — while not uncomfortable — was far from the glow of Arcadia.

ANDREW MARVELL

To His Coy Mistress (p. 849)

As involved in his way with the political issues of the middle years of the seventeenth century as Sir Walter Raleigh was with those around its beginning, Andrew Marvell wrote prose satires and metaphysical verse much admired and ultimately recovered for a twentieth-century audience by T. S. Eliot. Up until this time, Marvell was best known for having served as secretary to the blind poet John Milton. In a poem about Milton's composition of the epic poem *Paradise Lost*, Marvell reacts to Milton's writing process, describing his amazement as he watched the complex structure and lines of the epic take shape before his eyes. Therefore, as a reader in his own time, and later as an influence on early twentieth-century writers, Andrew Marvell is a poet's poet. Some readers of Marvell's lyric poems have speculated that his deceptively light touch, applied to what they see as his profound insight and skilled technique, came as a result of his years as a tutor. Even the most devoted readers of Andrew Marvell therefore concede that to skim the surface of his poetry is to miss an undercurrent that may run counter to the poem as it first appears. Some critics who have examined "To His Coy Mistress" in close detail maintain that the poem sends ambivalent, even confused, messages about love and that its ideas do not bear up under logical scrutiny.

The speaker's purpose in "To His Coy Mistress" is to persuade his reluctant audience to give up her virginity to him without further delay. His logic seems to be that if more time existed, then waiting would be okay; but since there is little time, we should not wait to make love. But the conclusion does not necessarily follow. It would be just as logical — or as illogical — to say, "Since there's so little time, we shouldn't waste it screwing around. I think I'll take that trip to pick up rubies in India before they are all gone." Good authority holds that the poet's argument "affirms the consequent" or commits the "fallacy of the converse." Although some students might know these terms for logical fallacies and enjoy taking a rhetorical analysis further, one could use their interest as a resource rather than expecting all students (or all literature instructors, for that matter) to identify examples of faulty reasoning by name.

What we might do is ask why so many readers love the poem in spite of our conviction that we would not be swayed by its argument. The answer would undoubtedly lie in its appeal to our emotions and the overwhelming beauty of its style, but even these can be called into question. The issues hidden within "To His Coy Mistress" are best discovered by close reading, something the class can do together. Even the title may confuse students who have never heard the word *coy* or who assume that the word *mistress* implies that she is already his illicit lover, a reading that throws her reluctance to make love into a different light. The woman addressed is assumed by the speaker to be a virgin, and her remaining so until marriage is the expectation of Puritan English society in the 1600s, though birth and marriage records call into question any universal adherence to prohibitions against premarital sex. If Marvell's speaker is meant to be the poet himself, an issue in itself, he is calling for a woman to sin or at best to marry. He assumes that she will be persuaded to do so by hyperbole, flattery, fear of death and decay, and violently erotic images rather than by logic.

The poem has three major sections, though the rhythm and sense often provide a sense of closure at the end of four lines and the rhyming couplets at the end of two. The first major section elaborates on the first premise of Marvell's argument, what he would do if there were world enough and time, and the final couplet (lines 19–20) sums up his warrant for this action, that she deserves it and he desires it. The second premise, that time prevents such a love, is described in the next section, again ending with a couplet that sums up and gives a warrant for his assertions by citing the finality of the grave (lines 31–32). The final section deals with the third part of the syllogism, with the word *therefore* appropriately used in its first line. He goes on to explain to her, repeating the word *now* at intervals, that he has proven his point, and now is the time to take action. He ends with a couplet that sums up the urgency of these last lines, proposing that though they cannot stop time, they can make it go faster, and this conclusion warrants the rushing violent images of this final part of the poem. The couplet that ends each part of his argument contains an opposition. The poem has a sense of desperation about it, with its images of violent birds of prey devouring time rather than allowing time to devour them, tearing pleasures through iron gates. He proposes that the lovers refuse to be victims, that they turn violently on the enemy, making love a frantic defiance of death.

Although some readers may see a threat toward his coy mistress in the last section, others may note that he does not propose that he should direct his violent energy toward her, but that they do these things together, pooling their "strength and . . . sweetness" (lines 41–42). And she seems ready to participate, if we are to believe his description of her body in lines 35 and 36. Students who have read Plato's *Symposium* may wonder from lines 41 and 42 if Marvell's reading of classical literature has included Aristophanes' description of divided human beings seeking their other halves, since he saw the original humans as round balls. Despite his fierce images, directed against time and death, the speaker of Marvell's poem seems to desire wholeness rather than rape. Still, readers can legitimately charge him with a rather rough approach to a virgin.

The third of our texts in the section on courtship, Marvell's invitation moves away from the original conventions quite a bit. Christopher Marlowe in "The Passionate Shepherd to His Love" (p. 846) entices the object of his desire by painting a picture of paradise, only hinting at the coldness for which he will devise clothing and shoes to protect her. Sir Walter Raleigh answers in "The Nymph's Reply to the Shepherd" (p. 848) with reminders of changing weather and with indirect references to aging. Marvell speaks of being pursued by an almost demonic time and graphically describes the end result of aging, the grave itself.

T. S. ELIOT

The Love Song of J. Alfred Prufrock (p. 851)

Students may be impressed to know that "The Love Song of J. Alfred Prufrock" is the work of an undergraduate student, published in part in the *Harvard Advocate* when T. S. Eliot worked on the publication in 1910 and 1911. The poem is considered by many literary historians to have invented a new way of writing poetry and to be one of the texts that launched the modernist movement in literature. Building on his education and wide reading, which was filtered through his own sensitivity and eccentricity of thought, Eliot anticipated in this poem his later theoretical ideas in the influential "Tradition and the Individual Talent" and other essays that later solidified into the New Criticism of the mid-twentieth century. His allusions to obscure bits of learning from the classics, French symbolists, Shakespeare, and multiple other sources can confuse even the most erudite of readers. Students need to be reassured that they do not have to understand every phrase. Although critics have maintained that "Prufrock" should not be read as simply a love poem, focusing our reading on this poem's relationship to the *carpe diem* poems in this cluster on courtship can make "Prufrock" accessible to students who are familiar with poems dealing with love and the passage of time. Unlike Andrew Marvell, who speeds up time in "To His Coy Mistress" (p. 849), Eliot slows time down to the pace of a lazy cat slipping like fog into the streets of a city. The speaker of the epigraph is in Dante's hell, where time does go on forever. And since his listener is in the same place, he says, he can tell his story without "fear of infamy," doesn't have to be ashamed. Eliot's narrator wanders through a city whose streets "follow like a tedious argument / Of insidious intent" (lines 8–9), and students who have suffered through dry lectures will agree that few things are more hellish than that. The speaker of Eliot's poem worries about shame, too, constantly asking if he "dares" and finally deciding that he probably doesn't dare, that the romantic adventure is not for him.

Prufrock may be asking himself if he dares to plunge into love as Christopher Marlowe and Andrew Marvell invite their lovers to do, even if there is, as Prufrock claims, plenty of time. Whereas Marvell's persona takes on the sun as an opponent, Eliot's wonders if he has the courage to "disturb the universe" (line 46). In contrast to Marvell's birds of prey devouring time, Prufrock is not sure he has what it takes "to eat a peach" (line 121), an image that evokes sensual pleasures. He worries about growing bald, a peculiar worry for a man so young, implying that he fears the changes that come with passing time. The idea of rejection, of being misunderstood, seems to keep Prufrock wandering through the streets and houses mumbling to himself. Students may conclude that he is afraid of life as well as love.

Prufrock has been sounding a great deal like Hamlet, vacillating about whether he will take action. But he hints that he is more like Polonius, "an attendant lord" who is characterized by faulty rhetoric, who talks and talks but is laughably unaware of what is really going on. Hamlet kills Polonius by mistake while Polonius is hiding, an unseen observer rather than a participant in the action. A Shakespearean fool, on the other hand, seems to be talking nonsense but sometimes speaks great wisdom. Eliot's tone is filled with irony, transforming the similes of romantic poetry in a startling way. Eliot's contemporaries who were steeped in the usual metaphors for natural phenomena must have been shaken by Eliot's unexpected image of evening as a patient having surgery. There's more than irony here, however, and students could make a case for other characterizations of the tone; certainly the self-mockery that permeates the whole poem begins in the opening lines. Prufrock seems to avoid relationships because he feels that he is not up to the task. His repetition that "the women come and go / Talking of Michelangelo" may imply that the women trivialize art, that superficial social relationships also get in his way. When he says that he "should have been a pair of ragged claws / Scuttling across the floors of silent seas," perhaps his isolation from this society reaches its extremity.

The urgent seductions of both Marvell and Christopher Marlowe would undoubtedly scare the timid and indecisive Prufrock into a corner. Eliot was a great admirer of Marvell, however, and brought his poetry into the literary canon. In fact, the repeated "there will be time" of "The Love Song of J. Alfred Prufrock" directly answers Marvell's argument in "To His Coy Mistress" that there is not "world enough and time" for waiting. The contention that line 92 is a direct allusion to "To His Coy Mistress" can be borne out by its juxtaposition with Lazarus returning from the dead, recalling Marvell's reminder that love cannot take place there. It is quite likely that, among other things, Eliot's poem is meant as a modern refutation of romantic love. Not only its ambiguous language but its experiment with form — its varying line length and rhyme in a way that is neither free verse nor closed structure — challenges conventions. This questioning of the sureties of love and poetry reflects the personality of one shy, sensitive, highly educated young man from St. Louis, but it struck a chord with writers on both sides of the Atlantic that sounded through most of the century.

THE APPEARANCE OF LOVE: A COLLECTION OF WRITINGS BY KATE CHOPIN (p. 856)

KATE CHOPIN

The Storm (p. 857)

Written late in her career, Kate Chopin's story of passion in the midst of a symbolic tempest, "The Storm," has a close relationship to two other Chopin texts: her novel *The Awakening* (1899) and the short story that first explored the characters of Calixta, Alcée, and Bobinôt, "At the 'Cadian Ball" (1894). In her novel, a sensuous and artistic woman moves toward independence from a stifling marriage into adultery, but more important, into seizing her own life. Although the novel's ambiguous ending invites debates about whether its protagonist pays for her sin with suicide or swims into a symbolic freedom, its complex characterization of her sexuality was bold for its time and was shocking to most of the literary community of 1899.

The short story "The Storm," too erotic to be published by a respectable woman during the writer's lifetime, deals with a similar subject but has some important differences. Chopin's female character in "The Storm" is not a member of the upper-class white plantation aristocracy, as is the protagonist of *The Awakening*, but is instead more closely related to the characters in her earlier local-color collections *Bayou Folk* (1894) and *A Night in Acadia* (1897). Although students need not read the earlier "At the 'Cadian Ball" to find issues to discuss, we should consider its perspective, which is often missed when "The Storm" is presented outside its cultural context in literature anthologies. The consideration of any of Chopin's texts must take into account the peculiarly French nature of social institutions in Louisiana in the nineteenth century and must deal with the issues of race, class, and religion that permeated the culture from which these stories arise. All women were bound to their fathers and husbands by the Napoleonic Code, which considered them chattels unable to enter into contracts. Their legal rights were reduced to a greater extent than in any other part of the nation, at a time when women's rights were limited at best. Equally repressive were the dictates of the Catholic Church and of a castebound plantation society still greatly influenced by the social abuses and prohibitions of institutionalized slavery.

A reading of the story that first introduced the characters we meet in "The Storm" goes far to explain the actions of its characters, revealing issues that may not arise when the story is considered out of context. The most startling realization, for those accustomed to reading the story in isolation, is that this text deals with love across the color line. Although she is light-skinned with blue eyes and "flaxen" hair, Calixta has African ancestry, and even a "drop of African blood" places her irrevocably outside of Alcée's life as an equal in the eyes of the culture. Yet, as someone who is also known for her fiery Spanish ancestry, she is at first beyond the reach of the adoring, dark-skinned sugarcane worker Bobinôt. However, according to the rules of this ethnically mixed but obsessively hierarchical society, Bobinôt is an appropriate husband, and the passionate storm of her relationship with Alcée can never be anything but an interlude in her life. The earlier story hints at "a breath of scandal . . . when she went to Assumption," a memory that the lovers share in both "At the 'Cadian Ball" and "The Storm," though we learn in the later story that Alcée had refrained from anything beyond kissing at that time, touched by her vulnerability. We discover that Alcée, a white planter, goes to the ball after he has first been rejected by his cousin Clarisse and later has lost a huge crop of rice in a hurricane. Clarisse comes after him, interrupting a flirtation with Calixta, and the story ends with both women proposing marriage to men they do not completely desire. Alcée, surprisingly for readers of "The Storm," is as smitten with the cold and rejecting Clarisse as Bobinôt is with the mocking and distant Calixta.

The events of "The Storm" take place five years later, as hurricane winds blow through the delta yet again. The sudden passion of Calixta and Alcée is inextricably tied to the symbolism of the storm itself; the cyclone is a natural phenomenon outside of the usual expectations of the weather, and the lovers' physical intensity falls outside the constraints of an ordered and constrictive society. Students may raise issues about the sort of love Calixta feels for Bobinôt, but there seems to be a feeling of tenderness in her attitude toward him. She is a solicitous housewife to him, though we might note that they seem to have separate sleeping arrangements. Whether what Calixta and Alcée share is love will also be a matter for debate. We might ask whether love and sex are necessarily linked in this story or if the story challenges conventions about love within marriage.

Chopin's contemporaries and many of our students may be bothered by the joyful tone of the ending. Unlike the female protagonist of *The Awakening*, Calixta does not suffer for her uninhibited claim to her sexuality; in fact, we are left with the impression that Bibi and Bobinôt have gained from the experience without being aware of it and that Calixta is able to love them more freely. Chopin's story thus runs counter to both the cultural truisms of the day and to the literary conventions she had accepted in the earlier text. Students familiar with soap operas and romantic fiction will recognize that such conventions still apply, since characters who transgress can expect to pay in some way. Chopin further frees Calixta from the *tragic mulatto* motif; rather than pining away for a white lover and dying tragically as a result, she moves effortlessly, without guilt and shame, back into her normal family routine. Although some may see "The Storm" as a celebration of adultery, Chopin seems to be saying much more than this, protesting not against marriage itself but against the legal and social restrictions imposed on human interactions. In a time when bodies were covered from head to toe, she insists that passion is a natural and joyful part — though only one part — of being a human being. The ironic ending, revealing that Alcée's wife Clarisse is happy to be free of the sexuality that Calixta has welcomed, underscores this point.

KATE CHOPIN

The Story of an Hour (p. 862)

Like "The Storm," the previous story in this cluster of Kate Chopin texts, "The Story of an Hour" was published after the author's death in 1904. Readers today are often as disturbed by Mrs. Mallard's emotions as Chopin's early readers were. Today, we hear students complain that if she felt so confined in her marriage, she should have just left. Readers at its first publication would have understood her unquestioning loyalty to her marriage while she knew her husband was alive but would have chided her for not adapting to her lot as a married woman. They might also point out that to be alone did not mean she would have the power to make her own decisions. Most widows, even if their financial means were considerable, would have found their husbands' estates in the hands of male executors.

It is interesting, however, that Kate Chopin's working title for her novel *The Awakening* was *A Solitary Life*. To Chopin, the very real difficulties — even dangers — of being a woman alone in the nineteenth century were more tolerable than the emotional confinement of most marriages. Divorce was inconceivable to most women around the turn of the twentieth century, although Chopin had less reason to be fearful of women's freedom than most. Her great-great-grandmother had been the first woman in St. Louis to receive a legal separation from her husband and had gone on to raise her five children and run a shipping business alone. Kate Chopin grew up surrounded by such strong women and herself became a widow, with six children, in 1882 after twelve years of marriage. Furthermore, her marriage was characterized by an unusual amount of freedom, with Oscar Chopin apparently not complaining about her smoking, riding streetcars, and walking alone through the streets of New Orleans, actions that scandalized "respectable" people.

"The Story of an Hour" may have its model more in the club women of St. Louis than in the Creole society of Louisiana. Either place, Louise Mallard may have been uncomfortably recognizable, as she would be in some circles today. Married people sometimes fantasize about the death of a spouse, but the thought seems not to have occurred to Mrs. Mallard until the events of the story.

Students sometimes judge the protagonist of this story harshly, seeing her as shallow and selfish, ignorant of the true meaning of love. To do this, however, is to miss Chopin's point that love cannot compensate for lack of freedom. Mrs. Mallard has been unaware of this, but we see her, after her initial grief at her husband's death, beginning to awaken. We see her as if she were a child sobbing in its sleep, her thoughts in suspension, with the joy of being her own person approaching her as if it were an outside force about to possess her. This happens to a great extent because she is a woman bound by cultural restraints, but it is not entirely gender-specific. She feels free, we are told, because she will no longer be oppressed by "that blind persistence with which men and women believe they have a right to impose a private will upon a fellow-creature" (para. 14). Within their cultural milieu, both partners in the marriage are trapped, even if they love each other. Like the stories of Guy de Maupassant and O. Henry, this Kate Chopin story depends on ironic circumstances for its action. This leads us to assign blame to a twist of fate or to the constraints of nineteenth-century marriage itself rather than to any of the characters.

Although some readers might wish to know something of Mrs. Mallard's life before or to hear the family's reaction to her death, the story's length seems appropriate to its title and its theme. It might, anticipating a Hemingway story about marriage, be called "The Short Happy Life of Louise Mallard," since her time as a free woman is so brief. The brevity of the story nevertheless allows us to see Mrs. Mallard as a dynamic character and to follow her quickly changing reactions first to her loss, then to her freedom, and finally to the loss of freedom that leads to her death. Some students will imagine that Mrs. Mallard is thinking about having a love affair or spending money without having to ask her husband's permission, but we should encourage them to go beyond such easy answers. Many students have experienced unwanted control from boyfriends or girlfriends. Although the status of women and the constraints of marriage have changed, even today, when in relationships, we sometimes intrude into areas our partners would prefer to keep private, feeling that even their thoughts belong to us. We want to control their movements and to tell them how they should feel. It is this intrusion that she is now freed from, and it is her autonomy, her self-determination, that she anticipates. The loss of her newfound self precipitates her death, and the reader understands the irony when the doctor says she has died of joy at her husband's return.

KATE CHOPIN

Désirée's Baby (p. 864)

"Désirée's Baby" is taken from Kate Chopin's first collection of short stories, *Bayou Folk*. Written in the genre termed *local color*, such narratives were a popular type of writing in which setting is an integral part of the theme. Whereas "The Story of an Hour" could have taken place in any number of settings throughout the United States and Europe in the 1890s, "Désirée's Baby" is best interpreted in the light of a specific time and place. Taking her readers back to Louisiana in the days before the Civil War, Chopin describes a society in which everyone knows his or her place. Masters have absolute power over the bodies and souls of their slaves, and men have a similar if more benign power over their women. To have even a hint of African ancestry places a person outside white society. Although Chopin's characters do not question the rules of this hierarchy, living in the certainty of what signifies their place in the order of things, Chopin holds these beliefs up to the light for her readers to examine.

Depending as it does on foundlings and mistaken identities, Chopin's plot stands in a long line of tradition with William Shakespeare and Charles Dickens, among many others. Around the same time as Kate Chopin used it, Oscar Wilde parodied this plot device in *The Importance of Being Earnest*. African American writers like William Wells Brown and Charles Chestnutt, though, were exploring the complications of mixed identity when applied to questions of race. Issues of passing, assimilation, and the separate cultural identity of people recently freed from slavery occupied the minds of many in the latter half of the nineteenth century. W. E. B. Du Bois was saying at the beginning of the new twentieth century that its major issue would be the troubling question of the "color line," of how the country would overcome the long abuses of slavery and bring Negro people into full equality. Much later, in mid century, studies would show that a major barrier to the integration of African Americans into full citizenship was the fear of white men that sexual relationships would develop between black men and white women. Sex had long been politicized between the races in the American South, with masters taking advantage of slave women, practicing the equivalent of rape under any of our current definitions of the term.

Throughout her narrative, Chopin subverts the assumption that a person may be defined or classified by race or heredity. As the story begins, we have only the hearsay testimony of Madame Valmondé that her husband has found a baby who calls him "Dada." The enigmatic presence just outside the story's action of La Blanche, the light-skinned slave at whose cabin Armand Aubigny spends so much time, raises unanswered questions about her paternity and that of her children. When Désirée finally realizes that her baby has African characteristics, it is because she compares him with the child of La Blanche, and the reader can infer that the children may look alike in some way. And the story ends, of course, with the ironic twist: though Armand has driven away his wife and child because of what he thinks is her tainted blood, he carries the inheritance he holds in contempt.

In addition to its challenge to the concept of race, this story, like many other Chopin texts, calls into question the definition of love. We are told that Armand fell in love at first sight, a trait that runs in his family. This statement links Chopin's twin themes, and the ridiculous contention undercuts cultural clichés about both love and heredity. Students will enjoy debating the question of whether love at first sight is possible. Some studies of flirting behavior seem to show that men are subconsciously attracted to women whose body language signals receptiveness and whose symmetry and other physical qualities indicate health and fertility. Moreover, some of these factors seem to be cross- cultural, even universal, with people in widely separated societies choosing the same indicators of desirability. Chopin, like many of her readers, might question whether such attraction constitutes love. Most of us would contend that Armand knows as much about love as he does about how to use his power over his slaves. In fact, Chopin explicitly links Armand's happiness in his marriage to his treatment of the people under his control.

We should beware of using Armand as an example of whether love can overcome racial bias, however, since his father undoubtedly came from the same culture but resisted its constraints, though not openly. Whereas Armand's character seems to show the inability of erotic love to overcome racial barriers, parental love, on the other hand, remains solid, even if, as in Monsieur and Madame Valmondé's case, the child is adopted. Racial prejudice wins in the case of Désirée, however, and we must assume that she allows her child to die with her in the swamps rather than facing life with Armand's rejection. Some readers may be reminded of Toni Morrison's novel *Beloved*, in which a mother kills her child to free her from slavery. For Chopin, too, this may have been a heroic act. Though Désirée has a foster mother with the power to prevent her child's enslavement, she is aware of the realities of plantation life and of her child's limited future. Speculations about Armand's future may range from suicide to freeing the slaves to fleeing to Paris, with most readers hoping that whatever course he takes will be miserable.

It may be more difficult to see how this story relates to breaking cultural taboos in our own time and place. We do not face such rigid role requirements. Still, class barriers based on money and education — and sometimes race and religion as well — are difficult for some to overcome. Many women, especially in certain regions and ethnic groups, are socialized to be subservient, and women often choose to give up their power to men much like Armand. Homosexuals face multiple barriers. Sometimes, babies do not fit the image that their parents have of the perfect child. In 1998, in a case in which babies were switched in a hospital nursery, one mother rejected her birth child as ugly and too black, a commentary on the persistence of internalized racial stereotypes and the self-hate they engender. Although times have changed to a great degree, it is still possible in many homes to bring the wrong type of person home for dinner. We could ask students to imagine what type of person this would be in their own families.

In the three stories in this cluster, the female characters feel quite differently about their husbands. Calixta, in "The Storm" (p. 857), understands the demands of the culture but retains a position of superiority over her husband. She is able to control the household: Bobinôt brings her shrimp and worries that she will be angry about their coming in dirty after the storm. And although she does not actively seek the passion of her lover, Alcée, it is her physical hunger to which he responds. Her husband seems to fit into the same category as her child, Bibi; she loves him, but as someone inferior to herself. Perhaps skin color plays a more prominent role than gender in the power relationships in their story, giving the light-skinned Calixta the upper hand. If so, readers may want to take Chopin to task for this, arguing that her text contains unconscious prejudice. Louise Mallard in "The Story of an Hour" (p. 862) on the other hand, seems to have possessed little power during her marriage. Her love for her husband is colored by this imbalance of power; she muses when she thinks he is dead that she has sometimes loved him, but sometimes has not. She has been the conventional wife of her social class, dependent and childlike, and finds freedom — or death — preferable to the emotional slavery of marriage.

We might ask if love is love when not freely given. In "Désirée's Baby," the young wife worships her husband but is fearful of him. Not only does her own welfare depend on placating his temper, but the welfare of the slaves — with whom she empathizes and perhaps identifies — depends on her keeping him happy in the marriage. She is much like the abused wife who thinks that taking the blows will protect her children. Again, we might ask if this is what our students want to define as love, or if Désirée's dependence on the whims of a tyrant is something closer to masochism. We might question the husbands' love as well. Although we know little of Mr. Mallard in "The Story of an Hour," we may infer that he has been paternalistic and emotionally controlling and probably loves her as he would love a favorite pet. Bobinôt in "The Storm" is in the opposite position; he adores his wife in a slavish but unequal way. While reading "Désirée's Baby," we question whether Armand's selfish and immature eroticism and pride can be categorized as love at all. The marriage of Bobinôt and Calixta seems the strongest of the three, an ironic fact, since theirs is the marriage that we would expect, according to the usual cultural norms, to find threatened by the wife's act of adultery. The faithful wives of the other two marriages are destroyed.

Chopin's texts consistently question the received wisdom about marriage and its effect on both men and women. Although her own marriage seems to have been a happy one, her fiction portrays the institution as destructive, especially for women. She does not offer answers, however, arguing against literature that preaches. If she could examine the present state of marriage, including divorce, we could expect her to approve gains in freedom, but perhaps she would focus on the ways in which power continues to elude women in many cases. She would undoubtedly be proud of the resurgence of interest in her fiction and in the way that women of the late twentieth century have received her ideas about their empowerment, ideas in many ways far ahead of her time.

AFFAIRS OF LOVE:
RE-VISIONS OF "THE LADY WITH THE DOG" (p. 869)

ANTON CHEKHOV

The Lady with the Dog (p. 871)

Chekhov's classic short story "The Lady with the Dog" raises many questions about the psychology of adultery. The limited third-person narration relates the thoughts of the upper-class Russian male protagonist, Dmitri Gurov, but no one else, requiring the audience to deal with Dmitri's self-absorption and eventual loss of emotional control during his infatuation and later obsession with the lady of the title. Although Dmitri is "under forty," young adult readers may be tempted to see him as a man in the grips of a midlife crisis, especially since his lover is younger and we are told on the first page that he has a twelve-year-old daughter and sons in school. We are also told that he has had affairs in the past and are invited to think of him as promiscuous and unlikely to fall in love with anyone but himself. He rationalizes his tendency toward infidelity by speaking of women disrespectfully as "the lower race" and by painting his wife as a mediocre human being. We are also told that he is "afraid of her" and that he is not comfortable with men. Therefore, only with his paramours, seemingly inferior creatures with whom he can feel attractive and interesting, does he claim to feel truly free. Yet he feels hatred and disgust when his lovers show signs of maturity or desire, and seems to have contempt for any woman who gets too close.

The issue, therefore, becomes not so much an ethical evaluation of adultery as a question of the public mask versus the private persona of a man who does not have satisfying, authentic relationships with his wife or his peers. When at the resort city of Yalta, he even becomes obsessed with stories of romantic encounters men tell of such things as "a romance with an unknown woman, whose name he did not know," he imagines having this sort of anonymous, objectifying nonrelationship with the young lady he sees walking the dog. We might ask students to speculate on why such an affair might be attractive. College students, with their busy lives and determination to remain free of emotional commitments, sometimes are attracted to a lifestyle in which they "hook-up" with virtual strangers just for a night. Others who are more idealistic about love and sex may be involved in intense emotional relationships for the first time and may in fact be contemplating marriage at about the same age that Dmitri married, in his second year of college. In either case, students may find it difficult to get past negative judgments of both Dmitri and Anna, who engage in an affair outside of marriage but get emotionally entangled. Anna is faulted for her "strange and inappropriate" emotion after their sexual consummation of the flirtation, while Dmitri seems foolish and self-centered in one way or another throughout the story.

The attraction of the love affair for Dmitri seems directed less toward a connection with Anna as a human being than toward building an image of himself within the alternative reality the affair allows him. Women, he says, "loved in him not himself, but the man created by their imagination," and the story's end finds both Dmitri and Anna in "intolerable bondage" to the double life that they lead. Because he leads this double life, Dmitri comes to suspect the authenticity of all human behavior and speculates, "All personal life rested on secrecy, and possibly it was partly on that account that civilized man was so nervously anxious that personal privacy should be so respected." Discussion in class may center on whether this is true for students. Are there private "alternate realities" in which we feel like entirely different people than we are in our "real lives"? College itself, a world of its own away from the hometown in which we know our place, may offer the opportunity to be a different person. Do students feel "freer" to forge new identities in this environment? How long do they think one might continue to step in and out of alternate realities before longing for an integrated sense of self? Does the fact that Dmitri and Anna meet on vacation in Yalta — essentially on a spring break for wealthy Russian grown-ups — add to their sense of inhabiting a temporary alternate reality in which unconventional behavior is permissible?

Trying to forget her adultery with Dmitri is for Anna much like obsessing about ice cream and pizza when on a diet. The more she tries to forget, the more he occupies her memory. Romantic fantasies work in much this way. When they are separated, the lovers can recall only pleasure, but they are tormented by its elusiveness and temporality, and new meetings bring only misery and incomplete satisfaction. Most readers are not sympathetic when Dmitri shares with a friend his romantic reminiscences about the affair in Yalta with Anna, but students who have engaged in summer romances might understand them. This premise begins the musical *Grease*, a play that is often performed in high school productions and familiar to most college students, and whose characters are confronted by the differences between their personas on summer vacation and those assumed in a tough high school environment. Dmitri may also remind readers of the adolescent narrator of James Joyce's "Araby" (p. 828), who is jarred by the trivialities of the tawdry world into an epiphany about the false idolatry of courtly love. But while Joyce's narrator is brought to the consciousness that his formerly naïve worship of his friend's sister has been foolish, Dmitri, who is old enough to know better, is angered when his friend responds to his revelations of his affair with Anna by commenting on the flavor of the sturgeon they'd had for dinner. His obsession is intensified by the challenge to his romantic idealization of Anna, and he takes action to find her and renew their love affair.

Chekhov does not seem to be on Dmitri's side but instead seems to hold the self-absorbed lover up for our ironic reflection; the tables have been turned, and Dmitri has become as determined to grasp at life as the older women he earlier held in contempt. The ending leaves the lovers trapped in the classic tension of wanting something they can never have — the integration of their public and private lives. The irony is that the double life that has created the excitement now becomes the source of discontent. Another ending would have missed this point. On the other hand, the ending does seem abrupt. Its resistance of closure leaves the characters trapped but leaves the reader dissatisfied as well.

Discussions of how we define the word *love* can lead to deep thought or to cliché, and we might want to pose the question of whether what Dmitri feels for Anna is truly love. If love involves mutual respect and a concern for the emotional and physical well being of the beloved, then Dmitri's seeking out of Anna in her hometown — an invasion into her public space during a concert — and his insistence that they continue their clandestine affair threaten to embarrass her and place her in danger. His feelings therefore fall short of *love* according to this definition. The danger, on the other hand, adds to the erotic dimension of the relationship for Dmitri. This perhaps is love as *eros*. It might be useful to have students research the various Greek words that are translated as the English word *love* and to explore whether the Russian language broadens or narrows the concept.

Dmitri's reasons for falling in love may have more to do with his own needs than the qualities of Anna. He seems to need the energizing effects of danger He may find it exciting that Anna remains emotionally connected to him even while she returns to her husband. Furthermore, his wife seems to be a forceful adult woman, while Anna seems more like a girl. In fact, Anna is first seen with a small dog — a position that is somewhat childlike — and is described as young. Dmitri is seen at one point to walk his daughter to school on the way to a tryst with Anna; Chekhov's juxtaposition of the two females cannot be accidental, and we might ask if Dmitri in fact shares the immature impulses that pedophiles demonstrate, leading to an inability to be excited by a woman who could be his equal. Evaluations of whether their behavior is acceptable will depend on the ethical convictions of individual readers, and we may want to confine discussions to the pragmatic societal reasons why their behavior is good or bad for them and their families. While historical context plays a part and could be profitably explored, the Joyce Carol Oates story (p. 883) that follows Chekhov's original in this cluster demonstrates that the characters can be moved forward a century or two and across a continent and an ocean with little damage done to the plot's basic conflict. Similar points could be made about the issue of divorce. Divorce is easier to obtain today, but adultery still occurs. The comment that times have changed — one so often made rather smugly by young adult readers — seems to be refuted by a deeper analysis.

JOYCE CAROL OATES

The Lady with the Pet Dog (p. 883)

By choosing the title that she does, Joyce Carol Oates immediately invites us to connect her story with Anton Chekhov's "The Lady with the Dog" (p. 871). Looking at the texts together provides us with the opportunity to discuss with our students issues about canon formation and intertextuality. At earlier points in the history of literary criticism, much scholarly effort was expended in search of the influences of the works of one author on a later author, tracing evidence of a writer's reading habits, cataloging the books of his or her library, or finding references in commonplace books, journals where thoughts about a person's current reading could be recorded. We may encourage our students to record their reading responses in a journal or a dialogical notebook in which they can talk to themselves about a piece of literature and attempt to make it matter in their own lives or in their writing. We often challenge the creative writers in our classes to respond in a literary way, to write a parody or a serious piece of writing in symbiosis with one or more of the texts in the anthology, to translate it into a different language or dialect, to move it into a different setting, or to change its point of view or its ordering of time.

Chekhov was an innovative writer, and many twentieth century writers in the genres of fiction and drama openly claim him as an influence. Oates makes the influence explicit. Yet while we recognize influences, current literary theorists often read for intertextual connections rather than one-to-one correspondences or influences. When we have students compare and contrast the writings in this cluster, therefore, we need to encourage them to go beyond the obvious to examine subtle ways in which the stories interact with each other and to think about how the often-used technique of *allusion* may work — how the cultural connotations of words and phrases from canonical texts reverberate in the minds of readers.

Much of the pleasure of reading a symbiotic text like Oates's "The Lady with the Pet Dog" comes from the title's invitation to read it in relationship to the classic Chekhov short story. It might be interesting to have some students read the Oates story first and compare their understanding of it with that of students who read the two in chronological order. Having read Chekhov first gives the audience some advantages but also causes expectations to be thwarted in unexpected ways. Readers who come to Oates's story with Chekhov's setting in mind, for example, find themselves imagining the couple in a nineteenth century Russian opera house as they read the first section of Oates's text. This view must quickly be revised as the reader realizes the setting is the northeast United States in the twentieth century, with Albany and Nantucket replacing Moscow and Yalta and the couple riding in a car rather than a carriage. Questions immediately spring to mind about how the differences between the two cultures will change the story and how clichés about changing times and universal truths will be challenged or confirmed.

While we do not notice these cultural and historical issues at the beginning of the Oates story, readers do find immediately that the author has altered both the style and the perspective of Chekhov's tale in a particularly twentieth century way. The first three sentences are visual, concise, and declarative and tell us that we are seeing a man through the eyes of a particular narrator. The first sentence occupies its own paragraph, illustrating the content by its structure: when we are told that the crowd seems to move aside for him, we find white space parting the first two statements of fact. The punctuation of this opening — periods, commas, and paragraph spacing — slows the narrative pace to achieve a slow-motion effect. By the end of the second short paragraph, we have seen the reaction of a female character and realize that we will experience the story from her point of view, since we are told that she thinks at first that she may have "imagined him," and we have subconsciously entered into the slowing of time that she experiences. Short sentences still predominate as we enter into her panic, and punctuation again plays a part as Oates continues to slow the action through white space, periods, commas, semicolons, ellipses, and dashes. She intensifies emotion as the female protagonist signals the man to *"no — no — keep away"* and allows the reader to enter into the consciousness of her body's reaction to seeing him. By foregrounding the body, Oates captures the modern American Anna's feelings from the beginning, as she attempts to negotiate the competing demands of heart and head.

The connection between the physical act of making love and the conflict and *panic* that ensue is dramatically brought home in Anna's interior dialogue: "How slow love was to drain out of her, how fluid and sticky it was inside her head!" While Chekhov presents a male protagonist who deals with the impact of romantic obsession on his own ego, Oates gives us a female protagonist who describes her conflict in sensory terms, describing a body and spirit have become separated. Each conveys a sense of alternate reality: the world of the affair involves a different self, one that at first excites the male by its secret nature but that eventually causes both participants in the affair to feel disconnected and unsure of who they are. We might ask students if the lovers truly wish to be married to each other or if they simply wish to regain an integrated sense of self.

Unlike Chekhov's Dmitri, Oates's Anna is motivated by a sense of shame in addition to the split in consciousness, and Oates again highlights her emotions by isolating the word in a sentence fragment in a paragraph of its own: "Shame." In Chekhov's story, on the other hand, we see Anna's shame through Dmitri's jaded viewpoint as a "strange and inappropriate" pose in which she "mused in a dejected attitude like 'the woman who was a sinner' in an old-fashioned picture." Oates allows us to see the twentieth-century Anna as solidly human. We are inside her head as she seeks out and endures a clumsy session of sexual intercourse with her husband while thinking of her lover, as she experiences love as "the fluttering of silky, crazy wings in her chest," and as she thinks desperately of killing both her lover and his blind son to escape the situation. While these thoughts may not make us sympathetic with Anna, they help us know her in a way that her lover cannot and illustrate the stretching of the emotions to extremes for the woman as well as the man in a love affair. The story would have a much different effect if Oates, like Chekhov, had chosen the male lover's perspective for her narration. This Anna, perhaps, would remain simply "a lady with a dog" — the object of a man's musings about himself. The two stories taken together — much like Christopher Marlowe's "The Passionate Shepherd to His Love" (p. 846) and Sir Walter Ralegh's nymph's reply (p. 848) — show a fuller picture, ironically with the man viewing the situation romantically and the woman conveying the physicality of her reactions to it. While some readers may find her emotions too extreme and question whether the lovers are really trapped, others will see them as serious people who have created a bond they find difficult to break.

The ending of Oates's story implies a breaking of the "intolerable bondage" that Chekhov's narrator feels at a similar point. The modern Anna finally comes to a sense of separation from the lover. She has first briefly defined the affair as a sort of "accomplishment she would take back to Ohio and to her marriage" before moving the sexual encounter into the realm of love and emotional dependency. She comes to feel at the end that their separateness is part of the of the "triumph" of their coming together. Rather than feeling alienated and shamed, she feels grateful and free. While the man still seems to feel the burden of their double life, the woman has accepted, through the Joycean epiphany of glimpsing him as he prepares to face his other life, the fact that "he existed in a dimension quite apart from her; a mysterious being." To be human is to be separate but whole, and love may consist of finding happiness in "the craziest of accidents" in which individuals come together for whatever time they have.

Rather than elevating romantic love into "the highest achievement" or "the ulti-mate goal," Oates's ending makes romantic love seem less desperately important and binding than the characters in both stories have made it be. It thus becomes more satisfying and freeing for those willing to accept it as merely a part of a whole and separate life. Oates's ending may suggest that Anna can love both her husband and this "other husband" and still remain a whole human being.

For Oates a split in the psyche and a longing for a more permanent union with the lover are not necessary consequences of a continuing affair. This is not the only way in which she challenges Chekhov even while being inspired by him. Oates changes Chekhov's chronological time line to allow the emotional movement in the woman's mind and body to take center stage. We follow her from most intense distress and shame to triumph and freedom. Oates begins by imagining Anna's panic as Dmitri encounters her at the concert, and the four characters of the two stories can be seen as occupying the same world; in fact, on later readings we can make them overlap. However, she quickly separates out her modern characters in a flashback to their first parting and the woman's emo-tions directly following their affair and does not describe their meeting until the third section. Unlike Chekhov, Oates allows the reader to meet the husband as something more than an obsequious "flunky" but as a man who perhaps works too hard (he goes to sleep at the dining table) and who is not a successful lover, perhaps because he senses his wife's emotional absence. He is more likely to inspire our pity than the contempt his parallel in Chekhov's story may evoke. The similarities to Chekov are closest in the concert incident, and Oates's tech-nique allows us to follow the protagonist's emotions and to accept the suggestion first implanted in the title that these characters have something in common. Because Oates veers from the similarities in their meeting — the dog, for exam-ple, belongs to the man's son and the son is present, though blind — we would be less likely to accept these as stories that inform each other. By the time Anna meets her lover, furthermore, we know much about her emotions and care about what happens, another good reason for leaving the actual beginnings of the affair for the middle of the story rather than the outset.

Shame plays a part in the Chekhov narrative mainly as we infer it from Anna Sergeyevna's behavior as described from Dmitri's point of view, but Oates imagines her Anna as dealing consciously with the issue of shame. It is interest-ing that the word *shame* is used rather than the word *guilt*. While guilt may be felt when one breaks the rules of his or her own ethical system, shame is said to be more closely related to how one imagines being seen by others and is felt as an intense sort of embarrassment: we blush with shame. It may be that guilt involves remorse for something we have *done*, while shame concerns our evalu-ations of ourselves as worthless or bad human beings and defines who we *are*.

The endings of both Chekhov's and Oates's stories may leave readers unset-tled. Chekhov leaves his lovers trapped in unsatisfying bondage to a double life they do not want, and while some may gain satisfaction from the irony of Dmitri's change of mind about the excitement of the secret life and enjoy see-ing the philanderer entrapped in obsessive love, nothing of the happy ending or even justice is to be found as we put down the story. Oates, on the other hand, manages what seems like a happy ending, with Anna's epiphany and her relin-quishment of shame, but her interruption of her lover's question with the answer

"Yes!" abruptly leaves the reader in a state of ambiguity, trying to figure out what each speaker really means to say.

BETH LORDAN

The Man with the Lapdog (p. 897)

In a 1999 interview with *The Atlantic* in conjunction with the first publication of "The Man with the Lapdog," Beth Lordan gave the advice to writers, "Read, read, read, read, read. I think that's how most writers get there. Your read enough and it begins to leak out." In this cluster, the advice would seem to be fitly enacted. Both Joyce Carol Oates (p. 883) and Lordan have read (perhaps read, read, read, read, read) Anton Chekhov's original (p. 871) and depend on their own readers' knowledge of the story for subtle nuances we might otherwise miss. On the other hand, Lordan's story works independently of Chekhov's text, and readers find it moving without picking up on the allusion to Chekhov at all. While Oates creates twentieth-century American characters and situations closely related to Chekhov's nineteenth-century Russian lovers locked in their secret double lives, even giving her protagonist the name Anna, Lordan ages the characters and keeps the love affair safely in the brief moments of her male protagonist's fantasy life.

Parallels remain teasingly indirect. The "lady" in the titles of Chekhov's and Oates's narratives becomes in Lordan's story a specific man — a sixty-seven-year-old American who has retired to his wife's home country of Ireland. Lordan relates in the 1999 interview that she had "spent last spring in Galway, Ireland" and, unlike many Irish-Americans, did not feel that she had finally come home but that she was in a "foreign place." She claims to have been surprised "when stories started showing up" with Irish settings. So we could speculate that her reaction was much like her character Lyle's resistance to romanticizing the place and playing the native. This resistance plays an ironic part in the plot. The American tourists, Laura and her dying husband, Mark, speculate about the life of the man they take to be an old Galway country gentleman and have a laugh when they discover he is American. Later he takes on the task of finding a map for the couple so that they can tour the Irish countryside. His connection to Ireland becomes sealed at the end of the story, however, as he responds to his wife's comment that the American couple are "lovely people" with the response in an unaffected Irish brogue: "They are so. And it's a sad thing, it is." He has "come home" to his wife, to Ireland, and to himself in a way that the characters of the other stories are unable to do in such a thorough way.

As the story begins, however, Lyle's attitude toward his wife resembles the mix of contempt and husbandly fear that Chekhov's Dmitri feels toward his "mediocre" wife. So while we catch no unfiltered glimpses of Dmitri's wife in Chekhov and know nothing of the wife of Anna's lover in Oates, Lyle's Irish wife, Mary, becomes an important character in Lordan's version of the tale and in a sense becomes "the lady with the dog" for her husband, whose love for her is renewed through their encounter with the younger couple. Lordan transforms the husband of the story into the sympathetic figure of a man dying of cancer rather than the unattractive "flunky" of Chekhov's tale or the clumsy, ordinary husband of Oates's. Yet the discontented husband meets a younger woman (this time one just "coming into middle age") walking by the sea in the presence of a dog (a dachshund who is a "pretty, girlish little thing") even though it is he, as in Oates's version, who owns the dog. While he doesn't even hint to Laura that he would like to have a love affair, he imagines a bed she has recently left and melds for a moment with her husband to "remember" touching her as they walked. Because Laura's husband will soon be taken out of the picture by death, Lyle imagines her returning to Ireland and sees a younger version of himself being with her. His dream is interrupted by his wife's return, however, and Lyle's love affair with Laura does not reach consummation even in fantasy.

As we have seen in the earlier two stories, the early attraction and the later tension between the lovers revolves around the conflict between the sense of another self that the affair brings to life and the desire to be whole again and not double. The invasion of the private into the public, as happens at the concert in both Oates and Chekhov, threatens the secret life at the same time it renews and prolongs it. When Lyle's wife, Mary, finds the map for Lyle and offers to go with him to deliver it, the invasion of reality, in the form of the public and private life of their marriage, shatters the alternate reality of the fantasy love affair. Lyle's tension is evident by his inability to look directly at Mark or Laura and by his speaking in a "voice too hearty for the words." What for Lyle has been a love story becomes reinterpreted as an act of kindness toward a dying man and toward a wife who is moving toward acceptance that her love and the trip to Ireland cannot bring herself and her husband "together in joy to the edge of life."

What may really be happening is a letting go both for Laura and for Lyle. The merging of his private fantasy and his real life cause Lyle to embrace married love and to recognize that he and his own wife are "lovely people" themselves who have much to live for together. This change of attitude is not what Lyle could have expected as a result of Mary's intrusion into his private fantasy relationship. His caution in telling his wife about Mark's illness is undoubtedly based on his knowledge that her compassion would inevitably lead to an invitation to tea that would threaten his secret love for Laura and cause reality to set in. Lyle has no real hope of ever being part of Laura's life, but the fantasy itself has formed an alternate reality that can cause his heart to thump when Mary walks in on him in the act of dreaming about Laura. His search for the map is symbolic of his desire to give Laura something, much as the young boy in James Joyce's "Araby" (p. 828) desperately tries to get a gift from the bazaar for his lady, a neighbor's sister who has shown no interest in him. Petrarch, the early Renaissance Italian inventor of the courtly love sonnet, wrote poems in worship of an unattainable lady named Laura, and we might speculate about Lordan's choice of names. Lyle's wife carries the name of the epitome of worship and chaste love, the Virgin Mary. Could Lordan's use of these names be ironically significant? Mary gives aid but is suspicious enough about her husband's desperate search for the map to change her bedtime habits and to accompany him to meet the couple the next day. But her presence and her reaction to Mark's illness change the situation entirely. While the meaning of the ending may become an issue, Lyle's solidarity with his wife seems sincere as they walk together, touching each other in the same way he had imagined himself touching and walking with Laura. The fact that he earlier "remembered" walking with Laura in just such a way indicates that he and Mary have walked in this way before as well. Rather than losing something, Lyle seems to have regained and enriched his love for his wife as a result of his imagined affair with Laura, a stranger on whom he may have been projecting his wife's forgotten qualities all along.

By reading all three of the stories of this cluster, readers examine love or imagined love from three different perspectives. The male protagonists in Chekhov's original and in Lordan's much later version are swept up in romantic fantasies. The center of consciousness in Chekhov's story is located in Dmitri's self-absorbed analysis of the alternate ego he acquires through the imaginations of women and the eventual trap this other self creates for him. In Lordan's story, the male character also uses the woman to picture himself in a new light, but the imagination involved is his own, and he does not enter into a sexual relationship with Laura, nor do we expect him to ever do so, in spite of his dreams of himself as a younger man with Laura in the future. Both men feel the need to dismiss the husband in some way in order to justify their adultery, whether real or imagined. Dmitri must view Anna's husband as inferior while Lyle imagines himself moving into Laura's life when Mark is safely dead. In Oates's story, however, the center of consciousness is Anna's less romantic, more physical, analysis. When we read Chekhov's text, we are invited to ponder along with Dmitri the psychological complications of this division of the world into public and private spheres, the paradox of the freedom and entrapment of the illicit love affair.

In Lordan's story, we similarly explore with the narrator the nature of romantic fantasy and the result when it comes into forced conflict with reality. Rather than remaining separate, we come to see that Lyle's two worlds may have overlapped all along, and that his thoughts about the imagined Laura may have been based on memories of the real woman Mary that can deepen their relationship in the remaining years of their lives. The disadvantage of the male perspective, of course, is that we can only guess at what the women may be thinking. We face a similar disadvantage in Oates's story when we try to imagine the feelings of her lover. We see the expressions on his face and suspect that he may feel a bitterness and frustration much like Dmitri's, but all of this is interpreted by Anna, so we cannot know. Lyle and Mary have been through a long life together, arguing about their children and dealing with the differences that come from growing up in different countries. The problem with their marriage may be that Lyle has lost his initial passion for Mary and must regain a vision of her as his lover rather than as the "mediocre" wife Chekhov's protagonist tells us he has married. At the end of the story he seems to have moved toward this renewal as he begins to speak her language and walk side by side with her. We know less about Dmitri's wife, because our only knowledge of her comes from a husband in the process of justifying his adultery, but it may be that Dmitri himself knows little about his wife and that this is the problem with his marriage.

With their wives, the male protagonists are unable to see themselves as they wish to see themselves. Both Annas seem unable to be truly there for and with their husbands. Not only do they physically escape to resorts and hotel rooms, but the Anna of Oates's story even absents herself during a sexual encounter with her husband that she has initiated. All of the lovers give to the person outside of marriage the attention that might be profitably given to the marriage partner. All become obsessed to a certain extent. All the attractions begin by the seaside, where people find themselves outside of their normal reality, and all must eventually deal with the conflict between that reality and the alternate world of the affair. The extent to which the protagonists feel themselves trapped or free differ greatly at the ends of each story, however. The optimism and the approximation toward the happy ending increase with successive versions of the story. Chekhov's original leaves the lovers entrapped, Oates's later retelling allows her female protagonist to accept her double life, and Lordan's version, the most recent evocation of Chekhov's tale, reinforces the strength of marital love.

ROMANTIC ILLUSIONS: CULTURAL CONTEXTS FOR DAVID HENRY HWANG'S *M. BUTTERFLY* (p. 908)

DAVID HENRY HWANG

M. Butterfly (p. 908)

Because both the play and the screenplay for the movie *M. Butterfly* were written by David Henry Hwang, the significant differences between the two can lead to fruitful discussions about revision and about adapting a text for a different audience and purpose. Although many classes will not have the time to view the video recording of the movie in class, watching it together provokes more immediate and open discussion than having students view it on their own time. Substituting a viewing of the film for a reading of the play, however, focuses its interpretation in a different direction, losing many nuances that only the original drama offers. The most dramatic differences come with the linear approach to time and the realistic settings and presentation of action used in the movie, a major departure from the play's flashbacks, surreal atmosphere, and first-person narration by Gallimard himself. The unveiling of Song Liling and the impact of the movie's wonderfully absurd closing scene, kept much as it is in the play, seem to be part of a different reality. Whether the jarring difference in tone at the film's conclusion is appropriate is an aesthetic issue that we can debate if we are familiar with both texts. I give students the option of reading the play before we see the movie or waiting to read it later, but set up response assignments to require comparison and contrast. It is also useful to give them some background information about Puccini's opera *Madama Butterfly* beforehand and to discuss the preconceived notions that most Westerners have concerning Asian culture. Asian American students in the class can contribute insights about the mixed messages they have received from their families about cultures in China, Japan, Korea, and other countries.

Hwang, like many children of immigrants, grew up knowing little about Asian culture, since his father was primarily American and fundamentalist Christian. He plays on the tendency of most Westerners to lump all Asians into one culture, having his French accountant, Rene Gallimard, see his Chinese opera singer as an incarnation of the Japanese geisha in Puccini's opera and himself as the American sailor Pinkerton. Gallimard's notions about "the Orient" are romantic and racially biased, with gender, culture, and geography linked in the drama, as they are in the colonial worldview. The geisha Butterfly in the opera is a male fantasy of dominance. She is fifteen, submissive and obedient, virginal yet eagerly in love, self-abnegating, and possessed of infinite patience. She is an exotic plaything whose adoration is encouraged and abused by the American sailor, who abandons her with empty promises when it is time to move on. At the end of the opera, Butterfly tragically commits suicide, giving up her child to Pinkerton's American wife in the same manner that she has earlier renounced her religion, the respect of her family, and the chance to marry a man of her own culture. Parallels with colonialism and with current Western domination of Third World countries seem obvious but may not at first occur to students. Hwang subverts the representation of Asia as an innocent and exotic plaything by the absurdity of his play, and he ends with the roles having been reversed, Gallimard becoming Butterfly. The Chinese character Song Liling plays the perfect Asian woman, innocent but possessed of esoteric sexual knowledge. Gallimard's self-deception is a factor of his selfishness; had he considered Song Liling to be a real person, rather than an objectified myth, he would not have remained ignorant of her (his) true nature.

Students, like most newspaper readers who first read about it, are shocked that Hwang's play is based on the true story of French diplomat Bernard Boursicot's twenty-year love affair with Shi Pei Pu, a singer with the Peking Opera. When Boursicot discovered after his trial for espionage that his lover, who he thought to be the mother of his son, was actually a man and that the whole world was laughing about it, he refused to believe it for a time and then unsuccessfully attempted suicide. The least believable parts of Hwang's plot line actually come from the historical accounts of Boursicot's life, first brought to the attention of Americans — including Hwang — in the *New York Times* on May 11, 1986. Hwang claims that Boursicot's self-deception puzzled him, as it does most of us, until he connected it with the myth that Asian women are like Madame Butterfly and with the principle of Asian theater that only a man can act the part of an idealized woman.

The mystery of Gallimard's ignorance of sex is partially explained by the coldness of his marriage in the play, a marriage of convenience. We are given glimpses of his inadequacy in sexual encounters with Western women. His first experience is shown in flashback, and his affair with an American student named Renee androgynously echoes Gallimard's. Renee, he says, is "too masculine." Only the relationship with Song Liling, which borders on sado-masochism and which gives him the illusion of absolute power, excites and satisfies him. It is hard to imagine how Gallimard can be fooled, and students have trouble getting past their inability to believe that the facts of human anatomy escaped Gallimard or his real-life counterpart Boursicot. The fact that Boursicot was only twenty in 1964 when his affair with Shi began does not convince people of the same age that he could have intercourse with someone and not be aware of his partner's body. His unconscious self-deception, however, is the point of the story, and Hwang provides much evidence for it.

The play's protagonist is fooled because he so deeply desires to be fooled. But the very definition of sexual identity is called into question; perhaps Gallimard desires in Song Liling the qualities he denies within himself. Whereas he thinks of himself as the active male partner in intercourse, Song Liling explains at the trial that Gallimard has been passive, letting Song do all the work. The play's title hints at the ambiguity: to whom does it refer — Monsieur, Madame, Mr., Ms., Gallimard, or Song Liling? In addition to raising issues of sexual and cultural identity, the structure of Hwang's play questions the constructions that we impose on reality. As Gallimard explains himself, we enter into his version of reality. The same actors obviously play several roles, further questioning identity. Perhaps this is why the play is more compelling than the more linear and realistic film, where we depend too much upon our own interpretations of what we see rather than relying on the narrator's point of view. In the courtroom scene in act 3, scene 1, Song Liling makes the play's point explicit when he maintains that men love the fantasy rather than the woman and when he suggests that this is true as well of international relations. Hwang deliberately draws the political analogy between sexual exploitation and imperialism.

Cultural Contexts:

PAUL GRAY, *What Is Love?* (p. 958)
ANASTASIA TOUFEXIS, *The Right Chemistry* (p. 961)
NATHANIEL BRANDEN, *Immature Love* (p. 964)

Students tend to be romantics. Many accept the concept of love and are surprised to find that scholars have questioned its universality. While debate rages among Western social historians about whether romantic love is an invention of medieval literature, students see the answer as self-evident: *Of course, it isn't,* they think; *what fool would think it was?* Evolutionary and biochemical "proofs" also strike them as a waste of time, an attempt to quantify the spiritual essence of human relationships. Some eagerly educate us on the matter, using as proof their personal experiences with the difference between infatuation and (their recently or soon to be found) undying love, their sincerity touchingly imprinting the page as they write. While remaining sensitive to their interpretations, we should hold them to more carefully considered evidence. Some may take the view that it's all about sex, with love being a rationalization or a trap. Classroom discussions of multiple definitions of love and of the issues raised by our texts should stress the complexity of love's social construction in cultures and challenge students to examine their first assumptions more closely. These essays lend themselves to assignments in critical analysis, since each presents a thesis about love that is supported by evidence. Students can examine and evaluate three professional writers' handling of a similar theme.

The texts in this cluster that provide contexts for the love of Rene Gallimard for his fantasy of Song Liling deal with playwright David Henry Hwang's native culture: the United States in the last decades of the twentieth century. This is appropriate, since Hwang's play (p. 908) speaks primarily to American attitudes toward love and difference, even though none of its main characters is American. Paul Gray (p. 958) and Anastasia Toufexis (p. 961) produced their articles for a *Time* issue focusing on love for the week of Valentine's Day in 1993. Nathaniel Branden's (p. 964) point of view is more scholarly but more problematic; as a psychologist he has focused on self-esteem, and as a social and political thinker he tends toward the extreme individuality of the objectivist and libertarian movements. Gray in "What Is Love?" begins with a questioning title, which is followed by a series of questions in an epigraph, as he engages song lyrics in syntactic wordplay. His essay doesn't provide answers. After tracing a bit of cultural history and touching on some scientific studies, he ends with another series of questions and a final surrender to love's seemingly "preposterous and mysterious" nature. Gray's words recall the tone and theme of M. *Butterfly*, with its paradox that Gallimard is unable to love the real person behind the fantasy of Song Liling. The ironic, black comedy of the play defines the Western male fantasy of love as pathetic (in more than one sense of the word) and absurd. Toufexis in "The Right Chemistry" grants, as does Gray, that we do not want our illusions about love explained by science. Like Gallimard, we prefer the fantasy to the reality. Hwang's protagonist and the historical French diplomat on which he is based practice incredible self-deception to keep love mysterious, illustrating the desire to which Toufexis refers in her closing sentence. Even anatomy is denied to retain the illusion of exotic romance.

Some students may protest that the homoerotic implications of the play's love story make the studies of heterosexual love to which Gray and Toufexis refer seem irrelevant. However, recent researchers of body language state that the same subliminal signals are exchanged by both homosexuals and heterosexuals. The movement of fingers on a drinking straw or the stem of a glass indicates "feminine" receptivity, for example, regardless of whether the person sending or receiving the signal is male or female. Such findings suggest to some scientists that human courtship behavior is learned rather than biochemical and evolutionary, though students may interpret the significance of these findings differently, drawing conclusions about the biological nature of homosexuality instead.

Branden's distinction between mature and immature love, based on psychological factors having their genesis in childhood, relates most directly to Hwang's characters in the play. Unlike Branden's mature lovers, whose strengths complement each other, Gallimard and Song are both essentially passive, seeking self-esteem from outside sources and from destructive behavior toward each other. Gallimard fantasizes that Song is a Madame Butterfly waiting to be rescued, but he is also an immature lover, seeing her only as a source of gratification and not as a human being. Branden says that one characteristic of immature love is "that the man or woman does not perceive his or her partner realistically; fantasies and projections take the place of clear vision" (para. 15). He goes on to say that the lover subconsciously recognizes reality but chooses not to see it, to play the game. Through most of the 1960s Branden was the lover and anointed successor of philosopher and novelist Ayn Rand, twenty-five years his senior, with the permission of both their spouses. After their break in 1968, precipitated by his adultery with the young woman who became his second wife, Branden went on to become a successful psychotherapist and writer. He departs from Rand's privileging of logos over pathos, arguing instead that emotions should be integrated into reason rather than suppressed. He retains many of her precepts, however, the most relevant here being the assertion that each human being has a right to exist for his or her own sake, neither sacrificing self to others nor others to self. Also important is the prohibition against force, whether exerted by individuals or by groups.

The relationship between the lovers in Hwang's play depends on illusions of sacrifice and force, and in this sense they are compatible lovers. And at the end, Gallimard, now in his true personality as the masochistic Butterfly, commits the ultimate self-sacrifice, suicide. In the final enigmatic scenes of the play, we see something of Song's needs as well. In analyses of the play, most critics tend to be so taken with Gallimard's self-delusion that we forget that Song also plays the game. He knows that the roles are reversed all along, that he is the one who exploits the innocence of Gallimard. The reversal becomes explicit at the end as he cries out for his Butterfly, his compatible immature lover.

IS THIS LOVE? (p. 968)

WILLIAM FAULKNER
A Rose for Emily (p. 969)

Just as Ann Petry's "Like a Winding Sheet" (p. 1603) gains much from an understanding of its time, William Faulkner's "A Rose for Emily" depends on a sense of place, of the social world in which the story's events occur. An intricate history of family relationships and social hierarchies structure William Faulkner's imaginary Mississippi town of Jefferson, the county seat of Yoknapatawpha County, where most of his fiction has its roots. Any outsider, anyone breaking the strict rules of conformity, is suspect here. On the other hand, belonging to the right family or having the right connections grants one indulgences, no matter how eccentric one's behavior seems to be. Readers may want to consider issues raised by such a world in which everyone is given a particular role. Love and courtship, like all other parts of life, are the community's business, and the community tells Miss Emily Grierson's story, appropriately using the unusual first-person-plural point of view, *we*. Faulker's story depends on character and plot, and its impact depends on its ironic ending.

Accustomed from childhood to stories of the macabre, today's students may be less impressed with the plot and its chilling conclusion than its first readers were in the 1930s, but they are quicker to spot the psychological implications of Miss Emily's strange and oppressive relationship with her father. They also enjoy recent critical speculations about Homer Barron's possible homosexuality, which are based on the narrators' statement that Barron likes the company of men, perhaps simply referring to his preference for barrooms and stereotypically male activities. On the other hand, students who see the recent dramatic presentation of the story on video are led into believing that Emily and Homer consummate their relationship, a reading that assumes facts Faulkner preferred to leave unresolved. Although we often cannot spare the time in class to read the story aloud, a skilled reader can highlight Faulkner's technique, demonstrating how flashbacks, suspense, and narrative pace enhance the story. The long, periodic sentence that closes Faulkner's narrative illustrates his strategy in microcosm, slowing the action for dramatic effect and providing us with an example of inductive organization.

Readers questioning Emily's actions need to consider her earlier denial of her father's death and to think about what might cause such dependency. She is desperate to find a husband in a time and place where women are failures if they do not attract a man, and Emily has been thwarted by her father's possessiveness at the age this might have happened. Emily has inherited or learned a family tendency to hold on past the time of letting go. Because we see their relationship through the limited vision of the town, we do not know what Homer's intentions are, nor do we know how much of the relationship exists in Emily's imagination. Our limited point of view also makes it hard to judge *when* Emily becomes disturbed. When she loses Homer through rejection perhaps? Or much earlier when her father dies? We can imagine cultures that would consider her to be not sick but evil, an aristocrat who is so determined to have her way that she kills out of pride and self-will rather than love. Most cultures would censure her poisoning of her beloved so that she could sleep with his corpse, but we might ask if she simply takes to extremes the dictates of her culture that she must have a man to have self-worth.

The story's perspective adds to the ambiguity of Emily's motives and allows the reader more room for speculation. To give the narration over to Emily might make it an interesting psychological study, but would rob the story of its mystery and irony. It would also remove an important collective character, the town itself. If Southern small-town culture determines who Emily Grierson will be, the influence is mutual. They own her and live through her; the adjectives at the end of paragraph 51 describe their ambivalence and her seeming omnipresence in their lives. The contention that Faulkner is writing less a personal love story than an allegory about the South seems credible in this context. The collective conspiracy to hide and overlook the corruption and the forced ownership of others — body and soul — that characterizes much of the South's history seems aptly symbolized by the events of "A Rose for Emily." And it is interesting that the only character who probably knows the whole story is the black butler who takes care of Emily and thus facilitates her insanity. Some readers might note that the maintenance of Southern society is thus dependent on the continuance of slavery, even after emancipation. Of course, the story could just as well be a warning about what happens to women who get mixed up with Yankees. Students with roots in the South may provide insights about how the South has changed or remained the same as Faulkner described it in 1930.

The African American male protagonist of Petry's "Like a Winding Sheet" and the aging Southern belle of Faulkner's "A Rose for Emily" both find themselves prevented from living out the roles that society says they must. Petry's protagonist cannot live up to his presumed role as the strong male provider and achiever because the same society that makes his sense of manhood depend upon this role denies him the chance to assume it. He is unable to deal with it and instead reacts to something in his wife that reminds him of his oppression. Emily, too, finds the ways blocked to filling her expected role in society and in marriage. She takes what she needs to feel like a woman, even though she must kill to keep the illusion. When we vote on possible punishments for Emily, "jurors" are quicker to send her to a mental hospital, and the black man of Petry's story is usually consigned to prison. Because many of our students are old enough to serve on actual jury panels, the issues raised by this difference are worth discussing. Do we forgive Emily more easily because she is a woman? Do race and social standing play a subliminal role in our assignment of responsibility? Or does she just seem more clearly insane in the legal sense of the term? The stories provide us also with an issue of the definition of *love*. In our evaluations of Petry's and Faulkner's main characters, Petry's protagonist usually wins. Students argue that he loves his wife, and his beating of her is more about his frustration than about their relationship. Others maintain that if he really loved her, he would not take out his frustrations on her, no matter what the circumstances. Most readers do not see Emily's feelings as love but rather as the obsession and fantasy of a sick mind.

RAYMOND CARVER

What We Talk About When We Talk About Love (p. 976)

Although earlier characterizations of Raymond Carver as a minimalist have been challenged as a result of his later work in the 1980s, the term still applies to the stories in the collection *What We Talk About When We Talk About Love*, including this one, which gives the book its title. Carver said of these stories that he cut them "to the marrow, not just to the bone." By using a first-person narrator within the story and limiting our knowledge of other characters to what that narrator experiences, Carver allows his readers little information from which to make interpretations, leaving many questions unanswered. Since we have defined an *issue* in this anthology as a question about which reasonable people may disagree, we should therefore expect to encounter many issues in our reading of Carver. When the narrator passes on to us the stories that Mel tells him, for example, we are limited to just what the narrator hears and observes and must further take into account the fact that Mel is probably drunk. Perhaps, because he is drunk, he is weaving fact and fiction or remembering things incorrectly. Or the old saying *in vino veritas* may instead come into play, and we can trust his word *because* he is too drunk to mind his words.

Carver's biography is relevant to "What We Talk About When We Talk About Love" because he lived many years as an alcoholic. His stories sometimes reflect the state of his first marriage as well, one that began too early — making him the father of two children by the time he was twenty — and that ended in divorce in 1982, the year after this story was published. His dialogue captures the realities of everyday life, but the prosaic details of conversations and commonplace actions mask turning points for his characters. Greatly influenced by the Russian writer Anton Chekhov, Carver leads his characters into a "Chekhovian moment," when the soul of the character is revealed in a subtle way. This moment seems to approach for the characters of this story as they come to see the gulf between their attempts at defining love and the glimpse of love Mel gives in his anecdote about an old couple injured in an accident. Perhaps pathos is a more precise answer to this issue of the definition of love than all the logic we can muster.

Ironically, we are told immediately that Mel is a cardiologist — a heart doctor — and that this ethos gives him the right to talk about love. He wants to think of love as the Greek *agape*, as something spiritual. His wife Terri, on the other hand, defines love in the context of an abusive relationship that she had in the past with a man named Ed. She can understand the sort of passion that leads one to kill or to die for what she calls love, and her insistence that Ed loved her implies that something is wanting in the sort of love Mel offers. Though Ed is not present and is, in fact, dead, his definition of love is the one with which the characters must contend. The narrator Nick and his wife Laura still bask in the warmth of newlywed bliss; their love is comfortably physical; they touch and kiss from time to time in response to the conversation. And love gets a bit too easy as the neighbors reassure each other that they are loved, cheapening the word *love* in the glow of the gin they are drinking.

The story of the old man who is depressed because they are both swaddled in casts and he cannot see his wife is juxtaposed with Mel's desire to talk to his kids and his fantasies about arranging a painful death for his ex-wife. The result is depressing, and the story ends with the narrator listening to their hearts beating as the gin runs out and the room gets dark. Whatever love is, we can conclude that they don't have it. Although Mel does not drag Terri through the kitchen by her ankles, an undercurrent of hostility and dissatisfaction runs through their conversation, and he sometimes becomes verbally abusive. If, as the cliché goes, love and hate are twins, the intensity of Mel's desire to let bees loose to kill his ex-wife indicates that he has strong feelings for her. His feelings for Terri, on the other hand, seem peculiarly bland. Terri longs for the passion of Ed. Students are likely to conclude that both are fairly sick puppies.

Mel's interest in knights may provide a clue to what Carver is saying about romantic love. Some scholars have maintained that romantic love as we define it comes from the courtly love tradition of medieval Europe. Carver undercuts the idea of a man performing feats of daring for his fair lady through sarcastic humor, profanity, and the increasing inebriation of the conversation's participants. Although the story of the old couple seems to indicate that true love exists, we have to remember that the story comes through Mel. Carver does not articulate a definition of love for us, nor does he come up with one answer for the question implied in his title. Because assigning Carver's story, we can ask students to come up with their own definitions and to relay their anecdotes of love. This will allow a more informed discussion of the subtexts of both their stories and Carver's.

Carver's "What We Talk About When We Talk About Love" allows us to see little of the motivation of its characters, letting us eavesdrop on a conversation. William Faulkner's "A Rose for Emily" (p. 969) also limits our vision, depicting the title character as a statue or idol observed from afar by a close-minded town. The characters who hurt others — Ed and Emily — are made frantic and desperate by something in their lives, and their strong emotions overflow into their personal relationships. Because we hear of Ed in the context of a discussion of love, we may accept the motive of his violence as connected with the power of his immature love for Terri, but perceptive readers will challenge this assumption as simplistic. Similarly, our views of Terri, and Homer as victims must take into account the tendency of immature lovers to find partners who play compatible games, as Nathaniel Branden points out in the essay "Immature Love" (p. 964) in the previous cluster. As instructors, we have done best by our students if they leave our discussion with a more complicated view of love than what they had at the beginning.

F. SCOTT FITZGERALD

Winter Dreams (p. 986)

In the first few paragraphs of F. Scott Fitzgerald's exposition, he develops the metaphorical context that informs the entire story. Dexter Green, an early draft of Jay Gatsby, is an ambitious romantic, longing for the rewards of the American dream. Students readily see the symbolic implications of a fallow golf course in wintry Minnesota, with the promise of a glorious future where "gay colors fluttered in summer" are suggestive of dreaming riches to come. Dexter longs for the immense possibilities of life, the "fleeting brilliant impression of the summer at Sherry Island." Unfortunately for Dexter, he meets a woman who embodies all his illusions and fantasies about the possibilities of a life with great wealth. Judy Jones, an early draft of Daisy Buchanan, becomes for Dexter a symbol of everything he can't have. Despite the trouble and pain she causes him, his desire for her grows stronger and more self-destructive. And although Fitzgerald writes that "The helpless ecstasy of losing himself in her was opiate rather than tonic," Dexter seems aware that yielding to Judy will bring him only agony. Indeed, when he goes off with Judy at the dance and in effect breaks his engagement to Irene, both Dexter and the reader know this is simply the beginning of the end of their relationship. The knowing helplessness of Dexter's infatuation certainly says something about America's dizzy infatuation with the surface glitter of the Twenties and our ongoing delusion that we can somehow buy happiness. Although the cultural implications of the story are rich indeed, most students will focus on the central love relationship, especially since we have placed the story in the context of dubious love affairs.

Is Dexter in love with Judy? The point of this problematic question is to have students construct their own answers as they argue what love might mean in this context. Surely he does, as he himself says. And surely he cannot, since he sees too clearly into Judy's flawed nature. College students can be both innocent and experienced about these kinds of contradictory emotional pulls, and their arguments can benefit from these nuances. Clearly Dexter loves what Judy represents to him — wealth, beauty, youth, and privilege — and yet few critics would want to be so dogmatic about anyone's reasons for loving another as to say that Dexter has simply symbolized Judy. Perhaps there is some of that in all deep loves.

Dexter is so fixated (along with America) on youth that he assumes he will someday be too old for love. It might be interesting to ask students if he is talking here about erotic love, although it might be painful or amusing for professors to hear college students assuming that once past forty (certainly fifty) sexual desire is a bit unseemly.

Dexter's passionate love is clearly volatile, as some but certainly not all intense relationships are. His relationship with Irene is unlikely to be as mercurial and probably is a good deal more stable. But this contrast is part of Fitzgerald's point here about the Twenties and its recklessness, its pursuit of excess and extravagance. Fitzgerald himself knew the price to be paid for such indulgence in his own life as represented in most of his fiction. One of my students noted, "If you play with fire, eventually you get burned." Prosaic but apt.

Dexter seems to be crying over his lost youth. Students ten yours younger than Dexter might see his sorrow over lost youth as poignant; middle-aged readers might see his moroseness as immaturity. It is fitting, says the middle-aged professor, that we give up the illusions of youth, of eternal summers and desire unending. But students are much more sympathetic to Dexter's loss — and rightly so. Perhaps more metaphorically, however, Dexter is sad over the loss of a certain passionate intensity, a certain sense of wonder and possibility, and this is sad, especially if we think of the last page of *The Great Gatsby* and its melancholy over the lost possibility of America's democratic promise. At least from the perspective of those in their forties and fifties, however, Dexter's world-sorrow will probably be short lived; he will probably dance again and love again.

Money and class, as mentioned in the story's first sentence, are crucial to these characters. Desire for more is the thematic center of the story. Of course, as Lacan reminds us, desire is an empty signifier that cannot be filled by money or power or Judy. But we beat on, boats against the current. Students will not miss the symbolic references to wealth here and the intimate and revelatory connections between Judy and financial success.

It might be interesting to speculate with students what "that thing" refers to in the last sentence. Lost youth is one obvious candidate but so are innocence, early infatuation, unbridled optimism, and a belief in the endless possibilities of life. Fitzgerald, of course, is often remembered as the writer who claimed that there are no second acts in America, and Dexter seems to think so also. Students might disagree.

People fall in love with dangerous people for numerous reasons, including fear of loneliness, desperation, a need for affirmation of any sort, a desire to be punished, and so forth. Students will be able to list many plausible motivations. Terri seems to need to be loved, Dexter needs to dream, and Homer probably just needs a temporary lover. But more important than these mundane explanations is to have students try to fit motivation to a specific character's behavior. When they do this, like the characters in Raymond Carver's story (p. 976), they will see the vast complexity of love and its infinite manifestations. We always want to remind our students that most of their notions are socially derived and historically situated. Indeed, all three characters are victims, at least in the most abstract sense that they inherit attitudes about love from a culture that rarely gives us a chance to shape unique destinies. Perhaps Emily, Judy, and Ed are also victims. But they act in human ways, as we all do. Terri, Homer, and Dexter are all children of complex, varied, and powerful social ideologies. Having students explore the sources of their notions of love seems more relevant than any specific idea they have about these characters. Stressing why over what usually pays off in critical depth.

TROUBLED MARRIAGES (p. 1003)

ANNE SEXTON

The Farmer's Wife (p. 1003)

Classes that read the fairy tales of the first cluster of Chapter 12, "Living in Families," of *Making Literature Matter* find themselves in a world that Anne Sexton shares. In her 1971 collection *Transformations*, Sexton retells Grimm fairy tales with a feminist slant, reinterpreting characters like Cinderella and Snow White. "The Farmer's Wife" comes from an earlier collection, her 1960 *To Bedlam and Part Way Back*, but it shares with the fairy tales a bitter ambivalence about women's roles in twentieth-century American society. Like Robert Lowell, whose "To Speak of the Woe That Is in Marriage" (p. 1005) directly follows "The Farmer's Wife," Anne Sexton is usually thought of as a confessional poet who used the facts of her own life in her poetry. For this reason, much attention tends to be given to both poets for their quite real psychological problems, and students are usually interested in knowing about Sexton's suicide. Nevertheless, each poet often assumes a persona in particular poems, and students who know their biographies should be encouraged to let the poems tell their own stories.

"The Farmer's Wife" is not Sexton, but she is a person whom Sexton understands. The poem is characterized by mixed feelings and unexpected turns of phrase. It begins with phrases that suggest oppressive boredom. The doubled idea of "hodge porridge" describes not married love but their "country lust," and conveys feelings of disorder, dreariness, and the unromantic hungers of the body. It continues in the same vein, referring to the wife as "his habit," and conveying the farmer's only snippet of dialogue, a trivial invitation that good-naturedly takes her for granted. She has flashes of sensual pleasure but no intimacy. The connotations of "sweat" and "the blowzy bag / of his usual sleep" disgust most readers, as Sexton surely intends. This sort of language is mild when compared with the language of Sexton's later poems, however, where she often directs more explicit terms for bodily functions and excretions toward herself.

The ending strikes many as extreme. "Why doesn't she just leave if she's so unhappy?" we hear students ask again, as they so often do of such texts. Surely the answer is that her feelings are complex, that her fantasies are the stuff of romantic fiction and soap opera but represent reasons why a person might *feel* something. Part of our consideration must be the times; the 1960s are beginning to open up options, though maybe not to some farmer's wives. She may not want to be free of him, but to shake him — and herself — into actually experiencing emotion.

The last line is difficult. Why does the speaker suddenly use the first-person pronoun when she has used third person in earlier lines? Some critics have suggested that the poet switches to her own voice, but this seems unlikely. Is the wife addressing her husband? If she is, "my lover" seems a strange way for a farmer's wife to address the husband who calls her "honey bunch," though we might understand her changing a husband into a lover in fantasy, something along the lines of crying out the wrong name during sex. And those who have read the stories of Kate Chopin in an earlier cluster (p. 857) will perhaps understand the motive behind wishing her husband dead, even if she loves him. Even grief is preferable to numbness. Perhaps she imagines that it would be better to dream romantically of a dead lover than to live with an emotionally dead husband.

Readers will say that we are being too tough on the farmer, however, and suggest that they talk it out. We might raise the issue of whether she is actually the one who is unable to get in touch with feelings. She enjoys sex but has no sense of being in love. Students may question whether there is a difference between the two, and how one can tell. The phrase "that old pantomime of love" and other terms she uses to show the habitual nature of the couple's relationship implies that they go through the motions of sex, both deriving pleasure from it, but that this is for her a hollow mockery of love.

Although Sexton's title tells us that this is a farmer's wife, the poem could refer to other relationships. A subtext of the poem is the wife's compliance when the husband yet again assumes his privilege of sex with his ever-available "honey bunch." Perhaps the perennial question does apply: If she is unfulfilled, why does she continue? And why does she keep her discontent to herself? Students might speculate about what his response would be if she did complain of being used. Probably he would be hurt and bewildered. Would she lose more than she gains by telling him? Could she suggest that they have sex less often to increase intimacy? If he agreed, would this help? Of course, one of the joys of poetry is that we can allow the couple to remain forever in the limbo of their farm in Illinois. We don't have to save this marriage. But we can learn from the debate, and it may be comforting for some readers to know that others have questioned whether sex is equivalent to intimacy. Though forty years after this poem's publication women feel freer to express their needs and men more often realize the importance of emotional closeness, it would be naive to think such relationships no longer exist.

ROBERT LOWELL

To Speak of the Woe That Is in Marriage (p. 1005)

Speaking of the particular style of poetry that he wrote in *Life Studies* (1959), the collection from which this poem is taken, Robert Lowell denied that all of his "confessional" poems were explicitly autobiographical. "This is not my private lash, or confession, or a puritan's too literal pornographic honesty, glad to share secret embarrassment and triumph," he explains. Well read and well educated, Lowell first followed and then broke with the New Critics of Kenyon College. He wrote poems that are often intertextual, drawing on his own experiences and on many other sources as well. The title of "To Speak of the Woe That Is in Marriage" echoes Geoffrey Chaucer's Wife of Bath as she begins her turn in *The Canterbury Tales*. After telling us of her marital adventures, wherein she keeps the upper hand until she marries a younger man who rules her, Chaucer's bawdy narrator goes on to give us the tale of a quest. Her protagonist must discover what every woman most desires. The answer to the riddle is that every woman wants to be in charge, to take the superior position. This raises issues about the relationship of the title to the poem; do they have any connection beyond the common theme "woe . . . in marriage"?

Lowell follows his title with an epigraph from Schopenhauer that links the joys of marriage to the continuance of families and the human race, an important element in Lowell's thinking. His poem seems to undercut both the title and the epigraph. Like the marriage in Anne Sexton's "The Farmer's Wife" (p. 1003), this marriage seems peculiarly unsatisfying and lacking in joy. The wife gains temporary mastery by finding a way to keep her husband from driving through the streets looking for sex, but she gains nothing from it. The last lines, comic if read as true rhyme but serious and threatening in the images of clumsiness and impotence they project, make marriage seem like a ridiculous and truly woeful exercise. The poem's forced, imperfect rhymes and slang expressions contrast absurdly with the violent images. The romantic magnolia blossoms of the second line quickly give way to dangerous pictures of a man on the prowl, and the poem ends by comparing him to a beast. He is an elephant, but he is also gored. Women usually experience a "climacteric," the end of their fertility; but Lowell applies the term to "his want," showing us a man without sexual powers. He "stalls." The woman holds the keys to the car, the great American symbol of mobility and power.

The wife says that the man is "unjust." Perhaps the reference is to the Wife of Bath's contention that it is a sin to deny sex to a partner in marriage; he does not give her what she justly deserves, his love. But perhaps what he denies her is mastery. Since we hear what happens through her interpretation alone, we can question the nature of their disputes. Line 5 presents a complex metaphor: the man goes "free-lancing out along the razor's edge." When a person free-lances, the implication is that he or she is independent, able to operate without controls. He breaks free of marriage. But if he owes her his love, he also spends it freely — and unjustly — on others less threatening, not on her. There may be sexual connotations to the "lance" as well. What's more, a surgeon might "lance" a boil with something not unlike a razor. The "razor's edge" implies danger and fear. The pledge she thinks he might take may be to no longer have sex with prostitutes. But the wife may fear he pledges to kill her.

Lowell teases us with multiple meanings and with the image of the money and car key tied to the wife's thigh. Students should follow the ramifications of their decisions about the possible meanings of this symbol. If we follow the Wife of Bath scenario, perhaps it is the woman's way of gaining mastery and getting what he owes her, but since he "stalls above" her, she hardly seems in a superior position. And what are we to make of the epigraph? Will they conceive a child as a result of this encounter forced by the wife? In 1958, many marriages did continue in spite of such woe, but two of Lowell's marriages ended in divorce. Some students will still contend that marriage is forever, no matter what.

Both Sexton's "The Farmer's Wife" and Lowell's "To Speak of the Woe That Is in Marriage" present pessimistic views of marriage. Sexton's married couple seems to have hope of continuing their relationship, since the husband at least seems content. The husband in Lowell's poem, on the other hand, seems on the verge of exploding. Yet some might argue that at least Lowell's female narrator speaks out, whereas Sexton's protagonist has unhealthy fantasies about her husband's death. It might be more useful to ask if all of the characters in these two poems are asking for fulfillment and self-esteem from their spouses rather than developing these qualities within themselves. If the wives in these poems from the end of the 1950s feel trapped, it may be because the culture told them they would be failures as women if their marriages failed. They feel compelled to stay with the situation, and they love their husbands less because of their inability to choose freely. The husband in Lowell's poem is trapped as well, and he responds to his wife's complaints by escaping in a way that is considered manly to many in the culture. His wife, on the other hand, may be accused of emasculating him symbolically by demanding her due. And most will agree that she is a whiner. Is this the sort of accusation the wife in Sexton's poem fears would fall on her if she spoke out?

Giving these poems to friends about to marry would be cruel. But oversimplifying the difficulties of marriage does no one any favors. We might consider the source of these pessimistic views of marriage. Both poems come from writers who had profound problems with psychological illnesses that perhaps could be treated now with lithium and antidepressant drugs. Personal issues may color their attitudes toward family relationships. Although aspects of marriage have at times been destructive for cultural reasons, the marriages in these poems are — as our title for the cluster indicates — troubled ones, and the institution itself may not be at fault.

DENISE LEVERTOV

The Ache of Marriage (p. 1006)

Denise Levertov's poem about a marriage in trouble seems more muted than either Robert Lowell's (p. 1005) or Anne Sexton's (p. 1003), perhaps because it depicts conflicts in more abstract and general terms. Instead of the explicit sexual frustrations of the previous two poems, Levertov simply says that there are attempts at "communion" that are "turned away." Clearly not as dramatically vivid as the "raucous bed" or tying "ten dollars and his car key to my thigh," but as the literary theorist Wolfgang Iser suggests, Levertov is inviting us to fill in the gaps from our own experience. Do they engage in long discussions about their relationship? Do they garden together, drink together, exercize together? Do their sexual encounters also end in frustration? Certainly these and dozens of other possibilities are reasonable ways to make concrete Levertov's general term — *communion.*

Perhaps also her use of *leviathan* to describe marriage is meant to connote not only the large space that marriage occupies in society and in the couple's life but also its religious association. The partners are caught inside the largeness of a metaphorical whale, unable to extricate themselves from difficulties but trying to make the marriage work. They are, after all, both searching for "joy, some joy." But the ambiguity in the word *some* can be read as trying to eke out a minimal amount of pleasure in, say, the togetherness of mutual pur-

pose and support. One can read the phrase "not to be known outside it" ironically or not. Hollywood representations are too mixed to give us a firm sense of
our culture's view, as movies represent marriage as both a sentence to be avoided and a refuge.

   Ache is not *pain* or *suffering*, words that probably would apply to our first
two poems. Levertov chooses this particular word carefully. Ache certainly is not
pleasant and is more annoying than an itch, but it probably will not destroy you.
Perhaps because marriage promises unity, the frustrations of achieving what
might not even be possible ensures a persistent ache. Levertov's tone avoids the
obvious emotions of sentimentality, lamentation, or romanticism that often
accompany poems of troubled marriages. She seems bent on simply recording a
fact of life: marriage is hard. The references to the leviathan and the ark rein-
force the antiquity of the dilemma of how we can be simultaneously separate
and together.

   This last point will probably resonate most with college students, since
Sexton and Lowell's views will seem too grim. Hope might be too strong a term
for this poem, but clearly it displays less histrionic complaining, less drama and
trouble than the other two. The couple here is looking; it is in process. Although
the couples in all three poems seem metaphorically trapped, clearly there are
degrees and levels to be discussed with students. Escape seems literal and necessary in Lowell's poem and unlikely in Sexton's. Perhaps Levertov's couple is
the least caught and has the best chance for happiness. Unity and duality can be
said to be true of all three, but again, the discussion should flesh out the degree
to which each couple is united in marriage but separated by boredom, fear, or
the difficulty of human connection.

A MARRIAGE WORTH SAVING?
CRITICAL COMMENTARIES ON HENRIK
IBSEN'S *A DOLL HOUSE* (p. 1008)

HENRIK IBSEN

A Doll House (p. 1009)

   It's been said that when Nora Helmer first slams the door on her marriage
in the final scene of Henrik Ibsen's 1879 play *A Doll House*, the windows shook
in houses all over Europe. Ibsen's contemporaries were shocked that Nora
leaves a loving, indulgent husband for what his first audience would have seen
as a difficult and shameful future. The husband's language and behavior,
which seem so patronizing and demeaning to current readers, would have been
seen as appropriate, even admirable. But Nora's desertion of her children
seemed to Ibsen's readers the most unnatural action a woman could take. In
some countries, the ending was changed, having her turn back and stay for the
sake of the children. This element will probably be the most difficult for our
students to understand as well. We need to explain or have them do research
on divorce in the nineteenth century so that they will realize that Torvald

Helmer has complete power over the lives and welfare of the children, just as he legally has control over Nora herself. Nora will have only the maternal rights he allows her, even if this means she will never see her children again. The first thought of readers, that she should take her children with her to ensure that they will not repeat the mistakes of their parents' faulty relationship, is anachronistic. This is not a choice for Nora.

What happens to Nora after the door closes behind her often dominates class discussions. Does she change her mind and return as soon as she realizes how hard life will be for her? Is Torvald capable of changing, as his words at the end of the play seem to indicate? What does happen to those children? The question of what happens after the door slams is so common in literature classes that the British comedy series *Monty Python's Flying Circus* was assured of an audience when it featured recurring scenarios showing Nora's possible fate. The funniest may be the scene that has her walk into the street only to be trampled by a passing parade of suffragettes. The ironic joke makes sense because we also realize that *A Doll House* invites feminist readings.

Although Ibsen denied that he had a feminist intent in writing the play, Nora's character can be understood only in the context of woman's position in marriage and in the financial world. To our students, Helmer's paternalism toward his wife seems inconceivably controlling, and her manipulation and lying painfully weak — embarrassing to watch. The character traits in Nora that current readers hold in contempt are those reflected in the title; we are disgusted that she behaves as a child, even a plaything. But she sees herself as taking care of her men. She leaves not so much because Helmer has behaved as a petty god but because he does not carry the "bargain" to its conclusion and rescue her, sacrifice himself for her completely. We cannot emphasize strongly enough that Torvald Helmer lives exactly as his culture told him he should. Students may know men today who live by a rigid code of honor and who control their families like tyrants, and they may in fact recognize their fathers in Helmer. Objections that the childish, manipulative woman stereotype is specific to the Victorian era can be forestalled by juxtaposing almost any 1950s episode of *I Love Lucy* with the scenes of Nora hiding macaroons and elaborately manipulating to hide her financial misdeeds. Lucy Ricardo is cute and dumb, always hiding things and disobeying her husband's rules; Ricky is indulgent and controlling, easily angered, concerned about what others might think. Nor should we assume that the childish role of the wife has disappeared. This writer knows of two young working mothers who have agreed to retrieve mail for each other so that their husbands do not see the credit-card bills until they get their stories straight. Although they deal with financial matters at work competently and honestly and go home to function as good mothers, both tend to slip into roles not unlike Nora's. Ibsen's use of the tarantella is often interpreted as "stage business" that is meant primarily to hold the attention of the audience. But taken symbolically, its frantic, abnormal energy aptly depicts the emotional strain of such relationships. When one partner "dances" as fast as she can to distract the other into allowing her a shred of autonomy, she reenacts the medieval phenomenon that lies behind the tarantella: bitten by a spider, the victim dances herself to death.

CRITICAL COMMENTARIES:

HENRIETTA FRANCIS LORD, From "The Life of Henrik Ibsen" (p. 1061)
CLEMENT SCOTT, "Ibsen's Unlovely Creed" (p. 1062)
HERMANN J. WEIGAND, From *The Modern Ibsen* (p. 1063)
KATHERINE M. ROGERS, From "Feminism and *A Doll House*" (p. 1065)
JOAN TEMPLETON, From "The *Doll House* Backlash:
Criticism, Feminism, and Ibsen" (p. 1069)

Henrik Ibsen's *A Doll House* (p. 1009) inspired controversy in its time and continues to do so. By examining some of the readings that have been applied to the play over time, our students get a sense of how historicist research and interpretation might be done. We are not limited to the immediate social and historical context of a text, nor must we consider it as an object to be evaluated as universal art, but we may also study how it changes over time and in different situations as readers interact with it. Henrietta Francis Lord (p. 1061) translated the play and wrote the introduction to the playwright's life in London in 1882; this small excerpt is taken from that introduction. Mrs. Lord — ladies of her generation, no matter how progressive, would expect the title Mrs. — acknowledges that her axiom about freedom is problematic. But she asserts that that Nora's husband, and by extension Western culture, has kept reality from Nora. Therefore, she does not have the knowledge to solve problems on her own. This seems reasonable. It also seems reasonable that love is not love if it is based on pretense. We might push our students beyond simple agreement or disagreement with Lord's axiom to suggest how authenticity may be learned, especially in marriages like the Helmers', in which playacting has solidified into habit. Do we always play roles, even when we think we are being forthright?

In the 1920s, Hermann J. Weigand (p. 1063) could not believe that Ibsen wanted us to take the character of Nora seriously. She is instead a silly, madcap little flapper. We might think ahead to *I Love Lucy*. How cute when Lucy has to admit her foolishness and beg forgiveness of Ricky. The majority of our student readers, especially women, will be insulted by Weigand's patronizing and naive indulgence, which we recognize as unconscious bigotry against women. Katherine M. Rogers (p. 1065), writing in the 1980s in the context of a women's studies course, would object, of course, to Weigand's talk of the inborn tendencies in women to engage in flirting and playacting to manipulate their husbands. She would maintain that these tendencies and the romantic fantasies about marriage that both Nora and Torvald Helmer hold through most of the play are learned and culturally determined rather than essential to being male or female. Furthermore, Rogers would suggest that our students would question how these and other assumptions still play a role in relationships.

As students search out the most useful and least useful comments in the five critical texts, they should avoid simply summarizing or woodenly comparing and contrasting the writers' opinions. Encourage them instead to create a synthesis that uses the ideas of the critics as a starting point for their own extrapolations, inviting them to enter into the academic dialogue surrounding Ibsen's play.

LOVE AS A HAVEN? (p. 1072)

MATTHEW ARNOLD

Dover Beach (p. 1073)

As the son of a famed headmaster of the English preparatory school Rugby, Matthew Arnold found himself in the midst of debates about social, political, and intellectual issues from the beginning of his life. In his prose, he tackled educational and literary issues directly. He felt that education would change society by changing the middle and lower classes, bringing culture to "the little ploughboy" who would as eventually hold the reins of political power. In his thirty-five-year tenure as an inspector of schools, Arnold was in a position to put his philosophies into action.

As a literary theorist, Arnold privileged the accessible diction and "high seriousness" that would uplift the reader. Religion was losing its power to transform, and he believed literature should possess qualities that would allow it to fill the gap. He wanted to bring "culture" to the class he called the "Philistines," people like those described by William Wordsworth as dulled by "getting and spending." For Arnold, culture could be defined as an awareness of the art, literature, philosophy, and so forth of Western civilization coupled with a mind unwilling to blindly defer to authority. These issues are reflected in his most lasting poem, "Dover Beach," in which a speaker proposes that human beings hold on to each other in lieu of a retreating faith in God.

The last half of the nineteenth century, and perhaps all of the twentieth, witnessed the ramifications of Charles Darwin's *Origin of Species*. Darwin's book appeared in 1859 to a storm of controversy, eight years before "Dover Beach" was published. We might ask students to consider how Arnold's poem addresses issues related to debates about Darwinism. Because students usually get a kick out of it, we like to use Anthony Hecht's irreverent parody "The Dover Bitch" to compare the earnest "high seriousness" of Arnold's text with the irony of a twentieth-century reinterpretation of the same scene.

In "Dover Beach" the sea serves as an extended metaphor for faith, as the poem explicitly states. Arnold saves this statement of his theme for the third stanza, however, using an inductive method to prepare the readers for his point. The opening stanza describes the sea itself — specifically the English Channel separating England from the continent of Europe. As the speaker calls his companion to the window to look at the sea, he asks her to listen to the effects of the waves on the shore. He ends by saying that a "note of sadness" is evoked by the ceaseless sound.

In the second stanza, the poet takes us back to ancient Greek drama for an allusion to Sophocles' same reaction to the sound of the sea. He refers to lines 656–778. of *Antigone*. Since the play appears on page 541, students should turn back to it and read the passage for themselves. Sophocles specifically refers to tragedy's reverberating consequences through the generations of a family like that of Oedipus. In Christian theology, the equivalent is the proverb that the sins of the fathers are visited on the children. The sea in *Antigone* is "a great mounting tide /

driven on by savage northern gales, / surging over the dead black depths / roiling up from the bottom dark heaves of sand." The sea's "moaning / echoes" bring to mind human grief. All this stuff keeps getting dredged up, Sophocles says. The sea does not keep still about family secrets. Arnold universalizes the allusion.

Though he has gone from sadness to misery, the third stanza makes the story literally worldwide. Faith once rolled up on every shore like the sea at high tide, hugging the hips of the land like a sash wrapped around the earth's body. But just as the sea rolls out at low tide — or as a woman might slowly unfurl her clothing for the night — faith is going away, leaving our souls as bare as the rocks on the shore or the unprotected body of the woman. This brings the speaker of the poem to his final point. Since we are now vulnerable without the authority of religion to make us feel safe, we have only our human love.

We discover at this late point that the speaker addresses someone he loves, probably a woman. The sounds of the ocean echo like the sounds of warfare as the speaker thinks of vulnerable humans alone "on a darkling plain" without the sure expectations faith once provided. Although the speaker calls someone to the window in the first stanza, revealing that the poem is a dramatic monologue overheard by us as he addresses another character whose voice we do not hear, we know little about the relationship. Anthony Hecht's parody "The Dover Bitch" assumes that this is a good way to get someone into bed, especially if the speaker is a soldier going off to war. Knowing something of Arnold's philosophy, we assume that he has higher motives. He is suggesting obliquely to his readers that we need to rely on our own critical thinking and good will to our fellow human beings rather than on authority. His vision of the world intensifies the value of love. The speaker wants to be in a relationship in which lovers are *true* to each other. Issues of definition may come up in class discussion about exactly what Arnold means by this. Students might enjoy writing their own scenarios for a soap opera about this couple.

The poem begins in the present tense, and the imperative sentences that invite his companion to the window and urge her to listen increase the sense of immediacy. But by the end of the first stanza, he raises the issue of eternity. At this point, he moves into the literary past "long ago" for a few lines before leaping back to the present again before the second short stanza is over. In the third stanza his movement back and forth in time is like the tide he describes. Finally, in the last stanza, he proposes a plan for the future, in view of the present condition of the human world, which he elaborates upon more fully. Misery is eternal; faith sufficed for a time as a counter to it; now faith is gone and we must counter it with love. We can't look to the world — or the sea of faith — for any of the positive values he lists in the final stanza. We therefore must look to each other as human beings. Perhaps the speaker places too great a burden on love, which most people today would say can't solve the problems of an individual. Some readers will feel that the speaker — and the poet — will be as disappointed in seeking comfort from love as he was from religion. Others will contend that he is on the right track as he seeks human solutions to human problems.

Arnold sees the solution to the decline of faith in a commitment to human love. Arnold's sea changes like Proteus; first it is a symbol of sadness and misery, then a symbol of faith, and finally a reminder of the contentious and dangerous nature of the human world of the mid-nineteenth century.

In a poem like Arnold's, where rhyme is irregular, readers tend to notice content before they notice form. The balance of Arnold's lines, however, gives the text a poetic cadence and rhythm reminiscent of the ebb and flow of the waves. Even though Arnold particularizes the changing perceptions of humanity by having his speaker address a lover, he still deals with the universal themes. Arnold's use of only two people does not mean that the poem is *about* these two people. Most readers will recognize that the poem is also about us.

MARK DOTY

Night Ferry (p. 1075)

The poem's sustained metaphor of life as a brief ferry ride across a lake at night is both conventional and arresting. Mark Doty's intensely poetic language immediately signals a text of sophistication and depth. To see life as a journey is certainly a longstanding trope in poetry and indeed in almost all the arts from painting to music. Doty, however, makes the journey motif an original and compelling symbol through his beautifully crafted and evocative imagery and the blending of clear and precise description with metaphors and similes — such as "like the patterns of Italian bookpaper lustrous and promising" and "liquid endpapers of the hurried water, shot with random color" — that suggest that life is also a narrative. Both ideas make sense in many world literatures both ancient and modern.

Students can probably suggest a number of plausible references for Doty's images. His "few lights vague," for example, can easily be connected to significant goals or ideas that help guide our journey; the "bookpaper" suggests the aesthetic pleasures of life, and the lines "no beautiful binding . . . shot with random color" suggest the transitory and shifting nature of reality. Here Doty sounds postmodern, eschewing a fixed, clearly chartered course for life's temporary, liquid nature.

The narrator speaks bravely, accepting the uncertainty of "no solid ground" (another favorite postmodern metaphor for intellectual life). Although the ferry is "launched into the darkness," the narrator is ready for the adventure, for what the "future" holds. He uses the phrase "almost not afraid" to suggest a knowing acceptance of life's difficulties that goes beyond mere bravado.

He understands the deep uncertainty of life but is able to appreciate its sensuous beauty, its good smells and warm winds. In pressing on, in embracing the future possibilities of life's journey, he comes on such a wondrous "scent so quick and startling" that it seems otherworldly, "of the stars." This highly romantic and transcendent image can be concretized in imaginative ways by students, including the general idea that when you are open to experience, surprising things can happen to you. Doty follows this image with something quite earthy, the promise (however accidental) of warmth on the chilly shore of our arrival. Sustaining the journey motif here could be challenging, but students will see plausible ideas in the idea of metaphorical arriving — that is, achieving one's goals or even the ultimate end for all of life's passages. And the fire? The ambiguity between warmth and pain should produce an interesting discussion.

Attentive students will see general and specific similarities between the two poems, including the sea at night, the emphasis on coasts and shorelines, the lights of the shore seen from afar, the condition of the sea, and, of course, the metaphorical play with the sea and its potential for a profound and perhaps inevitably melancholy reading.

But there are also differences. Matthew Arnold's "Sea of Faith" seems clearly a reference to an historical moment when religious faith was almost universal. Indeed an important theme of Arnold's "Dover Beach' (p. 1073) is the loss of faith and the resulting shock that we can depend only on ourselves for comfort. Doty's "faith" (line 17) seems more secular, more related to a vague hope that things will work out well. In lines 16 and 24, "night" is both literal and metaphorical, since Doty is playing with the idea that we usually move into the future blindly or at least without a clear sense of what lies ahead. But Doty's "love" (line 46) does seem to echo Arnold's famous "Ah, love." Doty's speaker, like Arnold's, does appear to be speaking to a loved one. Philosophically, Doty's postmodern "no solid ground" finds a companion in Arnold's last stanza, especially the phrase "which seems to lie before us like a land of dreams." And Arnold's "here on a darkling plain / Swept with confused alarms" certainly could have inspired Doty's "We are between worlds, between unfathomed water."

It is hard to be bleaker than Arnold is, perhaps because the loss of faith was still for him an open wound. Doty is certainly no Pollyanna, but he seems more measured and accepting of life's uncertainty. Perhaps this is the difference between a contemporary poet's look into the abyss and a Victorian's. Like Arnold, Doty does seem to put some emphasis on love, but he seems more open and accepting of the problematic nature of reality, more willing to gain pleasure from what he finds along the way. Both poets use beautiful imagery, but Doty seems more in tune with a contemporary aesthetic. As always, the point is to have students make these generalizations, making reference to specific lines as evidence to support their arguments.

15

Doing Justice (p. 1079)

DOING JUSTICE TO ANIMALS (p. 1081)

MAXINE KUMIN

Woodchucks (p. 1081)

Maxine Kumin's poem "Woodchucks" finds ironic parallels with the Holocaust in a woman's attempts to exterminate a clan of rodents from her garden. We can't be sure that the poem is directly autobiographical. Kumin does live in New Hampshire, on her PoBiz Farm, where she raises horses, sheep, and a variety of other animals. Now that her children are adults, she jokes that animals have become her family and that she writes more and more about them. But though she raises sheep and writes poems about butchers and "lambs for slaughter," she is virtually a vegetarian, and her poems ironically question the concept of nurturing animals only to destroy them. When she sells horses, she does so only after carefully screening new owners to make sure the animals will be treated well. Many of the animals on her farm have been rescued from inhumane conditions before arriving there. And she has protected the wildlife on her property — bears, foxes, and presumably woodchucks — by designating undeveloped land as a conservation area.

Perhaps this poem describes an actual experience from the family's early days on the farm. But we should remind students that poets often assume a persona and should not be confused with the poem's speaker. While the poem's narrator seems to approve the "quiet Nazi way," the poet ironically questions both the killing of woodchucks and, by implication, the Nazi atrocities. We may even go beyond the literal situation of the poem and its explicit Nazi parallels to see Kumin as raising issues about the taking of life under any circumstances. If the poet were not an animal lover, we could conjecture that "Woodchucks" is a mock epic that makes a trivial subject ridiculous through hyperbole and a more serious tone than is warranted. But she seems to be serious about both the humane treatment of animals and the lessons of the Holocaust. If anything, the speaker's self-righteousness is satirized.

Kumin has close connections with a number of poets of her generation who use the imagery of the Holocaust for their own purposes. Unlike Sylvia Plath, who compares her father to a Nazi in "Daddy" (p. 350), Kumin is Jewish. This perhaps gives her a more legitimate right to the "property" of the Holocaust as a poetic device. Still, some readers may criticize her for trivializing such horrors by juxtaposing them with the exterminating of garden pests. A close friend and collaborator with Anne Sexton on children's books, Kumin may be suspected by some readers of participating in a faddish appropriation of the historical pain and death of millions of people for a cheap effect. Others may argue that by including such references in their poetry, Kumin and her contemporaries keep Holocaust memories alive and show us how we may apply their lessons to our lives. We can read "Woodchucks" as a text that reverses the apparent tenor and vehicle of Kumin's metaphor. Rather than using Nazi atrocities to make us see the horror of killing woodchucks, she personifies woodchucks to remind us of the enormity of killing human beings. Just as the speaker of the poem is haunted by the baby faces of the woodchuck family, the reader sees that we cannot guiltlessly destroy people unless we dehumanize them and turn our faces away from our deeds.

The poet gives words a double meaning, raising additional issues. When she uses the word *case* in line 4 we can read this word to mean both a physical trap and a rhetorical or legal argument. If we stay with the specifics of the poem, most gardeners will understand the need for driving out the current inhabitants of the land so that the vegetables can grow and human beings benefit from the produce. We may know from Kumin's biography that the farm at the time of the poem's composition was simply a summer hobby rather than a source of sustenance for a subsistence farmer. But we can imagine a speaker with a more pressing need and thus justify the extermination of the woodchucks. Few readers would be opposed to hiring an exterminator to get rid of rats in an apartment building. But we may also recall that the Third Reich justified aggression against neighboring countries and implementation of the "final solution" to eliminate minorities by citing the need for living space for the German people. Many of the reasons given in the "case" against Jewish and Gypsy minorities were economic.

The poem's speaker begins by seeking a "merciful" method for eliminating the woodchucks, but when this does not work, she "righteously" finds excuses for exerting direct power using survival-of-the-fittest arguments. Her language hints at both the excitement of killing ("thrilling / to the feel of the .22") and the equivocation involved in going against one's ethics ("a lapsed pacifist fallen from grace / puffed with Darwinian pieties for killing"). But as the narrator kills the animals, they become more human and she becomes "the murderer . . . the hawkeye killer". She ends the poem as a stalker obsessed with killing the old woodchuck that refuses to die. The speaker's transformation has proceeded gradually, as such things do, and is now complete. If the poet had not used first-person, the voice of the poem would seem accusing, and the audience would be less aware of the changes that have taken place in the speaker's attitude. Third person perspective would allow us to be outside observers with the distance to be horrified at the killer's actions, just as we can be safely appalled by Nazi atrocities, sure of our inability to agree to such programs. As the poem stands, readers find it difficult to avoid the implication that we too are capable of the gradual metamorphosis that the poet describes.

Kumin's poem rhymes, but she does not use a conventional pattern, and the result echoes sounds rather than obtrusively imposing structure. Readers will find alliteration in several lines; the *s* and *sh* sounds of lines 5 and 6 are one example. In this example the sound interacts with the content, since we can imagine the speaker making shooing noises and hissing to drive the pesky critters away. Kumin draws deliberate parallels between the evolving attitude of the poem's speaker and the human propensity for becoming gradually tolerant of violence. She also raises issues about our willingness to accept killing we do not see as opposed to looking at the faces of those that we destroy. Some readers are more moved by descriptions of the killing of animals than they are of similar actions toward human beings. It would be reductive, however, to discuss this poem as simply about whether we should kill animals.

D. H. LAWRENCE
Snake (p. 1083)

Students interested in exploring the deeper meanings of D. H. Lawrence's "Snake" will find many critical studies. Since the snake is a phallic symbol in many cultures — even to some ways of thinking an archetypal symbol connected universally with male sexuality — the poem invites Freudian readings, and undergraduates are often surprised to find analyses of Lawrence's Oedipus complex as they look for interpretations of the poem. A reading of his novel *Sons and Lovers* may convince them that this is a reasonable assumption, though some Lawrence scholars contend that he'd written his way through the worst of his feelings about his father by the time he wrote "Snake" on a trip to Sicily in 1913. In a personal letter, Lawrence himself once wrote that human beings are freed by "phallic consciousness . . . [which is] the root of poetry, lived or sung." For Lawrence, sex was at the core of everything human, and such interpretations can usually be supported with ample evidence.

Critics who focus on Lawrence's ideas about women see in the poem's approach to nature a similar impulse to his desire for relationships in which the woman does not become submerged in the man but finds her own passion and integrity. This is a nature poem, but Lawrence tries his best to fight the cultural demands to subdue nature, to kill the symbol of evil. Lawrence privileges nature over received conventions in his work. He admires poets like William Blake and John Keats, whose work is characterized by structure, but Lawrence wanted to catch a sense of experience in the present rather than "recollected in tranquillity" as William Wordsworth taught. Readers will find this sense of immediacy in "Snake" as the speaker argues with himself throughout the poem, then acts impulsively, and ends with his spiritual task unfinished.

Critic Ross Murfin maintains that it is impossible for Lawrence or any other writer after John Milton's *Paradise Lost* to view a snake without making a conscious or subconscious intertextual connection with the biblical serpent and Satan. Murfin sees Lawrence as unsuccessfully trying to break free of this and other cultural connotations to interact with the snake in a natural way. Before reading the poem, we might have students brainstorm or free-associate their own connotations for words like *snake, serpent,* and *python,* and invite them to relate stories of encounters with snakes on camping trips or growing up in rural areas. Some may think of expressions like *snake in the grass* to describe someone who turns on us unexpectedly. We may recall the folktale of the "bosom serpent" in which a man befriends a snake only to have his kindness repaid with a poisonous bite. The moral is that we must be careful who we "pick up" and take to our

hearts. But some may connect Lawrence's presence on a Mediterranean island
with Greek stories that link the python with Apollo and his oracle at Delphi,
endowing the place where the god killed the snake with supernatural wisdom
and power. The python is usually taken to represent an earlier religion connected with mother earth and supplanted by the male god Apollo. Lawrence
would have known this.

Those of us who were fascinated with snakes as children recall a mixture of
fear and attraction that attaches to no other animal with the same intensity.
Lawrence reflects this ambivalence in his poem. He tells us that "the voice of
[his] education" says to kill the snake. He feels "afraid" of the snake but "hon-
oured" to be sought out by it. He hints at mythical allusions, the snake disap-
pearing into the underworld to be crowned as king. The nearness of the volcano
and the snake's withdrawal into the darkness of the earth remind us of hell and
the biblical (or Miltonic) connections of Satan and the serpent. Lawrence hears
the voice of logic and science first, telling him that "black snakes are innocent,
the gold are venomous." Then he hears the cultural voices that try to shame him
into proving his manhood by killing the snake. Since the Bible speaks of the
"enmity" between man and the snake, perhaps this is the voice of Judeo-
Christian religion that Lawrence so strongly resists in his work and his life. It is
the snake's "Deliberately going into the blackness" that impels him to throw
something at it. The horror that the speaker of the poem feels has something to
do with the blackness rather than with the snake, which he has continued to
admire. Perhaps for Lawrence this withdrawal is a rejection of relationship and
of life, but he blames his reaction to it on the "voices of [his] accursed human
education." He feels that he has momentarily done something unworthy. He
uses words like *paltry, vulgar, mean,* and *pettiness* to describe his action, comparing his throwing a log at the snake to the shooting of the albatross in Samuel
Taylor Coleridge's *The Rime of the Ancient Mariner.*

Reading portions of Coleridge's poem in class will help students unfamiliar
with it to understand the allusion. The ancient mariner must wear the dead
seabird around his neck until he has learned to appreciate the wonders of
nature; he is finally released from his penance when near the point of death
from thirst he takes joy in the beauty of the luminescent sea snakes. Some readers see Lawrence's judgment of his action as exaggerated and quite different
from the action of Coleridge's ancient mariner. The narrator of "Snake" is
thoughtful about nature and does not seem unthinking or unfeeling at all. But
he denies the snake his natural behavior, sees the darkness of the earth as a horror, and recoils from the union of the snake and the earth with its sexual connotations. Perhaps this is his sin that must be expiated. He has lapsed from faith
in nature because of the temptations whispered in his ear by the "voices of education." The biblical story wherein the serpent is the tempter is thus reversed.
Lawrence's use of the word *and* to begin many of his sentences recalls the syntax of the King James Bible. This usage also gives the poem a sense of ongoing
thought and spontaneity that contributes to Lawrence's purpose of communicating the present moment as it is happening.

If we compare the pettiness of the narrators of Maxine Kumin's
"Woodchucks" (p. 1081) and Lawrence's "Snake," the shooter of woodchucks
gets the award as most petty. Both wrestle with conflicting impulses, but Kumin's

protagonist wages an escalating war whereas Lawrence's acts on impulse, almost as an afterthought. And for most audiences, Lawrence's speaker could make a legitimate case for killing a solitary venomous reptile more easily than Kumin's can for killing mammals that seem like a human family. On the other hand, the snake does not really bother anyone, so attacking him is an arbitrary act of cruelty. The woodchucks interfere with a human activity, giving the narrator a warrant for getting rid of them; the cruelty is a side effect of the failure of the would-be killer's methods.

Although both speakers seem equally self-divided, the different tones of the poems make the internal dialogue of "Snake" seem sincere, whereas the conflict of the speaker of "Woodchucks" seems more like rationalizing. Both poets use a conversational style and allow the reader to share the thoughts of their narrators. Students may see Kumin's poem as more traditionally "poetic" than Lawrence's since it has rhyme and a more visible structure. Lawrence's poem is in free verse, but we should urge students to look for alliteration and other repetitions. His use of parallel structures is especially effective and may remind some readers of Walt Whitman.

ELIZABETH BISHOP

The Fish (p. 1086)

Elizabeth Bishop is known for her precise observations and evocations of objects in the world. She begins with something concrete and specific, as she does in "The Fish," and lets the imagery carry the meaning. She doesn't tell us what to think about it but simply paints the picture for her readers to interpret. For instructors using this anthology in a writing class, Bishop's poem provides an opportunity to discuss diction, syntax, and descriptive techniques. Students may notice that "The Fish" is really a sort of fish story, a narrative about the one that got away or rather the one that the narrator allowed to get away. It has unity, beginning with a straightforward statement of what happened and describing a series of observations that culminate in the narrator's letting the fish go. The details of the story build until she notices the evidence that this fish has already been caught five other times. This leads to what most critics have agreed is an epiphany, a sudden insight into reality spurred by some ordinary object or incident. There is a flash of joyful recognition as the concrete details converge for the speaker as "rainbow, rainbow, rainbow!"

We can ask students to look at the poem's diction, plotting words along a ladder of abstraction. For example, the word *tremendous* is fairly abstract and general, since readers' images of the fish may range from a foot long to something like the great white shark of the movie *Jaws*. When the poet says that the fish's "brown skin hung in strips / like ancient wall-paper," the image is more concrete, and the images that different readers have will come closer to being the same. Students can also be asked to find similes and metaphors like the wall-paper and to look for other ways that the writer provides precise descriptions. When she says that the fish "hung a grunting weight," several senses come into play, since we see the fish, but also feel the tug of holding it and hear the sound of grunting — whether from the fish or the fisher is unclear. Color plays an important role, too, coming together in the penultimate line with the rainbow. The phonetic qualities of words are important to poetic diction. We can read closely to find alliteration ("tarnished tinfoil," for example), assonance ("full-blown roses" or "green weed" or "frayed and wavering"), or unexpected rhymes and vocal echoes (like "shallower, and yellowed" or "backed and packed" or the unexpected couplet of lines 46 and 47, ending with "jaw" and "saw"). Students should also consider the syntax of the poem. The poet uses straightforward declarative sentences at first. There's a breathless quality to the series of short parallel sentences of lines 5 through 9. But the sentences get longer and more complex as the poem proceeds and the speaker becomes absorbed in her minute descriptions. She seems almost to look through a magnifying glass.

As the speaker observes the fish more closely in the course of the poem, her attitude changes. At first, the fish is a fairly abstract and undifferentiated weight, though the word *venerable* hints that the fish is elderly and worthy of respect, foreshadowing the insight that is to come. Gradually, the fish becomes even more real as the speaker mentally dissects it. Finally, the fish becomes personified, the old fishing lines in his jaw becoming "a five-haired beard of wisdom." Although her description is precise and seemingly unemotional before the outburst of passion at the end, the details she chooses to give reflect her values. The evidence of hard-won survival that the fish exhibits moves her. From her early description of him as "battered" to his "frightening gills, / fresh and crisp with blood" through many other images of his age and endurance, we finally come to the old fishing lines that prove his struggle to survive. She also values the precision of nature's machinery. For example, she is fascinated with "the mechanism of his jaw." She values the aesthetic, even when seen in the imagined internal organs of a fish; she sees beauty with an artist's eye. (We might note that Bishop was a painter as well as a writer.) When the poem's speaker uses the word *victory*, she refers to the fish but may also refer to herself. But rather than the victory of catching the grand old fish that myths are built on, hers is the victory of epiphany, of being struck by beauty and the will to live epitomized by the brave old fish. One critic has ironically termed Bishop's fish an "old man of the sea," alluding to Ernest Hemingway's character who tenaciously holds on to his catch, another symbol of endurance.

In a sense, the whole poem is about seeing. But the writer begins to make this explicit when she looks into the eyes of the fish in line 34. His eyes are like "tarnished tinfoil / seen through the lenses / of old scratched isinglass." Isinglass was used as a cheap substitute for window glass before the invention of plastics and is translucent rather than transparent. One sees through such a glass darkly. Like the other images of the poem, this one emphasizes age and endurance. The fish does not return her gaze. But later the speaker says that she "stared and stared." The rainbow itself has to do with visual perception, the breaking up of light into the colors of the spectrum. The speaker refers to the fish as *he*. Perhaps the only reason for the fish being male is the convenience of his having a beard made up of fishing lines. We have to admit, however, that if the fish were female, we might find her pathetic rather than enduring. The warrants for this reaction are worth discussing.

All of the speakers of the poems of this cluster use the animals they encounter for self-examination. Bishop's narrator seems more admirable than those of Maxine Kumin's "Woodchucks" (p. 1081) or D. H. Lawrence's "Snake"(p. 1083), since she releases the fish. But she has been just as willing at the beginning to take a fish as a trophy; she merely changes her mind as she gets to know him as a character in a narrative she imagines. Lawrence's narrator respects the snake as well, and seems no worse than Bishop's impulsive fisherman who opts for allowing the fish his life. The speakers of Lawrence's and Kumin's poems are more self-reflective than Bishop's, so they leave themselves open to our judgments. Lawrence lets us hear the internal dialogue as he examines his warrants for not killing the snake. Cultural assumptions tell him that he should kill it, and he eventually gives into them half-heartedly, and then feels guilty for caving in to the conventional pettiness that he has been socialized to exhibit toward snakes. Kumin's speaker also reveals her thoughts, but we feel that she has been caught up in actions she cannot stop. Some readers may feel that she reveals more than Lawrence, since she allows us into her dreams. Bishop is least explicit about her thoughts. She shares her observations, even the flash of joy, but she allows the reader to determine what these experiences mean.

Bishop's poem is a descriptive narrative that describes a single event. It makes sense to focus it into a structure that looks like one continuous block. Lawrence also describes a single event, but he describes his thinking process as the event takes place. This calls for the separation of thoughts into separate stanzas as he moves from one mind state to another. Kumin uses a closed structure of uniform stanzas with a fairly regular rhyme scheme. Each stanza tells of a different stage in her war on the woodchucks. Lawrence would be especially pleased if we recognized that content often suggests its own form. Good poets keep this in mind.

WILLIAM STAFFORD

Traveling through the Dark *(p. 1089)*

William Stafford's narrative, in which a speaker finds a pregnant deer dead beside the road, reads more like an objective newspaper account than a poem. This provides us with the opportunity to discuss his style and tone and the distance he maintains from his emotionally charged topic. When students write the obligatory autobiographical narrative in our first-year composition classes, they often have trouble separating themselves from the powerful feelings evoked by the events they want to write about. Our first instinct may be to tell them to postpone the telling of their loss of a high-school classmate or another traumatic experience until they have more distance. Their deeply felt emotions often come across to us as sentimental clichés.

The difference between emotion and sentimentality is difficult to communicate, especially to young people, for whom the experience and the expression of it are fresh and original from their perspective. The key to distinguishing the two has to do with focus. Sentimentality focuses on the feeling itself — something along the lines of being *in love with love*. There is a falsity to it, though it may be sincerely intended. A few years ago, when a young woman drowned her two young children by pushing her car into a lake, her acquaintances kept bringing up evidence of how much she had seemed to love the children. Her writings about them were revealing, however, showing a self-absorbed preoccupation with her own emotions about the role of mother rather than a sense of the children as separate human beings. Her voice when she spoke of them had a similar tone, and her comments were filled with clichés.

While some poets successfully focus on their own feelings, most twenty-first-century readers resist a solipsistic outpouring focusing on the speaker's emotions. A writer like Stafford can offer a useful counteracting example. Though some readers find him cold and unfeeling, he succeeds in making *the reader* feel something through his understated recital of this waste of life. He doesn't weep over the deer or preach at us, Look what happens when we carve roads through the wilderness! He lets his audience come to its own conclusions through the evidence he presents, and he trusts us to be perceptive enough to feel the emotions that are submerged beneath the details of the story. As a leader of creative writing workshops, Stafford emphasizes the need to communicate emotion without falling into the trap of sentiment. This is done, he teaches, by writing not about one's feelings but about the scene, the time of day, the sensory images that accompanied the emotion. If these concrete details are connected with emotion for the writer, they can evoke a similar reaction for the reader. The effect created is one of immediate, shared experience. Having said this, we should concede that many readers feel that Stafford goes too far in the other direction when he seeks to avoid sentimentality and to show rather than tell. When we assign the autobiographical essay, we urge students to go beyond narrative and description to ponder the significance of the event. But don't tag on a moral! we warn. The line is a fine one. But though he does it in a subtle way, Stafford places his narrative in a philosophical context by letting us see his momentary "swerving" from the necessary deed.

When Stafford uses the pronoun *us* in the final stanza of "Traveling through the Dark," he invites multiple interpretations of the word. He has just mentioned "our group" in line 16, seemingly referring to himself, the pregnant doe, the still-living fawn in her womb, and possibly the personified automobile with its purring engine and aimed lights. He also introduces the character of the wilderness, imagined as a silently listening audience. And then there is the reader, a sharer with the writer in a common humanity. All of these entities may be implied as he ponders the situation for "us." The poet frames the narrative with references to "swerving." Although it's possible that a hunter has seen the deer and shot for the joy of killing, the context of the poem seems to imply that the deer has been hit by a car. Most of us have swerved to avoid hitting animals when we travel roads through habitats and ranges, and we have all seen the mangled bodies of raccoons or opossums who did not successfully avoid their collision with civilization. Although some states have laws against taking road kill home to eat, presumably discouraging the deliberate use of an automobile as a weapon, few drivers would deliberately swerve to hit a large animal like a deer. If so, they would not leave the carcass. This is an accidental, arbitrary death — the result of the narrow mountain road and the deer occupying the same space in the wilderness. It's unclear when the speaker says that "to swerve might make more dead" if he means that people would be killed as the auto-mobiles swerved off the road or if more animals might be killed as the cars swerved to avoid this dead one. The ambiguity of the poet's diction implies equality between the two. But the swerving that he mentions in the final stanza is a figurative one. He knows what he must do — sacrifice this individual life within the dead doe to prevent further accidents — but he cannot do it without pause. The empathy implied in his swerving touches the reader most, though we may understand that the kindest act is to proceed as he does.

We might wonder if animals that see automobiles hurtling down the road interpret them to be fierce beasts of prey. Stafford personifies the car in "Traveling through the Dark" by making it seem like a large cat at rest after tak-ing its prey, the verb *purred* describing the sound of its engine. The verbs in this fourth stanza give the automobile credit for its "aimed" and "lowered" parking lights, conveying the impression of the eyes of a sentient being guiltily avoiding the sight of what one of its kind has done. The last sentence of the fourth stan-za also personifies the wilderness. The absence of sound becomes the wilderness "listening" as the human being, the only one with the power to take action, to accept responsibility for this clash of realities, hesitates. Those who object to the image might be asked if it is possible to hear silence or to see darkness. The lis-tening presence of the wilderness may be a key to the significance of the poem. It is as if humanity is on trial for this death. The judgment of the wilderness is implied in the stopped motion and the silence that surrounds the tableau on the mountain road. The action of the speaker is the most merciful course of action. The fawn will die slowly if he chooses any other alternative. But in the stillness, readers briefly mourn this collision between the natural world and the machine-driven world of human beings. Like silence, the word *dark* indicates an absence of something. Although the protagonist of the poem's narrative has stopped in his travels, the title may imply a figurative journey in which we always find our selves with insufficient light, making decisions we'd rather not make to redeem sins we have not ourselves committed.

For each of the writers in this cluster, a barrier exists between the human speaker and the animal he or she encounters. To varying degrees, the human protagonists of these poetic narratives respond to qualities that hint at a bond with nature that is almost, but not quite, possible. Maxine Kumin's (p. 1081) woodchuck killer sees their faces and allows them other human attributes, even as she tries to exterminate them, and explicitly draws parallels between this atti-tude toward nature and our ability to justify the killing of our own kind. D. H. Lawrence (p. 1083) resists the learned impulse to do harm to the representative of nature almost to the end, but instead demonstrates the power of the received ideas that would judge nature as evil. Elizabeth Bishop's (p. 1086) narrator at first sees the fish as an object, but enters into a bond through her close observa-tion and through this oneness is able to let the creature of nature go back into its own world. Stafford's speaker is forced to let go in a different way, but he too hints at a disjunction between the world of nature and the artificial environment of the human world that leads to the death of the natural creature. Had Stafford's speaker left the deer by the side of the road or made fumbling attempts to deliver the fawn, his act would have been unnatural. Except for Bishop's speaker, who comes to a moment of revelation, the human characters in these poems must deal with the guilt of knowing the cruelty of which human beings are capable. And even with Bishop's fish, it is the creature's many struggles with its human antagonists that reaches the speaker.

All of the texts in this cluster have an air of sadness and regret that their narrators are so separated from the natural world in which they live. All of these speakers think hard for all of us. Readers who admit that they also struggle with human cruelty and alienation from nature will get the most from these poems. The exercise of comparing the clarity of the poems with our aesthetic and reader-response evaluations of them will provide interesting insights into our own warrants as we read poetry. As instructors we should do this before we ask our students to try it, thoughtfully examining our own criteria but not imposing them on other readers in the classroom. If students do not like the texts that challenge them to look at unflattering facts about humanity or that demand close reading, we have the opportunity to discuss the purposes of literature. Do we want to read sentimental clichés that cover up the unpleasant issues of life or to face the conflicts involved in being aware human beings?

MILITARY JUSTICE (p. 1091)

FRANK O'CONNOR

Guests of the Nation (p. 1091)

Students and instructors will find many ways to discuss of Frank O'Connor's short story "Guests of the Nation." We first provide — or have students research — the historical and cultural context of Ireland's relations with Great Britain and the ongoing political and religious issues that motivate O'Connor's characters. We sometimes use intertextual connections with other Irish writers, perhaps bringing in William Butler Yeats's poem "Easter 1916" for another perspective on the same conflict that is taking place in O'Connor's narrative. Students may be confused by references to "the German War" in the dialogue of O'Connor's story, and they need to know that the war in the story takes place in Ireland concurrently with and continues after World War I. The British are involved in both, and the British soldiers here have been sent to curb what Great Britain sees as civil unrest in territory under their control.

The story takes place during the time usually referred to by the Irish as "The Troubles" — troublesome both because the British sought to stamp out Irish rebellion and because Irish factions engaged in armed combat about the way to proceed politically. The nation of Ireland had not yet gained independence, and independence was one of the issues involved. The partition of Ireland kept several northern counties as part of the United Kingdom and continues to be a source of conflict even now. Writing at the beginning of the 1930s, between World War I and the ideological upheavals in Europe that would culminate in World War II within a decade, O'Connor describes events and has his characters discuss debates that his contemporaries would have understood immediately. The British soldier Hawkins and the Irish Republican Noble echo in microcosm the major debates of the day. Many thinkers of the 1920s and 1930s, for example, saw communism or anarchy as the answer to economic and social problems. When Hawkins accuses the Roman Catholic clergy of collaborating with political forces to keep workers from complaining, he echoes Marxist rhetoric that labels religion the "opiate of the people." But for these characters the debates are merely theoretical arguments, not qualitatively different from the card games that fill their time, and they are surprised when patriotism and "duty" force them to play out the ideology of war in solid reality.

O'Connor wrote his story out of his own personal participation in this conflict as a young man. He had been held prisoner at one point because he disagreed with the treatment that his fellow Irish Republicans dealt out to women who transgressed. "Guests of the Nation" grew out of his chance hearing of the experiences of other participants (quoted in volume 162 of the *Dictionary of Literary Biography*) :

> One day, when I was sitting on my bed in an Irish internment camp, . . . I overheard a group of country boys talking about two English soldiers whom they had held as hostages and who soon got to know the countryside better than their guards. It was obvious from the conversation that the two English boys had won the affection and understanding of our own fellows, though it wasn't the understanding of soldiers who find that they have so much in common, but the understanding of two conflicting ways of life which must either fight or be friends. (255)

In addition to considering issues of historical, cultural, and biographical context, readers often evaluate "Guests of the Nation" in terms of aesthetic, philosophical, and ethical issues. Some critics consider this O'Connor story a flawless example of literary art. They praise the lyricism of his language, especially in the descriptive imagery of the final paragraph. The plot of the story lends itself to analysis, with the forces of cause and effect leading inexorably toward the climax and the final event being foreshadowed in earlier dialogue. Since the sections of the story are numbered, questions about narrative structure enter into our analysis as well.

Students might enjoy discussing the names of characters and comparing these with the traits that they reveal. In this context, it is interesting that O'Connor gives the rigid, duty-bound Donovan his own family name. (O'Connor was born Michael O'Donovan and invented a pseudonym from names in his mother's family to allow himself the freedom to express independent ideas as a writer and still retain his Irish civil service job as a library administrator.) "Hawkins" is a Kiplingesque name for a low-ranking British infantryman, and "Belcher" has similarly "common" connotations, while the Irish rebels carry mock heroic names like "Noble" and "Bonaparte."

Students can debate the extent to which these names and other aspects of the story are ironic. They might look at external and internal conflicts confronted by the characters. Issues of philosophical and ethical evaluation may arise as they discuss the conflicting codes of honor that drive the characters. Hawkins cannot believe that his "chums" would break the code of friendship by taking his life, and Donovan judges the situation by rules of patriotism and duty to God and country. Hawkins is even willing to change sides, since treason does not go against his ethics. Bonaparte and Noble, however, struggle with ethical dilemmas as these codes come into conflict. If they had known they would be called to execute their hostages, they would never have turned them into friends.

Donovan, Noble, and Bonaparte have been assigned the duty of watching the hostages Hawkins and Belcher. Noble and Bonaparte fail to realize, however, that their duty may eventually include executing their "guests." Donovan, on the other hand, seems prepared, even eager, to carry out this ultimate duty. Bonaparte responds to Donovan's comments about duty with the thought, "I never noticed that people who talk a lot about duty find it much of a trouble to them." And just before his execution, the English soldier Belcher says, "I never could make out what duty was myself." One point of the story is that the ethical concept of duty is problematic. Much depends on whether the warrants for interpreting a certain action as one's duty are based on loyalty to friends, religion, one political entity versus another, or some other nebulous concept of right and wrong action. Belcher takes on the duty of helping the landlady, whereas neither Hawkins nor the Irish soldiers feel an obligation to do so. Belcher may also demonstrate the duty a soldier owes to himself to die bravely. Perhaps soldierly ethics also explain why the hostages do not run, despite Bonaparte's desperate wishes that they would. The story makes no explicit judgments about which duties override others but implicitly critiques the blind duty that accepts without questioning. Anticipating by two decades the Nuremberg trials that condemned Nazi war criminals for simply "following orders" regardless of the atrocity of the orders, O'Connor's story asks whether in some cases individual human judgment should supersede political ideology.

Bonaparte and Noble are most upset because the killing of the prisoners has been for them an "unforeseen" occurrence. The word *unforeseen* becomes a refrain in Bonaparte's commentary on the events. The English soldiers have become like household pets, he implies at one point, and if the guards had realized they would have to kill their hostages, they wouldn't have become so attached to them. As we have seen elsewhere in this anthology, a recurring theme in many literary texts is the need to dehumanize before we can justify doing harm. Of O'Connor's Irish soldiers, only Donovan is able to shut himself off from acknowledging the humanity of the prisoners. When he is faced with Belcher's dignity in the face of death and can no longer ignore him, Donovan explains that he is only doing his duty, shielding himself from the emotion that the other characters cannot escape. Although the ending completes the narrative in a wonderfully satisfying way, and readers familiar with the short story will not be surprised, O'Connor allows us the full impact by keeping us in suspense. There's always the chance that they will run; after all, we have been told that Hawkins knows the countryside better than the Irish soldiers, and we could expect the landlady to hide Belcher if asked. Or perhaps a reprieve will come. But as it turns out, this story belongs to the narrator and is about the impact of deliberately killing men one has considered to be friends.

While Hawkins argues against religion and capitalism throughout the story, at the end he also argues against the betrayal of friendship. Readers will vary in their judgments about his sincerity and his depth of understanding of Marxist theory. His arguments fail both to convince his religion-bound listeners and to prevent his execution. Some may see his willingness to change sides as cowardly, whereas others will read it as an appropriate action for an anarchist to take. His only duty is to himself and his friends as individuals, not to the institutions he sees as oppressive. Most readers see Belcher as more admirable, especially as we finally hear his voice at the story's end. Hawkins has been the talker, but we know little of him as a person. Belcher reveals a great deal about himself in his few words at the story's end. The two English soldiers are revealed most by their actions and their attitudes toward their executions. Most revealing may be Belcher's kindness to the old woman and his placing of his own blindfold over his eyes. He is helpful to the end. Hawkins, on the other hand, does not go gentle into the good night of the bog. The English hostages are alike primarily in their lack of true commitment to the cause that has sent them to their deaths. Hawkins serves in one of the most controlled and conservative institutions in his world, the British army, yet he strikes the pose of a radical and turns out to be apolitical at best. Belcher admits that he has no real comprehension of the duty that sends him to Ireland, but he stoically accepts his death without really questioning its necessity. While Hawkins argues that the Irish are pawns of capitalism and religion, the two British soldiers epitomize such victimization: we are struck by their differences, but they are equally dead.

Undoubtedly, O'Connor's original audience of the 1930s needed less exposition to understand the context of the story. Although historical information is helpful, the story can stand on its own as an exploration of the competing claims of friendship and patriotism. Each generation of readers will think of its own parallels. Though we often hear of hostages coming to identify with their captors, "Guests of the Nation" shows that the bond can be powerful from the other side.

HARUKI MURAKAMI

Another Way to Die (p. 1100)

As we read Haruki Murakami's narrative of an incident that he imagines took place during the Japanese occupation of Manchuria in northern China, we might look at other war stories, like the preceding "Guests of the Nation" by Frank O'Connor (p. 1091) and "The Things They Carried" by Tim O'Brien (p. 1424), or we can illuminate cultural and historical issues through texts like Amy Tan's "Two Kinds" (p. 373) or David Henry Hwang's M. Butterfly (p. 908), in which stereotypes about Asians are skewered. The novel from which "Another Way to Die" is excerpted is called The Wind-Up Bird Chronicle. It takes a surreal journey through several generations of Japanese history, including elements of fantasy and science fiction that strike some readers as Kafkaesque. Murakami has been compared to Gabriel García Márquez in his attitude toward history, a subversion of chronology that compresses or elongates time and brings about impossible meetings and recurrences. Although "Another Way to Die" has a realistic tone through much of its action, the final scenes pick up a postmodern surrealism and a warping of time. Interested readers might compare Murakami's style to the text by García Márquez (p. 1465) in our anthology.

Readers of "Another Way to Die" may note the musical quality of its carefully paced action and its interweaving of visual imagery and narration. Some see Murakami as jazzlike, citing his occupation as the proprietor of a jazz club in the 1970s and 1980s. Other critics take issue with his subversion of genre, finding his inconsistencies confusing. Murakami likes to imagine alternate lives, and his texts are multilayered. For example, in *The Wind-Up Bird Chronicle* the protagonist moves in and out of dreams — sometimes dreams within dreams — in which other characters tell stories, act as mediums, or leave messages on the computer. But it is difficult to know which alternate reality is which or whether one character is actually living out another's experiences in a transformed way. At one point in the novel, the main character, Toru Okada, uses a baseball bat to beat his politically manipulative brother-in-law to death in a dream. In the part of the novel retold in "Another Way to Die," the baseball bat becomes a weapon in the hands of another character's father years earlier. The wind-up bird that is heard as this story ends is also a recurring motif. The bird screeches every morning as a sort of "wake-up call" that signals a day has begun, but it could as easily not begin. It symbolizes the tightly wound tension and the "inescapable ruin" that permeate life for human beings. In Murakami's story, the killing seems without real purpose. This is made clear by the instructions to kill the zoo animals, the most innocent and vulnerable victims one could imagine. War, like history, is as arbitrary and logical as a nightmare.

Although some readers may argue that "Another Way to Die" is too violent, we wonder if it is possible to communicate the effects of war on human beings without picturing the violence. Most readers would expect, as do the characters, that a killing with a baseball bat would be more physically brutal than an efficient bayonet thrust. The details of the story convince us otherwise. The second paragraph thrusts the reader immediately into the arbitrary nature of war with the pathos of the animals' silenced "voices" and the information that specific animals — tigers, leopards, wolves, and bears — have been "liquidated — eliminated." Alert readers will associate the month and year given a few lines down with the date near the end of World War II when the United States dropped atomic bombs on Hiroshima and Nagasaki, literally liquidating and eliminating innocent women, children, and other noncombatants. In the English translation, presumably a fair rendering of the original Japanese, the words have euphemistic connotations that remind us of Nazi doublespeak or current language that uses terms like "collateral damage" to refer to the injury and death of human beings not actively involved in fighting. Later, the narrator mentions Hiroshima in passing. The violence resonates.

The veterinarian sees himself in the hands of fate, and though the narrator characterizes him as "not passive," he becomes a literal bystander as atrocities are carried out. Later, he is called on to perform a duty because of his medical training, to pronounce the last Chinese victim dead. But he is literally "pulled into" the war against his will by the death grip of the soldier. We are told in the flashforward of the ending paragraphs that he will eventually die as a Siberian prisoner for his collaboration. But we also see that no action of his would change any of the events that take place, and honest readers may wonder if they would behave any differently. He is a Japanese national and would be guilty of treason by one code of ethics if he acted to prevent the deaths of either the zoo animals or the Chinese men.

We associate zoos and baseball with the innocent play of childhood. By interjecting these images into a war story, the author makes the events more nightmarish and horror-filled. The effect is heightened by the concrete details, a technique Murakami's narrator makes explicit: "This was reality — as real as the sink and toothbrush he saw in front of him." And we have the further juxtaposition of haikulike sensory imagery describing the natural setting. A similar voice of education is heard when the lieutenant explains to the veterinarian how a bayonet is used and when he instructs the young soldier in how to use a baseball bat. The coaching results in a perfect hit, but the suspense is agonizing as we wonder whether he will botch the job in some horrible way.

The visual incongruity of the Chinese men "disguised" by the numbered baseball uniforms reverberates with connotations. We think of the enhanced identification the uniforms have provided both the group and the numbered individuals, the "friendship" games these men have played, and the similarities and differences between sport and war. The zoo, also, where dangerous beasts have been imprisoned and then executed, echoes with implicit metaphors and analogies. It would be interesting to have students draw up free-associated lists of their own connotations for zoos and baseball games in relation to war.

Readers of the novel may have a different understanding of the symbolism of the wind-up bird than those who read just the story. This sudden switch to an alternate reality is interesting but puzzling. The ending of Murakami's short story may remind readers of the ending of O'Connor's "Guests of the Nation"; both suggest the impact of an event on the future of the characters. Murakami takes the postmodern approach of magical realists like García Márquez and allows his narrator, now taking the young soldier's point of view, to see or to imagine the future. But Murakami's text questions the very concept of reality, and we cannot be certain if the young man knows what will happen or if he is engaged in a dream or a vision of one of many possible futures. The symbol of the wind-up bird signals a change of reality, an enhanced awareness that is similar to the epiphany we see in writers like James Joyce and Flannery O'Connor.

We have thought to this point that the story belonged to the veterinarian, but it turns out to belong to the young man who wields the baseball bat. Like O'Connor's narrator Bonaparte, the naive young farmboy is profoundly changed by his participation in an execution in the midst of war. Both stories end with what amounts to a prose poem, with the language lyrical and dreamlike. Students proficient in Japanese may find it interesting to read the story in both languages. Murakami's books are best-sellers in Japan, selling millions of copies. Since most of his fiction crosses — cultural boundaries — *The Wind-Up Bird Chronicle* being his most Japanese text — he is also developing a following among readers of Jay Rubin's English translations of his work. Like American readers of the Vietnam War narratives of O'Brien, Robert Olen Butler, and others, Japanese readers may be uncomfortable with the brutally honest depiction of the behavior of Japanese soldiers during World War II. But the history of atrocity in war is documented by historical evidence, and all nations have been complicit in such activities at one time or another. Some readers may claim that cultural differences made Japanese soldiers more brutal than Americans. They fall into the prejudicial stereotypes of earlier generations who found it necessary to demonize "Japs" and "Gooks" to distance them as the enemy. "Another Way to Die" counters this image; the characters are human beings engaged in the ethical dilemmas and rationalizations of war, just as American readers can imagine themselves doing under the same circumstances. Furthermore, Western readers are reminded again that Asian cultures are highly diverse and differentiated, with histories that still influence attitudes.

Although O'Connor uses a first-person narrator in "Guests of the Nation" and Murakami uses a third-person narrator in "Another Way to Die," the differences in distance and degree of knowledge revealed are slight. Murakami limits the reader for much of the story to the perspective of one character, the veterinarian, and we know only what he knows. Later, he shifts the point of view very briefly to the lieutenant and then finishes the story with the young soldier whose knowledge seems to approach the omniscient. We stand at a greater distance through most of Murakami's story than we do in O'Connor's, since we — like the veterinarian — are primarily bystanders, whereas Bonaparte brings us intimately into his own thoughts and action.

We might also expect to feel differently about O'Connor's characters than we do about Murakami's, since their names give them individual identities. This individualization is undercut somewhat by the emblematic connotations of the names, however. It is more important that we hear the victims speak in a language we can understand, whereas Murakami's victims are silent for the most part and we never hear their words. We look in on the card games and the political debates of O'Connor's characters but are only told of the baseball games of Murakami's. We also notice that, as Hawkins has been willing to do, the Chinese soldiers change sides when the opportunity arises. Until they know the Soviets are on their way, the Chinese men have been training in a facility of the puppet government controlled by Japan. Perhaps their donning of the baseball uniforms is more symbolic than the action at first appears, since this seems to be where their true allegiance lies. They are a tiny army of their own.

The veterinarian uses the numbers on the uniform in an attempt to humanize them, making them separate individuals. But the killers are more distinctive, even though they are named by their function in the army rather than by their names. We know about the veterinarian's family and about the young farmboy's chasing dragonflies and playing sword games. We know that the lieutenant is inexperienced at killing. Perhaps more readers empathize with the narrator of "Guests of the Nation" since we see him struggling with his emotions. The theme of O'Connor's narrative has to do with his conflict between the duties of friendship and the duties of war. Murakami's characters do not make friends with their enemies, but underneath their attempts to distance and control their emotions their struggle seems equally real.

None of the characters really seem to want to kill. Donovan in "Guests of the Nation" and the lieutenant in "Another Way to Die" are the most rigid and most willing to follow the orders given them from authorities far from the immediate events. But even they attempt to shield themselves from the act. Their seeming coldness may be self-protection. There are distinct similarities between the reactions of Bonaparte and the veterinarian as they are gripped — one of them literally — by their experiences. There are major differences, however. Bonaparte is young and inexperienced. The animal doctor is older, reflective, and philosophical. Murakami's shift in perspective at the story's end provides a more likely candidate for comparison with Bonaparte: the young soldier who grew up on a farm. They are similar in their innocence and in their transformations. Both end with insights about the future, engage in a reverie filled with sensory imagery, and ponder the changes in perception that can occur as a result of participation in such an event.

COMMUNITY JUSTICE (p. 1113)

SCOTT RUSSELL SANDERS

Doing Time in the Thirteenth Chair (p. 1114)

Courtrooms provide excellent examples of the sort of rhetorical issues we deal with in our first-year college English classes. Since the advent of courtroom television, instructors can mine the presentations of lawyers and the responses of witnesses for both positive and negative illustrations of persuasion. With their opening and closing arguments, their critical questioning of opposing sides, and their hodgepodge of logical, emotional, and ethical appeals, the professional rhetoricians of the courtroom often surprise us by the means they use to achieve their purposes. Each witness imposes his or her own narrative line on events and sees the chain of cause and effect in a particular way. In the college classroom, as we teach our students to critique the arguments of other writers, we urge them to be on the watch for logical fallacies. Use the ABC rule, we advise: examine evidence for its appropriateness, its believability, its consistency and completeness. Make sure one idea follows logically from another. Be alert for emotional manipulation. Don't be fooled by false appeals to authority; judge the ethos of the writer for knowledge and trustworthiness. Question warrants and underlying assumptions.

But time after time, we find lawyers convincing juries through appeals we would never accept in academic discourse. The use of pathos, no matter how obvious and manipulative, often carries the day. Experts list their degrees, building a case for their ethical credibility, and bore everyone to tears with impressively detailed hard evidence; but showmanship, humor, and folksy anecdotes get everyone on the side of the expert with the most style. Jurors see the defendant and his or her community as foreign and terrifying; as a result, they distance themselves and make judgments that the evidence may not warrant. Although we want students to recognize and write cogent arguments in which the chain of reasoning is flawlessly connected, we need to point out that logic alone may not be as persuasive as we would like to believe. People are not computers, and most audiences are moved by subtle factors like tone and style. And sad to say, many are moved by prejudice, loaded and slanted language, or appeals to class, race, sexual orientation, gender, or religion. As writers, we face ethical decisions about how to present a fair and reasonable argument that effectively persuades without resorting to trickery or demagoguery. The stars, the really great lawyers, know the audience their particular brand of rhetoric can reach most effectively. They choose accordingly.

Scott Russell Sanders titles his essay "Doing Time in the Thirteenth Chair" and uses the time motif to unify the narrative. We hear the ticking clock in the first sentence, and the narrator imagines that there may be "bombs or mechanical hearts" inside the walls. The Poe-like image comes close to personification but leaves the impression of inhuman machinery instead. The bombs reappear later in the essay as some of the jurors relate a frightening incident in front of the courthouse, as we imagine the defendant's Vietnam experiences, and as the jurors come out of the room after finding Bennie guilty, looking like survivors of a mine explosion. We notice that the narrator's backpack reads "NO NUKES."

Time is important throughout the essay, along with the metaphorical expression "doing time." Sanders is losing his Christmas vacation, the other jurors lose time at work, and the defendant loses fifty-four years, presumably the rest of his life. "Time, time," Sanders intones, "it always comes down to time: in jail, job, and jury box we are spending and hoarding our only wealth, the currency of days." He brings up the image of a ticking heart again, recalling the sound of his unborn daughter's heart as heard through the stethoscope. Time is like a force of nature, "raining its tick tocks down on us." After he has been selected as the alternate juror, Sanders throws in the one-word sentence, "Ticktock." We notice that he is number thirteen and recall that both clocks and juries go up to twelve. This allows Sanders to occupy the perfect position for a writer, that of observer. But it keeps him out of what he sees as the final act of the play. Like anyone who has just escaped deliberating on a jury, the writer has mixed feelings.

Sanders portrays the jurors in a positive way and imagines that their conflicts about convicting the defendant resemble his own. We wonder, however, how they reach the conclusion that the evidence overcomes reasonable doubt, since it seems unconvincing as Sanders presents it. The social distance between the jurors and the defendant may strike readers as minimal, since several jurors are unemployed. The writer's keen observations individuate them, but they still remain somewhat anonymous, known mainly by their occupations. One he characterizes as "a boisterous old lady" and another as "a meek college student with the demeanor of a groundhog." Both comments seem slightly derogatory. We wonder if they resent not knowing that the law would require them to take away the rest of Bennie's life because of the habitual offender statute. Since we, like the narrator, are locked out of deliberations, we miss the most important details of the jury's interactions. This is a disadvantage for an observer, and readers may notice that the old men hanging around the courthouse and the young men doing "penance" seem more vivid than the jurors. The narrator sees them as akin to Bennie, at some point along the continuum from misdemeanors to long prison sentence to electric chair or lonely old age.

Sanders never truly becomes part of the "community" of the jury. He paints himself as an outsider from the beginning and is sure that this will keep him from being chosen to serve. He views Bennie and his "community" with a mixture of compassion and guilt, as almost but not quite an insider of this unsavory group. He has a great deal of insight about Bennie's situation; he identifies with him as an age-mate, as a person whose appearance defies the conservative norm, and as a reminder of his own working-class roots. Sanders's father comes from a similarly large working-class family; Bennie's little girls remind him of his childhood playmates; an uncle died on the railroad tracks and Bennie was arrested on the railroad tracks; Sanders has escaped the Vietnam experience that Bennie claims has damaged him. The writer/professor feels a there-but-for-the-grace-of-God-go-I bond with the part-time garbage collector on trial for selling drugs. At least twice, he doesn't want to look at Bennie, doesn't want to see his pain and common humanity. But his portrayal is not wholly positive. Bennie's supporters are "a parade of mangled souls." The defendant's "mate" is described with animal imagery: she is "tigerish," is as capable of retaliation as "snakes, bears, wolves," and "mountain lions." The jurors reveal their view of Bennie's community when they fear at first that "Bennie's mean looking friends" have thrown a bomb at the courthouse. Bennie seems to know an uncommon number of betrayers and "snitches," and his testimony is filled with shifted blame and excuses. Yet the representatives of the community called by the prosecution seem no better, and Bennie's arrest borders on entrapment.

The writer himself steps back from time to time and provides a contrast from his own real-life community. He presents a short dialogue with his son, who seems to have a romantic cops-and-robbers view of his father's jury duty. He reveals tacitly that he has been keeping up with the news: juxtaposing an item about the government's passive acceptance of the drug trade and elaborating on a prison suicide. He does not have to tell us that the relative weight of the damage and punishment in both cases, when compared with Bennie's case, seems ironic and hypocritical.

It would be interesting to have students vote on whether they agree with the jury's verdict against Bennie and to discuss the quality of the evidence pro and con. The judge claims to know additional information that leads him to believe that Bennie's conviction is justified. But readers may recall the facts of the case — characterized by the narrator as "a mess." According to the state's evidence, Bennie's gross income from the sale of drugs to I90 amounts to thirty-three dollars — even if we believe an informant's self-serving testimony and the garbled tapes and notes of a police officer. The jury learns even before they are surprised with the habitual offender issue that Bennie understands he can get over thirty years in prison. Few readers believe that the punishment fits the crime, even with his earlier convictions factored in. Others raise issues about the damage Bennie has done if he actually is a drug dealer, citing above all the effect on Rebecca's daughters of living in a house where drug deals occur. The jury is supposed to consider the law of the matter, however, and perhaps these are ethical issues. Has the prosecution proven its case through the evidence of I90 and his handler? The jury decides that it has. Although Sanders emphasizes the uncertainty of the matter, many readers could make a good argument for reasonable doubt.

JOYCE CAROL OATES

I, the Juror (p. 1127)

The title of Joyce Carol Oates's essay "I, the Juror" plays on Mickey Spillane's title *I, the Jury*, the novel in which his famous fictional detective Mike Hammer tracks down and wields his own brand of justice on the murderer of a friend. Spillane's character, in the first of several 1950s best-sellers, becomes the judge and jury as he pronounces sentence and exacts revenge. Oates links herself with Mike

Hammer through the allusion. Her attitude toward the African American male defendant is not vindictive, however. She goes along with the decision to find him guilty of a lesser charge, despite her feeling that his female victim is being blamed. But Oates ends her essay with a statement that indicates the real targets of her judgment, the jury system itself — and this jury in particular — as representative of a bigoted, classbound, "not serious" citizenry. Perhaps the essay itself is her revenge.

We ask students to examine the diction and syntax of Oates's narrative as they determine her attitude and tone. She begins by musing about the "abstract principle of Justice," using a capital letter J to emphasize the symbolic nature of the word. Abstractions and generalizations are problematic, since they invite divergent interpretations, and Oates foregrounds this fact. She begins with her own abstract notions and her conflicting emotions about jury duty, preparing us for the specific, concrete working out of the trial-by-jury concept in practice. She shares her thoughts leading up to this particular jury duty as a way of giving background and providing context for the crushing of her "romantic illusions" at the trial's end. As we assign the reading, we brainstorm our own definitions and metaphors for justice — writing on the board *Justice is . . .* and having students call out completing phrases. We find political and philosophical differences and discuss the possible reasons underlying responses.

Oates tells us her connotations for the word in her two first paragraphs, developing them further as the essay proceeds. Her syntax in the opening is poetic in its balance; she begins with a fragment and follows with a series of parallel repetitions of words and sentence structures. We find alliteration and assonance. This seems an especially appropriate way to begin a piece of nonfiction about the nature of justice, since we would hope for balance and satisfying order in the jury process. But even here Oates points out the conflicts. Her word choices in the essay critique the absence of the human touch in the system itself. She receives a "smudgily computer-printed summons," at first appreciating its "impersonality," doesn't explain her professional name because it might generate "a punitive misfiring in the unimaginative computer brain"; and tells us the jury list is "stored in the computer" and thus names cannot be removed. She refers to the system as a "gigantic grinding machine," and later repeats the image: "an antique machine clanking and grinding and laboring." The system is "archaic, cumbersome, inefficient, outmoded, punitive," characterized by "an air of menace and threat." The courthouse is "generic." The jury as first seen is "a rambling herd," and her view of them grows even more negative. Even without her overtly negative evaluations of her fellow jurors, the procedures, and the court workers — her "overseers" — Oates's loaded words alone make judgments.

One worker tells Oates, when she challenges the routine as "punitive" and "inefficient," that the process has been streamlined, that it used to be worse, and that people had to accept it. The worker, perhaps correctly in view of the writer's judgmental attitude, takes a defensive stance, feeling personally criticized. Some readers feel that through much of the essay Oates comes across as arrogant, negative, and inconsistent in her criticism of everything around her in the courthouse. Isn't it fair to speculate that juries, too, have changed as the culture has changed, that people are no longer as willing to shoulder the responsibilities of jury duty or to accept any discomfort outside their own self-interest? Like reluctant schoolchildren, potential jurors come unwillingly, and perhaps they must be pursued and punished when they play truant. Nevertheless, as Oates points out, the great majority of those called have been excused before these few are forced to show up. It has been ironically asked if anyone would want to be tried by a juror who was too stupid to avoid jury duty. Does the oppressive atmosphere of the courthouse make people reluctant, or does the resistance of citizens to participate and cooperate make such rules necessary? Oates criticizes both the informal dress of fellow jurors and the churchy trappings of the court. Isn't this inconsistent? She carps about both impersonality and bias.

Juries may have been even more biased in the distant past, before the two-week imprisonment the court worker describes or the systematic randomness of computerized selections. In some areas of the country in the past, the issue of bumping black jurors from the panel would not have existed because African Americans would not have been called for jury duty at all, most having been barred from voter registration by Jim Crow laws. The original "grandfather clause" was instituted in many localities in the 1890s, a generation after slavery was declared illegal, and prevented men from voting (and consequently serving on juries) if their grandfathers had not been qualified to vote. Oates herself would not have served in the past, since women were not called either. In the 1930s unemployed young men hung around the courthouse, hoping to be called for jury duty. It worked a bit like plasma donation. Local white men over the age of twenty-one could be pulled in off the street to serve and earn a dollar or so and, if sequestered, free room and board for as long as they could keep the hot debates going, taking whichever side was necessary. Would this sort of volunteer jury pool be preferable? Oates implies that African American jurors might have been able to try this case more fairly. Although few readers would condone racial loading of juries in either direction, we feel intuitively that cultural experiences play a part in judgments. However, African American jurors — even women — would be just as likely to blame the female victim. Trying to decide who in the jury pool is truly a "peer" of the victim or the defendant would be a risky and even more prejudiced approach than the current one. Readers who find Oates's complaints about the jury system persuasive should consider the ramifications of changes. Placing the justice system in the hands of a few judges or professional jurors, as some have suggested, seems especially conducive to elitism, a charge that could be leveled at Oates herself.

Some readers respond positively to Oates because she is a keen observer and an articulate, highly respected writer. She gets us on her side with balanced considerations of the pros and cons of jury duty and with self-revelations about her idealism and her fears. She seems to have compassion for the woman who has been beaten, for which most of us judge Oates positively. Her criticism of the jurors centers primarily around their willingness to condemn this woman and the others of her community because the jurors are unable to place themselves in the situations described. This is a major problem. Recently, in a televised trial in Texas, both the prosecution and the defense made shockingly open attempts to play on the jury's distance from the people of "that neighborhood" of Mexican Mafia members, glue-sniffing boys, "breeding" women, and careless girls. "Send a message to *those* people," the prosecutor actually said. "How could you expect this young boy to know how to behave given these role models?" the defense attorney countered, pleading for life in prison rather than death. The eighteen-year-old was sentenced to death row. Readers may find it frightening to contemplate that most jurors are more swayed by overt or unconscious race, class, and gender bias than by a careful consideration of the facts. Because it is a story that involves a black man beating his wife, Ann Petry's "Like a Winding Sheet" (p. 1603) makes a useful companion piece to "I, the Juror." Students can compare their possible votes on a jury panel that is trying Petry's character with the verdict in this case.

Readers sometimes feel that Oates judges the jurors too harshly, especially when she characterizes them as not taking the process seriously. Who is she to condemn their clothing and their offhand remarks? Others agree with Oates that justice for the victim should be uppermost in jurors' minds. Since Oates also participated in the deliberations, however, we wonder why she did not stand her ground if she wanted a harsher verdict. Her generalizations are questionable both because her experience may not stand as a representative example and because the writer herself may be biased in terms of class and education. Throughout her narrative, Oates seeks to separate herself from the other people in the courthouse. Only the judge — an articulate, educated woman who tells Oates later that she recognizes her — seems to be accepted by Oates as her moral and ethical equal. Some readers question the identification of the Princeton professor and award-winning writer with the black woman who is beaten, seeing Oates as taking merely an ideological stance. Those who know Oates's biography and work will perhaps see her position as consistent and sincere. Still, it hardly seems fair for one who stands aloof in her judgments of her peers to fault the jury for being equally distant from the world of the defendant and his victim.

Although Scott Russell Sanders (p. 1114) is less critical of his jury than Oates is of hers, the behavior of the Indiana and New Jersey panels does not seem qualitatively different. Both panels feel that the people they are judging are not their peers. Both juries engage in small talk. Sanders relishes the revelations of personality and common humanity in such exchanges as relieving the boredom, whereas Oates feels that this is time wasted and would like to contemplate the evidence. The ordinary, presumably respectable, people on the juries see a different world from their own in the drug- and violence-ridden world of the underclass. Oates's jury lashes out in judgment against the victim, while Sanders's jury — seen only from the outside view of an alternate juror — nervously jokes about bombs. Both narrators are professional writers and English professors and feel the intellectual's estrangement from the middle class and imaginative empathy with the underclass — Sanders with the scruffy defendant and Oates with the battered victim. Both writers have working-class roots that give this perspective some legitimacy, though no reader would believe either could have truly exchanged fates with the individuals with whom they identify. Although he does not criticize as harshly as Oates, Sanders supplies ample details for the reader to judge that what happens to the defendant in the Indiana trial is terribly unfair, and he makes it clear that the system and not the jury causes this injustice. Because Sanders dedicates more space to the defendant, his wife, and the witnesses from the lower-class community in the Indiana trial, they are more three-dimensional than Oates's emblematic abusive man and victimized woman in New Jersey. We have only Oates's judgment and the few glimpses that she gives us to decide whether the victim and the defendant in the New Jersey trial receive true justice.

By relating her story in the past tense, Oates gives a sense of having thought through the meaning of the events, but she also takes the chance that we will step back and observe her, as she does others. Sanders's use of the present tense allows the reader to share his observations and frustrations firsthand. He shows more than he tells. The use of the present tense seems especially effective when Sanders uses the time motif to unify his narrative. We hear the clock ticking along with him. Both writers use images that emphasize the inhuman, mechanical nature of legal institutions. Both feel limited by the waste of time and by their confinement in space. Oates speaks of the tedious nature of the testimony and the dead time when the jury is kept from hearing information. The trial "traced and retraced the same narrow terrain, like a snail with a motor imbalance," Oates says, linking the frustrations of time and space in the same simile. "The facts are a mess," Sanders generalizes, leading into his concrete metaphor. "They are full of gaps, chuckholes, switchbacks, and dead ends — just like life." Unlike the witnesses, each writer finds a way to focus the jury experience for the audience. Sanders uses the repetition of time images to impose a narrative line on the jumbled observations of an alternate juror. Oates structures her essay through a chronological arrangement. She first considers her thoughts about justice and jury duty before the trial, then shows her change and frustration as she finds that her ideals are far from reality, and ends with an "Afterword" that ponders the meaning of the experience and her changed views. She ends with a question rather than closure, projecting the issue into the future for the reader to consider.

MAXINE HONG KINGSTON

No Name Woman (p. 1138)

In 1976, Maxine Hong Kingston's *The Woman Warrior: Memoirs of a Girlhood among Ghosts* jumped straight off the presses into the multicultural literary canon in university classrooms. The book is interesting for many reasons. Its style is filled with metaphor and concrete imagery, often reading like poetry. Characters are as three-dimensional and dynamic as those of any short story, and they evoke a specific situation in a way that both insiders and outsiders to its culture can grasp. But perhaps most interesting is Kingston's interweaving of the nonfiction of autobiography with fictional leaps into imagination and myth. Just as the author lives in the borderland between her Chinese ancestral heritage and her American individuality, her narrative exists in the intersection where genres overlap.

In her adaptation of the stories of her childhood, Kingston critiques both American and Chinese cultural limitations, especially the racist assumptions of white America and the patriarchal structures of China that reduce women to shameful beings who are less than human. To be a girl is to be worthless and bad. Girls grew up to move into other families, so every mouthful of food given to a girl was stolen from the parents' true children, the boys. In China, where infanticide has long been accepted, female children were often disposed of, especially in times of starvation. So when the young Maxine Hong begins to menstruate, her mother tells her the story of her aunt, the No Name Woman of this narrative, an excerpt from *A Woman Warrior*. The assumption is that the warning is needed so that the young woman will not commit the sexual transgressions that will embarrass the family. But the author comes to see that the true punishment dealt to her aunt has been her erasure. Her fate has been a sort of "reverse ancestor worship" in which she continues to pay for her sin against the family. She has no name, and all memory of her has been wiped out, except as a bad example.

Kingston imagines scenarios that explain her aunt's shameful pregnancy, imagining at first that she was forced, then briefly that she had been promiscuous, and finally that she had sought out a lover, deliberately attracting and winning his love. She even realizes the possibility of incest. Kingston's aunt is one of the ghosts who haunt her girlhood and continues to haunt the woman twenty years later. Her affinity for this particular spirit is not altogether safe and wholesome, she admits at the end of her narrative. By filling in the gaps of her mother's cautionary tale to find the personality behind it, Kingston imagines her aunt's motives and explores her own assumptions about gender and society. The reader is invited to do the same because Kingston acknowledges the open quality of this mystery story.

The argument behind the narrative that Kingston's mother tells is that a woman is always being watched, and though she is prone to be bad, her punishment will be certain. Women students who read the story may be able to recall such exemplary warnings by their mothers against forming relationships too early or having unprotected sex. Often, parents see such warnings backfire, as children say, "Well, I guess I take after that aunt you told me about." Like Kingston, most young people find that such anecdotes make them curious to know the reasons behind the behavior the parent disapproves. Most contemporary parents might ask daughters to consider how focusing on a sexual relationship will interfere with education and the chance to establish a career. "Don't give up your power," we tell them, pointing to women who are abused or otherwise dominated by men. Most American students will not have comparable punishments to share with the class and will think of the aunt's treatment by the villagers and her family as unforgivable abuse. Some American parents shun adult children for choosing the "wrong" partner or lifestyle, cutting off communication entirely, but this is rare among our students. Some girls in any given class may have ended unplanned pregnancies with abortions, either by their own choice or because of their parents' insistence. Sometimes they mention this privately to the instructor, but usually they keep silent. We might want to keep this in mind as the class enters into the discussion of sensitive matters, maintaining a noncondemning atmosphere. Young men might be asked to consider what they would do if they realized they had impregnated someone; can they imagine covering this up by joining the villagers who invade the woman's household? Although discussing their punishments for minor infractions may seem trivial in the light of what happens to No Name Woman, this is an illuminating way to discover the values of our families and to think about the warrants we bring into adulthood. Students also might want to share the stories their parents tell, usually to laughter, about their childhood or adolescent infractions. Have fathers shared with sons their college drinking escapades? Or an arrest at a political demonstration?

Sometimes, Kingston tells her readers explicitly that "No Name Woman" is a tale of gender inequality. For example, she tells us in paragraph 15, "To be a woman, to have a daughter in starvation time was a waste enough." But the whole story is implicitly about the greater burden that sex places on a woman. She is punished by the family and the village, must bear the child and give birth alone, and is driven finally to commit murder/suicide because she cannot provide a respectable life for the baby. We can believe the part of the story told by Kingston's mother, though she leaves many gaps. We can also trust the information the author provides about herself and her own childhood experiences. Her facts about Chinese customs can be verified. But she only guesses about her aunt's experiences and motives, often signaling this with the word *perhaps*. When she speaks of her aunt haunting her, she speaks metaphorically, but in an emotional and psychological sense this may be equally as true as the numerical fact that there are only one hundred surnames in all of China.

As we have seen in many of the texts of this anthology, writers often distinguish between things that are true in a human or spiritual sense and things that are merely factual. Kingston's imagined events give flesh to the sparse facts of her mother's cautionary tale and her knowledge of her Chinese family and history. Kingston reiterates the assertion that the crime of No Name Woman was severe because it happened in the context of famine. "Adultery is extravagance," Kingston says of the Chinese view. Thirty or forty years ago in America, a daughter's pregnancy would have brought shame to her family in most regions and subcultures. Girls were sent away to "homes for unwed mothers" and their babies disappeared into the adoption market. Neighbors often guessed the reason for the young woman's absence, but secrecy reigned. Sometimes, family members found ways to quietly claim the child as their own, and there are tales of people discovering in adulthood that the woman they thought was an older sister or aunt was their biological mother. Those with cooperative family doctors often had a "D&C" to discover why their periods were "irregular," effectively removing any fetal tissue that happened to be there without anyone outside the family knowing for sure. And, of course, we have all heard stories of illegal abortions. For contemporary women, pregnancy does not usually carry a stigma as a sign of sexual activity, though peers may judge harshly the failure to use birth control or safe-sex measures. Church members who once might have been condemning of unmarried pregnant women find themselves in the incongruous position of praising them for not choosing abortion, though premarital sex and adultery are still considered sins. An American woman in the position of Kingston's aunt would probably be able to get help with the support of her child, but keeping the name of the father a secret would not be encouraged, since he would be expected to contribute financially. While sexual transgression is shrouded in moral and religious prohibitions, economic factors may be the most important underlying reasons for cultural taboos against sexual activity outside of marriage.

Whereas Scott Russell Sanders (p. 1113) and Joyce Carol Oates (p. 1127) were involved in the cases they report, Kingston heard about her aunt's death many years after the event. This difference is relevant to a certain extent, since the juries play a similar role to that of the villagers who judge Kingston's aunt, exacting the justice prescribed by the culture in which they live. Kingston is not a member of the jury and participates in the punishment of her aunt only by maintaining silence. But the narrators of the other two essays position themselves as outsiders to the jury as well: Sanders is an alternate and identifies with the defendant, and Oates sees the trial from her own ideological perspective and chooses to distance herself from the other jurors.

All three writers seek to fill out stories that are presented to them in an incomplete form. Kingston's mother gives her only the details that suit her purpose, to admonish a pubescent girl to avoid situations that could shame her family. The prosecutors, defense lawyers, and witnesses at the court trials give slanted and incomplete narratives as well. The jury members in Sander's account are surprised to find that their guilty conviction will lead the defendant to spend virtually the rest of his life in prison for a minor drug offense, since the man is a repeat offender. The judge implies that their verdict is fair because he knows dangerous details about the defendant's character, but the jurors leave the courtroom knowing only the conflicting stories they have heard in court. They catch glimpses of the lives of the "mangled souls" in the courtroom, but "some of them remain offstage, summoned up only by the words of those who testify." Like Kingston, observers and participants in the courtroom may continue to replay the meager, conflicting facts of these lives, imagining scenarios but never having a cohesive narrative. The story continues to be as "full of gaps" as ever. Sanders gropes toward a narrative by linking the defendant and witnesses to his own experiences — seeing childhood neighbors in the faces of the children, comparing the informant's large family to his own father's, and flashing back to the memory of an uncle who died on the railroad tracks — as he hears the details of the defendant's arrest. Kingston does much the same, seeking out a connection between herself and her dead aunt. Oates also finds herself frustrated by the incomplete information given to jurors, parenthetically complaining that "as a juror, denied virtually any contextual information, and made, from time to time, to leave the courtroom, one is absorbed in trying to figure out what *really* happened, what the *real* story is." Like the incomplete drama Sanders observes and the story Kingston tries to piece together, the narrative Oates seeks to grasp remained elusive during the trial as "witnesses supplied wildly varying details, each convinced he or she was remembering correctly."

Like Sanders, Oates wonders if jurors are capable of leaping across the cultural divide that separates them from the victim and the witnesses. Oates thinks that the jury members may even see themselves as a different "species, wholly distinct from the blacks of Trenton's underclass whom they were empowered to judge." When we take these cultural differences into account, it may be that Kingston, as a member of the close-knit Chinese American community, depends no more on hearsay than Sanders and Oates and actually has more knowledge of her characters' emotions and challenges to work with. All three stand outside of the story, seeking to identify with the accused, the families, or the victims. Furthermore, all three stand outside of the jury or seek to do so.

Kingston allows herself more room for speculation, perhaps because the gaps are greater in the narrative she is given, perhaps because as a family and community member she is more rather than less involved in the "case" she describes.

Because we have such a cultural distance, we tend to see the community that judged Kingston's aunt as less rational than the American juries. The word *rational* implies reasoned, logical thought. The court system is supposed to be built on rationality, and judges instruct juries that they must determine the facts and act in accordance with the law. Kingston does a good job, however, of explaining the warrants for the actions of the villagers who act as judge, jury, and executors of punishment against her family. She explains that people in China think in terms of enduring famine and conserving orderly family traditions. It is telling that members of the crowd who splatter blood and destroy the home of the adulterous woman's family are crying as they enter the compound. Kingston repeats this fact, imagining that "they sobbed and scolded while they ruined our house." They cry with outrage but perhaps also with compassion and grief. Not all members of the group feel good about what they are doing, but they all feel that they must do it, just as jury members must follow the law and turn in a reasoned verdict.

In the trial Sanders describes, three jury members weep when they realize that they must place their stamp on a conviction of at least fifty-four years. Had they known this in the early stages of deliberation, they could have brought in a less "rational" not guilty verdict. In both Kingston's rural China and Sanders's small town Indiana, rationality, based on cultural and legally established warrants, seems to dictate more serious consequences than the jury or the village would have chosen.

In her more diverse New Jersey county, Oates continues to grieve over the situation she has observed, even though she has participated in the verdict. What seems to bother her the most is the lack of rationality, the lack of seriousness, she observes in her fellow jury members. She feels that by taking a superior attitude toward the female victim, they undercut their ability to judge the facts of the case. The system is far from rational, Oates maintains: "the jury itself, though the fabled glory of our American criminal justice system, resembles nothing so much as a large, ungainly, anachronistic beast with one eye patched over, a gag in its mouth, cotton stuffed in an ear, a leg shackled. Yet the delusion persists, the jury judges 'facts.'" Prejudice colored the ability of her jury to function, Oates feels, and she argues that "if the victim had been, not black, but a young white woman, they would surely have seen the charge differently." Discussion is not logical but based on "gut-level" intuitions and efforts to distance themselves from members of the frightening crime-ridden community glimpsed in the courtroom. She points out that the true peers of the victim and the defendant have been excluded by peremptory challenges.

For American readers, "No Name Woman" in its entirety describes an egregious invasion of privacy. We do not see sexual transgression among consenting adults as a reason for punishment to be dealt out by the community and usually consider what happens behind closed doors to be a matter of concern only to the parties involved. Yet the villagers feel compelled to tramp through the bedrooms of the offender's house. Certainly we would not punish the whole family for the sins of one member, we think. We might recall, however, that "No Name

Woman" lives in China in the 1920s. In the United States at that time, many laws regulating sexual behavior were on the books, and women pregnant outside of marriage were ostracized in most communities. Furthermore, while laws now shelter rape victims from having their previous sex lives displayed in the court-room, Oates's jury shows that the behavior of women victims still raises suspi-cions, even if judgments about their characters can only be inferred from appearance and demeanor. As this entry is being written, the trial of an accused child murderer in California has also made public details of the "swinging lifestyle" of the child's parents that have nothing to do with her death. While cultural and historical contexts shape definitions of *private* and *public* and defi-nitions of crimes against the community, trials by their very nature cause public and private spheres to overlap.

PSYCHIATRIC INJUSTICE: CULTURAL CONTEXTS FOR CHARLOTTE PERKINS GILMAN'S "THE YELLOW WALLPAPER" (p. 1148)

CHARLOTTE PERKINS GILMAN

The Yellow Wallpaper (p. 1149)

The narrator of Charlotte Perkins Gilman's 1892 short story "The Yellow Wallpaper" — a married woman who has a young baby she is not required to care for — writes a series of surreptitious journal entries while undergoing treat-ment that prescribes complete rest from physical, social, and mental activity. The context of the entries, separated by spaces, suggests that there are eleven of them, written over the course of the summer. As the narrator records her thoughts, they become increasingly disordered and her tone becomes gradually more manic. The change is particularly evident when the story is read aloud by a skilled actor. Our class listens to an especially good audiotape, allowing the voice of the narrator to sweep the audience inexorably into her delusion. Gilman's narrator is unreliable, and readers question her interpretations of the situation. Is the narrator in a country house with her husband, or is she actually in an insane asylum? Is she delusional, or does her early comment that the house may be haunted indicate that this is a ghost story in which the figure of a woman really does come out of the wallpaper? Would she be crazy anyway, as students sometimes contend, or does her condition become worse because she is treated as a foolish child and forbidden intellectual activity?

Gilman's sensory imagery creates an impression of gradually altered per-ception. The wallpaper has unattractive and ominous connotations from the beginning. The narrator's first description of its color uses words like *repellant, revolting, smouldering, unclean, lurid orange,* and *sickly sulphur.* Her reaction to the pattern is even more revealing. Curves "suddenly commit suicide" and "destroy themselves in unheard of contradictions." Two weeks into the summer stay, in the second journal entry, the narrator has begun to personify the wall-paper, suspecting that it has knowledge of its effect and a will of its own. She begins to see horrible faces in it; "the pattern lolls like a broken neck and two bulbous eyes stare at you upside down." As her solitary confinement and forced idleness continue, the narrator comes to believe that a woman is imprisoned in the wallpaper, and she takes action to help the woman get out.

At a point late in the narrator's illness, the images become synesthestic — melding two senses into one as sometimes occurs with schizophrenia. The wall-paper now has a "yellow smell." By this time, the narrator claims off-handedly to have been the woman in the wallpaper, who has finally been released, in spite of Jane and the husband. This is the first time we have heard this name; Mary is credited with caring for the baby, and Jennie does everything else. The logical conclusion is that Jane is the name of the narrator, whose derangement we have followed through most of the story. Now, the narrator implies, the woman behind the wallpaper has escaped. Where then is Jane?

The narrator moves from a cheerful though frustrated attempt to submit to the authority of her husband/physician and other male authority figures to a determined, single-minded "creeping" that takes her right over the husband's prostrate body, which has collapsed in shock. Read strictly in a psychological way, her story is one of a slide into madness, brought on by society's denial to her of any real fulfillment of her intellectual and emotional needs as an adult. But some readers feel that she achieves a victory of sorts, is finally freed from oppression and has become her own person. No longer can her feelings be waved aside and dismissed with baby talk. Students usually enjoy diagnosing her psychological illness. Postpartum depression is certainly indicated, though bipolar disorder and schizophrenia are sometimes suggested. Research on neurasthenia, a faddish diagnosis for women with vague symptoms around the turn of the twentieth century, will turn up interesting facts for students with medical and psychological interests. Similar symptoms in recent years have resulted in increased labeling of patients with hypoglycemia, chronic fatigue syndrome, fibromyalgia, and so on . By the end of the story, the narrator has the symptoms of an obsessive-compulsive disorder; she focuses on the need to tear down wallpaper, chew up the furniture, and creep along the edge of the wall.

Although critics like to emphasize the cultural and historical issues of patriarchy and women's societal position in the 1890s and beyond — a focus consistent with the author's concerns — it is possible to read Gilman's story as a psychological thriller like those of Edgar Allan Poe. Readers find ample evidence that the narrator reveals the truth of her illness to us in bits and pieces, sometimes misleading us because she herself does not realize the truth. From her earliest musings about the house, we wonder whether it has been used as a madhouse before or if she has been here longer than she indicates. There is a locked gate at the top of the stairs, bars on the windows, and "rings and things in the walls." Although she assumes that the room has been a nursery and a gymnasium, we do not have to accept this evaluation. Even at the beginning of the story, the wallpaper "is stripped off . . . in great patches all around the head of my bed, about as far as I can reach." We see that the bed is damaged long before we see her take a bite out of it. Some readers question whether she has already begun to damage the furnishings or if the room has housed a previous resident who rips wallpaper, perhaps a woman who is now trapped in the wallpaper. To read the story in this way is to enter into her madness, but it provides a valid perspective.

The wallpaper becomes a symbol of the circumstances of the narrator. Forbidden the order of work and adult activity, the narrator's mind is as confused and disordered as the lines of the paper, and she feels as sick as its colors and as full of poison as its nasty fungi. She is trapped within the constraints of dependency and societal rules and frantically grasps for the action that will allow her to be free and whole. She feels suicidal — at one point thinking of jumping out the barred window — and the wallpaper writhes with images of choked people and women behind bars.

The joy of reading "The Yellow Wallpaper" with a new class each semester is the opportunity to read the story from multiple perspectives. Students who choose to write papers about Gilman's story could experiment with playing a believing-and-doubting game with the text, first completely trusting the narrator's words that these supernatural events are taking place and then questioning everything. Though some readers see Jane as a freakish madwoman who is merely displayed for our horror, many others find her persistence in the face of patriarchy admirable. We empathize with her resistance to forced isolation and insulting condescension and are able to imagine our own reactions to such abuse. Students who dismiss her as simply crazy might be asked to consider if this is proper treatment for her even if she arrives at the house mentally ill. Isn't Gilman correct in her contention that being forbidden to work, exercise, read, or see friends makes a depressed person feel worse?

Through her use of the present tense, Gilman allows us to observe the progression of the narrator's reading of the wallpaper and to be startled by the sudden inconsistency and disjunction of certain remarks. At the end of the fourth entry, she sees the shape of a woman, or many replications of the same woman, and she says, "I wonder — I begin to think — I wish John would take me away from here." We are not told what it is she wonders about, but we know that at this point it frightens her. By the ninth entry, the present tense allows her to nonchalantly drop her own method of "creeping" into her musings about the woman she now believes she sees creeping outside every window. We do not know what happens after her husband awakens from his fainting spell. If the story were told from the past tense, we would sense a narrative line being drawn to explain either her recovery or her continuing illness. As it stands, the reader must decide what happens next and ultimately must decide the meaning of the story.

"The Yellow Wallpaper" lends itself to a discussion of symbolism, cause and effect, theme, and social and historical context. Most critics take the story to be a condemnation of the cultural barriers that work against equal treatment of women. By creating a composite character in the narrator's husband John, making him both her husband and a physician, Gilman broadens her critique to include not only the medical profession but also marriage and, by implication, the other institutions of a patriarchal society. John's paternalistic control over his wife is complete. She has no power and no voice, since she is virtually imprisoned and all of her thoughts are dismissed as foolish. Readers doubt whether John could really understand what love between equals entails. He is his wife's keeper, and she is his pet. Yet in her time, many of Gilman's contemporaries would wonder what the woman has to complain about. She lives like a princess, they would think. She is even robbed of the conflict that women of past generations felt between the need to do meaningful, creative work and the need to nurture and love husbands and children. She is allowed neither and instead must occupy the position of a fragile doll. She is expected to be cheerful and docile, denying any of the feelings that she needs to work out.

CULTURAL CONTEXTS:

CHARLOTTE PERKINS GILMAN, "Why I Wrote 'The Yellow Wallpaper'" (p. 1162)
S. WEIR MITCHELL, From *The Evolution of the Rest Treatment* (p. 1163)
JOHN HARVEY KELLOGG, From *The Ladies' Guide in Health and Disease* (p. 1168)

Young men and women in college in the twenty-first century might find it difficult to imagine the inferior position to which women were relegated in the 1890s, when Charlotte Perkins Gilman was facing gender discrimination as a writer and as a person. Students tend to blame the victim in "The Yellow Wallpaper" (p. 1149) for the distress she feels as a result of her limited options for self-expression and meaningful work, dismissing her as her husband does as foolish and weak. Because Gilman was subjected to S. Weir Mitchell's "rest cure" in the wake of her own postpartum depression, many readers have assumed that the events of the short story are autobiographical. In her response to such hasty conclusions in her own time, Gilman states unequivocally that although she and the narrator of "The Yellow Wallpaper" share some experiences, they are not the same person. "I never had hallucinations or objections to my mural decorations," she quips.

Gilman mentions Mitchell by name in the short story, keeping him in the distance as a threat to the narrator but not a person directly involved in her treatment. In the nonfiction piece "Why I Wrote 'The Yellow Wallpaper'" she does not give his name; however, she does cite "friends" of the "specialist" who say that he "admitted" to changing his treatment methods after reading Gilman's story. He may have done this privately, but the public speech that is excerpted here (p. 1163) gives no indication that he has abandoned his methods.

Health professionals today would agree with some of Mitchell's techniques — the use of massage, perhaps — but would be horrified by the lack of exercise and the insistence on "overfeeding" in his regimen. This alone tends to make Gilman's objections to his advice seem reasonable to modern readers, despite what Mitchell says. Gilman's evidence for her statement that Mitchell has been influenced by her story is weak, however, since it is based on hearsay and not attributed to a specific, reliable source. This possibly erroneous statement of the doctor's views, undoubtedly without his permission, comes across to some readers as a false use of authority in her defense of her story.

The physicians she answers in this piece raise two issues. One praises her description of insanity as believable and asks if it is autobiographical. She responds to this by a frank admission that it is true to her life to an extent, but then counters Mitchell's methods by maintaining that going directly against his advice saved her. In response to the doctor who says that her story could drive people crazy, she insists that "The Yellow Wallpaper" has achieved its purpose of saving people from mental illness. She gives a single example of a woman whose family was influenced to stop such treatment, but presumably her final statement refers to the alteration in Mitchell's program, a fact in question. The core of Gilman's explanation, like the main idea of her story, remains convincing, however: she speaks from experience. Mitchell's advice to avoid intellectual stimulation and to give up her creative activity almost sends her over the edge, and she emerges from the experience convinced that work empowers women.

In Gilman's day, a woman of her social class was often denied work and education and was then seen as inferior — perhaps underneath it all as "a pauper and a parasite" — as a result of her dependence. Some readers may raise the issue that Gilman's experience is not necessarily representative and that the failure of Mitchell's cure in her case keeps her from fairly evaluating its efficacy for others. If a person is mentally ill, such readers insist, it is difficult to know whether poor treatment causes decline or whether the disorder would have taken the same course in any event. Nevertheless, for most readers, Gilman's firsthand knowledge of depression and of the "rest cure" lends weight to her story. Her clarification about the extent of her illness is especially useful, her "escape" from the fate of her narrator giving her a survivor's credibility and distance. Biography is most helpful when the reader is able to see the world of the story as informed by the facts of the writer's life but as not identical to them.

Although he does not acknowledge feminist and fiction writer Gilman, that by the time Mitchell discusses his methods in "The Evolution of the Rest Treatment" in 1904, he has come under a great deal of attack from other quarters. His tone in the essay is defensive. He has been labeled a charlatan. He says in his closing paragraphs that he has "suffered keenly" from accusations that his methods are unscientific. In this passage, he emphasizes his discovery of massage as an adjunct to the rest cure and defends his method as pragmatic but also "defensible in the end by scientific explanatory research." He separates himself from "quacks" like osteopaths and Swedish massage practitioners, whom he judges as too rough. He describes several cases in which his cure has been successful but does not provide the evidence of controlled studies that we would expect today. Students find it ironic that one proof of success is weight gain, an effect that many people today would see as a sign of an unhealthy lack of exercise. Mitchell takes his patient's illness seriously, and we may approve his defense of her against the label of hysterical woman. He recognizes the pejorative quality of the word *hysteria*, maintaining that "calling names" and labeling don't really lead to recovery.

Mrs. G. is like Gilman and the narrator of "The Yellow Wallpaper" in that she is essentially placed in solitary confinement and forbidden to work, but Mitchell emphasizes massage and "electric passive exercise" in which the muscles are stimulated by mild electric shocks. She gets better, he claims, and he is able to "overfeed" her and to sneak iron supplements into her food. Everything about her treatment is decided for Mrs. G., but readers do not sense the level of condescension that Gilman's narrator receives from her husband. Perhaps this is because we hear Mitchell's tone as he addresses other doctors and not as he speaks to Mrs. G. Unlike Gilman, she stays with the program and unlike the narrator of Gilman's story, she does not slip into madness. Mitchell takes full credit: the woman remains at the time of his speech "what I made her." Implied in the description of Mrs. G., however, is the notion that she suffers from exhaustion because she seeks to go beyond her strength. There is no way to know from this distance what Mrs. G.'s problem was or why Mitchell's treatment worked in her case and not in Gilman's.

Mrs. G. is offered as evidence of success, not as a case study that gives detailed observations from which his audience can draw their own conclusions. The gaps make comparison difficult, and readers are usually too influenced by our reading of Gilman and our knowledge that isolation and lack of exercise are debilitating. Still, we may appreciate the need of busy people to have some respite from the duties of life and the recognition that it is not a good idea for a woman to have babies too often. Mrs. G. may recover in spite of Mitchell's treatment.

Modern readers cannot miss the signs of anorexia and bulimia that would indicate a need for more calories and mineral supplements and would cause weakness that might require bedrest. It may strike young working mothers as appropriate that this woman's case comes up in a speech that also describes what we would now call post–traumatic stress syndrome in American Civil War soldiers. Today's women often feel embattled. When stress is the cause of illness, rest alone may bring relief. Mitchell's description of the male patient with "locomotor ataxia" is more puzzling, since some physiological condition seems to be involved. The gaps in his description are too great to draw any real parallels with Mrs. G. or Gilman's character. From the details we are given, the woman's care is managed more closely. Students may find it significant that Mitchell distinguishes between his male and female patients. In speaking of men with battle fatigue, which he sees as a variety of "Neurasthenia," Mitchell says that such cases are "more certainly curable than are most of the graver male cases which now we are called on to treat." Does this imply that female cases are less grave or that male cases are taken more seriously? One wonders too if Mrs. G. would have received such solicitous, albeit intrusive, attention from the famous doctor if she had been of a lower social class.

In the passage from John Harvey Kellogg's 1882 *The Ladies' Guide to Health and Disease,* (p. 1168) women are advised about their responsibilities as childbearers. Like today's nutritionists, who encourage women of childbearing age to eat a diet high in folic acid and other nutrients that prevent birth defects, Kellogg encourages a healthy diet and exercise, arguing that these should begin even before conception occurs. But his tone reveals warrants close to those of the eugenics movement of the nineteenth and early twentieth centuries as he uses words like *stock-breeder* and *propagate*. Prenatal care for mothers focuses on the breeding of superior children. He assumes as fact some notions about prenatal responsibilities of mothers and fathers that modern readers find laughable. The mother's "mental condition" at the time of conception is important, Kellogg says, though he states with no apparent fear of contradiction that the father's condition as the couple is having sexual intercourse is naturally more important in forming the child's character. One is reminded of medieval descriptions of homunculi, tiny beings implanted in the mother's womb wholly through the father's influence, though women were blamed, of course, if the child was the wrong sex. With no real understanding of genetics and prenatal development, Kellogg reveals his warrants as he suggests reasons for symptoms of fetal alcohol syndrome and perhaps other birth defects in the opening paragraph. If the child is retarded, both parents must have been "in a state of beastly intoxication" when the child was conceived. Because the child can be further marked during gestation, the mother "should not yield to the depressing influences" of pregnancy. The assumption is that she should be happy to find herself pregnant, her opportunity of "molding a human character" being a "God-given" one.

Although Kellogg differs from Mitchell in his emphasis on a vegetarian diet, exercise, and "interesting conversation, reading, and various harmless and pleasant diversions," he agrees with the avoidance of excitement and the need for the woman to think happy and calm thoughts. If she wants her child to acquire high culture, the pregnant mother must concentrate totally on the art in which she wishes her child to excel. One presumes that if the child is born without talent, she didn't think hard enough. If she does not want her child to crave stimulants, she should avoid spices, coffee, tea, and so forth. But throughout his list of suggestions, Kellogg gives the impression that women must be saved from their emotional tendencies and that husbands should gently control the lives of these flighty bearers of their children if they want healthy progeny. When he goes on to discuss "puerperal mania" — or postpartum depression — the connection of this text with Gilman's "The Yellow Wallpaper" is evident. They seem to be describing the same woman. We might ask students considering majors in medical or social science fields to research current knowledge about this condition. Some readers will recall the biography of poet Anne Sexton, whose psychosis following postpartum depression led both to a career as a writer and to her ultimate suicide. As late as the middle of the twentieth century, Sexton insisted that her work as a poet kept her alive rather than contributing to her psychosis, even though her intellectual activity was not able to keep her from suicide. Although the condition is taken seriously in Kellogg's 1882 quotation from a medical expert, the wording borders on the pejorative; there is a "sullen obstinacy," for example, and a shocking "immorality and obscenity" sometimes occurs in patients' speech. This "insanity of childbirth" is characterized by "active mania" much like that of Gilman's narrator. Kellogg's text implies paranoia in the frequent suspicion that one's food is being poisoned, whereas Gilman's protagonist centers her paranoia on the wallpaper and the house.

In both texts, however, postpartum symptoms may trigger underlying tendencies. Gilman's narrator tells of childhood experiences in which she saw her surroundings in an imaginative way that may either reflect the fantasies or presage mental illness. Whereas Gilman's narrator is freed from the responsibility of caring for her child and doesn't seem to think much about the baby, Kellogg describes the rejection of the child and even its attempted murder that we sometimes read about in court cases today. One of the ironies of Gilman's story is the husband's unwillingness to accept his wife's condition as real. Many mental illnesses are now being recognized as having a physiological basis in brain chemistry and function. Although Gilman's narrator blames her treatment for driving her over the edge, Gilman did not try to raise her own child. Given the climate of divorce at the time, perhaps she had no choice. It is more likely, however, that she feared the recurrence of her illness or her inability to function as both mother and writer. Like Mitchell, Kellogg advises isolation during the manic phase of the disorder and counsels against excitement. He prescribes a change of scene, as the husband of Gilman's narrator has provided for her. But Kellogg ends with the suggestion that a "dear friend" could be called on to visit. Readers wonder if his wife's obsession might have been avoided if John had allowed her to have her cousins visit, as she so greatly desired.

If Kellogg's text were published today, readers would find a great many of his assumptions faulty. We know that genetic and congenital factors play a large part in the development of a child but not in the naive ways assumed by Kellogg. Still, many pregnant women cultivate a peaceful atmosphere for the unborn child, playing classical music to influence developing neural pathways. Many of Kellogg's insights about eating whole foods and vegetables rather than meat are more accepted today than they were in his time. We are horrified when Gilman's character is forced to eat meat and to avoid exercise and when Mitchell fattens up his patients as they lie idle. We find Kellogg's ideas about sex a bit odd, however, and would not prohibit sex during pregnancy for fear that this might make the children more prone to sexual activity. We usually allow diet and exercise to naturally take care of constipation and do not fear poisoning by the "effete products" of digestion. While his warrants may be outdated, many of Kellogg's ideas about diet, exercise, and the avoidance of stimulants during pregnancy would be accepted today. Most modern readers find his assumptions about the treatment of mental illness in women to be more problematic, however.

RACIAL INJUSTICE (p. 1173)

COUNTEE CULLEN

Incident (p. 1174)

Countee Cullen's poem from 1925 can be placed in the context of a long tradition of racial incidents involving public transportation. Asian, Irish, and African workers were exploited, in virtual and sometimes actual slavery, in the building of the railway system of the United States, and lawsuits demanding reparations have been filed recently against some railway companies because they purchased or rented the labor of slaves and thus benefited from the institution of slavery to the detriment of the descendents of these slaves. As transportation systems developed, regulations kept economic power in place while limiting the capacity of enslaved people to travel. Nineteenth-century narratives by escaped slaves tell of heart-pounding experiences: a dark-skinned husband travels as the servant of a light-skinned wife passing for white on a train going north; a man escapes to Canada as freight in a packing crate. In both of these examples, oppressed people subvert the economic structures in which transportation plays a part. They take advantage of their status as property to steal their own lives from their "owners." After emancipation and reconstruction, Jim Crow laws confined black riders of trains to crowded cars, often open to dust and soot, that kept them separate from whites. And later bus and streetcar systems in many cities continued racial segregation by assigning separate sections to blacks and whites.

In the second line of the poem "Incident," Cullen gives readers an image of a fully carefree child, whose heart and head are "filled with glee." By referring to both intellect and emotion, the poet implies that prejudice works through both logos and pathos. We are persuaded by what seems to be the logic of prejudice. For example, the white person who remembered the black woman on the bus punishing her child for an innocent act might have extrapolated from this and other representative experiences that black women are violent toward their children had she not been provided with an explanation that took into account the reality of the woman's situation. Many "logical" arguments surround the subject of race, with some scholars arguing for differences falling along a bell curve that shows African Americans to be intellectually inferior to Americans of European and Asian extraction and other thinkers maintaining that the concept of race is itself based on logically flawed assumptions. That emotions play a large part in the development of race consciousness is even more evident, with fear, guilt, and shame playing large roles.

But a child, Cullen implies, is at first unaware of the thoughts and feelings that prejudice conveys. While the cliché that children must be taught prejudice may be true and may be implied by the second line of Cullen's poem, it also is true that in a society with a history of racism this prejudice must be untaught. Much prejudice is unconscious and unacknowledged, absorbed from the culture rather than overtly taught. Eight-year-old children, therefore, have their innocence taken — from both head and heart — through the agency of other eight year olds.

The child who insults Cullen's speaker is a "Baltimorean." The use of this rather lofty word may be significant in several ways. The effect, taken with the poem's sing-song rhythm, approaches mock epic. These are children, so their experiences can be assumed to be trivial, but the word sounds important. Since mock epic often has a satirical purpose, we may notice that the prejudiced child is set up as the pompous figure to be taken down. This doesn't happen in the poem, however. Instead, the speaker himself is permanently changed and has been robbed of his "glee" — a silly, naïve happiness based on lack of knowledge. It is also worth noting that the city of Baltimore is near the Mason-Dixon line, which divides the North from the South.

It might be interesting to ask students if they recall when and where they first became aware of racial issues. Minority students may be interested to find that many white classmates recall injustices they have seen directed toward others and have learned to oppose prejudice through reading or watching the news on television. This is an important factor to consider as readers, since some students will claim to be unable to relate to the experiences of the narrators in this cluster because they are not African Americans or because "times have changed" so radically. The speaker does not have to be the poet himself for his voice to be effective. Cullen's speaker does not share his feelings but implies that the experience was important because he remembers this and nothing else of Baltimore. His reticence invites the reader to imagine his emotions and thus to become more involved with the poem. We might question whether he has chosen to hide his emotions or whether he has suppressed them from himself, as well.

The sing-song rhythm of the poem is appropriate for a child's voice, giving the impression that the speaker relives this loss of innocence with the raw emotions of childhood. The simple diction and style of "Incident" is not typical of Cullen's poetry. However, we might speculate that when Cullen's speaker recalls the racial epithet, he becomes a child again, experiencing the hurt for the first time. This reluctant memory of a life-changing experience, often a tragic one, is similar to what African American Nobel laureate Toni Morrison calls "rememory" in her novel *Beloved* — a memory that keeps returning despite a person's efforts to distance herself from it.

Born in 1903, Cullen was still a young man when this poem was published in 1925. Like his contemporary Langston Hughes, Cullen was one of the new Negro voices of the Harlem Renaissance at this time. But Cullen was less overtly African American in his poetry than was Hughes, desiring most of all to be considered an important literary figure for his art rather than his race. It is telling that he addresses at least two poems to the English Romantic poet John Keats. If Cullen is the child riding public transportation in Baltimore, the adult seems unwilling to accept the prejudiced view of himself. On the other hand, he may be a man struggling with the double consciousness of a Negro poet who sometimes "[h]eart-filled, head-filled with glee" imagines himself as Keats.

LANGSTON HUGHES

Let America Be America Again (p. 1175)

During the 1930s, like many other literary figures, Hughes became interested in anti-Fascist movements, visiting Spain during that country's civil war and traveling to communist Russia as part of a young troupe of artists and entertainers. The trip to Russia was not especially successful in terms of building solidarity with socialist movements to organize the working classes of the world, and "Let America Be America Again" may reflect the ambiguity of his thinking at the time about the relationship between class and race.

The phrase "let America be America again" has the ring of flag-waving demagoguery or the naïve acceptance of such rhetoric. But the speaker of the opening stanza can be assumed to speak out of a heart-felt desire. He really does desire an America in which all people are free. The parenthetical line that forms the second stanza, therefore, seems to come from a different source. This may be a dialogue or the speaker may be at odds with himself. The result is not to challenge the plea for America to live up to the American dream for everyone but to challenge the glowing national self-congratulation that ignores the truth of inequality.

The speaker who challenges the unrealistic rhetoric is accused of obfuscation rather than common sense, of hiding rather than revealing. In response, abstract concepts like "equality" and "liberty" (and their absence for oppressed people) are brought down to earth as Hughes concretizes the history of America's "dog eat dog" capitalism and goes on to speak for a multiplicity of people oppressed in America, ending with a forceful voice that turns the glittering generalities of the opening stanzas into a call for action to "make America again." The patriotic tone of the beginning becomes first a protest and then a manifesto. The whole poem thus becomes a critique of the warrant implied by the opening line, the assumption that America was once the America that our patriotic rhetoric imagines it to be. He literally calls for redemption, for a new birth for the nation.

The difference between the opening and closing lines is telling. While the phrase "let America be America again" has been a key repetition in the poem, it undergoes subtle changes as the dialectic of the poem proceeds and is quite different in tone and substance from the idea of workers uniting to "make America again." Rather than being an immoveable entity, America becomes something people re-create. It has, in fact, been built and hammered out by the very people to whom the dream has been denied. Other repetitions are important in the poem, as well, especially the response that "America never was America to me" and the parallel constructions of stanzas in which lines repeatedly begin with the words "I am." Readers with biblical knowledge will be reminded that the God of Exodus when asked his name tells Moses, "I am that I am" — also translatable from the Hebrew as "I shall be doing what I shall be doing." In this poem calling for the re-creation of a nation by its workers, the oppressed take matters into their own hands and declare their existence: "I am."

It might be useful to consider the verbs of the poem in this context and to discuss the implications of verbs of being versus verbs of action. The re-creation and redemption that Hughes suggests in "Let America Be America Again" seem to occur at the intersection of action and being. Seen in this context, the poem is a discourse on the ontology of America and its working people.

Issues will arise in class about whether all of the people said to lack freedom in Hughes's poem are equally chained. He mentions the poor white first and emphasizes that he is "fooled and pushed apart." We might ask students to think about the hatred that many poor whites — the classic "rednecks" — have harbored toward African Americans. How might this separation and traditional competition among segments of the working class benefit those in power? He identifies Native Americans and immigrants as oppressed along with "the Negro bearing slavery's scars." We might ask if restrictions on the freedom of these people are the equivalent of those imposed on the "young man" of the following stanza, who seems to be enslaved by his own compulsion to exploit others for his own gain. While the oppressor can be seen as trapped in the system, some readers may feel that the inclusion of the money-grubbing capitalist as a victim weakens the argument. Others may feel that it strengthens the argument that America has become a place that is bad for everyone and therefore needs to be remade into something that more closely approximates the dream of equality of opportunity.

In addition to examining the verbs of Hughes's poem, students should look closely at pronouns. The speaker or speakers of the poem usually speak in the first-person singular. The individuality implied is both American and modernist and is particularly characteristic of Hughes, with the capitalized "ME" of line 65 epitomizing his style. His shift to the plural "we" in line 55 lasts for only one stanza. Thinking in terms of the whole community — "the millions" — seems more in line with socialist thought. But this stanza comes at a turning point in the poem. First there has been the idealistic voice of the dreamer, interrupted by the voice of reality, followed by the challenge and the multiple voices in response. At this point, the speaker pulls himself up short because he has fallen back into the false rhetoric of unquestioning patriotism. After he chastises himself for this, he reminds himself and the reader of the millions of oppressed. Some will feel that this is inconsistent, perhaps revealing the didactic purpose of the poem as a Marxist text. Others may feel that the effect is to remind the reader that the individuals who are oppressed add up. He has personalized oppression and now he universalizes it or at least reveals the magnitude of the problem. The use of the personal pronouns *I* and *me* comes across to some readers as childlike or even childish — a trivialization of a weighty matter — and many readers may feel that Hughes could have used less egocentric diction. The dream, however, is not the dream of one individual but "our mighty dream," and the land is ours, as well. In the last stanza, as he calls for action, the speaker again uses the first-person plural, giving it additional connotations as he says, "We, the people" — echoing the Preamble to the Constitution of the United States.

The poem was written during the Depression and reflects the times, but it often refers back to earlier times, especially evoking early immigrants and pioneers. (Some alert readers will note the title of Willa Cather's frontier novel in line 36.) The cultural milieu of the poem may be revealed most compellingly in lines that refer to poverty; lines 34 and 35 repeat the word "hungry" and make us think of soup lines. A reference to strikes also lends a 1930s flavor. Many readers will agree that the "dog eat dog" world still exists and that some people still never get ahead and are "bartered through the years." In the wake of the terrorist attacks of September 11, 2001, patriotic rhetoric of the vague, sentimental sort has again become the norm, and those who question it come under suspicion of disloyalty. While phrases like "homeland of the free" would have sounded humorously old-fashioned a few years ago, such high-sounding abstractions are now common, and President Bush can speak of "the evil ones" while keeping a straight face. As Hughes suggests, perhaps we need to work toward the ideals of democracy while demanding that warrants be examined and while questioning what generalities really mean, if they reflect reality or wishful thinking and self-deception.

While Countee Cullen's poem "Incident" (p. 1174) easily falls into the category of "memory poem" and might best be discussed by asking students to call on their own memories of hate speech and observations of racial injustice, Hughes's "Let America Be America Again" is less clearly of this genre. What we might recall are elementary and even high school experiences with American history. Textbooks today are more multicultural, but the attitude toward America in most classrooms may still reflect the unquestioning hero worship and moralistic jingoism of earlier generations. We might listen to the lyrics of "America the Beautiful," "America," or "God Bless America" to discover language of the sort — embedded in our memories — that Hughes recalls and questions in his poem. In the line "America never was America to me," Hughes might be said to remember injustices that he has experienced or the inequality of opportunity that he has had to overcome. Certainly, Hughes has "sung the songs" that he talks about in line 57 and has accepted at some point in his life the American dream that he wants to rebuild for everyone.

If we seek to categorize both Cullen's and Hughes's texts as "protest poems," we can make a stronger case for "Let America Be America Again" than for "Incident." The oppression in Hughes's poem is organized into a massive system that seems to entrap the oppressors themselves. He passionately advocates a rebuilding of a faulty America from scratch. This is especially evident in the final stanzas in which he insists that the people must redeem a land filled with "rack and ruin . . . rape and rot of graft, and stealth, and lies." The line in which he addresses his reader (or another speaker) by saying "Sure, call me any ugly name you choose" is reminiscent of the incident Cullen's speaker recalls in which he is called a "nigger," but the scale of the two poems is vastly different. Hughes ranges through history and geography and identifies with people of many classes and ethnic groups. Cullen, on the other hand, tells of one small incident between two small individuals. Even when Hughes individualizes, his characters are representative of groups — stylized and allegorical and therefore two-dimensional for the most part. The individual voice, though it is present, is mixed with this larger aggregation of voices in dialectical conflict with each other. Cullen's characters, on the other hand, have particularity. Even though he does not explicitly protest racial prejudice, by revealing the lasting effect of the racial epithet and the reality it symbolizes he does protest implicitly. Because we identify with the hurt the gleeful little boy experiences, the impact of his protest may even be stronger than that of Hughes's more openly rhetorical text. Cullen's text centers on the single issue of racial prejudice as expressed in hate speech, carelessly and perhaps ignorantly delivered. Hughes arguably takes on much more, raising issues so large the reader may get lost in them. He critiques the oppressive capitalist system that has caused the Depression, but he also raises issues of definition and symbolism surrounding America and its stated ideals of liberty and opportunity, bringing in hints about oppression of the poor, of African Americans, of Native Americans, of immigrants, and of workers of all sorts. Ironically, for readers familiar with the body of their works, Cullen comes across as more straightforward and Hughes as more elaborate.

AUDRE LORDE

Afterimages (p. 1178)

When Audre Lorde speaks of afterimages, she is drawing on the knowledge that the history of racial violence in the United States has become imprinted in our minds, often without our being aware of it, much as an afterimage occurs physically in the human eye. In the scientific study of optical illusions, the word *afterimage* refers to the phenomenon that we experience after staring at an image like a photographic negative; the image becomes temporarily imprinted on the retina so that when we then stare at a blank page, the opposite colors of the image seem to appear on that surface. The image is similar but not exactly the same. This is also true of Lorde's poem. She views television news reports of floods occurring in 1979 in Jackson, Mississippi, when the Pearl River inundated streets, destroying homes and shops, even threatening the archives in the buildings of the state capital. Viewing an interview with a white woman who has lost her home reminds the poet of the white woman whose husband instigated and participated in the torture and killing of a young black boy, Emmett Till, who attempted to flirt with her, perhaps giving a wolf whistle as a reckless act of male bravado. Lorde changes the Tallahatchie River of the Emmett Till murder twenty-four years earlier to the Pearl River — the white connotations arguably chosen for irony — and places it in Jackson rather than in the small town of Money, Mississippi, a few counties north.

The psychological afterimages of racial violence become "dragonfish" that recall the inkblots of Rorschach tests. Lorde's repetition of this image invites the reader to see it as an important issue in the poem. The speaker begins by telling the reader that her eyes are "rockstrewn caves where dragonfish evolve / wild for life, relentless and acquisitive / learning to survive / where there is no food." Connotations of poverty that will resurface later in the poem are subtly introduced here, but the usage is also symbolic: her eyes seek out the memories of hate as a starving animal might seek out food. The animals that grow out of the environment of hate are monstrous, like the creatures one might find deep in the ocean or in the pools of caves where light cannot reach. The image of dragonfish occurs again as she makes the context of the poem a bit more explicit at the end of the first numbered section, referring to a white woman and "a black boy hacked into a murderous lesson" as the food the dragonfish eat and as "fused images beneath my pain." As a black woman, Lorde must deal with the ramifications of the Emmett Till incident from conflicting yet "fused" perspectives of gender and race. The thought of dragonfish eating the murdered boy conjures up the recognition that because Till's bloated body had been in the river for some time before it was discovered, it had undoubtedly been mutilated further by fish or turtles. We think of dragons as reptilian, and anyone familiar with Southern rivers will picture snakes writhing in the dark recesses of Lorde's underwater caves. While the syntax is ambiguous and invites several interpretations, her final use of the word in the penultimate stanza implies that she and the woman of the flood interview have become fused and are "becoming dragonfish to survive the horrors we are living." This last section of the poem brings together the images that have been introduced in the earlier three parts.

Part I of the poem introduces issues; we know that vision will play a major role and see a white woman who has suffered a loss and a black boy who has been "hacked into a murderous lesson." Lorde mentions the dragonfish twice and uses the words "fused images beneath my pain." Therefore, the first and last sections of the poem serve as a frame for the middle sections. Part II gives a more specific vision of the white woman, showing her to be ground down by poverty and her husband's violence and insecurity and placing her in the particular context of the 1979 Pearl River flood. Images connected to vision continue to appear in this stanza: the television projects a "flickering afterimage of the nightmare rain" and the woman's children are shown "hanging upon her coat like mirrors." The introduction of the violent white man ends Part II with bestial images of "ham-like hands" and "snarling" words that are compared to "rotting meat." In Part III the speaker takes the reader back to an earlier historical event, the murder of Emmett Till in 1955. The flood and the murder are tied together by the presence of the white woman in the flood and the "white girl" in the earlier crime. The implications are that they could be the same person and that for Lorde they are the same type of person. By conflating the two, she emphasizes the interactions between the issues of race and class. The white man in the flood interview violently denies his inability to provide for the economic needs of his family. His misplaced sense of honor causes him to be bestial toward his wife. In the third part of the poem, this warped sense of manhood results in the death of a boy who breaks the rules by assuming the same sort of manhood, one that denigrates women. That the men in Part III take "their aroused honor" to a brothel after the murder brings home Lorde's contention that their crime is not only a crime against African American men but a crime against all women. She emphasizes the part that poverty plays as she leads into Part IV. She implies, though, that the floods are a sort of revenge for the hate and misplaced pride that caused the murder of Till and other murders like it and that she cannot forgive and forget. "I can withhold my pity and my bread," the speaker says, and the dragonfish are last seen "adapting to breathe blood."

Although the people of the poem — the white woman, the white girl, the speaker, Emmett Till — become linked, the result is not sweetness or even empathy, although student readers will be tempted to search for a happy ending. The afterimages of violence and hate continue to be monstrous and lasting. The woman of the poem is willing to admit that her life has been harder than she thought it would be, and her husband sees this as a criticism of his ability to provide. The ideal of the Southern man — no matter what his social class — who protects and honors his lady not only does not come to fruition but leads to murder and perhaps to violence against the woman herself. A sense of disappointment and inferiority is hidden beneath the exchange between the husband and wife. In a news magazine article about another highly publicized manifestation of racial hatred, the killing of three civil rights workers in Mississippi in the early 1960s, one of the conspirators was quoted as asking, "If I ain't better than a nigger, what am I better than?" The words reveal a motive that seems much in the same spirit as that of the white men in Lorde's text. The issue seems to be one of definition: what are the qualities that define manhood? This issue might be raised before we discuss other issues in the poem, since it seems to be at the heart of the matter. Emmett Till is trying to do what he thinks men are supposed to do, and the relatives of the white woman he "insulted" can be seen as doing the same thing.

The ghost of Emmett Till "rides the crest of the Pearl" at the beginning of Part IV and is compared to "the shade of a raped woman." He seems to exact revenge on the woman who caused his death at the same time he is connected subtly to white women who, like African American men and women, suffer from the violence of men trying to prove their manhood. The persona of the poem, presumably a black woman able to identify with both the white woman and the black boy, seems close to the poet herself. It is quite likely that the poet, who would have been twenty-one years old when Emmett Till was killed, wrote the poem (first published in 1981) as a direct response to news reports of the 1979 floods. Her use of the first-person pronoun makes this identification more credible and emphasizes that the afterimages of the poem are real, linked to historical events one can read about in newspapers. Because the poet includes herself in the cycle of hate that creates the afterimages of dragonfish, the poem's effect is dramatic and personal, inviting the reader to think about the afterimages in his or her own mind. The distance of third person would have blunted the immediacy of this effect.

While the first three poems of this cluster all employ the first-person perspective, the visual imagery of Lorde's "Afterimages" is more dramatic than that of Countee Cullen's "Incident"(p. 1174) or Langston Hughes's "Let America Be America Again" (p. 1175). The poem is actually *about* a visual phenomenon that is expanded to become a symbol of the psychological impact of visual images of historical events. Cullen's poem ends with the word "remember" and can thus be linked closely to Lorde's theme. "Incident" gives a vivid snapshot of one small event, whereas "Afterimages" moves among multiple "flickering" images of both personal and historical significance. It is almost possible to feel Lorde's images in one's eyeball, especially since readers today are familiar with television and other moving images that produce optical illusions. Living in an earlier era, Cullen is more two-dimensional, and memory seems for him more straightforward, though he finds it striking that one memory of hate can cancel out all other memories of a particular time and place. Hughes is more abstract, rhetorical, and distant than either Cullen or Lorde. His poem reads like a speech. His image of the "poor white, fooled and pushed apart" and the worker's "hand at the foundry. . . [and] plow in the rain" are visual but do not approach the specificity of Lorde's poor white woman poignantly touching the chimney of her flooded home as she speaks in a "voice like Pearl River mud / caked around the edges." Even sound in "Afterimages" works synaesthetically with vision. The white man's "lie hangs in his mouth / like a shred of rotting meat," evoking not only sound and sight but smell. In Lorde's poem, students will have many visual details from which to choose examples, while their choices in the other texts will be limited.

When considering the emotions of the speakers, readers will encounter similar experiences. Cullen's episode is specific to the speaker or to the poet himself, and while he hints at emotional impact, he keeps a certain distance, telling rather than showing that he remembers. The reader is left to extrapolate this one small incident into a historical context that includes an accumulation of thousands, perhaps millions, of such individual insults. Hughes, on the other hand, shows only the big picture, and while his rhetoric is meant to stir emotions in the reader, the voice seems distant and not really personally involved as it assumes various identities of oppressed peoples. The speaker of "Let America Be America Again" tries hard but seems to be playing roles and perhaps oversimplifying complex issues. Lorde allows the reader into the agonized psyche of the speaker, portraying emotions that are complex and intensely emotional. Many students will find the less ambiguous emotions of Cullen and Hughes more persuasive than the raw, divided honesty of Lorde's speaker.

Because Lorde is dealing with the multiple effects that a racial incident may come to possess as time adds new connotations, the title "Afterimages" — a plural construction that semantically compresses the theme — is much more apt than the title "Incident" would be. Given this title, the reader would be limited to choosing one of the incidents mentioned in the poem, most likely the murder of Emmett Till. The title "Incident" does fit the limited event described by Cullen, however. While Till's murder and Cullen's experience with hate speech are not equivalent events, both are part of the same problem — the tenacious racism that continues to plague America long after the end of slavery as an economic institution. Both also begin with a boy's naïve assumptions, and both involve speech. Because students often do not believe that speech has consequences, it might be useful to spend some time discussing situations in which words have caused events to take place. We might want to speculate about what might have happened to Cullen's speaker if he had responded in kind. Conversely, Emmett Till might have had a full life — though arguably less influence on American culture — had the young woman who was insulted by his attempt at flirtation simply scolded him as the impertinent fifteen-year-old he was and kept the incident to herself. The line between an "incident" and a historical event may be a fine one, subject to chance decisions made on the spur of the moment. To apply the title of Hughes's "Let America Be America Again" to Lorde's poem would seem at best to detract from the subtle connotations of the events she describes.

CORNELIUS EADY

Who Am I? (p. 1183)

In much the same way that Audre Lorde weaves newspaper and television images of historical events into poetry in "Afterimages" (p. 1178) Cornelius Eady uses the 1994 murder of two small boys by their mother to raise issues about racial injustice. The poem "Who Am I" is the third poem in Eady's book *Brutal Imagination,* a poetry sequence about the Susan Smith case, which has subsequently been adapted by Eady into a drama. In both the book and the play, Eady deals with racial stereotypes and speaks in a number of voices. For example, Uncle Tom, Uncle Ben, and Stepin Fetchit are all characters used to perpetuate subservient images of African Americans — inviting readers to think about their complexities. He imagines what will happen to the loveable, small boy of the "Our Gang" comedies, Buckwheat, when he grows to be a man. He speaks as Aunt Jemima's "do-rag" that covers, as does the knit cap of Susan Smith's imagined villain, "the hair / The world seems to dread." The speaker of the poem "Who Am I" is a persona Eady calls "Mr. Zero." Like Ralph Ellison's Invisible Man, Mr. Zero lives out the stereotype of the black man who is seen by everyone as a symbol rather than as an individual human being.

After the young white woman Susan Smith pushed a car with her children strapped into their safety seats into a South Carolina lake on October 25, 1994, she convinced most people in the nation by way of her televised pleas that a black man had stolen her car and kidnapped the little boys. For nine days, concerned citizens called police when they saw men they thought might be the suspect, with sightings occurring as far away as Seattle, Washington. A local man was detained for several long hours.

Based on Smith's description, the police drawing of the supposed perpetrator of the crime was a virtual caricature of the minstrel-show black — very dark-skinned and large-lipped, wearing the cloth cap and flannel shirt of a field worker. Perhaps subconsciously, the Southern white woman created a typical "profile" of the dangerous black man that a white audience would be likely to accept — also subconsciously — as capable of such a nightmarish act. Eady's poetry sequence takes this fact and imagines the stereotype coming to life for the nine days during which he exists in the public imagination. And, as the speaker says in the poem, if he is alive, then the boys are alive for these nine days, as well. He thus creates an alternate universe that exists until Susan Smith confesses.

Eady's title asks the question, "Who am I?" By posing the question, he forces the reader to pay attention to the speaker and to see him as an individual rather than as a stereotype. Read out of context, the issue may be one of fact, since we would be unlikely to connect him with the Susan Smith case. The question is really asked twice, since the first line has the little boys repeating it. The repetition emphasizes the need to imagine the African American man from a different perspective than that of the nine days before Smith's confession. The man's overall tone as speaker of the poem is gently nurturing. He is glad that he exists because it means the boys can be alive too. His use of the pronoun we in the penultimate line indicates that he and the boys share an existence. They are in fact kept alive by the "brutal imagination" of Susan Smith and perhaps her believers. The words "brutal imagination" have interesting connotations, since Smith imagines a stereotypical brute to cover her crime, but by killing her children she shows herself to be the brutal one. The imagination that takes advantage of racism is brutal, as well. The imaginary character comes to life in Eady's book, but we might ask if the stereotype can come to life in reality when it is believed to be true. Do men sometimes become brutal because they see brutality as masculine? We might think back to Lorde's description of white men in "Afterimages." When the speaker of Eady's poem imagines that the boys might find him familiar, he takes on the role of their mother, driving as they sit in the "eternal back seat."

It would be a mistake to think Susan Smith did not nurture her children or show them love, even though she perhaps saw them at the same time as extensions of herself. Not only does Mr. Zero merge with the boys; he also merges with the mother and is in fact a figment of her imagination. At one point in the book, the speaker merges with the perpetrator of an earlier murder, Charles Stuart, who in 1989 in Massachusetts killed his pregnant wife and shot himself, claiming that a gun-wielding black man attempted to steal his car. Mr. Zero says that he comes when he is called and exists because the killers and an unintentionally racist public make him exist. The word *secret* is repeated to emphasize the nature of this existence. The world of the speaker exists only as a lie told by a woman with a horrible secret, and he is therefore part of her secret. Once her secret is in the open, he no longer exists. The secret is shared only with the dead children, who experience the "secret thrill of hiding" and who have now become ghosts who know all their mother's secrets. The poem and the larger text from which it is taken, *Brutal Imagination,* thus play with the paradoxes of reality and ask that we examine the power of lies and secrets, especially when the public is swept into them.

Once the context is known, Eady's poem seems as "realistic" as any poem, though its protagonist has never existed. It seems to occupy the same surreal world as Lorde's "Afterimages": both take historical events and show how they are something perceived by the human mind. The reality of the original event shifts within the poems, just as interpretations of our personal experiences change as new information comes to light or as our perspective is altered by experience. The news media play a large part in defining reality for the speakers of both Lorde's and Eady's texts. Isolated incidents become national news and affect the thinking of thousands of readers and viewers. Susan Smith's slanting of her story can be seen as an exaggerated example of the slippery nature of the reality we see on television, while the display of the dead body of Emmett Till shows the power of the press to effect social change through pathos. The events that both poems discuss are about as real as events can get, but the speakers challenge us to think critically about their interpretations. Countee Cullen's "Incident" (p. 1174) is more overtly realistic, only hinting at the mystery of interpretation when the speaker points out that he remembers the racial epithet but nothing else about Baltimore. Langston Hughes's poem (p. 1175) also questions "reality": his speaker debates with himself about the truth of the rhetoric of American patriotism, challenging readers to bring the dreams of equality and opportunity into reality for the first time. To the extent that they question the concept of reality, these poems invite readers to do the same. Students should especially be encouraged to question how far their sense of reality is shaped by images filtered through news and entertainment media.

The "brutal imagination" of Eady's poem could clearly apply to most of the white characters in the other poems. These characters and their counterparts in the "real world" define reality as a place in which African Americans are inferior and must be kept in their place. Emmett Till imagines that he is part of the male fraternity allowed to flirt with women of any status, but his killers' brutal imaginations sort people using a different paradigm. The "brutal imagination" of Cullen's eight-year-old white boy sees the black boy as a target for ridicule rather than an equal. But the naïve way that Cullen's speaker imagines the world is as brutal in its own way, since it does not prepare the young boy to withstand prejudice and to deal with its impact. Hughes's speaker might see the denial of injustice implied in American rhetoric as brutal and certainly as imaginary. He does not want his readers to imagine but to take action and "make America again."

Most readers are able to recognize the Cullen and Hughes poems as having been written before the Lorde and Eady texts. Sophisticated late twentieth-century readers tend to prefer the subtle nuances of poems that throw us into a surreal world rather than poems that tell us what to think. However, while most instructors will prefer Eady and Lorde, many students will choose the earlier poems because students are more certain about where the speakers of those poems stand and what their own stance is expected to be. Hughes may strike readers as preachy, and some readers argue that "Let America Be America Again" does not speak to today's situation. On the other hand, others will argue that economic inequities still exist in both America and the wider world. The childlike persona of Cullen's "Incident" still speaks to readers, with African American students insisting that the poem is relevant today. They appreciate its simplicity.

In fact, the major difference between the earlier two poems and the later ones may be in the demands they make on the reader to deal with complexity and ambiguity. Though the African American speakers of the poems all seek to understand the other, all force the reader to see that there are no easy answers. Cullen's speaker identifies with the white boy as being the same age as he is, but he becomes the brunt of a racial slur and must admit that the effect is lasting. Hughes seeks to place himself in the shoes of all the individuals cheated by an unequal system in America, but his call for action at the end shows that the dream of solidarity is still unfulfilled. Lorde openly admits that her attempts at empathy for the white woman fall short, that what they have most clearly in common are the "dragonfish" evolved through a history of racial hatred. Eady's narrator exists only because of a woman much like the women of Lorde's poem, and the reader must recall that, empathetic as he is, he exists only because of a "brutal imagination" and a murder. While Cullen and Hughes would probably not have found publishers for these particular poems today, readers can bring a twenty-first-century complexity to their interpretation, refusing like Eady and Lorde to accept oversimplifications of complex issues.

BRINGING MURDERERS TO JUSTICE (p. 1185)

WILLIAM SHAKESPEARE

Hamlet, Prince of Denmark (p. 1185)

With the possible exception of Sophocles' *Oedipus the King* (p. 495), William Shakespeare's *Hamlet* is the West's best-known play about an effort to bring a murderer to justice. Point out to students, though, that it is by no means the only revenge drama written in Renaissance England. Shakespeare was working in a tradition that was already well established and that would continue after him in the form of lurid Jacobean revenge tragedies. Even though your students probably won't know other examples of the genre, you might still ask for their ideas about what makes *Hamlet* distinctive. Another possible move is to have them relate the play to contemporary pursuits of retribution such as the pursuit of Osama Bin Laden and his followers after the mass murders of Americans on September 11, 2001. Your class might also think of local police investigations and trials. In any discussion of contemporary examples, the talk is bound to be more profitable if it focuses on the values that a society has in mind when it distinguishes between just and unjust revenge or between brute revenge (e.g., lynching) and more deliberate judicial processes.

Four hundred years after Shakespeare's tragedy examining the dynamics of a royal household was written, we still find issues that relate to the family and political events. During the impeachment trial of President Bill Clinton, a student from a particularly authoritarian family called the situation disrespectful, arguing that one does not ask impertinent questions of the leader of one's country. This was for her the equivalent of defying the authority of one's father, something that ran counter to the conservative values she had been taught. Although other family values were in conflict with the president's actions, this one seemed paramount to her, especially since her father had recently died. Having been created before the American and French Revolutions and the social and political changes of the twentieth century, the characters of Shakespeare's play wrestle with prohibitions against reversing the order of family or kingdom.

Although we may debate the many reasons for Hamlet's delay in obeying his dead father's urgings to kill the usurper, we can see that his values are in conflict. Any decision he makes will cause him to challenge a person in the position of father, in the personal and the political sense. He is "a little more than kin, and less than kind" (line 65) — a position that will require him to go against what he considers to be natural, both as a son and as a subject. Furthermore, Hamlet is also dealing with a supernatural world, and he dares not strike as Claudius prays because he wants to send the false father literally to hell.

Hamlet's feelings about his mother are more complex, and Freudian issues are often raised to explain them. Does he unconsciously wish to do as Claudius has done, to kill his father and marry his mother, acting out the Oedipus complex? Students may want to examine various productions of the play available on videotape to see how act 3, scene 4, is staged and what tone is used to deliver Hamlet's harsh words to his mother. Some interpretations have a decidedly incestuous slant.

Our argument-based approach to reading the play might best consider how the families deal with their own issues. The royal family in *Hamlet* acts in an emotional frenzy, and all is pathos as they go about making their decisions. The men of Polonius's family are petrified in logos, reasoning out their lives in rhetorical clichés. Questions of ethos arise as values are questioned and characters seek for people who can be trusted. It's all too much for Ophelia, who escapes into incoherence. The play abounds with examples of flawed reasoning and logical fallacies as its families struggle, and for the most part fail, to work out their conflicting issues.

SUSAN GLASPELL

Trifles (p. 1290)

Students are likely to find Susan Glaspell's *Trifles* an interesting play, especially if they read it aloud or even stage it. Each of these things is easy to do, given the work's brevity. Perhaps some of your students will object to Glaspell's implication that men and women differ markedly in their values, ideas, and experiences. Alternatively, some might argue that gender divisions are much less evident today than they were in the early twentieth century. If your class does debate gender relations today, try to focus the discussion on actual events in the news; otherwise, comments may remain on too general a level to be useful. Perhaps students will think of a recent case or two in which a woman murdered a domestic partner gained sympathy from members of the public.

Fictional analogies may work just as well. For instance, your class may be familiar with the film *Sleeping with the Enemy*, in which the character played by Julia Roberts initially flees her abusive husband and is later forced to destroy him. Students may also have seen *Enough*, a recent Jennifer Lopez film with a similar plot. Understandably, the class may want to distinguish between physical abuse and psychological abuse, with John Wright in *Trifles* evidently being guilty of the latter. But can psychological abuse ever be comparable to physical abuse? You might raise this issue.

Try, eventually, to bring the class's attention back to the gender dynamics actually operating in the play. In addition to the play's treatment of distinctions between men and women is the issue of how loyal the two women "detectives" should be to Minnie Wright. Their decision to cover up evidence of her act is, in a sense, the climax of the play, so Glaspell clearly is concerned about the degree of responsibility that they feel toward her. A worthwhile issue of defini-tion to raise is how we should define justice by the end of the play. If you com-pare *Trifles* with *Hamlet*, invite your class to consider which play presents a more clearly drawn definition of this important term.

PUNISHMENTS (p. 1302)

ROBERT BROWNING

My Last Duchess (p. 1302)

One of the most anthologized poems in the literary canon, Robert Browning's "My Last Duchess" epitomizes the dramatic monologue form and opens up our class discussion to issues of persona. As an audience of drama, a genre Browning tried with little success, we easily accept the notion that the actor who delivers the lines may differ a great deal from the character being por-trayed. And in fiction, readers understand that the *narrator* and the author are not one and the same. In poetry, however, students tend to have more difficulty separating the voice we hear in the poem, usually called the "speaker," from the poet. This may be because we are accustomed to reading confessional poetry or texts inspired by William Wordsworth's romantic dictum that poetry should relate intense emotional experience "recollected in tranquillity." When students say that they do not like poetry, this is often the sort of poetry they mean. Dramatic monologues, with their links to the soliloquies and dialogues of drama, help students to recognize that poetry too may have a fictional element. The Greek word *persona* originally referred to the masks worn by actors in clas-sical dramas like Sophocles' *Antigone* (p. 541). When the speaker of the poem is obviously not the poet, we usually refer to the character we hear speaking in the poem as a persona. Usually, the speaker of a poem is not called a "narrator" unless the poem tells a story.

Although Browning's biography does not play a direct part in the interpre-tation of this poem, since it presents a persona quite distant from his own per-sonality, students may find it interesting that the dramatic monologue was an experimental form in his time. Browning was a bit out of step with other Victorian poets like Alfred, Lord Tennyson, and Browning's wife Elizabeth Barrett Browning was more popular than her husband for her lyric poetry.

Students usually enjoy researching the romance between the Brownings. When he was thirty-four, Robert rescued Elizabeth, six years older, from a life as an invalid, hovered over by a domineering father. Students who have read Charlotte Perkins Gilman's "The Yellow Wallpaper" (p. 1149) will recognize the sort of inactivity that was imposed on Elizabeth Barrett before her marriage to Robert Browning, which was followed by a fifteen-year residence in Italy and the birth of their son. All evidence indicates that they were an extremely happy cou-ple from the early days of their courtship until her death. Because "My Last Duchess" is about a bad husband, to put it mildly, Browning's biography thus provides an interesting contrast to the poem. Though the 1842 poem predates his romantic marriage to Elizabeth and their time in Italy by several years, it shows Browning's ability to imagine the subtleties of power and sex in an Italian Renaissance setting where a rich man could do whatever he pleased.

Some scholars have pointed out that the dramatic monologue affords Browning the safety of speaking indirectly, forcing us to read the implicit meaning hidden beneath the actual words of the poem's persona. Because we want our college students to do just this, to go beyond the literal or reductive interpretations of textbook reading to explore less obvious issues in literature, "My Last Duchess" serves as a good starting point. Browning's complexity of characterization and his colloquial and experimental style have been linked to his literary ancestors William Shakespeare and John Donne; his contemporary Victorians, novelists Charles Dickens and George Eliot; and future modernist poets like T. S. Eliot and Ezra Pound, who both admired and parodied him. Because Browning's speaker suggests to his unseen auditor, the marriage broker about to get another young woman into a fine mess, that he "read" the portrait of his first wife, we may further use this poem to discuss the concept of reading a text. We like to bring in prints of paintings and have students read them from different perspectives. They can then write descriptions or narratives, think of personal and intertextual connotations, make aesthetic evaluations, and/or discuss historical, sociological, or psychological issues. In class, we look for gaps and oppositions, consider audience and purpose, and talk about any other interpretive aspects of reading particular paintings. We define a "text" at this point as anything that can be read and interpreted, ranging from the anthropologist's reading of a cultural group to a jury's reading of the evidence in a court case to our various interpretations of literary works in a college literature class. We also explain that although it may be possible to misread a text, there is seldom only one valid reading of a given text and our interpretations often tell us as much about the readers — ourselves — as the text. Browning's poem connects well with this exercise, since the Duke of Ferrara, as the poet imagines him, seems to have had his young wife killed because of his reading of her demeanor with other men. As we listen to his reading, we judge him more critically than we do the young woman he describes.

The speaker of Browning's poem is based on the historical Alfonso II, Duke of Ferrara, who lived in Renaissance Italy in the 1500s, at the height of the flowering of art taking place in that country's city-states. The duke's very young first wife, Lucrezia, died mysteriously in 1561 after just three years of marriage. Soon after her death, the duke began negotiations with representatives of the Count of Tyrol, whose capital was in Innsbruck, to marry the count's niece. Here, the duke is expecting to replace the dead beauty with a count's daughter. In the dramatic monologue, we are to imagine the shocked wedding negotiator as he listens to a cool description of the preceding wife's shortcomings and the duke's response to them. Her sin has been what may be a pretty woman's tendency to flirt or simply a sweetness and kindness that reaches out to everyone. Her husband feels that such attention should be saved only for him and seems to be especially bothered by her pleasure when the portrait artist compliments her beauty. She is not discriminating enough, he feels. He insists that it would be beneath his dignity to complain about her lack of decorum or to give her a chance to explain. There seems to be no suggestion that she has committed adultery or betrayed him in any way, though some readers can't resist blaming the victim, suspecting her of hidden sins. He tells the marriage broker that it is because she smiled at people more and more that he "gave commands; / Then all smiles stopped together." The reader is left to conclude that the speaker has ordered his wife killed because she is cheerful and friendly to people other than her aristocratic husband. Readers familiar with studies on spousal abuse see symptoms of a typical abuser in the duke. But unlike many abusers, this man possesses the power to get away with the ultimate abuse of murder. Some readers may be reminded of court cases in which wealthy defendants with skilled lawyers evade punishment. This is not even a question for the Renaissance nobleman in Browning's poem, since no one will dare call him to account. His complaints seem petty and arrogant to most readers, and his discussion of this topic with the agent of a potential bride's family has ominous implications. He's a scary, menacing man.

Although it is difficult to think of any positive qualities about the duke, some readers may admire his power and decisiveness. The duke is an art lover, obviously. But one wonders what happened to the fictitious Frà Pandolf, the artist Browning imagines creating the portrait of Lucrezia. Titian painted the duke, but there is no known painting of his young wife. Ironically, the duke now controls who gazes at her beauty; only he pulls the curtain aside. The duke may be warning the family of his new bride that he will be in complete control this time. Perhaps the first instinct of the count's agent is to bolt from the horror of what he has learned; the duke at one point feels the need to verbally pull him back and tell him that they should leave together. But another motive for revealing the painting may be to show off this object of art to the representative of an equally cultured household, the duke seems just as interested in pointing out the statue of Neptune by an artist from the count's own city. This is the duke's own private stash of art for his eyes only, and he thinks of wives in the same terms. The count's daughter will simply be an addition to his private collection of aesthetically pleasing objects. The duke speaks of these things matter-of-factly, almost off-handedly.

The monologue may be read in a conversational tone as one long speech, as Browning's choice of keeping it as one undivided stanza invites. Syntax and meter fight against each other in "My Last Duchess" in a way that submerges rhyme. If we follow the sense, we do not pause for a full stop at the end of lines but let enjambment take us to the end of a sentence, often in the middle of a line. The poem is written in heroic couplets; that is, two successive lines in iambic pentameter rhyme with each other. Instructors might want to introduce definitions of poetic terms as we listen for the effects of Browning's stylistic choices. Because a dramatic monologue works best if it sounds as if a real person were speaking to an unseen listener, the poet may sacrifice some of the lyrical effects of poetry when he chooses this genre. Many of Browning's Victorian contemporaries frowned on what they judged to be his clumsiness. Reading poetry in the wake of modernists who take their lead from Browning and others who were willing to be colloquial, and with a post-Whitman appreciation for free verse, today's readers usually are not as bothered by the conflict between syntactical rhythms and counted meter. The dramatic monologue allows Browning to develop a character who reveals himself through his own words.

The poet trusts his readers to work through the difference between the message of the poem and the words of the villainous character, just as we deal with the disjunction between traditional meter and conversational sentence rhythms. As twenty-first-century readers of a nineteenth-century poem about a sixteenth-century character, we might expect barriers to understanding.

Students inexperienced with reading poetry sometimes do feel at a loss when they first read the poem. It helps to provide the sort of context we've touched on here. We could show students a few examples of Renaissance portraiture to set the mood. Reading the poem aloud may give the best grounding and allow the instructor to choose an emphasis; for example, the word *last* in the title and the first line needs to be read in a way that lets us know another duchess is waiting in the wings. Once they catch the character of the speaker, today's readers recognize the sort of snobbish, self-absorbed person that still exists and certainly existed in the 1800s. Although few men in Browning's time had the power of a Renaissance nobleman, we read of many autocrats who terrorized their wives and children. Later, when Browning would defy Elizabeth Barrett's father, he would be dealing with a similar sort of authoritarian man who felt he owned the women in his family body and soul. The laws in most countries in the nineteenth century, including the United States, would have allowed or even encouraged a man to beat his wife. We often read of women today who are in abusive relationships, "punished" by husbands or boyfriends for actions no less innocent than Lucrezia's seem to be. Browning's duke is more psychologically interesting than the ordinary bully, however. Rather than lashing out in anger, he acts in secret, never really approaching his wife with his dissatisfaction with her. Misplaced pride often keeps a person from revealing true feelings to a partner, and we often insist that the other person guess what is upsetting us, to anticipate our needs without our having to "stoop" to express them. Our students may have stories to share about when this has happened in their relationships, though it will be easier to recall when others have done it to us than when we have been guilty of it. Both men and women sometimes build scenarios in their minds that interpret innocent behavior according to a suspicious narrative they have imposed on a partner.

CAROLYN FORCHÉ

The Colonel (p. 1304)

Poet and peace activist Carolyn Forché calls her prose poem "The Colonel" a "documentary poem" and considers her work a "poetry of witness." We ask students to consider the possible reasons for Forché's use of these terms, exploring the ways in which "The Colonel" fits this description. Like a reporter with a video camera, the political poet records injustices for her audience to view. Although she provides some commentary, she primarily presents the details of what she sees, challenging the reader to make judgments about the subject. As a witness, she passes on the facts and holds them up to the light. She makes no apologies for having a political purpose, however, and does not pretend — as some writers might — that she is an objective observer. Like a photographer who aims the camera, the writer directs our gaze by the details she selects.

But the topics chosen by Forché and other poets who write about social and political issues strike some American readers as inappropriate to poetry. Perhaps this is a reaction against moralistic and didactic literature that relegates art to an inferior position as the means to a political end. Most readers do not believe Forché's poetry sacrifices the subtleties of imagery and metaphor for the sake of her message. They feel that the poetry is more vivid because of its strong purpose. Forché reminds us that literary artists in many countries occupy a place of influence and respect, often holding positions of leadership in government or resistance movements. The way she usually tells her story, Forché stumbled into international affairs, naively landing in El Salvador in 1978 just as war was breaking out and later finding herself in Beirut, Lebanon, as strife was heating up there. The fact is, however, that she has consistently taken stands for human rights, and as a commentator for public radio and an investigator for Amnesty International, she often finds herself in hot spots, since these are the places where human rights are likely to be abused.

As a teacher in the creative writing program at George Mason University and in workshops for writers in various parts of the country, Forché sees her job as equally proactive. She says that such programs play a subversive role in the academic world, "democratizing" education by privileging the voices of students. For her, teaching means involving students in creative and critical thinking. She advises students to learn to write by reading, suggesting to potential poets that they keep books of poetry in the bathroom and use their time there to read at least one poem a day. She conducts programs in which writers in graduate school creatively document in words and photographs the particular issues of an economically depressed region or move outside the university to research the experiences of Holocaust survivors. In 1998, Forché received the Edita and Ira Morris Hiroshima Foundation for Peace and Culture Award, an international prize recognizing her work for human rights and the "preservation of memory and culture."

In "The Colonel" Forché describes an arrogant man who would undoubtedly judge her work for human rights as without value. He mocks the power of the poet to accomplish any change that will stop men like himself: "Something for your poetry, no?" he says as he shows off his trophies, a batch of severed human ears. His action seems crude and sophomoric, reminding instructors of students who think they will shock us with lurid descriptions of adventures with drugs, alcohol, and explicit sex. He is "mean," both in the word's connotation of willingness to cause pain and in its sense of pettiness and poverty of spirit. The poet uses the natural symbolism of the ears, however, to catch our attention, to shake us into awareness of present tyranny — "this scrap of his voice" — and to be alert for approaching tyranny, with our ears "to the ground." The ending calls us back to the opening line of the poem, which suggests that we have "heard" something about the colonel's brutality and perhaps have dismissed it as folklore. The poem makes him seem ordinary at first, simply a family man having dinner. But we soon learn that he is cruel to the extent of turning even his house into a weapon. The colonel controls and dominates language. He is even compelled to silence the parrot, and the narrator's friend warns her to keep quiet as well, knowing that the colonel is getting ready to show off his trick with the ears.

Although the narrator's — and therefore the reader's — awareness of the colonel's barbarity escalates as the poem goes on, we feel his menace from the beginning lines. For example, the presence of a pistol is juxtaposed with details of everyday family life and with a poetic metaphor that compares the moon to a light bulb in the interrogation room of a prison. As we argue about whether Forché's text is really a poem, we should consider its use of metaphor, symbol, and imagery. The vivid visual image of the ears looking like peach halves and then coming to life in the water is not lyrical, but it is a simile that has symbolism and sensory power. Its conversational tone does not preclude its definition as poetry; compare, for instance, Robert Browning's "My Last Duchess," (p. 1302), which directly precedes Forché's poem.

One aspect of poetry is compressed language that distills experience into a few carefully chosen words. This is therefore a poetic text, and the prose quality is more a factor of typography than genre. The short sentences could have been lines. Small groups of students might work together at a computer station to make "The Colonel" look more like a traditional poem, explaining to the class their decisions about where lines should end. Part of Forché's method is to make this poem of witness a documentation of the egotism and terrible small-mindedness of a military dictator. Not only does she make it look like prose, but she justifies margins so that they are perfectly straight, as a legal document would be. By turning his attempt to shock into a poem that reveals his character, the poet takes back the power of speech that the colonel seeks to undermine and control. He has meant the *text* of the ears to symbolize his power, but the poet uses it to ask her audience to listen attentively. Her decision to bury his words in her poem without quotation marks further emphasizes her linguistic coup. His words are no more important than the television commercial or the parrot's meaningless *hello*. We give him our attention only because we know he must be stopped and that others like him must be listened for. Although the story of the colonel has the ring of folklore, Forché claims that this incident really happened, that the man was notorious for entertaining dinner guests in this way. Like narratives about war atrocities, the details seem too outlandish to be true, and we don't know whether to believe the author or not. Although it is fair to assume the colonel is based on someone the writer met in El Salvador, it is a good strategy to keep his exact identity generic. Tyrants exist in many times and places, and the colonel's universality helps us remember to be alert for them wherever they crop up.

The twentieth-century Central American dictator of Forché's poem and the sixteenth-century Italian nobleman of Browning's "My Last Duchess" could be the same man. Each seeks to subtly bully a guest, to send a warning that he has the power to command violence and will not hesitate to do so on the smallest pretext. Although we do not know who the victims of the colonel are, our knowledge of the arbitrary nature of political murder in El Salvador, especially the brutal killings of priests and other noncombatants, causes us to see their deaths and mutilations as unwarranted. A man who would coldly have a wife killed for smiling too much would have no trouble carrying out political executions or bragging about them at the dinner table.

The listeners in both poems are forced by caution to be passive. Nothing would be gained by challenging the dangerous tyrants of these poems. Forché's listener is the speaker of the poem, a persona who may be very close to the poet herself. Although she has the sense to remain silent in the presence of the

colonel, she goes on to write a poem, a political action of potential consequence. We know less about the listener of Browning's poem, since it is the menacing duke whose voice we hear. There is a hint that the listener makes a move
to leave, perhaps involuntarily; but he does not possess the power. Perhaps, he
will advise the count to keep his daughter in Innsbruck, but we will never know.

Our students find Forché's diction easier to understand, since its simple,
declarative sentences have an American directness that we are accustomed to
hearing every day. Browning takes more work, both because his nineteenth-century British poetic style is more formal and because he is portraying a
Renaissance character. Even though Browning's poem rhymes and has an
underlying meter, both poems have the effect of conversational prose. Both writers deliberately choose this style to suit their content and the dramatic situation
they have imagined. With their block form, the two poems even have a similar
visual appearance.

SEAMUS HEANEY

Punishment (p. 1306)

In Northern Ireland where poet Seamus Heaney grew up, large areas are
covered with peat bogs. Heaney tells of being fascinated even as a child with the
amazing variety of objects that fall or are thrown into the bogs only to be found
years later, preserved by the unique chemical properties of the watery, vegeta-
tion-rich soil. He recalls that people would store butter under the peat in the
days before refrigeration, keeping it fresh for long periods of time. In his earlier
poem "Bogland" Heaney mentions butter being discovered after hundreds of
years still "salty and white," and he describes the quality of the bogland as "itself
. . . kind, black butter." He remembers as a child the recovery of a prehistoric
skeleton of a "Great Irish Elk" from a local bog and the newspaper pictures of
his neighbors posing with the huge antlers.

This land had a habit of remembering, and Heaney himself came to see history as something that still exists in the present, each object reverberating with
it and each human being echoing a heritage and mythology that does not die.
As a Roman Catholic living in Northern Ireland, Seamus Heaney would have
been hard put to avoid a sense of history and politics. Students may be aware of
religious and political issues that have plagued Ireland for centuries. They may
have read poetry by the late nineteenth-/early twentieth-century writer William
Butler Yeats, like Heaney a Nobel Prize laureate who wrote about Ireland's
unique culture and history. Some may know about Irish culture from background reading on James Joyce. Instructors may need to remind many students
of the social and historical context of Heaney's texts, however. Classes that have
read Frank O'Connor's short story "Guests of the Nation" (p. 1091) in which
Irish Republican soldiers are called on to execute their English prisoners will
find intertextual connections. We may recall from O'Connor's biography his
imprisonment by an Irish political faction because he spoke against the brutal
punishments dealt out to women who were judged too friendly to men of opposing political or religious groups. Heaney's poem "Punishment" refers to similar

treatment in modern Belfast. Irish Republican Army sympathizers have been known to humiliate women who date British soldiers by shaving their heads, stripping them, coating them with tar, and then handcuffing them to railings for public ridicule.

With his knowledge of such politically motivated actions, his contact with history and mythology, and his personal experience of growing up near the peat bogs of Ireland, Seamus Heaney's reading in 1969 of *The Bog People* by Danish archaeologist P. V. Glob led to a powerful convergence of interests that energized Heaney's writing. The book contains photographs of preserved bodies from bogs in various locations in northern Europe. The details that remain of faces, bodies, and artifacts are stunning. Glob's book, was published by Cornell University Press in 1969. If the book is available to you, take it to class; nothing can replace seeing the photographs themselves, and students will understand why Heaney was impressed by them. Glob sees some of the bog people as human sacrifices, offered to a pre-Christian earth mother deity, and Heaney makes that connection in some poems in his sequence inspired by Glob's book: for example, "Bog Queen" and "The Tolland Man." The poet sees "an archetypal pattern" in these deaths and explains in his nonfiction "Feelings into Words" that the photographs of these ancient victims converge for him with similar images of "atrocities, past and present, in the long rites of Irish political and religious struggles" (58).

Glob goes to first-century Roman historian Tacitus for a hint about the girl who inspires Heaney's poem "Punishment." His account describes a situation chillingly like that of her Irish counterparts. "Tacitus names a special punishment for adultery by women," Glob writes, "but says nothing about male adultery. The adulterous woman had her hair cut off in the presence of her relatives and was then scourged out of the village. This calls to mind one of the bog people in particular, the young girl from Windeby, in Domland Fen. She lay naked in her grave in the peat, her hair shaved off, with nothing but a collar of ox-hide round her neck and with bandaged eyes" (153). Elsewhere in the book, Glob describes her burial in minute detail, telling us that she was around fourteen, that her hair was originally light blonde and had been chopped off and shaven unevenly, that her hands and facial features were "delicate," that she hadn't been getting enough to eat. Pollen samples show that she was roughly contemporary with Tacitus. Her woven blindfold would have been bright red and yellow at the time she died. She wore only this and an ox-hide collar. She had been drowned and covered with birch branches and a large stone. Glob includes with his description three photographs: one of her body, one of her face, and one of her remarkably preserved brain (112–14)

Heaney weaves many of the details from the archaeologist's written and visual texts into his poem. The scientist's account is written for a popular audience rather than for experts; he even includes in his introduction letters from a group of English schoolgirls interested in his discoveries and dedicates his book to them and his own daughter, Elsebeth. It is not surprising, therefore, that we detect empathy in his descriptions. These are real people for him, and we cannot look at the photographs without feeling their individuality. Seamus Heaney uses sensory imagery that empathizes even further, evoking the physical sensations she must have felt, especially the cold. He shows us her fragility; her rib cage is "frail," she is "Little" and "undernourished," and she is like a "sapling" — a slender young tree. He shows her as vulnerable, using the word naked and referring to parts of the body we think of as tender, her "nipples" and the "nape / of her neck." She is passive, since we feel and see what is done to her but not what she does. We feel compassion for her and perhaps a touch of sexual or aesthetic attraction. The poet does not address her directly until the sixth stanza. This shifts the perspective somewhat, now focusing on the feelings of the speaker while the reader has previously envisioned the girl herself. This allows a movement in time. He first projects us into the past and brings the individual victim to life. After we have felt something for the first-century woman, we are more prepared to hear the comparison with the political present and the speaker's status as a "voyeur," a silent witness to modern "tribal" vengeance. For Heaney, the bog woman drowned for sexual transgressions, the Belfast girls tarred for similar crimes, the speaker of the poem, and the reader who joins him as a bystander are all part of the same story.

A key to one possible theme for the poem is Heaney's use of the word scapegoat in the seventh stanza and his allusion to "stones of silence" in the eighth stanza. Both are biblical referents that symbolize the shifting of the sins of a culture to a selected victim. The scapegoat in ancient Israel was driven into the wilderness, carrying the evils of the community, as a way of acting out repentance and absolution. We have come to use the word to refer to a person or group unfairly punished for the misdeeds of others, often the person or persons exacting the punishment. The "stones of silence" may refer to an incident in which Jesus defends a woman accused of adultery, a crime punishable by stoning. He implies that no one really has the right to judge and punish the personal behavior of another since no human being can claim moral perfection. The allusion may also relate to another biblical stoning in Acts 7:58 in which Saul, not yet transformed into the Apostle Paul by a dramatic conversion experience, stands by and holds coats as a mob murders the first Christian martyr, Stephen. The poem's speaker feels that he engages in a similar complicity in which he does not fully participate in political violence but understands the emotions that underpin it. Heaney has lost friends to terrorism, and, as a Roman Catholic raised just thirty miles northwest of Belfast, he understands the reasoning behind the rage against British occupation and those who go along with it. But he shows the victim in the bog and her future sisters in Ireland to be incongruously fragile and pathetic targets.

The speaker calls himself "an artful voyeur." A voyeur is usually defined as a person who obtains sexual gratification from observing the sexual activities or the bodies of other people. The reader joins the speaker in looking at the naked body of the victim. (Who wouldn't find the image of her nipples as "amber beads" irresistible?) But we go even further to invade the "darkened combs" — the valleys — of her "exposed" brain and to inspect her skeleton. In a sense, to read is to be a voyeur, and to write is to be an artful one. The poet uses her for his art, and we find pleasure in the images he creates. But whereas the speaker may do nothing about the violence that he witnesses, this cannot be said of the poet, since he does not stand idly by. He takes the action of writing the poem. By exposing our own voyeurism to us, he may challenge us to act.

In the speech Seamus Heaney gave when accepting his Nobel Prize for literature in 1995, he relates the story of a busload of men stopped by a masked band of gunmen in Northern Ireland. When the men, presumed to be Protestant terrorists, shouted for the Catholics to step forward, the lone Catholic in the group felt the passenger next to him squeeze his hand to pull him back with the silent promise that his Protestant friends would keep his religion a secret. The Catholic decided to stand up for his faith and stepped forward anyway. He was the only survivor. The terrorists pushed him to the side and opened fire on the Protestants, and the Catholic lived to tell of this small gesture of peace. It is this squeeze of the hand that Heaney calls for, the small sign of friendship and solidarity that refuses to hand over the scapegoat for condemnation.

In the last stanza of "Punishment" Heaney admits that the issues that divide are complex. The poem's speaker faults himself for being willing to "connive / in civilized outrage." The word connive implies an action that disregards or tacitly consents to a wrongdoing. The word has pejorative connotations. If we called someone conniving, we would be hurling an insult. But his usage is ironic. He leaves some question about the act he takes himself to be silently condoning. Is it the "revenge" that he sees as the wrongdoing? Or is it his own sense of "outrage" that he sees as a betrayal? Does he connive when he shares the outrage directed at the woman who has sinned against the community or the world's outrage against his fellow Catholics who punish her? The tarring of the woman who has committed treason by sleeping with the enemy is an act against one's own: A "tribal, intimate revenge" that the speaker claims to understand. Though readers tend to romanticize such relationships as Romeo-and-Juliet situations, we might have students imagine scenarios in which we saw our nation occupied by an oppressive enemy. Would we easily forgive someone who willingly formed relationships with the men who abused our fathers and brothers?

As a writer, Heaney is sometimes criticized for being disloyal to his own Northern Irish Catholics, failing to take a strong stand against oppression. Others fault him for raising such political issues in poetry at all. Still, by linking the treason of the Irish women with the presumably less political adultery of the bog woman and by painting her with such compassion, Heaney makes the brutality toward these women seem to be directed primarily toward their sexual transgression. Seen in this way, the revenge of the "tribe" reminds readers of the Chinese villagers who punish the whole family of an adulteress in Maxine Hong Kingston's "No Name Woman" (p. 1138) or of the men of some Muslim cultures who execute daughters and sisters who go against their sexual mores. Rarely are men punished for having sex that does not involve violence, but women often are.

Seamus Heaney uses down-to-earth language — no pun intended — to describe the woman in the bog. Many words are one syllable. He ends the fourth stanza with the hyphenated "oak-bone, brain-firkin," reminiscent of the Anglo-Saxon rhythms of Beowulf or the inventions of Gerard Manley Hopkins, a favorite poet of Heaney's. A firkin is a small cask. She is therefore a container for the brain whose complexity he admires with voyeuristic interest in a later stanza. Because his diction consists mostly of strong, terse nouns and verbs, the adjectives he does use stand out vividly: naked, amber, frail, drowned, and so forth. Rather than depending on meter and rhyme, Heaney's rhythm emerges as a natural consequence of word choice and content. Much of the sound depends on subtle assonance and alliteration. Notice in stanza 9, for example, the repetition of the consonant b and the vowel o, with the deliciously mouth-filling vocalic echo of combs and bones filling in for formal rhyme. If the poet had substituted the synonym valleys for the more localized English word combs, much would have been lost. The single-syllable words of the poem's first line literally pull us into the poem, communicating a feeling of forced movement that exactly fits the sense.

In the three poems we have read in this cluster, punishments seem far more brutal than the crime would warrant, and all are even more disturbing because they continue after the victim's death. Robert Browning's "My Last Duchess" (p. 1302) describes a murder that seems to have been prompted by nothing more than a young girl's pleasure in social interactions. Her blush may as easily have been interpreted as modesty that honored her husband. But her husband degrades her memory by describing her supposed sins to a stranger who will provide her replacement. Carolyn Forché's bully in "The Colonel" (p. 1304) goes beyond merely killing his opponents to mutilating them and desecrating their memories with a tasteless show. The women of Heaney's "Punishment" are stripped naked before the community, subjected to attacks on their beauty, and held up to public humiliation. The bog woman is drowned and weighted down, perhaps being sacrificed in a religious rite meant to return the community to proper order.

In each poem, control is maintained through the extreme exercise of power, and the language is controlled as well. The subject of silence is implied in Browning's poem, since we hear only the voice of the duke. He has ownership of language in his world, and the listener in the poem cannot escape it. He has silenced even the nonverbal expressions of his wife. The listener will have to decide, however, if he will share the information he is given with the father of the duke's new bride. The theme of listening is foregrounded in Forché's poem from beginning to end. The colonel seeks to control language, the severing of ears being a symbolic image of this attempt. But the final image of ears pressed to the ground subverts his power, as does the poem itself. Again, the reluctant audience must make a decision to listen alertly and to act on what is learned. The speaker of Heaney's "Punishment" gives us the metaphor "stones of silence" and the image of himself standing "dumb" as he watches the humiliated women. To keep silent is sometimes to take an action, he implies. To stand aside may be to assist in wielding a weapon.

It is difficult to imagine such extreme punishments taking place in the contemporary United States with the approval of the community. However, students may suggest examples of subtle ways that we punish individuals, symbolically overreacting to transgressions or opposition. Do they know people who have been punished by their families for forming relationships outside of their religion or ethnic group? Do American subcultures enforce silence on some, seek to control language, or hold transgressors up to humiliation? Perhaps class members can offer examples from their own experience of the double standard that punishes women for sexual behavior accepted as the norm for men.

SHERMAN ALEXIE
Capital Punishment (p. 1308)

Sherman Alexie, a Spokane/Coeur d'Alene Indian, likes to challenge stereotypes and genres: he is first a poet, but his poetry edges into narrative and prose poetry, whereas his short stories — some of the "sudden fiction," short-short-story genre — have the feel of poetry. He has been called "a storyteller with a poetic streak." Alexie says that his poems are essentially stories and acknowledges a "strong, narrative drive" in all of his work. In the introduction to his screenplay for the movie *Smoke Signals*, published in paperback by Hyperion in 1998, Alexie talks about genre:

> When people ask me, and they do ask me, how I feel about making the difficult transition from writing novels to writing screenplays, I am not always sure what to say.
> I mean, screenplays are more like poetry than like fiction.
> Screenplays rely on imagery to carry the narrative, rather than the other way around. And screenplays have form. Like sonnets, actually. Just as there are expectations of form, meter, and rhyme in a sonnet, there are the same kinds of expectations for screenplays.
> Of course, free verse poetry subverts all expectations of formalist poetry.
> So, I wonder aloud, who is writing free verse screenplays? (x)

Though his movie is not free verse, it begins and ends with poetry and includes songs, some of them written by Alexie and his cowriter Jim Boyd. For Alexie, songs are people's poetry. One of the songs in *Smoke Signals* bears the memorable title "John Wayne's Teeth." *Smoke Signals*, loosely based on Alexie's 1993 book of interconnected short stories *The Lone Ranger and Tonto Fistfight in Heaven*, breaks new ground as a movie written, directed, coproduced, and performed by Native Americans.

Like his poetry, Alexie's movie challenges stereotypes of American Indians as necessarily shamans or warriors, and his texts exist in the present rather than a romantic *Dances with Wolves* past. His characters are not magical holy men and women who turn into deer or possess supernatural spirituality. Alcohol and poverty play a part in their lives because these are realities of reservation life, but his characters are not pathetic victims who say, as Dustin Hoffman's character does in *Little Big Man*, "Today is a good day to die." Alexie says that there is no such thing as a good day to die, and he parodies the line: "Today is a good day to play basketball" or "Today is a good day to have breakfast," his characters quip. Humor and irony energize all of Alexie's work.

His work also takes an argumentative rhetorical stance. This is an angry young poet, and he has a right to be. The first peoples of the Americas have endured a Holocaust, and Alexie and other Native American writers represented in this anthology do not intend to let anyone forget this fact. Consider the texts, biographical headnotes, and instructor's manual discussions (in the order in which they appear) for N. Scott Momaday, Linda Hogan, Richard Rodriguez, Leslie Marmon Silko, and Gabriel García Márquez. In addition to the "should be simple" equation in line 98 of "Capital Punishment" (1 death + 1 death=

2 deaths"), Alexie has suggested a more complex equation: "Survival = Anger x Imagination" or sometimes "Poetry = Anger x Imagination." Ironically and appropriately, we may interpret his variation to mean that no one simple answer exists to any problem, or we may notice that the equations suggest another truth for Sherman Alexie and other forthright voices in current Native American literature: Poetry = Survival.

Alexie argues against the death penalty in his poem "Capital Punishment" first by raising the issue of racial inequities in the system. He goes on to bring up the implicit point that the electric chair constitutes cruel and unusual punishment by relating the story of "a black man" — reiterating the inequality — who was executed twice because the chair malfunctioned. Readers may recall true horror stories of the flames, smoke, and other physical atrocities Alexie describes in the lines following line 74. The speaker eats from the plate of the man to be executed and hopes to be with him in his death. He develops this idea further in the last three stanzas of the poem to imply that "any of us" — the speaker and the reader united in the first-person plural pronoun but alone in the unique *any* — could be connected with the executed man, that we have all "sinned" and all are equally vulnerable to death. The arbitrary connotations of being struck by lightning add to his argument against the unjust selection of those to be executed.

Since any of us in a college classroom are likely to be called for jury duty during the next few years, it makes sense to think about our attitudes toward the death penalty. We might have students look back at this point to Joyce Carol Oates's observations of jury bias in "I, the Juror" (p. 1127). Ironically, people who admit to being against capital punishment are not allowed to serve on "death-qualified" juries when such a verdict is legally possible, a fact that may skew judgment more surely against mercy for the defendant. Students may recall the furor from usually vocal advocates of the death penalty like Jerry Falwell who were protesting the 1998 execution of a pretty, white, born-again Christian woman on death row in Texas for the pickax murders of two robbery victims. Gov. George W. Bush refused to pardon the woman. Alexie questions why we feel that one person's death is more acceptable than another's. Some readers may not change their minds about the death penalty no matter how rhetorically effective they concede the opposing argument to be.

One of Alexie's most compelling points revolves around the definition of the word *kill*. Proponents of the death penalty when challenged with the biblical commandment *Thou shalt not kill* contend that the Hebrew word should have been translated *murder*, referring to guidelines in the Bible for carrying out capital punishments. The term *capital punishment* is itself a euphemism, as is *execution*. Alexie describes the procedures linguists use to edit dictionaries, a process students may not realize is based on studies of how words are actually being spoken in social and written contexts rather than on prescriptions for proper speech. In line 82, the poet repeats the word *kill*, refusing to gloss over the reality of what is taking place. We may try to sugar-coat it, but killing is killing.

Alexie refers to the divisiveness of the issues surrounding victimization and punishment with the observation that we "throw the killers in one grave / and victims in another. We form sides / and have two separate feasts." In most traditions, funerals are accompanied by eating. Readers may recall Hamlet's ironic observation that it was thrifty of his uncle to make the funeral feast do double duty as a wedding reception. Alexie is equally ironic in making his speaker a cook who prepares the last meal for the execution victim. He imagines a vestige of his own being reaching the body of the man as he is dying, a sort of communion.

Just as he demands an honest definition of the word *kill*, the speaker questions the meaning of the word *witness*. We recall that Carolyn Forché (p. 1304) calls hers a "poetry of witness." Alexie has a political agenda as surely as she does; he may in fact have more legitimacy because he is a person of color who realizes the part prejudice plays in deciding who goes to the electric chair. The speaker's first claim that he is not a witness simply seems to differentiate the role of official witness to an execution from the role of cook. But he moves soon after this first denial into an assertion about the racial inequality of execution and tells us that this can be proven by the facts — hard rhetorical evidence that we can verify. We remember that a witness may be someone called on to testify, to offer proof. In line 22, the denial that he is a witness becomes a refrain, a line that will echo throughout the poem. This time, the context indicates that he will not stand as a witness against a man who loves another man, that he does not pass judgment. The next negation of his witness status comes after he has told "a story" about a failure of the electric chair and the subsequent double execution of a man. This is hearsay evidence and is anecdotal, so we would not be expected to give it as much rhetorical weight. He does not have the authority of a true witness. The irony, of course, is that such evidence tends to be extremely persuasive, though we like to think we are more swayed by logic and facts. The next repetition comes when the speaker is trying desperately to block out the reality of what is happening by sitting in the dark and chanting to himself "not to look at the clock." At this point, the claim that he is not a witness has the panicky tone of a prayer or a mantra: *Please God don't make me be a witness*, he seems to say underneath the words. After powerful imagery describing the body's reaction to the jolt of electricity, he again claims not to be a witness, though he sounds like someone who knows what he is talking about, and we now trust the ethos he projects. Finally, in line 102, he admits to being a witness to the culture's denials, curiosities, and divisions, if not to the execution itself. He witnesses with his anger and imagination from the pit of the stomach of the executed man.

It cannot be denied that race is a factor in the dealing out of punishments in the United States. Some readers will find that Alexie's ethnicity lends authority to his argument, whereas others may feel he has an ax (a tomahawk?) to grind and his ethos is therefore undermined by his lack of objectivity. Some readers see Alexie's argument against inconsistency as more persuasive than his argument against capital punishment per se. Whereas the movie *Dead Man Walking* juxtaposes the faces of the victims with that of the executed man as he dies, Alexie's speaker imagines himself as present through the sharing of food. This is not a story about the victim or the crime but about the execution and the nature of witnessing. The victim in Alexie's poem is mentioned matter-of-factly, in spite of the violence of the image describing his death, and the speaker follows quickly with a joke about the stereotype of Indians gambling. The humor works on multiple levels, since casinos are one of the few sources of economic power that tribal governments have, but gambling can be a seductive addiction like alcohol.

Games and sports took the place of war in the history of several tribes, and the "Indian killer" in the poem stands ironically in a tradition, even as we laugh at Alexie's subversion of the stereotype. This particular use of humor is typical of Alexie's style, deflecting pathos, bitterness, and prejudice with irony. In the notes to his screenplay for *Smoke Signals*, Alexie praises actor Irene Bedard for ad-libbing a "very Indian moment" as Suzy Song. As she hands over the can of ashes containing the cremated remains of Victor Joseph's father, she jokes deadpan, "This is Arnold. He ain't looking so good." Alexie's conclusion is that filmmakers should learn from this: "Cast Indians as Indians, because they'll give better performances" (162). At the end of the poem "Capital Punishment," Alexie offers another image that readers could interpret as ironic. Electricity is electricity, whether in a chair or in lightning, just as killing is killing whether it is done by an Indian or a government. We — the speaker, the poet, and the reader — are not qualitatively different in our humanity from the man who is brought by just one of his sins through a system as arbitrary as lightning to "headlines and ash." Although readers may vary in their guesses about their possible epitaphs after standing on a hill in a thunderstorm, an appropriate one might be, "We knew she didn't have enough common sense to come in out of the rain."

Both Alexie in "Capital Punishment" and Forché in "The Colonel" assume readers who critically question what they are told. We want convincing evidence, so they offer it. But they also trust their readers to think for themselves as they consider the images the poets project, to come to as reasonable conclusions from the implicit messages as we would from more overt polemics. Like the word *witness*, the word *tribal* has divergent connotations. For the first peoples of the American continent, identification with a tribe is both legally and culturally important. Different tribes require different degrees of genetic inheritance for full tribal membership and the benefits that now accrue from belonging to a separate nation within the nation of the United States.

Such identification has had its drawbacks in the past, to say the least. Writers wishing to describe ethnicity constantly rephrase to keep from saying *Native American* yet again, knowing that editors will probably cut out references to *American Indians*. But some people within these ethnic groups object to the pretentiousness of the term *Native American*; one Internet Web site of the Choctaw Nation, for example, proclaims "No Native Americans here, just Indians!" Using tribal names seems more precise, but this doesn't help when a person is qualified by ancestry to register as a member of more than one tribe. Nevertheless, the word *tribal* in this sense has an objective connotation, serving simply as a descriptor.

As a person becomes involved in the characteristics that make his or her particular group unique, *tribal* can take on positive cultural undertones, can be a source of self-esteem. When Seamus Heaney (p. 1306) uses the word to describe the actions of his own Irish "tribe" of Roman Catholics, however, the word takes on pejorative connotations. Just as non-European or non-Christian societies were long considered "primitive" and without culture, Heaney's characterization of the extreme revenge carried out against women as *tribal* implies negatively critical connotations. The division he describes by the word is similar to the one Alexie evokes by his image of separate funeral feasts. In Forché's poem, too, the colonel acts tribally, in Heaney's sense of the word, as the leader of a faction who feels justified in any action taken against the opposing tribe.

The taking of ears may remind us of scalping, of accounts of ancient Assyrians piling up body parts as trophies, of heads of Catholics or leaders of peasant revolts impaled on the railings of London Bridge.

Whereas the first two poems of this cluster confine their documentation of a character's speech or action to a one-stanza block, Heaney and Alexie allow more white space to separate the phrases in their speakers' stories. When white space is used, whether at the line or stanza breaks of a poem or at the beginning of a paragraph of prose, the pace slows down the words nearest the white space are emphasized. Like the spaces within the geometric solid shapes of a sculpture or the rests in a piece of music, the pauses of a literary text count. Students might be asked to note the words that come just before a break in Alexie's two-line stanzas to determine if they tend to convey important images. One result of the slowing of pace is an increased sense of spontaneity and intimacy. Rather than demonstrating a character's control of language, the poet gives space for our entry into the issue, allowing a dialogue between reader and speaker as we think about what is said. This means not that the poems of Heaney and Alexie are more or less effective in communicating their message than those of Browning and Forché but simply that their method and purpose are different.

REVENGE (p. 1314)

EDGAR ALLAN POE

The Cask of Amontillado (p. 1314)

Most students have read Edgar Allan Poe in high school, perhaps the spooky novella *The Fall of the House of Usher,* short stories like "The Telltale Heart" and "The Black Cat," or the much-anthologized poems "The Raven" and "Annabel Lee." They may even be familiar with "The Cask of Amontillado." Rather than covering territory with which they may already be familiar, we invite students to address issues they may not have considered before. If they have studied the story in high school, they may have considered its suspense and other narrative elements. In a college class, they may explore instead how the story illustrates the issue of carnival, in which the rules of society are turned upside down. Or they may consider the implications of class in nineteenth-century America and speculate about the writer's decision to set his story in an anonymous European setting.

Students enjoy researching and debating details of Poe's various and conflicting biographies and relate to the problems that he experienced as a young man with his foster father, John Allan. Since the writer sensationalized himself, and readers often have difficulty separating the creator of his texts from their narrators, issues remain open about his addictions, his romances, his family relationships, and the extent of his genius and his madness. His parents were itinerant actors, just a step up from vagrant gypsies in the eyes of polite society in 1809, his father was an alcoholic unwilling or unable to take responsibility for his family and both parents died before he was three. To understand nineteenth-century views about parental influence on character and the implications for Poe's self-image, we might turn to the theories of John Harvey Kellogg (p. 1168) in the cluster of background materials for Charlotte Perkins Gilman's "The Yellow Wallpaper" (p. 1149). His heredity must have presented cause for concern as Poe came of age and his artistic temperament and eccentricity began to manifest. The carnival quality to his life before he came into the aristocratic Allan household would surely have been seen as a foreshadowing.

Some critics believe that "The Cask of Amontillado" reflects Poe's relationship with his foster father. Conflicts with Allan had begun before Poe flunked out of West Point: he felt his allowance was inadequate and the military atmosphere was oppressive and therefore stopped attending classes. Poe had already seen some literary work published by this time and turned to writing as a profession after it became apparent that he would be disinherited. Perhaps the flighty, alcohol-soaked Fortunato, with his carnival trappings of a fool, represents the ungrateful son in a bit of ironic self-parody, and the bitter and revengeful Montresor represents the rigid, unforgiving father tormented by a "thousand injuries." The hyperbole of the narrator marks him as unreliable, and the reader is left to wonder if Fortunato has truly insulted Montresor or if the narrator is simply paranoid. Interested students might compare this narrator with other insane protagonists in Poe's fiction. The symbolic walling up of a victim is a recurring motif, appearing in both "The Telltale Heart" and "The Black Cat" — stories in which the narrator imagines himself to be clever but gives himself away.

Montresor seems to be successful, however, and much more in control of himself than the usually manic and hallucinating madmen of the other stories. He is actually quite funny to some readers; we laugh at his ironic assurances that Fortunato will not die of the cold and niter, his toasting of Fortunato's "long life," and his revelation of the trowel underneath his cloak as proof that he is a mason. He ridicules the secretive Masonic brotherhood, itself an elitist organization, reversing the ceremony in which the initiate moves from darkness into light. The narrator's echoing screams and laughter can be imagined as hilarious if the reader decides to agree with Montresor that Fortunato deserves his fate. They are nightmarish otherwise. Readers may decide to read the story first in total agreement with Montresor and a second time with doubts.

Dramatic irony is added to Montresor's verbal irony because the audience understands that Fortunato's unknowing descent into the bowels of the earth is a descent toward death. The niter reminds us of hellish brimstone, and the flambeaux — the torches — are described by a word that reminds us of flames. Montresor's coat of arms makes a visual allusion to a verse in the Bible directed toward the serpent who tempts Eve to disobey God in the Garden of Eden. When God expels humanity from the garden in response to this original sin, he also curses the serpent, saying that Eve's offspring "shalt bruise thy head and thou shalt bruise his heel" (Genesis 3:15). This gives Montresor a Satanic aura. His family motto — *Nemo me impune lacessit* — means "No one wounds me with impunity," a sinister threat but also the motto of Scotland and the Stuart kings. Some scholars see in this yet another connection to John Allan, a man of Scottish descent and a Scottish Rite Mason. By this interpretation Poe would be the hapless Fortunato.

The name is symbolic, indicating that Fortunato has been blessed. Perhaps, like Poe, he has been fortunately rescued into privilege. Whether or not we believe that he has really harmed the narrator, we recognize Fortunato as an elitist. His pride in his ability to judge fine wine marks him as an aristocrat who needs to be taken down a notch. Seen in this way, it may be Fortunato who symbolizes Allan and other moneyed representatives of the upper class and Montresor who fulfills Poe's fantasies of revenge. When Poe ends the tale with the epitaph "*In pace requiescat!*" he continues the irony. The words traditionally mean, "Rest in peace," but experts have pointed out that *In pace* can also describe solitary confinement in a monastic prison.

As students think about who the narrator may be addressing, they may recall the dramatic monologue of another nobleman, Robert Browning's Renaissance duke in "My Last Duchess" (p. 1302). Although they are writing in different countries, Browning and Poe offered the two texts to a public audience at roughly the same time. Perhaps Poe's narrator has a similar motive to Browning's; he may be giving the listener a sinister warning that he is a person to be feared. If he is speaking fifty years later, however, he may be justifying his actions to a confessor or another person attending his deathbed. Montresor accuses Fortunato of adding insult to injury, but he keeps to these abstract, general descriptions, so the audience does not know what Fortunato has done. No matter what the crime, we cannot envision its being severe enough to warrant being buried alive. Therefore, it is best left unexplained.

Like Browning's Duke of Ferrara, Poe's nobleman does not stoop to discuss the matter with the person he sees as challenging his pride. This would give him away. But unlike Browning's character, Montresor feels that revenge must be carried out personally with the full understanding of the offending victim. The carnival setting makes possible the image of the ridiculous victim, drunk and dressed like a clown going foolishly to his death. He is amazed by the luck of finding such fine wine during carnival and is drunk enough from his Mardi Gras revels to accept as sincere the false flattery praising his expertise. Montresor uses reverse psychology to entrap Fortunato into volunteering. Poe establishes early that Fortunato is a con man but that he knows his wine. Montresor's victory is sweeter for his success in conning a con. Perhaps he uses the word *amontillado* so much to parody the name dropping of rare vintages engaged in by pretentious foreign charlatans who make a living from "imposture upon the British and Austrian *millionnaires*," as the narrator describes this Italian *quack*, Fortunato.

When Fortunato pleads with Montresor at the end of the story, saying "For the love of God," Montresor mocks him by throwing the words back. Students may feel that this blasphemy indicates that Montresor is completely evil. Others may argue that he feels so justified in his revenge that he believes God is on his side against the sinful and frivolous Fortunato. Readers may recall that in the second paragraph of the story the narrator anticipates the "immolation" of his enemy. The word *immolation* refers to a human sacrifice. Fortunato does not answer Montresor's final mockery, and Montresor throws a torch into the wall with the imprisoned man. At this point the bells jingle in reply, perhaps as Fortunato moves involuntarily to avoid the flames. When this sound sickens the narrator's heart, he attributes his reaction to the atmosphere of the catacombs and leaves. With the jingling of the bells, Fortunato has the last word, since the narrator cannot echo him in ridicule.

Many readers will identify with Fortunato because he seems merely foolish whereas the narrator commits premeditated murder in a heartless manner. Hardier souls may temporarily abandon their morality and identify with the ironically single-minded Montresor. A case can be made for Montresor as satanic. Others may see him as the wildly insane epitome of an Edgar Allan Poe unreliable first-person narrator.

LOUISE ERDRICH

Fleur (p. 1320)

Most readers of Louise Erdrich's short story "Fleur" in our college classes will approach it as a self-contained text. Instructors who have read Louise Erdrich's complex series of interwoven novels, composed of interrelated short stories about several interconnected families, may be tempted to explain more about the characters than students are ready to hear. Instead, we can invite interested readers to explore the longer fiction on their own, noting how the author makes changes to fit her new purposes. "Fleur" becomes a chapter of the novel *Tracks*, for example, and another short story that deals with the narrator of "Fleur" as an adult — "St. Marie" — makes its way into the novel *Love Medicine*.

The narrator of "Fleur" is Pauline Puyat, who grows up to be the cruel nun, Sister Leopolda. Perhaps in the story here we glimpse the source of the child's bitterness and rage as an adult. The narrator speculates that Fleur might have been compelled to stop in this particular town because of the spire of the Catholic church. But although this may be a symbol of power for Pauline, there is no indication that Fleur is attracted by this particular brand of the supernatural. Fleur, at least in the reading of the people of around her, is connected with forces in nature that are fatal to men. The author, Erdrich, is affected by both the Roman Catholicism and Black Forest witchiness of her European ancestry and the windigos, water monsters, and transformed animals of her Chippewa side. It's intriguing in this context that Erdrich's contribution to a feminist book about rape issues includes a photograph of herself in her white confirmation dress and veil. "The veil is the mist before the woman's face that limits her vision to the here, the now, the inch beyond her nose," Erdrich writes. "It is an illusion of safety, a flimsy skin of privacy that encourages violation. The message behind the veil is touch me, I'm yours. The purity is fictional, coy. The veil is the invitation to tear it away" (in Emilie Buchwald et al., *Transforming a Rape Culture* [Minneapolis, MN: Milkweed, 1993], 335–39).

The issue has been raised that this story might better be titled "Pauline" since she is the narrator who exacts revenge for the brutal rape of Fleur by Pauline's stepfather and the other men at the butcher shop. But Fleur Pillager is the central figure of the story. In Pauline, we have the sort of child narrator often used in fiction to give a fresh perspective to the activities of adults. Pauline is less naive than is usually the case with such narrators, and we may notice that the date of the story indicates that she is recalling this from the distance of old age. One element of the story is Pauline's pathetic understanding of her own invisibility to the men. She, like the title character, is a female who is shunned by her community.

But it is Fleur who affects everyone around her so strongly that they die from her influence or avoid her in fear or rape her to take revenge on her for exerting power and independence. The supernatural elements of the story keep the power in Fleur's hands; otherwise, she'd be a pathetic victim. We do feel compassion for her, since from her childhood she seems to have been blamed for things that are not her fault. The "results" of the curse of saving her life on the hapless Chippewa men are laughable to the reader just plunging into the story. But most readers come to accept her special relationship with nature and may notice that the animal imagery connected with Fleur begins in the first paragraph, where she shivers like a dog.

The narrator frames the story of Fleur's sojourn off the reservation in the mean little town of Argus with scenes of Fleur at Lake Turcot. The story recalls recorded legends of monsters in lakes. In one story, a girl strikes off the tail of a "lion" in Leech Lake and it turns out to be pure copper, which her father sells, making the family's fortune. Some folklorists speculate that the use of the word *lion* to describe a creature already in Native American mythology comes from contact with the British coat of arms. Its stylized lion may have reminded the Chippewa and others with this legend of the copper-scaled lake spirit. Erdrich's description is vivid, and we're willing to believe that Fleur's children bear a family resemblance to Misshepeshu.

Fleur herself is changed by her drownings or perhaps by the reactions to them, and she becomes a woman who breaks the rules of female decorum and tribal tradition. This repels the Chippewa and attracts and eventually enrages the lecherous white men of Argus. As Pauline describes her, Fleur seems like a lake creature herself, "her hips fishlike, slippery, narrow." She wears a green dress that clings to her body, and she is variously described as like a bear or a wolf. Her teeth curve and her braids look like animal tails.

The narrator prepares us for the violence that erupts when the men will no longer tolerate Fleur's strength and supernatural luck. We follow the plot as Lily gets angrier about Fleur's teasingly winning only a dollar each night. The setting, in a place where animals are butchered and boiled, smoked and hung in an ice-lined compartment, seems overwhelmingly brutal and disrespectful of nature, and readers may question Fleur's willingness to throw herself into such work. It may remind us of historical accounts of buffalo hunters piling up stripped carcasses to rot. Readers of Native American mythology will be reminded of windigos, men turned into mad, voracious, cannibalistic giants. But whereas the men seem to be brutalized by this atmosphere, Fleur shows that she can gently give the young girl respectful bits of attention.

Erdrich foreshadows Pauline's betrayal of Fleur by having the child describe herself as "the shadow that could have saved her." While racial differences are foregrounded by Lily's exaggerated whiteness, the inability to see Fleur's supernatural power is where the white men exhibit their difference from Native Americans. Although the Chippewa do not treat Fleur well, they recognize her power. When the white men finally see that she has tricked and beaten them at a man's activity, they want to destroy her. But this reaction may be less about race than about gender.

Ironically, the narrator describes the rape in one sentence. She concentrates instead on the forces of nature unleashed by the attack. Erdrich thus makes use of a cultural stereotype that links nature with both women and the indigenous people of a land. She can always blame this on the narrator. Pauline believes that Fleur is magic. She describes Lily's violent encounter with the sow as a sort of dance, wrestling match, and knife fight combined. Later, when the tornado approaches, it has a similarly bestial aspect. "The odd cloud became a fat snout that nosed along the earth," Pauline says, "and sniffled, jabbed, picked at things, sucked them up, blew them apart, rooted around as if it was following a certain scent, then stopped behind me at the butcher shop and bored down like a drill." She watches a surreal movement of weird objects, reminding the audience of a scene from *Alice in Wonderland* or *The Wizard of Oz*.

Pauline has landed in a nightmare, and she judges herself more harshly than most readers do at this point. We question how she could have stopped the men. Perhaps, by calling attention to herself, she too would have been raped. Most of us even applaud when she takes the revenge of locking the men in their death chamber, ensuring that they will remain after the tornado buries them alive. We may notice that the child has remained out of sight and mind as the men have selfishly taken shelter without concern for her safety. We recall that the stepfather has forced the girl to leave school to do the tasks her dead mother would have done. And these men are rapists, a fact that for many readers fully justifies Pauline's act. The cold selfishness of the whole town is revealed when we discover that they have not even noticed that the men were missing. They are even less concerned about Fleur, presumably because she is an Indian.

Pauline blames herself for Fleur's rape, and revenge is her way of making amends. It also brings her into solidarity with Fleur and the natural elements that conspire to see that her rape is avenged. Their continued connection when both return to the reservation indicates that Fleur does not condemn Pauline, though one of the scanty details the narrator gives of the rape has Fleur calling out her name. The events bring them together.

Although the narrators of both Edgar Allan Poe's "The Cask of Amontillado" (p. 1314) and Erdrich's "Fleur" entomb their enemies, we understand Pauline's motives more clearly than we do Montresor's. This is partly because we observe the "injuries" the men at the butcher shop inflict, whereas Fortunato's sins against Poe's narrator remain vague. Also, Pauline's act, although premeditated and unrepented, is less deliberate and planned than Montresor's. Finally, she is a child, numbed by several traumatic experiences in a row and by what modern readers see as ongoing abuse and neglect. Most readers are therefore more horrified by Poe's narrator. Others, however, dislike the explicit violence and images of death at the butcher shop in Erdrich's more realistic horror story. It is harder for some readers to distance themselves from the animal heads boiling in Fleur's pot than from the human figure in motley jingling his bells in the wall of the catacombs.

Both stories use a framing technique in which the first-person narrator looks back on an event from the distance of old age. When we leap forward at the end of Erdrich's story, we do not advance to the present but to the same location that we saw in the beginning. The time period is later than the major action of the story but still takes place in the past, when Fleur's children are young. Pauline is reflective and does not seek to justify herself or to impress the reader with her own cleverness as Montresor does. Poe's narrator ends with the ironic "Rest in peace" whereas Erdrich's ends with an aura of the supernatural. Erdrich has her narrator offer an assertion at the beginning of her closing section, placing her characters in a continuum of family or tribal inheritance. Poe's narrator is concerned with family pride, too, but the effect is negative. Montresor has not been able to rest in peace about his murder of Fortunato, since it still preys on his mind fifty years later, but there is a sense of closure in his remark. Erdrich's story projects us into a possible future, however, with the knowing smile of Fleur's little girl, an omen of things to come, we suspect.

Throughout her story, Erdrich has shown people reading the text of Fleur's life and coming up with various interpretations. But she remains a mystery with no one solution. We enjoy this for the same reasons we enjoy TV shows such as the *The X Files*: the eerie mystery provides the delicious thrill of wondering if we are surrounded by an invisible world with different rules. When the men speak of "not knowing," we recall the blindness of the men at the butcher shop to the women in their world. As we read both Erdrich and Poe, readers need to cultivate a tolerance for ambiguity. Students often prefer texts that give all the answers. We can help them appreciate that writers show respect for their readers when they allow us to imagine some of the answers for ourselves, even if this means we find different interpretations each time we read the same text.

ANDRE DUBUS

Killings (p. 1330)

By giving his short story about revenge the one-word plural title "Killings," Andre Dubus subtly avoids the definite or indefinite article that would particularize one of the specific killings that occur in the story. This universalizes the situation he describes. Any parent or spouse can imagine taking action to avenge a child or to save a partner from agony. Young people can imagine their own fathers desperately taking such matters into their own hands. But the title, like the story at its end, does not allow the interpretation that revenge murder is without cost. The two murders of the story share equal billing. He implies, as Sherman Alexie does in "Capital Punishment" (p. 1308) with his equation "1 death + 1 death = 2 deaths," that killing is killing, no matter what the warrant.

This does not mean that Matt Fowler does not face an ethical dilemma or that he would act differently given another chance. This is the true conflict of the story. He is left knowing that his action has cut him off from his family. His wife has not participated in the act of revenge physically, and she wants to use their lovemaking as a celebration and communion in vengeance. But for Matt, everything is now literally anticlimactic. He has also robbed himself of a full relationship with his living children, since he cannot make them accessories and he knows that they will think, as he has arranged for outsiders to conclude, that his son's murderer has run away. The reader is complicit in the killing, since we go along for the ride and agree with him that this boy does not seem as worthy of living as Matt's son, especially since we are sure he will not be punished severely. Revenge is not sweet but empty, Dubus tells us with his narrative.

Dubus introduces a collection of short stories with a quotation from Flannery O'Connor. "The man in the violent situation reveals those qualities least dispensable in his personality," O'Connor said, "those qualities which are all he will have to take into eternity with him." Ironically, Dubus once told an interviewer that he doesn't read O'Connor because she *frightens* him. Like O'Connor, Dubus is a Roman Catholic — it is her religious symbolism that scares him rather than the violence in her stories — and he has been characterized as a profoundly moral writer. He realistically portrays ordinary Americans who struggle with definitions of moral behavior and sometimes lose their spirituality in the process. Dubus maintains that the foregrounding of violence in his fiction has to do with being American, that "violence is a reflection of American consciousness." But the acceptance and action of killing goes against nature, Dubus believes; Matt Fowler at the story's end is therefore "forever removed" from nature, and he will never recover the life destroyed by his son's death and his own surrender to anger and revenge.

In his justification of the premeditated murder of Richard Strout, Matt Fowler uses the warrant of protecting his wife. This is what a man must do, take charge of the evil that has been directed toward his family. Everywhere she goes in their town, Ruth sees the killer of her son, and Matt takes action as a good husband. But he is also angered by the young man's apparent flaunting of his freedom to enter a new relationship with a woman, to go out drinking, and to otherwise boldly continue his life. Richard Strout may not be capable of feeling the remorse that Matt Fowler will endure for killing him, and this is part of the story's irony and perhaps part of Fowler's motive for murder. We read the story from Matt Fowler's point of view and tend to agree that he has reason to take revenge. We sympathize with the grieving father and admire the cleverness of the plan to make it look as though the murderer has fled.

Strout is humanized for us, however, by the details of his room, his obedient packing, and his respectful attitude as he addresses the older man as "Mr. Fowler" like one of his son's high-school friends might have done. The audience has been led to think of Strout as defiant, but here — in the situation of violence described in the Flannery O'Connor reference — he is touchingly vulnerable. His own killing of Matt Fowler's son has been more impulsive, and he has been wronged. Though this does not excuse his actions, we see a qualitative difference between the murder that American society would once have condoned as a "crime of passion" and the calculated execution that the wronged father carries out.

Readers may point out that Strout epitomizes another American attitude of the past that sees women as chattels legally owned by men. In both murders, men use the feelings or actions of women as the warrant for their own violent actions. We are back to the Garden of Eden, with Adam making the excuse that Eve handed him the apple. The younger man tries to reason with the avenging father as he pleads for his life: "I'll do twenty years, Mr. Fowler; at least. I'll be forty-six years old." He assumes that his life will essentially be over by then, but the older man sees this from the perspective of fifty-five. Twenty years in prison does not seem just punishment for the loss of his son and the family's way of life. Earlier, Strout argues that he had reason to kill Matt's son Frank, because he had violated Strout's marriage and was keeping him from pulling his family back together. Neither man takes the step of seeing how the other's family has been sinned against.

Willis Trottier's motives are even more questionable, since he makes revenge possible and participates fully, though he does not have the excuse of family as a warrant. Perhaps he represents an outraged community with law-and-order values, the type of vigilante who takes action when the courts are seen as weak. He may even have baser, more criminal assumptions about the validity of personal revenge. We do not imagine him wrestling with guilt. Ruth, too, is not troubled by the act of murder, has encouraged it, and has known what her husband would do in response to her expression of her needs. She does not realize yet the impact that this second killing will have on her marriage and family.

Interested students can trace the attitudes toward women that the men demonstrate in Dubus's story. Matt is less judgmental of Mary Ann than his wife is. He defends her marital unfaithfulness and the fact that she is older than Frank. He too finds Mary Ann attractive, but he also feels compassion for her. The Fowler family is gradually accepting the young woman and her boys when their son is killed in front of Mary Ann's children. Dubus keeps this fact from his readers at first, delaying our judgment of Strout on this account. It makes less credible his claim that he was trying to reestablish his family, and it reflects on his character.

It would be interesting to explore whether the theme in "Killings" relates as much to what it means to be a good husband and father as to judgment and revenge. Strout is neither a good husband nor a good father. Matt Fowler, on the other hand, mourns the loss of "the quietly harried and quietly pleasurable days of fatherhood" even while he recognizes that he has "wandered through" most of these days. As he carries out his obsessive act of revenge, his life becomes focused. Dubus focuses his story at this point as well, slowing the narrative pace and taking us step by step through the deliberate murder, thus matching style to content.

Focus obtained through obsession dehumanizes a person. Edgar Allan Poe's narrator in "The Cask of Amontillado" (p. 1314) is chillingly focused on his revenge, and we see him as evil to the point of the demonic. Dubus's avenging father in "Killings" does not know that he is robbing himself of the human connections he has so highly valued, and he earns our compassion, even as we realize he has taken the wrong action. The narrator of Louise Erdrich's "Fleur" (p. 1320) acts more impulsively, but if we go beyond the context of the short story to look at her future as Sister Leopolda, we realize that she too will pay with a loss of humanity. On the other hand, readers may say that the treatment of women to which Pauline responds with revenge is actually what dehumanizes her. Because she realizes that she is burying the men alive, terrorizing as well as killing them, her alliance with the avenging forces of nature comes across as equally cold and brutal to the murders committed by the men in the other stories in this cluster on revenge. In law, we are told that premeditation does not have to take very long; it just requires a deliberate action taken with the knowledge of the consequences to the victim. Pauline is young and acts quickly, but she is not innocent. Whether we agree that the men at the butcher shop are worthy of death is another issue.

Of the three narrators in this cluster, only Matt Fowler in Dubus's "Killings" seems to truly approach remorse. Poe's Montresor feels a momentary twinge as he immolates Fortunato but brushes it aside as attributable to the atmosphere of the catacombs. Pauline is able to keep quiet for days about her entrapment of the men in the debris of the tornado and coolly enters the meat locker to observe the dead bodies. Dubus is the most realistic of the three writers in the attention to verisimilitude that convinces the reader this could have really happened. He shows everything from the socks and underwear neatly in Richard Strout's drawer to the meticulous details of the location and organization of the gravesite where Matt Fowler and Willis Trottier shoot the young man. We feel the gun kick and watch the victim die. Erdrich's settings, on the other hand, seem dreamlike and selective in the details they give. We learn in more detail than we would wish the inner workings of the sweat- and-tallow filled butcher operation. But we know little of the neighbors who shrug at Fleur's disappearance, don't think to look for several missing men, and are not even considered as possible avenues of help as Pauline blames herself for Fleur's rape. It seems reasonable that a young girl would block out the details of the rape itself, but Pauline's concise description conveys what is symbolic to her — Fleur's crying out in her Chippewa language and the incantation of the narrator's own name. The fight between the swinelike Lily and the sow stands in for other details of the rape. The details are nightmarish. Other scenes are similarly surreal as Pauline watches cows and other objects flying past her in the tornado or weaves folklore into Fleur's experiences at Lake Turcot.

We are aware in Erdrich's story that the narrator communicates events in the light of her own interpretations and that her vision of Fleur is permeated by the supernatural. We cannot trust her reliability. Poe, of course, is the modern inventor of the unreliable narrator along with the American short story, and his self-satisfied murderer is the least trustworthy of all. We know that such catacombs exist under Italian estates, but the journey he describes feels like a descent into hell, and the temporal setting of carnival adds to the unreality. With Poe's story, the reader is entitled to have grave doubts about the existence of the setting outside of the narrator's nightmares. We willingly suspend disbelief, however, because we recognize the genre of the Edgar Allan Poe tale of horror.

CONFRONTING SIN: A COLLECTION OF WRITINGS BY NATHANIEL HAWTHORNE (p. 1345)

NATHANIEL HAWTHORNE

Young Goodman Brown (p. 1346)

Nathaniel Hawthorne's "Young Goodman Brown" invariably raises issues of historical and biographical context and intertextual relationships with other treatments of the Puritan struggle against perceived manifestations of sin and evil. Students may have read Hawthorne's frequently anthologized story in high school and perhaps have read his novel *The Scarlet Letter*, itself a famous text dealing with the issue of outsiders. Arthur Miller's drama *The Crucible*, a retelling of the Salem witch trials, also appears on high-school reading lists. Less familiar, but recommended to students interested in an alternate fictional view, is *I, Tituba, Black Witch of Salem* by Caribbean writer Maryse Condé. This novel tells the story of the Salem witch trials from the perspective of the Barbadian cook whose stories and Afro-Caribbean lore may have interacted with Puritan credulity about evil to fascinate a group of young girls into hysteria. Colorful and imaginative in the midst of the mostly humorless and somber members of the Salem congregation, Tituba, a black servant, was the first person blamed for the strange behavior of the bewitched girls. Sarah Good, a woman whose behavior and appearance may sound to current readers like a description of a "street person" — annoying respectable people with her smelly pipe, her pleas for food, and her neglect of her children — was accused soon after Tituba. Those claiming to be tormented also pointed out Sarah Osburne, a woman who was known to have lived with her husband for several months before their marriage. Each of these women was an easy target, since each was in some way an outsider, a transgressor against the accepted views of proper demeanor and behavior for a woman. Most readers will know the story of how the hysteria spread and how, to use the words of the seventeenth-century Boston preacher Cotton Mather, "some of the Witch Gang ... [were] ... Fairly Executed." Ironically, Mather's study of the matter may have stopped the hysteria, since he argued against the use of "spectral evidence" in which victims claimed to see various members of the community behaving like witches. Since he maintained that evil spirits can take any shape, claims to have seen a neighbor in a manifestation of evil were not proof.

Hawthorne uses these ideas and others about witches in "Young Goodman Brown." Hawthorne, writing in the 1830s, long after the 1690 trials, knew the history well, since his family had been intimately involved with the prosecutions. In the generation preceding the witch trials, Hawthorne's ancestor had become known for fighting heresy, forcing a Quaker woman to be whipped out of town. Students can read about this in Hawthorne's autobiographical preface to *The Scarlet Letter* called "The Custom-House" or in various biographies and critical studies of the author's life and work. Like James Joyce would later do with Dublin, Hawthorne found himself inextricably bound to writing about Salem, even though he was happiest elsewhere. Hawthorne takes his witch lore from both oral and written sources, including official Puritan doctrine like Mather's. Mather mentions the "multitude and quality" of the accused and speaks of a woman "who had received the devil's promise to be queen of hell," words Hawthorne uses in his story. Names of his characters come from actual people who were brought to trial; for example, Goody Cloyse and Goody Cory both appear in the historical record. Hawthorne's ancestor John Hathorne interrogated Goody Cory. The recipe for witch ointment was published — one hopes as a joke — in a popular magazine Hawthorne was connected with, but it is interesting that brave souls who have tested a mixture of smallage (hemlock) and wolfsbane (aconite) say that it produces a sensation of flying. The inclusion of the "fat of a new-born babe" perpetuates a common belief about witches as baby killers, a story still heard today. There are also hints that Young Goodman Brown has made an agreement with the devil before the story begins, another motif that we recognize from multiple adaptations of the Faust legend and other sources.

In allegory, abstract ideas are represented as people, objects, places, and so forth that play symbolic roles. Hawthorne read John Bunyan's early Puritan allegory *Pilgrim's Progress* many times, and he also enjoyed the long allegorical poem *The Faerie Queen* by Edmund Spenser. He employs the genre in a less ambitious way than the writers of these classics of English literature, but Hawthorne's narrative does have many qualities of allegory. Names are most obviously symbolic. The narrator refers to the protagonist always as "Goodman" and the implication is that he represents the quality of goodness, as Bunyan's "Everyman" stands for the ordinary human being. We may need to point out to students that "Goodman" is the character's title, similar to *Mr.*, rather than his name. "Goody" is short for *Goodwife*. But ironically, the people who seem to be good are revealed in Young Goodman Brown's nightmare — or his actual experience — to be evil. The good man of the story is actually a hypocrite who goes out for a night of adventure or in response to a bargain made earlier. He goes on an evil quest, unlike Bunyan's hero, who perseveres toward salvation. The Puritan husband expects that he may leave his good wife alone long enough to indulge in evil this one night and then return to the "arms of Faith." His wife's name is equally symbolic. In fact, readers may find that the double meaning as he cries, "My Faith is gone," lays it on a bit too thickly. He ultimately finds a vision of evil that causes his alienation from all goodness and joy, and the report of his funeral indicates that he goes on to eternal damnation.

Our interpretation of his discovery depends on our answer to the narrator's question: "Had Goodman Brown fallen asleep in the forest and only dreamed a wild dream of a witch meeting?" The reaction of his wife and neighbors as he returns to town after his night out gives no indication that they have seen him or have been engaged in secret ceremonies. If we recall Cotton Mather's warning about accepting "spectral evidence," we have further evidence for believing that Young Goodman Brown has not actually seen his neighbors. He may have dreamed it, but it is equally possible that evil spirits have fooled him, disguised as his wife and fellow church members. Whatever has happened, the protagonist makes a case against the townspeople, holding them to a higher standard than he demands of himself. He feels betrayed, but he had been willing to sin, in spite of all his wavering.

Later, Hawthorne would write about Herman Melville's unresolved crisis of faith that Melville had "pretty much made up his mind to be annihilated; but . . . will never rest until he gets hold of a definite belief. . . . He can neither believe, nor be comfortable in his unbelief; and he is too honest and courageous not to try to do one or the other." Puritans agonized over whether or not they were truly of the elect. One record tells of a woman who threw her baby into a well, explaining that now she knew without a doubt that she would go to hell, and the misery of doubt about her salvation was over.

Goodman Brown wants it both ways: to have Faith, both the wife and the abstract quality of character, but also to have the adventure of sin. The anticipation of those traveling to the meeting in the woods hints that they may expect experiences of a sexual nature, since women are excited about the new young man they have heard will be inducted, while men look forward to a new young woman. We may remember that Faith has begged him not to leave her alone, but he rejects her for his errand. Even if she has been at the devil's meeting, she is at least as reluctant as her husband. But he does not grant her this virtue. As a result of his experience, the earnest young man cuts himself off from faith and fellowship and lives as a bitter misanthrope, unable to trust.

We might suggest to him that he think of alternate readings of his experience, that he consider evidence that the neighbors and his wife have not attended the Witches' Sabbath. But he sees the text as fixed, much as Puritans see their interpretations of the Bible and the predestined salvation of a selected few as not to be questioned. The devil in Hawthorne's story doesn't allow the shifting of blame. *Evil has a human face* is a cliché because our experience says this is true. When the devil relates the sins of Brown's neighbors, he lists secret sins that happen within the family: incest, wives poisoning husbands, sons killing fathers, infanticide. When he describes his knowledge of Brown's family, he claims to have helped his grandfather as he "lashed the Quaker woman so smartly through the streets of Salem" or his father as he burned an Indian village. The religious and racial bigotry of Hawthorne's Puritan ancestors are thus characterized as evil, ironically so since they believed they were taking a godly stand against evil.

Young Goodman Brown's naiveté hides an arrogance that is based on either/or reasoning: people are either saints or sinners, rather than having elements of both good and evil. Students may recall President Clinton's impeachment trial as they consider the standards we require of leaders. Although the scandals involving television evangelists are old news by now, we may want to recall them. The public judges such figures harshly perhaps because we hold them to a higher standard of conduct than we do ourselves, much as Young Goodman Brown does church leaders. But we may also be angry with such role models when they tell us how to behave but fail to follow the rules they set for us or to be honest about their own shortcomings.

NATHANIEL HAWTHORNE

The Minister's Black Veil (p. 1365)

It will most likely be unproductive for class discussion of Nathaniel Hawthorne's "The Minister's Black Veil" to focus on the issue of "What does the veil *really* mean?" or "Why does the minister wear it?" More talk is apt to be generated when the class considers how the veil and the minister's wearing of it are ambiguous — that is, subject to multiple interpretations. Indeed, a good catalyst for discussion might be the various *performative effects* of the veil, both on the minister and on his Puritan parishioners. You might point out that for most of the story the minister's own thinking is rather opaque. We learn that he himself is frightened by the veil, and we read his speech about veils at the end, but otherwise he seems unsure why he wears it. We can't be certain that his final speech expresses ideas he had from the beginning; perhaps the significance he attaches to the veil has changed over time. One possible angle is to see him as a post–Goodman Brown figure (p. 1346). Perhaps, like Brown, he is newly conscious of humanity's sinfulness and can no longer live as he did before. Moreover, like Brown, he increasingly isolates himself from society and dies a largely solitary man. Of course, were his motives perpetually clear to himself, the effects of the veil on others might still be different from what he intended. At any rate, remind your class that an early effect is that his previously tepid sermons come across more forcefully, which indicates that the veil serves the minister at least as a rhetorical strategy.

Students can relate to this story by thinking about contemporary uses of veils. Ask them to identify circumstances, both cultural and personal, in which people cover their faces. This question may lead to an interesting discussion about forms of religion. Students are apt to know, for example, that many Islamic women wear a chaldor, and you might even have one or two students report on the reasons why. The whole class is likely to be familiar with the wearing of bridal veils, but you might have students investigate and report on the origins of this practice.

It you wish, ask the class to identify ways in which this story — as well as, perhaps, literary texts in general — is comparable to the minister's black veil. You may fear that this critical move is too sophisticated for undergraduates. Actually, though, a student may have little trouble seeing literary works as resembling the black veil insofar as they, too, are ambiguous and often tinged with despair. Then another interesting question becomes "How is Hawthorne's story *different* from the minister's wearing of the veil?"

NATHANIEL HAWTHORNE

Ethan Brand (p. 1366)

Like the main character in "Young Goodman Brown" (p. 1346), Nathaniel Hawthorne's Ethan Brand has investigated sin and experienced despair as a result. While "Young Goodman Brown" focuses on its title character and even sticks largely with his point of view, "Ethan Brand" introduces its title character only after introducing Bartram and his son Joe. Indeed, the middle of the story presents several additional characters, and the conclusion centers on Bartram and Joe again. Only for a climactic stretch are we with Brand alone. Have your class think about why, despite the title, Hawthorne includes so many other people in the story. In some sense, the story is about them just as much as it is about him. More specifically, what does their reaction to him say about them?

Brand's unpardonable sin seems to be his utter divorce from humanity, which involves the metaphorical death of his heart. Much discussion can result when you ask students to nominate other candidates for the unpardonable sin. You might have students identify various kinds of sins and vote on how to rank them. Such a discussion touches on religious issues, including matters of doctrine you may prefer not to raise. Nevertheless, it is possible to consider relative degrees of sin without getting denominational, and you might begin by saying as much to your class.

One of the most interesting elements of this story is Brand's laugh, which does not seem to express merriment. Try drawing your students' attention to those moments when Hawthorne mentions this laugh, and ask them to come up with phrases that capture its essence. The class may be able to provide analogies from current movies and TV shows, especially those from the horror genre.

Don't overlook moments and characters that initially seem minor but may assume symbolic import. One event you might draw your class's attention to is the dog's frenzied chasing of his own tail. In what ways is this equivalent to Brand's pursuit of the unpardonable sin? Also, you may want your class to ponder the role of the Jew in this story. Hawthorne implies that the character is comparable to the legendary figure of the Wandering Jew, which many people today see as an anti-Sematic myth. Is Hawthorne, in fact, propagating anti-Semitism in this tale? If so, how much does such caricature interfere with the artistry of the story? If you wish, you might invite your students to compare this work with William Shakespeare's *The Merchant of Venice*, a play with which they may be familiar.

MISFIT JUSTICE: CRITICAL COMMENTARIES ON FLANNERY O'CONNOR'S "A GOOD MAN IS HARD TO FIND" (p. 1378)

FLANNERY O'CONNOR

A Good Man Is Hard to Find (p. 1379)

Flannery O'Connor's texts mix comedy and tragedy in a manner usually termed Southern grotesque. "Why don't you ever write about any *nice* people?" a relative not unlike the grandmother in "A Good Man Is Hard to Find" once asked her. Like the ghoulish and ridiculous figures perched on medieval cathedrals, O'Connor's characters lurk on the crumbling rooftops of the Christian religion and in the shifting shadows of the American South of the mid-twentieth century, both repelling and fascinating us with their odd humanity. Readers who have grown up in the South laugh, cry, and blush with shame at the perfection of her characters' obsessions and their dialogue. We know these people. They are the mothers, grandmothers, aunts, and cousins we don't talk about in company. To say this is not to sentimentalize or forgive them. Students will find many critical studies of O'Connor's work, and the author herself has commented on her stories, often confusing readers more than clarifying the ambiguities of the text. Critics who disagree with O'Connor's interpretation of a character or event often remind us of D. H. Lawrence's advice to trust the art rather than the artist. After the writer is finished, the story has a life of its own, and the author's opinion is no more authoritative than any other, according to this view. When O'Connor comments about the meaning of her work, she speaks as a Roman Catholic theologian rather than a writer, some contend. And often, she perversely compounds the mystery, purposely deflating people who analyze and dissect her stories.

Each reader will have his or her own opinion of "A Good Man Is Hard to Find" and its ambiguous protagonist. In fact, students sometimes differ over whom they identify as the protagonist. Usually, we think of the grandmother as the main character. We see most of the story from her point of view, and she is the only character whose thoughts we overhear. But a few readers argue that The Misfit is the protagonist, since the whole story belongs to him, beginning with the foreshadowing of the opening paragraph and ending with his existential pronouncement about life in the final sentence. Even minor characters ring true in a Flannery O'Connor narrative. Students will enjoy the connotations of names. Bailey, for example, may get his name from "Bill Bailey Won't You

Please Come Home?" — a song in the same blues/jazz genre as the one that gives the story its title. (One can begin discussion with a recording of Billie Holliday singing "A Good Man Is Hard to Find" and point out its second line: "You always get the other kind.") The rude son who supplants the authority of the father has the name of the founder of the Methodist Church, John Wesley, certainly a dig at the Protestant usurpation of Catholic authority. The Misfit explicates the meaning of his name; rather than describing his outsider status as we expect, his name is a philosophical statement on the misfit between sin and punishment.

The Misfit engages in rationalization about his violence, but he seems to do this for his own purposes rather as an excuse for his actions. He attempts to construct a logical argument with evidence that convinces him that his punishment is warranted. He is frustrated because, although written documentation exists — "They had the papers on me" — it does not clarify matters for him and he has no memory of his original sin. Therefore, his punishment seems out of proportion to him, does not fit. Because of this, he makes sure that he signs his work, leaving clear evidence of his crimes, so that he will know when the claims made about him are valid. When the psychiatrist tells him that he was really killing his father when he committed his crime, The Misfit interprets this literally instead of symbolically, refuting the doctor's assertion with evidence. He provides specific facts as proof, offering the date, the diagnosis of his father's final illness, and the precise location of his grave. This is hard evidence, he maintains, because "you can go there and see for yourself." Jesus is a logical conundrum for The Misfit. He attempts a theological decision based on his own brand of logic: if Jesus raised the dead, then we must give up everything and follow him; but if Jesus did not raise the dead, then any "meanness" that gives pleasure is permitted. But The Misfit is frustrated again by the lack of concrete evidence to guide his decision about Jesus. An essential step in the chain of logic is missing. Since he has not observed with his own eyes whether Jesus raised the dead or not, he finds no pleasure in anything. By raising the issue, if not the dead, Jesus "thown everything off balance" and makes reasoning impossible.

The grandmother, too, encounters problems as she attempts to create persuasive arguments. When we first meet her, she is trying to convince her family to go to Tennessee instead of Florida, using appeals to fear. She further attempts to manipulate, unsuccessfully employing the non sequitur that going to East Tennessee will broaden the minds of the children. Later she will persuade the family to seek out the old mansion by appealing to the self-interest of the children and winning them over to her side but ironically bases her argument on an assertion that is false. At the trip's beginning, she convinces herself that the cat might turn on the gas in the house and die, an improbable hypothesis, so she ignores opposition and sneaks the cat into the car, including it on the trip, along with her other hidden agendas. As they leave town, she collects statistical data — the mileage and how long it takes to get out of Atlanta. She passes on information to an unheeding audience, makes aesthetic observations, and reveals her racist and class-driven assumptions. The ethos of Red Sammy Butts's credentials along the roadside may lead her to draw the hasty conclusion that he is a good man, though her evaluation of him may simply be an ingrained tendency to use the fallacious false-flattery appeal. The conversation in Red Sammy's "filling station and dance hall" is sentimental and filled with cliché. These people and the grandmother understand the discourse of small talk. The Misfit, on the other hand, finds such conversation difficult, fumbling around for comments about the weather, and he uses the grandmother's attempts at sentimental flattery and manipulation to discuss theology and philosophy.

The end of the story raises issues for critics. Some think that the grandmother mistakes The Misfit for Bailey because he now wears the shirt that she has last seen him wear. Her disorientation and her obvious distress about Bailey — she keeps calling his name — lend credence to this interpretation. Others insist that she feels compassion for The Misfit, recognizing him as vulnerable, and reaches out to him as a mother. She has noticed his thin shoulder blades, and she hears the crack in his voice. He seems to her to be on the verge of crying. Some readers take her statement that he is her child as a cowardly, desperate attempt to persuade him not to kill her, the strongest argument saved for the crucial point just before the conclusion. O'Connor has increased the ambiguity by insisting that this final scene between The Misfit and the grandmother is a "moment of grace" that has religious significance. In O'Connor's stories, as in James Joyce's, characters move toward epiphanies, moments of clarity. Just before she calls him her child, the text says that "the grandmother's head cleared for an instant." How we interpret the ending depends on our interpretation of the grandmother. Students often feel that her sins do not warrant the punishment she receives, but The Misfit would say that this squares with his experience as well.

Religious orientation, or the absence of it, will also enter into the reading. It has been seriously argued that the grandmother confuses The Misfit with Jesus at one point or that she speaks with the authority of God when she claims her killer as her child. O'Connor abhorred hypocrisy and arrogance. Just before the grandmother dies, the falseness and self-centered pride that have characterized her throughout the journey have, by some interpretations, been stripped away. If this is true, The Misfit is correct when he implies that it has taken this crisis to make her a "good woman." The grandmother goes through her whole repertoire of persuasive appeals and finds them wanting as she tries to save her life, but we don't see her using any of them to save her family, not even the baby. Her obsessive drive to get her way leads her family to death, and her impulsive identification of The Misfit seals their fate. As the epigraph to the story suggests, The Misfit has been the dragon by the side of the road that this sinful pilgrim must pass on her way to God. How does one deal with a dragon?

The ending of O'Connor's story shocks most student readers, especially those who love their grandmothers. They usually see the other characters as nasty and the grandmother, whose perspective we have followed throughout the story, as perhaps foolish but the best of a bad lot. But the shift in tone is what makes the story so compelling, and it drives home O'Connor's point that both good men and good women are hard to find and that those who think they are good are perhaps the ones in greatest danger of being forever lost. As in most of O'Connor's fiction, the comedy sets us up for the shocking truth as the tragedy is revealed. This moves her writing out of the realm of cute, regional tales of quaint rustics into the world of theology and questions of eternal life and death. Readers tend to either love the ambush or resent it.

The irony of the story is wrapped up in competing definitions of the word *good*, which has a different meaning for the author than it does for the characters. Through the simplistic views of the grandmother, O'Connor presents the shallow, optimistic view of the sentimentalist. It is much harder to be good than this, O'Connor implies; in fact, her narrative follows Christian theology by claiming that no human being is capable of being good and that it is only people who realize their total depravity are capable of becoming good. Because to God, O'Connor insists, we are all misfits, creatures who do not fit into the perfection he requires, the sanctimonious hypocrite and the confused murderer are on an equal footing and are equally eligible for salvation. An openness to our unredeemable lack of goodness is our only hope of redemption. While the grandmother's eyes may become opened to her lack of goodness, the Misfit is left in confusion about his own redemption. He may have completely cut off any chance he has of becoming good, since he insists on relying on reason rather than self-renunciation and faith. O'Connor does not resolve all the issues of fact because she feels that this would change God's rules: giving the Misfit — and the reader — all of the facts about life after death would make goodness a matter of logic rather than of faith. The mystery must remain.

Some students feel that none of O'Connor's characters has any redeeming qualities. Less severe judges argue that all are products of their past experiences, shaped by their families and their cultural assumptions. The Misfit seems at times to contain some intellectual and spiritual depth, certainly when compared to the mundane Bailey, his dull wife, and their self-absorbed children, and O'Connor herself sees him as the character with the greatest spiritual potential, someone destined to become a "prophet." The grandmother, with her childlike qualities, may be just as selfish as her progeny but also may have the innocence to change, given a loving environment. Readers may point out, however, that goodness for the old woman is tied up in social hierarchies that are essentially non-Christian. She is able to overcome her constant evaluations of others at the end of the story when she classes the Misfit as an innocent child with whom she is connected in a human chain. While the Misfit must reject this, as he must reject God at this point, he recognizes that the grandmother has been redeemed by her epiphany. While the reader's degree of knowledge about and agreement with Christian theology must inevitably color his or her pleasure in reading "A Good Man Is Hard to Find," anyone can relate to shifting definitions of goodness and think about how an attitude of self-righteousness can blind people to their own shortcomings. Christian readers, in fact, often find the story disturbing, taking it as a criticism of their faith rather than as an insider's demand that Christians take the ideals of their religion with brutal seriousness. As a character in a C. S. Lewis fantasy replies to a question about the safety of the lion representing Christ, "He's not tame, but he is good." There is nothing tame or easy about O'Connor's version of Christianity.

CRITICAL COMMENTARIES:

Flannery O'Connor, From *Mystery and Manners* (p. 1392)
Martha Stephens, From *The Question of Flannery O'Connor* (p. 1393)

Madison Jones, From "A Good Man's Predicament" (p. 1397)
Stephen Bandy, From " 'One of My Babies': The Misfit and the
Grandmother" (p. 1399)

Martha Stephens (p. 1393) believes that her interpretation of "A Good Man
Is Hard to Find" is compatible with Flannery O'Connor's view outlined in the
excerpt from *Mystery and Manners* included in this cluster (p. 1392). O'Connor
emphasizes that the unexpected turn that the plot takes is crucial, that every
good story contains "some gesture . . . both totally right and totally unexpected."
This small bit of the action connects the character and the reader with a "mystery" that is linked with the "grace" of God. She suggests that her contemporary
audiences have problems understanding the story perhaps because they no
longer believe in the existence of evil or in the need to be saved from it, and we
might speculate that half a century later our readers will have an even larger
chasm to leap. O'Connor contends that because people no longer recognize
grace (the undeserved action of God to redeem human beings who cannot possibly deserve or earn such favor), it takes extreme violence to make her characters and her readers see this reality. Stephens seeks to elaborate on O'Connor's
explanations, which often leave readers as confused as they began. Stephens's
most useful analysis begins with a quotation from T. S. Eliot in which he suggests that while choosing good is best, choosing evil is better than remaining
apathetic. Stephens claims that the deaths of the family members in O'Connor's
story are unimportant in the final scheme of things since they are people "who
have lived without choice or commitment of any kind, who have in effect not
'lived' at all." Although she acknowledges the difficulties in O'Connor's story
and the worldview it reflects, admitting that grace for O'Connor is "rather an
expensive process," she joins O'Connor in placing the problem squarely in the
lap of the bewildered reader: "O'Connor's statement about the story, taken as a
whole, only further confirms the fact that the tonal problem in this tale is really
a function of our difficulty with O'Connor's formidable doctrine."

Students often accuse instructors of "overreading" texts, of taking simple
stories and making them say more than could possibly be intended by the author
or logically defended within reasonable parameters. Stephen Bandy (p. 1399)
and Madison Jones (p. 1397) suggest that O'Connor does exactly this as she
seeks to explain her interpretation of the story to puzzled readers. Bandy make
the excellent point that "[t]here is no 'later on' in fiction." When O'Connor
imagines that her Misfit will go on to become a prophet, she therefore makes
new rules for the game, and readers have a right to complain that the story does
not suggest any such thing. Creative writers among the audience will agree that
the writer is often surprised by the direction a story takes and may be in the same
position as other readers as they discover symbolic meanings and recurring
motifs. To participate in an active writers' workshop is to undergo something like
group psychoanalysis. Critics therefore can legitimately question the writer's
explication of her own work, especially when the explanation enters territory
outside the text. Bandy critiques O'Connor's later comments about the grandmother as an interpretation that weakens the character by making her merely a
harmless, sentimental Southern grandmother; she must be more essentially
depraved than a "cranky maiden aunt," he contends, for her to equal the evil of

the Misfit. He reads her final actions as evil and cowardly in the extreme, an interpretation that gives the Misfit's recoil more credibility. The grandmother sinks to "stratagems of sentimentality" that play on her status as a mother, and Bandy finds O'Connor's comments about grace to be a sort of wishful thinking, her afterthoughts about the text she wrote. (In this context, another critic has proposed that this reference to motherhood invites connotations that recall Jesus and Mary, arguing that the grandmother intercedes at this point for the Misfit, a human being now linked with her son.) But O'Connor and readers who buy the theological interpretation are wrong, Bandy insists, implying that the author does not understand her own story.

Jones similarly takes issue with the story's climax. Raising issues of definition about the meaning of *grace* for secular readers, he posits that epiphany is possible in the human psyche without any link to religion. He sees the story's ending scene as describing the opposite situation to that proposed by O'Connor in *Mystery and Manners*. Far from bringing the Misfit to a sudden recognition of God's grace in which he becomes spiritually uplifted, the grandmother's comment and his reaction in the text of the story demonstrate the Misfit's horror at being classed with the repellently dull and spiritually lifeless (now literally lifeless) Bailey. As Jones points out, this categorizes him "among the world's family of vulgarians." Who would want to be this woman's child?

Many readers will agree that O'Connor's narrative is strong enough to hold together as a great story even when we read against the author's stated intentions. Because she includes religious themes in both her story and her interpretations of it, it is difficult to read "A Good Man Is Hard to Find" outside of this context. Most readers in our college classrooms do not have such a context, however, and may even be hostile to Christianity, holding all its adherents in contempt. Students who choose to write about this story and who therefore will be inclined to read it more than once might try playing the "believing and doubting games" — shifting subject positions as they read it first with full acceptance of the religious assumptions and again with an attitude of skepticism or as much objectivity as possible. Others might choose to ignore the theological implications and read the narrative much as we do Geoffrey Chaucer's *Canterbury Tales*, savoring O'Connor's three-dimensional characterizations of aptly named Southern stereotypes.

SUPERNATURAL JUSTICE: RE-VISIONS OF "THE DEMON LOVER" (p. 1403)

ANONYMOUS

The Demon Lover (p. 1403)

ELIZABETH BOWEN

The Demon Lover (p.1406)

The demon lover motif that Elizabeth Bowen calls on in the title of her short story is an ancient one, going as far back symbolically as the temptation of Eve in the Garden of Eden. More explicit connections can be made with the Scottish border ballad that begins this cluster. "The Demon Lover"(p. 1403) first appeared in broadsides of the seventeenth century, an example of a genre that was one of the first popular uses of the medium of print. Many British and Appalachian folk singers have recorded the song, based on texts collected in Francis James Child's *The English and Scottish Popular Ballads* of the nineteenth century, other collections, or versions in oral tradition. An audiotape shouldn't be difficult to find if instructors want to add it to the class context for reading Bowen's short story. Readers interested in British literary history will enjoy the discovery that both Samuel Pepys and Sir Walter Scott wrote down versions of the ballad being sung in their times.

In its many versions, the story is basically the same: a vulnerable and naive young woman exchanges vows with a dangerously attractive and mysterious man that she barely knows; events occur that cause the lovers to be separated; the woman goes on with her life, marrying and perhaps having children; the lover returns after many years and carries the woman off, often to an evil fate, in punishment for her broken vows. Sometimes the lover is a man, but more often he is supernatural, an evil revenant returned from the dead or the devil himself.

Readers over time have undoubtedly been attracted to the supernatural qualities of the story, in the same way that readers and viewers of visual media enjoy spine-tingling tales today. The ballad begins like a love story, as the young wife is seduced by an old lover into abandoning her husband and children to follow him on a romantic adventure. We may think back to Leslie Marmon Silko's "Yellow Woman"(p. 820), in which a Native American woman takes a similar journey into adultery. But we soon find the story taking a turn (as does Silko's narrative) as the woman finds herself suddenly with a sinister character who has a "cloven foot," recalling stories like Flannery O'Connor's "A Good Man Is Hard to Find" (p. 1378) or Tobias Wolff's "The Rich Brother" (p. 391) in which unsuspecting protagonists suddenly find themselves face to face with a sinister stranger who may be evil incarnate.

In addition to the thrill of vicariously encountering evil, however, the audience may also respond to the underlying theme: women who transgress can expect to be punished. If you have sex outside of marriage, girls, you will go to hell, the message reads, especially if your motives include an elevation in class. The young wife is attracted to the taffeta sails and the masts of gold as she steps into the ship of her demon lover. Because she is so easily bought and because she abandons her children for sexual freedom, early audiences undoubtedly felt that she got what was coming to her. The ending would be satisfyingly appropriate. Ironically, the end of the wife in Bowen's version may bring satisfaction to a later audience for the opposite reason: she has chosen the safe path and become boring. We may be satisfied to see her taken away to her death because she has so zealously avoided life.

These stories offer a reading experience that does not involve sympathizing with the characters. Women who do identify with the female protagonists who fall in love with the dark hero may feel that the fate that they suffer is unfair. People seldom choose their first loves with care, and the vows made during these relationships, no matter how sincerely felt at the time, are seldom kept. But vows were important when the ballad was popular, and the warning to young girls to take care would have been taken seriously. While we recognize wedding vows as speech acts that have legal consequences, though less irrevocable than in the past, the more casual promises of courtship are usually taken less seriously. We seldom hear of "breach of promise" suits anymore. But in a day when one's word was one's bond, the events of the ballad make more sense.

We might recall the incident in Angela Carter's "In the Company of Wolves" (p. 673) in which a woman pays dearly for remarrying after her first husband disappears into the woods. In fact, the ballad form may remind us a great deal of folk tales like the ones about Little Red Riding Hood (pp. 666, 669), in both their worldview and their form. Repetitions occur in both the folk tale and the ballad genre, and both are limited to traditional themes, having grown out of oral tradition. But they form a template from which modern writers can develop their own elaborations, drawing on archetypes most readers will recognize, if only subliminally.

Of the repetitions in the ballad, the reader will first notice the traditional rhyme and meter, and our more literary students may want to discuss the effects of these, as well as of repeated lines that create thematic echoes or enhance narrative pace. When the demon lover repeats the complaint three times that he could have married "a king's daughter," he plays on the young wife's guilt about not waiting for him but also on her pride and class consciousness. Though she seems to dismiss this claim, she quickly moves to thoughts of leaving her children for what he is able to offer her. She also repeats the image of her "two babes," driving home for the reader that she has abandoned her maternal responsibilities and has therefore damned herself in spite of her tender parting from them. A man might leave his children for adventure, but a woman should not. When the line "They had not sailed a league, a league" is repeated, however, the effect is less thematic than narrative, since the action is thus slowed to emphasize the startling revelation we are expecting, that her lover is a devil. Other repetitions — the hills of heaven, the mountain of hell — seem to function in the same way.

Many student readers claim to have little tolerance for strange dialects and old-fashioned forms of poetry and may find the ballad structure limited. But the repetition and the step-by-step unraveling of the story can enhance the supernatural feeling of the narrative if read aloud properly or heard performed by good interpreters of folk music. While the cloven hoof indicates that the demon lover may be the devil himself, he may instead by a revenant, an evil manifestation of a once living person, now returned from the dead. Either way, goose bumps are in order.

Current readers will not have to leave the twenty-first century to find parallels. Students will be able to think of many examples from popular literature, film, and television. For example, soap-opera viewers will testify that characters who die cannot be expected to stay buried for long but will return after recovering from miraculous plastic surgery to complicate the lives of heroines who have established new love interests. Fans of slasher movies know that the killer will return like any good zombie in time for the next sequel. The vampires of Anne Rice, the diverse ghouls of Stephen King, and the eerie psychopaths of Dean Koontz may occur to other readers. Audiences of every generation have enjoyed being frightened by the idea that those presumed dead may return to exact vengeance, that the forbidden lover will show up when least expected, to ensure that the faithless one's sins will find her out.

The beginnings of the novel in English have been analyzed as belonging to this genre. The seducer of Samuel Richardson's *Clarissa* or Thomas Hardy's *Tess of the d'Urbervilles*, Bram Stoker's Count Dracula, the darkly brooding men of the novels of the Brontë sisters, and their many descendents in the gothic romance genre all represent the demon-lover type, the dangerous and romantic man a woman is powerless to resist. Repressed women need an excuse to indulge in sexual passion, and the demon lover provides a devil-made-me-do-it out. But the culture demands that the woman pay for her sins — perhaps the breaking of vows but more likely the unwise making of vows in the first place. Therefore, the satisfying ending demands that her leaving of home and family, whether willingly or through deception or force, leads to her ultimate destruction. Sex and horror go hand in hand because undomesticated love is forbidden but oh so tempting.

Bowen structures her version of the demon-lover tale in a way designed to build suspense. The title signals us to look for sinister clues from the beginning, and the diction further builds the atmosphere of danger. Even before the lady of the house enters her closed London home she notices the "unfamiliar queerness" of the street. We are told that "no human eye watched," inviting the question of whether supernatural eyes might watch instead. A cat, often a symbol of the occult, walks the rooftops, and the word *dead* is used to describe the air. The description of the house is oddly violent: The wallpaper has a "bruise," and the floor has "claw-marks." As the language paints its eerie atmosphere, the narrative action is paced so that suspense slowly builds. Just before she spots the letter, for example, she stops "dead" — that word again — and a dash further slows the pace.

Suspense is further heightened by the gaps in the text. We do not hear her promise to her lover, and the flashback provides few clues to its exact nature. The scant details about her demon lover only increase the sense of danger. We are told that this flashback takes place twenty-five years earlier, during World War I. During wartime, girls frequently promise to wait for their soldiers, just as the soldiers promise to return. These promises tend to be broken more often than they are kept. But the details hint that this is not a sweet wartime romance.

He is cold, "without feeling," and even causes her physical pain. She seems to be in a trance during this time, and her mother interprets his interest as obsession rather than love. He has a stalkerlike quality and hints that he will be near her even when he seems far away. At one point, she pictures his eyes as "spectral glitters," making us wonder if he is human.

Our students may want to discuss the issue of distinguishing between obsessive relationships that make us uncomfortable and healthy love relationships that bring out our strengths. Mrs. Drover may be having this experience now because World War II evokes the same feelings. Her life seems to have been quite boring and safe. She is called a "prosaic woman," a description we might want to explore in class discussion. She seems to have married because this is what one does and because there had been some concern for a time that she would not attract a suitable husband. She wears a string of pearls, a seemingly timeless indicator of conventional good taste. But overall she does not seem to be a very pleasant person. She is the sort of woman who comes to the house without announcing the visit because she hopes to catch the caretaker in suspected neglect of duty. We are told that her "most normal expression was one of controlled worry, but of assent." We are told her exact age — forty-four — which is about as middle-aged as one can be. Student readers, perhaps to the consternation of some instructors, will see this age as particularly sexless and boring. Though we may identify with her growing perplexity and sense of dread, most readers will not see her as sympathetic. She may look in the mirror to check on the reality of the situation but also may be concerned about how she looks.

Throughout, she seems conscious of being watched, and there are hints that this may be a recurring experience since her separation from the demon lover years earlier. Alert readers will note that the letter's presence in the house suggests the supernatural character of this experience, since she has had to force the door open. The enjoyment of reading "The Demon Lover" comes with our questioning of whether this really happens or if she simply imagines it in response to the crisis of the London Blitz. One arguable theory may be that the sinister taxi driver is actually Death, as he may have been all along. This reading might compare Mrs. Drover's taxi ride with Emily Dickinson's carriage ride in "Because I could not stop for Death —" (p. 1452). Mrs. Drover has been unable to recall her lover's face but sees with terror exactly who is driving the cab at the story's end. It is a good narrative strategy to leave the face a mystery, since description would have robbed the story of its ambiguity.

This ambiguity about the lover's exact identity is one of the elements that Bowen's short story shares with the ancestral ballad of the same name. Just as the wife in the ballad realizes slowly that the man is not a wealthy admiral of a golden fleet but a manifestation of evil, Mrs. Drover comes slowly to the realization that she is being courted by a supernatural being and is gripped with fear when the taxi driver, a figure she has fantasized will be a consoling, protective presence, is actually the horror she fears. The narratives also share the elements of a promise made long ago that has been broken by marriage to another man but now must be kept. Both men are exciting but do not really demonstrate love and are, in fact, the sources of damnation. Both women may have transgressed sexually, though this remains off stage in both versions of the story. When Mrs. Drover recalls how her lover has exacted her promise to wait for him, she pushes the thought out of her mind, and we are left to imagine that she may have succumbed to passion, a likely reason for her uncharacteristic "trance" just before his departure. Both have allowed themselves to be seduced at some point by a dangerous man, a stranger who poses a threat to family harmony. While the woman in the ballad goes willingly on her lover's fantastic ship, Mrs. Drover is abducted in a dark, enclosed taxi against her will. But neither has any choice once the journey begins; the men insist that their vows be kept.

Unlike the ballad, Bowen's version is set in an identifiable time and place, London during the two wars of the early twentieth century. This lends a sense of verisimilitude. It has been said that good stories usually place an extraordinary person in ordinary circumstances or an ordinary person in extraordinary ones. This story exemplifies the latter; as we have discussed, Mrs. Drover is "prosaic." She does not go on adventures. While the war could be expected to lead to extraordinary events, London is eerily silent, and the adventure forces itself on her supernaturally from her one brief period of recklessness. The realistic setting and the ordinary protagonist heighten the *Twilight Zone* atmosphere. The specific, mundane details help the reader to enter the alternate universe of the story. Like the ballad, Bowen's narrative also increases the suspense and the delicious spookiness of the plot by slowing down the action to allow maximum impact when the truth is revealed. However, we never quite see "the truth" of the eerie presence in Bowen's "The Demon Lover." Even at the end, though she finally sees his face and moves into a state of terror, we do not. The effect is more chilling than the one produced by the cloven hoof of the ballad's evil presence. We hear his voice, perhaps understand how the wife might be seduced. Kathleen Drover's obsessive suitor, on the other hand, is silent and unseen and therefore as terrifying as any stalker.

16

Confronting Mortality (p. 1413)

THE PASSAGE OF TIME (p. 1415)

JOHN KEATS
Ode on a Grecian Urn (p. 1416)

John Keats knew a great deal about confronting mortality. When he was a child, his father died in a riding accident. His mother died of tuberculosis when he was fourteen, and he would later nurse his brother through the same illness. Keats himself would die of tuberculosis in 1821 when he was barely twenty-five years old. Perhaps it was with the pale, delicate young poet with so much unfulfilled life and promise that the disease itself began to take on romantic connotations. The myth would develop that people with tuberculosis were too gifted, too intense, too intelligent, too sensitive and fine for this world. Keats perhaps served as a model for this stereotype of the consumptive artist. During a five-month period in 1819, he produced an amazing amount of original, creative work, including the poem we include here. Like his critical writings proposing the idea of "negative capability," "Ode on a Grecian Urn" reflects Keats's belief that we should leave ourselves open to uncertainty rather than reducing all of life to logic and reason. We might encourage our students to follow his lead, especially in the early stages of examining an issue, encouraging a tolerance for antithetical beliefs, a willingness to speculate, and a skepticism that does not make up its mind too quickly.

Keats was the youngest and last great writer of the Romantic movement. Romantic poetry sounds old-fashioned to most of today's readers, and its passionate, lyrical outpourings about nature and art may strike our students as mannered, even silly. Much of the poetry of the modernists of the twentieth century reacts against the style and attitudes of the Romantic poets and those who followed them in the nineteenth century. But we need to remind our students that the revolutions of one generation quickly become solidified into the idols that the next generation must topple. The Romantic poets, responding to the American and French revolutions and to newly discovered knowledge about Greek and Roman "antiquities," were doing something fresh and exciting. Keats was insisting on ideas that we now take for granted: that we can process personal experiences, emotions, and realizations about life into poetry; that images should be concrete and sensory; that poetry may be suggestive and ambiguous; and that intensity and control can interact to "surprize by a fine excess."

After having students try to visualize or draw the vase described in the poem, we might look at examples of this genre of Greek ceramics. Scholars theorize that the "Grecian urn" of the poem is a composite of several that Keats might have seen in a London museum. Some details may come from the poet's imagination. The surface of the vase would be rather crowded if it depicted all that the poet sees. His words catch the essence of the original but go beyond the details to imagine the scene as a moment frozen in time. This idea is familiar to current readers, since we can pause time on a videotape or freeze the frame of a film, but even photography did not yet exist for Keats and his contemporaries. Most readers will see his description as imaginative and subjective rather than objective.

Both the first and the fourth stanzas of the ode ask questions about the people in the scene. The poem's speaker seeks to place the myth or the ceremony in context, to historicize it. In fact, he addresses the vase as a "historian" in line 3, asking the personified object to explain itself. Like the scenes described by Christopher Marlowe and others in Chapter 14, "Loving" (p. 810), Keats's images of love recall the conventions of pastoral poetry where lovers live in rural bliss in the rural fields of ancient Greece. But some readers might question whether this sort of love is blissful for everyone described. The "maidens" of the first stanza seem to be fleeing rape. Even the designation "unravished bride" may have violent connotations. But all of this is forestalled, stopped in the moment of desire for the male lover and in the moment of flight and intact beauty for the female. Ironically, Keats became engaged to Fanny Brawne later in the year these words were written, but he may not yet have realized that he had contracted the tuberculosis that would keep the physical expression of their love in a similar suspended animation.

Though the poem sounds passionate, even seeming to prefer the urn's suspended love to "breathing human passion" in the third stanza, he calls the image a "Cold Pastoral" in the final stanza. Perhaps his mention of the empty town prepares us for this antithesis. It comes just after a description of human passion in the third stanza that sounds more like tuberculosis than love. In the long run, the object is empty, cold, and even reminds us of eternity and old age, though he still seems to value it as "a friend to man." Many conflicting explications exist for this ambiguous poem, reams of paper being expended to discuss just the last two lines. In the course of discussing the inconsistencies in the poem, students may raise many of the issues that literary scholars have brought up in the past, and we should resist imposing our own interpretations. The poem resists definitive answers. We cannot even be sure who is speaking in the final line, the poet or the urn. We may guess that the concrete images of the poem define what the speaker means by "beauty," but we may raise an issue of definition about the meaning of "truth." We may raise issues of theme: is the poem about beauty, truth, love, art, mortality, immortality, or some combination of all of these? It seems useful to consider the ode in terms of Keats's own literary criticism of William Shakespeare in which he privileges the open mind that allows opposite meanings to coexist.

GERARD MANLEY HOPKINS
Spring and Fall (p.1418)

Writing in the nineteenth century but remaining virtually unpublished until the twentieth, Gerard Manley Hopkins consciously wrote as a poetic innovator ahead of his time. Hopkins chose to keep his poems out of print partly because he was a Catholic priest whose superiors in the church were unlikely to have approved of his writing, but he also may have realized that the literary world would not have fully appreciated his poetry either. Later generations, however, have embraced his experimentation with rhythm and language, seeing them as an antidote to the mannered lyricism of the Romantic poets and the structured forms of the Victorians. Readers of "Spring and Fall" will notice the accent marks Hopkins supplies to make clear what he called the "sprung rhythm" that characterizes his poetry. Rather than counting the regular beats of meter in a line as the conventions of English poetry dictated, he aimed for rising and falling patterns of speech that borrowed from the time and tempo of music, as well as those of the Welsh language.

His language is experimental, too. He coins new words, like "wanwood leafmeal" (line 8). Or he uses words in unexpected ways, like "unleaving" (line 2). The reader's mind searches for definition. At first, *unleaving* seems to connote permanence — something that doesn't leave — but then we realize that it refers to the trees divesting themselves of leaves. The opposing definitions interact as we read the poem. We often find such puns in Hopkins's poems. The meanings become complex as all of a word's possible connotations intertwine. Alliteration, internal rhyme, and other devices that depend on sounds further elaborate the connotations. Odd syntax forces the reader to see meanings in new perspectives, to follow a tortuous path to interpretation. Hopkins believed strongly in the power of words, attributing to them an essential, spiritual quality. He aimed in his poetry for something he called "inscape," an inward pattern of language that exactly expresses a specific reality.

The subtitle, perhaps the dedication, to the poem "Spring and Fall" is "To a Young Child." The seasons of the year provide a source of natural symbolism. In some parts of the world, fall stands for passing time, old age, and approaching death, and spring is associated with youth, fresh beginnings, and life. We easily associate Margaret with springtime, though the scene and most of the poem's images reflect autumn. Aside from her "fresh thoughts" (line 4), there is little of spring. The words for both seasons have double meanings, however. Adam and Eve lost their innocence in another garden, and forever after we have called the results of their actions the "fall." Some, perhaps including the poet, believe that every human being lives out that particular fall as he or she goes through the seasons of life. Margaret will come to the knowledge of good and evil and eventually recognize that she is grieving over her own mortality. And there are other meanings for "spring," one of which Hopkins juxtaposes with sorrow in line 11. The springs of her sorrow are in her spirit and are an inevitable consequence of being human.

Although the speaker seems to address a young child, the issues may be raised that most adults would not actually say these words to a child and that most children would not understand them. Overhearing the speaker as he seems to speak to Margaret herself has more impact on the actual audience for the poem, however. Imagining how we might explain the sorrows of life to a child or defend our reasons for distracting or lying to her instead leads Hopkins's readers to contemplate our own humanity from the perspective of adulthood. Telling us about the passage of time and the accompanying sorrows using Margaret as an example might seem too preachy, might even reduce the poem to trite cliché. When Hopkins compares the "things of man" to dead leaves, he may be revealing his religious philosophy about what endures and what does not. The view of human life is pessimistic, seeing sorrow, perhaps even death, as "the blight man was born for."

As a Jesuit priest living in working-class sections of large industrial English cities in the late 1800s, Hopkins saw more than his share of human suffering. In other poems, Hopkins celebrates the power of God — as revealed in simple, natural objects — to overcome man's blight. Some readers may feel, however, that the implied separation between the child and nature that will come with adulthood reflects a stance in this poem that removes humanity from nature and is thus against what they consider to be truly religious. Students will differ in their definitions of the word *religious*. Do they see it as having similar meanings to the words *spiritual* or *mystical*, or do they define it in terms of established systems of ethics, worship, or belief?

In looking at alliteration, rhyming, and unusual words, students have much to choose from. We might ask them what they think "wanwood leafmeal" means or if "Goldengrove" is likely another coinage rather than a real place. Have them dig for how the words sound, other words they are reminded of, connotations, and even how the words feel in the mouth as they are spoken aloud. In addition to the alliteration of the *g* and *v* consonants in line 2, for example, the assonance of the repeated *o* vowel sounds makes reading the line a physical experience beyond hearing and seeing the words, perhaps bringing the reader close to the "inscape" the poet seeks.

Though readers differ, most will probably respond more easily to Hopkins's "Spring and Fall" than to John Keats's "Ode on a Grecian Urn" (p. 1466), for a number of reasons. Even though the narrator of the Keats poem allows us to experience his emotions and thoughts as he addresses an object of art, he is separated from us in time, and the object itself is even more distant. The scene he describes, furthermore, is static; time stands still. The speaker's excited utterances and animation may seem exaggerated to many student readers. They may be disturbed by his ambiguity and seeming inconsistency, feeling that the whole exercise is artificial and worked up. Hopkins speaks to a child in a garden and contemplates the passage of time in an understated, gentle tone. The scene is dynamic, since he imagines Margaret's growing up into real sorrows that will replace this vague feeling of grief she does not yet understand. His tone, though sad and pessimistic, is consistent. The scene depends less on context than experiences common to many readers. Most readers will relate more easily to a child than to an artifact, even though people are represented on the vase.

Others may think it morbid to speak to a child as Hopkins's narrator does and will be more comfortable with Keats. The scene in Keats's poem is an eternally fixed spring in which leaves will never fall as they do in Hopkins's autumn

Goldengrove. In "Spring and Fall" even the springtime of childhood foreshadows the inevitable, symbolic changes of season. When Hopkins uses the word "colder" in line 6, therefore, he reminds us that winter will follow. Dead bodies are cold, and death will eventually come to young Margaret. Keats uses the word "cold" in line 45 of his poem, referring to the scene on the urn as a "Cold Pastoral." At first, we might not connect his meaning with the cold of winter and symbolically of death. Yet the urn is not alive, nor is the scene of young vitality on the vase. Nothing about them is warm. They rest among the marble monuments in the British Museum. His juxtaposition of the word "eternity" with "cold" invites the reader to consider the inevitability of the grave. Ironically, this cold thing — this art — lives long, while the lives of truly warm human beings pass away generation by generation.

A case could be made that the two poets reveal similar attitudes toward the passage of time and the mortality it symbolizes. Keats sees the figures in the painting as blessed because they are spared the changes of time, even the sexual consummation of the lover's chase. Hopkins sees Margaret as grieving because, though she does not realize her reasons, she senses the changes of time. The implication is that she will gain knowledge (truth?) but lose her connection with the beauty of nature. As a child, however, she senses a truth in the beauty of falling leaves. Whether we believe that Keats really equates truth with beauty in his ode depends on which of the many possible readings we choose. Readers can successfully argue that both the poems are about mourning, although Hopkins is more clearly so. Keats mourns the things of life that do not remain by praising an object that contrasts with the world of the living in its unchanging permanence.

A. E. HOUSMAN

Loveliest of trees, the cherry now (p. 1419)

Like the poems by John Keats (p. 1416) and Gerard Manley Hopkins (p. 1418), this A. E. Housman lyric from *A Shropshire Lad* speaks of the passage of time in the graceful language of poetry. While his reputation with critics has gone up and down with changing ideologies about poetry, Housman's seemingly simple lines have remained popular with readers since their first publication when the poet was a Latin professor and textual scholar in his thirties. He openly opposed writers like T. S. Eliot and Ezra Pound, who broke with the traditions of English and classical poetry. Students interested in British literature and culture might enjoy following up on some of the characters in Tom Stoppard's 1997 play *The Invention of Love* to catch the flavor of the Victorian and aesthetic movement Oxford milieus of the late 1800s that helped to shape Housman's (and his contemporary Hopkins's) strong opinions. The most important influence in a biographical sense may have been Oscar Wilde, who was imprisoned for acts of homosexuality. Housman therefore repressed his own homosexuality, and his unrequited love for a young athlete lends pathos to his poetry for many readers. But such knowledge is not necessary for appreciating the ironic sadness and spare beauty of his verse, and it has been said that many soldiers carried a thin copy of A *Shropshire Lad* with them to the trenches of World War One. We can imagine one of these soldiers reading "Loveliest of trees, the cherry now" on a bloody winter's day in a bombed out field and thinking of the landscape of home, hoping to live past twenty to experience the longer passage of time that the words anticipate.

Fifty years seems little time to Housman's speaker, however, because the beauty he experiences in the moment is so intense. Greedy for time, he says that the twenty years he has already lived leaves him "only" this much more time. He emphasizes this by repeating the word "now" in the opening lines of the first two stanzas. We must savor every moment, he says, because a lifetime is not long enough for this keen joy. We can't lose *now*, not so much because beauty is fleeting but because — as with any intensely positive emotion — we can't imagine ever tiring of it, can't imagine ever being filled up. Perhaps Housman emphasizes the present, however, because he knows that loss and unrequited desire are a part of life and that death eventually interrupts all such experiences. When we are in the midst of a fully lived moment, therefore, we need to give it our complete attention. None of the vicissitudes of time can take that moment from us.

According to the second stanza, the speaker is twenty years old. His use of calculations here stresses even more strongly the sense that each moment is important. He could have gone further and figured out how many minutes or seconds he might have left if he lived the biblical span of "threescore years and ten" (seventy years). But as the soldiers who carried his book keenly realized, we may not have even that much time. Added irony accrues to the speaker's words when we consider this fact, since we see the twenty-year-old making the naïve assumption that he has exactly this much time. The bookkeeping contrasts with his aesthetic appreciation of nature. The contrast is interesting biographically when we picture the atheistic, pedantic, picky textual critic writing his beautifully simple, hymnlike, bittersweet lyrics. Yet the two go together.

Housman's poems are beautiful partly because they grow out of his scholarly classical studies (he uses models from Greek and Latin poetry) and because their structure is carefully crafted or calculated. His diction, too, reveals evidence of careful art. His use of the word "snow" when he could have described the cherry blossoms as simply "white" is a choice he makes precisely because it contrasts with the springtime image associated with "Eastertide." He ends with a word filled with connotations of coldness, reminding the reader of death, even in an image of newly blossoming life. The word "Eastertide" is also filled with connotations, some of them religious. Easter is a church feast that celebrates life, specifically the resurrection of Christ from the dead; so while it is biblically and theologically linked to the Jewish Passover, which also occurs in the spring, its date in the traditional church calendar is apt. The dating also links the Christian holiday with pre-Christian European religions more closely tied to nature. When Housman describes his cherry tree as "Wearing white for Eastertide," he calls on all these connections. But he also personifies nature as a young girl going to her first communion, dressed in a color that symbolizes unspoiled innocence, thus linking her with the young man who can't get enough of her beauty. Housman, neither Christian nor heterosexual, uses cultural symbolism that draws on knowledge of both. The tone and structure of the poem are linked to this ironic play of youth and maturity, craft and simplicity.

Much of our pleasure may come from sensing the great depth that is beneath the seemingly simple, childlike rhyme scheme and quatrain form reminiscent of those used in hymns and folk ballads.

We can infer a symbolic connection between winter and death, spring and life, in Housman's poem, just as we can in those by Keats and Hopkins in this cluster. All invite this interpretation by referring to nature and to the passage of time. Spring has a bittersweet quality because we know it will not last, and Hopkins emphasizes this by setting his poem at the beginning of autumn and explicitly making spring (the season) the *spring* (the beginning, the source) of sorrow. Spring and youth are small parts of life — not celebrated seasons to pro-long. Keats, on the other hand, finds beauty and truth in a perpetual youth that can never be lost. He privileges spring, perhaps sensing that he will not live to experience old age. But he will pass away, as intervening generations between his speaker and the ancient Greek models for the urn's images have and as later ones will. Housman, too, sees spring as something to be valued. But rather than eternal, his spring is more natural — more living — because it leaves but will return. Even when he is seventy, we can imagine the speaker — no longer a Shropshire lad but a man who continues to savor each moment — experiencing spring yet again. In this sense, while the acknowledgment of death and the pas-sage of time are present in his poem, the symbolic linear analogy is deliberately broken.

A *carpe diem* quality is common to all of the poems, but an active *seizing* of the day characterizes Housman's attitude, recalling more closely the metaphys-ical poets he hated. All emanate a sense of loss, but Housman seems to offer more hope as he collects images of spring to hold him through fifty more win-ters. While Keats hints at Platonic ideals that outlast humanity and Hopkins seems to see death and a fallen world (though God as well) in the most tender buds of spring, Housman implies that this is it: this keen, fleeting beauty is all we have, so we'd best enjoy the physical, natural here-and-now world with each returning spring while we live. Both Housman and Hopkins set their poems in woodlands, but Hopkins sees the "wanwood leafmeal" of the forest floor and the trees' "unleaving" — a word inviting images of the dying fall — while Housman sees their blossoms.

Housman also hints at the coming winter by ending his poem with the word "snow" and by having his narrator calculate how many springs he has left. Housman lived to seventy-seven, reaching the biblical span of seventy years that is calculated in his poem. Keats, on the other hand, died at twenty-five and may have suspected when he wrote "Ode on a Grecian Urn" that the tuberculosis that had taken other family members would soon lead to his early death as well. Hopkins died shortly before his forty-fifth birthday, but the conflicts that he felt between religion and art led him to burn his early poems — those from his springtime years — when he became a priest. Their lives therefore ironically enact the attitudes we infer from the poems.

Some students prefer to approach poetry through biography, considering poems — often erroneously — to be spoken by the poet rather than an assumed persona. We cannot warn them often enough to avoid such a trap. People who knew the testy, critical, professorial Housman, for example, found a very differ-ent voice in his verse. He does not deliberately place himself in his poetry and would have seen this as improper. The speaker of Housman's poem seems closer to the young soldiers who carried his book during World War I than the scholarly professor himself. His speaker does not keep his distance from the world he describes. By using the first person, the poet makes the poem say more about the speaker than it says about nature or death. Keats, on the other hand, has his (very Keats-like) speaker address an artistic image; he is saying something philosophical, and he reveals this when he uses the abstract words *truth* and *beauty* in his final line. Therefore, while we hear an involved speaker, he nevertheless stands outside his subject. Hopkins, too, couches his poem in the observations of a witness who addresses the subject of the poem rather than in the words of an active participant in its action. The poem is about Margaret but more clearly about the death that will eventually come to Margaret and everyone else. Even when the poems have them keep a safe distance, however, we have seen that many of the speakers' (and the poets') attitudes are revealed.

ROBIN BECKER

The Star Show (p. 1421)

The title of contemporary writer Robin Becker's third collection of poetry, *All-American Girl*, has ironic undertones. Growing up in Philadelphia in the 1950s, Becker is American, certainly, though she has traveled widely. But writing about being middle-aged and the accompanying task of confronting mortality, she is hardly a "girl" in the traditionally youthful definition of the word. Writing as a lesbian, she sometimes crosses gender, giving the word *girl* a double irony. In one poem, she shares her desire as a young girl for the freedom of "the boy across the street / who hung upside down from a tree / and didn't care / that his shirt fluttered over his bare / chest." Or after making love with another girl in a Philadelphia hotel room as a teenager, she is "happy as the young / Tom Jefferson." Her poems deal with the totality of life, however, not about issues of gender and sexuality alone. Becker looks back on a lifetime of experiences honestly and reflectively, exploring her losses and gains, her winding journey toward self-definition and insight. She writes about her Jewish grandmother who wants to have her granddaughter's nose fixed (she declines) and about her sister who commits suicide. In "The Star Show" she recalls a childhood experience in Philadelphia, the transformed reality of a visit to the planetarium, but the poem may be *about* much more.

The poem begins with the writer's present situation. Becker has spent a good deal of time in the American West, where it is possible to look up at "the enormous sky." In years when meteor showers are active, groups of people often get together at night to watch shooting stars, and her poem may describe such an experience in the first stanza. She establishes here that she is no longer a child but an adult having an experience with a real star show. Unlike the narrated, scripted excitement of the planetarium that she will remember, a star show is something you glimpse, something words cannot really keep up with or explain in the present tense. If the beginning had been omitted, the most recent scene of the poem would be the ending, where the children jarringly leave the other world of the planetarium and the spell is broken. With the opening scene, the sense of wonder is recovered before we know it is lost, and the poem is significantly different in tone. The night sky and the planetarium are of one substance; it is the "autumn afternoon" into which the children are thrust after the planetarium show that seems out of place. The planetarium lecture takes the children through the seasons of the year, beginning with winter night and ending with autumn day. This seems more to reflect the way such lectures are conventionally done in planetariums rather than a cheap use of symbols of time by the poet. The adult voice that begins the poem pinpoints the time at midnight, perhaps a logical place for an adult narrator at the end of life. But midnight can as easily be the beginning of something as the end of something. And autumn, usually associated with middle age, is still with the children as they leave the planetarium, far too early to fit the usual metaphor.

The seasons and other signs of the passage of time do not seem to be used in a conventional refers to trite way. The interlude of night is religious and mythic in quality. The speaker refers to it as the "miracle spreading overhead" and the "sky's mysteries." She compares the lecturer with a rabbi discussing Moses and then brings up Galileo and the Inquisition. But we soon move away from established religion into the wonder of the Native Americans, the climax of the story that causes the child to weep "for what I'd lost." The lecturer turns out to be a sort of Wizard of Oz, a false god who gets the students caught up and then rewards them with the mockery of "a grown-up laugh" as he takes the heavens away from them. We suspect at this point that the narrator knows something about feeling betrayed by grown-up laughter, has felt let down by religion. That she compares him to a rabbi makes us wonder if she has lost her faith. But the wonder of the sky remains.

Memory is always selective; we impose a narrative line on the elements of our experiences, making them match up with the story we have taken for our own. The story of the planetarium star show belongs to the woman lying at midnight out west watching a meteor shower, and she interprets the child's experience through the filter of the years since third grade. But the details may be the ones the child stores up; maybe the woman who would travel out west is shaped by the child who hears stories of the Hopis in a planetarium in Philadelphia. Maybe the woman adds stories that she heard much later, traveling out west. Many writers maintain that a story may be true without being factual, and vice versa. The poem does not have to be realistic. A case may be made that the theme of the poem is not the stars but the language used to discuss them. Words are inadequate, the narrator tells us at the outset. Words are seductive, she tells us during the planetarium star show; they can bring us into wonder but toss us as quickly out again. And words are inadequate, she tells us again at the poem's end; they are meaningless, ordinary, derisive, destructive.

Both Gerard Manley Hopkins (p. 1418) and Becker attribute more wisdom and religious sense to a child than may seem warranted. Hopkins assumes in Margaret the foreknowledge of a fact of life that surfaces in the child as vague emotion. He sees the child as an innocent but intuitive being who will grow into the knowledge of sorrow. Becker gives her narrator — perhaps herself as a child — a spiritual and intellectual experience in which she recalls connections to major religions, Hopi myth, changing seasons, and loss of faith. But she is able to return as an adult to the wonder of the sky. The child of Becker's poem seems more aware, but this may be because we see Hopkins's Margaret from the outside.

These two poems and John Keats's "Ode on a Grecian Urn" (p. 1416) may end on a note of despair. It would be hard to make a case that the Hopkins poem does not end with despair, though there is a sense of appropriateness about the grief that the protagonist, like all humankind, will come to know. The narrator may feel acceptance rather than despair. On the other hand, "Ode on a Grecian Urn" (p. 1416) is ambiguous. Some readers might see it as transcending despair by maintaining the immortality of beauty. Others interpret the ending as filled with despair, especially if the writer's close acquaintance with sickness and mortality is taken into account. Becker's ending startles the reader with its brusque quality after we have experienced the wonders of the sky with her. Yet we may read it as only temporary, citing the beginning as closer in time to the adult narrator, who seems less despairing than matter-of-fact as she watches the meteor shower and admits that it cannot be narrated.

Becker's commentator is like Hopkins's at the beginning: he is calm as he speaks to the children, sad as he describes Galileo's trial for heresy, cold as he moves them into winter. But he is like Keats's narrator in his changes and in the way he woos them with beauty that we think for a while might be truth. The sky in the planetarium is a great teaching tool but is not the real thing. Without her words telling us that she felt "bereft," we would see Becker's lecturer at the planetarium as a wonderful teacher and storyteller. In fact, her complaint may be that he is too good. Keats's narrator might talk about the timeless circling of the sky, and he might ask questions and make exclamations about the figures he saw in the constellations. He might point out that Polaris stands still and shines steadily, unlike the flickering candles of our daily lives. Hopkins's narrator might notice the young girl who is so moved by the trip through the seasons and remind her that she will feel this again looking at the stars as a middle-aged woman. With either Keats or Hopkins, style is important to content. Students who attempt to write a commentary for Keats should use a lyrical style, whereas those imitating Hopkins might create new words or combinations of words to describe the night sky.

A tone of despair characterizes the endings of all four of the poems in this cluster. Although Keats seems to say that beauty and truth will survive forever, they survive in a naïve image fixed in a "cold pastoral" in a museum while the poet reminds us that we will surely die. Hopkins uses words throughout his poem that could be construed to symbolize lifelessness, decay, and disease; even his use of the word *golden* in the name of the grove, with its connotations of the rich, warm, pure sunlight of spring, could as easily apply to turning leaves and the despair of coming winter. His last line underscores this despair, saying that Margaret cries for her own mortality as she grieves over the changes in nature. A. E. Housman (p. 1419) leaves us with the image of snow, a word encapsulating winter and death, even as his speaker seizes the day, driving home the point he has made in the earlier stanzas that life is too short, even if we live out the full span. Becker ends with despair as her speaker sits "bereft" after the mundane world reenters the planetarium and her consciousness. She has been "wooed" by the voice of the planetarium commentator to follow him into the sweep of nature and life as he talks the class through the heavens.

Like the speakers of the poems by Keats, Hopkins, and Housman, Becker's commentator uses "plain English" to make profound points. The speaker reminds her of her rabbi, and the poems in this cluster also speak at times with the authority of religion and philosophy, though they also "whisper" to us in a tone of intimacy — almost in the "still, small voice" with which Moses hears the voice of God speak in a burning bush in the wilderness. But like the other authors, Becker uses the image of cold as the commentary proceeds into winter. Her commentator reminds us of the chill of death, as have the earlier poets in this cluster. At the end, she hears his "grown-up laugh" and feels betrayed and manipulated. We might imagine the narrators of the other poems doing the commentary in different ways. Keats might "*oooh* and point / and say *over there*" along with his audience, reminding us of the lasting beauty of the stars and telling us that though the Native American hunters are gone, Becker's child narrator should not weep for what is lost but appreciate the immutable truths generations of human beings have drawn in the sky. "Go ahead and cry, little Robin," Hopkins might say. "I'm glad you caught a 'glimpse of the sadness to come.' This is why you are really so moved; you realize that you and the whole mortal world are dying. But there is beauty in seeing the deep-down reality of things, the real decay rather than the pretend ideal, and God is really in it all." Housman, perhaps, would sound much like himself, the professor who woos us in the voice of the poet, ironically laughing at the naïve reader who misses the immaturity of a speaker who thinks he can figure it all out and actually hold on to ephemeral life. "Enjoy what you see now," he might say. "Go out and look up at the sky every night. Don't lose a second of the time you have."

FIGHTING FOR SURVIVAL (p. 1424)

TIM O'BRIEN

The Things They Carried (p. 1424)

In a sense, the stories in Tim O'Brien's collection of interrelated narratives about the Vietnam War are stories *about* stories. One piece has the title "How to Tell a True War Story" and begins by swearing to the reader that the story is true. But the narrator will later explain that "a true war story cannot be believed. If you believe it, be skeptical." At times, O'Brien will tell the same story with differing endings, confiding to the reader at one point that the first ending is true and later insisting that another one is what *really* happened. In his mystery novel *In the Lake of the Woods*, he leaves the reader with no resolution of the plot, maintaining that the point of the story is the impossibility of ever knowing the secrets that people keep within themselves. Imagination and memory interweave in autobiography or fiction, and the fact that they do is part of the story for O'Brien.

Like many writers we have encountered in our anthology, O'Brien distinguishes between facts and truth and insists that we must sometimes lie in order to tell the truth. "Stories save us," he believes. This may especially be true about

Vietnam War experiences, since conflicting political narratives about that war have been part of our culture since the 1960s. People like O'Brien, who were eyewitnesses and (often reluctant) participants, find their actual experiences so bizarre and surreal that they foreground the incredibility of the account. And like Kiowa in "The Things They Carried," they find that the incredibility compels repetition. The story must be told again and again to be confirmed as true.

It would be futile to attempt a sorting of the fact and fiction in a Tim O'Brien narrative. Much of it is certainly autobiographical, and there can be no doubt that the war still haunts him. He says it was an image of himself, still loaded down with the physical and spiritual burdens he carries from Vietnam, that prompted his writing of this story, though he has written about the war both before and since. Ironically, given his teasing of readers with the fuzziness of the line between truth and fiction, O'Brien says that he does not write for catharsis but for communication. He is a perfectionist about his writing, working long hours and editing out much more than he keeps in a story. Students sometimes complain of the long catalogs in O'Brien's story, missing the subtle shifts of emphasis and the connotations and wry puns that layer meanings. Assure them that every line of "The Things They Carried" is crafted in minute detail. Much will be missed if they rush through it.

The lists of things carried have a cumulative effect that builds as the story humps on, interweaving physical, mental, emotional, spiritual, cultural, and political burdens. The story presents itself as a sort of factual account of items carried. From time to time, there is white space as the narrator takes a breath and renews the rhetorical tone of nonfiction. At times, the tone is of the formulaic classification paper that students too often use for every possible occasion. You can almost see the numbered outline: things carried out of necessity, things carried as a function of rank, weapons, variations by mission, things carried out of superstition, and so on. By the time we get to the last bit of separating white space, the narrator can be obvious about the complex meanings underlying the concept of carrying things and tells us how the soldiers carried themselves. The last sentence ironically includes the military jargon "Carry on," which we now recognize as full of meaning. But soon into the story, the coolly objective narrative voice unexpectedly varies the pattern; for example, in the midst of describing "odds and ends" like New Testaments and vitamins, the narrator throws in, "They all carried ghosts."

His delivery continues to be deadpan, even when he slips in bit by bit the central event of the story, the death of Ted Lavender. Buried in the middle of a list of things they carried from necessity, we first hear of this in past tense, as if it were just another trivial detail. Yet it is the event that effects the change in the dynamic character First Lieutenant Jimmy Cross. It seems unlikely that Cross's daydreaming about Martha is the cause of Lavender's death. Scared, high, concentrating on urinating and zipping his fly, Lavender is as much to blame as anyone. In the long run, none of the soldiers is at fault: the war is beyond their control, and death for some is a given. But Cross must exorcise his consciousness of the things of the other world in order to carry on as the leader of these men. We may question whether his change will be for the better.

In the mid-1990s O'Brien returned to My Lai, where his platoon had been stationed a year after the much-publicized burning and killing of civilians by

American soldiers. Writing about the trip and the implications of the massacre, he suggests that lost love and the insanity of war interact to produce such atrocities. In the light of this, it is interesting that the platoon in "The Things They Carried" carries out just such an atrocity after Lavender is killed.

The story is set up in a way that encourages the reader's identification with Cross as the main character of this story. We are allowed to know what he is thinking. Perhaps he is preoccupied with Martha's virginity because he needs her as an ideal, a fantasy to contrast with the reality of war. He may reflect the mores of the times: contrary to stereotype, many young people of the 1960s had conservative ideas about premarital sex. We have no reason to believe that she does not love him, since he is an unreliable judge of her feelings. Some students might use the word *paranoid* to describe his obsession. Others might point out that he is in an insane situation and that his seeming paranoia is understandable. We might also keep in mind O'Brien's preoccupation with the shifting nature of any narrative, even fantasy. His point may be that the story Cross tells himself about Martha is destructive. Or he may instead be saying that fantasizing about Martha is the thing that keeps Cross human. Or he may be saying that both readings are true, that for Cross and his men to survive under the insane conditions of war, he must give up the story that makes him vulnerable and thus human.

Other members of the company become more rounded in other stories of O'Brien's intertextual group of narratives. Kiowa, for example, will later die in a shit field, smothered in excrement. In the realistic details of "The Things They Carried" readers will find a cross section of young American manhood. Characters are clearly distinguishable from each other. As a group, they are protective of their pride, filled with bravado, irreverent and mocking in the face of death. The best word to describe them might be *burdened*.

The best comparisons to make between O'Brien's story and the stories of earlier wars might be found in Ernest Hemingway. In his nonfictional *If I Die in a Combat Zone*, O'Brien says that he is greatly influenced by a Hemingway character who has the courage to walk away from war in *A Farewell to Arms*. "Henry was able to leave war being good and brave enough at it, for real love," O'Brien writes, "and although he missed the men of war, he did not miss the fear and killing. . . . Henry, like all my heroes, was not obsessed with courage; he knew it was only one part of virtue, that love and justice were other parts." But the Vietnam War challenges such abstractions, and "The Things They Carried" is the epitome of the concrete. The brutality and lack of idealism in O'Brien's characters bring home the ugliness of war. This is an antiwar story because it shows the dehumanization of the men involved and the meaninglessness of the activities in which they are engaged.

JAMESON CURRIER

What They Carried (p. 1438)

The fight for survival described by Jameson Currier in "What They Carried" and in his 1998 novel *Where the Rainbow Ends* has much in common with the dogged effort of men to stay alive in Tim O'Brien's war stories (p. 1424). Lost love, fear, the indignities of death and dying, and — perhaps above all —

the loss of autonomy and control over the simplest things of life are common to both war and the catastrophic illness AIDS. Currier points out, however, that medical advances of recent years have somewhat lessened the grim death sentence that the diagnosis of HIV signified at the time this story was published in 1993. Nevertheless, the story reflects the early days of the AIDS epidemic of the 1980s, times that shaped the lives of many people who were coming of age, especially in the homosexual communities of large cities. Currier, a southerner transplanted to Manhattan, remembers the first time he heard about the disease that would take many of his friends, business associates, and lovers. "I clearly remember the day in Central Park," he writes in the *Lambda Book Report* (February 1999), "a summer morning in 1981, waiting to meet my friend Kevin and reading an item in the *New York Times* about a rare cancer being found in gay men. That morning is ingrained in my consciousness. My immediate reaction was one of confusion and skepticism, but I was also aware of being caught up in an historical moment, yet uncertain how the future would play itself out." He goes on to speak of being haunted by his first few friends who contracted the disease and by the fear that he remembers as he visited them. Like O'Brien in his concentration on themes of war, Currier finds himself writing about AIDS not only because its existence has been a central conflict to be dealt with in his life but because its stories are the stuff of literature.

Some readers may miss the fact that a flashback is framed by the activities of Adam's funeral. We are not explicitly told at the beginning that Adam is dead, and the reader might assume that the flowers are for someone who is still in the hospital after a long time. Rereading explains John's confusion and Danny's help. Still, the flashback does take us back to an earlier time, when Adam checks himself into a hospital as his disease moves into a more severe stage. Flowers are carried at the story's beginning, and we are told that Adam carries only his briefcase to the hospital. All of Adam's friends wind up carrying food to him, and the story ends with Danny carrying plates to the table as they get together after the funeral. They bring him things to read and changes of clothing to replace those he keeps throwing away. Danny carries lists of things to carry, mostly medicines and other items to help Adam feel better. He carries the most, eventually including items for his own needs as he stays by Adam's bed, even though John is Adam's partner. This seems to be because Danny has done this before. When Adam goes home, medical equipment is carried into the apartment, and paperwork and insurance forms are soon carried there as well. But some things that are carried are not physical. At first, everyone carries hope. Later, when a doctor speaks of people carrying the virus, Danny responds angrily that they know this: "It's the fear every gay man carries today." Finally, Danny carries the ashes of Adam's body, surprised at how heavy they seem.

Although Adam's disease brings about the major conflicts of the story, Danny seems to be the main character. Most readers will probably identify most closely with Danny, since we experience the story through his perspective. He is a hero of sorts, giving a great deal of time and energy with no apparent hope of reward. We tend to feel pity for Adam, who seems to bravely fight the disease. John is more problematic. We understand that he is grieving, but he seems to distance himself from Adam; it is Danny who is available. And Danny is there for John when Adam dies. Much is left out of the story. We wonder why Danny is so dedicated and why he has so much time to give. Why does John keep his distance? Where is Adam's mother during the illness? We know little of the other members of the circle of friends, but they seem supportive, and this may be what counts. The narrator is objective, telling the story in third person, but the point of view seems to be limited to Danny's perspective. We know his thoughts and feelings, but not those of other characters. This, and the lack of direct quotations, allows a distance that keeps the emotions of the story in check. We do not get bogged down in pathos, though it permeates the situation. Perhaps the writer intends for us to observe the impact of AIDS on a circle of friends and specifically on the caregiver. A first-person account or a narration that focused on Adam or John might cause us to see the disease as something affecting an individual or a couple rather than an interconnected community of people who care and try to help.

If Currier borrows O'Brien's idea about the physical and spiritual burdens of war, applying it to the battle against AIDS, he tempers it a bit. For example, he doesn't constantly repeat the phrase *They carried*, as O'Brien so effectively does. To do so would border on plagiarism, no matter how sincere the motive. Surely, Currier would have been aware of a book that was a finalist for the Pulitzer Prize and other major awards in 1990, only a few years before this story's publication. If he borrows the concept deliberately, the metaphor adds to Currier's story. Fighting AIDS is like fighting a nasty war, he implies, and the friends of the victim are the troops. And someone, like Lieutenant Cross or Danny, must be there to take the lead, to give up something to carry others.

Readers will accept or resist the characters of O'Brien's "The Things They Carried" and Currier's "What They Carried" based on their own biases, though some may protest that they are not prejudiced, *but.* . . . Listening to others in a discussion group may allow unconscious assumptions to surface. Cross's romantic vulnerability and his weeping with guilt may surprise readers who see soldiers as grim fighting machines, while the brutal aspects of war portrayed by O'Brien undercut sentimental views of "our boys overseas." People who see homosexuals as predatory and promiscuous exploiters may be surprised by the solidarity of the friendships and the altruistic actions of the caregiver described by Currier. Unexamined warrants may come to light as students discuss their emotional reactions to the two stories. The violent images and harsh language of O'Brien's narrative might offend some readers, preventing their involvement with the characters. They may, in fact, be repelled by the characters themselves and feel angry at O'Brien for portraying the soldiers of the Vietnam War in this way. Many of our current college students are the children of O'Brien's contemporaries and do not like to think of their fathers in this way. Others may recognize some of the realities of war for the first time, feeling compassion for soldiers who are about their age. Currier's characters are human beings surviving the death of a friend. Many readers have known people with catastrophic illnesses and can relate to the universal experience of losing someone to death. We can usually head off homophobic reactions by matter-of-factly introducing the story and tacitly setting the tone for a tolerant atmosphere. Although ignoring the issue of AIDS as a "gay disease" may go against the stance of Currier's narrative, each instructor has a sense of a particular class's dynamics and how much confrontation falls within his or her own comfort zone.

Imagining the End: A Collection of Writings by Emily Dickenson (p. 1448)

EMILY DICKINSON

I like a look of Agony, (p. 1448)

As instructors using *Making Literature Matter* in composition classes, we encourage students to discover analysis techniques that work for them. Students often have no idea how to begin. Some feel that only one correct way to approach a text must exist, and since they do not trust their own ideas, they lean too heavily on research or safe but superficial interpretation. To help young writers realize that analysis involves creativity and intellectual risk-taking, we often share our real-life writing tasks at different stages, assuring students by example that invention and organization involve personal choices. We want them to catch the excitement of becoming actively involved in reading, researching, and writing about literary and academic texts.

One of the writers of this instructor's manual shared her writing process for the entry on Emily Dickinson with a group of first-year composition students to help them understand how such decisions may take place with a real audience and purpose in mind. She emphasized to them that another writer would undoubtedly read Dickinson's poem from an entirely different point of view but that we all have an opportunity at college to enter into the academic dialogue already in progress and to make our voice heard. We cannot do this by simply repeating the received wisdom of experts. The surprising response of many students was that they simply did not realize they were "allowed" to explore their own original thoughts about a literary work. Written in an informal "I-Search" style, in the present tense, the remainder of this entry is one teacher's idiosyncratic approach.

In the midst of finding my way into Emily Dickinson, another part of my mind chews on how best to guide my freshman composition students in their current task of writing an argumentative research paper. They are having trouble choosing an issue to write about, narrowing it down, and finding their way into the research. I wonder how my process might inform theirs as I fish for my angle. So much has been written about Dickinson. How do I best serve the needs of my audience of college professors and adjunct lecturers and graduate teaching assistants without covering ground they may know more intimately than I do?

So as I nag my students to do, I begin by writing, starting with sentences that sound a bit like turning over the engine of a car on a cold winter morning. I've underlined the second line of each stanza of Dickinson's "I like a look of Agony" because these phrases seem to express a main idea or theme. The speaker of the poem — perhaps Dickinson but perhaps another persona — does not like hypocrisy. I have done some background reading on Dickinson, as I have instructed my students to do on their topics, and I know that the poet valued intellectual honesty, especially in religion. I know that she resisted the sort of Christian conversion that demands a total renunciation of self in return for the promise of victory over death, even though most of her friends and family publicly made this religious commitment and urged her to do the same.

As I think about how to present this text to students, I realize that many have been brought up in fundamentalist religions much like Dickinson's, though 1990s culture is not permeated with religion in the way that Amherst, Massachusetts, was in the poet's time. I know that Emily Dickinson lived from 1830 to 1886, an era when many people died young of diseases like tuberculosis and women were expected to maintain a watch over the dying. And I know that she often wrote about death, though she wrote about many other issues as well. I've also read about her love of metaphor, what she called telling things "slant." From reading other Dickinson poems I know that the poet herself is not always identical to the speaker in the poem. So I go back to the poem again, with this in mind.

This time, I notice the word *Convulsion* in the third line. It strikes me as odd that the speaker says people "do not sham Convulsion." I'd just been looking through the index of a biography of the poet, searching for the word *conversion*, along with other words that might help me find pages that discuss her attitude toward religion and death. The words are so similar that they raise an issue for me. People cannot pretend *convulsion*, but under circumstances like the fervent revival meetings that took place regularly in Dickinson's church, family, and schools when she was in her teens, a person could be mightily tempted to fake a *conversion*, if for no other reason than to get everyone off her back. Could the poet be playing with the configuration and phonetic echoes of the two words, punning or otherwise counting on the connotations of one working with the other, with most readers subliminally absorbing the "slant" vibrations between the two? If I were writing an argumentative research paper, I would now have an issue about which I could make an assertion.

As I think about the issue of Dickinson and her deliberate decision to resist the surrender of autonomy that comes with conversion, it strikes me that the voice of the poem might be an ironic persona, expressing her idea of a perverse and unloving God's attitude toward death and suffering. From what I have read, I believe that I could make a case for this interpretation. At this point, if I were going on to write an argumentative research paper on this poem, I would direct my reading toward its being Dickinson's ironic protest against a God who demands suffering and death. One critic has described the voice in this poem as "almost a hysterical shriek." Reasonable people may disagree! I think it is an ironically defiant mockery of either God or the angel of death. Given this, how might I refute the characterization of Dickinson's poem as *hysterical* — a word full of pejorative, sexist connotations?

First, I would point out that the word is loaded and that the critic's assertion is inconsistent with what we know of the poet's wry humor and defiance of death. I would try to find evidence of other times that Dickinson takes an ironic tone in relation to death and times when her content is boldly heretical. I would keep in mind my first reaction, that Dickinson does not like hypocrisy any more than God does, but would argue that she often hides behind the protective coloration of metaphor. I'd have to work out the seeming inconsistencies of this statement, perhaps arguing that Dickinson knows she cannot fool God and simply throws his absurdity back in his face. She is totally honest with God, herself, and any reader who cares to discover the joke. One Dickinson biographer makes the point that Dickinson believed in the existence of God because she was convinced by evidence of design in the physical universe but that for equally logical reasons she had difficulty believing God has humankind's best interests at heart. To Dickinson, the evidence of suffering and death supports the thesis that the designs of God, as interpreted by Protestant theology, are less than loving.

Whether the poem is a "hysterical shriek," a satire describing a harsh god's view of suffering and death, or the sincere though brutal imagery of an honest woman who has seen many people die, the speaker's attitude toward hypocrisy is clear. Taken at face value, the poem seems monstrous, but there is something to be said for reaching the point where pretense is shed. If the tone is ironic, the agonizing deaths of the Civil War are simply historically specific examples of exactly what the poet is talking about. Is agony the price of authenticity for this speaker?

The poet capitalizes most of the nouns. By doing this, she implies personification in some cases: "Agony," "Convulsion," "Throe," "Death," and "Anguish" become entities. They also become emphasized as emblems or symbols, as do "Eyes" and "Beads upon the Forehead." They seem to shout or stand out on the page. The first stanza describes pain and critical sickness or injury; the second stanza takes one step further and describes death itself. Anguish is described in the second stanza " homely." This word, and others in the poem, may have both denotations and connotations that are unfamiliar to students, and we might look them up in small groups in different dictionaries. In the first definition in most dictionaries, *homely* denotes unattractiveness. However, since the speaker claims to "like a look of Agony" and other forthright manifestations of suffering and death, the secondary definitions may be more apt: "simple; plain; or unpretentious" — even "comfortable in the manner of home; cozy."

We might be reminded of the women of Dickinson's day, who sat up with dying relatives in the home and then prepared the body for burial. We may picture Anguish as a grieving aunt or sister, keeping her hands busy in the death watch, placing beads one by one on a string as she patiently waits, and finally placing them on the dead face. The image may refer to the beads of perspiration that might linger after a sick person has finished a death struggle. If Dickinson were Catholic, we might think of a rosary, since this would be an appropriate emblem to place with the dead. On first reading, we might expect the image of death to end the poem, and readers may fault the last two lines as anticlimactic. On closer reading, however, we may see the honest sweat that clings to the body after death — put there by authentic, down-to-earth anguish — as an appropriate concluding image.

EMILY DICKINSON

I've seen a Dying Eye (p. 1450)

Emily Dickinson observed death from multiple perspectives in her poetry. In the well-known poem that begins "My Life had stood — a Loaded Gun — " the speaker may be the angel of death himself, according to some critics. In many of her poems, including the two that follow "I've seen a Dying Eye" (pp. 1450, 1452), the speaker is the person who has died. In "I've seen a Dying Eye" the narrator observes as a person who looks frantically around the room as he or she dies. It has been pointed out that the phonetic coincidence between the word *eye* and the first-person pronoun *I* is sometimes used by Dickinson to evoke a double meaning when speaking of death. When the eyes close for the final time, this also signals the end of the "I," the human individual that Dickinson values so highly.

In an era when people usually died at home under the watch of the women of the house, Dickinson had seen many close friends and relatives as they lay dying. Her letters to family members often include lists of the sick and dying or accounts of the deaths of friends, including the young woman who had been her college roommate at Mount Holyoke Seminary. Of an age-mate who died when they were thirteen, Dickinson wrote a friend two years later,

> There she lay mild & beautiful as in health & her pale features lit up with an unearthly — smile. I looked as long as friends would permit & when they told I must weep no longer, I let them lead me away. I shed no tear, for my heart was too full to weep, but after she was laid in her coffin & I felt I could not call her back again I gave way to a fixed melancholy.

Poetry may have been Dickinson's way of dealing with this close acquaintance with death and dying.

"I've seen a Dying Eye" tells as much about the speaker as it does about the person who dies. We do not know what the dying person searches for as he or she looks intently around the room. The effect as the speaker describes it is desperate, purposeful, but helpless. The dying eye does not seem to find what it seeks. The speaker does not flinch. Like the thirteen-year-old Emily Dickinson, who must be led from the room by the adults as her friend lies on her deathbed, the narrator of the poem observes the stages, not looking away until the eyes are "soldered down" — welded shut forever. Some might find this attitude morbid, ghoulish, or sick. Others might find it brave, honest, and realistic. Perhaps the speaker simply reveals a probing, curious mind that wants to know the whole business of death. She observes with an almost scientific detachment. The active verb *run* describes the eye, not the dying person. The contrast creates a tension between dying and searching for something or someone just before death. This seems to be something important to the dying person in the speaker's view. Her language makes it seem as if this search is something the narrator may have seen more than once.

Part of the mystery of death is that we do not know and the dead person can never tell. This seems to be the point of the poem. The poet does not make clear whether the blessing comes to the dying eye. There is no smile, which perhaps means both the speaker and the dying person are left unfulfilled. The *m* sounds are clustered in the middle of the poem as the search comes to an end and the vision is obscured. This is the moment of dying, and perhaps the hum describes the last breath, like the sound of a fly buzzing that we will hear in the next poem of this cluster. "I've seen a Dying Eye" focuses on vision throughout, however. The word *seen* of the first line is repeated in the last, but the perspective is quite different. At the poem's outset, the verb describes the keen observation of the speaker, whereas its use in the final line occurs within a verbal structure that leaves unclear whether the dying person has *seen* anything or not. The movement of vision in the poem follows the same progression as death, from clarity to obscurity.

The eye darting around the room in "I've seen a Dying Eye" seems to be more conscious and purposeful than the look of agony described in the previous poem in this cluster. This eye searches for "Something," whereas the person in "I like a look of Agony," seems absorbed in his or her dying rather than looking around. The word *look* is ambiguous. The narrator of "I like a look of Agony," seems to like the way the dying person appears, the sincerity of the look of death, not the way the person looks around the room. A case might be made for either interpretation. The moment of death itself seems the same, however. One poem describes the way the eyes "glaze," and the other says that the eyes "obscure with Fog," both implying the end of the ability to see. Both death scenes are vivid, and the people who are dying have business to do. The differences are subtle, but the death scene in "I like a look of Agony," seems more violent, and its dying protagonist seems to be busy with the illness itself. The dying person in "I've seen a Dying Eye" looks outside of herself, and we do not know why — perhaps for help, perhaps to search out the angel of death, perhaps to find a familiar face or to take care of unfinished business with the living.

EMILY DICKINSON

I heard a Fly buzz — when I died — (p. 1450)

Like the two poems that precede it in this cluster, "I heard a Fly buzz — when I died — " catches its subject at the moment of death. But whereas the other poems show the dying person from the perspective of an observer, this one lets us into the mind of the person who dies. The image of the fly subverts any romanticizing of death. Rather than flights of angels or something else as elegant and high-minded, the poet gives us an image that conjures up absurd and down-to-earth connotations. We do not see the painful death throes of "I like a look of Agony" (p. 1448) or hear the serious tone of "I've seen a Dying Eye" (p. 1450). For people of the nineteenth century, the fly could be a homey, everyday image. A children's song of the time was "Baby-bye, Here's a Fly" in which a mother playfully invites her child to watch a fly with her. A fly is a trivial irritation that one might brush away. It has no sting. But the fly can have other connotations as well. We associate it with decay and physical death, and a biblical demon is named Beelzebub, the Lord of the Flies. The humming sound of the fly in this poem may remind readers of the *m* sounds that we noted in "I've seen a Dying Eye" just at the moment of death. "I heard a Fly buzz — when I died — " could be a companion piece to the preceding poem, providing a view from the deathbed to explain the observations of the watcher. The progression is similar, and the buzz of the fly may be the source of a noise that the dying eye seeks before the vision is finally obscured and she cannot "see to see."

Because the poem minimizes both the horror and the romanticism of dying, some readers will find a grim humor in it, almost a ridiculing of death as something insignificant that we might brush away from our face. The understatement implied in the calm voice that speaks of death as a failure of vision lends an ironic tone that some will read as amusing. Rather than giving us an inside view of the look of agony described in an earlier poem, the speaker relates the business of making a will, though this may be meant symbolically. Death seems rather prosaic here. Others will find the poem horrifying and oppressive. The juxtaposition of the fly with death may call up images of rotting bodies. They will note the deadly stillness in the room and the onlookers steeling themselves for the end. Part of the poem's irony is the use of the dead person as a speaker. Literal-minded people may find this too improbable. Others will argue, however, that we do not know at what point death actually comes or what it is like. It may be that Dickinson, with her intimate acquaintance and keen introspection about death, makes as good a guess as any.

The repetition of the word *stillness* in the first stanza explicitly communicates the sort of feeling some of us have experienced in the eye of a hurricane. We can feel the weight of the air and perhaps are reminded of the stillness that awaits in the heavy airlessness of the coffin. The word denotes an absence of both movement and of noise and is a uniquely appropriate word to use in connection with death. The word *see* also has a double meaning, referring to both vision and understanding or logical thinking. For Dickinson, loss of the "eye" and loss of the "I" — the self — are related. When the speaker says she "could not see to see," she may mean that she no longer has the vision to engage in rational thought. This loss of conscious self is death.

The poet frames the business of death that relates to the others in the room, the living, with the actual dying of the first and last stanza where she hears the fly. The middle stanzas convey a different sort of reality, the part that concerns the living. This provides a sort of flashback to earlier observations and even earlier activities. It provides suspense of the sort that we saw in earlier poems before the eyes glaze over, but it allows the actual dying to be a personal experience. Death here is not *about* the survivors, and it is a profoundly different experience for this speaker than for the witnesses of the preceding poems.

To refer to the eyes as the windows of the soul may have been a cliché even in the 1860s, and to argue that the final image of the poem is such a metaphor may be an oversimplification, though it is often read in just this way. Dickinson may use the obscured view implied when the "Windows failed" to be consistent with the image of the fly. Most readers have seen a fly beating itself against a window to get out. Perhaps the windows give way to the fly, allowing the dying person to break past the barrier between life and death. In a similar poem "I felt a Funeral, in my Brain" the speaker experiences her own funeral, with the final stanza implying a similar crash, this time through "a Plank in Reason." The poem ends as does "I heard a Fly buzz — when I died — ," with one of Dickinson's enigmatic dashes. Because the poems are so closely related in persona and theme, some readers might find it interesting to compare and contrast the two. In both, the loss of vision may be important, but the loss of reason seems to concern the poet most.

The difference in point of view between this poem and the two preceding ones produces an ironic effect. "I like a look of Agony" is horrible to read, its speaker perhaps an evil God who glories in the authenticity of the death struggle. "I've seen a Dying Eye" is more compassionate but still evokes pathos for the dying person. It is difficult to feel sorry for the matter-of-fact narrator of her own death in "I heard a Fly buzz — when I died — " because we hear her tell her own story. The last line is poignant but not horrifying. Like a place we have read about for years and finally visited, death has an everyday quality when seen from this more familiar perspective.

Most Christian readers will assume that the king is Jesus Christ, since he is sometimes called the King of Kings in the Bible. If the poem had been published in the Amherst, Massachusetts, of her time, Dickinson might have kept her silence and allowed this safe interpretation. But most Dickinson scholars think that the title probably refers to a personified angel of death or death itself. Some might read this as the "Something" that the dying person searches for in the room in "I like a look of Agony."

The poet's use of "eyes" in all three poems of this cluster is consistent with her connections between vision and the ability to think. Dickinson insisted on her own vision, her own independent worldview. When a person dies, he or she loses vision in this symbolic sense. If this poem was written in the early 1860s, as it is usually dated, Dickinson was experiencing some frightening vision problems, almost going blind. The thought of not being able to read was horrifying to her. Perhaps this threat to her access to texts and the critical thinking they provoked explains her linking of literal and figurative vision in her poetry. Her focus in these death poems on vision and on stilled breath peels away the things of the body, focusing our gaze on the essentials of death — the loss of voice and the power to see, to understand.

EMILY DICKINSON

Because I could not stop for Death — (p. 1452)

In 1847, when Emily Dickinson was sixteen years old, a friend just a few years older, Olivia Coleman, died from complications of tuberculosis. This happened as Olivia was taking a carriage ride. Perhaps the memory of this death, one of many among Dickinson's friends and relatives, underlies the imagery of "Because I could not stop for Death — ." It is perhaps her most anthologized poem, and many students will have read it in high school.

The poem describes a courtship or, more likely, a marriage. It has been popular in recent years in our town for the bride and groom to ride from their wedding to the reception in a horse-drawn carriage. Royal weddings in England may also come to mind. Readers may also recall images from state funerals in which a carriage carries the body to a place of burial. Although readers a century and a half distant from Dickinson have no everyday associations with carriage rides as the poet would have had, perhaps our images are even more appropriate to the poem. Weddings and funerals are ceremonial occasions, and we understand the sort of "Civility" that ironically accompanies these most dramatic of events. When a death in the family takes place, we tend to be surprised for a while that life goes on, that children still play and the sun is still in the sky. The allegory of the believer as the bride of Christ may also be implied in the poem. Some readers see Death as merely the driver of the carriage, with the bride going to wait for the bridegroom who will come to receive his bride at a later time. By this interpretation, she is still waiting at the poem's end. The speaker does not reveal any strong feelings about this. Though the poem implies no horror, the speaker's eerie passiveness equally denies ecstasy.

The active life implied in the first line sharply contrasts with the timelessness and stillness of the final stanza. As early as the fifth line, we find the elongating of time. And we are given to understand the change in the speaker from busy movement to total stillness when she reverses her perception of the sun's movement between the third and fourth stanzas. At first she speaks of the sun's standing still as she passes it, then corrects herself to describe the transformed reality: it is she who is stopped in place. Like an observer who watches a moving train and feels as if she herself is moving, though actually standing still, the poem's speaker realizes that the world is literally passing her by.

Immortality is personified in the poem but seems a strangely static character. If the speaker is immortal, it may be because time no longer has the same meaning. Centuries of death do not contain as much time as one day of life. Some may read the final stanza as an expression of contentment of a time-flies-when-we're-having-fun quality. Others may argue that this person who so filled her time that she could not stop for death is now cheated of both time and activity, a reading that rejects the implied optimism of a romantic view of death as a contented marriage. The adjectives that readers choose to describe their images of death in the poem will depend on their interpretation of the poem as optimistic, perhaps even Christian, or as an ironic challenge to this traditional view. The speaker has "passed" away, and the poem describes the things she has passed in her passing: the school, the fields, and the sun. But each is described oddly. Rather than seeing the children at the school as they played, the speaker remembers that they "strove," a word implying struggle. Rather than gazing at the grain in the field, she sees the grain as gazing at the carriage as the passing takes place. And she realizes that it is the sun that moves rather than the carriage. All that she passes contrasts with her new position as one who can no longer strive, see, or move. This is not a marriage she has chosen, but she has lost the vital powers she needs for resistance.

The grave is a house in the last two stanzas, continuing the extended metaphor of death as a wedding procession. At thirty-three, Dickinson would have been considered in her day to be a spinster, an old maid too old for marriage. She had seen many deaths of people younger than herself. Current college readers may consider her to be about the right age for marriage, certainly too young to die. There is no warmth to this macabre marriage. Some might find it comforting. Others will question as overly sentimental the assumptions that find a happy ending here.

The death described here, unlike those of the earlier three poems in this cluster, is sudden. The dying protagonists of "I like a look of Agony," "I've seen a Dying Eye," and "I heard a Fly buzz — when I died — " die in the presence of witnesses who observe the stages of death. They have business to deal with — going through the agonies of sickness, searching the room with frantic eyes, making wills — so perhaps the difference is one of perspective. Here, death is a journey that takes place outside of the sickroom. Perhaps the protagonist actually dies on a carriage ride, as Olivia Coleman had many years before at the young age of twenty. Perhaps, like the speaker of "I heard a Fly buzz — when I died — ," her experience of dying has a different focus from that assumed by her observers.

Unlike the other deaths, this one involves the whole body, and we have a change in perspective rather than a blurring of vision. Some readers will find this incompatible with the descriptions of death in the earlier poems. Others might argue that the first two lines of "Because I could not stop for Death — " summarize the experience described in the earlier poems. Now we are beyond the actual dying, journeying to the place death takes us to. Perhaps the journey described here takes place at the time vision blurs in the earlier poems. The images of this poem are sunnier, but we also feel the chill of death. A case could be made for this poem's metaphor being even more horrible than the honest imagery of the earlier poems. It is difficult to see the Dickinson of the earlier poems really meaning us to take it at face value.

Students are entitled to their favorites, but they should examine their reasons for ranking certain poems higher than the others. "Because I could not stop for Death — " will be the favorite of many because they find it more optimistic. Experienced readers often like it the least, finding it a true horror story, much like William Faulkner's "A Rose for Emily" (p. 969) or other stories that reek of necrophilia.

CONFRONTING THE DEATH OF A STRANGER (p. 1454)

KATHERINE MANSFIELD

The Garden-Party (p. 1455)

Like most young people, the main character of Katherine Mansfield's short story "The Garden-Party" is in the midst of constructing her view of reality and finding her place in the social structure of her society. The music, the clothing, the activities, and the attitudes that surround her all contribute to Laura's developing worldview, deliberately and subliminally telling her who to be and what to believe. In the world in which the garden party takes place, reality has a predetermined order that remains unquestioned by most of the characters. They accept the social constructs as givens and do not examine the reasons underlying class-determined behavior. This world is not unlike the colonial hierarchies of the New Zealand of Mansfield's childhood. The British empire imposed its own structure on the lives of its colonized peoples, and the lines between social classes continue to rule manners among the children and grandchildren of settlers. A garden, with its courteously blooming roses, its potted lilies, and its manmade constructions obscuring the karaka trees, symbolizes the taming of nature by the hand of "civilization."

Mansfield, in her life if not her fiction, resisted this imposition of societal rules. An early marriage lasted only twenty-four hours, and two affairs resulted in miscarriage or abortion. She lived with John Middleton Murry for several years before their marriage in 1918. By this time, she had manifested the tuberculosis and heart disease from which she died in 1923 at the age of thirty-four. Although she spent her adult life in England and other European locations, she recalled her South Pacific childhood with pleasure. Like the protagonist of "The Garden-Party," she grew up with sisters and shared a special bond with her brother, Leslie Beauchamp, whose early death she felt as a great loss.

Although she read and wrote about her contemporaries in the early modernist movement, enjoying T. S. Eliot but finding James Joyce vulgar, Mansfield — like the later student of middle-class manners, Raymond Carver — was most influenced by the Russian master of characterization, Anton Chekhov. Writing to her husband just weeks before her death, Mansfield may have been referring as much to herself as to Chekhov: "We know he felt his stories were not half what they might be. It doesn't take much imagination to picture him on his deathbed thinking, 'I have never had a real chance. Something has been all wrong.'"

Students, like critics, will interpret Laura's reaction to death differently, since her newly found definition of "life" is left unfinished. Many readers find her shallow, seeing Laura as fixed in the unreality of romanticism. The woman at the dead man's house has perhaps expected to shock the young aristocrat by forcing her to look at the body; Mansfield describes the woman's movement as "sly." Instead, Laura sees him through the same glowing filter through which she has earlier seen the workers in the garden. Her reaction recalls the sentimental Victorian song her sister sings earlier with no thought to the meaning of its words, and our discussions will gain much from a consideration of the lyrics. The prosperous family members have no understanding of how "weary" life might be for those who do the actual labor of their household and seem able to interpret life only in relation to their own concerns. This superficiality also includes Laura.

At the story's beginning, Laura indulges in poses and generalizes romantic views of the workers as they go about their work and she plays at directing them. In the grieving household, she must appear as incongruously decorative as the trappings of the party. But there are hints that she recognizes this, as she asks the corpse to "forgive" her hat, and she makes assumptions throughout the story that reveal her view of the workers as people with feelings similar to her own. Although she sees her family as "heartless" in having the party despite the man's death, she too may seem to some readers to have very little substance at her core. She is easily distracted from her empathy by her own appearance in the new hat. The implication of the word *heartless* may be that the upper-class family live on the surface because they are hollow, lacking in real emotions. Some readers will maintain that it would be unrealistic for the family to change their plans because a worker has died, arguing that Laura is romantic and impractical. Warrants may reveal attitudes about social class but may also be related to experiences with death and varying ways in which subcultures and families deal with it.

Laura clumsily tries to ignore class distinctions, but her efforts are naive, since the workers and their families have their own concerns. She exaggerates her own importance to them. They look at her "queerly," and a woman speaks to her with an "oily" voice. Although she fantasizes that they are more natural, making much of one worker's sniffing a sprig of lavender, a worker suggests placing the marquee in front of the karaka trees, hiding their natural beauty. Some students might point out that if the family had called the party to a halt, it would be at best a hollow gesture, and the band, at least, would be out of a job. Despite its title, the story shows little of the party itself, since the events that affect its protagonist occur in the encounters with workers that take place before and after the party.

We see the family's attitudes toward the people they consider inferiors, there for their own comfort and amusement; for example, a household servant is referred to fondly as "good little Hans" and the band is laughingly compared to frogs. We are told that Laura's sister Jose "loved giving orders to the servants, and they loved obeying her. She always made them feel they were taking part in some drama." This contrasts sharply with Laura's naive, democratic fantasies, which make everyone uncomfortable. Although readers may applaud her intentions, it is unclear whether Laura will grow beyond her immature attempts at finding common values with the people across the road to a philosophy based on true respect. In the long run, the story is *about* the impact of the working class on the consciousness of an aristocratic character. She tells her brother that her confrontation with mortality has been "simply marvelous," a comment that seems to trivialize the death of a human being, turning it into a learning experience for a silly girl. However, at the point when language fails her, Laura may reveal the dynamism of her character: no longer able to reduce life to romantic cliché, she is silenced by its complexity.

GABRIEL GARCÍA MÁRQUEZ

The Handsomest Drowned Man in the World (p. 1465)

In 1955, a small Colombian destroyer ran into heavy seas on its return to Cartagena. Several sailors were swept overboard and lost, and all died except one, who survived for ten days at sea, clinging to a life raft. When he eventually washed ashore, the castaway became a national hero. The government of dictator Gustavo Rojas Pinella immediately claimed him for propaganda purposes. The man traveled the country making speeches and starred in advertisements for watches and shoes. Eventually, however, a guilty conscience led the sailor to confess that the cargo of his ship had been contraband and the sailors had fallen overboard through their own incompetence. There had been no storm. When the story was offered to *El Spectador*, a newspaper in Bogotá, the assignment fell to Gabriel García Márquez to act as the ghostwriter of a serialized narrative. The dictator was furious, and García Márquez's editor felt that it was time for his reporter to serve for a time as a European correspondent. Soon after this, the government shut down his newspaper, but by this time García Márquez was beginning to see his fiction published.

Considering the surreal nature of most of his work, it is interesting to read that this master of magical realism says that his starting point for any story must be a *real fact*. Although he includes texts that he has read as real facts — for example, the flying carpets and genies of *The Thousand and One Nights* — he insists that such adventures correspond somehow to real-life experiences. His grandfather's experiences in the Banana Wars and his grandmother's superstitious tales equally serve as material for his fictional worlds. Readers could make a case for "The Handsomest Drowned Man in the World" as prompted by the real facts of the sailor's tale first written as nonfiction in *El Spectador*. Beyond the bare fact that a man has been washed up on shore, however, the fictional tale may owe more to the reception the sailor received. Like the drowned man of the story, whose character and narrative are imagined by the villagers, the surviving sailor became a text to be read and rewritten by the government, the adoring populace, and finally the newspaper reporter.

Like its companion story "A Very Old Man with Enormous Wings," in which a winged man appears after a storm, "The Handsomest Drowned Man in the World" is subtitled "A Tale for Children." Both stories may have elements inspired by the lurid, superstitious tales the writer heard from the grandmother with whom he spent his first eight years in the coastal Colombian town of Aracataca. He confesses that her stories so frightened him that he was afraid for a time to venture outside the house. These were the folktales of *mestizos* and *costeños*, racially and culturally mixed descendents of Spanish pirates, African slaves, and indigenous peoples of the Caribbean coast of northern South America — an ethnic heritage García Márquez wears with pride.

His subtitle is certainly ironic. These are stories that question the warrants of adults as they seek to read the strange, new text of a godlike drowned man or a winged ancient, and children would perhaps have nightmares or, at best, would be unlikely to understand them. Yet the real irony may be that because he was not protected from such tales, the frightened little boy grew up to become a Nobel laureate. He has related the breakthrough that led to his mature style when he realized on a trip out of town that the key to the narrative he wanted to write should be the perfectly deadpan style of his grandmother as she told the most incredible of tales. He turned around, went home, and began to write like a madman. This matter-of-fact acceptance of the most unlikely of circumstances is the essence of magical realism.

In "The Handsomest Drowned Man in the World" the appearance of the dead man is presented as a fact. The story is about the unfolding reactions of the villagers to him. All are in awe of his size and manliness, and we are told that after they see his face, their imaginations cannot contain him. As the women lovingly clean and clothe him for burial, he becomes an object of desire as they compare their husbands unfavorably with him. They give him the name *Esteban* — Stephen — the name of the first Christian martyr, who in Acts 6:15 is portrayed as having the face of an angel as he preaches the new religion in the temple just before the mob stones him for blasphemy. The first African man named as a traveler to the Caribbean, perhaps a symbolic ancestor for the writer, is also *Esteban*.

Whatever the name's significance, the women have given him further definition by giving him a name. They come to love him for his vulnerability, now seeing him as like their husbands. The men are equally awed, but as the women delay, they become jealous and call him names that degrade and dehumanize him. However, even the men come to love him. At the beginning and later at the end, he is compared to a whale, and they come to pity him, seeing him as ashamed and sincere. Readers may be reminded of Herman Melville's *Moby-Dick*, a text quite familiar to García Márquez, in which the whale becomes a symbol for characters and readers alike. The drowned man becomes a kinsman to the villagers, forever identified with the town. Like a god — or a text — he becomes a mirror reflecting the people who interpret him. This is not unlike the funerals of friends and relatives; sometimes we hardly recognize the person we knew as we listen to the various glosses on his or her life.

There is a great deal of ironic humor, almost slapstick comedy, in the story. The godlike creature is an object of awe, but the children play at burying and reburying him in the sand, the women imagine householders fearing that he will break their chairs, and the doting women almost make the men trip over him as they delay the parting with their big toy. At first, the children even think he is a ship! The manner of telling is realistic, and the villagers seem naïve but believable, but the drowned man is fantastic. Long sentences give a breathless quality to the prose. For example, after the one-sentence paragraph in which the women praise the Lord that the drowned man has not been claimed by another village and thus belongs to them, much of paragraph 8 is made up of one long sentence in which the women delay and the men get irritated. We are told at the paragraph's end that "the men were left breathless too," and the style models this breathlessness.

At a recent funeral, the minister made the statement that the woman being buried had died peacefully because no mortician could have artificially placed such an expression on her face. Some of his listeners knew, however, the distress that her husband had felt when he saw the distortions of her face in the hospital after the medical team's strenuous efforts to resuscitate her. The clergyman's interpretation revealed more about his own views or perhaps his purpose in comforting mourners than they revealed about the manner of the woman's death. Much the same thing happens as the characters of Katherine Mansfield's "The Garden-Party" (p. 1455) and García Márquez's "The Handsomest Drowned Man in the World" view the dead.

In both stories, the observers of the dead engage in idealistic fantasies. Readers whose warrants involve the view of death as a rest from one's labors may find Laura's view sensible. Others may see her reaction as similar to her earlier submerged attraction to the worker who smells the lavender. To find the reactions of the villagers sensible requires that the reader enter the fantastic world of the story. We assume that there must be some good reason behind all of the villagers seeing Esteban as desirable in some way, but we also realize that the story may be about the projection of desire onto the blank page of the dead man's face. The villagers are forever affected by their encounter with the drowned man, since they are now identified with him; their village is now Esteban's village. We are not as certain about Laura, since the story ends ambiguously. Perhaps her new understanding of the complexity of life will keep her from conforming to the social distinctions and shallow selfishness that characterize her mother and sisters.

At the garden party of Mansfield's story, even the flowers defer to the upper-class family. Roses bloom on cue. Lavender can be plucked from the lawn. There is a "lily lawn," and the mother has even more lilies brought in. Even

Laura's hat is flowered. She realizes instinctively that taking the flowers to the house of mourners will be pretentious on top of the "scraps" from the party. As Laura looks at the body, she knows that he has no need of flowers. By contrast, the seacoast village is barren of flowers, is like a desert. But neighbors bring flowers for Esteban's funeral, and later the villagers paint their houses bright colors and plant so many flowers on the cliffs that people far out to sea can smell their aroma and see the sunflowers. The whole village has come to life.

DON DeLILLO

Videotape (p. 1470)

When John F. Kennedy was killed in 1963, Americans felt for the first time the full impact of television in creating the shared experiences that define a culture. A generation now middle-aged and older can recall exactly where we were when the news came. Although we did not see Kennedy's death at that time — the Zapruder film was released later — many of us saw Jack Ruby's killing of Lee Harvey Oswald as it happened. Later, after viewing the videotape of the parade made from the film — women wearing head scarves milling about, the blow to the head, the wife in her pink suit reacting in panic — many of us think we have a memory of the scene itself. Not only is the videotape real to us, it seems somehow more real than living memory, has the official stamp of reality on it. It is hard evidence that we can go back and verify, unlike our own experiences, by comparison vague impressions with the quality of dream about them. Walker Percy wrote about the phenomenon in his 1961 novel *The Moviegoer.* Describing a scene in which a young man lights movie star William Holden's cigarette, Percy tells us, "The boy has done it! He has won the title to his own existence, as plenary an existence now as Holden's. . . . An aura of heightened reality moves with him and all who fall within it feel it."

In the forty years or so since Percy's novel and Zapruder's grainy film, the power of the visual image has continued to increase exponentially. Today, the twenty-four-hour news channels on cable television compete for images in the wake of school shootings and bombings in Israel and Afghanistan. We weep at the funeral services of children we have never met and ache for homeless refugees. The beheading of a journalist is videotaped by his murderers and released for television and Internet viewing. A few years ago we watched Rodney King beaten by police officers, and we argued about the guilt or innocence of O. J. Simpson, whose dead ex-wife we know on a first-name basis. Dr. Jack Kevorkian assisted at the suicide of a man on a weekly television newsmagazine and was convicted of second-degree murder for doing so. Audiences watched the man die. The boys who murdered classmates at Columbine and then killed themselves are said to have been inspired by images from video games, German techno-rock, and the Internet.

News analysts debate how censorship can protect kids, but electronic images have become the materials from which we construct our reality, determine common sense, and explain our judgments of the world. Don DeLillo writes most of his fiction about the power of the image to dominate reality. His novel *Libra* retells the Lee Harvey Oswald story, the first major example of the bizarre, unreal reality of the televised news event. The short story "Videotape" examines the effects of this easily accessible technology of the image on its audience.

As digital technology advances, students will probably see videotape as only a step along the way, as dated as cassette tapes have become in the days of compact discs. But DeLillo's point may be less about the technology itself than about easy access to the creation of images that are forever fixed and about the impact of such images on the audience. The story points out that the creation of videotapes no longer belongs exclusively to trained cameramen supervised by directors. This gives the videotaped point of view vivid authenticity. Having said this, however, we should note that computer technology in which images may be altered, morphed into forms that never existed in the real world, may lead to a questioning of the image. Seeing is no longer believing when editing takes over.

Readers might judge the narrator to be unusually morbid and nothing like themselves. The need to look tragedy in the face may be human nature, however. He philosophizes about the nature of videotape, speaking almost as a literary critic. He says that it makes children "see things twice," that it defines, that it can have a "jostled sort of noneventness." He views the victim as an actor, mentioning his "underplayed reaction" as he waves nonchalantly to the child. He discusses suspense and the event's lack of accompaniment. The death has become a drama by virtue of the medium of its telling.

The narrator assumes that the audience shares common assumptions and reactions with him and repeats the direct address "You know" to establish common ground. Having a child as the creator of the videotape gives the event an added horror, since we imagine the effect on the young witness who, as the narrator has pointed out, sees this horrible thing twice. Imagining her emotions makes it more real to the narrator.

He wants his wife to witness it with him and speculates about his reasons for doing this. He is absorbed by the tape's authenticity. Like Walker Percy in *The Moviegoer*, DeLillo has his narrator ponder the nature of the reproduced and fixed image: "The tape is supperreal, or maybe underreal. . . . The tape has a searing realness." Videotape is significant for its recurring quality; the viewer can rewind and rerun it again and again. The serial killer is a particularly apt sort of murderer to appear on videotape, since his crime has a similar recurring quality, is like a taped-and-played event. The story itself is much like a videotaped documentary in which the narrator interweaves commentary with the visual images of the tape. However, it more closely resembles a movie review in its synthesis of criticism and textual evidence, although it is a brutally personal one.

The settings of the three stories in this cluster are extremely different. Katherine Mansfield (p. 1455) sets her garden party in a realistic setting, suffused with the romantic glow of its young protagonist's point of view as she sorts out issues of social class and the manners surrounding death. Gabriel García Márquez (p. 1465) provides a setting appropriate to the magical realism genre in which he writes; the setting is realistic enough, though exotic to most readers, but the events have a fairy-tale quality, as his subtitle allows. Setting in DeLillo's story is confined to the videotape and its double audience, the narrator and the child as he imagines her. Ironically, because it is closer in time and experience to current readers, DeLillo's taped event may seem most real. Although most of us have never seen a murder, we have witnessed thousands in the way that DeLillo's narrator describes this one. Not every story that includes children is a tale *for* children, though we may argue that García Márquez means his title ironically.

All of these stories assume a sophisticated audience able to catch the irony and fill in the gaps of the text. Both DeLillo and García Márquez may in fact be writing about how we interpret texts, bringing our own character and emotions into the reading. Dead bodies are palimpsests, like old parchments that have been written on, layer after layer. Since they cannot speak for themselves, we fill in the gaps with our projections, our unquestioned warrants and assumptions. The characters of the three stories in this cluster write their own lives onto the silent image of the corpse, revealing themselves by their interpretations. The less we know about the dead person, the more the living characters tell us about themselves.

DISRESPECTING DEATH (p. 1475)

JOHN DONNE

Death Be Not Proud (p. 1476)

As an Anglican priest who was a contemporary of William Shakespeare, John Donne wrote sermons, satires, and a great many highly original poems. His major themes are religion, love, and death. His *Holy Sonnets*, considered his most skilled work, reflect these concerns. Like many of Donne's poems, "Death Be Not Proud" personifies an abstract concept, death, in the kind of extended metaphor called a *conceit*. The sonnet is constructed as a rhetorical argument, a refutation of the power of death. Addressing death directly, the speaker summons his evidence with an analogy comparing death to rest and sleep, something that human beings welcome. What's more, death is the final agent of the soul's *delivery*, its deliverance to God or perhaps its final rebirth. He goes on to characterize death as a mere tool of other powers and ends his argument with the paradox that because the Christian wakes to eternal life, death itself will die.

Death was an ever-present reality for the people of Renaissance England, and Donne had experienced the deaths of many family members. The wife he passionately loved gave birth to a new child almost every year in a time when women frequently died from the complications of childbirth. She died after sixteen years of marriage in 1617, soon after their twelfth child was delivered stillborn. Six of Donne's children preceded him in death. His letters often speak of his own illnesses, and he once wrote a friend, "I am afraid that Death will play with me so long, as he will forget to kill me; and suffer me to live in a languishing and useless age. A life that is rather a forgetting that I am dead, than of living." Death for Donne in his later years seems like an aging cat, toothless, forgetful, and arbitrary. But the letter is from a later date than the poem, which may have been written as early as 1611, the same year that the King James Version of the Bible was published. The *Holy Sonnets*, subtitled *Divine Meditations*, owe much to his own translations of the biblical Psalms and may be read as religious and philosophical exercises that explore the Christian faith. Perhaps the true intersection of his obsession with death and his personal history would come later.

In many of his poems, Donne has his speaker address someone or something in a dramatic monologue that readers are expected to imagine overhearing. The situation is much like a formal debate in which the opponents each seek to persuade not each other but a listening audience. Donne, as both a clergyman and a member of Parliament, would have been familiar with both direct and indirect ways of swaying an audience. He uses an Aristotelian argument that seeks to prove the opposition completely in the wrong. Because it is impossible to present an argument without revealing something of oneself, the speaker shows that he is proud of his defiance of death. His tone is mocking, almost jeering in its sarcasm. Perhaps its strong language is merely bravado, a cover for fear. Or the speaker may seek out death, taunting him into striking.

The poem assumes that the audience will share the speaker's warrants about eternal life after death. But even readers who do not believe this may relate to the concept of death as a rest from life. The intellectuality of the speaker and his skill with language are not consistent with naïveté, and we trust such an ethos. But considering his argument in terms of logos, we might charge him with begging the question. Before we can believe that death should not be proud, we must believe the doctrine that Christ has conquered death and the grave. Donne preaches to the choir, to people who are already supposed to believe that death is powerless.

The poem flows so well as an argument that we may not notice its Shakespearean sonnet structure or its traditional rhyme scheme. For modern readers, the final couplet does not rhyme, though it would have rhymed in many Elizabethan dialects. The final line may be read with the rhythms of iambic pentameter, since it is perfectly regular in its meter. Imagining Donne in the pulpit or in Parliament, however, we might hear a strong voice emphasizing each syllable of the final phrase for a strong, sermonic ending.

As a starting point for death's answering sonnet, we might share with students Donne's fears of old age as expressed in the letter above. Recalling how deeply the poet loved his wife, death might taunt him with their separation. Perhaps death's sonnet will show us a picture of what it would be like to live forever in a decaying and tiresome world. Considered in this light, especially in view of T. S. Eliot's admiration of John Donne's poetry, perhaps "The Wasteland" and other pessimistic texts of the modernist movement of the twentieth century provide a reply from death much like that proposed by our question.

DYLAN THOMAS

Do Not Go Gentle into That Good Night (p.1477)

Like Elizabeth Bishop's "One Art" (p. 790), Dylan Thomas's "Do Not Go Gentle into That Good Night" is written in the highly structured form called a villanelle. The villanelle began as a French verse form that originally addressed trivial and lighthearted themes. Thomas uses it for the serious purpose of responding to his father's death, thus transforming the form and making it his own. Always experimental in some way, Thomas's dramatic readings of his poetry in the 1950s made him an important voice in twentieth-century poetry. He plays not only with the conventions of form but with language as well. Although "Do Not Go Gentle into That Good Night" does not fracture syntax or use words in the unusual ways that characterize many of his more ambiguous poems, he uses rich imagery and highly metaphoric language to express his deep emotion as he exhorts his dying father to resist death.

Repetition is extremely important to the effect of the poem. It is like an incantation or perhaps like one of the Welsh sermons the poet heard in childhood. In a villanelle, specific lines must be repeated according to a set pattern. But Thomas employs parallelism in numerous other ways. He repeats the word *rage* at the beginning of the repeating imperative sentence. It is difficult to read the line aloud without clenching one's fists and speaking from the gut. He parallels different sorts of men in a sermonic fashion: "wise men", "good men," "wild men," "grave men," and finally the particularized "you, my father." The sermon builds rhetorically to its strongest point. Implied comparisons and puns give the poem complex layers of meaning. The word *grave* speaks of both seriousness and mortality, and the sight of dying men is "blinding," implying both enhanced light and the loss of it at the same time. Students might enjoy tracing the contrasting images of light and dark in the poem.

The meanings of various images may become less clear the more closely they are examined. Some metaphors have an odd negativity. For example, "wise men" resist the dark because of the absence of "lightning" in their words, and "good men" resist for the equally empty reason that their "frail deeds might have danced." For the speaker of Thomas's poem, blessing and cursing are ironically linked as expressions of his father's life force; either or both are desired as representations of the rage that resists death. Each line of the poem is suffused with paradox.

People who are freezing to death tell of a seductive impulse to curl up and go to sleep. Others tell of near-death experiences in which they have a great desire to remain in the peaceful passivity of the moment rather than return to the voice of the people calling them back to consciousness. In Sophocles' tragedy *Antigone* (p. 541), the heroine reaches out to her dead family in the underworld, finally free from the suffering and shame brought about by curses on her father Oedipus. Although it is doubtful that Dylan Thomas envisions a loving reunion between his father and his father's loved ones, he concedes the desire that human being feel for death, even as we dread or fight it, by calling it "good." The frightening opposition to the "dying of the light" mentioned in the most significant refrain would be an awakening into darkness. Light symbolizes a power in the human being, and Thomas refers to other images of light or something like it in all but last stanza. But it has been pointed out that these references have a strange negativity. Thomas says in the first stanza that "Old age should burn," but the word *should* leaves open the possibility that his father's old age will not catch fire. In the second stanza, the "wise men" apparently could have "forked lightning" but didn't. The "good men" of the third stanza might have seen "bright" deeds dance, but they do not. The "wild men" of the next stanza, did something with the sun, but it seems to have been the wrong thing. The "grave men" of the penultimate stanza "see with blinding sight" a potential conflagration that is compared to "meteors," but this has not yet happened. Consequently, all of them resist death.

Thomas goes through the list of different types of men their failings before revealing that the poem is a dramatic monologue to the speaker's father. Most of us cannot remember the first time we heard or read this poem, and its familiarity makes it difficult to imagine the effect of leaving this information to the end. It will be interesting to look at student responses to the question if some are reading it for the first time. We might intuit that the impact is greater because of this technique of seeming to address the audience in the abstract at first and then particularizing the message. Both the tantalizing ambiguity of the poem and the technical diffi- culty of writing a villanelle make this an impressive text. Attempting to write in structured forms may be a good exercise, but a better strategy for writers may be to keep forms like the villanelle and the sonnet in mind for use when content seems suited for them. For most us, putting the form first limits creativity.

John Donne's poem (p. 1476) assumes a Christian faith that sees death as conquered, even though human beings die physically. Therefore, death is not to be feared, and it probably is not to be fought as strongly as Thomas suggests. Donne might not advise the dying father to resist death so strenuously. Thomas, on the other hand, sees death as a "dying of the light," an end of human under- standing. He might not see the hope of life after death as a consolation, certainly not as a victory. Donne sees it as a paradox that when death seems at its most tri- umphant, the human being saved by God's grace enters into eternal life. Thus, when death wins it loses. Thomas's poem, as we have seen, is filled with para- dox when examined closely, each stanza containing opposites. Which use of paradox readers see as more effective will depend on their religious faith, per- haps, and their tolerance for ambiguity. The diction of the two poems also influ- ences the reader's understanding. The conventions of the 1600s called for pro- nouns like *thee* and *thou* when addressing God and archaic forms like *think'st*. The vernacular of Thomas's poem, on the other hand, uses words we hear every day. Their syntax also gives a hint about time period. Both poems use impera- tive sentence, but Donne's word order — "Death be not proud" where we would say, "Death, don't be proud" — separates current readers from the speak- er. Although Thomas's sentences are difficult, they are fairly straightforward in their word order. Finally, the worldviews of the speakers help us to date them. Attitudes toward death change in literary circles, and the foregrounding of reli- gion would be less likely in a twentieth-century poem than in one written three hundred years earlier.

WISLAWA SZYMBORSKA

On Death, without Exaggeration (p. 1478)

In 1996 at the age of seventy-three, a Polish woman named Wislawa Szymborska won the Nobel Prize for her poetry. She has been called a poet of the ordinary and has said that she aims for a style that is without artifice.

Deceptively simple, her poetry often deals with war, especially World War II. The Warsaw Ghetto and Auschwitz are part of her personal experience, and her confrontations with mortality begin there. She brings war down to earth with her irony. Postwar Europe is seen through the eyes of a worker: "After every war / someone has to tidy up. / Things won't pick themselves up, after all," she says in one poem. In "On Death, Without Exaggeration" she catalogs the things that death cannot do, giving the homely art of "baking cakes" and the human quality of a sense of humor equal importance with astronomy and engineering. And again, she tells us that it can't "clean up after itself." Like John Donne in "Death Be Not Proud" (p. 1476), Szymborska jeers at the incompetence of a personified death.

By referring to death throughout the poem by the neutral pronoun *it*, the poet simultaneously dehumanizes death even as she personifies it. Death is like a programmed robot, lacking all creativity and spontaneity. Furthermore, she spends most of the poem telling us what death can*not* do, her negative definition elaborating the vitality that surrounds the hollow impotence of death. Her technique models her title, using understatement rather than hyperbole to make death look foolish. When we stop to think about the reality of death, especially the sort of death Szymborska knew during the war, it seems ironic to think it possible to exaggerate death. How could we make death seem more dreaded and fearful than it really is? Some readers might charge Szymborska and Donne with denial. When Szymborska uses the word *exaggeration*, perhaps she means the sort of attitude we see in Emily Dickinson's "I like a look of Agony" (p. 1448), in which death seems to have the upper hand.

To Szymborska, life lived in the present moment overcomes death, who always arrives too late to steal the time we've already lived. Death is never retroactive. The speaker criticizes humanity for "lending a hand" to death, but even this does not overcome the constant regeneration of life. Like a good argument, Szymborska's poem gives specific examples, saving her most vivid ones for last. She grants death's strengths but goes on to continue her recital of its failures. Like Donne in "Death Be Not Proud," she ends with paradox. Just at the point of what seems its greatest victory, death is defeated by its very nature.

All three of the poems in this cluster speak of death without exaggeration. The strong emotion of Dylan Thomas's "Do Not Go Gentle into That Good Night" (p. 1477) might seem exaggerated at first reading. Yet death is seen as something that can be resisted, raged against. In Donne and Szymborska, death is ridiculed as awkward and clownish. In all three poems, death is an absence of power: Donne denies death any pride, Szymborska subverts the concept of death as omnipotent, and Thomas makes it analogous to the absence of light. Szymborska's poem seems more lighthearted than the other two. She sets the stage for this by saying that death "can't take a joke," implicitly inviting us to laugh at death with her. Donne takes a similar tack, but a full acceptance of his argument requires a leap of faith. Szymborska, on the other hand, privileges earthly existence. Rather than defeating death by awaking to eternal life, everyday people defeat death just by living. Because she foregrounds everyday life and overcomes death by persistence rather than struggle, we might recognize Szymborska as a woman without reading the prefatory notes. The description of growing embryos seems especially female in its concerns. But as we have seen with many texts, writers often use personas quite different from themselves. It would be interesting to spring the poem and the author's name, impossible for English speakers to identify as male or female, on students at the beginning of the unit, asking them to guess the age and gender of the poet.

REFLECTING ON KILLING ANIMALS (p. 1481)

GEORGE ORWELL

Shooting an Elephant (p. 1481)

George Orwell's "Shooting an Elephant" recounts an arguably true story of an event that took place during the writer's tenure as a colonial policeman during the 1920s in British-controlled Burma, now the country called Myanmar. Orwell's essay was published in 1936, the year Rudyard Kipling died. Kipling had written many stories and poems set in colonial territories, usually from the point of view of the ordinary British soldier. Students undoubtedly know *The Jungle Book* and other Kipling stories still read by children, and they may have encountered Orwell's *Animal Farm*, a vastly different animal tale that satirizes totalitarian government. Because Kipling's texts do not overtly question the assumptions of empire, interested readers might wish to compare them with Orwell's critique of British domination in Burma in the essay we include here. Enterprising instructors might begin the discussion of "Shooting an Elephant" by playing a tape of a musical rendition of "On the Road to Mandalay" or reading the Kipling poem that has a retired soldier in London longing to return to the "Burma girl" he imagines still waits for him where "the dawn comes up like thunder outer China 'crost the bay." This context can be used to encourage students to question the warrants of imperialism, and some may draw parallels with the American economic or military presence in various parts of the world.

Most current readers will have no trouble finding animal rights issues in Orwell's essay, though they may not immediately recognize the elephant as a metaphor for an unwieldy British empire. Recently reopening the country to Western tourism, the oppressive dictatorship of Myanmar capitalizes on images of working Asian elephants, now considered to be an endangered species because of human exploitation, to emphasize the relatively untouched simplicity of a romantic, exotic Burma that can still be sold to visitors. Eric Blair, who later renamed himself George Orwell, joined the Indian Imperial Police at the age of nineteen in 1922. Burma had been annexed into the British empire as a province of India in 1886. At first, relations were friendly, but British injustices quickly led to resistance by the Burmese, with Buddhist monks leading strikes and protests. Exclusive clubs, like the Gymkhana, were strictly off limits to people of color, no matter what their social station.

While Orwell recognizes the abuses of imperialism and hates them, he does not romanticize the Burmese either. He feels trapped between his guilt for being part of the colonial system and his shame and anger in the face of the contempt and manipulation of the oppressed people. In the fictionalized *Burmese Days*, he relates the autobiographical story of an inspection of a suspect to determine whether the man is a repeat offender. As the policemen check the buttocks of the prisoner for bamboo scars from earlier beatings, a missionary chances by and says, "I wouldn't care to have your job." It was brought home to the writer that, in spite of his seemingly superior position, the colonial effort was at base an unmanly enterprise. "Shooting an Elephant" captures a similarly degrading situation in which the policeman, as an agent of empire, is forced to behave shamefully in order to maintain a façade of superiority.

The writer begins the essay by discussing his frustration with the double bind he finds himself in. He tells the reader that his guilt about "doing the dirty work of Empire at close quarters" oppressed him, even while he fumes against "the evil-spirited little beasts who tried to make my job impossible." It is a truism of oppression that the oppressors become as trapped in their roles and as shaped by the system as the people who are oppressed. The essay illustrates this helplessness to escape the predetermined role. It also reveals the strong motivating force the fear of shame has in the human psyche.

For young men, especially, the fear of being laughed at for a lack of masculinity, for a failure of power, may also be significant. Perhaps it is no coincidence that the concept of honor and the march of conquering armies tend to go hand in hand. Orwell's introspective description of his internal conflicts shoots down pretensions about the glories of empire and masculinity more surely than his bullets fell the elephant. The younger Orwell, Eric Blair, can see the Burmese as beastly, can fantasize about stabbing a Buddhist priest in the gut, but the older Orwell has the 1930s perspective of one who has studied poverty and oppression on a larger scale. For this reason, he is able to describe the young policeman's struggle to recognize the evils of imperialism with some distance.

The shooting of the elephant could have been avoided at several points. His primary motive for responding to the problem in the first place is curiosity. Later, he comes close to abandoning the search for the elephant when rumors become confusing and he thinks the story may be a hoax. Events take on their own momentum when he accepts a rifle. He could have justified not shooting the animal because of the elephant's value or because it has calmed down, but by this time the crowd expects him to do it. In paragraph 7, Orwell explains eloquently why the young man feels he must do this, tying his individual dilemma to the hollow hypocrisy of empire. He compares the imperialist to "an absurd puppet . . . a sort of hollow, posing dummy," and says that the oppressor "wears a mask, and his face grows to fit it." (A quick survey of the art of South Asia will provide interesting visual parallels for these images.)

Like the British empire in Burma, the elephant dies slowly, painfully, and awkwardly. The narrator emphasizes the "senility" that overcomes the enormous beast. Orwell's language does not spare us the ugliness or the brutality of the elephant's agonizing death, and he makes it clear that the whole effort is characterized by incompetence. Throughout the description the reader realizes, because the narrator makes it painfully clear, that arrogance and lack of knowledge have caused this specific death just as similar attitudes have caused the ugliness and brutality of empire and the clumsy dismantling of empire.

Colonialism is a huge, unwieldy monster gone mad, and its end is not graceful. Orwell is a master of language and has written about the subject in both fiction and nonfiction. Perhaps it is this mastery that makes "Shooting an Elephant" a popular essay for anthologies. The essay provides good examples of narrative technique. It has vivid descriptions and comparisons, a clear sense of cause and effect, suspense, and specific narrative action paced to carry readers along quickly at times and to slow us down at others. The essay may also be popular because students weary of ambiguity appreciate Orwell's clear explanation of the issues he is addressing.

ANNIE DILLARD

The Deer at Providencia (p. 1487)

Because excerpts from Annie Dillard's nonfiction frequently appear in anthologies, students may have encountered her piercing honesty about nature and life. For readers brought up on the cute bunnies of Walt Disney cartoons, Dillard's attitude may come as a shock. Although she often finds mystical significance in nature, she seldom romanticizes it. In an earlier chapter of *Teaching a Stone to Talk* titled "Living like Weasels," Dillard gropes toward her philosophy for living. She would like to live as she imagines the weasel does, she says, "open to time and death painlessly, noticing everything, remembering nothing, choosing the given with a fierce and pointed will." She does not flinch as she observes the world, and she accepts the paradox of "choosing the given." There is a steeliness to this refusal to sugarcoat life. Life is not sweet, as she sees it, and she has no patience with attempts to pretend that it is.

In her autobiography *An American Childhood* (1987), Dillard compares life to standing under a roaring waterfall:

> It is time pounding at you, time. Knowing you are alive is watching on every side your generation's short time falling away as fast as rivers drop through air, and feeling it hit. . . . Knowing you are alive is feeling the planet buck under you, rear, kick, and try to throw you; you hang on to the ring. It is riding the planet like a log downstream, whooping. Or conversely, you step aside from the dreaming fast loud routine and feel time as a stillness about you and hear the silent air asking in so thin a voice, Have you noticed yet that you will die? (125–26)

Perhaps "The Deer at Providencia" comes at a time of stillness, but its stillness does not bring peace but a tense, bitter irony. In *Pilgrim at Tinker Creek*, the book that won her a 1975 Pulitzer Prize, Dillard ponders whether the earth has been created "in jest or in earnest." "Cruelty is a mystery," she says, "and a waste of pain." But she goes on to say that human beings almost universally recognize "beauty, a grace wholly gratuitous." It is a mystery that the world contains both in outrageous plentitude. Dillard's original and creative style and her keen skill with metaphor and description attract experienced readers, but many students find her tedious, morbid, and incomprehensible. They may find "The Deer at Providencia" especially uncomfortable to read. We might prepare them by having them create their own metaphors for life and then write responses to

Dillard's observations about the prevalence of both cruelty and beauty in the universe.

In "The Deer at Providencia" the North American men on the trip to the South American jungle expect a North American woman to have a tearful, sentimental reaction to the cruelty they see. Most readers, both male and female, would feel impelled to free the animal and may be angered by Dillard's enjoyment of the deer meat. She describes eating a fish with relish, but the images remind us that she is eating something that was recently alive, and with the pain and fear of the little deer in our minds we are reminded that the eating of meat always involves an act that is essentially heartless. Not only does she resist the cuddly animal images of Disney, but she rubs them in, comparing the entangled deer to the less cute but familiar childhood tale of Brer Rabbit and the Tar Baby. Most readers do not find this image humorous and wonder why she has been willing to watch for fifteen minutes as the animal struggles. We may ask why she chooses to tell this story.

The experience of Alan McDonald, a man who has been burned twice, is obviously connected in Dillard's mind, and both stories are examples of the same mystery, the mystery of cruelty, the "waste of pain" she had addressed a few years earlier in *Pilgrim at Tinker Creek*. After she relates McDonald's story and her fascination with it, she states her lesson in an enigmatic sentence: "This is the Big Time here, every minute of it." Dillard looks at the cruelty of life and forces us to look with her, not because she does not care but because she cares fiercely and refuses to flinch. *This* is life, she insists, just as surely as beauty: this mysterious excess of pain. In describing these stories as mysteries rather than issues, Dillard takes them out of the arena in which reasonable people may disagree. She implies that the unfairness of pain exists as a fact and can be wondered at but not argued. Such arbitrary cruelty cannot be justified by any proofs. After we have felt the impact of this truth, she allows us to see her pity for the deer at the end of the story. But she refuses to admit even this moment of pathos, hinting that such feelings are absurd in a world in which such things routinely happen. The Spanish word *Providencia* calls us back to her questioning of God, the divine providence that created such a world. The word implies that God may be a blind and unfeeling force of nature, a sort of fate, rather than a kind and loving father.

Dillard, like George Orwell (p. 1481), finds herself in a culture that is vastly different from her own. She seems less narrow-minded than Orwell. Rather than seeking to impose her values, she observes and accepts the givens of her hosts. She is not an imperialist. Still, she is keenly aware that others are observing her behavior. She is pleased to shock the men with her difference from most North American women. Left on her own, we might expect her to free the deer, though she would coolly watch it being eaten by a jaguar or struggling in quicksand. And even then, we could expect her to imagine the reader observing her, even in solitary moments. After all, she even allows us to watch her at her mirror. Perhaps she is not as different from Orwell as we might think at first. Both narrators seek to prove to an audience how tough they are. Seen from this perspective, both writers are willing to reveal qualities their readers may hold in contempt. Both allow us to watch them as they grapple with hard realities. Whereas Orwell tells a traditional narrative as an illustration of his disillusionment with empire, Dillard takes a more cinematic approach, cutting from one scene to another, with brief commentary to hint at connections between her stories of arbitrary cruelty. Each is dramatic and intense in its own way.

Gender is important to both essays. Dillard proves that she does not share the weakness, or perhaps the compassion, of most women of her culture. Orwell suggests that imperialism forces men to behave in ways that maintain a facade of power but that the results are recognized as impotent and thus laughable. Not only is the colonial policeman trapped into proving he is a man, but he is trapped into acting as a *white* man is scripted to act. Both writers must contend with both gender and culture as they decide how to behave.

BRUCE WEIGL

Spike (p. 1491)

Whereas George Orwell's (p. 1481) and Annie Dillard's (p. 1487) essays deal with animals in exotic settings, Bruce Weigl's piece may lead students to recall experiences with their own pets. Given what happens to Spike, they may especially remember those that met untimely ends. Feel free to encourage such personal accounts, for they can enrich the class's appreciation of Weigl's writing and bring meaning to this cluster. At the same time, be aware that some students may be upset over a beloved pet's death and won't enjoy speaking about it. Quite possibly some students will recall times when their family had to put a pet to sleep. In any case, the class may want to debate whether Spike indeed had to die. This may indeed be an interesting issue to consider, but make sure students realize that the writer himself seems to condone the shooting of his dog. As chilling as Spike's death may be, the essay doesn't seem to argue against canine euthanasia.

Whatever personal experiences your students bring to Weigl's piece, have them identify some of its own distinctive features. Readers are likely to be struck right away by the intensity with which Weigl evokes his boyhood, but ask your class to cite particular sentences that contribute to this effect. Linger on passages in which he describes Spike. Consistently, you might point out, Weigl depicts his dog as a whirligig of energy, though this becomes demonic energy when the dog turns rabid.

Despite the impression of immediacy, this essay is retrospective. Weigl is now an adult who is looking back on his earlier years. In particular, he puts his ownership of Spike in the context of his working-class boyhood, which he more or less associates with a general despair. Indeed, though Weigl is mostly known for his poetry about the Vietnam War, this essay suggests that even an American city can be an economic battle zone. You might have your students write about their own childhood experiences with a pet from the point of view of their older and presumably wiser selves. His relationship with Spike aside, Weigl seems especially haunted by his relationship with his father, and you might ask your class whether gender is important here. Would the essay be significantly different if written by a woman looking back on her girlhood?

ESCAPING LIFE: CRITICAL COMMENTARIES ON MARSHA NORMAN'S *'NIGHT, MOTHER* (p. 1497)

MARSHA NORMAN

'night, Mother (p. 1497)

To illustrate inductive organization, in which evidence mounts in increasing importance and the claim is asserted as a concluding statement, we might use a cumulative folktale with the double title "No News Is Good News; or, What Killed the Dog." A traveler returns home and asks his servant if there has been any news. The servant begins with the bad news that the master's dog has died. Then in the process of telling what killed the dog he reveals that the dog has died from eating burnt horse flesh, that the horses have been killed when the house burned down because of candles around his mother-in-law's coffin, and that the mother-in-law has died of shock because the traveler's wife ran away with his best friend. "But other than that," the storyteller drawls in an Appalachian accent, "there ain't been no news."

From Kentucky, a traditional hotbed of the storytelling art, Marsha Norman uses inductive organization in a similarly ironic way as she cumulatively reveals more and more about the oppressive relationship between Jessie Cates and her mother, Thelma, in the course of the play *'night, Mother*. In the midst of household details that are trivial in the extreme, Jessie reveals in a matter-of-fact way that she is going to kill herself after handling the chores on her list and giving her mother a manicure. This sets up a situation that builds suspense as the audience wonders if Jessie will really go through with the suicide or if her mother will be able to talk her out of it. As the play proceeds, Thelma comes up with reasons for Jessie to live, but her argument is refuted at every point by Jessie, who takes each piece of evidence as another reason to go ahead with her suicide plans. Ironically, the audience comes to believe that Jessie may be correct in her decision as her mother gradually reveals the extent to which she has controlled her daughter's life in a misguided attempt to protect the family from the shame of what she sees as Jessie's disability, having "fits." We learn that Thelma has even manipulated Jessie's marriage and that other family members have suffered from the repercussions of Thelma's surreptitious control. For the first time, Jessie is actually *taking* her own life, a life that has been dominated by Thelma. When Thelma points out that Jessie does not have to commit suicide, Jessie declares that this is exactly why she likes it. She claims her autonomy in this way, finally having her say.

Although a synopsis of the story might give the impression that Thelma is the villain of the drama, she seems to be misguided rather than evil. After hearing the gunshot from behind the closed door of Jessie's bedroom, she cries for her daughter and asks her forgiveness. "I thought you were mine," she explains. And this truth about motherhood, the destructive power of the assumption that children belong to their parents, is the point of the story. Ironically, Jessie says early in the play that she wants the gun for protection, but she has been unable to protect herself from her mother's protection, the mother's failure of trust that has prevented the child from becoming her own person. Yet in spite of its serious themes of codependency and suicide, there is a grim humor to Norman's dialogue. At one time, Thelma offers to sing all night to keep Jessie alive. Later, when she finally accepts her daughter's decision, she decides that she will not go to her son's house after the deed is done, since "All they've got is Sanka." Most of the humor comes from the ironic juxtaposition of everyday triviality with the desperation of the suicide situation and of the lives that have led to it. Ordinary actions and comments take on a wryly humorous quality in the light of Jessie's impending suicide.

Although her mother assumes that Jessie wants to commit suicide because of her epilepsy, both Jessie and the audience realize that it is Thelma who is troubled by her daughter's condition, not Jessie herself. Thelma has kept this a dark secret, even from Jessie, as she has her husband's similar condition. She has managed her guilt and shame about the "fits" her daughter and husband have by working to hide the epilepsy from everyone. This motherly appropriation of their lives, hiding the information they need to be fully functional human beings, steals Jessie's life from her as it may have stolen her father's life earlier. Jessie knows that suicide is her only way to be independent, but it ironically becomes the avenue through which the two women are able to truly communicate for the first time.

The dialogue makes it clear that Jessie's suicide is a positive move on her part and that the control of her epilepsy has given her the clarity of mind to make this independent decision. She kills herself because she is well, not because she is troubled about being sick. Thelma at first argues that the gun won't work and the bullets are too old, but Jessie shows that she knows what she is doing, has acquired new bullets, and has an alternative plan if this gun doesn't suffice. When Thelma threatens to call Jessie's brother, Jessie answers that she will go ahead and kill herself now, then moves to hang up the phone, explaining that this is "private." Mama implies that Jessie will not succeed, that she will have one of her fits and miss, shooting her ear off or winding up a vegetable. Jessie assures her that she can do the job. Thelma brings up the conventional objections that everyone is afraid of death, that we don't know what death is like, that suicide is a sin. These objections support Jessie's assertion that suicide is right for her. She is always cold anyway, Jessie insists, and she likes quiet; death is profound privacy, and — surprising herself — she realizes that Jesus could be considered a suicide, so sin is not an issue. Thelma counters that Jessie can't use the towels, the gun, or the house to kill herself, since these belong to Thelma. Jessie offers to make coffee. Mama's suggestion that she wait to see what she gets for her birthday opens up the important revelation that Jessie can predict exactly what each relative will give her, each present patently lacking any sense of Jessie as an individual. (Later, Jessie will leave gifts for these relatives that reflect her keen sense of who they are and what she wants them to learn.)

Thelma spends much of the play making wrong guesses about Jessie's unhappiness and offering solutions based on them. She continues to try to fix things for Jessie and eventually assumes that she is the cause. Jessie will not allow her mother to appropriate the suicide as something that is about Thelma rather than Jessie. When Thelma insists finally that she cannot let Jessie go because she is her child, Jessie refutes this: "I am what became of your child," she counters. Although some readers will insist that now that the issues are out in the open Jessie could go on to live differently, most will see Jessie as winning the argument. She can only be her own person, really be heard, if she goes through with the suicide.

Unlike many plays, *'night, Mother* takes place in real time, with clocks ticking away the time onstage. This foregrounding of time keeps the audience aware of the limited amount of time the characters have to complete their dialogue and hints at the ending when Jessie decides that her time is up. Once, Thelma even postulates that death, rather than being quiet, may be like a ringing alarm clock that you can't shut off, and at another point she picks up one of the clocks and winds it. The prominent place of time adds to the sense of panic as Thelma looks for ways to persuade her daughter to continue living. As the emptiness of Jessie's life becomes apparent, however, the audience comes to expect that she will carry out her plan. If the play ended differently, most readers would feel a sense of despair and defeat for Jessie. Thelma, on the other hand, has expressed her desire to go on rather than to think about things. It is clear that she is capable of surviving, and though stunned, she ends by taking care of the business of telephoning her son. The ending is not tragic; rather it is honest, perhaps even triumphant. Jessie wins the argument, asserts her autonomy, and will finally express herself by this final, decisive action.

The presence of only two characters on the stage focuses our attention on their claustrophobic relationship. Jessie insists that her privacy be maintained for once, and this allows the full story of her mother's domination of her life to surface. But offstage characters are important. We first hear of Jessie's father as she searches for his gun, and we're told that the gun may be in the shoebox that held the shoes he died in. She would prefer to kill herself with his gun. We hear that he once dropped the gun in the mud, a fact that takes on new importance when we learn that he, like Jessie, had seizures that were covered up by the protective Thelma. Daddy is Jessie's soul mate, a quiet man who has an artist's soul, to his wife's great frustration. He is laughable to others because he only pretends to fish and instead makes figures from pipe cleaners. Because they are so closely linked, understanding something of Daddy's place in the family helps us to understand both Jessie and Thelma. Also absent, but important to the relationship between Thelma and Jessie, the ex-husband Cecil seems from one angle to be a pawn of the mother and from another to be a factor in the daughter's decline. Although Mama has caught Cecil in adultery, she has kept this from Jessie. For all her neediness, however, Jessie claims to have chosen smoking over Cecil when forced into a choice. She values smoking for its quietness, the quality she loved in her father.

Other characters, though kept offstage, help to develop the main characters. Dawson and Loretta seem to be lacking in imagination, though not in pretension, and Jessie resents their intrusion into her privacy. A hint of sibling rivalry may be indicated, though as the man of the family, Dawson has a great deal of influence in this household. Jessie faults her brother both for not really knowing her and for knowing too much about her. This is especially telling when Thelma reveals that Dawson is routinely called to carry Jessie to her bed after she has had a seizure. Thelma's friend Agnes, like Loretta, can be brought up as a subject of humor, but she also helps us to see how outsiders may see Jessie. Agnes is afraid to come to the house because of Jessie, perhaps for the same reasons she loses her job at the hospital. Jessie's strangeness goes beyond anything that could be attributed to the epilepsy Thelma finds so shameful. Jessie's son Ricky, like her father, helps us to understand Jessie, because she sees him as similar to herself.

Some readers may criticize Norman for painting a positive picture of suicide, but she provides her own answer to this when Thelma says that Jessie's son, Ricky, will think that killing is not wrong. "[It's] only a matter of time, anyway," Jessie answers, perhaps glancing at a clock. If she thought she could influence her son, she would not kill herself. Jessie draws an analogy between death and getting off the bus at a bus stop. Jessie wants to choose her own stop. Because many people fantasize about making a statement by means of suicide, it might be useful to discuss whether outsiders read suicide in the way that the suicide victim would hope. Jessie does not care, but perhaps most readers do.

CRITICAL COMMENTARIES:

LISA J. MCDONNELL, From "Diverse Similitude: Beth Henley and Marsha Norman" (p. 1531)

SALLY BROWDER, From " 'I Thought You Were Mine': Marsha Norman's *'night, Mother*" (p. 1531)

JENNY S. SPENCER, From "Norman's *'night, Mother*: Psycho-drama of Female Identity" (p. 1531)

Within the literary text, readers can explore with safety many contradictory experiences we would never emulatein our own lives. We can follow Emily Dickinson's narrator into eternity (pp. 1448, 1450, 1452), follow Tim O'Brien's soldiers into the killing fields (p. 1424), or watch the slow dying of George Orwell's elephant from the perspective of postcolonial theory (p. 1481). From the same sort of perspective, we can understand Jessie' s suicide in Marsha Norman's in *'night, Mother* as a declaration of independence, a gaining of self, even while we admit the paradox that such an act in real life would be a loss. We may agree with Lisa McDonnell (p. 1531) that death is Jessie's only avenue to "peace and dignity as an individual." In the midst of what McDonnell characterizes as an "adversarial" relationship, Jessie seems to seek silence most of all. It has been silence that Thelma resents in her husband and in her daughter, and both have illnesses that thrust them into silence; both finally retreat from Thelma into the silence of death. Yet it is Thelma's silence that has caused much of the damage to her daughter's psyche.

Many of our college students are beginning to experience the almost surreal transition that occurs as parents begin to accept them as adults. In the happiest of circumstances, they come back to school after Thanksgiving or Easter break and relate the strange sensations of being treated as familiar, but honored, guests at the family dinner table, lingering for after-dinner coffee with their parents to toss around ideas they've encountered at school. Some instructors have experienced this change as parents, realizing with inexpressible satisfaction that our former adversaries have become interesting young adults we would gladly choose as friends. As Sally Browder (p. 1531) points out, Jessie has failed to find herself as a person who is independent of her mother, has never developed "a sense of self . . . power . . . meaning in life." Unlike the lucky ones among our students and children who have parents who facilitate their equality, Jessie has been unable to free herself from what Browder calls "the security of an unequal relationship."

Thelma's silence, her inability to be honest with her daughter from an early age, makes suicide seem the only alternative. Browder does not cast blame but insists that the belief that the mother is solely responsible for her daughter's happiness leads to the dependency that Jessie feels only suicide will cure. The converse would be just as destructive, when children are made to feel responsible for their parents' self-esteem. Readers who have not considered such issues may be influenced by the psychoanalytic view to read the play in terms of autonomy rather than suicide. Classes might brainstorm ways that daughters — or sons — can find independent identities and develop honest relationships with parents before suicide seems the only option.

Certainly, most women do identify with the mother/daughter struggle in *'night, Mother*, and the play is, to a great extent, gender specific. As Jenny S. Spencer (p. 1531) points out, men may react to the play differently because they are accustomed to seeing women as objects of sexual desire rather than as complex human beings. Before reading this commentary, we might want to survey male and female students for their gut reactions to the play. Generational differences may appear as well, since many women of college age have little patience with other women who remain dependent.

REVIEWING SOMEONE'S LIFE: RE-VISIONS OF "RICHARD CORY" (p. 1535)

EDWIN ARLINGTON ROBINSON

Richard Cory (p.1537)

Several of your students may already be familiar with this poem. Admittedly, it is something of a "warhorse." Yet you might find that it is new to a significant portion of your class, while for others it is still worth rereading and discussing. Edwin Arlington Robinson's poem is well known especially because of its shocking ending, where we discover that the title character has killed himself despite his outward life of luxury and ease. Indeed, the poem is often taught or cited as an exemplary case of irony, and you may wish to emphasize this element in your approach. If so, take the opportunity to point out that the term *irony* can be defined in various ways. For instance, it can refer to instances when we readers know something that one or more characters don't: in *Oedipus Rex*, for example, the audience knows but Oedipus does not know that he has murdered his father. With Robinson's poem, we are no wiser than anyone referred to in the text. The poem seems designed to surprise us at the end, and because the "we" who narrates the poem is speaking after Richard Cory's suicide, the "we" can be thought of as knowing more than we do.

Considerations of irony aside, your class may be tempted to "thematize" too simply, reducing the poem to clichés such as "Appearances can be deceiving" or "Money can't buy happiness." While these hoary messages can, in fact, be extracted from the poem, encourage your students to mine it for greater complexity. Among other things, press them to think about why and how the townspeople were deceived by Richard Cory in the first place. To what extent, evidently, did he lead people to misconstrue him? To what extent do the townspeople seem responsible for their misconceptions? Worth pondering, too, is the fact that the poem is spoken by a "we" rather than an "I." This remains a fairly unusual narrative technique, so ask your class to specify the effects it creates.

As we suggest with our Web-based assignment related to Kurt Cobain, students might think of contemporary analogies to Richard Cory. Invite examples, reminding the class that celebrities may self-destruct without actually ending their lives. You might even ask how we learn nowadays about celebrities. Richard Cory was a local figure, studied by his town's citizens; through what sorts of media texts do we now become familiar with the public and private lives of the famous?

PAUL SIMON

Richard Cory (p. 1538)

This text will have more impact on your students if you are able to play Paul Simon and Art Garfunkel's recording of the song. Nevertheless, Paul Simon's adaptation of Edward Arlington Robinson's poem (p. 1537) will interest your class even if the recording is unavailable. Although you may be familiar with Simon's work, some of your students may not have heard of him, while others may be only hazily acquainted with his name. Therefore, take a little time to review who he is, perhaps commissioning a student report on him.

The most striking feature of Simon's adaptation may be that he continues Robinson's text past its original ending. In Simon's version, the townspeople seem to have learned little or nothing from Richard Cory's suicide. They still want to be like him. Ask students whether they think Simon's townspeople are ignoring Cory's self-extinction completely. If they are at least somewhat mindful of his death, how might they make sense of it while continuing to admire him? You might also ask them whether Simon's ending seems more pessimistic than Robinson's, given Simon's emphasis on the townspeople's seemingly unchanged behavior.

As you probably know, many of today's students look to rock music for inspirational messages. If you are like us, you have read many student papers that begin with lyrics that the writer considers profound. The discussion of Simon's text can be an occasion for inviting students to identify lyrics that they have found memorable. Put these in abbreviated form on the blackboard so that the class can then categorize the various messages they put forth. Then point out that Simon's text ends with the townspeople apparently *not* getting the message that Cory's death presumably conveys. Finally, ask whether Simon's song is thereby quite different from the songs containing the students' favorite lyrics.

W. D. SNODGRASS

Richer Quarry (p. 1539)

W. D. Snodgrass's "de/composition" of Edward Arlington Robinson's poem (p. 1537) needs to be constantly juxtaposed with the original text so that your class can see Snodgrass's specific changes. Also, have both texts read aloud, so that students can better detect Snodgrass's rhythmic alterations. Remind the class that Snodgrass is an accomplished poet and deliberately alters Robinson's poem for the worse so that readers can see the original text's virtues.

Your students may not discern right away the various changes that Snodgrass has made. Moreover, they may not sense why each of his departures from Robinson's poem harms it. A good place to begin the comparison is the two poems' endings. Your class should be able to see that Snodgrass has made the ending more abstract; "committed suicide" is vaguer than "put a bullet through his head." If students fail to see immediately that Robinson's ending is better, don't push. Instead, ask how the two endings differ in effect. With each of the differences between the two texts, class discussion will be productive merely if the specific contrasts are noted and pondered. Any elaboration of aesthetic standards that takes place is a bonus.

Try using Snodgrass's text as a springboard for your students' own de/compositions of various other poems. Rather than making them just admire his inventiveness, let your class be as playful as he is.

REVIEWING YOUR OWN LIFE (p. 1562)

PERCY BYSSHE SHELLEY

Ozymandias (p. 1542)

A few years ago the Rameses exhibit from Egypt toured the United States. The museum had reassembled the huge statue of the monarch that had been shipped in pieces and stood like a redwood tree for one's admiration. It illustrated one point of the poem "Ozymandias" — the irony of *how the mighty have fallen,* exhibited in the person of a boasting Egyptian monarch of the thirteenth century B.C.E. Even the readers of Percy Bysshe Shelley's poem are subject to the eroding changes of time, however, and we will all die and risk having our words read differently in new contexts. The judgment of a life is complicated by the perspectives of those who interpret it.

Students are usually interested to learn that Shelley was expelled from Oxford University for writing a pamphlet praising atheism and distributing it to his professors. The eighteen-year-old expected to stir a logical debate in which the issue would be hammered out. He was surprised when his academic audience judged him rather than the idea he had presented for discussion. Interested students might delve more deeply into Shelley's biography for judgments leveled against the poet's radical lifestyle. They will be interested in his complicated relationships with women, in his radical political activities, and in his death in a boating accident at age twenty-nine. If we believe Reynolds Price's quotation in the "Before You Read" prompt that precedes "Ozymandias" on page 1542, Shelley was a little over ten years shy of being able to understand that we owe much of who we are to those who have gone before us. Shelley lived as if he truly thought he'd invented both life and poetry. Although the Romantic poet is still studied extensively, it is ironic in the context of this poem that many undergraduate students may not recognize his name but can immediately identify his second wife, Mary Shelley, as the author of the Gothic novel *Frankenstein*. Shelley, a man with supreme confidence in his own genius, has become for popular readers merely a footnote. In this respect, he resembles his Ozymandias. Perhaps this is because he finds himself in a barren desert in terms of readers.

"Ozymandias" is less emotionally charged and has less of the dizzying sequence of poetic images and hyperbole than do most of Shelley's lyrical poems. Because it speaks more directly to emotions we can understand — pride and folly — "Ozymandias" is frequently included in anthologies, and students may have read the poem in high school. If so, we might ask them to challenge any definitive readings they came to then by looking for oppositions that complicate their judgment of the Egyptian monarch's life. Or they may decide instead that the poem is really about the artist who created the statue. Some readers interpret the ambiguous line 8 to refer to the creator of the monument instead of its subject.

Although "Ozymandias" follows some of the conventions of a sonnet, meaning is not sacrificed to rhyme or to meter and traditional divisions. Rather than taking a sharp turn after the eight lines of the octave, the sestet continues to elaborate on the scene, seemingly without pause. But by reading closely we find that subtle divisions do exist. The early lines tell what the traveler saw, describing the statue but also making the observation that the artist who did the work was a perceptive reader of the "passions" he represented. The sestet moves outside of the original text of the statue and its subject and creator to quote the words of Ozymandias. There is a cause-and-effect relationship between this "caption" to the work of art and the ending lines of the poem. We obey the king's command and see only an empty desert. We might therefore read his quotation with irony, interpreting it to mean that he thought rival rulers would continue to be cowed by his kingdom after his death. We can see that a discrepancy exists between his expectations and the reality of the wasteland in which he stands. But a less orthodox reading might argue that he predicted rightly. The mighty should look and see that it all comes to nothing in the end, and for this reason they should "despair."

Ozymandias might be seen as scornful or supercilious, judged by his "wrinkled lip, and sneer." His "frown" would indicate that he is disapproving or judgmental. The word *cold* shows him to be insensitive to those to whom he issues his orders. Words like *warlike, arrogant, proud,* and *boastful* come to mind to describe the man who issues the words of lines 10 and 11, though some might choose to see him as a confident, bold, in-your-face leader. We may describe his present state as powerless, impotent, or broken.

Shelley begins the poem as if he is already engaged in a conversation with the reader and uses this anecdotal evidence to elaborate on a point he is making. Perhaps the discussion is about art, and the speaker who is the *I* of the poem wants to say something universal about the creative process, that the artist has to be acquainted with the emotions he conveys in his art. Or he may want to talk about the fact that art does not remain intact, either, but lasts only somewhat longer than life. Line 8 gives the artist power over the monarch, since his hands are able to mock — both to imitate and to ridicule — the passions of a king. As the English proverb says of a cat, an artist too may look at a king.

Shelley and the ancient Egyptian sculptor both understand the passions of others because they are acquainted with passion. There is no doubt that this is true of the intense Shelley, and he imagines it for the sculptor. In our literature or writing classes, we often emphasize to students that a text can be anything one reads, from anthropologist Clifford Geertz's Balinese cockfights to a work of art to the books we read at school. We also read each other. To create a work of art, the sculptor or painter or writer must first interpret what he or she sees. The audience, in turn, reads the reading. In "Ozymandias" Shelley reads the tale by a narrator who reads the statue that represents the artist's reading of the king. And it may be that his frowns indicate a reading of a situation in his world that we no longer have the context to understand. Little survives in the poem but the sands of the desert, but the poet is able to read the shattered ruins, and it could be argued that he makes the memory of the Egyptian king and his sculptor last a few centuries longer. Recently, the footprint of what seems to be a boy of about twelve years old was found in a cave believed to have been sealed for 20,000 years. The art nearby has lasted that long, as has the sign of his living presence. Art seems to last pretty long, after all.

STEVIE SMITH

Not Waving but Drowning (p. 1563)

Biographies of Stevie Smith, whose real first name was Florence, always contrast her limited personal life with the energy and turmoil of her mind. From a family reduced to lower-middle-class circumstances, she worked for many years as a secretary, lived in a London suburb with an elderly aunt, and didn't marry. But as a writer she was a woman gifted with multiple personalities, using many different personas. Most of her poetry mixes tragedy with satirical wit in a style that has been characterized as what you'd get if you crossed William Blake with Ogden Nash. Perhaps the paradox behind "Not Waving but Drowning" is the knowledge that more is usually going on beneath the surface of an ordinary life than one might think.

Some readers have had the experience of being caught in a rip current, trying simultaneously to remember to swim parallel to the shore while desperately trying to get the attention of swimmers who had the good sense to stay in the shallows. We speak metaphorically of "getting in too deep" before we realize we are "out of our depth" in a given endeavor. We don't know what the drowned man was attempting that proved to be more than he was capable of handling, but apparently he'd been faking nonchalance for a long time.

There are three parts to the situation that leads to his drowning. First, there's the cold, suspected of causing a heart attack by its suddenness. But the drowned man says that "it was too cold always." We can only guess, but perhaps the cold-ness represents a lack of real love in his life. This could affect one's heart, in a symbolic sense. People can be "alone in a crowd" — getting no real warmth from human relationships even though from the outside they seem to be doing okay, with plenty of friends and lovers. The second difficulty involves being out too far, a situation the man declares has been a lifelong habit. Maybe the drowned man is one of those people who to this point has been unable to say no and winds up overextended. In his moaning, he now reiterates the word *no* as he seeks to explain his death. Or perhaps he is one of those people recognized for his talent and ability, inexplicably to him, and he feels the need always to prove himself or to fake his way through, pretending wisdom he knows he lacks. Since he has a reputation for "larking," he may plunge into play too enthusiastically, getting into things that are risky, and this is what he means by going too far. Or finally, the risk may be an emotional one; perhaps he has been drowning in his intense feelings, even while pretending to be a light-hearted clown. Whatever the details, he tends to excess. Finally, he drowns because he is "not waving but drowning."

This image is funny in an ironic sort of way, and the words have surely been spoken many times at beaches every summer, though not by dead men. Bystanders at the scene of the tragedy say, "We thought he was waving!" Smith's protagonist was drowning and now is dead, but he's still "moaning" to let his companions know that he has been terribly misread. But if we fake it all our lives, how does anyone know — how do we even know ourselves — when we are being real? We all have known the class clown who covers his insecurities with laughter, and many comedians claim to be shy people at heart. This is a version perhaps of waving *while* drowning.

Although the basic scenario is presented in the first stanza, the second stan-za lets us hear how the people around the drowned man view him. We under-stand why they didn't take him seriously and hear their guess about the cold. This invites his elaboration in response. In the third stanza we get the important information that the drowning is the result of a lifetime pattern, not something ironic that just happened one day at the beach. The dead man attempts to explain himself, and his moaning implies hidden misery. Now that he's dead, he wants everyone to know. It's ironic to have a dead man speak, but somehow it doesn't feel unrealistic in the poem. It's like a dream of attending one's own funeral or like writing an epitaph or a sealed letter to be opened *in the event of my death*. Writing one's own epitaph is an interesting exercise in trying to define who you are in a few words, and we might suggest that students voluntarily give it a try.

Comparing the words of Smith's drowned man to Percy Bysshe Shelley's "Ozymandias" (p. 1542) shows the modern character admitting his shortcom-ings, perhaps realizing the irony of his crossed communication, whereas the Egyptian monarch tries to ensure that the pose continues after his death. Most readers feel closer to the drowned man, and feel that this is the sort of stupid thing that would happen to us. He seems honest enough after death to admit that he has made mistakes. We have more trouble relating to the bravado of Ozymandias, partly because such boasting is chillingly dangerous in a man with the power to carry out his threats. On the other hand, Ozymandias may arouse our pity because he is so blind to the fact that death will end his power. It isn't likely that the man in Smith's poem has the same power as the Egyptian king, though a member of British royalty might have this combination of overreaching and insecurity. He seems more of an ordinary fellow, though — perhaps like a lower-middle-class poet who fakes her way using wit in the circles of the literary elite. In Shelley's poem, the equivalent of the people who speak of the drowned man is the glimpse we get of the artist who "mocks" the king's arrogant features. By creating a portrait, he makes judgments, giving the man's personality his own particular reading. We can realize, by the way, that the Egyptian artist of the thirteenth century B.C.E. was working within strict conventions at the dictates of the government, whereas Shelley read the artist and his art through the eyes of a nineteenth-century Romantic. Unlike the drowned man, the sculptor doesn't get to tell us that Shelley misread his intentions.

CARL DENNIS

The God Who Loves You (p. 1544)

This poem was published recently but has already received a fair amount of attention, especially because Carl Dennis won the 2002 Pulitzer Prize for the book in which it appears, *Practical Gods*. If you are unfamiliar with this poem, you may hesitate to have your students discuss it. But it is worth their consideration, and the issues that it explores are perennial. For example, many people have wondered how their life might have been different — a subject that comes up in literary works as familiar as Frost's "The Road Not Taken" and in films as recent as *Sliding Doors*.

Because this poem is one long stanza and includes some sentences that span several lines, students may have difficulty grasping the text's developing logic. Be sure to have the poem read aloud, and encourage your class to analyze it slowly and carefully. A good overall question to pursue is how we should characterize the "you" of the poem, who has had certain definite experiences. Yet another worthwhile question is how we should describe the tone of the speaker who addresses the "you." Make sure your class understands that the speaker is, in fact, different from the "you," at least on the surface (for it is possible to interpret the poem as a dialogue between parts of the same self). Point out that the last line of the poem isn't necessarily its "moral." Even if the poet does want us to believe that we largely choose the lives we lead, his poem dramatizes the tension between fate and free will we may feel as we consider what shapes our existence.

Students's responses to this poem may be influence by whether they believe there is indeed a god who loves them. You might invite your class to enumerate the various kinds of deities that people worship today. At the same time, try to prevent discussion from lapsing into personal testimonies about who is saved and who isn't. You might note that one can enjoy the poem without subscribing to any particular religion.

WHEN DISASTER STRIKES: CULTURAL CONTEXTS FOR BHARATI MUKHERJEE'S "THE MANAGEMENT OF GRIEF" (p. 1547)

BHARATI MUKHERJEE

The Management of Grief (p.1548)

Tragedy brings people together, but it also divides, bringing individuals and groups of people into conflict as they deal with grief and anger in different ways. Issues arise about how problems should be addressed or where blame should be assigned. After a 1999 school shooting near Denver, Colorado, gun-control advocates protested at a National Rifle Association convention and asked for tougher laws. Others looked for the genesis of the Columbine High School violence in video games, music, and the Internet. Some survivors celebrated forgiveness, and others choked on frustration. One father took down crosses erected for the young killers and called for the teaching of absolute right and wrong in the public schools. Speakers at televised funerals called for Christian conversion. A generation that demanded autonomy in the 1960s and 1970s advises parents to search the rooms of their adolescent children and read their diaries. Parents, school administrators, police, magistrates, and "the media" were castigated for various sins of omission. A famous, controversial lawyer contacted the only African American family among the victims but soon began fishing for guilty parties to sue, moving away from specifics into pathos about the tragedy. Each individual or group found evidence in the tragedy to support widely divergent assertions. Like any disaster involving violent death on a large scale, the 1985 Air India bombing and the later TWA 800 crash raised issues of their own.

For Bharati Mukherjee, brought up in India, for many years a Canadian, and now a U. S. citizen, multiculturalism is a primary issue. Like many vocal members of "visible minorities" in Canada, Mukherjee sees that nation's official government policy as destructive and insensitive, in spite of its intent to be respectful of ethnic diversity. To a certain extent, her position is based on personal experience. Mukherjee values the autonomy of the individual, an attitude in many ways antithetical to the culture of her native India, where everyone knows his or her place and is expected to live accordingly. Even her name, Mukherjee points out, sends an immediate message that she is of a specific caste and culture — in her case a Bengali Brahmin of the highest caste. But even these fortunate circumstances are limiting and isolating, in Mukherjee's opinion. Her father's game plan had her earning her M.F.A. in Iowa and then returning to India to marry a man of her father's choosing. Instead, Mukherjee married a Canadian classmate, Clark Blaise, thus choosing individuality over culture.

Speaking of her years as a professor in Canada, Mukherjee describes the underlying racism of the dominant culture: "I was frequently taken for a prostitute or a shoplifter, frequently assumed to be a domestic, praised by astonished auditors that I didn't have a 'singsong' accent. The society itself . . . routinely made crippling assumptions about me, and about my kind." She believes that the "multicultural mosaic" of which Canada is so proud encourages such stereotypes, along with a separatism that amounts to de facto segregation. In both Canada and the United States, she maintains, official multiculturalism does not allow for the inevitable changes that take place when cultures come into contact. Instead, it "implies the existence of a central culture, ringed by peripheral cultures. . . . the establishment of one culture as the norm and the rest as aberrations." Because she feels that individual differences become absorbed into the stereotypes of the group, Mukherjee rejects "hyphenation" as an "Asian-American," resisting such categorization. This stance sometimes brings her into conflict with others of Indian descent, who see her as having abandoned her heritage, and with some members of the academic establishment, who see her views as reactionary. Mukherjee's protagonist in "The Management of Grief" begins as a somewhat more conventional woman of the ethnic subculture of Indian immigrants in Canada, but by the end of the story she has worked her way through grief into the beginnings of autonomy.

In many ways, "The Management of Grief" is a story about culture. In the *American Heritage English Dictionary*, the primary definition of culture is "the totality of socially transmitted behavior patterns, arts, beliefs, institutions, and all other products of human work and thought." Other definitions emphasize that culture consists of shared patterns that identify the members of a culture while excluding nonmembers. The loss of close relatives or friends to death is an experience that is common to all human beings. But responses to this loss are not universally the same. The management of grief is to a great extent culture specific. Still, as Mukherjee would remind us, responses of all individuals within an ethnic group are not necessarily the same. One widow finds comfort in her swami, whereas the protagonist chooses Valium. The Indian culture dictates that "it is a parent's duty to hope" and reminds the men that they have a duty to remarry. But the disaster changes cultural configurations. As the narrator describes it, they have "been melted down and recast as a new tribe." Because of a family history that has caused her parents to reject traditional culture, the protagonist is between two worlds even before the tragedy occurs.

Judith Templeton, the naive social worker assigned by the Canadian government to lead the survivors through the stages of grief and bureaucratic paperwork, has trouble fitting her charges into the little boxes of managed grief. She has her chart detailing the stages of grief — rejection, depression, acceptance, and reconstruction — and she busily goes about her job of checking off each stage for the victims. But she cannot see that the Indian survivors handle grief differently, that if the stages are the same, their manifestations may not appear in ways she will recognize.

Shaila seems to be handling her grief well because on the surface her behavior seems closer to that of the mainstream culture. At first, she is numb, surprised to be so calm and controlled. This "normal" first stage, she tells us, is not what the Indian culture would consider normal. In Ireland, she thinks her sons may still be alive. Western psychologists would call this denial, but the Indian community understands it as the duty to hope. Shaila goes through depression, evidenced by not eating or brushing her teeth. But her friend's swami says that depression is selfish. She explodes in anger, must deal with her feelings about the Sikh bombers, feelings that Western culture would find understandable as part of the grief process. Perhaps she comes to acceptance in a vision of her husband, something if related to the social worker might cause alarm. His instructions to carry on bring about action on her part, but her final release and reconstruction begin at the story's end. Instead of finishing what she has begun with her husband and sons, the voices tell her *"Your time has come."* She is now through the stages of grief, and she is on her own. She is particularly culture-free at this point, able to act without preconceived notions, Canadian or Indian, of how she must proceed.

The title is ironic. Grief should not be managed, Mukherjee implies. Those most connected with cultures, official or traditional, seem most concerned with getting the grief of others safely under control. Templeton has her list, the traditional families in India find wives for the men, and the Hindu religion offers escape for Kusum. Templeton tries her best but is unable to see past her own culture of social work. Mukherjee may use her as a metaphor for Canada's official policies of multiculturalism that manage the complexities of constantly transforming human groupings and regroupings into a reductive mosaic, each tile hardened in place. The intentions are good, but the results, according to Mukherjee, are deadly to the individual.

From the opening lines, gender is important in the story. It begins with the strangeness of having other women in the kitchen and ends with a woman striding through the park alone. For a mature woman, there is no pressure to remarry, as there might have been for a man. It is less likely, too, that a man would need permission to move into acceptance and to *"Go"* and *"be brave."*

CULTURAL CONTEXTS:

CLARK BLAISE AND BHARATI MUKHERJEE, From *The Sorrow and the Terror: The Haunting Legacy of the Air India Tragedy* (p. 1561)

The American public did come together in the days following the September 11, 2001, attacks on the World Trade Towers, the Pentagon, and the plane that crashed in Pennsylvania. However, tragedy also brings individuals and groups of people into conflict as they deal with grief and anger in different ways. Issues arise about how problems should be addressed or where blame should be assigned. While the enormity of September 11, 2001, still haunts us as this second edition of *Making Literature Matter* comes together, the solidarity felt during the early weeks following the disaster is beginning to weaken. Questions have been raised about knowledge that government agencies may have had before the attacks took place, charitable organizations have been accused of mishandling contributions earmarked for families of victims, and some New Yorkers have bickered with their new mayor over which day of the week to hold memorial services to commemorate the end of the clean-up efforts. In each disaster, groups and individuals find evidence to support widely divergent claims. Like any disaster involving violent death on a large scale, the Air India bombing raised issues of its own.

Verisimilitude is achieved as Bharati Mukherjee creates composites and compresses and shifts details of the actual tragedy for use in her fiction. Unlike the short story (p. 1548), which explores the impact of the tragedy on one woman and on others as seen through her eyes, the chapter from the nonfiction book emphasizes the process of identifying bodies on a variety of representative survivors. This account begins by describing in an objective voice the horrifying business of accurately matching recovered corpses with the identities of people known to be on the Air India flight. Although the fact is not brought out in the Clark Blaise and Mukherjee text, it is now known that one of the many careless errors made by the regional Canadian airline that checked the luggage containing the bombs through was the failure to match luggage with passengers. The terrorists had never even boarded the planes on which they indirectly planted the bombs, insisting that their bags be directed to Air India flights. With this in mind, it is supremely ironic that the bureaucracy works so tediously to correctly account for each dead body. In the short story, Shaila is never able to find the bodies that match her family, but in the actual incident every body is identified.

Like the social worker in the short story, the Canadian bureaucracy is characterized as more interested in efficiency than in compassion. Whereas criticism of this seemingly cold approach is implied in the short story, it is explicit in the nonfiction narrative. Irish acts of compassion are held up in contrast to Canadian paper shuffling. It is telling that officials are unwilling to provide temporary visas for Indian citizens, seeming to suspect an immigration scam. It has been pointed out elsewhere that when the Air India flight went down, then Canadian Prime Minister Mulrooney sent a letter of condolence to his counterpart in India, even though most of the people lost were *Canadian* citizens. The underlying assumption seems to be that members of ethnic minorities still belong to the home country, are somehow not *real* Canadians. Grief must be managed so that emotional remarks do not set off riots or emphasize problems with airport security.

The authors make the tragedy specific and concrete by using examples of survivor experiences and reactions, often quoting them at length, and using their pathos to critique the official handling of the disaster. Both the story and the book chapter have as one underlying purpose Mukherjee's position that Canadian multiculturalism policies hide unquestioned warrants that are fundamentally racist and arrogant. Students who wish to explore the validity of this position will find articulate arguments on both sides. Some authors provide convincing evidence that readings of the failure of Canadian multiculturalism like Mukherjee's are based strictly on anecdotal impressions. They maintain that such judgments can be disproved by statistics showing increased applications for Canadian citizenship among ethnic minorities, their active participation in established political parties with increased representation in Parliament, the lack of evidence that people vote as members of ethnic blocs, overwhelming interest in English and French second-language programs among immigrants, and increased acceptance of mixed marriages like that of Blaise and Mukherjee themselves.

Nevertheless, Blaise and Mukherjee are convincing in their descriptions of actions that fail to consider cultural differences in attitudes toward death and mourning. They characterize the survivors as "private and noble, in their terrible grief," reminding readers that we have been allowed to listen in on Shaila's thoughts, realizing that she is often feeling something quite different from what she appears to be feeling on the surface. We might also remember the older couple who have lost their adult children but refuse to fill out the forms that will put the estate in order. They continue in their "duty to hope" and will not allow the government to manage their grief. The attitude of the writers is implied throughout by the details that they choose to include. For example, the repetition of the symbolic "Pink and Yellow forms" speaks volumes about what the writers see as the actual focus of those who set themselves up to help the survivors. Although they let examples of Irish kindness and family grief speak for themselves, with little commentary, they select from the many possible anecdotes the ones that effectively carry out their purposes.

PAUL GESSELL

Revealing the "Family Man" Terrorist (p. 1570)

North Americans tend to ignore the politics of other nations until we are thrust into the midst of them. Several years ago, few people had heard of the Taliban, and Afghanistan was the Soviet Union's Vietnam. Before terrorist attacks shocked our country, few ordinary citizens could have predicted how enmeshed we would become in the politics of this faraway place. Yet in the 1980s, according to Clark Blaise in this excerpt, much of the money and military equipment that the United States pumped into Afghanistan to oppose the Soviet Union wound up in Pakistan, where the highest and most frequent bidders were Sikhs, who were fomenting revolution in India. The Sikh goal, one that Sikhs had supported since the formation of Pakistan as a Muslim-majority nation in 1947, was a separate homeland called Khalistan, which was to be carved out of the Indian state of Punjab. In those early days and later, the predominantly Hindu government of India violently opposed such a state, manipulating borders to avoid allowing a Sikh majority to gain group power. In 1984, the Indian Army attacked the Sikh Golden Temple in the Punjab city of Amritsar, a shrine that the government claimed harbored terrorists. This became one violent, symbolically charged event in a series that included both the assassination of India's then Prime Minister Indira Ghandi and the Air India bombings of 1985 described in the writings of Bharati Mukherjee (pp. 1548, 1561) and Blaise (p. 1561).

Much like the escalating Palestinian suicide bombings and Israeli army revenge attacks of 2002, such violence between Hindus and Sikhs claimed thousands of lives during the last two decades of the twentieth century. Despite these Sikh acts of terrorism, television news reports immediately following September 11, 2001, assured the American public that not everyone wearing a turban was a Muslim terrorist. Interviews were done with presumably harmless Sikhs to discourage vigilantism, with no hints at all given — as perhaps they should not have been at a time when all Middle Easterners and South Asians were in danger of retaliatory actions — that this group has its own terrorists, some of whom allegedly perpetrated history's deadliest act of aviation sabotage before the September 11 attacks. In fact, more North American citizens were killed in the 1985 Air India bombings than in any single disaster before the more recent events in the United States. While most Sikhs, like most Muslims, are not terrorists, their issues tend to be ignored by Americans, and few know of the Air India disaster. Perhaps this is because arrests were long in coming, and the trial date of suspects has been postponed several times. At this point, the trial of three men held in custody in Canada (the interviewee Ripudaman Singh Malik since October 2000) is slated to begin in March 2003. While news reports may surface at that time, especially since twenty-four-hour news channels are now relentless in their search for programming, Canadian judges usually require that nothing occurring in the courtroom be published by the press; therefore, this tragic event may continue to be an obscure historical footnote unless other noteworthy events occur to focus our attention on Indian and Pakistani affairs.

Gessell's discussion with Blaise centers primarily on the interview that Blaise and Mukherjee conducted with Malik in 1986, long before his arrest. Blaise admits that he and Mukherjee engaged in duplicity when they interviewed this suspected terrorist and when they changed his name in their book. Details in Gessell's report hint at possible reasons for this. Our first view of Malik in this article identifies him as both a religiously fervent and a physically threatening person. He keeps his hand on his *kirpan*, the ceremonial knife/weapon that Sikh men traditionally carry. For safety alone, the writers would want to protect themselves from possible retaliation by this dangerous man. In fact, though Gessell does not mention it, one of Malik's codefendants is also charged with the attempted murder of a newspaper publisher (also Sikh). The Indo-Canadian newspaperman had opposed the Khalistan movement and the terrorist group, known by a name best translated "Tigers of the Faith," that had sworn to avenge the Indian Army's assault on the Sikh's Golden Temple in 1984 and similar violent acts.

By singling out Malik as a possible terrorist, Blaise and Mukherjee place their lives in danger. But they may seek to deceive Malik for other reasons, as well. They need to gain and maintain his trust to get information from him. Like police officers, who are allowed to lie in the interest of obtaining confessions, the reporters feel justified in doing something similar. Malik's information network allows him to catch on to the reporters, though he grants the interview anyway. Readers might question more rigorously the decision to protect Malik's confidentiality by altering his name. Some may feel that Blaise and Mukherjee delay justice by protecting a man who has helped to kill over 300 people.

The title of this entry, "Revealing the Family Man Terrorist," communicates the irony of Malik's persona. Reading recent news articles, we find that when he was finally arrested in 2000, fourteen years after the Blaise/Mukherjee interview, Malik was at a fundamentalist Sikh parochial school that he supports near Vancouver, British Columbia; and accounts of his bail hearings mention the supportive presence of his wife and three eldest sons. The image of this Canadian millionaire is of a family man who is devoted to teaching principles of faith to younger generations. He participates in community projects, coming across as a dedicated philanthropist. He tells Blaise and Mukherjee, however, that he is "a machine for converting Sikhs," exhibiting a fervor they describe as "Dostoyevskian." Defining their term, they point out Malik's "zealous commitment to courses of action rooted in piety." The contrast between his benign demeanor as he sits with his children, who watch *Star Trek* on television —

details that seem consolingly North American — and the menace implied in the almost-drawn kirpan are ironic and chilling. These details also invite comparisons with the families whose children are dead, probably because of this man and others like him. When he says that he wants to leave "his mark" on the world, current readers may be reminded of the mark that terrorists made at the site of the World Trade Towers. But Gessell uses this scrap of dialogue also to link Malik and Blaise, both of whom wish their lives to be meaningful.

One of Blaise's ongoing projects is the revelation of racism in the public and private life of Canadians, an endeavor he shares with his wife. For readers who know how deeply racism is embedded in the history and culture of the United States, it seems ironic that Blaise and Mukherjee would choose to come to this country to escape Canada's racism. We think of Canada as the land where African Americans escaped from slavery and found freedom. Today, issues arise about Canada's liberal amnesty policy that allows people who claim refugee status to enter the country with little proof of their good will. Some analysts of terrorism in the United States fear that our open-border policy with Canada poses grave danger because of such practices. Blaise has observed, "The great sin of Canada has been complacency: that we're too small or too good or too honest to ever be taken advantage of. We have always played so fair with everybody that no one would ever treat us with contempt." This would seem to indicate an attitude the opposite of racism. But as Mukherjee and Blaise demonstrate in many of their writings, racism in Canada is more insidious for being denied. All North Americans run such risks. One reason that the Air India crash did not engender the sort of agonized grief and widespread attention as September 11 or the TWA Lockerbie crash was that most of the people on the plane were of Indian descent; as brown-skinned people they were not accorded the same focused empathy as victims of European ancestry. Similar racist attitudes affect investigations in the United States. If the perpetrators are foreign (read *not European*), we demonize them, especially if the victims are white. If victims are black or brown, however, the pursuit of justice may be less rigorous. In 2002, massive searches were conducted for young, blond girls abducted from affluent neighborhoods, and the entire country became absorbed in the televised coverage. Yet the kidnappings of children who are black or poor do not earn the same attention and concern. The degree to which we deem an event a "disaster" seems closely linked to issues of race and social class.

SAM HUSSEINI

Profile in Unfairness (p. 1573)

Whereas some critics of the airport incompetence that led to the Air India bombing in 1985 might insist that any Sikh traveling on June 22 should have been detained and searched, others, including Bharati Mukherjee (pp. 1548, 1561), remind us that the bomb was not planted by the terrorists because their religion or ethnicity made them evil, but because this was part of their agenda as Khalistan activists. It is even possible to support the formation of a Sikh homeland without believing that this must be achieved by violent action. Bharati

Mukherjee has her protagonist in "The Management of Grief" (p. 1548) recognize that her anger toward Sikhs unrelated to the bombing is unjustified, though understandable. Her point, in fact, is that stereotypes are destructive. For the same reason, the profiling of people who typically commit certain crimes depends upon stereotype.

An American of Jewish descent who looks vaguely Middle Eastern tells of uncomfortable experiences in airports. A single woman and a university professor who looks younger than her age, she often travels alone and travels light, sometimes with just a backpack. At Heathrow Airport in London while making connections on a flight from New York to Israel, she describes an experience that was frightening — her detention and questioning apparently based on nothing other than appearance and destination. Currently in the news are assertions that police should be stopped from profiling drivers as possible criminals based on profiles that often foreground race, and conflicting contentions that schoolchildren should be profiled to predict their potential for violent actions as adolescents.

At the end of his article Sam Husseini describes profiling as "brazenness." He might have easily said *racial and religious prejudice*. Although the crash of TWA 800 turned out to have been caused by mechanical failure rather than terrorism, Husseini claims that fear and prejudice generated by theories for its cause have led to measures that discriminate against certain groups. He begins by relating three anecdotes, tied to current events and presumably representative examples, and follows this with his own personal experience. He points out the equivocation of defenders of profiling, who euphemistically label it "passenger analysis" instead, and he questions the warrants underlying criteria for added questions and searches. He refutes the notion that profiling is an important tool of security, maintaining that it does not do the job. As evidence for this he mentions one case in which a "white seminarian" — doubly eliminated from racial and religious profiling — was discovered to have grenades. The example seems particularly unrepresentative of those who have been convicted of terrorist attacks in recent years and fails to consider that Timothy McVeigh or Unabomber survivalist types might also fit current profiles. He further uses air accidents to refute the idea that profiling will prevent air disasters. He appeals to the authority of Supreme Court Justice Thurgood Marshall and relates as his last piece of evidence a news reporter's approval of El Al's policy, which includes "young, dark-skinned men" as needing a second look.

Still, when contrasted with the anecdotes that Clark Blaise and Mukherjee (p. 1561) relate about the effects of terrorism, the indignities of those subjected to airport searches for whatever reason may seem like an acceptable tradeoff to readers who travel often. When we realize that alert employees could have spotted the Sikh nationalists who sabotaged the Air India flights — did, in fact, remember them in retrospect as suspicious because of their behavior and demeanor — we may find Husseini's arguments weak and self-serving. Unlike William Carley in the *Wall Street Journal* article mentioned in connection with the previous text in this cluster, Husseini does not suggest alternatives, but perhaps this is not his point. Although it would increase time in airports greatly, perhaps everyone should be checked as thoroughly as those who fit a profile, thus eliminating the prejudice factor. When an Arab criticizes El Al, we might be tempted to ignore his argument as based on traditional enmities and religious bias. Readers may also note that he is paid to have just this opinion, though this does not mean he does not hold it personally.

We may walk a fine line between maintaining civil rights and ensuring safety. Certainly, all people of good will would want to eliminate prejudice, but a good case may be made for being realistic about the dangers of a world filled with people willing to die or kill over political, social, religious, or simply personal issues. Students might want to develop an anonymous survey or questionnaire that seeks out the warrants people might use for determining if a person poses a threat, asking respondents to describe the sort of behavior, demeanor, or appearance that would put them on guard. Would their criteria be the same in an airport as on a deserted street or in their dormitories?

MAKING LITERATURE MATTER FOR SEPTEMBER 11, 2001 (p. 1577)

WILLIAM BUTLER YEATS

The Second Coming (p. 1578)

Because for many experienced readers, especially English professors, this poem has become so familiar that we can quote lines from memory, we may see it as a given of our culture that needs little explaining. Its lines resonate with meaning and powerful allusion. Yet students born in the 1980s often find William Butler Yeats's "The Second Coming" incomprehensible and may need to deal with issues of fact before moving on to deeper discussion. It therefore calls for a close reading that examines the meaning of words and ideas that Yeats draws on and transforms. We might encourage students to picture Yeats's powerful images literally as they first read the poem. For the spiral of the "widening gyre" we might have them imagine the dark, whirling winds of a tornado, blizzard, or whirlpool shrieking so loudly that nothing else can be heard. While we have seen images of billows of dust rushing down streets between buildings as the twin towers collapsed on September 11, 2001, those of us who were not there can only imagine the sounds and the choking smell, taste, and feel of dust particles from burned and pulverized materials of many types rushing into the lungs.

As they reach the third line, some students will notice the title of Nigerian author Chinua Achebe's novel *Things Fall Apart*, a text often assigned in global studies and postcolonial history and literature courses. As in Achebe's novel, Yeats's poem hints at a world in which all of the commonsense assumptions of a culture suddenly come into question as the unthinkable happens and philosophies and ideologies implode. For example, readers paying attention immediately after September 11, 2001, will have noted changes in rhetoric and political debates as critical thinking and freedom of discussion became less valued than expressions of solidarity and patriotism. Formerly impatient travelers submitted to long lines and searches in air terminals, and uniforms denoted heroes, whether they were police officers, firefighters, or soldiers. Perhaps in fear of "Mere anarchy," Americans were comforted by the simplifications of order and safety.

Yeats expresses well the lack of complexity and critical thinking in his imploding society: blind rage, evil, apathy, and fanaticism are the antitheses of diplomacy, reasoned discussion, problem solving, and exchange of ideas. Yeats follows Christian eschatology and its variations in Western thought in seeing such evil and chaos in human affairs as signs of the times that presage the "Second Coming" of Christ and the coming of the Anti-Christ. Students may be familiar with these ideas by way of music and popular culture, though some may have read the last book of the Christian New Testament, called the Apocalypse or the Book of Revelation, out of curiosity if not religious conviction.

Yeats's account is not simplistic, however; it raises as many questions as it answers. Because the sphinx image is notably lacking in human compassion and mercy — its "gaze blank and pitiless as the sun" — it seems soulless and unreachable by argument or persuasion and is thus more terrible than a human enemy. The being who comes is not the innocent baby Jesus but a "rough beast" — an image not of a human being walking through the desert but instead a thing that "slouches toward Bethlehem." We might raise the issue of dehumanization and demonization at this point: have students encountered evidence that news media and government spokespeople may be asking us to see Islamic or ethnically Middle Eastern terrorists as similar to the inexorable "nightmare" forces in "The Second Coming"? Are Israelis seen this way by Palestinians? The odd syntactical structure of the final interrogative sentence of the poem has been examined by critics, and we should ask our students also to speculate about the reason for the question mark at the end. Unlike the unthinking, inhuman forces of his poem, Yeats's speaker problematizes and opens up the poem for the reader to question.

By using the imagery of Bethlehem, the birth of Jesus, and the Apocalypse, Yeats invites the reader to interpret the poem in terms of Christian theology. He complicates matters, however, by following the prophetic days of tribulation not with the expected triumphant second coming of a risen Christ coming to judge with justice and mercy but with the birth of a "rough beast" preceded by the coldly indifferent image of the Egyptian sphinx. Nor does the poem offer an avenging messiah who heads an army or leads a people toward material salvation. No salvation is offered, in fact — only terror. The first stanza describes a world spinning in a maelstrom of inhumanity, while the second stanza purports to speculate on the possible prophetic meaning of such a world. The second stanza has a more personal tone, beginning as it does with an exclamation of hope for revelation and ending in doubt and dread, with a question and a confused sentence enacting the realization that the opposite of revelation may be coming instead. By leaving his audience with uncertainty and questions, Yeats forces us to think. Though some students may want to explore Yeats's convoluted spiritual system, such a search often proves counterproductive because students who do a bit of reading will tend to expound definitive answers to questions about *Spiritus Mundi* and other Yeatsian concepts. The unanswered questions make the poem more effective for most readers. Students familiar with the resurgence of fundamentalism in Christianity and Islam may feel that the often quoted lines ending the first stanza apply most clearly to this phenomenon. Others will offer examples from politics, business, or personal relationships.

Certainly, issues involved in combating terrorism and achieving peace apply. The first definition of *apocalypse* in one dictionary indicates the biblical meaning of "divine revelation" and goes on to extend the meaning to include "a grand or violent event resembling those described in the Apocalypse." Both meanings are alluded to in the poem. The violent events and images presented by Yeats are apocalyptic, but though the speaker explicitly refers to revelation, only uncertainty and additional images of horror are revealed.

W. H. AUDEN

September 1, 1939 (p. 1579)

A quick reading of the first stanza of "September 1, 1939" by W. H. Auden makes apparent the poem's popularity after the events of September 11, 2001. The poem begins in New York, and its images of "darkened lands of the earth / Obsessing our private lives" and "the unmentionable odor of death [that] / Offends the September night" could as easily refer to the aftermath of the terrorist attacks in New York, Pennsylvania, and Washington, D.C., as to the 1939 Nazi invasion of Poland to which Auden refers. The poet looks to the history of religious prejudice and anti-Semitism for reasons to explain the rise of Nazism and Fascism in the 1930s, referring to Martin Luther, the founder of German Protestantism who also wrote treatises that advocated the persecution of Jews. Interested students might briefly delve into the history of anti-Semitism in Europe beginning in medieval times. Others might be interested in how the established churches of Germany supported Nazism, perhaps reading a biography of Dietrich Bonhoeffer or Martin Niemoller, Lutheran clergymen who opposed Hitler's appropriation of religion to bolster his philosophy of Aryan superiority. The reference to the city of Linz in the second stanza of the poem may refer to Hitler's birth, which took place near Linz, or to the annexation of Austria announced there in 1938.

Auden uses the word *imago* in the psychological sense of the idealized image that a child creates of his parents and relates this image to the sort of idol that European culture came to construct — perhaps in its own image — of a "psychopathic god" who would allow such hate. He goes on to deconstruct the biblical Golden Rule that instructs the believer to "do unto others as you would have them do unto you" into a pessimistic boomeranging of evil. Going further back into history to the Athenian historian Thucydides of the 400s B.C., Auden borrows the authority of the ancients to critique dictators, imperialism, and empty rhetoric. Yet we are all much like Hitler, he implies later in the poem, seeking to be worshiped as petty gods; the dictator's "windiest militant trash" is loftier than the desire of ordinary human beings to be the unique object of love. His reference to dancer Vaslav Nijinsky's words about ballet producer Segei Diaghilev makes his point: "Some politicians are hypocrites," Nijinsky said, "like Diaghilev, who does not want universal love, but to be loved alone." Instead of seeking to fulfill this desire, Auden argues, we must learn to "love one another or die."

Certainly the urban setting of Auden's poem makes it meaningful in the context of September 11, 2001. The strongest argument for the importance of the urban setting might begin with the lines in stanza 4 in which "blind skyscrapers . . . / proclaim / The strength of Collective Man." We might ask students to speculate about the effect of capitalizing the term "Collective Man" as he emphasizes the use of language for propaganda and futile self-aggrandizement rather than communication and the willed self-deception that the events of war threaten to break down. The business (busy-ness) of the city and the constant activity of daily work, the tavern, and "helpless" governing become a "compulsory game" as people "To make this fort assume / The furniture of home." While he compares this frenzied, communal denial to the situation of children "Lost in a haunted wood," the city scenes underscore the failure of civilization to satisfy human needs for happiness, goodness, safety, and peace.

Except for the poem's title, Auden refers to his topic, the invasion of Poland by Nazi armies on September 1, 1939, only obliquely. Knowing the topic, the first and second stanzas can be related to war and to the roots of Nazism, but even then the connection is not direct. Auden's poem becomes universal because this specific event is alluded to but not spelled out. Readers of any time can relate to the sensory images that communicate terror, dread, and blind denial. We have felt our bodies swept by "Waves of anger and fear" — an image that links the emotional and the physical — and we can imagine the "unmentionable odour of death" and hear the self-justifying rhetoric of both Hitler and the citizens of the city that represents Western civilization. We see the skyscrapers and the lights of the city, and the visual sense ends the poem with its "points of light" and "affirming flame," although the warmth implied in the word *flame* appeals to the body as well. Some readers will argue for the primacy of the sense of hearing in the poem, however, since the poet's voice is presented as a possible tool to release the deaf and dumb, deliberately unthinking masses. However, he proposes to "undo the folded lie" with his voice, thus bringing in other senses as we visualize the abstract "lie" as a concrete garment or piece of paper and as we feel our hands unfolding such a material thing.

Perhaps by the time these poems are read, the class will have encountered the concept of irony in discussions of texts in this anthology that are clearly ironic, challenging our expectations or letting us in on secrets hidden from characters. It can be useful to read definitions of *irony* from handbooks of literary terms and to remind them of familiar examples. To counter the cacophony of the competing "excuses," the "militant trash," and the "lie of Authority" of an imperialistic and warlike Europe and North America, Auden offers the visual image of messages sent out by "the Just" as "ironic points of light." Added irony accrues for readers who remember the elder President George H. W. Bush's call for a "thousand points of light" — volunteers from the private sector who were expected to take over from government the work of helping people in need. Although Auden is writing much earlier, his phrase undoubtedly inspired the Bush speech writers. Perhaps the irony comes from the unexpected nature of this quiet communication that can take place only in the dark. If darkness is a natural metaphor for evil, then the irony may lie in this paradox. Because these positive messages of hope and love are visible only in the midst of "negation and despair," they are ironic rather than sentimental.

The ending of the poem invites oversimplification for many inexperienced readers. We might ask students to examine the more problematic aspects of posing a vague and abstract solution in Rodney King's "why can't we all just get along" manner. Does love mean listening to competing opinions, ignoring differences, or trying to save others by converting them to our side? Would love have persuaded Hitler not to invade Poland?

Because Auden ends with a wish rather than a question like William Butler Yeats uses at the end of "The Second Coming" (p. 1578), this poem leaves the reader with more hope. By offering a solution, however, Auden may take away some of the reader's autonomy. In sharing his desire to combat evil with his poet's voice and by sending a subversive message to other people who desire justice, he calls for readers to be one of the individual points of light rather than one of the deaf and dumb of city commuters who ignore the problem. This sounds good but confusingly abstract. Readers may find his words inspiring or oversimplified. Yeats, on the other hand, challenges the reader by giving no solutions and perhaps negating even the hope of one. While both poets pull images from history, Auden does this more explicitly by referring to specific historical people and events. One of these people, Thucydides, was a historian himself. Yeats draws on the Bible and images from Middle Eastern and Egyptian history and religion. Both, however, emphasize the blindness and inhumanity of the forces that threaten to destroy us.

ADAM ZAGAJEWSKI

Try to Praise the Mutilated World (p. 1583)

One suggestion for writing at the end of this cluster suggests that students imagine Adam Zagajewski's title as being advice that he writes to William Butler Yeats (p. 1578) and to W. H. Auden (p. 1579). The premise seems attractive to students, who often like poetry to take a positive turn and find Yeats to be especially pessimistic. We find that comparing the tones of the three poems is useful. Writing in the bleak, modernist, postwar period of the early twentieth century, Yeats seems to offer only dark, inhuman images and confusing questions, and he certainly does not praise the mutilated and terrifying world he imagines to be looming. Students may understand this view better if we situate the poem in the period following World War I, a conflict that shocked Europe and America into seeing the horrors of war and the inequalities of class and power that sent young men to die in the thousands. Auden, at the beginning of World War II, depicts the world of human beings, the city, to be a place where people have moved back to the blindness that preceded World War I. His American city-dwellers desperately try to deny the horror of war and the oncoming Nazi oppression that threatens the world. While a few points of light shine in the darkness, no one has the energy to praise the mutilated world, as they expend all their efforts trying to pretend that all is normal or groping for ways to speak out. Much later, after growing up in the devastation of postwar Eastern Europe and under the Soviet hegemony that characterized much of it, Zagajewski writes from a perspective that looks back at the wasteland of the twentieth century with open eyes, admitting that the world is scarred by the violence of the past. He does not pretend that it will be easy to praise the mutilated world (we are ask just to *try*), but he calls for increased awareness through which praise — perhaps what Auden calls love —

can arise. He repeatedly asks his readers to remember, reminding us of what we have witnessed and shared.

By using the second-person pronoun, addressing the reader directly as *you*, the poet invites the audience to enter into conversation with him, persuading us to listen to his request. Often, this usage leads student readers in a different direction, however. Because the writer asks that we recall specific incidents, literal readers assume that the poem is directed toward a specific person — a lover, perhaps, who shared the white room where the curtain fluttered — and these students may resist the poem's wider application to human relationships that they might have shared with someone in a different but analogous situation. The things that we are to recall and praise involve the senses, sights, or activities good or bad that we have experienced in our bodies. Many of these images place us as human beings in the world of nature, but some remind us of death and homelessness. The first line is repeated as a refrain, but it changes slightly throughout the poem. The speaker first pleads with us to *try* to praise the mutilated world. Later he tells us that we *must* praise the mutilated world, perhaps because we have an obligation to do so, perhaps because the praise might ward off the bad luck that surrounds this line — preceded as it is by a reference to thorns taking over the former homes of exiles and followed by the possibility of shipwreck and images of refugees and joyful executioners. Then he insists that we *should* praise the mutilated world, with the implication that we have a moral responsibility to do so, perhaps because we have experienced the good luck of survival, human contact, and the sensory experience of beauty in spite of the "earth's scars." Finally, the sentence becomes imperative, a gentle command rather than a plea, a suggestion, or an attempt at persuasion. The poem's argument becomes more insistent with each repetition.

This "issue of pattern" can thus be seen as a clue to the meaning of the poem. Just as student readers sometimes insist that the *you* of the poem does not refer to them, they may also protest that they have not known executioners or refugees. The poet might feel that if one human being has experienced this, then we all have. The poem insists that we have the empathy to enter into the experiences of others. Certainly, we know that some people, if given the opportunity, would joyfully carry out the chore of execution. But perhaps soldiers and policemen, with a license to kill under certain circumstances, could also be seen as joyful executioners; movies of fighter or bomber pilots exulting in battle are perhaps relevant here. And are homeless people on the streets of large American cities not refugees of a sort? Students will have witnessed such things either directly or on television. Details of the poem may be taken as symbols or analogies that go beyond their surface meanings. The movement in the poem from June to autumn may be symbolic as well, taking us through longer periods of time in the seasons of the world or in individual lives.

The word *mutilated* seems particularly applicable to the worlds presented in the poetry of this cluster, though the mutilation is perhaps more a numbing of the human soul than physical destruction like that of terrorist attacks. Yeats speaks of a world of confusion spinning in a deafening tornado-like gyre, and the world left in the aftermath is imagined as a desert inhabited by monsters. This world is not so much mutilated as soulless and dead. The image is one of a barren hell in which there is no compassion or hope. In Auden's poem, the skyscrapers and the speech and activities described seem to express human arrogance and narrowness of vision reminiscent of the civilization in the Bible that built the tower of Babel in an attempt to become gods, leading to a confusion of languages. Only a few people are imagined to transcend self-love to send messages of hope to each other. If this world is mutilated, it has been mutilated by the creation of the city itself and by humans' willing abdication of the responsibility to see beyond their own petty needs and desires. Zagajewski, on the other hand, humanizes the world and presents it as an object worthy of our compassion, regret, and praise. Like a human individual, the world in the autumn has scars, and we are called on to imagine both moments of joy and moments of sorrow and oppression that take place over time.

All three poems are characterized by concrete details, and students will find many lines to use as examples. The beautiful sensory images of "Try to Praise the Mutilated World" evoke praise in the reader. A tender love affair can be inferred from the presence of a couple in "a white room [where] . . . the curtain fluttered," while "the gray feathers of a thrush lost" can serve as a synecdoche for the mutilated world itself. The cold, unfeeling stare of the sphinx in Yeats's "The Second Coming" can be read as a powerful image of the inhuman forces of war and evil. And Auden's poem paints a picture of the desperation of the city on the verge of war by virtue of its details. On the other hand, Auden's poem is the most abstract and therefore perhaps the least effective. Terms like "love" are vague and mean different things to different people, and while the "points of light" and the "affirming flame" of the final stanza are pretty, their meaning too is unclear, and they are more abstract than they may appear to be on first reading. Coming at the end of Zagajewski's poem, a similar line describing "the gentle light that strays and vanishes / and returns" seems somehow more concrete than Auden's image because the poem has described the ebb and flow of human experience throughout. Yeats's poem, though it calls on culturally charged abstract ideas like apocalypse and Yeatsian terms like *Spiritus Mundi*, is visually concrete to a terrifying degree once the reader enters into its world. Although we do not know what the "rough beast" looks like, we can vividly call up the picture of its "slouching" movement toward Bethlehem: no other verb could so concretely convey the monstrous and depraved image.

Because most teachers are more familiar with Yeats and Auden, the more recent poem may have a fresh quality that makes us prefer it. Its speaker has the advantage of knowing what we do — that the world, though mutilated, somehow survived the two major wars of the twentieth century and others besides. We know, as Auden did not, that the tall buildings of New York can come to symbolize human altruism and individual losses and that we can speak of rebuilding not from the motive of arrogance and denial but as a celebration of courage and the value of the sort of human experience Zagajewski describes in his poem. Volunteers responded to need in the thousands, without rhetoric about "points of light" being needed, though something like it certainly was evident. A new project involves planting thousands of daffodils in a park near the destroyed twin towers, and the Netherlands has contributed bulbs. These efforts, whatever the motivation behind them, makes the tone of "Try to Praise the Mutilated World" suddenly seem very contemporary, whereas the pessimism of Yeats may have carried the day before September 11, 2001.